THE DEVIL, HERESY
AND WITCHCRAFT IN
THE MIDDLE AGES

CULTURES, BELIEFS AND TRADITIONS

MEDIEVAL AND EARLY MODERN PEOPLES

Editorial Board:

ESTHER COHEN, Hebrew University, Jerusalem
WILLIAM BRINNER, University of California at Berkeley
FLORIKE EGMOND, Leiden University
GUSTAV HENNINGSEN, Danish Folklore Archives
MAYKE DE JONG, University of Utrecht
MIRI RUBIN, Pembroke College, Oxford University
ELI YASSIF, Tel Aviv University

VOLUME 6

Jeffrey B. Russell

THE DEVIL, HERESY AND WITCHCRAFT IN THE MIDDLE AGES

Essays in Honor of Jeffrey B. Russell

EDITED BY

ALBERTO FERREIRO

BRILL

LEIDEN · BOSTON · KÖLN

1998

For this new series Cultures, Beliefs and Traditions *manuscripts and manuscript proposals are invited by the editors and publishers. Please send these to Professor Esther Cohen, Department of History, Hebrew University, Jerusalem, Israel.*

This book is printed on acid-free paper.

Library of Congress Cataloging-in-Publication Data

The devil, heresy, and witchcraft in the Middle Ages : essays in honor of Jeffrey B. Russell / edited by Alberto Ferreiro.
    p. cm. — (Cultures, beliefs, and traditions, ISSN 1382–5364 ; v. 6)
    Includes index.
    ISBN 9004106103 (cloth : alk. paper)
    1. Heresies, Christian—History—Middle Ages, 600–1500.
2. Witchcraft—Europe—History. 3. Devil—History of doctrines–
–Middle Ages, 600–1500. 4 Europe—Church history—600–1500.
I. Ferreiro, Alberto. II. Russell, Jeffrey Burton. III. Series.
BT1319.D49   1998
273'.6—dc21
                                      98–12748
                                      CIP

Die Deutsche Bibliothek - CIP-Einheitsaufnahme

The **devil, heresy and witchcraft in the middle ages** : essays in honor of Jeffrey B. Russell / ed. by Alberto Ferreiro. – Leiden ; Boston ; Köln ; Brill, 1998
    (Cultures, beliefs and traditions ; Vol. 6)
    ISBN 90–04–10610–3

ISSN 1382–5364
ISBN 90 04 10610 3

© *Copyright 1998 by Koninklijke Brill NV, Leiden, The Netherlands*

All rights reserved. No part of this publication may be reproduced, translated, stored in a retrieval system, or transmitted in any form or by any means, electronic, mechanical, photocopying, recording or otherwise, without prior written permission from the publisher.

Authorization to photocopy items for internal or personal use is granted by Brill provided that the appropriate fees are paid directly to The Copyright Clearance Center, 222 Rosewood Drive, Suite 910 Danvers MA 01923, USA. Fees are subject to change.

PRINTED IN THE NETHERLANDS

CONTENTS

PREFACE

Jeffrey B. Russell has had and continues to have a distinguished career in the field of medieval studies. Over the decades he has left a deep mark through his scholarly work and numerous graduate students. Moreover, the interdisciplinary nature of his work has enriched the work of historians of Christianity, art, ideas, and theology of the church. The essays contained in this Festschrift exemplify the wide range of topics that have been advanced by Russell's scholarship. The authors also represent the levels of relationships, personal and professional, between themselves and Russell. Some have known him only through his written work, others have had occasion to meet him at professional meetings, and still some of us have enjoyed in addition a personal friendship with him. We all, however, desire to present these essays to Jeff as a tribute to his scholarship, friendship, inspiration, and the many challenging novel ideas that have enriched our professional and private lives.

Jeffrey B. Russell was formally educated at the University of California, Berkeley (B.A. 1955) and at Emory University (Ph.D. 1960). He also spent a year of his graduate training at the Université de Liège, Belgium in 1959–60 as a Fulbright Fellow. He began his teaching career at the University of New Mexico (1960–1961) followed by a Junior Fellowship at Harvard University (1961–1962). From 1962–1975 he taught at the University of California, Riverside where he achieved the promotion to Full Professor, and where he served as Associate Dean of the Graduate Division (1967–1975) and Chair of the Religious Studies Program (1972–1973). From 1975 to 1977 he was Director of the Medieval Institute and Grace Professor of Medieval Studies at Notre Dame. In 1977–1979 he went back to an administrative position as Graduate Dean at California State University, Sacramento. His final academic move occurred in 1979 when the late Professor C.W. Hollister brought him to the University of California, Santa Barbara. Before his recent retirement in 1996 he was a member of both the History and Religion departments at Santa Barbara while at the same time serving as Adjunct Professor at Pacifica Graduate Institute.

Among his other academic achievements are the numerous major fellowships which he has been awarded. Fulbright Fellow to Belgium (1959–1960), Harvard Junior Fellowship (1961–1962), Guggenheim Fellow in England (1968–1969), NEH Senior Fellow (1972–1973), Fellow of the Medieval Academy (1985), NEH Summer Research Seminar Directorships (1991 and 1993), and most recently the Erick Nilson Award (1996). He also participated or has been invited to speak at literally hundreds of seminars, congresses, symposia, and colloquia. Jeff has participated in major popular media interviews and presentations with the BBC, ABC, the Australian Broadcasting Corporation, Discovery Channel, NPR, A&E Network and others. He has also appeared in *Time* and *Newsweek* magazines on several occasions. In short, his research and expertise has given him the rare opportunity among academic scholars to reach a broad spectrum of academic and non-academic audiences.

He began his scholarly inquest into heterodoxy with the publication of two articles: "Les Cathares de 1048–1054 à Liège," *Bulletin de la société d'art et d'histoire de diocèse de Liège* 42 (1961) 1–8 and "A propos du synode d'Arras en 1025," *Revue d'histoire ecclésiastique* 57 (1962) 66–87. His first major published essay in English is "Interpretation of the origins of medieval history," *Medieval Studies* 25 (1963) 23–53, which placed him at the forefront of medieval heterodox dissident religious movements studies. In 1965 his book *Dissent and Reform in the Early Middle Ages*, Berkeley, 1965 became a major study that many scholars have built upon ever since. In 1968 appeared *A History of Medieval Christianity: Prophecy and Order*, a fascinating interpretive monograph which is still widely used and in print. Jeff's fascination with marginal medieval religious groups, resulted with another important work, *Witchcraft in the Middle Ages*, Cornell, 1972. He was already at that time working on and publishing articles on the Devil in Christian thought and related themes. That work resulted in the publication of *The Devil: Perception of Evil from Antiquity to Primitive Christianity*, Cornell, 1977. The topic would occupy his attention over the next ten years or so and resulted in subsequent volumes. *Satan: The Early Christian Tradition*, Cornell, 1981, *Lucifer: The Devil in the Middle Ages* (1984), *Mephistopheles: The Devil in the Modern World* (1986) and *Prince of Darkness: Evil and the Power of Good in History*, 1988, all published by Cornell. These works, although mainly historical in their approach, boldly delve into questions of philosophy and theology and they are exemplary of his interdisciplinary scholarships. Another breath of fresh air about his work is that Jeff does not shrink back from expressing his personal beliefs, but in a way that is not overbearing. Although some critics have taken him to task on this point the overwhelming positive response from lay and academic audiences has vindicated his methodology time and again. After devoting so many years to the "Evil One"—as Abraham Friesen with joking fondness has remarked acting as the "Devil's biographer"—Jeff has once again impacted the scholarly community with his acclaimed new study, *A History of Heaven: The Singing Silence*, Princeton, 1997 [Italian edition, 1996]. Fortunately, for all of us, Jeff is on track on several other book projects which I and so many excitedly await.

I wish to thank firstly the authors of this volume for their unhesitant enthusiastic response to contribute to a *Festschrift* for Jeff, a sign of their deep respect. I also wish to extend my gratitude to the editors of the *Cultures, Beliefs, and Peoples Series* for readily endorsing the book. Lastly, the valuable technical and production contributions of Theo Joppe, Gera van Bedaf, and Julian Deahl, Brill Senior Acquisitions Editor, are enormously appreciated.

Alberto Ferreiro
Seattle Pacific University
November 6, 1997

LIST OF CONTRIBUTORS

Alan E. Bernstein is Professor of Medieval History at the University of Arizona. He is a specialist in the history of belief in hell. His most recent book is *The Formation of Hell: Death and Retribution in the Ancient and Early Christian Worlds* (Ithaca, NY, 1993).

Richard K. Emmerson is Professor of English at Western Washington University. He is a specialist in medieval apocalypticism, drama, and illustrated manuscripts. His recent publications include *Antichrist and Judgment Day: The Middle French Jour du Jugement* (with David Hult), *The Apocalypse in the Middle Ages* (with Bernard McGinn), and *The Apocalyptic Imagination in Medieval Literature* (with Ronald Herzman).

Alberto Ferreiro is Professor of European History at Seattle Pacific University. He has published some 30 articles in both patristics and medieval studies and *The Visigoths in Gaul and Spain: a bibliography A.D. 418–711*. Brill, 1988. He is currently working on a book entitled *Simon Magus in the Early Christian and Medieval Tradition*.

Neil Forsyth is the Professor of Modern English Literature at the University of Lausanne. He is the author of *The Old Enemy: Satan and the Combat Myth* (Princeton, 1987). He is now preparing a book on Milton. His latest publications are both in electronic form: one is an essay on Chaos theory and its application to literature at <http://www.richmond.edu/~creamer/mr11.html> and the other is an essay on the biblical subtexts of Milton's rebellion myth at <http://voyager.cns.ohiou.edu/~somalley/milton.html>.

Abraham Friesen is professor of History at the University of California at Santa Barbara. He specialises in European history of the later medieval and early modern periods as well as in the history of Christianity from the later middle ages. His recent publications include: *Thomas Müntzer, a destroyer of the godless* (Berkeley, 1990), *History and Renewal in the Anabaptist/Mennonite Tradition* (North Newton, KS, 1994) and *Erasmus, the Anabaptists and the Great Commission* (Grand Rapids, 1998).

Karen Louise Jolly is Associate Professor of History at the University of Hawaii at Manoa. She is a specialist in Anglo-Saxon history with interests in popular culture, religion and magic. Her recent publications include *Popular Religion in Late Saxon England: Elf Charms in Context* (1996) and an edited volume of source readings, *Tradition and Diversity: Christianity in a World Context to 1500* (1997).

Henry Ansgar Kelly is professor of English and director of the Center for Medieval and Renaissance Studies at the University of California, Los Angeles (UCLA). He is a specialist in literary, intellectual, and legal history. His recent publications include "The Right to Remain Silent: Before and after Joan of Arc," *Speculum* 68 (1993) 992–1026; *Ideas and Forms of Tragedy from Aristotle to the Middle Ages* (1993); *Chaucerian Tragedy* (1997); "Statutes of Rapes and Alleged Ravishers of Wives: A Context for the Charges Against Thomas Malory, Knight," *Viator* 28 (1997) 361–419.

Richard Kieckhefer is professor of Religion and of History at Northwestern University. He is a specialist in late medieval religion, in particular mystical theology and the history of witchcraft and magic. His recent publications include *Magic in the Middle Ages* (Cambridge University Press, 1989) and *Forbidden Rites: A Necromancer's Manual of the Fifteenth Century* (Stroud: Alan Sutton, 1997).

Beverly Mayne Kienzle is Professor of the Practice of Latin and Romance Languages at Harvard Divinity School; she also currently serves as President of the International Medieval Sermons Studies Society. She is a specialist in twelfth-century preaching by Cistercians and dissident movements. Her recent publications include: "Hélinand de Froidmont et la prédication cistercienne dans le Midi, 1145–1229," in *La prédication en Pays d'Oc (xiie–début xve siècle)*. Cahiers de Fanjeaux, 32 (Toulouse, 1997): 37–67; "*Operatrix in vinea Domini*: Hildegard of Bingen's Preaching and Polemics against the Cathars," *Heresis* 26–27 (1997): 43–56; and "Tending the Lord's Vineyard: Cistercians, Rhetoric and Heresy, 1143–1229, Part I: Bernard of Clairvaux, the 1143 Sermons and the 1145 Preaching Mission," *Heresis* 25 (1996): 29–61. She had also edited *Models of Holiness in Medieval Sermons* (Louvain-la-Neuve, 1996) and (with Pamela Walker) *Women Preachers and Prophets through Two Millennia of Christianity* (Berkeley, 1998). She is currently completing a guide to *The Sermon* for the Typologie des source du moyen âge, a bilingual edition of the Gospel homilies of Hildegard of Bingen, and a history of twelfth-century Cistercian preaching against heresy.

Gary Macy is professor of Theological and Religious Studies at the University of San Diego. He is a specialist on eucharistic theology and practice in the Middle Ages. His recent publications include "The Dogma of Transsubstantiation in the Middle Ages," *Journal of Ecclesiastical History*, vol. 45 (1994), pp. 11–41; "Demythologizing 'the Church' in the Middle Ages," *Journal of Hispanic/Latino Theology*, vol. 3 (1995), pp. 23–41 and "Was there a 'the Church' in the Middle Ages?" *Unity and Diversity in the Church*, edited by Robert Swanson, Studies in Church History, vol. 52 (Blackwell: Oxford, 1996), pp. 107–116.

Bernard McGinn is Naomi Shenstone Donnelley Professor of Historical Theology and the History of Christianity, at The Divinity School of the University of Chicago. He works in the history of Christianity and the history of Christian thought, primarily in the medieval period. He has written extensively in the areas of history of apocalyptic thought and most recently in the areas of spirituality and mysticism. His current long-range project is a five-volume history of Christian mysticism in the West under the general title of *The Presence of God*, two volumes of which have appeared, *Origins of Mysticism* (1991) and *Growth of Mysticism* (1994).

Edward M. Peters is Henry Charles Lea Professor of History, at the University of Pennsylvania. He specializes in the early history of Europe, from the second to the seventeenth centuries. His chief interests are political and constitutional history, including church history, intellectual and legal history, and historiography. His current research deals with various aspects of crime and punishment, on the one hand, and with the idea of curiosity and the limits of intellectual inquiry, on the other. His book *Torture* appeared in a expanded edition with supplementary original documents in translation and a bibliographical update in 1996 (UPenn Press).

Cheryl A. Riggs is Chair of the Department of History at California State University, San Bernadino. She is a specialist in medieval church history, spirituality, and mysticism. Her recent publications include

"Julian of Norwich and the Ecstatic Experience", in *Tradition and Ecstasy: The Agony of the Fourteenth Century*, Nancy van Deusen (general editor), Claremont Cultural Studies (Ottawa, Canada: The Institute of Medieval Music, 1997); *The Global Past*, co-authored with Lanny Fields and Russell Barber (Boston: Bedford Books of St. Martin's Press, 1997).

Larry J. Simon is an assistant Professor of History at Western Michigan University in Kalamazoo. He has published articles on medieval slavery, the mendicant movement and Muslim-Christian-Jewish relations, and is the editor of *Iberia and the Mediterranean World of the Middle Ages* (Brill, 1995).

Laura Ackerman Smoller is Assistant Professor of History at the University of Arkansas at Little Rock. She is a specialist in late medieval science and religion, with particular interest in astrology, apocalypticism, sanctity, and miracles. Her recent publications include: *History, Prophecy, and the Stars: The Christian Astrology of Pierre d'Ailly, 1350–1420* (Princeton, NJ: Princeton University Press, 1994); "Defining the Boundaries of the Natural in the Fifteenth Century: The Inquest into the Miracles of St. Vincent Ferrer (d. 1419)." *Viator* 28 (1997): 333–59; and "Miracle, Memory, and Meaning in the Canonization of Vincent Ferrer, 1453–54." Forthcoming in *Speculum* (1998).

Catherine Brown Tkacz is an independent scholar in Spokane, Washington, currently on fellowship from the Pew Trust for her book in progress on Susanna, the heroine of the Book of Daniel. She is a specialist in Patristic and Medieval Studies. Her recent publications include *The Key to the Brescia Casket: Typology and the Early Christian Imagination*, forthcoming in two series: Études Augustiniennes—Antiquité (Brepols) and Christianity and Judaism in Late Antiquity, University of Notre Dame Press; "Susanna as a Type of Christ", *Studies in Iconography* 20 (1998); "Ovid, Jerome, and the Vulgate," *Studia Patristica* 33 (1996) 378–82; "*Labor tam utilis*: The Creation of the Vulgate," *Vigiliae Christianae* 50.1 (1996) 42–72; and "The Seven Maccabees, the Three Hebrews, and a Newly Discovered Sermon of Saint Augustine," *Revue des études augustiniennes* 41.1 (1995) 59–78.

John V. Tolan is Maître de Conférences d'Histoire Médiévale at the Université de Nantes. His specialty is Muslim-Jewish-Christian relations and polemics in twelfth- and thirteenth-century Europe. He is author of *Petrus Alfonsi and his Medieval Readers* (Gainesville: University Press of Florida, 1993) and editor of *Medieval Christian Perceptions of Islam: A Collection of Essays* (New York: Garland Press, 1996).

HOSPITALS AND POOR RELIEF IN
RAMON LLULL'S MAJORCA[1]

Larry J. Simon

Jeffrey Russell's brilliant five-volume study of the devil from antiquity to modernity, his work on witchcraft in the Middle Ages, and, more recently, his monograph on the invention of the flat earth have tended to mask his more general contributions to the history of the medieval church or medieval civilization, and some of his earlier work on heresy. It is Russell, however, as much as any other scholar, who has emphasized the intimate links in the High Middle Ages among heresy, religious and intellectual dissent, the ideal of apostolic poverty, and church reform.[2] The role of the mendicant orders in combatting heresy in the thirteenth century via preaching, evangelical example, and staffing of the medieval inquisition is well known, as is their role in adopting and adapting the ideals of earlier reformers, and channeling and directing attitudes toward poverty.[3] Less well known is the role played by Christendom's thirteenth-century profusion of hospitals in shaping the spiritual climate of the age and altering the institutional orientation of the church. Because hospital administrators and employees seldom if ever became bishops or popes, dominated university life, lapsed into heresy, or put quill to parchment at a rate approaching the medieval mendicants or Professor Russell, the significance of hospitals as religious and social institutions in the thirteenth century is more difficult to study than the growth and importance of the mendicant orders.

[1] This paper was originally presented at the 26th International Congress on Medieval Studies, May 9–12, 1991, at Western Michigan University in Kalamazoo. I thank Alberto Ferreiro for the opportunity now of revising it for publication.

[2] I am thinking of his monograph *Dissent and Reform in the Early Middle Ages* (Berkeley and Los Angeles: University of California Press, 1965); his edited collection of sources and studies entitled *Religious Dissent in the Middle Ages* (New York: John Wiley, 1971); and his recent survey *Dissent and Order in the Middle Ages: The Search for Legitimate Authority* (New York: Twayne Publishers, 1992). His two general surveys are the lavishly illustrated and printed *Medieval Civilization* (New York: John Wiley, 1968), and *A History of Medieval Christianity: Prophecy and Order* (New York: Thomas Y. Crowell, 1968).

[3] See especially Lester K. Little, *Religious Poverty and the Profit Economy in Medieval Europe* (Ithaca: Cornell University Press, 1978), in particular pp. 146–219 and 249–61.

The starting point for any study of hospitals and poor relief in the Middle Ages is the work of Michel Mollat. The years from 1962 to 1976 of his Sorbonne seminar on "The Poor and Poverty" were, in Mollat's own words, "years of joint research with my students and colleagues, graced by some 90 seminar papers and 220 articles, to say nothing of several theses."[4] Some of this research is available in ten mimeographed Cahiers which are next to impossible to locate in this country; and some of it is located in a more accessible two-volume collection of thirty-five articles published in Paris in 1974.[5] In 1978 Mollat published a scholarly synthesis on the topic, and Yale University Press in 1986 published an accurate, if occasionally comic, English translation of this seminal work. The "freres des sachets," formally the Order of the Penitence of Jesus Christ, appear not as the Friars of the Sack, as they are more commonly known, but as the "Brothers of the Bag." Neither Mollat nor his students were much concerned with things Iberian; since the 1970s, however, much of the most exciting work on hospitals and poor relief concerns Iberia and the Mediterranean, perhaps owing to the survival of rich archival material.[6] Roberto Rusconi has pointed out the way in which municipal, especially archival, sources have shed "new light on the phenomenon of women (and men) who gave themselves as oblates in the service, not of a monastery, but of a hospital: an expression of religious choice whose social consequences were immediately tangible."[7] James Brodman has recently surveyed a number of works and provided

---

[4] Michel Mollat, *The Poor in the Middle Ages: An Essay in Social History*, trans. Arthur Goldhammer (New Haven: Yale University Press, 1986), p. vii; this is a translation of *Les pauvres au Moyen Age: Etude sociale* (Paris: Hachette, 1978).

[5] *Cahiers de recherches sur l'histoire de la pauvreté*, ed. Michel Mollat (Paris, 1962–1977); and *Etudes sur l'histoire de la pauvreté*, ed. Michel Mollat, 2 vols. (Paris: Publications de la Sorbonne, 1974).

[6] I am thinking especially of Philip Gavitt, *Charity and Children in Renaissance Florence: The Ospedale degli Innocenti, 1410–1536* (Ann Arbor: University of Michigan Press, 1990); Maria Pia Alberzoni and Onorato Grassi, eds., *La carità a Milano nei secoli XII–XV: Atti del Convegno di Studi, Milano, 6–7 novembre 1987* (Milan: Jaca Book, 1989); Manuel Riu, ed., *Pobreza y la asistencia a los pobres en la Cataluña medieval*, 2 vols. (Barcelona: Consejo Superior de Investigaciones Científicas, 1980–82); Luis Martínez García, *La asistencia a los pobres en Burgos en la Baja Edad Media: El Hospital de Santa María La Real* (Burgos: Diputación Provincial de Burgos, 1981); and Agustín Rubio Vela, *Pobreza, enfermedad y asistencia hospitalaria en la Valencia del siglo XIV* (Valencia: Diputación Provincial de Valencia, 1984).

[7] Roberto Rusconi, "Women Religious in Late Medieval Italy: New Sources and Directions," in *Women and Religion in Medieval and Renaissance Italy*, ed. Rusconi and Daniel Bornstein, trans. Margery J. Schneider (Chicago: University of Chicago Press, 1996), 305–326 (308), citing especially Marina Gazzini, "Uomini e donne nella realtà

a useful synthesis of the growth of the hospital movement in medieval Catalonia.[8] The history of the island-kingdom of Majorca's hospitals and poor relief efforts has seen a few articles and short studies, mostly focussed on the fourteenth and fifteenth centuries, and occasionally as part of a broader or tangential topic.[9] As a contribution to this burgeoning bibliography I offer the following study, based on archival documents but augmented especially by a fascinating literary source, of Majorca's thirteenth-century hospitals and attitudes toward poverty and poor relief.

Ramon Llull's *Blanquerna*, a utopian romance rich in description of the social world of the thirteenth century, offers a unique view of hospitals, the poor, and of the testamentary procedures which transformed thirteenth-century poor relief.[10] Llull, scion of a wealthy merchant from Barcelona who accompanied Jaume I of Aragon on the crusade which wrested Majorca from the Muslims in the years 1229–32, was apparently born on the island in 1232. *Blanquerna*, the

ospedaliera monzese dei secoli XII–XIV" (pp. 127–44), Maria Grazia Cesana, "Uomini e donne nelle comunità ospedaliere di Como del Duecento" (pp. 145–60), and Gian Maria Varanini, "Uomini e donne in ospedali e monasteri del territorio trentino, secoli XII–XIV" (pp. 259–300), in *Uomini e donne in comunità*, ed. Giuseppina De Sandre Gasparini, Grado G. Merlo, and Antonio Rigon, Quaderni di storia religiosa, 1 (Verona, 1994).

[8] James W. Brodman, "The Origins of Hospitallerism in Medieval Catalonia," in *Iberia and the Mediterranean World of the Middle Ages: Studies in Honor of Robert I. Burns, S.J.*, vol. I: *Proceedings from Kalamazoo*, ed. Larry J. Simon (Leiden: E.J. Brill, 1995), 290–302.

[9] See Gabriel Llompart Moragues, "La población hospitalaria y religiosa de Mallorca bajo el rey Sancho (1311–1324)," *Cuadernos de Historia Jerónimo Zurita*, 33–34 (1979), 67–98, esp. 68–75; Pablo Cateura, *Sobre la fundación y dotación del Hospital de San Andrés en la ciudad de Mallorca por Nuñp Sans* (Palma de Mallorca, 1980), 29 pp.; Alvaro Santamaría, "La Asistencia a los pobres en Mallorca en el bajomedievo," *Anuario de estudios medievales*, 13 (1983), 381–406; and José María Tejerina, "La medicina medieval en Mallorca," in *Historia de Mallorca*, ed. J. Mascaró Pasarius (Palma de Mallorca, 1978), 8:278–432, esp. 289–306.

[10] There are several Catalan editions; I quote from the modern English translation of the 1920s by E. Allison Peers (London: Jarrolds, n.d.). For studies on *Blanquerna* see the extensive bibliography in Roberto J. González-Casanovas, *The Apostolic Hero and Community in Ramon Llull's Blanquerna: A Literary Study of a Medieval Utopia* (New York: Peter Lang, 1995), 129–53. González-Casanovas, describing *Blanquerna* as a "hybrid genre of hagiographic fiction and novel-sermon," generally follows scholars such as Martí de Riquer in emphasizing ideal and utopian elements in the text. In contrast, however, compare Antoni Carbonell, Anton M. Espadaler, Jordi Llovet and Antònia Tayadella, *Literatura catalana: Dels inicis als nostres dies* (Barcelona: Edhasa, 1979), 52: "De tots els llibres de Ramón Llull, és el que reflecteix amb més detalls i precisió fidedigna els ambients de la societat de l'época"; and Eamonn Rodgers, "The Realism of Ramón Llull's *Blanquerna*," in *Hispanic Studies in Honour of Geoffrey Ribbans*, ed. Ann L. Mackenzie and Dorothy S. Severin (Liverpool: Liverpool University Press, 1992), 37–41.

most famous and one of the earliest of Llull's more than three hundred
Catalan and Latin works of polemic, disputation, apologetic, logic,
philosophy, science, mysticism, poetry and fiction, was written in 1283
in Montpellier, then one of the mainland southern French holdings
of the Crown of Majorca.[11] The first book of Blanquerna concerns
the protagonist's parents—the full title of the entire work is, in fact,
the *Libre d'Evast e d'Aloma e de Blanquerna*—and is devoted to the topic
of matrimony; subsequent books address broadly religion, prelacy,
the apostolic estate, and the life of the hermit and art of contemplation.
The narrative opens with the marriage of Evast, "a goodly youth, of
right noble lineage, the son of a gentle burgess [who] became through
the death of his father very wealthy in temporal riches," and Aloma,
a "damsel [who] ruled and directed all her [widowed] mother's house."
In character, Aloma is described as "right virtuous," as her mother
had kept her busy lest "foolish and evil thoughts should enter her
mind through overmuch leisure and incline her to base deeds." There
was not only prayer and devotion on the day of their wedding mass,
but "a great feast for the poor of Jesus Christ, who praise and bless
God when alms are given to them."

Through these poor Jesus Christ is represented at weddings and
such wealthy men turned away "as bear not in mind the Passion of
the Son of God, wasting and squandering those temporal goods which
the poor sorely need, and spending them in the service of men full
of worldly vanity, like unto themselves." On the day of their wedding
Evast and Aloma, "in remembrance of the humility of our Lord Jesus
Christ," washed and kissed the hands and feet of thirteen poor men,
and provided them with new garments. It was "proclaimed throughout
the city that every poor man who desired to receive alms for the
love of God should come to that wedding feast." The couple dined
at the table of the thirteen poor men, and the "kinsfolk and the
friends of Evast and Aloma likewise served the poor of Jesus Christ."[12]

---

[11] It is only accurate to say this of *Blanquerna* because it contains as book VI the
Libre d'amic e amat (*Book of the Lover and Beloved*), by far the most widely circulated and
often printed, translated, and anthologized of Llull's works. For a listing of Llull's
many works see "A Chronological Catalogue of Ramon Llull's Works," in *Selected
Works of Ramon Llull*, trans. and ed. Anthony Bonner, 2 vols. (Princeton: Princeton
University Press, 1985), 1257–1304. For a more general orientation to some of Llull's
work see Mark D. Johnston, *The Evangelical Rhetoric of Ramon Llull: Lay Learning and
Piety in the Christian West around 1300* (New York: Oxford University Press, 1996).

[12] All of the above is found in Book I, chapter i, the latter quotations from para-
graphs 8 and 9.

The two of them lived in charity, patience, and humility, and they produced a son, Blanquerna, who enjoyed a pious and idyllic childhood. Approaching adulthood, Blanquerna resists the temptation of a local maiden Natana, becomes enamored of the hermit's life, and departs from his home "to contemplate God in the rustic places and in regions uninhabited by man."[13] His parents then devise a very detailed rule for their lives which commends all their goods to a "faithful religious lay brother" for distribution to Christ's poor, money enough for their necessary expenses alone to be kept for their own private use.

Evast and Aloma encounter difficulties in finding a friar to whom they could commend their property. They resist the idea of "kinfolk [who] are wont to have overmuch pleasure in possessions commended to them, and think and plan how they may be made the heirs," settling eventually on "a monk who was a priest, an old man of good life and a native of other parts." It was soon after that Evast fell deathly ill, and proceeded to draw up a last testament, seeking his wife's counsel. "Among the things that men do in this world for the love of God," Evast announces to his wife, "it is worthy of praise to give alms in perpetuity to the poor of Christ; consequently, I wish to leave all my possessions for the building and endowment of a hospital where the poor and destitute may be tended, and I would that thou aid in the administration of this hospital and in the service of the poor, to the end that by thy merits God may have mercy upon me a sinner and continue His blessing upon thee and upon Blanquerna." The hospital's chaplain and administrator is to be the administrator of their goods, and after his death "some other religious man" is to be placed in charge of the hospital. Aloma gives her approval to this plan, and Evast makes his testament, commending the hospital to the care and protection of the prince of the land, the bishop, and important men of the city. He makes humble provisions for his burial, receives the sacraments, and sleeps until, "by the virtue of God and the merits of Aloma and Blanquerna, who prayed to God for him daily, God restored to him his health."

A few days later, while searching for a letter in his trunk, Evast chances upon his last will. Marvelling at "the good which would have been done to the poor of Christ had I passed from this life,"

---

[13] Chapter ii details Blanquerna's birth and education, iii concerns Evast's desire to pursue the religious live, vi Natana, and viii Blanquerna's farewell.

Evast tells Aloma that merely "because God has been pleased to lengthen my life it is not just that injury should result to those who beg for love of Him," and they resolve to execute the testament's provisions immediately.[14]

Evast proceeds promptly to sell his house and build a hospital "in the most convenient part of the city." They live as servants of the poor of Jesus Christ in the hospital, Evast making "the sick men who lay in the hospital his care, and Aloma the women." After they had tended to the needs of the sick the couple would dine together, not on food which belonged to the hospital but on food which they had "begged for the love of God." Through the merits of their worthy lives God "heard the prayers of many sinners in that city, and healed many sick folk in the hospital."[15]

Evast and Alomas's actions prompted such remorse of conscience in those people who encountered them that they "mortified in sinners the seven deadly sins." In the succeeding chapters which cover gluttony, lust, covetousness, pride, sloth, envy, wrath, and vainglory—eight deadly sins according to my reckoning, though the walls separating pride from vainglory and covetousness from envy are porous ones—Evast and Aloma accomplish marvelous works, and the historian catches a greater glimpse of their ideal hospital.[16]

By their example the bishop of the city turns from gluttony to moderation, two couples mismatched by age but attracted by lust—the young for money, the old for carnal pleasure—grow to love chastity and religion, and a money-changer jettisons the "bondage of avarice" to become a "generous and liberal friend to the poor of Christ." A draper who had suffered from such pride and haughtiness that he sought "to give his daughter to a man of greater honour than befitted her" frees himself, as a result of the great humility shown by Evast among the poor tarrying at the draper's house for alms, from the "bondage of pride," and gives his daughter in marriage to another draper.

In the chapter on sloth, we see "two women whom Evast and Aloma had dowered," and we are told the cautionary tale of a man so slothful that "he had no wife, nor was fain to have, and whose possessions were a profit neither to himself nor to anyone

---

[14] All of this is in chapter ix.
[15] Chapter x.
[16] Chapters xi–xviii, which concludes Book I.

else." The man encounters Evast and Aloma's hospital where there were "many poor, and many servants who served them with great diligence; each one of the poor therein lay in the fairest of beds, with as much food before him as he needed." Conscience-stricken, the man realized that all the alms he had given in his life were not "in value as great as the food which the sick folk in the hospital had before them on that day." Becoming ill the man takes himself to the end of one of the rooms where he found "two beds that were made but of branches of the vine, together with a small quantity of straw, and one covering only." Evast returns to encounter the man in his bed, and to pray with him, later leading him before the altar of Sant Andreu, where the man offers "himself in person, and with all of his possessions, to be for all time a servant of the hospital."

In the chapter on envy a wealthy man covetous of the great house which Evast and Aloma sold to build their hospital is led to donate his own house to the hospital. In the chapter on wrath "a sick man who suffered from an ulcer in the leg and could not be cured" is in Evast's hospital "constrained by illness," and cursing God and most anyone close at hand. Evast, "together with the physician, tended his leg," applying powder and dressing the sore, while admonishing him to suffer and endure patiently which results in the man's "beseeching pardon of God and rejoicing in His mercy." A vainglorious friar is humbled, in the final chapter of Book I of *Blanquerna*, by the realization that Evast and Aloma's example nets a larger spiritual catch than his hortatory preaching. The story of Evast and Aloma ends with God removing them "from the perils and misery of this world."

Llull's *Blanquerna* is as valuable for its prosaic details as for its evocation of thirteenth-century ideals; it is a fascinating read, and it most certainly is not improved in the partial retelling here of the first of its five to seven, depending upon one's edition, books. The transition, however, from the graphic language of Llull's entertaining novel to the brief, formalized expressions of public piety and concern for the poor contained in our limited documentary record is an abrupt one. No Majorcan documents or histories, at least for the thirteenth century, relate the piety of analogous though real-life Evasts and Alomas. Only one foundational charter or reasonable facsimile thereof apparently survives for any of Majorca's thirteenth-century hospitals. This document, edited and studied by Pablo Cateura, details the endowment on January 16, 1234 of a "hospital of the

poor of Santa Eulàlia of Majorca."[17] It was issued by Nunyo Sanç,
lord of Roussillon and Cerdagne, a leading noble who participated
on the Majorcan crusade, and played a major role in the land
repartiment following the conquest. Nunyo received property not only
in Majorca City but extensive lands around Bunyola and Valldemossa,
and he later participated with Guillem de Montgrí, sacristan of Girona
cathedral and archbishop-elect of Tarragona, in the conquest of Ibiza
in 1235. The hospital's endowment was to include half of a *rahal*
next to the city, the *alqueria* or farm hamlet of Santa Eulàlia in the
city's *terminus*, a *rahal* identified as being between one belonging to
the bishop of Barcelona and one belonging to Bernat d'Olzet, ten
jovates of land near Manacor in the island's interior, and the land
and houses of the hospital itself, as well as 100 cows and 100 goats,
four suckling pigs, and four pairs of oxen. The rector of the hospital
is identified by name, the hospital is to be limited to twenty beds,
and the bishop of Majorca retains powers of oversight.

There are no stray account books or chartularies extant, or at
least of which I am aware, from any of Majorca's hospitals until well
into the fourteenth century, and no run of even terse and legalistic
notarial documents apparently survives from hospital archives for the
thirteenth century, though a few scattered references have come to
light. In 1243, for example, Fray Berenguer de Cervera, identified as
the commander of the Hospital of San Andreu, purchased for sixty
Melgorian sous a baptized slave Jaume from Garcia Ferrer and his
wife Raimunda. Berenguer subsequently sold, with the slave's consent,
half of the legal right to Jaume, to a Ramon de Costogia, for the
same sixty Melgorian sous.[18]

The historian of Majorca's thirteenth-century hospitals must rely on
the paltry and fragmentary data contained in wills to reconstruct even
a limited history of these institutions. There is, fortunately, valuable
evidence to be gleaned from these wills: Majorcan testators evidenced a
high degree of concern for the poor and various categories of the poor,
and from the surviving legacies one can show that hospitals were an

---

[17] Cateura, *Sobre la fundación y dotación*, gives full details on pp. 16–23 and edits
the charter on pp. 24–25; the documentary appendix includes two other documents
of 1375 and 1376.
[18] Palma, Arxiu del Regne de Mallorca [hereafter ARM], Reial Patrimoni,
Escrivania de Cartes Reials 342, fols. 167 and 167v. For a study of the whole
question concerning Majorcan church ownership of and attitudes toward slaves, see
Larry J. Simon, "The Church and Slavery in Ramon Llull's Majorca," in *Iberia and
the Mediterranean World*, pp. 345–363.

important urban presence from early in the thirteenth century.

One of the first Majorcan testaments, that of Jaume de Muell in 1233, containes no *pro anima* bequests, but Guillema, wife of a Guillem whose surname is illegible, includes several significant legacies in her will dated 12 September 1234. Among them are ten sous for the ransoming of captives, ten sous for the hospital of Santa Eulàlia, and fifty Melgorian sous for the hospital of Santa Maria Magdalena.[19] This is less than five years from the date Majorca City was conquered by Christian crusaders. The hospital of Santa Eulàlia is the hospital endowed by Nunyo Sanç, and apparently took its initial name from the church whose parish it was in or from the *alqueria* near Majorca City which provided it with a major source of its income; sometime in the 1240s it ceased to be referred to as Santa Eulàlia, but, rather, was known as Sant Andreu, the name of a chapel in the hospital and, appropriately enough, the name of the altar in Llull's fictional hospital as well. It successfully attracted other legacies. Ramon Desvilar, in his will dated 29 December 1237, left three sous to the Franciscans, ten sous for the ransoming of captives, three sous to the hospital of Sant Antoni, and two sous each to the hospitals of Santa Maria Magdalena and Santa Eulàlia.[20]

The testament of Sanxa Teobalda illustrates well the degree to which Majorcans supported their hospitals. Sanxa made few *pro anima* bequests beyond a substantial one to her parish church, Santa Maria de Valldemossa, where she desires to be buried. She made, however, donations of two sous each to the hospitals of Sant Andreu, Santa Maria Magdalena, and Sant Antoni.[21] It is noteworthy that Sanxa was a resident of Majorca's rural mountainous region, yet still left legacies to these urban hospitals. Arnau de Sala, obviously a resident of Majorca City, makes his will in August of 1240. He leaves three sous each to the cathedral, the Franciscans, and the Dominicans, as well as ten sous to the parish church of Santa Eulàia, where he wishes to be buried. Arnau leaves two sous each to the hospitals of Santa Maria Magdalena and Sant Antoni, and eight sous, a substantial sum when compared to his other bequests, to the hospital of Sant

---

[19] Madrid, Archivo Histórico Nacional [hereafter AHN], Clero, pergs. carp. 76, no. 15: "Item dimito hospitali Sancte Eulalie X solidos predicte monete. Dimito etiam hospitali Sancte Marie Magdalene L solidos malgorienses. Item dimito ad redempcionum captiuorum X solidos predicte monete."

[20] Palma, Arxiu de la Catedral de Mallorca [hereafter ACM], pergs., Miralles 7766.

[21] ARM, pergs., reial patrimoni, s. XIII, no. 53.

Andreu. He also leaves three sous, though precisely to whom is not
clear, for the ransoming of captives.

The will of Genís de Reus informs us that by 1256 there were not
only the three main hospitals in Majorca City, but one in the city of
Inca as well, in the center of the island. In addition to the twelve
sous which he leaves the four hospitals, Genís also leaves three sous
to the Mercedarians, two hundred sous for the clothing of the poor,
and four hundred sous for the dowering of orphaned girls.[22] Martí
de Frau's bequests in 1252 are a little more modest; in addition to
legacies for several rural parishes and for the cathedral, Franciscans
and Dominicans, Martí leaves two sous to the convent of Santa
Margarida, a total of thirteen sous to the "three hospitals of Majorca,"
and twelve diners for "captives."[23] Bernat de Fàbrega makes similar
bequests in 1260. Bernat leaves five sous each to the Franciscans and
the Dominicans, and two sous to the cathedral, the sisters of Santa
Margarida, and to the Poor Clares, founded in Majorca City in the
mid-1250s. He bequeaths two sous to each of the hospitals of the
poor in Majorca City, and he arranges for six paupers to be clothed
at his expense.[24] The very wealthy Pere Serra leaves many legacies
in 1270, including five sous to the "house of the captives," by which
I assume is understood the Mercedarians, fifty sous to the "ashamed
poor," and one hundred sous for the dowering of poor girls.[25]

Jaume Geniz in 1282 leaves three sous to each of the hospitals of
Majorca City and Inca, and three sous for the maintenance of the
chapel of Sant Bartomeu at the Inca hospital.[26] Jaume is a wealthy
man, but many of his bequests are modest; he leaves, for example,
only twelve diners to the Mercedarians. Guillem Cadireta in 1279
leaves five sous each to the three hospitals of the poor of Majorca
City, and two sous each to the Mercedarians and to the Barcelona
order of Sant Sepulcre.[27]

---

[22] ARM, pergs., reial patrimoni, s. XIII, no. 115 (5 December 1256): "Item dimitto
unicuique hospitalium pauperum mayoricaium et dincha iii solidos. Item dimito
fratribus de mercede captiuis redimendis iii solidos."

[23] ARM, pergs., reial patrimoni, s. XIII, no. 105 (13 August 1252).

[24] ARM, pergs., reial patrimoni, s. XIII, no. 126: "et unicuique hospitalium
pauperum civitatis maiorice et Sancte Clare et Sancte Margarite cuique ii solidos"
and "item dimito ad sex pauperes induendos. . . ."

[25] ARM, pergs., reial patrimoni, s. XIII, no. 163 (15 May 1270).

[26] ARM, pergs., reial patrimoni, s. XIII, no. 217 (1 May 1282): "Item hospitali
de Incha tres solidos. Item operi capelle Sancti Bartholomei eiusdem loci tres solidos.
Item unicuique hospitalium pauperum ciuitatis maiorice tres solidos."

[27] ACM, pergs., Miralles 7967 (21 August 1279): "Item dimitto unicuique trium

Almost all residents of Majorca City made bequests to the hospitals of the poor, and a surprising number of rural and village residents did so as well. The hospital of Sant Andreu was the most prominent among these hospitals, and like Evast's hospital was built in "the most convenient part of the city." It sat on the same site where today the *ajuntament*, or municipal government, is located: in the upper part of the old city, close to both the cathedral and Santa Eulàlia. The hospital of Sant Antoni Abad was, according to later choniclers, founded by Jaume I soon after the conquest in 1230; located in the street of Sant Miquel, north of Sant Andreu, it was run by Augustinian canons. The hospital of Santa Maria Magdalena was situated near the parish church of Sant Jaume, and close to the site of a later nunnery by the same name; its initial endowment may have come from Pons Huc, count of Empúries. All three institutions are mentioned by name in a papal bull of Innocent IV in 1248 which enumerated the parishes of Majorca's diocese. José Tejerina makes reference to a hospital of Sant Esperit dels Rossos, specializing in abandoned children and run by Trinitarians. It was apparently founded in the parish of Sant Jaume but immediately moved to a location in the parish of Sant Miquel; the first charitable bequest Llompart could find for it was in the will of A. Ricolf in 1282.[28]

Among various pious causes which could be classified as poor relief the ransoming of captives figures prominently in these Majorcan wills. Even the poorest of testators usually left twelve diners for "captives to be ransomed," and the Mercedarians had both a house and an attached church in Majorca. The reverse side of ransoming captives was the freeing of one's own slaves, and several Majorcan testators freed their slaves, usually baptized ones. On August 18, 1267, for example, Pere Calafat, a resident of Valldemossa, who wishes to be buried at the church of Santa Maria of Valldemossa, declares his last will. He frees both his slave Pere "the baptized," and Pere's sister Romia "the baptized," further leaving Pere ten and Romia twenty sous.[29] In addition to the Mercedarians, both the Templars, who accompanied the crusaders in 1229 and received extensive lands,

hospitalium pauperum ciuitatus maiorice quinque solidos et domui captiuorum et Sancto Sepulcri unicuique duos solidos."

[28] Tejerina, "Medicina Medieval," 300; and Llompart, "Población Hospitalaria y Religiosa," 71.

[29] *Diplomatari del Monestir de Santa Maria de La Real*, I: 1232–1360, ed. Pau Mora and Lorenzo Andrinal (Palma de Mallorca: Impremta Monàstica, 1982), no. 84.

and the Hospitallers, who arrived soon after the initial success of the crusade, receive legacies in these wills. Pere Ortiz, for example, donates two sous to each of Majorca's hospitals, five sous to the church of Santa Eulàlia, and five sous to the "work and church" of the Hospital of Sant Joan.[30]

A few Majorcans were clearly more troubled by the poor than were their fellow citizens. Dulcia Trobat in 1248 makes *pro anima* bequests totalling no more than three hundred sous, yet twenty of these are designated for the clothing of the poor and another twenty for the "ashamed poor."[31] Some, like the wealthy Domingo de Rubió, could afford to give as much as one hundred sous for the clothing of the poor.[32] Likewise the knight Ramon de Valle Leprivi left fifty sous to clothe the poor, fifteen sous for the ransoming of captives, and various other bequests to Majorca's hospitals.[33] In keeping with his station in life, Ramon also makes substantial bequests to both the Templars and the Hospitallers. Other Majorcans, like Berenguera widow of Pere Ponç, make their bequests conditional; if her legitimate testamentary heir dies, then she institutes the poor of Christ.[34]

The largest amounts donated to the poor are probably those to which we cannot attach a figure. Valença, wife of Pere Gerard, designates the residue of her *pro anima* bequests to go for the dowering of poor girls, the ransoming of captives, and the clothing of Christ's poor.[35] The previously mentioned Pere Calafat leaves the remaining approximately eighty or ninety sous of the six hundred he sets aside *pro anima* for his tomb with the rest of the remainder "to be given to the poor of Christ for the salvation of my soul."[36] Ramon Albert leaves ten sous for the poor of Christ and likewise leaves a residue of one hundred sous to be divided among masses for his soul and alms for the poor of Jesus Christ.[37]

The most generous donors to poor relief were canons of the cathedral and rectors of the city's parishes, most of whom had handsome

---

[30] AHN, Clero, pergs., carp. 79, no. 6: "et unicuique hospitali maiorice ii solidos, et operi Sancte Eulalie quinque solidos, operi et ecclesie hospitali Sancti Johannis v solidos."

[31] ACM, pergs., Miralles 7822 (24 April 1248): "Dimitto ad pauperes induendos viginti solidorum. . . . Dimitto pauperibus verecundantibus viginti solidorum."

[32] ARM, pergs., audiencia, s. XIII, no. 29 (26 November 1259).

[33] ACM, pergs., Miralles 7834 (30 November 1249).

[34] ARM, pergs., reial patrimoni, s. XIII, no. 228 (6 October 1285?).

[35] *Diplomatari*, no. XX (11 February 1281).

[36] *Diplomatari*, no. 84 (18 August 1267).

[37] ACM, pergs., Miralles 7995.

incomes and either no children to be recognized, or which they cared to recognize. Several of them, such as Ponç de Puigserver and Guillem Graciós, instituted the poor of Jesus Christ as their main testamentary heirs.[38] An analysis of these wills indicates that this was not merely social convention, but that substantial sums of money were being donated. Social convention of course had its role to play in thirteenth-century Majorcan poor relief. However repulsive the prosperous and upright may have personally found the sick and indigent, they were seldom loathe to provide for them in their last wills and testaments.

The ubiquity of testamentary donations is not only notable for what it reveals of pious convention, but was of great and immediate social significance. John Mundy has demonstrated that the hospitals at Toulouse were dependent upon testamentary bequests for their operation, and that the profusion of thirteenth century hospitals was a product of changes in testamentary provisions—a recognition of a testator's desire in Paul Freedman's memorable phrase, to "diversify one's intercessory portfolio."[39] The documentary record of the thirteenth century may not offer any likely candidates for real-life Evasts and Alomas, but two hospitals of the fourteenth century and one of the fifteenth century were specifically endowed by testamentary bequest. In his will of 1343 the merchant Ramon Salellas gave more than 4,000 royal Majorcan pounds to endow Santa Caterina dels Pobres, the first Majorcan hospital specifically devoted to serving the poor.[40] In 1377 Sayt Mili, a Majorcan Jew, set aside 300 pounds in his will for the foundation of a hospital in the Jewish *call*, the sacking of which fourteen years later resulted in the murder of several hundred Jews.[41] In 1475 Antoni Lana founded a hospital, situated in the

---

[38] Puigserver's will is located in ACM, pergs., Miralles 7961 (12 August 1278), and Graciós's will is in ACM, pergs., Miralles 7966 (27 March 1279). One canon who did acknowledge offspring was a Mestre Joan, described as a Provost of the Majorcan see; he freed two female baptized slaves, and left to Bernat de Vinero, his "natural" son, the *alqueria* of Porreres with all of its vineyards and moveable and immoveable property, including an unspecified number of male and female Muslim slaves. See ARM, Reial Patrimoni, Escrivania de Cartes Reials 348, fols. 346–349v. (April 26, 1276).

[39] See John H. Mundy, "Charity and Social Work in Toulouse, 1100–1250," *Traditio*, 22 (1966), 203–87; and Freedman, *The Diocese of Vic: Tradition and Regeneration in Medieval Catalonia* (New Brunswick, New Jersey: Rutgers University Press, 1983), 60.

[40] See Santamaría, "Pobres en Mallorca," 386–87; and E.K. Aguiló, "Fundació i documents relatius a l'hospital de santa Catarina dels pobres," *Bolletí de la Societat Arqueològica Lulliana* [hereafter *BSAL*], 10 (1903–1904), 365–88.

[41] Santamaría, "Pobres en Mallorca," 387, where he unfortunately has the date wrongly listed as 1387; and E.K. Aguiló, "Testament de Sayt Mili, jueu, fundador

neighborhood of the Almudaina in Majorca City, by the name of Sant Pere and Sant Bernat for poor priests.[42]

To return by way of conclusion to Ramon Llull, it is interesting and instructive to see how hospitals and poor relief made out in the testamentary provisions of Majorca's most famous citizen. Was the portrait of piety and charity idealized in Llull's *Blanquerna* translated into reality in Ramon's own will, dated 26 April 1313? The document containing Llull's will has never in modern times been housed in public or ecclesiastical archives, and its present location is unknown. Francesc de Bofarull studied the testament in 1896, and his study contained a transcription, and, more importantly, a photograph of the orginal document.[43] This photograph is usually missing when one orders the volume via interlibrary loan service, but the editors of a magnificent *Diplomatari* for the Cistercian monastery of Santa Maria de La Real have produced a new and accurate transcription based on that photograph.

Llull begins his last testament by proclaiming himself healthy—he was perhaps eighty-one years of age at the time of its writing—and by appointing his son-in-law Pere de Sant Menat, Guillem Arnau d'Església, Francesc Renovart, and Jaume de Aies as executors, leaving each of them a bequest of twenty sous for their labors. Llull gives as their legal inheritance twenty sous each to his son Domènec and daughter Magdalena, wife of Pere de Sant Menat. Lull then bequeaths ten sous each to the Dominicans, Franciscans, Poor Clares, Sisters of Santa Margarida, Sisters of Penitence, and to orphaned students. He leaves five sous to each of the parish churches of Majorca City; by this time there were five of them, Sant Nicolau in the center of the city having been added to the original four urban parishes. Llull also leaves ten sous to the See of Majorca.[44]

---

d'un hospital en el call de Mallorca," *BSAL*, 9 (1901–1902), 203–4. For a recent study of Jewish wills drafted by Christian notaries, see Robert I. Burns, S.J., *Jews in the Notarial Culture: Latinate Wills in Mediterranean Spain, 1250–1350* (Berkeley and Los Angeles: University of California Press, 1996).

[42] Santamaría, "Pobres en Mallorca," 387–88; and E.K. Aguiló, "Testament de Antoni Lana, fundador del hospital de preveres de sant Pere y sant Bernat," *BSAL*, 7 (1897–1898), 201–5.

[43] See F. de Bofarull y Sans, "El testamento de R. Lull y la escuela luliana en Barcelona," *Memorias de la Real Academia de Buenas Letras de Barcelona*, 5 (1896), 453–79.

[44] *Diplomatari*, p. 441: "In nomine Domini nostri Dei Iesu Christi qui solita pietate neminem uult perire immo saluat sperantes in se ac perducit ad gaudia paradisi. Ego magister Raimundus Lulli sanitate perfruens corporali meo pleno sensu [atque

Llull declares that he has deposited 140 pounds and two sous in the coin of Majorca with his executor Francesc Renovart. After Llull's death and the paying of legacies and debts, Llull wants all of his remaining money to go towards copying a number of his many works, which he specifies by name, into new books made of parchment. One copy is to be sent by his executors to Paris to the monastery of Chartreuse; another copy is to be sent to Genoa to Master Perceval Spinola.[45] From the remaining funds, books are to be made and sent by his executors to whatever religious house, church, or other location they deem appropriate. Llull then leaves his trunk, which would normally have been filled with clothing but in Llull's case contained books, to the Cistercian monastery of Santa Maria de La Real; he identifies the trunk as being located in the hospice of Pere de Sant Menat. The standard formulae of ratification close the will; Llull

memoria] in[tegra] cum firma loquela meum facio et ordino testamentum. In quo eligo manumissores meos videlicet Petrum de Sancto Minato generum meum, Guillemum Arnaldi de Ecclesis, Franciscum Renouardi et Iacobum de Aies. Quibus rogando supplico ac plenam confero potestatem quod si me contigerit mori antequam aliud michi liceat condere testamentum ipsi omnes, seu illi qui presentes fuerint de eisdem, diuidant et distribuant omnia bona mea prout in hoc meo testamento scriptum inuenerint ac etiam ordinatum tamen sine dampno eorum et rerum suarum. In primis quidem dimito cuilibet predictorum manumissorum meorum viginti solidos regalium Maioricenses minutorum pro eorum labore huius manumissorie. Item dimito Dominico Lulli filio meo et domine Magdalene filie mee vxori dicti Petri de Sancto Minato, utrique ipsorum, viginti solidos in quibus et in eo quod eis et cuilibet ipsorum dedi ipsos filium meum et filiam meam michi heredes instituo. Item dimito fratribus Predicatoribus et fratribus Minoribus et dominabus Sancte Clare et dominabus Sancte Margarite et dominabus de Penitentia et scolaribus orfanis, cuilibet istorum locorum, decem solidos. Item dimito operi cuiuslibet istorum locorum, decem solidos. Item dimito operi cuiuslibet ecclesiarum parrochialium Ciuitatis Maioricarum quinque solidos. Et operi Beate Marie Sedis Maioricarum decem solidos."

[45] Ibid., pp. 441–442: "Item recognosco in ueritate quod predictus Franciscus Renouardi tenet in [sua ta]bula campsorie in mei deposito et comenda centum quadraginta libras et duos solidos regalium Maioricenses minutorum, quas pro me et nomine meo habuit et recepit de bonis meis usque in hunc presentem diem, de quibus quidem predictis centum quadraginta libris et duobus solidis et etiam de omnibus aliis denariis quos habebo tempore obitus mei solutis inde prius legatis predictis volo et mando quod fiant inde et scribantur libri in pergameno in romancio et latino ex illis libris quos diuina fauente gratia nouiter compilaui, videlicet, De vitiis et virtutibus et De [n]ouo modo demostrationis et De quinque principiis et De differentia correlatiuorum et De secretis Sacratissime Trinitatis et incarnationis et De participatione christianorum et sarracenorum et De loqutione angelorum et De virtute veniali et vitali et De peccatis venialibus et mortalibus et De arte abreuiata sermonitandi. Sermones autem ibi scripti quos perfeci et compilaui sunt in summa centum octuaginta duo. Item est ibi liber De sex sillogismis. De quibus quidem libris omnibus supradictis mando fieri in pergameno, in latino, vnum librum in vno volumine qui mitatur per dictos manumissores meos Parisius ad monasterium de Xartossa, quem librum ibi dimito amore Dei. Item mando fieri de omnibus supradictis

himself signs it, referring to himself as magister; seven individuals witness it; and the Majorcan notary Jaume Avignon writes and closes the document in the office of A. de Sant Martí.[46]

Llull's strong ties to his son-in-law are striking. So, too, is the degree to which Llull appears to place the importance of furthering his life's work over and above the passing on of acccumulated wealth to his son and daughter. Parents were not at liberty to disinherit children, and Llull does remember Domènec and Magdalena. It is also possible that Llull had endowed his children through donations *inter vivos* long before filing his last testament, for wills represent only one stage of a larger inheritance process. Llull's children were of course well into adulthood, and they possibly had children or even grandchildren of their own. None of this is apparent, however, from Llull's last will. Also missing from Llull's testament is any effort consonant with the ideal presented in *Blanquerna* of serving or giving to the poor; hospitals, for instance, are strikingly absent.[47] Michel Mollat cited

---

libris vnum alium librum in vno [vo]lumine in pergameno scriptum, in latino, quem dimito et mando miti apud Ianuam misser Persiual Espinola."

[46] Ibid., p. 442: "Et residuum predicte [totius] peccunie mee et residuos alios libros qui fient per dictos manumissores meos de mea peccunia supradicta, dimito et mando dari ac distribui per eosdem manumissores meos ad eorum notitiam amore Dei pro anima mea et pro animabus omnium illorum quibus in aliquo iniurior quoquo modo et domibus ordinum et aliis locis, ita quod ponantur in armario cuiuslibet ecclesie in qua illos dabunt cum catena ita quod quilibet ipsius ecclesie volens illos legere possit ipsos legere et uidere. Item lego monasterio de Regali vnum coffre meum, cum libris qui ibi sunt, quen habeo in hospitio dicti Petri de Sancto Minato. In quibus quidem omnibus et singulis supradictis, que superius dimito et mando fieri atque dari, instituo michi heredes vniuersales Deum omnipotentem ob cuius amorem predicta facio et ordino et animam meam atque animas predecessorum et animas insuper omnium aliorum fidelium in plenam deliberationem nostrorum omnium peccatorum. Hec est autem ultima voluntas mea, q[uam] laudo et concedo ac uolo ualere iure testamenti mei et iure ultime voluntatis mee, que si non ualet uel ualere potest iure testamenti saltim ualeat ac ualere <uolo> iure testamenti mei et iure ultime voluntatis mee, que si non ualet uel ualere potest iure testamenti saltim ualeat ac ualere volo iure codicillorum aut alio quolibet iure ultime uoluntatis. Actum est hoc Maioricis sexto kalendas may anno Domini millesimo trecentesimo tertiodecimo. Sig+num magistri Raimundi Lulli testatoris predicti, qui hoc meum presens testamentum laudo, concedo et firmo. [Testes huius testamenti] sunt uocati et rogati [Berengarius Ianuarii], Guillemus Malleoli, [Guillemus Belhevim], Petrus Podioli, Fortunus Delso, Petrus de Podialibus et Petrus Jofre. Sig+num Iacobi Auinionis, notarii publici Maioricarum, qui hoc testamentum scripsit et clausit in scribania A. de Sanctomartino, connotarii sui, cum raso et emendato in linea .xvi. ubi dicitur lego."

[47] There is little justification for the cloying praise of E. Allison Peers, *Ramon Lull: A Biography* (London: Society for Promoting Christian Knowledge, 1929), 366: "Certainly Justice, Prudence and Charity [this is an allusion to Llull's *Tree of Love*] were among Llull's executors; and many, both rich and poor, must have been the better

Llull, along with the Dominican Taddeo Dini and the Barcelona Carmelite Bernat Puig, as one of several orthodox thinkers, as opposed to chiliastic heretics, who had realistic attitudes toward poverty and its consequences, and who appeared to advocate justice for the poor.[48] A study of Llull's references to poverty and the poor remains a desideratum; there are intriguing references elsewhere in *Blanquerna*, and several fascinating discourses in Llull's other major novel *Felix*.[49] Though Llull had labored energetically and enthusiastically for his philosophical system, the conversion of Muslims and Jews to Christianity, and various crusade projects until he was well into his eighties, he was still not satisfied and it was his Lullian "art" and his other lifelong projects, rather than concern for the poor, which took precedence in his testament. The final legacy of this peripatetic and restless propagandist was to ensure yet more copies of his written works and a wider audience for them; while the moralist, Christian or non-Christian, may wish to cast blame, who among scholars and students would possibly wish to cast the first stone?

---

for his dying as for his living." Peers does quote on the preceding page an interesting line from Llull's *Desconort* or *Desconhort*, completed while in Rome perhaps eighteen years earlier: ". . . Never did I see/ Or think on wealth or honour graspingly;/ And with the heritage that fell to me/ Ever have I been liberal and free:/ My very children are in poverty."

[48] See Mollat, *Poor in the Middle Ages*, 184–86, where "*Evast et Aloma*" and "*Blanquerna*" are cited as separate works.

[49] In Book III where Blanquerna becomes a bishop, the Canon of Tears weeps for women allegedly driven to prostitution by poverty; later, the Canon of Affliction runs through the city with a multitude of poor folk to the houses of wealthy men, crying "Hunger, hunger!" There is an English translation of *Felix* by Bonner in his *Selected Works of Ramon Llull*, 2:659–1105. In Book VIII, chapter 65, on "Charity and Cruelty," the hermit responds to Felix: "For lack of charity men prefer white bread, good wine, money, clothes, women, children, cities, castles, and honors, to God. Through excess of cruelty people are disinherited, women become widows, and poor people die of hunger, thirst and cold while begging for alms for the love of God." Chapters 70 on "Generosity and Avarice," 72 on "Diligence and Accidie," 83 on "Wealthy and Poverty," 106 on "Alms," and, among others, 110 on "Buildings" all offer further insight into Lull's views.

ELVES IN THE PSALMS?[1]
THE EXPERIENCE OF EVIL FROM
A COSMIC PERSPECTIVE

Karen Louise Jolly

In 1952, J.H.G. Grattan and Charles Singer published an edition and translation of the eleventh-century medical text the *Lacnunga* with an extensive introduction to Anglo-Saxon ideas of healing, under the title *Anglo-Saxon Magic and Medicine*.[2] For the frontispiece, they reproduced a picture from the mid-twelfth-century *Eadwine* (or *Canterbury*) *Psalter* illustrating Psalm 37 (38): *Domine, ne in furore tuo arguas me* (*Lord, reprove me not in your wrath*). [See Fig. 1.][3] Grattan and Singer identified the portrait of spritely creatures plucking at the arrow-filled psalmist as a "diseased elf-ridden man" and noted that "there is confusion between [Christ's] arrows and elf-shot." More recently, M.L. Cameron in his 1993 book *Anglo-Saxon Medicine* cited this picture as an example of elfshot, an affliction found in Anglo-Saxon medical texts in which humans or animals suffer illness caused by invisible elves who have shot them with arrows.[4] If this attribution by Grattan/Singer and

---

[1] I am grateful to the University of North Carolina Press and its art designers, who inspired me to pursue this project by putting "clip-art" images of these so-called elves all over my book *Popular Religion in Late Saxon England: Elf-Charms in Context* (Chapel Hill: University of North Carolina Press, 1996); on pp. 137–38, I made a short excursus into this image and briefly suggested its problematic nature. My thanks to Carol Langner, slide curator and art historian in the University of Hawai'i Art department, for her encouragement and to Alison Sproston, Sub-Librarian at Trinity College Cambridge, and her excellent staff for their assistance. Special thanks also to two scholars, Phil Pulsiano and Timothy Graham, who willingly read drafts, made cogent suggestions, and corrected infelicities. Most of all, I offer thanks to Jeffrey Russell for inspiration. The more I read and reread his words, the more I realize the debt I owe him.

[2] *Lacnunga* (BL MS Harley 585, ca. 1050); J.H.G. Grattan and Charles Singer, *Anglo-Saxon Magic and Medicine* (London: Oxford University Press, 1952).

[3] *Eadwine Psalter* (Cambridge, Trinity College MS R. 17.1, fol. 66r); facsimile, M.R. James, *The Canterbury Psalter* (London: Percy Lund, Humphries, & Co. for Friends of Canterbury Cathedral, 1935). Psalm 37 is the Vulgate number, Psalm 38 the Hebrew. For simplicity, this essay refers to Psalm 37 throughout.

[4] Grattan and Singer, *Anglo-Saxon Magic*, frontispiece; M.L. Cameron, *Anglo-Saxon Medicine*, Cambridge Studies in Anglo-Saxon England 7 (Cambridge: Cambridge University Press, 1993), p. 142.

Cameron is correct, then the *Eadwine* Psalm 37 illustration is a rare picture of an elf, and the only representation of Anglo-Saxon elfshot affliction that we possess. The image would then be a unique portrait of these invisible, amoral creatures of Germanic and Scandinavian lore at a time when they were undergoing a Christian transformation into devils, a demonization process evident in Anglo-Saxon remedies for elf-afflictions.[5] The *Eadwine Psalter* would thus represent a fascinating portrait of this process of merging Germanic and Christian conceptions of spiritual agencies. However, a more likely explanation that this essay offers is that the later iconography of elves as delightfully mischievous little figures playing tricks on people has caused scholars such as Grattan and Singer to read an Anglo-Saxon elf into this picture of demonic affliction. Nonetheless, these demons, if not elves, present an intriguing view of human experience within an early medieval Christian cosmology.

The kind of problem presented by this image is not wholly resolvable, and yet a consideration of what this image represents, however ambiguous, may shed some light on the construction of early medieval world views. The elf-demon identification, while perhaps erroneous in this case, does raise the general issue of acculturation between Latin and non-Latin (i.e. "Germanic") traditions in Europe: the demonic creatures in the illustration are not found in the psalm itself but are embodiments of an interpretation of the psalm; and the way they are drawn reflects a specifically European understanding of the Christian concept of demons.[6] More than anything else, this is an illustration of the problem of evil in the Christian world view that highlights the inherent dualities of this belief system: the symbiotic relationship of body and soul in human experience, the dual perspectives from earth and heaven, the relationship of microcosm and macrocosm, and the literal and figurative modes of interpretation. The system of signs in this one psalm and its illustration reveals the complexities of Anglo-Saxon and Anglo-Norman views of life and humanity.

---

[5] See Jolly, *Popular Religion*, pp. 136, 142, 163–64.

[6] Germanic in a generic sense describes the non-Latin traditions of European peoples such as the Anglo-Saxons. Clearly Scandinavian traditions are related and Celtic influences play a role, however the term Germanic (or Teutonic) serves as a shorthand for the non-Roman cultural factors in medieval European history. The term Germanicization is a way of indicating the processes whereby non-Latin cultural factors of Europe transformed the Latin cultural heritage of western Europe.

The following analysis compares the illustration of Psalm 37 in the *Eadwine Psalter* (1155–60) to other illustrations of demons within the same manuscript, and to the manuscript's near relations, its source the *Utrecht Psalter* (816–835), the earlier *Harley Psalter* copy of *Utrecht* (1000–1025), and the later *Paris* copy of *Utrecht/Eadwine* (1170–1190).[7] Since the problem of evil is central to the text this picture illustrates, this analysis considers the variant versions of the Psalm (the Gallicanum, Romanum, and Hebraicum) and the relation of the text and glosses to the illustrations as a way of exploring the cosmology implicit in this picture. These comparisons demonstrate that the "demons" in the *Eadwine Psalter*'s Psalm 37 are different in character from the same picture in the *Utrecht, Harley,* and *Paris* manuscripts and that their difference is a deliberate change in interpretation on the part of the artist based on his reading of the text and glosses.

Demons in the Psalter?

Recent work on liturgical and quasi-liturgical manuscripts, particularly by Anglo-Saxonists, has made the study of these varied texts easier; however, considerably more work needs to be done on the purposes and uses of Psalters and other manuscripts produced in ecclesiastical and monastic scriptoria.[8] In particular, a full study of demon iconography in these manuscripts and of individual psalms would be fruitful, if only because the very presence of demons in the illustration when they are nonexistent in the literal text of the Psalms suggests an interpretive tradition rooted not only in the written glosses but also in early medieval iconography. Curiously, demons do not appear in Christian art before the sixth century, but their representations multiplied from the ninth century on, as Jeffrey Russell articulates so well.[9] This preliminary study, preparatory to a full-scale research project into the demon iconography of the *Eadwine*, suggests that, whatever one chooses to call these grinning creatures, they do represent

---

[7] See C.M. Kauffmann, *Romanesque Manuscripts 1066–1190* (London: Harvey Miller, 1975), no. 68 for a brief overview of the provenance of these manuscripts.

[8] *The Liturgical Books of Anglo-Saxon England*, ed. Richard W. Pfaff (Kalamazoo, MI: Medieval Institute, 1995), especially Phillip Pulsiano, "Psalters," pp. 61–85; M.J. Toswell, "Anglo-Saxon Psalter Manuscripts," *Old English Newsletter* 28.1 (Fall 1994), A23–A31.

[9] Jeffrey Russell, *Lucifer: The Devil in the Middle Ages* (Ithaca: Cornell University Press, 1984), pp. 129–133.

a conception of spiritual agency that is distinctly the product of a Germanic Christian cosmology. My argument is that the ambivalence of this image precisely captures the mood of the Saxon conversion process and early Anglo-Norman cultural adaptation in which Germanic folk custom and Christian belief intermingled. Specifically, this picture illustrates the problem of evil in medieval world views: it attempts to combine the cosmic view of divine causation with the experiential view of evil as caused by specific agents operating under God's oversight.

The Gallicanum version of Psalm 37 as rendered in the *Eadwine Psalter* (ff. 66r–68r) reads:[10]

1   P[salmus] d[aui]d in rememoratione diei sabb[at]i

2   Domine ne in furore tuo arguas me; neq[ue] in ira tua corripias me.

3   Quonia[m] sagittae tuae infixe sunt michi; et confirmasti sup[er] me manu[m] tuam.

4   Non est sanitas in carne mea a facie irae tuae; non est pax ossib[us] meis a facie peccatorum meorum

5   Quoniam iniquitates meae sup[er]gresse sunt caput meum; sicut onus grauae grauatae sunt sup[er] me

6   Putruerunt et corrupte sunt cicatrices meae; a facie insipientiae meae.

7   Miser factus sum et curuatus sum usq[ue] in finem; tota die contristatus sum ingrediebar.

8   Quoniam lumbi mei impleti sunt illusionib[us] et n[on] est sanitas in carne mea.

9   Afflictus sum et humiliatus su[m] nimis; rugiebam a gemitu cordis mei.

10 Domine ante te omne desiderium meum; et gemitus meus a te non est absconditus.

11 Cor meum conturbatum est dereliquit me uirtus mea; et lumen oculorum meorum et ipsum non est mecum.

---

[10] The Gallicanum is the main (large) text; the narrower Romanum column is glossed in Old English, while the Hebraicum column is glossed in Anglo-Norman. Verse numbers are those used in the Vulgate, which numbers the psalm attribution as verse 1; brackets mark expanded abbreviations and punctuation follows the manuscript. Parallel column view of the psalm is on the web at http://www2.hawaii.edu/~kjolly/ps37.htm. A color image of the illustration is on the main page (~kjolly). Edition of the Anglo-Saxon with Romanum: Fred Harsley, *Eadwine's Canterbury Psalter*, EETS o.s. 92 (London: N. Trübner, 1889).

12   Amici mei et p[ro]ximi mei; aduersum me app[ro]pinquauerunt
     et steterunt. Et qui iuxta me erant de longe steterunt;

13   et uim faciebant qui querebant animam mea[m]. Et qui inquirebant
     mala michi locuti sunt uanitates: et dolos tota die meditabantur.

14   Ego autem tanquam surdus non audiebam; et sicut mutus non
     ap[er]iens os suum.

15   Et factus sum sicut homo non audiens; et non habens in ore suo
     redargutiones.

16   Quonia[m] in te domine sp[er]aui: tu exaudies domine d[eu]s
     m[eu]s.

17   Quia dixi nequando sup[er]gaudeant michi inimici mei; et dum
     co[m]mouentur pedes mei sup[er] me magna locuti sunt.

18   Q [uonia]m ego in flagella paratus sum; et dolor meus in conspectu
     meo semp[er].

19   Q [uonia]m iniquitatem mea[m] annuntiabo; et cogitabo p[ro]
     peccato meo.

20   Inimici aute[m] mei uiuunt et confirmati s[un]t super me; et multi-
     plicati sunt qui oderunt me iniq[ue].

21   Qui retribuunt mala p[ro] bonis detrahebant michi; quoniam
     sequebar bonitatem.

22   Non derelinquas me domine. d[eu]s m[eu]s ne discesseris me.

23   Intende in adiutorium meum; domine deus salutis meae.

In the *Eadwine* illustration of this text (Fig. 1), the psalmist gazes
heavenward, looking to Christ who holds bow and arrows (verses 2–3).
The stooped and weary figure (verse 7) points to his head (verse 5)
or eyes (verse 11) to indicate his weakened physical state. Meanwhile
the psalmist's body is afflicted not only by arrows (verse 3) and sores
(verse 5), but also by winged figures whose appearance varies between
the Psalters from vaguely angelic to demonic and who are either
placing a burden on the back of the psalmist (verse 5) or besetting
him as illusions (verse 8). The psalmist's worldly friends, to the left,
abandon him (verse 12) and he also suffers from the ill will of evil
men portrayed on the right (verse 20). All of this experience of evil
is set in the context of a Christian cosmology dominated by a monotheistic deity presiding over the psalmist's fate (the ruling *Dominus* of
the psalm). The psalm itself is then an appeal that seeks to cross the
boundary of these two perspectives, a boundary represented by the
cloud-bordered heavenly realm impinging on the experiential world.
  How the psalmist's suffering as described in some of the verses in

Psalm 37 came to be interpreted as divine, demonic, or elfin in causation is a difficult puzzle to unravel, but says a great deal about both modern constructs of the medieval past and the development of European medieval theology. This essay deconstructs these layers of interpretation, beginning with the modern and moving back into the medieval. The first section examines the modern historiography of the illustration to locate the origins of the erroneous elf interpretation. The second, and longest, section carries out a textual and iconographic investigation of the *Eadwine* and related Psalter manuscripts by comparing the illustrations and analyzing the texts and glosses. The third section concludes with a discussion of the Christian beliefs represented in this interpretation of Psalm 37 and what they may mean for a twelfth-century Christian conception of body and soul in relationship to the experience of evil.

Historiography

The problematic modern interpretations of this illustration have their roots in the nineteenth century and its preoccupations with both a scientific approach to history and with the recovery of folklore. Combined, these two trends often sought to unravel the "origins" of the earliest Anglo-Saxon beliefs by stripping away the layers of post-conversion accretions.[11] The scientific approach often reflects a progressivist orientation in which magic gives way to superior religion, which itself is supplanted by the more rational thinking of science. These views persisted into the middle part of the twentieth century. History-as-science scholars, such as Grattan and Singer, endeavored to isolate the strands of popular legend, theology, and true medicinal science, privileging the more rational elements and judging any mixture of so-called magic and religion as "confusion." On the other hand, scholars coming from a primarily folklorist orientation, such as Wilfrid Bonser, or those studying the iconography of the manuscript illustrations, such as M.R. James or C.R. Dodwell, focused on the mixture of Germanic and Christian and the ease with which this transformation from pagan to Christian, from sprite to demon, took place, as well as the implicit logic of combining the two traditions. To the

---

[11] An error brilliantly exposed by E.G. Stanley in *The Search for Anglo-Saxon Paganism* (Cambridge: D.S. Brewer, 1975).

scientist historian, the *Eadwine* illustrator of Psalm 37 has a confused theology because he mixes magical elements with religion, sullying the more rational elements of Christian theology with the superstitions of Germanic lore. To the folklorist or art historian studying the *Eadwine* text, the illustrator is representing his own coherent reality in light of a complex set of theological traditions, however incoherent this representation may seem to later eyes.

These two strands of scholarship are evident in treatments of elf-affliction in the first half of the twentieth century. The folklorist Bonser, writing in 1926 and 1939, was quite happy to point out the convergence of Germanic and Christian traditions evident in the demonization of elves in Anglo-Saxon medicine.[12] While asserting that we can learn a great deal about paganism from studying Anglo-Saxon medical texts written down in Christian monasteries, he carefully acknowledges the self-conscious hegemony of the Christian view: elves become demons.[13] Godfrid Storms (1948), however, taking a more scientific approach, endeavored to unravel the intertwining strands of pagan and Christian, magic and medicine, to get at the origins of each.[14] This approach is fundamentally flawed because in combining various Germanic and Christian traditions the Anglo-Saxon authors/compilers effectively and permanently altered both traditions. The error of trying to glean "original" paganism from these texts by eliminating the Christian "layers" lies in the false metaphor: we are not dealing with layers, but complex constructions exhibiting a particularly Anglo-Saxon way of representing a Christian cosmology.

In this context of a scientific approach to the search for origins, it becomes clear why Grattan and Singer included the *Eadwine* Psalm 37 illustration as an example of elfshot. In their careful edition of the eleventh-century medical text *Lacnunga*, the authors employ scientific caution in second-guessing the medicinal identification of herbs in the remedies. In the section "Semantics of Anglo-Saxon Plant Names," they highlight the instability of Latin to Anglo-Saxon identifications and discount the possibility that the Anglo-Saxons knew all of the herbs found in the medicinal texts.[15] While their work shows admirable

---

[12] Wilfrid Bonser, "Magical Practices Against Elves," *Folklore* 37 (1926), 350–63; "Survivals of Paganism in Anglo-Saxon England," *Transactions of the Birmingham Archaeological Society* 56 (1939), 37–70.

[13] It remains to be seen whether demons become elves.

[14] Godfrid Storms, ed. and trans., *Anglo-Saxon Magic* (Halle: Nijhoff, 1948).

[15] Grattan and Singer, *Anglo-Saxon Magic*, pp. 80–90. For a positive analysis of

restraint in the area of medicine (often based upon a negative view
of the Anglo-Saxons' intellectual capacity), the same caution is not
evident in their treatment of religious beliefs, folklore, or iconography.
Their survey of elf references in Anglo-Saxon medical materials rightly
points to the gradual demonization process and the sublimation of
elves as lesser, meaner demons; however they view this process as
confusion rather than seeking an internal logic to this representation.
Instead, they make an imaginative leap forward to Olaus Magnus'
1550 illustration of a bow-and-arrow *counter-attack* against elves, which,
combined with their frontispiece of the *Eadwine* Psalm 37 illustration,
implies a continuous iconographic tradition of elf imagery.[16] However,
the historical and cultural distance between sixteenth-century notions
of elves, a mid-twelfth-century Psalter, and an eleventh-century medical
text is too great to bear the weight of this interpretation.

Further, the illogic of their explanation of the Psalm 37 picture is
evident from a cursory examination of the *Eadwine* illustration itself.
Elves in Anglo-Saxon lore, as evidenced in the medicinal remedies,
were invisible arrow-shooting agents of illness. However, in the Psalm
37 illustration, the spritely figures cannot be responsible for the arrows
penetrating the psalmist's body from the front, since they are flitting
behind him and carry no bows. Christ is the only possible arrow-
shooter, holding a bow and arrow above and in front of the psalmist.
Moreover, the arrows clearly illustrate verses 2–3 of the Psalm: *Domine
ne in furore tuo arguas me; neque in ira tua corripias me; quoniam sagittae tuae
infixe sunt michi* ("Lord, do not reprove me in your wrath, nor in your
anger chasten me, since your arrows are fixed in me"). Grattan and
Singer apparently thought that the illustrator did not understand this
reference and "confused" elfshot with it. But there is no reason to
think of these demons as elves, unless one extrapolates from much
later iconography, as Grattan and Singer appear to have done. Because
they approached the Psalter text from a study of Anglo-Saxon magic
and medicine, and because they tended to devalue the interpretive
capacity of the Anglo-Saxon authors, they failed to see the context
of the Psalter manuscript and its cosmological framework.

When one turns from a study of elves and medicine to the scholarship of Psalter iconography, a very different picture emerges, more

---

Anglo-Saxon knowledge of plant identifications, see Linda Voigts, "Anglo-Saxon Plant
Remedies and the Anglo-Saxons," *Isis* 70 (1979), 250–68.

[16] Grattan and Singer, *Anglo-Saxon Magic*, pp. 60–61 and illus. 25 on p. 52.

in tune with the interpretations of Bonser: these figures are demons, with perhaps elfin characteristics. M.R. James, in his facsimile edition, describes the illustration with reference to the psalm text, and notes that "five demons in air place a burden on his back (my loins are filled with illusions, Lat.)."[17] As for *Eadwine*'s model, the *Utrecht Psalter* (Fig. 2), art historian E.T. De Wald describes the winged beings in that manuscript as "four elf-like 'illusiones' (verse 8,7), or 'iniquities' (verse 5, 4) . . . placing a heavy sack over his back and shoulder ('as an heavy burden they are too heavy for me,' verse 5,4)."[18] Accordingly, C.R. Dodwell notes a gradual transformation of these beings from vaguely angelic in the *Utrecht* to demonic in the *Eadwine*: "In U, it is not clear that the small figures besetting the psalmist are devils— they are small winged figures, not like the usual demons of U, and they may perhaps be meant for emissaries of the Lord sent to tempt the psalmist with tribulation. . . . In E they have clearly become devils/ imps, and the trend is continued in P[aris] where they have assumed monstrous form."[19] Dodwell's note accounts for differences between the sketchy *Utrecht* figures and the tightly drawn little imps of Eadwine, but is not an extended analysis of how this transformation may have taken place in the iconography of such beings. To do that, we must turn to a consideration of the Psalter manuscripts themselves.

Iconographic and Textual Analysis

The *Eadwine Psalter* is a unique manuscript in its combination of so many disparate features. It has a triple layout of three versions of the Latin, enhanced by the commentaries of the *Glossa Ordinaria*, as well as both Anglo-Norman and Anglo-Saxon interlinear glosses, elaborate illustrations of each psalm and canticle, richly decorated initials, and several other noteworthy illuminations (not to mention the magnificent picture of the apparent genius guiding the text's production, *Eadwine*, and the famous waterworks plan). All of these features, and more, have earned *Eadwine* a prominent place in scholarly

---

[17] M.R. James, *Canterbury Psalter*, p. 20.

[18] E.T. De Wald, *The Illustrations of the Utrecht Psalter* (Princeton: Princeton University Press, 1932), p. 19. Facsimile edition, *Utrecht-Psalter*, ed. R. van der Horst and J.H.A. Engelbregt, Codices Selecti 75, 2 vols (Graz, 1984).

[19] C.R. Dodwell, "The Final Copy of the Utrecht Psalter and its Relationship with the Utrecht and Eadwine Psalters," *Scriptorium* 44 (1990), p. 42.

analysis of medieval manuscripts.[20] The extraordinary quality of this Psalter extends beyond just its complex interweaving of multiple texts; the illustrators and scribes were also engaged in an interpretive exercise in which they altered, made choices, and shifted emphases from their sources. Consequently, *Eadwine* captures a moment in time in the evolution of a Christian cosmology, a window onto a mental landscape. The fact that we can compare *Eadwine* with earlier and later manuscripts in this tradition allows us to see the processes of interpretation more vividly.

The Manuscripts

Eadwine belongs to a family of Psalters:[21]

Utrecht Psalter: Utrecht, Universiteitsbibliotheek MS 32 (Script. eccl. 484) produced at Rheims, 816–835.[22]

Harley Psalter: London, British Library MS Harley 603, an incomplete copy of *Utrecht* produced at Canterbury, 1000–1025.[23]

Eadwine (or *Canterbury*) *Psalter*: Cambridge, Trinity College, MS R. 17.1 (987), the only complete copy of *Utrecht*, produced at Christ Church Canterbury, dated either circa 1147 or 1155–1160.[24]

---

[20] Other features found in this manuscript are a calendar, the canticles and creeds, prognostications, waterworks plan, and a drawing of a comet; four leaves of biblical illustrations removed from the manuscript are now in three places (London BL MS add 37472 (1), London Victorian and Albert Museum MS 661, and New York Pierpont Morgan Library MSS M. 521 and 724). These features, combined with its large size leaves (approx. 460 mm × 330 mm) and initials in gold and silver, put *Eadwine* in the top category of expensive, luxury manuscripts.

[21] For a listing of Anglo-Saxon Psalters, see Pulsiano, "Psalters," pp. 61–70. The most recent definitive publications on each manuscript are given below.

[22] Two major works based on the 1996 Utrecht exhibit of the four manuscripts are: *The Utrecht Psalter in Medieval Art: Picturing the Psalms of David*, ed. Koert van der Horst, Willam Noel, and Wilhelmina C.M. Wüsterfeld (The Netherlands: HES Publishers, 1996), hereafter referred to as van der Horst, et al., *Picturing the Psalms of David*; and a complete CD of the images, *The Utrecht Psalter: The Psalms of David*, Koert van der Horst and Frits Ankersmit (Universiteit Utrecht, 1996).

[23] William Noel, *The Harley Psalter* (Cambridge: Cambridge University Press, 1995).

[24] *The Eadwine Psalter: Text, Image, and Monastic Culture in Twelfth-Century Canterbury*, ed. Margaret Gibson, T.A. Heslop, and Richard W. Pfaff (London: Modern Humanities Research Association; University Park, PA: Pennsylvania State University Press, 1992), hereafter referred to as Gibson, et al., *Text, Image, and Monastic Culture*. The latter favor the 1155–1160 date on scribal grounds (pp. 22–24, 209) and reject the traditional argument of circa 1147 that is derived from the comet on f. 10r, a view which C.R. Dodwell defends in *The Pictorial Arts of the West 800–1200* (New Haven: Yale University Press, 1993), pp. 329–40.

Paris Psalter: Paris, Bibliothèque Nationale, lat. 8846, an unfinished copy of *Eadwine* and *Utrecht* produced at Canterbury, 1170–1190.[25]

Although these latter three Psalters are related through borrowing from the exemplar of *Utrecht* while it was in Canterbury, they differ from one another in both the text and illustrations. Of the three, *Eadwine* has the most complex set of content changes. The comparisons below show how *Eadwine*'s choices reflect its design and orientation as a study book that incorporates both contemporary and traditional sources into a master Psalter.

While *Eadwine* copies from *Utrecht*'s illustrations, it incorporates a complex set of psalter textual traditions to form a unique psalter manuscript emphasizing study apparatus. The *Utrecht Psalter* contains only the Gallicanum version of the Latin psalms, the revision that was dominant in the Carolingian Empire and later superseded the Romanum version. *Utrecht*'s psalm text is arranged in three columns on a page, with an accompanying illustration above the text that spans the three columns, a pattern copied by *Harley*. *Eadwine*, on the other hand, is a triple Psalter with parallel columns of three different versions of the psalms in Latin (the Gallicanum, Romanum, and Hebraicum, all attributed to Jerome). *Eadwine* gives prominence to the Gallicanum (a revised Latin based on Greek and Hebrew versions) by locating it centrally in a larger hand and with more space than the other two Latin versions, which are in smaller hand and narrower columns. The Romanum (the dominant Latin tradition of the early medieval period) contains an Anglo-Saxon interlinear translation or gloss, while the Hebraicum (supposedly a direct translation from the Hebrew) has interlinear Anglo-Norman. Moreover, *Eadwine* adds in the generous margins surrounding the Gallicanum a set of commentaries known as the *Glossa Ordinaria*, a compilation and distillation of patristic interpretations that emerged in a standardized form in the twelfth century.[26] The other outstanding difference that sets *Eadwine* apart as more than a copy of *Utrecht* is found in the illustrations,

---

[25] Not to be confused with what Anglo-Saxon scholars call the *Paris Psalter*, BN Lat. 8824. The relationship of this "Paris" copy of *Utrecht/Eadwine* (called the *Paris Psalter* by art historians) to *Utrecht* and *Eadwine* was defined by C.R. Dodwell, "The Final Copy of the Utrecht Psalter."

[26] Beryl Smalley, *The Study of the Bible in the Middle Ages* (Notre Dame, IN: University of Notre Dame Press, 1964), pp. 46–82; Margaret Gibson, "The Latin Apparatus" in Gibson, et al., *Text, Image, and Monastic Culture*, pp. 108–109. *Eadwine* also has a prologue before and a collect following each psalm.

which are tinted or lined in rich color, compared to the monochrome of *Utrecht*, and are in a "hardened" Romanesque style, as compared to the impressionistic sketchiness of the Rheimsian style found in the Carolingian *Utrecht*.[27] [Compare Fig. 1 and Fig. 2.] *Eadwine*'s pictures do more than merely illustrate the psalm, they are themselves a form of interpretive commentary vitally connected to the psalm text and, in some cases, the glosses; although major changes from the *Utrecht* model are few, they can reflect differing interpretations available to *Eadwine*.[28]

All of these features—the triple Latin text, the interlinear translations, the glosses, and the interpretive illustrations—make *Eadwine* a preeminent study text, rather than a liturgical text. Its use was not in the Divine Office for the performance of the psalms but in the library for meditative and study purposes; nor is this apparatus suitable for teaching students Latin or novices the psalms. It was clearly designed for study by scholarly monks or a wealthy patron.[29] Moreover, its inclusion of both Anglo-Saxon and Anglo-Norman suggests that it represents a synthesis of Canterbury's traditions, an effort to incorporate an exegetical history into one state-of-the-art manuscript. In the concluding words of Margaret Gibson in the current definitive study of this manuscript, *Eadwine* is "the Psalter that has everything" and hence is "unclassifiable" in comparison to other Psalters.[30]

Eadwine was not the only child of *Utrecht*, however. Its siblings, the earlier *Harley* and the later *Paris*, help place *Eadwine*'s significant differences from *Utrecht* into a broader context of copying at Canterbury. All three Canterbury productions endeavored to create a study Psalter, but they incorporated different textual traditions based upon the

---

[27] Kauffmann, *Romanesque Manuscripts*, p. 97 describes the stylistic change in *Eadwine* as "hardening." Because of the influence of *Utrecht*, *Eadwine*'s Principal Illuminator cannot fulfill his Romanesque leanings or follow the St. Alban's style he favored when on his own. The newer style, constrained here in the psalm illustrations of *Eadwine*, tends to create a narrative across the picture and favors hierarchical representations. The influence of the St. Alban's Psalter is evident in the decorated and historiated initials in *Eadwine*, a novelty not found in *Utrecht*. For a general discussion of style, see C.R. Dodwell, *The Canterbury School of Illumination 1066–1200* (Cambridge: Cambridge University Press, 1954), pp. 41–47.

[28] Wormald, *Utrecht Psalter* (Utrecht, 1953), pp. 1–2 as cited in William Noel, *The Harley Psalter* (Cambridge: Cambridge University Press, 1995), p. 168. Noel makes this same argument on behalf of the *Harley Psalter*, asserting that the *Harley* illustration's deviations from *Utrecht* can reflect textual readings of specific verses.

[29] Gibson, "Conclusions," in Gibson, et al., *Text, Image, and Monastic Culture*, p. 211.

[30] Ibid., p. 213.

perceived use of their manuscript and they employed artistic styles of their own time while borrowing from *Utrecht*'s layout and style.

The incomplete *Harley Psalter* (early eleventh century) and the later *Eadwine* (mid-twelfth century) represent two separate responses to *Utrecht*, in that *Eadwine* uses *Utrecht* as a model without reference to *Harley*.[31] *Harley* contains a primarily Romanum Latin version of the psalms, unlike the Gallicanum of *Utrecht*, but follows the layout of *Utrecht*'s page with an illustration of the psalm above all three columns of the text; its native style contains the impressionistic elements of *Utrecht*'s sketches, but adds Anglo-Saxon elements and color.[32] According to the recent analysis of William Noel, the *Harley* production gave precedence to the illustrations, drawing them first and using them as a way of explicating verses from the psalm text in a way significantly different from the *Utrecht* design.[33] *Eadwine* appears to have a similar raison d'être, that of producing a study Psalter in which illustrations were an essential tool of interpretation; unlike *Harley*, though, *Eadwine* includes the *Glossa Ordinaria* from which to draw these interpretations. Both *Harley* and *Eadwine* are more than mere copies modifying their original; they both have design and purpose that cause them to pick and choose from their main model and draw on other manuscript traditions as well.

The later, unfinished *Paris* copy used both *Utrecht* and *Eadwine* as models and thus can serve to highlight changes and differences that *Eadwine* made to *Utrecht*.[34] The *Paris Psalter* is, like *Eadwine*, a triple Psalter with Anglo-Norman glosses of the Hebraicum and Latin commentaries on the Gallicanum; however, it has only a few Anglo-Saxon glosses on the Romanum, perhaps an indication that the value of the Anglo-Saxon tradition had faded since *Eadwine*. The illustrations of the *Paris* copy (Psalms 1–52, with six only in under-drawings) follow

[31] For stylistic comparisons, see T.A. Heslop, "Decoration and Illustration," in Gibson, et al., *Text, Image, and Monastic Culture*, pp. 25–61, specifically pp. 51–52. The *Harley* does differ from the *Utrecht* in other ways, such as modernizing the style of dress or reinterpreting a portion of text.

[32] The *Harley Psalter* contains Psalms 1–143.11, illustrated except for Psalms 49–99; Psalms 100–105.20 are Gallicanum. See Pulsiano, "Psalters," no. 11, p. 64.

[33] Noel, *The Harley Psalter*, pp. 150–202. Janet Backhouse, "The Making of the Harley Psalter," *The British Library Journal*, 10, no. 2 (1984), 97–113, established the contention that the *Harley* illustrations preceded the text and were designed as a study aid to the text.

[34] The Paris copy contains Psalms 1–98.6 (Pulsiano, "Psalters," no. 24, p. 67); see Dodwell, "The Final Copy," for the argument that *Paris* derives from both *Utrecht* and *Eadwine*.

to some degree *Eadwine*'s Romanesque illuminations but are in a
"sumptuous" Byzantinizing style with a burnished gold background
that, according to Dodwell, may be the work of hired secular artists,
a twelfth-century departure from the tradition of monastic artists in
the earlier Canterbury copies of *Utrecht*.[35]

The Psalm 37 Illustration

A comparison of the four Psalters in the way they illustrate Psalm 37
presents an interesting cosmological shift in the representation of
spiritual agencies, specifically those impish demons assaulting the
psalmist in the central and hence most important part of the illustration. Since *Harley* remains closer to *Utrecht* in format and general
style, while *Paris* is influenced by *Eadwine*'s choice of content and
Romanesque style, the interesting shift, at least for this illustration, is
between *Utrecht* and *Eadwine*.[36] *Eadwine*'s Principal Illuminator is responsible for this psalm, and, as Heslop points out, he is capable of interpretive departures from the *Utrecht* illustrations even in the midst of
faithfully reproducing its general format.[37] The Principal Illuminator's
style is a mixture of his model's Rheimsian characteristics, such as
tapering legs and spindly ankles, and his own Romanesque style.[38]
Eadwine's Principal Illuminator turns the sketchy bodies of *Utrecht* into
firm, often more compact but larger, figures. With these general stylistic considerations in mind, the following similarities and differences
can be noted in comparing the little figures afflicting the psalmist in
Utrecht, Harley, Eadwine, and *Paris* (Figures 3–6).

    Utrecht (Fig. 3) shows four winged beings attacking the psalmist
from behind, with one at the top left appearing to pour from a small
sack (presumably the burdens of verse 5) into the opening of a large
sack slung over the shoulder of the psalmist, while the other beings
help hold it open. Most editors treat this area of the illustration as a

---

[35] Dodwell, "The Final Copy," pp. 22–23.
[36] Van der Horst, et al., *Picturing the Psalms of David*, pp. 156–57, in a chapter
comparing the illustrations of the four manuscripts, includes this psalm, reproducing
all but *Harley*.
[37] Heslop, in Gibson et al., *Text, Image, and Monastic Culture*, pp. 45–47, 49–51, 59.
[38] The influence of the St. Alban's Psalter is evident in early illustrations in the
manuscript, where the Prinicpal Illustrator added something entirely different from
the *Utrecht*, and in the decorated initials; see Heslop, in Gibson et al., *Text, Image,
and Monastic Culture*, pp. 26–30.

conflation of both verse 5 (the burdens) and verse 8 (the illusions) and call the winged beings demons; Dodwell characterizes the attackers as vaguely angelic as opposed to demonic in comparison to other demons in the manuscript.[39] *Harley* (Fig. 4) is very close to *Utrecht*, with four winged beings placing a burden on the psalmist's back, but the artist colors all of the figures in a way that Noel asserts is a more visual representation of the text in verses 4–5.[40]

Eadwine (Fig. 5), on the other hand, has five winged beings whose appearance is much clearer and more impish than *Utrecht*; the additional "demon" is at the bottom, while the other four appear in roughly the same position as *Utrecht*. The major change, though, is that *Eadwine* omits the small sack that the *Utrecht* winged beings use to pour burdens into the large sack on the psalmist's shoulder and also the staff on which the psalmist leans in *Utrecht*.[41] Instead, the focus of the attackers' activities seems to be the large "sack," which now appears more like a cloak, still furled open, but now not used to pour things into. Oddly enough, the *Paris* copy (Fig. 6) goes all the way to making the burden/sack a hooded cloak tugged at by four (again) demons, rearranged completely so that only one is on the left on the back of the psalmist while the other three are on the right facing him. These *Paris* demons are non-humanoid in appearance, with animalistic features (two are brown and two are reddish). The crippled psalmist now has a scroll which he offers up as his prayer. At least, then, the *Paris* artist, working from the *Eadwine* but with access to the *Utrecht*, thought the *Eadwine* illustrator meant to show a cloak pulled at by demons, whereas the *Harley* maintained closeness to *Utrecht* in portraying a sack and four angelic beings.[42]

The changes in the representations of these winged beings needs to be seen in the context of Psalter demon iconography. A comparison of these little figures with other demons in the *Eadwine Psalter* and

---

[39] Dodwell, "The Final Copy," p. 42.

[40] Noel, *Harley Psalter*, pp. 38–39.

[41] Noel, in his contribution to the celebratory *Utrecht* volume (van der Horst et al., *Picturing the Psalms of David*, p. 156), argues that the representation of the psalmist's bodily weakness is effectively portrayed in *Utrecht* through the staff (missing in *Eadwine*) and through a stooped and bent body in *Paris*, but that *Eadwine* fails to convey this weakness with any artistry.

[42] Other differences: The middle being in *Utrecht* appears to be bracing its feet against the psalmist, leaning back (tricky, since it appears to be flying), while in *Eadwine*, the middle being retains the effect of leaning back, but without as much sense of bracing itself in order to pull open the cloak. Also, two of *Eadwine*'s figures have red lines coming out of their mouths, apparently flame-like tongues.

their counterparts in the *Utrecht, Harley*, and *Paris* reveals a range of types, from black monstrous demons to the cute sprites evident in this psalm illustration. Beat Brenk classifies two types of demons in the ninth through eleventh centuries, the *Eidola*—which Russell prefers to call imps—and the *Hadestyp*, a muscular humanoid type.[43] After the eleventh century, as Russell notes, a third form emerges, the monstrous and animal shapes. Examples include the furry monsters in *Eadwine's* Psalm 1 (by the Superbia Master, not the Principal Illuminator) and the demons throughout the *Paris* illustrations, including Psalm 37 (Fig. 6).[44] Louis Jordan refers to this change toward monstrosity in demonic appearance as "demonization" of demons, an awkward anachronism that nonetheless conveys the basic shift from earlier impishness, through humanoid figures, to animalistic monstrousness.[45] Clearly *Eadwine's* Psalm 37 demons fit into the impish category and are basically humanoid, if somewhat childlike in appearance, and not animalistic (although some have tails).[46] Demons similar to these appear elsewhere in *Eadwine*, and in *Utrecht* and *Harley*, in association with evildoers or the condemned. These impish figures frequent hellmouth scenes, prodding the wicked into the gaping maw or pit (Psalm 27, Fig. 7), but they also flit about the heads of the wicked, as forms of temptation.[47] For example, *Eadwine's* Psalm 25 (Fig. 8) has three small, almost child-sized demons who hover over some sinners on the right of the picture, seemingly whispering in their ears (the far right one extends off the margin of the frame). In Psalm 75 center bottom, (Fig. 9), three horsemen each have overhead a winged

---

[43] Beat Brenk, *Tradition und Neuerung in der christlichen Kunst des ersten Jahrtausends* (Vienna: Hermann Böhlaus, 1966), pp. 196–97. He cites examples from the *Utrecht Psalter*: Eidola on fols. 8r and 16v and the Hadestyp on fols. 53v and 79v.

[44] Russell, *Lucifer*, p. 130.

[45] Louis Jordan, "Demonic Elements in Anglo-Saxon Iconography," in Paul Szarmach, ed., *Sources of Anglo-Saxon Culture* (Kalamazoo, MI: Medieval Institute Publications, Western Michigan University, 1986), pp. 283–317.

[46] Within the *Eadwine* Principal Illuminator's work, Ps. 142 (fol. 251v) has a good example of the muscular humanoid type of demons. These are full-sized, standing, wingless, with spiky upright hair, and pitchforks. Three on each side of the mound are leading away captives, while two below surround the Psalmist's soul rising from a casket in a cave. The demons have characteristic shredded loin cloths. The six appear to have flames or tongues coming from their mouths, similar to Psalm 37's sprites.

[47] Psalms 5 and 6 also have imps in hellmouth scenes in both *Utrecht* and *Eadwine*. These two psalms introduce some unusual dynamics into any comparisons because these are part of the experimental set of illustrations done by the Principal Illuminator where he departed radically from the *Utrecht* model by adding scenes across the top. This experimentation does not appear to affect the presentation of the imps.

sprite similar in appearance to those flitting around the heads of their victim in Psalms 25 and 37. The impish appearance of these demonic figures in these psalms (25, 27, 75) is consistent in *Utrecht, Harley,* and *Eadwine,* and yet *Utrecht* and *Harley* do not utilize this impishness in their illustrations of Psalm 37 in the way that *Eadwine* does.

Two anomalies are thus apparent in the iconographic comparisons between *Eadwine, Utrecht,* and *Harley.* First, this is a rare instance in *Eadwine* of such an imp attacking the psalmist himself, as opposed to the wicked. Second, the Psalm 37 figures in *Utrecht* and *Harley* do not look like the imps of *Eadwine* or the imps found elsewhere in their own pages, but seem ambivalent. These two observations lead to the conclusion that the Principal Illuminator *chose* to substitute the impish demons, a type available in *Utrecht* and *Harley,* for the unclassifiable winged beings in *Utrecht*'s Psalm 37. Again, the *Paris* version confirms this choice by moving the figures even further over into a demonic type, a more frightening animalistic form characteristic of twelfth-century demon iconography.

Interpretive Changes

Although it would be easy to attribute these changes from divine agents to demons and from sack to cloak to a misunderstanding of *Utrecht* (which the Principal Illuminator is guilty of on occasion), it is entirely possible that he used the Psalm or its glosses to arrive at a different interpretation of the text. A conscious change in content seems more likely than misunderstanding *Utrecht.* The addition of an extra winged creature is clearly not due to misreading *Utrecht*; it may be simply an attempt to fill in the space left by the Principal Illuminator's usual stylistic omission of the surrounding lines of shrubbery found in *Utrecht.*[48] Furthermore, the Principal Illuminator was capable of noticing even finer detail in the *Utrecht* illustration than the possibly ambiguous sack: the five arrows piercing the psalmist's

---

[48] This is typical of the Romanesque style evident in *Eadwine*: background landscaping present in the Rheimsian art of *Utrecht* or other early medieval styles is omitted in favor of an exclusive focus on the foreground representation of the textual narrative (see Heslop, in Gibson et al., *Text, Image, and Monastic Culture,* pp. 45–47 and Dodwell, *Canterbury School,* pp. 46–47). At this point, I can find no numerological basis for the change from four to five imps, nor does the *Paris* copy treat it as significant since it returns to four.

body, although hard to locate amid the sketchy lines of *Utrecht*, are duplicated in exactly the same position in *Eadwine*.

The changes, then, to a more demonic appearance in the attackers and the omission and alteration of the sack of burdens suggest that the Principal Illuminator had a different representation of the Psalm text in mind. Heslop does question whether the artist had time to contemplate the text, but notes that the artist certainly knew the Psalms well enough from memory.[49] What I am suggesting here, though, is that the Principal Illuminator's alterations to the demons reflect a reading of the glosses present in *Eadwine* but not in *Utrecht*, and hence represent not only a change in interpretation but also a shift in world view.

A similar line of argument was taken by Noel in his analysis of the *Harley Psalter*, that the changes reflect a conscious response to the text. He reasons that "just one example of textual understanding in the image-making process demonstrates an interest in it and an involvement with it."[50] One of Noel's examples of this kind of conscious interpretive change is found in the Psalm 37 demon iconography, as noted above, where *Harley* adds color and flesh to accentuate the suffering of the psalmist as described in the Psalm text. Noel's footnote to this interpretation comments briefly on the *Paris* changes and *Eadwine*. Noel sees the hood added by *Paris* as a clearer representation of the verse 5 burdens placed on the psalmist than *Eadwine*'s hoodless cloak (although a hood pulled at by demons seems a peculiar way to represent burdens); he then contrasts this "imaginative" handling of the verse by *Paris* to the "less inventive" version in *Eadwine*.[51] However, since *Eadwine* precedes and is a model for *Paris*, it is more likely that the interpretive change—and inventiveness—is found in *Eadwine* and that *Paris* elaborated on it. If we follow Noel's main line of argument that changes in the illustration reflect rereading of specific verses of the text and also note that *Eadwine* and *Paris*, unlike *Utrecht* and *Harley*,

---

[49] Heslop, in Gibson et al., *Text, Image, and Monastic Culture*, p. 50 notes a few rare instances where the Principal Illuminator errs through misunderstanding the *Utrecht* picture in ways that a reading of the Psalm could have corrected. Both Heslop (pp. 45–46) and Dodwell (*Canterbury School*, p. 42) suggest that the artists had recourse to the text and glosses, but confine this observation to the early, experimental psalms where additions to the illustration and consequent change in style are obvious enough to substantiate such a use of the text by the artist.

[50] Noel, *Harley Psalter*, p. 12.

[51] Noel, *Harley Psalter*, p. 39, note 26; see also Noel in van der Horst, et al., *Picturing the Psalms of David*, p. 156.

contain the *Glossa Ordinaria*, then we are led to an examination of the
glosses. These reveal a major shift: *Eadwine* chose to illustrate a different verse, not the burdens of verse 5, but the illusions of verse 8.
The following textual analysis demonstrates this shift and also locates
this interpretation within the larger framework of the world view
evident in the commentaries.

The Glossa Ordinaria

The relevant text for this central image of the besieged psalmist is
verses 3–8 which describe the psalmist's personal state. Psalm 37 is
a penitential psalm of David in remembrance of the Sabbath and
this penitential motif is the strongest element in the commentaries
and glosses. The notations from the *Glossa Ordinaria* discuss the interconnection of bodily and spiritual affliction and cure, as well as the
divine and demonic dimensions of the psalmist's experience.[52] The
world view explicated in these glosses helps make sense out of
the illustration, so recourse to the fuller expositions of the Psalms by
Augustine and by Cassiodorus (the main sources for the *Glossa Ordinaria*)
clarifies the meaning of the abbreviated comments in *Eadwine*.[53] In
part, these commentaries explain why *Eadwine* chose to demonize
the figures as representations of illusions that afflict the psalmist.

The divine perspective and causation are established in the early
verses of the Psalm. The arrows of verse 3 obviously come from the
hand of Christ above (*Your arrows have pierced me*). The *Glossa Ordinaria*
commentary on the passage (fol. 66r, to the left of the Gallicanum)
indicates that the psalmist's afflicted state is a permanent condition
inherited from Adam and cites the Genesis curse (*in the day that you
eat you will surely die*), a comment derived from Augustine.[54] The commentaries on this verse, also based on an interpretation from Augustine's exposition, move from the corporal to the spiritual level by

---

[52] Quotations from the *Glossa Ordinaria* are taken from *Eadwine* with comparison
to the *Biblia Latina cum glossa ordinaria* facsimile, ed. K. Froehlich and M.T. Gibson
(Turnhout: Brepols, 1992).

[53] Augustine, *Enarrationes in Psalmos*, CCSL 38: 382–401; Cassiodorus, *Expositio
Psalmorum*, CCSL 97: 342–53.

[54] *Eadwine*, f. 66r, left, on *sagitte: Vindicte quas minabaris ade[,] dicens[:] In q[ua]c[um]q[ue]
die comed[eritis] m[orte] m[oriemini] q[uia] comed[it] infixe sunt [et] nob[is] [et] non ad horam
s[ed] confirm[asti]. ut sint usq[ue] ad fine[m] s[æ]c[u]li. a potestate iudicis. non est sanitas ab
infirma p[er]sona.* Cf. Augustine, CCSL 38: 384 (sect. 5).

identifying the arrows with the words of God piercing the soul of the psalmist, words that remind him of his sin. The affliction of body and soul in this life is a reminder, according to Augustine, that ultimate soundness of health will be found only in heaven.[55] Thus the lack of physical health in verse 4 (*there is no health in my flesh*), is attributed first of all to God's anger at his sins (*in the face of your ire*), expressed as the weight of His hand on the psalmist (*your hand presses down on me* in verse 3, and in verse 5 *my iniquities hang over my head*).

These burdensome sins are represented in *Utrecht* and *Harley* by a weighty sack, with more burdens added by the winged beings. Since neither of these two texts have the glosses and commentaries, the artists may be rendering a standard and literal interpretation of verses 3–5 as the burden of sins that are part of the human condition as a result of the fall. Hence the vaguely angelic appearance of the beings in *Utrecht* and *Harley* may reflect this general sense that the sufferings of the psalmist are imposed by God through His messengers, just as the arrows are reminders of the psalmist's fallen state.[56]

In rendering this central scene, *Eadwine* bypasses the *Utrecht/Harley* view based on verses 3–5 in favor of a representation of verse 8: *For my [loins] are full of illusions and there is no health in my flesh.* Further, he takes a demonic view of this reference, for reasons found in the glosses. This verse presents some interesting problems of interpretation in light of differences between the three variants of the Latin available in *Eadwine*. The Gallicanum has *lumbi* (loins), glossed as *carnalitas* (flesh), the Hebraicum has *ilia* (bowels), while the Romanum and the Anglo-Saxon have *anima* or *sawl*.[57] While this may seem to be a significant

---

[55] *Eadwine*, f. 66r interlinear on *sagitte: uindicte d[e]i dolores animi [et] corp[or]is. V[e]l u[er]ba d[e]i que infixa cordi faciunt recordari sabb[at]i [et] q[uia] nondum h[abe]t q[uod] amat. gemit [et] cognoscit non e[ss]e salutem carnis comp[ar]atione futuri.* Eadwine, f. 66r right comment on *sagitte: Quonia[m] sagitte. Num[er]at que patitur ut quia multa satis sint d[e]o. ne peiora patiat[ur]. portat [enim] corp[us] mortale tot miseriis subditu[m]. quod [et] cum sanum d[icitu]r. n[on] uere san[um] est quod leuit[er] pot[est] ledi. Vn[de] non est sanitas in c[arne] A facie ab instantia uindicte in adam exerte. V[e]l timore future ire. terret[ur]. sicut non sit sanitas in c[arne] more uerecundi qui futuris flagell[is] iam affligit[ur].* Cf. Augustine, CCSL 38: 385–86.

[56] As noted above, scholars vary in their description of these beings in the *Utrecht* and *Harley*, some calling them demons outright (Noel for example), others referring to them as vaguely angelic (Dodwell). Consequently, I have referred to them throughout as "winged beings."

[57] The Hebraicum also has *ignominia* instead of *illusionibus*. Since the glosses only offer commentary on the Romanum and the Gallican versions, it is hard to know what effect the Hebraicum could have on interpretations of this passage. The Anglo-Norman closely translates the Hebraicum.

difference in meaning—whether one's flesh is the source of ill or the soul—it is not that difficult to understand the interconnection given the context of this psalm and the glosses. The psalmist has already established that his physical illness is caused by sin; the repetition from verse 4 of *there is no health in my flesh* in verse 8 makes this connection explicit, and is glossed at verse 8 with a reference to Romans 7:24, *quis me lib[er]abit d[e] c[orpore] m[ortis] h[uius]* (*who will free me from this body of death*).

The Augustine-derived comment to the right of the Gallicanum verse 8 (fol. 66v) explains the reason for both *lumbi* and *anima* in this passage by pointing out that both body and soul are components of the whole man; soundness in both is essential for the experience of joy. In order for a person to experience such joy, *the soul must be stripped of illusions* and *the body clothed with health*. In the commentary, these illusions are defined as mental images that rush into the soul, sometimes inhibiting prayer—obviously the kind of thing with which monks would struggle. According to this interpretation, this mental confusion will cease only when the person reaches heaven and sees the Truth as it really is, without any of these inhibiting illusions.[58] Augustine's full commentary in his *Enarrationes in Psalmos* recommends contrition as a way of divesting the soul of its illusions. He acknowledges that everyone is afflicted by stray thoughts primarily because all thought is made up of visual images; the power of association in the mind brings in other pictures that cause those praying to forget what they were originally thinking about. The antidote for such illusions, Augustine propounds, is found in Truth, brought through the Incarnation. Christ came in the flesh, and the reality of his presence dispels the illusions blinding human beings.[59] Consequently, the cure for these illusions is to contemplate Christ, which is what the psalmist appears to be doing in the Psalm 37 illustration.

The demonic explanation for the experience of evil, beyond the burden of sins or the illusions of the mind, comes not from Augustine but from Cassiodorus' *Exposition on the Psalms*, reproduced in brief in *Eadwine* in a comment on verse 8, begun interlinear and carried on

---

[58] *Eadwine*, f. 66v, line 8, right: *Lumbi [v]el Anima impleta est [et] ita non e[st] in toto homi[n]e un[de] sit leticia donec anima exuat[ur] illusionib[u]s [et] corp[us] induat[ur] sanitate. Illusiones anime infinite sunt q[uae] aliq[ua]n[do] uix orare sinunt. Imagines occurr[unt] [et] t[ra]nsis de hac in illam. Venit obliuio, recordaris hoc pro illo. [et] h[uius]m[od]i he pellentur cum uidebimus ueritatem ut est.*

[59] Augustine, CCSL 38: 389–90 (sect 11).

to the left of the Gallicanum on fol. 66v: It is *the devil who afflicts the body and vexes the soul through vain imaginings, whereby there is again no health, just as above* [v. 3] *on account of the arrows.*[60] This gloss makes clear that the source of illusions is demonic and that the attack is both physical and spiritual. It falls in line with the above Augustinian explanation of the illusions as distracting mental images by identifying them as "vain imaginings." The illusory, deceptive quality of demonic temptation to sins of the flesh occurring in the mind is a commonplace in hagiographical literature, evident for example in Gregory the Great's well-known *Life of St. Benedict*. Benedict himself is tempted with illusory women; and, as a consequence of his recognizing this deception as demonic in origin, he can see clearly through demonic illusions that afflict his monks (the imaginary kitchen fire, for example).[61] There is also the whimsical story about St. Macarius, who sees through the mass hallucination of some villagers who think a girl has turned into a horse.[62]

This Cassiodoran gloss on verse 8 implicating the Devil also connects the verse to the arrows of verse 3, linking the two sources of affliction, Christ's arrows and the Devil. To attribute sufferings to both divine and demonic sources seems problematic, but is consistent with early medieval theology and the dual world view presented in this picture: the upper cloud-bordered region expresses divine causation, while the temporal sources of affliction in the experience of the psalmist are portrayed in the lower, and main, portion of the illustration.

Thus, the winged figures besetting the psalmist represent to the *Eadwine* Principal Illuminator the demons of the verse 8 glosses. Consequently, he omits the idea of sacks and burdens and instead portrays these figures as spritely demons either tearing at a cloak or engaging in some form of temptation or illusion. *Utrecht* and *Harley*, operating without the glosses and comments, do not read demons explicitly into this psalm, although demons are certainly present in their illustrations of other psalms. Thus the more elongated somewhat angelic bodies of *Utrecht* and *Harley* stand in sharp contrast to

---

[60] *Eadwine*, f. 66v, line 8, interlinear on *Quoniam* . . . and carried to the left: *Non solum mea infirmitate pecc[at]o* {Left} *s[ed] [et] diabolus qui corp[us] afflig[it] [et] animam fatigat uan[is] imaginationib[us], [et] [per] hoc non est i[teru]m sanitas. sicut [et] supra per sagittas*. The *Glossa Ordinaria* (ed. Froelich and Gibson) attributes this comment to both Cassiodorus and Augustine, however I did not find it in Augustine's *Enarrationes* but only in Cassiodorus, CCSL 97: 347 (sect. 8).

[61] Gregory the Great, *Dialogues* Book 2, Chapters 2 and 10.

[62] *Ælfric's Lives of the Saints*, ed. Walter Skeat, EETS 76/82, vol. 1:470–71.

the child-sized, chubby and mischievous looking imps of *Eadwine*. The *Eadwine* Principal Illuminator was working with a highly annotated text with three versions of the Latin that present a conflict of interpretation (*lumbi vel anima*); in reflecting on these verses and their interpretation, he chose to represent the temporal, experiential cause of evil, mental delusions, rather than the cosmic, divine cause of affliction from the inherited sin nature expressed in verses 3–5 and portrayed in *Utrecht/Harley*. In so choosing, the *Eadwine* artist is relying on a native tradition of demon iconography evident elsewhere in the manuscript.

Although it is premature to draw conclusions from this initial survey, it would appear that the Principal Illuminator of *Eadwine* chose to use imps flitting around the humans to indicate temptation or mental deception. Psalm 37, however, appears to be one of the only instance where this kind of demonic attack is directed at the psalmist himself, rather than, as is more usual, the wicked. This form of physical-spiritual affliction is rooted in the Augustinian Christian view of the whole man as composed of body and soul, such that the health of both is intertwined; consequently, spiritual attack had physical qualities, even if illusory. The illusions of the "loins" may imply sensual temptation, but the battle is spiritual. The view that this illustration gives of the human condition, when seen in light of the glosses, is a coherent one, not incoherent as Grattan and Singer contended. Since the *Eadwine* was designed for study and meditation, its apparatus—including the illustrations—shows us the interpretive framework of twelfth-century Canterbury. That framework was innovative and yet incorporated historical traditions important to Canterbury, in the same way that the Principal Illuminator both followed his model and yet added new views. The result was a Psalter that presented each psalm with a full range of interpretations for the monastic scholar to contemplate. Thus the *Eadwine Psalter* is a way into the monastic mentality and the cultural landscape of Anglo-Saxon and Anglo-Norman Canterbury. The Psalm 37 pages reveal a complex world view that seeks to integrate experience and belief, micro and macrocosm, temporal and eternal, body and soul to foster the health of the whole man.

World View

The dualities inherent in this world view are evident throughout early medieval literature and have both Christian and Germanic European roots. We see this correlation between the Psalm 37 illustration and other literature in two ways: the tension between body and soul, with the consequent desire for reintegration; and the dual perspectives of temporal experience versus the eternal divine view, with the need to shift from one to the other to make sense out of the human experience of evil and suffering.

The tension between body and soul and the desire for reintegration is evident in the Anglo-Saxon poem *Soul and Body*, albeit in a crude fashion in the aesthetic judgment of some scholars.[63] In the first portion, found in both the Vercelli and the Exeter Book versions, the harsh language of the soul blaming its body highlights the disjunction between body and soul for the fallen or unsaved. However, when the *halige sawl* speaks to its body in the Vercelli manuscript version, its theme is reintegration. For example, in lines 38–41, the lost soul bewails its unfilled thirst for *godes lichoman, gastes drynces* (the body of God, the drink of the spirit); while in lines 142–43, the "hallowed" or "whole" soul praises its body for fasting on earth and filling itself instead with *godes lichoman, gastes drynces*. The body and blood of Christ, the eucharistic meal, transcends body and soul, unites them, and fulfills them. As with relics, the eucharist channels heavenly might; rather than sanctified bones, words activate the divine power in the natural realm.

The need for a shift in perspective from temporal to divine is the remedy for the disjunction of body and soul in the experience of evil. This experiential view of human life does resonate with early European traditions—particularly the psalmist's abandoned state as one who is forsaken by his comrades and is tormented by non-human assailants (whether elves, demons, dwarves, or other invisible creatures known to cause ill).[64] The shifting perspective, from the suffering of this life to the joy of the eternal is evident in the Anglo-Saxon poem *The Dream of the Rood*.[65] In the poem the alternating appearance of the cross between blood-stained agony and bejeweled

---

[63] S.A.J. Bradley, pp. 358–59 says of *Soul and Body II*: "morbid, coarse, near-superstitious, unintelligent Christianity, weak poetic technique." Citations are from *The Vercelli Book*, edited George Philip Krapp, The Anglo-Saxon Poetic Records 2 (New York: Columbia University Press, 1932), pp. 54–59 and *The Exeter Book*, ed. George Philip Krapp and Elliott van Kirk Dobbie, Anglo-Saxon Poetic Records 3 (New York: Columbia University Press, 1936), pp. 174–78.

[64] Similar to the elegiac *ubi sunt* found in such poems as *The Wanderer* and *The Seafarer* (also in the *Exeter Book*, ed. Krapp and Dobbie, pp. 134–37, 143–47).

[65] *The Dream of the Rood*, in the *Vercelli Book*, ed. Krapp, pp. 61–65.

glory is in part a visualization of the theology of Christ's simultaneous humanity and divinity. The typological meaning of the Old Testament Scriptures sometimes invokes a Christological interpretation of the psalmist as suffering servant. Christ's dual nature reflects the human condition and suggests that his life experience—manifested in the incarnation, crucifixion and resurrection—bring reintegration for the human soul.

In a similar fashion the recitation of and meditation on the psalms brings about a shift in perspective from temporal to divine; the psalms portray the disjunction of body and soul and the possibility of reintegration and wholeness through appeal to God. The iconography of these Psalters illustrates how the cosmic and earthly dimensions overlapped in one visual representation: a heavenly realm hovers at the top, indicating the cosmic perspective; sometimes in the lower portion, devils drag victims down to hellmouth to be digested, the ultimate eternal disintegration of body and soul, as Caroline Bynum so aptly describes.[66] But in-between, in the middle or main portion of most psalm illustrations, is the experiential, temporal "now," where the psalmist or monk struggles with various difficulties—from his own sin, from physical illness, and from perpetrators of evil, both human and demonic. Thus the experiential perspective of the psalm and the illustration portrays a multiplicity of agencies and experiences of evil, from wicked men, indifferent friends, physical ailments, sins, and, some kind of invisible spiritual agency represented in the impish creatures surrounding the psalmist. It is this middle-earth that reflects the specific cultural environment of the European monks involved in this manuscript and its traditions. In human temporal experience, physical and spiritual ills are often indistinguishable. Causation is also ambivalent: in one sense of the psalm (verses 3–5), all of the suffering of the psalmist comes from God as the result of sin; while in another sense (the glosses of verse 8), the source of evil is embodied in externally manifested ills, such as the attacking demons. Thus the troubles emanate not only from the specific earthly circumstances, but are also in some way under the direction of the divine hand at the top of the picture.

The psalms function in a monastic context as prayers that seek to transcend temporal experience and give meaning to life in this world

---

[66] Caroline Walker Bynum, *The Resurrection of the Body in Western Christianity, 200–1336* (New York: Columbia University Press, 1995).

through achieving a divine, eternal perspective. The illustration of
Psalm 37 shows the relationship between materiality and spirituality,
temporality and eternality, experiential and cosmic realities. What is
intriguing is the iconography used to explore the temporal, material,
experiential side of life. The picture reveals how European conceptions of temporal life relate to the Christian belief in a spiritual, eternal, cosmic reality that governs the life of the psalmist in the here
and now. The psalm and its illustration serve as an explanation for
the experience of evil under a presiding omniscient, all good deity.
Through identifying with the earthly experience portrayed in the main
portion of the picture, the readers who meditate on this manuscript
are drawn upward to a contemplation of the divine dispenser of fates
above.

FIGURES 1–9*

*Figures 1–9 belong to *Elves in the Psalms?* by Karen Louise Jolly.

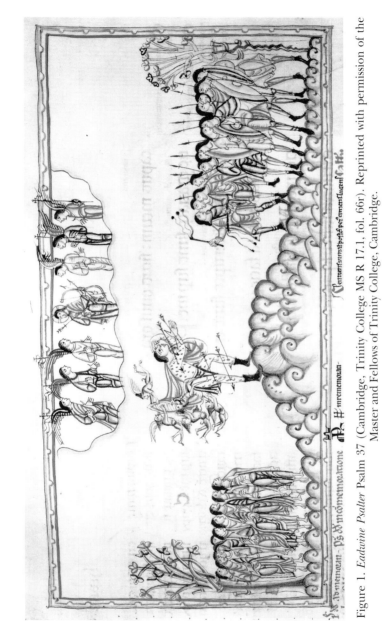

Figure 1. *Eadwine Psalter* Psalm 37 (Cambridge, Trinity College MS R 17.1, fol. 66r). Reprinted with permission of the Master and Fellows of Trinity College, Cambridge.

Figure 2. *Utrecht Psalter* Psalm 37 (Utrecht, Universiteitsbibliotheek MS 32, fol. 22r). Reprinted with permission from Utrecht University Library.

Figure 3. *Utrecht Psalter* Psalm 37 center (Utrecht, Universiteitsbibliotheek MS 32, fol. 22r). Reprinted with permission from Utrecht University Library.

Figure 4. *Harley Psalter* Psalm 37 center (London, BL MS Harley 603, fol. 22r). By permission of the British Library.

Figure 5. *Eadwine Psalter* Psalm 37 center (Cambridge, Trinity College MS R 17.1, fol. 66r). Reprinted with permission of the Master and Fellows of Trinity College, Cambridge.

Figure 6. *Paris* Psalter Psalm 37 center (Paris, BN Lat. 8846, fol. 66r). By permission of the Bibliothèque Nationale, Paris.

Figure 7. *Eadwine Psalter* Psalm 27 bottom center (Cambridge, Trinity College MS R 17.1, fol. 46v). Reprinted with permission of the Master and Fellows of Trinity College, Cambridge.

Figure 8. *Eadwine Psalter* Psalm 25 right side (Cambridge, Trinity College MS R 17.1, fol. 43v). Reprinted with permission of the Master and Fellows of Trinity College, Cambridge.

Figure 9. *Eadwine Psalter* Psalm 75 bottom center (Cambridge, Trinity College MS R 17.1, fol. 132r). Reprinted with permission of the Master and Fellows of Trinity College, Cambridge.

FIGURES 10–16*

*Figures 10–16 belong to "*Simon Magus, Dogs and Simon Peter*"
by Alberto Ferreiro.

Figure 10. Late Antique sarcophagus in S. Giovanni in Valle, Verona, Italy. Alinari/Art Resource, N.Y.

Figure 11. Late Antique sarcophagus in Mantua, Italy, with permission from the *Direzione dell'Archivio Storico Diocesano di Mantova. Curia Vescovile.*

Figure 12. Line sketch of Late Antique sarcophagus at Nîmes, France, now lost. After E. Le Blant, *Les sarcophages chrétien de la Gaule*. Paris, 1886, fig. 136, p. 114.

Figure 13. Late Antique sarcophagus in the Krakow Museum (inv. Num. DMNKCz, 2167) with permission from Dr. Janusz A. Ostrowski, Director of *Princes Czartryski Museum*, Krakow.

Figure 14. Simon Magus acussing Peter and Paul and Peter meeting the dogs of Simon Magus. Sessa Aurunca Cathedral, with permission from Dorothy F. Glass, *Romanesque Sculpture in Campania. Patrons, Programs, and Styles*. Pennsylvania State University Press, 1991, figure 165, p. 139.

Figure 15. Latin Passional no. 8541 (XIV century). *Biblioteca Apostolica Vaticana.*

Figure 16. Fresco in the Cloister Church of Müstair, Switzerland. Reproduced from Beat Brenck, *Die Romanische Wandamalerei in der Schweiz*. Bern, 1963, figure 21.

"SIMON MAGUS, DOGS, AND SIMON PETER"

Alberto Ferreiro

One avenue of research that holds immeasurable opportunity for exploration is the proliferation and usage of Christian apocryphal writings in the patristic and medieval eras.[1] This material has been preserved in patristic and medieval homilies, liturgical texts, hagiographies, theological tracts, vernacular literatures, poetry, chronicles, and in art. Simon Magus, an important figure in apocryphal literature, captured the attention of Christian exegetes and is a central character in the *Actus Petri cum Simone* (*Acts of Peter*), a source known also as the *Actus Vercellensus*, and the *Passio Sanctorum Apostolorum Petri et Pauli* (*Passio*).[2] In this brief essay, it is not my intention to engage all of the legends about Simon Magus, even though each merits specific attention.[3] I wish to focus my efforts here on two specific legends found in the *Acts of Peter* and the *Passio*.

---

[1] A version of this paper was presented at the *12th International Conference on Patristic Studies*. Oxford, 21–26 August 1995. I wish to thank Seattle Pacific University for making my attendance possible. My heartfelt thanks to my friend and colleague Luke Reinsma, Seattle Pacific University, who took the time to read and critique this manuscript. Also, to Professors Robert Faerber and Barbara Fleith, University of Geneva, for useful information on key sources. Consult the research activities of the *Association pour l'étude de littérature apocryphe chrétienne*, (Institut des sciences bibliques) at the University de Lausanne, Switzerland.

[2] In this study I am using the standard editions as found in: *Actus Petri cum Simone* = *(Acts of Peter). Acta Apostolorum Apocrypha* (ed.) R.A. Lipsius and M. Bonnet. Verlag: Hildesheim-New York, 1972, pp. 45–104, and in the same volumes *Passio sanctorum apostolorum Petri et Pauli = (Passio). Acta Apostolorum Apocrypha* (ed.) R.A. Lipsius and M. Bonnet. Leipzig, 1891, pp. 119–177. The standard translation of the *Acts of Peter* is in the *New Testament Apocrypha* (ed.) W. Schneemelcher and (trans.) R. McL. Wilson. Vol. 2. Philadelphia: Westminster Press, 1965, pp. 279–322. There is a translation of the *Passio* in *The Ante-Nicene Fathers*. Vol. 8. Grand Rapids: Wm.B. Eerdmans, 1951, pp. 477–485.

[3] This article is part of my ongoing monograph, *Simon Magus in the Early Christian and Medieval Tradition*. See also my preliminary articles, "Sexual Depravity, Doctrinal Error, and Character Assassination in the fourth-century: Jerome against the Priscillianists," *Studia Patristica* 28 (1993), 29–38; "Jerome's polemic against Priscillian in his *Letter* to Ctesiphon (133, 4)," *Revue des Études Augustiniennes* 39 (1993), 309–332 and "Simon Magus and Priscillian in the *Commonitorium* of Vincent of Lérins," *Vigiliae Christianae* 49, 2 (1995), 180–188. For an overview of the major Simon Magus legends see my, "Simon Magus: The patristic-medieval traditions and historiography," *Apocrypha* 7 (1996), 147–165.

Scholars conversant with the *Acts of Peter* and the *Passio* are familiar with the fascinating encounters between Simon Magus and Simon Peter involving ravenous dogs.[4] Evidently these apocryphal dog stories found a place in the imagination of patristic-medieval writers and artists.[5] A survey and analysis of these episodes in the *Acts of Peter* and the *Passio* in the ensuing centuries will reveal the extent of their influence and the place that they held in the broader typological usage of the image of the dog.

In the *Acts of Peter* a dog plays a prominent role in the conflict between Simon Magus and Simon Peter.[6] The first reference involves the arrival of Simon Peter to Rome to combat the magician. Simon Magus had brought Rome under his magical influences, including the prominent Senator Marcellus in whose house he was staying and who had been "persuaded by his charms" (morantem in domo Marcelli senatoris persuasum 8.32–33, p. 54).[7] Marcellus had a well established reputation as a generous almsgiver to widows, orphans, pilgrims, and the poor (8.1–5, p. 55). In a sudden turn of events, a group of repentant followers of Simon Magus sought out Peter to plead with him to come to Rome to rescue Senator Marcellus from the deceptions of Simon Magus and the "bitterness" that the Senator

---

[4] The few modern studies that have touched upon these episodes have carried out primarily internal critical analyses. Two fundamental studies on the *Acts of Peter* are by G. Poupon, "Les Acts de Pierre et leur remaniement," *Aufstieg und Niedergang der Römische Welt.* II, 25, 6 (1988), 4363–4383 and C.M. Thomas, "Word and Deed: The *Acts of Peter* and Orality," *Apocrypha* 3 (1992), 125–164, on the dog story, at 138–143 for a brief discussion. Both articles contain copious bibliography and address many issues surrounding this document. It comes somewhat as a surprise that the *Passio* has not received the same scholarly attention. I hope that this study will help to alleviate this inattention.

[5] A study that explores the image of the dog in a broad global context is in, P. Dale-Green, *Dog.* Rupert Hart-Davis, 1966, on the Middle Ages see pp. 123–125 and 150–155.

[6] For discussion on the dog incidents in the *Acts of Peter* see, R.A. Lipsius, *Die Apokryphen Apostelgeschichten und Apostellegenden* 2.1. Braunschweig, 1887, pp. 174–194, at 178–180. G. Ficker, *Die Petrusakten. Beiträge zu ihrem Verständnis.* Leipzig, 1903, pp. 19–20. J. Flamion, "Les Actes apocryphes de Pierre," *Revue d'histoire ecclésiastique* 9 (1908), 233–254, 465–490, and for further general discussion, by the same author 10 (1909), 5–29, 245–277; 11 (1910), 5–28, 223–256, 447–470, and 675–692; 12 (1911), 209–230 and 437–450. An important study that is fundamental still is by L. Vouaux, *Les Actes de Pierre.* Paris, 1922. A discussion on textual matters is in Schneemelcher, *New Testament Apocrypha,* 2:259–275, with relevant bibliography. For a consideration of redaction problems in the dog story see, Thomas, "Word and Deed," pp. 138–143.

[7] There is an interesting parallel and modification in the *Acts of Peter* of the Simon Magus account in the Acts of the Apostles 8:9. The latter text reads, "Now for some time a man named Simon had practiced sorcery in the city and amazed all the people of Samaria." Samaria has been replaced with Rome, the spiritual seat of Simon Peter, and its environs.

now harbored in his heart against God, (sed si qua in te domini nostri misericordia et praeceptorum eius bonitatis permanet, succurras huius errori, qui tam magno numero in serbos dei aelemosynas fecit 8.20–22, p. 55). Moved by the insistent rogations of the brethren Peter traveled to Rome, where he condemned Simon Magus before a large crowd in a passionate speech. In his sermon, however, Peter identified the "real" culprit working within Simon Magus, the Devil, arch-enemy of God and of His Church, after which he elaborated a lengthy inventory of the Devil's crimes, chiefly: the Fall of Adam and Eve (8.27–30, p. 55) and the betrayal of Judas (8.30–32, p. 55), both damnable examples of prideful treason against God. In fact, the Devil and Simon Magus are likened by Peter to ravenous wolves, (lupus rapax, uorator et dissipator uitae aeternae! 8.26–27, p. 55); towards the end of the homily, Peter again rebuked the Devil/Simon Magus for attempting to carry off as a wolf the "sheep of Christ",— (tu enim, lupe rapax, uolens abripere pecora quae tua non sunt, sed sunt Christi Iesu qui custodit ea diligenter summa cum diligentia 8.16–18, p. 56).[8] Peter's preaching touched off a new wave of converts who abandoned Simon Magus, and the newly converted brethren now zealously encouraged him to further confront the magician. Stirred by the enthusiastic crowd, Peter immediately set off towards the house of Senator Marcellus to seek out the false magician (9.19–24, p. 56).

When Peter arrived at the gate of the house of Marcellus, he commanded the doorkeeper to inform Simon Magus, who was hiding in the house, that he was waiting for him at the entrance. The doorkeeper who was unable to lie to the apostle returned immediately and told Peter that Simon Magus had instructed him not to tell Peter, whether it was night or day, that he was hiding in the house, (praeceptum autem habeo: recognouit enim te externa die introisse in urbem, dixit mihi: "Siue interdius siue noctu adque hora quae uenerit, dic quoniam non sum intus" 9.28–31, p. 56). Apparently, Simon Magus already had been tipped off that Peter was looking

---

[8] Once again, the allusions to the New Testament are prominent, particularly Jesus's thrice admonitions to Simon Peter to "Feed my sheep," in John 21:15–18. Also, wolves as a type of evil in scripture are noteworthy: prophets as wolves in sheep's clothing (Mt. 7:15) and the world as wolves, Mt. 10:16. The shepherd, in this case Simon Peter in the *Acts of Peter*, as protector of the sheep from wolves, John 10:12. Finally, the wolf as a dividing influence of the flock (the Church) Acts 20:29 requires little effort on our part to apply it to the schismatic activities of Simon Magus in the *Acts of Peter*.

for him. Sympathetic to the doorkeeper's obligations to the master of the house, Peter turned to the crowd and promised them that they would witness a "great and marvelous wonder" (Magnum et mirabilem nostrum uisuri estis 9.33–34, p. 56).

Peter noticed that a dog had been chained at the entrance to Marcellus's house. Whether Simon Magus personally placed the canine there or whether it was a watchdog belonging to Senator Marcellus is unclear. In any case, Peter unchained the dog. To the amazement of all, at that moment the dog miraculously acquired a human voice and asked of Peter, "What do you wish for me to do, servant of the ineffable living God?" (Quid me iubes facere, seruus inenarrabilis dei uiui? 9.3, p. 57). Peter ordered the dog to go into the house to tell Simon Magus to come out immediately and face him. The dog obediently carried out Peter's command. When Simon heard the dog speak, he and those with him were dumbfounded at the sight of this speaking canine, (Audiens enim haec Simon et respiciens incredibilem uisum, excidit a uerbis quibus seducebat circumstantes, omnium stupentium 9.11–13, p. 57).

The focus of this section of the narrative is not on Simon Magus stupefied, but on Marcellus converted. When Marcellus witnessed the miracle of the speaking dog, he went straightway to the doorway, threw himself at Peter's feet, and pleaded that he not experience eternal fire with Simon Magus, (non me tradidi cum peccatis Simonis igni aeterno 10.23–24, p. 57). Praying the mercy of God upon Marcellus and his entire household, Peter in full view of the crowd embraced Marcellus as a sign of his re-entry into the Church (10.11–24, and 11.26, p. 58). Suddenly, a man in the crowd began to laugh mockingly, at which time Peter recognized that he was demon possessed called him out of the throng. Still under demonic control the man ran into the courtyard of the house and gave out a shout and slammed himself against a wall. Then in a loud voice he proclaimed that Simon Magus was in the house arguing with the dog, who was giving the magician an earful; the dog would die, he prophesied, as soon as his work for Peter had finished (11.25–31, p. 58 and 11.1–4, p. 59). In order to further display the power of God and to expose the weakness of Simon Magus, Peter exorcised the demon out of the young man—the inference being that he had also been under the magical influences of Simon Magus.[9]

---

[9] This incident is analogous in one detail to the demon possessed young man

The dog once again comes to center stage as we get further details about the conversation at Marcellus's house between the dog and Simon Magus. Having recovered from the shock of a speaking dog, Simon Magus commanded the dog to tell Peter that he was not in the house. The dog refused to obey Simon, however, and harshly rebuked Simon as a shameless man who would not even listen to a dumb animal with a human voice sent by God to uncover his deception (12.1–4, p. 60). In the *Acts of Peter* no hope is held out whatsoever for Simon's repentance, however. The dog makes it clear that this extraordinary display of divine intervention was intended only to effect the redemption of those who had been deceived by his magic and false teachings, (et hoc non tui causa, sed horum quos seducebas et in perditionem mittebas 12.8–9, p. 60). After his eloquent speech the dog immediately ran out of the house, and the people who had been led astray by Simon Magus likewise abandoned him (Simone solo derelicto, 12.13, p. 60).

The dog went to Peter, now with the former disciples of Simon Magus, to report to him the details of his conversation with the Magus. The dog seized the occasion to prophesy that a great contest would take place between Simon Magus and Peter, which would result in many more converts to the faith (12.13–18, p. 60). As soon as the dog finished prophesying, he sat at Peter's feet and died, (haec cum dixisset canis, caecidit ante pedes apostoli Petri et deposuit spiritum 12.19–20, p. 60), just as had been predicted earlier by the demon possessed man, (et postquam perfecerit mysterium quod illi praecepisti, ante pedes tuos morietur 11.3–4, p. 59). Although the story ends with the dramatic conversion of numerous people who heard the dog speak, there still remained some in the crowd demanding even more "signs" from Peter. In the end, however, the apostolic mission accomplished the rescue of Marcellus and the throngs from the magical deceptions of Simon Magus.

The second major episode between Simon Magus and Simon Peter involving dogs is found in the *Passio*.[10] The confrontation in question takes place in the presence of the Emperor Nero, who had been

---

that Jesus exorcised as recorded in Luke 4:33–35. In each case respectively the young men sarcastically mock Jesus and Peter in public.

[10] R.A. Lipsius, *Apokryphen Apostelgeschichten* 2.1, pp. 366–390 for a consideration of the various versions of the *Passio*. A brief comparison of the *Passio* with the *Acta Nerei et Achillei* is in, J. Flamion, "Les actes apocryphes de Pierre," *RHE* 11 (1910), 447–470.

swayed by Simon's magical powers to favor the magician and to
persecute the apostles Peter and Paul. Peter told Nero that Simon
Magus could not, as he had claimed, read the minds of those around
him. Peter proposed to the Emperor a test to prove once and for
all the false claims of Simon Magus. Peter asked Nero to have a
loaf of barley bread brought to him secretly, that is, unknown to
Simon Magus. When they had all gathered together for the "contest," Peter pressed Nero to ask Simon Magus what Peter had been
doing and thinking prior to their meeting. Unable to reveal the
truth, Simon Magus attempted to turn the tables on Peter by asking
him instead to reveal what was on his own mind at that moment.
Undaunted by this trickery, Peter continued to press Simon Magus
once again to disclose his own thoughts and deeds earlier that day
(27.5–6, p. 143). In an aside, the narrative reminds the reader that
Peter had secretly blessed and broken the bread into several pieces,
which were hidden up his sleeves from Simon Magus's view, (Petrus
enim benedixerat panem quem acceperat ordeaceum et fregerat et
dextera atque sinistra in manica collegerat 26.3–4, p. 143).

At this critical juncture in the confrontation a visibly humiliated
and frustrated Simon Magus, having failed to reveal Peter's thoughts
and deeds, became uncontrollably enraged and cried out, "Let Great
Dogs come forth and devour him before Caesar,"—(Procedant canes
magni et deuorent eum in conspectu Caesaris, 27.6–7, p. 143). Instantly, large growling dogs miraculously appeared and lunged at
Peter to bite him. Peter unshaken by the sight of the ravenous dogs
maintained his composure, stretched out his hands in prayer, offered
the dogs the blessed bread which he had in his sleeves, and the
dogs upon eating [the bread] vanished as suddenly as they had
appeared, (27.7–11, p. 143). Turning to Nero, Peter reminded the
Emperor that he had proven by his own deeds that he knew in advance what Simon Magus had all along been plotting against him.
Peter also asked Nero to recall that Simon had promised to command a group of angels to come against Peter, but instead because
of his inferior magical sorceries could only muster up dog(like) angels, (nam qui angelos promiserat contra me esse uenturos, canes exhi-
buit, ut se ostenderet no diuinos angelos sed caninos habere 27.13–
14, p. 143). The story moves on to more confrontations between
Simon Peter and Simon Magus before Nero that do not involve any
canines. The apostle eventually vanquishes Simon Magus and although
Peter will suffer martyrdom at the hands of Nero at the end of the
story, his death is clearly displayed as a triumph for the Church.

The dog stories in the *Acts of Peter* and the *Passio* survived in the patristic and medieval centuries and were invoked or adapted in creative fashion. The image of the dog, however, as a type for evil or good as found in these apocryphal documents is only a part of a much larger tradition. The image of "Dog" as metaphor became exceedingly useful for biblical exegetes who used it repeatedly to combat heresy, magic, and moral lapses. There are three clearly identifiable usages of the dog in the *Acts of Peter* and the *Passio* summarized in our comments above which became integrated into the broader tradition and which are the focus of the remainder of this article: (1) The dog as preacher or messenger of God's Word; (2) The portrayal of dogs as "enemies" of the Faith; and (3) The use of bread by Simon Peter to pacify the hostile dogs.

1. *Classical and Biblical Images of the Dog*

Unique to the apocryphal narratives is the appearance of talking dogs, a feature that becomes even more extraordinary when compared to Greco-Roman and biblical references to canines.

The most famous dog in all of Greco-Roman literature is, of course, Cerberus, the guardian of Hades, found in a wide range of sources.[11] Hesiod in the *Theogony* described him as a beast who, "eats raw flesh, the brazen-voice hound of Hades, fifty-headed, relentless and strong." Homer and Apollodorus, describing Heracles's capture of Cerberus, did not even mention his howling.[12] Ovid, however, in the *Metamorphoses* said that, "Cerberus reared up his threefold head and uttered his threefold baying." Horace mentioned only that "foul breath" came

---

[11] For general discussions and background on Cerberus see, R. Mitra, "On the origin of the Myth about Kerberos," *Proceedings of the Asiatic Society of Bengal* (May, 1881), 91–97. M. Bloomfield, *Cerberus, The Dog of Hades. The History of an Idea.* Chicago, 1905. H.J. Rose, *A Handbook of Greek Mythology including its extension to Rome*, 4th ed. New York, 1950, pp. 31, 41, 210–212, 214–216 and 228. O. Immisch. "Kerberos," in *Ausführliches Lexikon der griechischen und römischen Mythologie*, II, I. (Ed.) W.H. Roscher. Hildesheim, 1965, cols. 1119–1135. Dale-Green, *Dog*, pp. 85, 89, 91–92. P. Grimal, *The Dictionary of Classical Mythology*, (trans.) A.R. Maxwell-Hyslop. Blackwell, 1986, pp. 96 and 478. T.H. Carpenter, *Art and Myth in Ancient Greece: A handbook.* Thames and Hudson, 1991, pp. 129–130 and illustrations references at 251.

[12] Hesiod, *Theogony*, 311–315, pp. 100–103 and 768–775, pp. 134–135, in *Hesiod. The Homeric Hymns and Homerica*, (trans.) H.G. Evelyn-White. Loeb Classical Library. Harvard, 1970. Homer, *The Iliad* 8.366–370, pp. 364–365 in, *Homer. The Iliad* (trans.) A.T. Murray. Loeb Classical Library. Harvard, 1978. Apollodorus, *Library* 2.5.12, pp. 99–100, in *Gods and Heroes of the Greeks: The "Library" of Apollodorus*, (trans.) M. Simpson. University of Massachussets, 1976.

forth from his mouth.[13] Apuleius focused vividly on the voracious appetite of Cerberus.[14] Virgil, in the *Aeneid*, took notice of Cerberus's loud barking, presumably amplified by his three throats.[15] In none of these and other references, however, is Cerberus endowed with the ability to speak with a human voice. Even in the medieval centuries, the imaginative Dante uses the insatiably hungry Cerberus in Canto VI of the *Inferno* to symbolize the vice of Gluttony. Although, Cerberus, according to Dante, "bays in his triple gullet and doglike growls," not once in the Canto does he utter so much as a syllable.[16]

In the Old and New Testaments the dog has no small place: references spanning from Exodus to the Revelation of St. John.[17] The citations are many and not directly relevant to the question of talking dogs; they do reinforce the fact that canines do not speak as humans do in these biblical texts. The only animals in the Bible fortunate enough to speak with a human voice are the serpent in Genesis (3:1–5) and Balaam's donkey in the book of Numbers (22:21–34).[18] The appearance of dogs in the Bible is strictly in the metaphorical sense—either to affirm virtue as in (Luke 16:21) or to condemn vice (Proverbs 26:11).[19]

Like the canines in Greco-Roman and biblical sources the dogs as

---

[13] Ovid, *Metamorphoses* 4.450–463, pp. 208–211 and a shorter reference at 7.406–412, pp. 370–371 in Ovid, *Metamorphoses*, vol. 1, (trans.) F.J. Miller. Loeb Classical Library. Harvard, 1984. Horace, *Odes* 2.19.29–32 and 3.11.17–21, pp. 162–163 and 216–219, in Horace, *The Odes and Epodes*, (trans.) C.E. Bennett. Loeb Classical Library. Harvard, 1978.

[14] Apuleius, 6.20. in Apuleius, *The Golden Ass*, (trans.) W. Adlington. Loeb Classical Library. Harvard, 1928, pp. 276–279.

[15] "Cerberus haec ingens latratu regna trifauci personat adverso recubans immanis in antro," *Aeneid* 6.417–418, p. 138 in, *The Aeneid of Virgil. Books 1–6*, (ed.) R.D. Williams. MacMillan, 1972.

[16] Dante, *Inferno* 6.14, p. 104 in, *The Comedy of Dante Alighieri the Florentine. Cantica I Hell "L'inferno"*, (trans.) Dorothy L. Sayers. Penguin Books, 1977.

[17] Young's *Analytical Concordance* lists 40 references to dogs, with 31 in the Old Testament and 9 in the New Testament, in Young's *Analytical Concordance* to the Bible (ed.) Robert Young. Wm. B. Eerdmans, 1974, p. 267. All references to the Bible are from the *New International Version*.

[18] The Devil is twice called "that ancient serpent" in the book of Revelation 12:9 and 20:2, a cross-reference to Genesis 3:1–5. Likewise in the New Testament there is a direct citation of Balaam's talking donkey in 2 Peter 2:15–16, a text that chastises evildoers. On Balaam and the donkey see, Elena Conde Guerri, "Interpretación de la escena de Balaam y su Burra (Via Latina B, F y C?) En las fuentes patrísticas y nuevas vinculaciones iconográficas," in *Miscellanea del Prof. Alejandro Recio Veganzones. Historiam Pictura Refert.* Città del Vaticano, 1994, pp. 141–174.

[19] It is telling that there is not a single instance in the Old Testament of a clear positive reference to dogs. The New Testament follows this tradition with only two exceptions, the reference in Luke already cited, and in Matthew 15:27, when the woman responds to Jesus, "Yes, Lord," she said, "but even the dogs eat the crumbs

depicted in the *Passio* are beasts of terrifying character, symbolic of the enemies of the Hebrews in the Old Testament and of the Church in the New Testament. In the *Passio*, we recall, the dogs do not have the ability to utilize human speech. In sharp contrast, the canine in the *Acts of Peter* is quite unique for its speaking ability as it assists Simon Peter in his contests with Simon Magus. In either case the dog as a faithful help-mate of Peter [the Church] is a common theme in patristic-medieval literature.

The dogs in the *Acts of Peter* and the *Passio*, although used distinctly, are both intended to be seen metaphorically as "preachers" of God. In the *Acts of Peter* the added touch is that, much like Balaam's donkey, the dog is given human speech to convey God's message. But the dogs in the *Passio*, who do not possess human speech, are no less the "messengers" of God's will in that they serve as a warning to beware of the enemies of the faith, as in the frequently cited Proverbs 26:11, "As a dog returns to its vomit, so a fool repeats his folly." In the Early Church the Fathers and even sources extraneous to the Bible did not fail to use the image of the dog as either a positive or negative type.

2. *Dogs in the Patristic Era*

The dog in the *Acts of Peter*, messenger of God and helpmate of Peter [the Church], is part of a "positive" image perpetuated by some Church Fathers.

In *Enarrationes in Psalmos*, Augustine praised the good dog for being faithful to its master and guarding his home from potential enemies through incessant barking.[20] Ambrose in the *Hexameron* echoed this point noting how the barking of a dog is given by God to protect their masters and their homes. The bishop of Milan, then, admonished Christians to imitate the dog by using their "voices" [barking] for Christ to protect the Church from ravenous wolves, a type of the enemy of Christ. Like the Christian who does not witness to others Christ's truth, a silent watch-dog, then, is slothful.[21] In *Explanation of*

---

that fall from their master's table," even so, this latter example is still not a generous portrayal of the dog.

[20] "Canes laudabiles, non detestabiles; fidem servantes domino suo, et pro eius domo contra inimicos latrantes," 67.32. *MPL* 36:833.

[21] "Quid autem de canibus loquar, quibus insitum est natura quadam referre

the Psalms Cassiodorus compared converted Jews to dogs who "now converted defend the city (that is, holy Church)"; this type of dog is further representative of the faithful believer, for the Canaanite woman says, "Yes Lord, . . . even the dogs eat the crumbs that fall from their masters' table," (Matthew 15:27).[22] Like zealous converts, Cassiodorus wrote, good dogs, "never cease to bark for the Lord and guard His house with the most prudent intelligence"; thus these formerly evil dogs have been transformed [converted] by the Lord into faithful dogs now in his service.[23] Caesarius of Arles harkened to the image of a shepherd and his barking dogs, ever alert in protecting their flock (Church) from the wolf (the Devil) who approaches with the intent of devouring them.[24] Gregory the Great compared the dogs that licked the wounds of Lazarus (Luke 16:19–21) to the Church which mends and heals the sins [open sores] of those gone astray.[25] In *Moralia in Iob* Gregory provided a long list of well-known heretics that had been rebuked by the Church [dogs] through their diligent preaching [barking].[26] And in the *Hexameron* Basil praised canines

---

gratiam et sollicitas excubias pro dominorum salute praetendere? unde ad inmemores beneficii et desides atque ignauos clamat scriptura: canes muti, nescientes latrare. canes ergo sunt, qui nouerint latrare pro dominis, nouerint sua tecta defendere. unde te tu disce uocem tuam exercere pro Christo, quando ouile Christi incursant lupi graues, disce in ore tuo uerbum tenere, ne quasi mutus canis commissam tibi fidei custodiam quodam praeuaricationis silentio deseruisse uidearis," *Exameron.* 6.17. *Sancti Ambrosii Opera. CSEL* 32.1. Vienna, 1897, p. 213. Ambrose cited the dog which the angel Raphael led to follow the son of Tobias, in *Tobias* 6.1; 3.8; 8.3; and 11.3 (9) in the Old Testament apocrypha, pp. 213–214.

[22] "In eadem comparatione permansit. Canum enim consuetudo est illa loca defendere, in quibus se norunt alimoniam reperire: ita et Iudaei iam conuersi *civitatem*, id est sanctam Ecclesiam defendunt, quam correctis praedicationibus *circuibunt*," *Psalmo* 58.196–200.7. Magni Avrelii Cassiodori, *Expositio Psalmorum. 1–LXX. CCSL*, 97, pars II,I. Turnholt, 1958, pp. 523 and 596–597.

[23] "Isti enim *canes* pro Domino latrare non desinunt, domumque eius cautissima sagacitate custodiunt," and "quia prius inimici fuerunt, qui postea clamosis latratibus Ecclesiae Domini uindicarunt. Sed hoc ipsum a quo fieri potuisset, adiecit, id est *ab ipso*," *Psalmo* 67.479–484.24, p. 597.

[24] "Lupus venit ad ovile ovium, quaerit invadere, quaerit lacerare, quaerit devorare: vigilant pastores, latrant canes: nihil potest, non aufert, non occidit; sed tamen lupus venit, lupus redit," *Sermo* 140.4, in *Caesarii Arelatensis, Sermones. CCSL*, 103. Pars I. Turnholt, 1953, p. 578.

[25] "Quia ergo praedicatores sancti peccata damnant, confessionem vero peccatorum approbant, dicentes: Confitemini alterutrum peccata vestra, et orate pro invicem ut salvemini (Jac. v, 16), ulcera Lazari canes lingunt. Sancti etenim doctores dum gentilium confessiones accipiunt, mentium vulnera saluti restituunt," *Homiliarum in Evangelia*, 2, *Homilia* 40, *MPL* 76:1303.

[26] "Patres vero haereticorum dicimus, eos videlicet quos haeresiarchas vocamus; de quorum perversa praedicatione, id est locutionis semine, sequentes sunt populi in

because, "the dog is grateful and constant in friendship." As proof he repeated the story of how some dogs were reported to have remained with the bodies of their murdered masters, and had even assisted in identifying their assassins.[27]

Among the Church Fathers, John Malale in the *Chronographia* recalled the encounter of Peter in the *Acts of Peter* in order to assert the spiritual authority of Peter over and against the false magic of Simon Magus. The extraordinary intervention of the dog through the exercise of its human voice is highlighted. The brief narrative triumphantly proclaims that in "all things Simon Magus was vanquished and that many believed Peter and were baptized."[28] John Malale affirmed the superiority of apostolic faith by having the dog declare Peter as the servant of the Most High God before a large crowd and with a human voice. What is missing is the dog's debriefing Peter on the details of his conversations with Simon Magus and its dying at Peter's feet. Only two other patristic texts have preserved scantily the basic elements of this episode from the *Acts of Peter*: Commodianus, in a few lines of his lengthy *Carmen de duobus populis*, (Et, canem, ut Simoni diceret: Clamaris a Petro!); a Syrian text in a single line, (Ingressus urbem ad ianuam domus Simonem canem invenit et ei.)[29] Another patristic

errore generati. Sancta ergo Ecclesia cum canibus gregis sui haereticorum patres ponere dedignatur, quia inventores errorum dijudicando respuit, eosque inter veros patres numerare contemnit," 20.6.16. *MPL* 76:116.

[27] *Homilia*, 9.3 and 4, in *Basilii Magni Opera Omnia*. *MPG* 29:191 and 198.

[28] *Liber* 10, *MPG* 97:383–386. For studies on John Malala see, Lipsius, *Apokryphen Apostelgeschichten*, 2.1, pp. 207–217. Vouaux, *Actes de Pierre*, pp. 188–196 and Flamion, "Les Actes Apocryphes de Pierre," *RHE* 12 (1911), 437–450.

[29] *Commodiani Carmina. Carmen de dvobvs popvlis* (ed.) I. Martin. *CCSL*, 128. Turnholt, 1960, lines 626 and 629–630, p. 96. These verses have been the subject of some scholarly scrutiny, see G.B. de Rossi, "Conferenze della società di cultori della Cristiana Archeologia in Roma," *Bullettino di Archeologia Cristiana* 4 ser. 1 (1882), 105–109, at 107–108. Ficker, *Die Petrusakten*, p. 20. H. Brewer, *Kommodian von Gaza. Ein Arelatensischer Laiendichter aus der Mitte des fünften Jahrhunderts*. Forschungen zur Christlichen Literatur und Dogmengeschichte, 6. Paderborn, 1906, pp. 317–318. Flamion, "Les Actes Apocryphes de Pierre," *RHE* 11 (1910), 228. Vouaux, *Actes de Pierre*, pp. 142–143. G. Stuhlfauth, *Die apokryphen Petrusgeschichten in der altchristlichen kunst*. Berlin-Leipzig, 1925, pp. 8–9. G. Turcio, "San Pietro e i Cani," *Ecclesia* 7 (1948) 297–299, at 298. Relevant also, K. Thraede, "Beiträge zur Datierung Commodians," *Jahrbuch für Antike und Christentum* 2 (1959), 90–114. A broader discussion about Commodianus is in, J. Fontaine, *Naissance de la poésie dans l'occident chrétien*. Études Augustiniennes, 1981, pp. 39–52. Schneemelcher has recently argued that mention of the dog and infant by Commodianus prove that he knew *only* about the speaking animals in the *Acts of Peter*, but that it does not demonstrate an acquaintance with the entire work, in *New Testament Apocrypha*, vol. 2, p. 261. Are we then to believe that the *Acts of Peter* circulated in snippets that fell into the hands of interested readers here and there?

source that heavily depended upon the *Acts of Peter* and which gave significant place to the dog stories is the *Acta Nerei et Achillei*, believed to have been written in the fifth and sixth centuries. This text incidentally appended important novelties that were incorporated into medieval versions of the *Acts of Peter* and which are discussed below.[30]

In the preceding summary of select Church Fathers there are specific character traits attached to dogs that are congruent with those found in the *Acts of Peter*. Augustine, Cassiodorus, and Caesarius of Arles stressed the faithfulness of a dog towards its master and its willingness to act as guardian. In the *Acts of Peter*, the converted dog remained unwaveringly faithful to Peter; and as a symbolic act of humility once having completed its mission, the canine sat at Peter's feet and died. The image of Peter as Shepherd with his faithful sheep-dog is conveniently extrapolated into the *Acts of Peter*, where the metaphor is

The entire tone and content of the *Carmen* suggests strongly that Commodianus was well versed and had more than a passing acquaintance with most of his sources, including perhaps the *Acts of Peter*.

For the Syrian testimony see the critical edition by, A. Baumstark, *Die Petrus- und Paulusacten in der litterarischen ueberlieferung der Syrischen Kirche*. Leipzig, 1902, pp. 76–77. For the diffusion of the *Acts of Peter* in the Near East see, Flamion, "Les Actes Apocryphes de Pierre," *RHE* 12 (1911), 209–230 and 437–450.

[30] There are two standard editions of the Greek text, A. Wirth, *Acta SS Nerei et Achillei graece edidit*. Leipzig, 1890 and H. Achelis, *Acta SS Nerei et Achillei*. Leipzig, 1893, who corrects and adjusts Wirth's edition. F. Schaefer, argued persuasively that the original text was in Latin, "Die Acten der heiligen Nereus und Achilleus," *Römische Quartalschrift* (1894) 89–119, and that text is in the *Acta Sanctorum*. Maii, vol. 3, (ed.) G. Henschenio and D. Papebrochio. Paris, 1866, chapter 3.13, p. 10. Commentary on the *Acta Nerei Achillei* is in, de Rossi, "Di tre antichi edifici componenti la chiesa dei ss. Cosma e Damiano; e di una contigua chiesa dedicata agli apostoli Pietro e Paolo," *Bullettino di Archeologia Cristiana* 5 (1867), 66–71, at 70–71. Lipsius offers a detailed analysis, *Apokryphen Apostelgeschichten*, pp. 200–206. Brief yet relevant comments are in, Ficker, *Die Petrusakten*, pp. 47–51. Flamion carried out a marvelous comparison with the *Acts of Peter* in, "Les Actes Apocryphes de Pierre," *RHE* 11 (1910), 447–470. Vouaux presents a summary of the scholarship up to that time, *Actes de Pierre*, pp. 155–160. C. Schmidt demonstrates further dependencies and similarities between both texts, "Studien zu den alten Petrusakten," *Zeitschrift für Kirchengeschichte* 43 (1924), 321–348. See also, Stuhlfauth, *Apokryphen Petrusgeschichten*, p. 7, note 2. For pithy insightful remarks see Schneemelcher, *New Testament Apocrypha*, vol. 2, p. 268.

An example of a medieval commemoration of the *Acta Nerei et Achillei* which omits the dogs, but does mention Simon Magus is the liturgical twelfth-century poem by Adam of St. Victor, which reads:

Ibi Priscus et Furius
Simonis Magi complices
Avertebant attentius
A sana fide simplices

(lines 29–32)

strengthened by the fact that twice in the narrative Simon Magus is depicted as a ravenous wolf (lupus rapax—8.26–27, p. 55). In the second reference, Simon Magus is called again a ravenous wolf desirous of carrying off the sheep [of Christ] that are not his own; rather they belong rightfully to Jesus Christ, who cares for and protects them, (tu enim, lupe rapax, uolens abripere pecora quae tua non sunt, sed sunt Christi Iesu qui custodit ea diligenter summa cum diligentia 8.16–18, p. 56).

Ambrose of Milan called upon Christians to protect the Church from wolves by preaching God's truth with their own voices, as dogs bark incessantly to protect their owners and their homes. Similarly drawing attention to the deep and abiding friendship between a dog and its master, Caesarius of Arles and Basil employed in their *Sermons* the full range of imagery: the shepherd, barking dogs, sheep in need of protection, and the wolf as predator.[31] The dog in the *Acts of Peter*, too, continually "barks" with a human voice against the wolf, Simon Magus. And Gregory the Great, too, recalled with pastoral concern the compassion that the dog demonstrated toward downcast and sickly Lazarus, so as to stress once again the healing mission of the Church; the same lesson was echoed by Augustine and Caesarius.[32]

Cassiodorus, as noted above, used Psalm 58 to argue that converted Jews were like tamed dogs committed to the service of the Church, as evidenced by their ceaseless barking to protect their Lord and to guard His Church. Prior to their conversion the Jews had been "evil dogs," he reminded his readers. In his interpretation of Psalm 67 he again turned his attention to previous enemies of the Church who had been converted to the cause of Christ; they are dogs now defending the Lord's Church with noisy barking [preaching]. The psalmist, according to Cassiodorus, emphasized that the source of their conversion was *ab ipso*, meaning the Lord, who changes bitter to

---

with an English translation, in D.S. Wrangham, *The Liturgical Poetry of Adam of St. Victor: from the text of Gautier.* 2 vols. London, 1881, 2:60–65, at 62–63.

[31] Caesarius of Arles, *Sermones. CCSL*, 103, pars 1. *Sermo* 140.4, p. 578. Basil, *Homilia* 9.3, *MPG* 29:191.

[32] "Canum etenim ligua vulnus dum lingit, curat, quia et doctores sancti dum in confessione peccati nostri nos instuunt... ulcera Lazari canes lingunt," *Homiliarum in Evangelia*, liber 2, *Homilia* 40, *MPL* 76:1302–1303. Augustine, "Canes ergo qui ea lingebant, Gentes sunt, quos homines peccatores et immundos dicebant Judaei, et tamen passiones Domini in Sacramentis corporis et sanguinis ejus, per totum jam orbem suavitate lambunt devotissima," *Quaestionum Evangeliorum*, liber 2.38, *MPL* 35:1352. Caesarius of Arles, *Sermo.* 158A.1 and *Sermo* 164 in its entirety, and *Sermo* 183.3, in *Sermones. CCSL*, 104, pars 1, 2. Turnholt, 1953, pp. 648–650, 672–675, and 745–746.

sweet, sadness to joy, cursed illness into sound health.[33] In the *Acts of Peter* we witness a similar spiritual liberation or conversion of the guardian dog at Marcellus's house. Apparently the dog was there at Simon's biding to prevent Peter from entering Marcellus's home since he already knew ahead of time that Peter had arrived at Rome the previous day, (praeceptum autem habeo (the doorkeeper speaking): recognouit enim te externa die introisse in urbem 9.28–29, p. 56). When the account says that Peter walked up to the dog and let him loose, it entailed a "conversion" or release of the dog from spiritual bondage to Simon Magus into the service of Simon Peter and release from the flesh of animal to human intelligence, (Et respiciens Petrus canem magnum catena grande ligatum, accedens soluit eum 9.34 and 1, pp. 56–57).

One of the most fascinating adaptations of the Marcellus story in the *Acts of Peter* is found in a document known as the *Toldoth Jeshu* (Generations of Jesus)—a Hebrew anti-Christian work. Its editor, Hugh J. Schonfield, has noted, "This document can hardly be described as a Gospel, and rather resembles the sectional Passion stories in Christian apocrypha."[34] The resemblance goes beyond such a casual similarity in literary genre, however. Schonfield has demonstrated convincingly the direct borrowings and adaptations of the life of Simon Magus as found in the *Acts of Peter* and the *Passio* into the *Toldoth Jeshu*. Although the *Toldoth* did not reach Europe until the beginning of the ninth century, Schonfield has established that it was originally written in late-fourth-century Tiberias.[35]

My focus in the *Toldoth* is on the passages that have a direct bearing on the theme of dogs. According to the translation by Schonfield, the account reads in part:

> And in the temple was the foundation-stone . . . and on it were graven the letters of the Ineffable Name . . . Dogs of brass were bound to two pillars of iron at the gate of the place of burnt-offerings, so that whosoever entered and learnt the letters, as soon as he went forth the dogs bayed at him: if he then looked at them the letters went forth from his mind. . . . And as he [Jesus] went forth the dogs of the pillars bayed at him, and the letters went forth from his mind.[36]

---

[33] "*Ab ipso* utique Domino, qui amara mutat in dulcedinem, tristitiam uertit in gaudium, aegritudines detestabiles in salutem," Cassiodorus, *Expositio Psalmorum, CCSL*, 97, pars II,1. *Psalmo* 58.196–200.7 and *Psalmo* 67.480–486.24, pp. 523 and 597.

[34] *According to the Hebrews.* London, 1937, p. 32.

[35] Ibid., pp. 214–219.

[36] Ibid., Chapter 2, sections 1–7, pp. 39–40. The editor notes that in one version of the *Toldoth Jeshu*, lions are in the place of the dogs, p. 39 note 5.

It does not take very long for the reader of this text to realize how extensively the Marcellus account has been altered: here Jesus is Simon Magus, the place of burnt-offerings is Marcellus's house, instead of one, two brass dogs act as guardians of this temple of special knowledge, the dogs howl and do not speak with human voices. Jesus (Simon Magus) overcomes the dogs by learning the mysterious "letters," and the howling appears to be an act of acknowledgment and submission to Jesus (Simon Magus). In fact, in a rather curious way the *Toldoth* recounts the arrival of Simon Magus to Marcellus's house *before* Peter in the *Acts of Peter* shows up to call Simon Magus out for their contest. In the final analysis, the dogs in the *Toldoth* are not necessarily portrayed as ravenous canines, nor are they "converted" at any point to righteousness. Like the mythical Greek dog Cerberus, the guardian of Hell, they act solely as guardians of the place of burnt-offerings. Given the abhorrence of dogs in Judaism, coupled with their consistently negative portrayal in the Old Testament, the association of Jesus (Simon Magus) with these dogs was hardly intended to flatter.

There is also a dark side to the image of the dog in the writings of the Church Fathers and congruent with that in the *Passio*. Frequently biblical exegetes used dogs to symbolize the enemies of the Church. In *Liber Formularum spiritalis intelligentiae* John Cassian used dogs metaphorically to denigrate the devil, Jews, reprobates, tepid believers, and unbelieving Gentiles. Tertullian in *Adversus Marcionem* cited Revelation 22:15, which states that outside of the New Jerusalem are the "dogs" "who practice magic arts, the sexually immoral, the murderers, the idolaters, and everyone who loves and practices falsehood."[37] Augustine turned to Matthew 7:6 in which Jesus told his followers not to give to dogs [hardened unbelievers] what is sacred [the gospel]. The dogs in this passage, according to Augustine, are people guilty of turning away from God and of embracing idolatry, and he voiced similar sentiments in his *Faith and Works*.[38] In the *Enarrationes in Psalmos* the negative association of Jews as a type of faithless dogs did not escape

---

[37] "Canis, diabolus, vel Judaeus, vel gentilis . . . Hic leonem diabolum, canem vero gentilem, vel hominem peccatorem accipiendum putant: quod ille ad fidem vel poenitentiam possit venire, ille autem non veniat," Cap. 5, *MPL* 50:733. Tertullian, "Jam hinc ad queastiones omnes. Canes, quos foras Apostolus expellit (Apoc, XXII, 15), latrantes in Deum veritatis," 2.5. *MPL* 2:289. The text in Revelation 22:15 reads, "Outside are the dogs, those who practice magic arts, the sexually immoral, the murderers, the idolaters, and everyone who loves and practices falsehood."

[38] Canis es, una es ex Gentibus, idola adoras," *Sermo* 77.6.10. *MPL* 38:487. Sancti Avreli Avgvstini, *De fide et operibus*, 3.4.; 4.6; 5.7; 6.8, and 16.30. *CSEL*, 41. (Sect. V, pars III). Vindobonae, 1900, pp. 38–44 and 73–74. See also Paulinus of Nola, who

the notice of the bishop of Hippo.[39] As evidenced by his typlological use of the hostile dog, Cassiodorus repeatedly portrayed the Jews as enemies of the Church. To his commentary on Psalm 21:17, "For many dogs have encompassed me," he added, "So the Jews are most justly compared with them," and he expressed more anti-Semitic comments elsewhere. The dogs in the *Passio* do not experience any transformation of character or conversion and as such are symbolic of the hopeless reprobate.[40]

Embracing doctrinal heresy and lapsing morally were sins meta-phorically identified by the Church Fathers with evil dogs. Augustine called tepid members of the Church weak in the faith—dogs to be tolerated for the sake of the peace of the Church, a rather creative adaptation of the parable of the Wheat and the Tares (Mt. 13:29).[41] Cassiodorus said that Psalm 21:21, referred to a deliverance of the soul from the sword—from the hand of the dog—to which he added bluntly, "He [the psalmist] compares heretics to dogs."[42] Paraphras-ing Proverbs 26:11, Augustine compared morally lapsed Christians to dogs that have returned to eat their own vomit,[43] and Caesarius similarly admonished his flock not to lapse into their former sin and vice as a dog returns to its own vomit.[44] The bishop of Arles compared lukewarm, careless, and fearless [of God] brethren to dogs bound in chains [to sin], easy prey for the Devil.[45] The perilous state of the weakened soul from the wiles of worldly pleasure and the Devil are likened respectively by Caesarius to "the dog's power" and "the lion's mouth," and these inconstant persons he sternly called "defiled pigs and dogs" not worthy to be accepted into the Church.[46]

---

called nominal Christian Gentiles "hounds of God," and whose fate is with the unbelievers because of their empty tepid faith, in *Epistola* 50.1.8. *MPL* 61:411 and Caesarius of Arles, *Sermones. CCSL*, 103, pars I. *Sermo* 93.1, pp. 382–383.

[39] "Canes Gentes Judaei dixerunt, tanquam immundos. Nam inde et ipse Dominus, cum post eum clamaret Chananaea quaedam mulier . . .," 58.15. *MPL* 36:702.

[40] *Expositio Psalmorum, CCSL,* 97, pars II, I. *Psalmo* 21.17 and *Psalmo* 58.7 and 15, pp. 198–200, 523 and 527.

[41] "Nos uero ad sanam doctrinam pertinere arbitramur ex utrisque testimoniis uitam sententiamque moderari, ut et canes in ecclesia propter pacem ecclesiae tole-remus et canibus sanctum, ubi est pax ecclesiae tuta, non demus," *De fide et operibus,* 5.10–13.7. *CSEL,* 41 (Sect. V, pars III), p. 42.

[42] *Expositio in Psalmorum, CCSL,* 97, pars II, 1. *Psalmo* 21.503–504.21, p. 202.

[43] *De fide et operibus,* 25.18–20.47. *CSEL,* 41 (Sect. V, pars III), p. 92.

[44] *Sermones, CCSL,* 103, pars I. *Sermo* 81.2 and *Sermo* 97.5 and *Sermo* 135.6., pp. 334–335, 399–400, and 558–559.

[45] *Sermones, CCSL,* 103, pars I. *Sermo* 121.6, p. 507.

[46] *Sermones, CCSL,* 103, pars I. *Sermo* 136.7, pp. 563–564 and *Sermones, CCSL,* 104, pars I, 2. *Sermo* 229.3, pp. 907–908.

In a final passage, Caesarius, turned to Proverbs 26:11 to chastise clerics, monks, and virgins for having become proud, disobedient, and lukewarm. These are religious guilty of abandoning abstinence for gluttony, vigils for sleeping, humility for pride, obedience for disobedience, and patience for wrath. In them is fulfilled, the bishop declared, the proverb, "The dog returns to its vomit."[47]

In the *Acts of Peter* the entire episode with Simon Magus and Marcellus is one of rescuing not just a single lapsed believer, but an entire throng that had abandoned the true faith and come under the spell of the magician. The *Acts of Peter* identifies the brethren at Rome as those who are now spiritually "scattered" and Peter's opening statement in his sermon to the crowd clearly identifies them as former believers. Peter even refers to his own triple denial of Christ (7.2–3, p. 54), as reported in all four Gospels, to illustrate that there is opportunity for repentance and hope for re-entry into the Church; his own tearful repentance through God's grace is powerful testimony of redemption. Likewise, when Peter approached Marcellus's house, the crowd gave witness concerning the Senator's virtuous life and his subsequent fall into the deceptive spells of Simon Magus, which explains why they pleaded with Peter to show the Senator mercy (8.31–34 and 1–5, pp. 54–56). Although the *Acts of Peter* never quotes Proverbs 26:11, nor even alludes to it, the example of believers lapsing into heretical error is firmly embedded in the story. The account, however, does end with the victorious redemption of both Marcellus and the brethren at Rome, thanks to the intervention of Peter and his faithful, loquacious dog. Even in their harshest polemics against heresy and moral depravity, the Church Fathers always left open the gate for lapsed believers to return to the fold through repentance and God's grace. Like the Judas figure, however, Simon Magus is never given the possibility of redemption in the *Acts of Peter*; like Satan, he is a being whose will is hopelessly turned against God.

The dog scene at the house of Marcellus did not escape the notice of artists in the Early Christian period. Aside from the artistic interest of these rare pieces, the most striking feature is that all of them are found on sarcophagi. Two are from Verona and Mantua and are dated by scholars between the years A.D. 390–400.[48] (Figs. 10 and 11.)

---

[47] *Sermones, CCSL*, 104, pars I, 2. *Sermo* 237.3, pp. 946–947.
[48] One of the earliest and productive studies of these two sarcophagi is in Stuhlfauth, *Apokryphen Petrusgeschichten*, pp. 3–9, and he offers only a photograph of the Mantua piece, at 4. G. Wilpert published two splendid photographs of the Verona

A third sarcophagus, at one time deposited at Nîmes, France, but very likely from the Transalpine, is now missing and is known only from a drawing. (Fig. 12.) The object may be more the victim of being misplaced than actually being lost, and it would be worth the time and effort to try to locate it anew.[49] The fourth piece is deposited at the National Museum in Krakow and according to its discoverer Professor Janusz A. Ostrowski, it also likely originated in Gaul and dates between 390–400.[50] (Fig. 13.) We should not rule the possibility that there may be other artistic representations of this and other apocryphal themes since no one has ever carried out a full inventory of this material.[51]

In content the Verona, Krakow, and lost Nîmes sarcophagi are strikingly similar one to another: all three have Peter on the left and the dog on the right of the relief. The dog is wearing a visible collar around its neck, presumably where the heavy chain had been attached, according to the *Acts of Peter*, (catena grande ligatum 9.1, p. 57), although a chain is not visible. They all depict the scene in front of Marcellus's home as evidenced by the arcade and columns in the Verona and Krakow pieces, but in the drawing of the lost Nîmes

and Mantua sarcophagi, but with little commentary, in *I Sarcofagi Cristiani Antichi*. Testo, vol. 2. Roma, 1932, pp. 348–351. For the Mantua sarcophagus, plate 30, p. 39, and the Verona piece, plate 150.2, p. 177. Neither piece escaped the attention of G. Turcio, "San Pietro e i Cani," p. 299. See also the succint discussion by, M. Sotomayor, *S. Pedro en la Iconografía Paleocristiana*. Biblioteca Teologica Granadina, 5. Granada, 1962, pp. 30–31 and 161–162. See note 50 below.

[49] E. Le Blant was the first scholar to widely publicize the lost sarcophagus from Nîmes, in *Les sarcophages chrétiens de la Gaule*. Paris, 1886, p. 114, no. 136. For further notices and commentary see, Stuhlfauth, *Apokryphen Petrusgeschichten*, pp. 5–6, with a reproduction of the LeBlant drawing, p. 5. Wilpert took notice of the Nîmes piece, *I Sarcofagi*, 2:350. See also, Turcio, "San Pietro e i Cani," p. 299 and Sotomayor, *S. Pedro en la Iconografía*, pp. 31 and 161.

[50] The article contains photographs of the Verona and Nîmes sarcophagi, "Apocryphal and Canonical Scenes. Some remarks on the Iconography of the Sarcophagus from the Collection of the National Museum in Krakow," *Études et Travaux* 13 (*Travaux du Centre d'Archéologie méditerranéenne de l'académie polonaise des sciences*, 26) (1978), 305–309. A photograph of the Krakow sarcophagus is at, p. 308. I wish to thank the Director of the *Polish Academy of Sciences*, (Warsaw) Dr. Karol Mysliwiec, for sending me a copy of this article. Also relevant, J.A. Ostrowski, "Unknown fragments of Early Christian Sarcophagi," *Meander* 28 (1973), 326–331.

[51] In my own search of the *Princeton Index of Christian Art*, which I consulted as a summer fellow at UCLA in 1992, and through other sources I have identified at least 60 artistic representations of apocryphal scenes of Simon Magus. The Princeton collection which depends on the contributions of researchers is not as yet to be considered exhaustive, although ultimately that is the goal. Prof. Agustín Hevia Ballina, director of the Diocesan Archives of Oviedo, Spain, informed me about the uncatalogued Simon Magus relief in the cathedral which I researched in the summer of 1995. Results are forthcoming in *Hagiographica*.

object the column is there without the arcade. One wonders if the drawing of the Nîmes relief has fully captured the entire scene contained in the original. The Mantua sarcophagus has all of the elements found in the other sarcophagi with some basic differences, however: here the dog is on the left, Peter, on the right. Like its companions, the dog, has a prominent muzzle but no chain, and as in the others the entrance has an arcade without any columns or building blocks. All four depict the dog with his fore-paw in the air, which I believe demonstrates his submission and friendly disposition towards Peter or the "conversion" of the dog that I described earlier. Although the dog still has a growling face in all the reliefs, let us recall that ancient and medieval reliefs usually collapse into one scene a sequence of events, in this case: the initial hostility of the dog, the blessing of Peter, and the conversion of the animal to God's service.

There is still the question as to the identification of the person standing with Peter in the Mantua, Nîmes, and Krakow sarcophagi, yet absent in the Verona sarcophagus. In the *Acts of Peter*, when Peter approached the house of Marcellus, a great crowd followed him, and he alone walked up to the doorway where he was met by a doorkeeper who engaged him in conversation, (Petrus de synagoga ibat in domum Marcelli ubi Simon manebat. sequebantur autem eum turbae magnae. ut autem uenit ad ianuam, uocans hostarium dixit ad eum 9.23–25, p. 56). It is certain that the figure with Peter in these sarcophagi is none other than the doorkeeper. Professor Ostrowski has maintained that the man with Peter in the Krakow sarcophagus is a young male, and this fine detail is noted in the *Acts of Peter*.[52] In fact, Peter addresses the doorkeeper as a "young man", (Petrus autem ad iuuenem dixit 9.31, p. 56). The doorkeeper is not portrayed at all in the Verona sarcophagus, and this omission does not in any significant way alter the story in that relief. The one episode that is absent in all of the iconography of the Early Church is the feeding of bread to the dogs by Peter in the *Passio*.

3. *Dogs in the Middle Ages*

As a result, when the Dominicans were given the nickname *Domini canes* in the Middle Ages, it was part of a well-established metaphorical

---

[52] "Apocryphal and Canonical Scenes," p. 306.

tradition. Furthermore, the image of dogs continued to be used in earnest by numerous medieval writers as "types" of both good and evil. In this section I will explore select medieval sources that exemplify two major ways in which dogs were invoked in medieval polemics: (1) the dog in Christian anti-Jewish/Muslim and Heretical literature; and (2) the dog both as symbolic of moral sin and as preacher of God's word. The *Acts of Peter* and the *Passio* enjoyed extensive diffusion among medieval writers, and these apocryphal texts have a central place in the medieval, metaphorical uses of dog.

Christianity had already established a long, precarious, and inconsistent relationship with Jews when in the seventh century Islam emerged to further challenge the religious hegemony of the Church. The polemical weapons that Christianity had aimed against Judaism were now put into action to combat Islam. In view of the overwhelming negative view of dogs in Judaism and Islam, it is hardly surprising that Christians utilized them metaphorically to belittle both faiths.

Two major ninth-century western anti-Islamic texts will suffice to illustrate how "dogs" were effectively used by Christians to insult Islam in general, and Muhammad specifically: the *Song of Roland* and the Spanish text *Istoria de Mahomet*, of Andalusian origin, that eventually found its way north into the province of Navarra.[53] A third document, the *Liber Apologeticus martyrum* by Eulogius of Cordoba borrowed verbatim from the *Istoria de Mahomet* and deserves at least passing mention because of its popularity among the Mozarabs.[54]

In section 29 of the *Song of Roland*, which describes Marsile at Saragossa, we read at lines 2590–91:

> Throw the idol of Muhammad into a ditch,
> And pigs and dogs bite and trample it.

---

[53] The Oxford text with English translation that I am using for this article is in, *The Song of Roland: An analytical edition.* 2 vols. (ed.) G.J. Brault. Pennsylvania State University, 1978. The text of the *Istoria de Mahomet* is translated with brief commentary in K.B. Wolf, "The earliest Latin lives of Muhammad," in *Conversion and Continuity. Indigenous Christian communities in Islamic Lands. Eighth to Eighteenth centuries*, (ed.) M. Gervers and R.J. Bikhazi. Papers in Mediaeval Studies, 9. Pontifical Institute of Mediaeval Studies, 1990, pp. 89–101.

[54] The authoritative edition is in, *Corpus Scriptorvm Mvzarabicorvm*, vol. 2 (ed.) I. Gil. Madrid, 1973, pp. 483–486, the dogs at, "Statimque uice angelica ad eius foetorem canes ingressi latus eius deuorauerunt," 16.53–54, p. 485 and, "et ob eius uindicandam iniuriam annis singulis canes occidere decreuerunt.... Digne ei quidem accidit ut canem uentrem tantus ac talis propheta repleret," 16.55–58, p. 486.

(E Mahumet enz en un fosset butent
E porc e chen le mordent e defulent).

The equal revulsion of pigs in Islam explains their presence along
with the dogs in this passage. G.J. Brault has identified the similarity
between Muhammad's fate here and that of Achab and Jezebel in
the Old Testament.[55] In Scripture dogs eat their own vomit or are
fed leftovers from the meal table; there are perhaps even further
biblical allusions that may be read into this passage.[56] The fact that
Muhammad's body is in a ditch decaying is a Christian denial of the
belief by Muslims that the Prophet ascended into heaven, as Christians believe about Christ. We witness here, in sort of a twisted
manner, the use of dogs in the service of the Church, as they bite
and trample upon Muhammad's body.

Section 30, entitled "Baligant's Arrival" has yet another instructive
reference to dogs at lines 3526–27, which describe:

The men of Occiant bray and whinny,
The men of Argoille yelp like dogs
[Cil d'Ociant i braient e henissent,
Arguille si cume chen i glatissent]

The yelping dog-like howling attributed to Emic Baligant's men are
sounds associated with pagans and devils. Scholars have long noted
that in Old French literature certain animal sounds were attributed
metaphorically to pagans. In this reference the Muslim message is
likened to the annoying sounds of whining dogs as opposed to faithful barking dogs and as such reveals openly the pagan nature of a
false prophet. In the *Acta Nerei et Achillei* Simon Magus, too, is described as a howling wolf as he is chased out of Rome, "quamdiu
illum cum ululatu quasi lupum extra muros civitatis ejicerent."[57]

An equally relevant document, the *Istoria de Mahomet*, found in the
eleventh-century Codex of Roda, yields more dogs that oppose Islam.[58]
According to this text, as Muhammad contemplated his own imminent

---

[55] *Song of Roland*, section 188, 2:158–159. I Kings 21:23–24 reads, "And also concerning Jezebel the Lord says: 'Dogs will devour Jezebel by the wall of Jezreel.'
Dogs will eat those belonging to Ahab who die in the city . . .," and there are cross-
references at 22:38 and 2 Kings 9:36, Ibid., 1:270.

[56] Proverbs 26:11, See Brault, *Song of Roland*, 1:425–26 note 23 on the meanings
and nuances.

[57] Brault, *Song of Roland*, section 255, 2:214–215. On the symbolic meaning of
howling see, 1:304, and 408 note 10, and *Acta Sanctorum*, chapt. 3.13, p. 10.

[58] Wolf, "The earliest Latin lives," text and translation at, pp. 96–99.

death, he predicted that on the third day after his death he would
be resurrected from the dead by an angel [Gabriel]. His followers
waited faithfully for the miracle to take place, but soon realized on
the awaited third day that his body was beginning to rot. They reasoned that their presence had scared the angel Gabriel away, so they
left the body alone to allow the heavenly messenger to effect the
miracle. At that moment, however, wild dogs sniffed out the stench
of the decaying body and began to eat it. The writer of the *Istoria de
Mahomet* was quick to add how appropriate it was for these wild dogs
to fill their bellies with the remains of this [false] prophet, who had
sent his own soul and that of many others [his followers] to hell.[59]
Once again, as in the *Song of Roland*, the thrust of this polemic was
to discredit any Islamic claim of a resurrection of Muhammad, and
wild dogs devouring his corpse dramatically undermine his claims to
deity. Similarly, the dogs are again depicted in the service of God
exposing the false prophet of Islam; they also served the double
purpose of validating for the writer the Christian claim of Jesus's
resurrection. The assault against Islam continued vigorously in the
Middle Ages, and there are other precise adaptations of the Simon
Magus legends in anti-Islamic polemics which will be dealt with in a
separate study.[60] The dog in the *Acts of Peter* served precisely the
same purpose, helping Simon Peter reveal the false claims of Simon
Magus. Likewise, the wild dogs of Simon Magus in the *Passio* were
unable to inflict any bodily harm upon Simon Peter. Peter's victory
over the magician in that latter contest vindicated his apostolic authority, while Simon Magus is exposed as a fraud, as are all subsequent
false prophets, including Muhammad.

The patristic condemnation of Jews—via the image of the dog—
continued with unabated vigor in the Middle Ages. Raban Maur in
Allegoriae in universam sacram scripturam dedicated a section to dogs
wherein he explained the varieties of allegorical canines. Among these
he cited Psalm 21[22]:16, "Dogs have surrounded me," which he

---

[59] "Digne ei quidem accidit ut canum uentrem tantus hac talis propheta repleret, qui non solum suam, sed et multorum animas inferi tradidisset," Ibid., p. 97 = Eulogius, *Liber Apologeticus Martyrum*, 16.57–59, in *Corpus Scriptorvm Mvzarabicorvm*, p. 486.

[60] The figures of Simon Magus and Nicolas of Antioch are both utilized in the Christian anti-Muslim propaganda of the High Middle Ages. I intend to explore in a separate study this fascinating medieval Islamic-Christian confrontation. For the patristic use of Simon and Nicolas see, Ferreiro, "Sexual Depravity," pp. 29–38 and "Jerome's polemic against Priscillian," pp. 309–332.

likened Jews to a pack of wild dogs that are hostile to the Church.[61] Abbot Rupertus, a twelfth-century writer, employed the same psalm to describe the enemies of the Church in general, but in his work on the *Trinity* he metaphorically associates Jews with dogs.[62] Garnerius of Paris in the *Gregoriarum*, another twelfth-century work, succinctly identified the three chief enemies of the faith: heretics, Jews, and Gentiles. Of the Jews, he said they were dogs who persecute the Lord [and his Church] and he invoked Psalm 21[22]:17.[63] In the thirteenth-century *Ancrene Riwle*, Psalm 22:16–17 is once again used broadly to describe the hostility leveled at the Christian faith [by Jews, too] and to censure sin. The same psalm is found in the *Acts of Peter* in Peter's speech directed at the followers of Simon Magus in which the apostle affirms how the Lord rescued him from such wicked dogs, (erant enim qui me circumuenerant canes inprobi sicut prophetas domini 7.4–5, p. 54).[64]

The early fifteenth-century Irish source known as the *Leabhar Breac* (c. 1411), which also recounts the passion of the apostles Peter and Paul, is the only source that I have found which uses the *Passio* specifically to link the Jews directly to Simon Magus. When the apostle began to convert many people away from Simon, "the leaders of the Jews (Iúdaide) and the priests of the Gentiles (pagans)... praised Simon Magus in the presence of Nero Caesar," and they also heaped blame upon Peter and Paul. As the confrontation between Simon Magus and apostles escalated, the magician voiced his concern that so many people were turning away from his teachings. Simon laments

---

[61] "Per canes, Judaei, ut in psalmo: 'circumdederunt me canes,' id est, invaserunt me Judaei," *MPL* 112:883.

[62] "Respondit turbam et dixit: Daemonium habes; quis te quaerit interficere?' 'Ecce isti sunt canes, de quibus hic opprobrium hominum et abjectio plebis propter nos factus, in psalmo dicit:' Quoniam circumdederunt me canes multi (Psal. XXI). 'Frustra laborat hic intentio describentis.' Neque enim hunc latratum nequissimorum canum verbis posset ullo modo consequi," *In evangelium S. Ioannes Commentariorum Liber* 7. *MPL* 169:513 and, "Propheta dicit: Lingua canum tuorum ex inimicis ab ipso (Psal. LXVII): non, inquam, inveniebant copiam escarum apud inimicos Christi Judaeos, ex quibus et ipsi secundum carnem erant, paucos quippe ex illis manducare, id est, convertere, et sibimet incorporare poterant," *De Trinitate* 7.8. *MPL* 167:453.

[63] "Canum nomine Judaei Dominum persequentes designantur, sicut a Domino per Psalmistam dicitur, 'Circumdederunt me canes multi,' (Psal. XXI, 17)," 3.12. *MPL* 193:103. Concerning Gentiles he says, "Canum nomine gentiles designantur, sicut in Evangelio Dominus mulieri Chanauaeae dicit. 'Non est bonum sumere panem, et mittere canibus (Matth. XV, 26)," Ibid.

[64] *The Latin Text of the Ancrene Riwle*, (ed.) C. D'Evelyn. Early English Texts Society, 216. London, 1944, pp. 124–125.

with alarm, "This clique of men have turned away all the Jews (Iúdaide) from believing on me." A comparison of the terminology of the *Passio* and the *Leabhar Breac* shows that the latter text substituted "Judea" (Iudaeam, 17.6, p. 135) for "Jews" (Iúdaide), thus introducing into the account a significant shift aimed at Jews specifically and away from a generic reference to the peoples of Judea.[65] The collaboration between the Jews and Simon Magus was firmly established as well as their persistent rejection of apostolic truth as preached by Simon Peter. Thus, the ensuing defeat of Simon Magus and his ravenous dogs by Peter in the *Passio* is also to be viewed as a victory against the unbelieving Jews.

Many other texts could be harnessed to illustrate the usefulness of the dog image to attack Jews in general and to perpetuate the perception that they were enemies of the Lord and of his Church. How the Church decided to be rid of such ravenous dogs (Jews) depended in the Middle Ages upon the winds of religious fervor, anti-Semitism, and politics. And, as in the case of Islam, the association of Jews (Judaism) with dogs was a serious affront to Jewish communities a message that Christians had every intention of conveying. Like the anti-Muslim polemic, the use of Simon Magus by the *Leabhar Breac* was meant to attack directly Jews and censure their rejection of Christianity. The propaganda sometimes worked in both directions; for it was the Jews, as we saw earlier, who turned the tables on Christians and used Simon Magus in the *Toldoth Jeshu* to ridicule the claims of Christianity.

The watch-dogs of the Church, the Dominicans (*Domini canes*), were kept busy not only by Muslims and Jews; but heretics as well. We have noted in the above discussion how the linking of wild dogs with Islam served in part to reveal the heretical nature of that faith, and it delivered a similar message in regard to the Jews. The heretics, too, became the object of attack by the orthodox community. The ninth-century writer Paulinus of Aquilea, while rebutting the adoptionist heretic Felix of Urgel, declared heretics as not being worthy of even being in the same company with dogs, a clear allusion to Job 30:1.[66] An exemplary twelfth-century text depicting heretics as

---

[65] *The Passions and the Homilies from Leabhar Breac.* (ed. and trans.) R. Atkinson. Todd Lecture Series, 2. Dublin, 1887. For the Irish text, pp. 86–95, and a translation pp. 329–339, at 333–334. For a brief discussion of this text see, M. McNamara, *The Apocrypha in the Irish Church.* Dublin, 1975, pp. 11–12.

[66] "Isti igitur famosissimi canes, qui ingressus Dei sunt visi, pastoris officium erga caulas ovium non immerito certum est procul dubio modo fungi mirabili: qui

dogs is once again Garnerius of Paris in the *Gregoriarum*, in which he quoted Proverbs 26:11, accusing heretics of returning to their own vomit, "Canum nomine haeretici designatur, sicut scriptum est: 'Sicut canis revertitur ad vomitum suum, sic stultus ad stultitiam suam'."[67] Amatus of Montecassino, in his lengthy poem in praise of Simon Peter, included the major incidents with Simon Magus, and he invoked Proverbs 26:11 to describe the magician's lapse into heretical error [vomit], "Sed canis ad vomitum pollutus sorde reversus."[68]

This same proverb was combined at times with additional biblical texts to address the ever-present disturbing moral lapses that continually plagued the Church. One such passage is the popular verse found in Luke 16:21 that describes the gentle dogs which licked the sores of the incapacitated beggar, Lazarus. The story from Luke became a catalyst to promote a more positive view of canines: the dog as preacher against moral sin and of God's benevolent grace. Along these lines, while Raban Maur preached that a shameless sinner is like a dog who returns to his own vomit, "Canis est peccator impudens, ut in Parabolis: "Canis reversus ad vomitum suum," diligent preachers are to be compared to the good dogs who "heal" [lick] through preaching the sins of the people as the dogs healed the open sores (sin) of Lazarus, "Per canes, praedicatores boni, ut in Evangelio: 'Canes lingebant ulcera Lazari,' quod sancti praedicatores sanabant peccata gentilis populi."[69] These preachers are the antithesis of evil preachers who are silent like a dog that does not bark, "Per canes praedicatores mali, ut in propheta: 'Canes muti, non valentes latrare,' quod mali praedicatores vitia corripere nolunt."[70] Garnerius of Paris echoed a similar message in his *De canibus* entry, in which he reminded his readers that the tongues of God's preachers heal the disease of moral sin.[71] For every positive usage of dogs to extol those

---

crudelium belluarum rabiem sanctis, si dici liceat, procul a mandrilibus gregum coercere latratibus non pertimescunt," *Sancti Paulini Contra Felicem* 1.2. *MPL* 99:351, this is also a cross-reference to Gregory the Great's *Moralia in Iob* 20.9. Job 30:1 reads, "But now they mock me, men younger than I, whose fathers I would have disdained to put with my sheep dogs."

[67] 3.12. *MPL* 193:103.

[68] *Il Poema di Amato su S. Pietro Apostolo*, (ed.) A. Lentini. Miscellanea Cassinese, 30–31. Montecassino, 1958, 2.7.4, 1:84.

[69] *Allegoriae in Universam sacram Scripturam*, *MPL* 112:883.

[70] Ibid., the second reference is a partial paraphrase of Isaiah 56:10.

[71] "Canum nomine sancti praedicatores designantur, sicut in Evangelio scriptum est: 'Sed et canes veniebant et lingebant ulcera ejus (Luc. XVI, 21). Quid enim per

faithful to the Church, a negative image of dogs was not too far behind. In two twelfth-century Goliardic texts Simon Magus is presented as a dog barking falsehood:

> Decanus canis est archidiaconi
> Cuius sunt canones latratus dissoni
> Canens de canone discors est Simoni[72]

and in the second Goliard poem *Ecce Sonat in Aperto*, Simon appears as a frustrated howling dog that does not get its way [against Peter], a sure sign of the prideful reprobate:

> Si non datur, Simon stridet
> [Simon howls unless he wins].[73]

In a twelfth-century *Book of Beasts* we find two contrasting images of the dog taken from Luke 16:21 and Proverbs 26:11. In the first, the commentator praised the righteous dog: "In licking a wound, the tongue of a dog heals the same. . . . In certain ways, Priests are like watchdogs. They always drive away the wiles of the trespassing Devil with admonishments. . . . The tongue of a dog cures a wound by licking it. This is because the wounds of sinners are cleansed," In contrast, "The fact that a dog returns to its vomit signifies that human beings, after a complete confession, often return incautiously to the crimes which they have perpetrated."[74] In *De silentio clericorum* Philip of Hawering brought together the Lazarus story with Proverbs 12:18, the latter reading, "but the tongue of the wise brings healing," to emphasize the spiritual medicinal outcomes of preaching; he also contrasted this positive image by rebuking the mute dogs—silent preachers—for failing to oppose sin.[75]

---

canes nisi praedicatores intelligimus? Canum etenim lingua vulnus dum lingit, curat.' Quia et doctores sancti dum in confessione peccati nostri nos instruunt, quasi vulnus mentis nostrae per linguam tangunt," 3.12. *MPL* 193:102.

[72] O. Dobiache-Rojdestvensky, *Les Poésies des Goliards*. Paris, 1931, p. 107.

[73] G.F. Whicher, *The Goliard Poets. Medieval Latin Songs and Satires*. New Directions, 1949, pp. 150–151. Simon Magus is mentioned in another Goliard poem that condemns simony, pp. 132–133.

[74] T.H. White, *The Book of Beasts: being a translation from a Latin Bestiary of the Twelfth-Century*. New York, 1954, pp. 66–67.

[75] "Et supra: 'Lingua, inquit, sapientium sanitas est (Prov. XII).' Cum autem lingua sapientium sanitas sit, quis dubitet eam non debere silentio cohiberi, sed imperitis et infirmantibus adhiberi, ut vice canum lingentes ulcerum foeditatem, dolorem mitigent, pellant morbum, revocent sanitatem? . . . In cujus typo rei putrescentem Lazarum canes in Evangelio lingere perhibentur, quia sapientes quique minus sapientibus

The thirteen and fourteenth centuries witnessed a no less vigorous use of the dog to encourage virtue and to denounce vice. The dog Cerberus in Dante's *Inferno*, Canto 6, is symbolic of gluttony and more. When the poet speaks of, "three sparks from Hell—Avarice, Envy, Pride" (line 74), he refers to the three heads of Cerberus which bark forth the three vices. The thirteenth-century *Speculum Laicorum* deals with virtue and vice by comparing noble and ignoble dogs to noble and ignoble women.[76] Simon Magus, incidentally, in the *Acts of Peter* and the *Passio* is portrayed as embodying all three major vices and of even setting himself up as a "god."[77] A friar, Nicole Bozon in *Les contes moralisés* (c. 1320), creatively coupled the Devil with eight hounds, who obediently go out and do his evil bidding, one of which, *Havegyf*, is portrayed as perpetrating the sin of Simony.[78] In this passage Simon Magus is associated directly with a devilish dog through the vice named after him.[79] In its entry on luxuria the *Speculum Christiania*, a fourteenth-century Middle English work, used the image of a dog.

---

adhibentur, ut oris medicamine, et multifaria verbi cura tanquam ferro, oleo, potione, malagmate, ligaturam, et nocentia resecent, et adhibeant diligentius profutura," cap. 14. *MPL* 203:969.

[76] "Bays in his triple gullet and doglike growls," (line 14) in Sayers, *Comedy of Dante Alighieri*, p. 104 and line 74 at 106. Further comments on Cerberus are at, pp. 107–108. For exhaustive references see, P. Toynbee, *A Dictionary of Proper Names and Notable Matters in the Works of Dante*. Oxford, 1893, p. 147. "Canum duo sunt genera, quidam enim sunt nobiles, quidam ignobiles. Nobiles vero taciti sunt et simplices, ignobiles iracundi et latrantes. Ita est de mulieribus; nobilium filie sunt simplices et tacite et solitudinis amatrices, ignobiles vero tumultuose et per plateas discurrentes," *Le Speculum Laicorum*, (ed.) J.Th. Welter. Thesaurus exemplorum, 5. Paris, 1914, p. 33, other references to dogs in this work are at, pp. 39–41 and 96–97.

[77] "Roga ergo pro me tamquam bonus procurator dei, non me tradidi cum peccatis Simonis igni aeterno, qui me tantum suasit ut statuam illi ponerem, subscribtioni tali: 'Simoni iuueni deo.' si scirem," *Acts of Peter*, 10.22–25, p. 57. The reference to the inscription comes from Justin Martyr, *Apologia* 26.2. In the *Passio* we find a similar charge that Simon Magus claimed some status of deity, "Cumque perlecta fuisset epistola, Nero dixit: Dic mihi, Petre, ita per illum omnia gesta sunt? Petrus ait: Ita, non te fallo; sic enim est, bone imperator. hic Simon plenus mendaciis et fallaciis circumdatus, ut putet se qui homo est, etiam hoc esse quod deus est," 22.4–8, p. 139.

[78] *Les contes moralisés de Nicole Bozon frère mineur*, (ed.) L.T. Smith and P. Meyer. Paris, 1889, pp. 29–37.

[79] "Puis al venour descouplé un autre chien, qe est apellé Havegyf, ceo est a dire 'pernés et donez,' qel est descouplé sur les abbés, priours e chivalers e damez qe ont esglises en lur donisoñ, qe pensent en donant de doner e prendre: de doner un esglise de lur doneisoñ e lur seignurage, e pur lur doun receyver ascun avañtage," Ibid., p. 31. In the ensuing lines are partial quotes from the Acts of the Apostles 8:21–22 where Peter rebukes Simon Magus for attempting to buy the power of the Holy Spirit.

The writer cited Augustine's statement that a rotten dog is more tolerable than a sinful soul that is in mortal sin and at the very door of hell.[80] Charged with seducing a wealthy Senator such as Marcellus and milking him of enormous financial resources Simon Magus is damnable proof of *luxuria* in the *Acts of Peter*. This accusation of deceiving the wealthy for financial gain is reinforced at, (Marcellus furens paenitetur in benefaciendo, dicens: "Tanta substantia inpendi tanto tempore, superuacuo credens in di notitiam me erogare!" 8.13–16, p. 55). Along these lines there is absolutely no doubt regarding Simon's impure intentions with the wealthy woman, Eubula. Peter explicitly refers to her wealth and Simon's theft by way of his "spells" on the woman (17.1–27, p. 63).

Another well-known source is the fourteenth-century *Gesta Romanorum* (c. 1300), in which through the use of moral stories dogs appear in creative fashion.[81] In Tale 142, "Of the snares of the Devil," the story talks about a traitor who used eight dogs—virtually the same ones found later in Nicole Bozon, as noted above—to spoil the forest of a benevolent king. In the application of this story, the writer explains, "The traitor is any evil Christian; the dogs and nets are vices."[82] Simon Magus at one time walked with the apostles Peter and Philip, but then filled with pride, betrayed the faith and became its greatest enemy, as the tradition of the hopeless reprobate unfolded. In the *Passio* Simon Magus attempted to use his evil dogs to destroy the messenger of God, Simon Peter. Tale 12, "Of bad example," is a lengthier story which features a, "putrid dog with its mouth wide open, and its teeth black and decayed, through which the whole fountain gushed in a surprising manner."[83] "As this water,

---

[80] "A roten dogge stynkez more tollerable to men than a synful soule to god . . . Thei that be in dedly synne ben as at helle gate," (lines 7–8 and 11–12), p. 72. The Latin text reads, "Tollerabilius fetet canis putridus hominibus quam anima peccatrix deo . . . Qui in peccato mortali sunt, quasi ad portam inferni sunt," (lines 7–8 and 11), p. 73 in *Speculum Christiani. A Middle English religious treatise of the 14th century*, (ed.) G. Holmstedt. Early English Texts Society, 182. London, 1933. There is a second reference to dogs in the section on *Ira*, "Ther-for a man so wrethede es to be flede, as a woode hounde or ellys as a cruel lyon broken louse," (lines 15–16), p. 62, for the Latin (lines 14–15), p. 63.

[81] *Gesta Romanorum: or entertaining moral stories*, (trans. and ed.) C. Swan and W. Hooper. Reprint of 1876 edition. Dover, 1959, pp. 22–26; 137–139; and 248–249. For a continuing use of dogs as images of vices in the late Middle Ages, see *The Fantasy of Pieter Brueghel*, (ed.) A.J. Barnouw. New York, 1947, pp. 18–23.

[82] *Gesta Romanorum*, p. 249.

[83] Ibid., p. 23.

gushing through the mouth of a putrid dog, is neither polluted nor loses aught of its natural taste or colour," continues the tale, "So is the celebration of Mass by a worthless minister."[84] In the *explanatio* it is taught that the putrid dog is an evil preacher, and that dog is used because of four "excellent qualities" not found in other animals: a medicinal tongue, the Lazarus story; a distinguishing nose, to sniff out heresy and moral error; an unshaken love, the faithfulness of priests to the Church, and unremitting watchfulness, which protect from thieves (the Devil) by barking.[85] In the much shorter Tale 79, "Of presumption," a certain king showed partiality for "little dogs that barked loudly," (p. 137). In this tale the yelping little canines are identified in the moral "application" as zealous preachers and the king as Christ.[86]

The late medieval Catalán preacher Vincent Ferrer (1350–1419) kept alive the positive image of dogs in Sermon 24, "Dominica prima post Trinitatem," dedicated to Lazarus the wounded beggar. In the exegesis of Luke 16:21 he made the following observations: the dogs who licked his wounds are like those who preach the healing doctrine of God, (aquests cans són los preycadors, e menors, e agostins, e tots aquells qui preyquen bona doctrina, lines 13–15, p. 269).[87] Vincent quoted Job 30:1, as had Paulinus of Aquilea in the ninth-century, but he integrated the text into Luke 16:21 on the medicinal benefits of the dog's tongue. According to Vincent Job's dogs are preachers who possess spiritual healing powers through preaching, (Aquests cans són los preycadors. Mas més hi ha: que los cans han lengua medicinal, lines 31–32, p. 269). Through their tongues the preachers are able to bring healing to souls inflicted by mortal sin, (E axi han a fer los preycadors, car ab la lengua han a lepar les nafres del peccat mortal, lines 1–3, p. 270). In the remaining section, Vincent listed all of the major sins the Devil inflicts upon the people of God: superbia, avaricia, simonia, and more.[88] In all cases it is the tongue of the preacher which brings the opportunity for redemption and forgiveness, even as Christ forgave the very people who crucified him, (e quan tal persona ve a la preycació, e hou com nostre senyor Déus

---

[84] Ibid., pp. 23–24.
[85] Ibid., pp. 24–26.
[86] Ibid., p. 138.
[87] Sant Vincent Ferrer. *Sermons*, 6 vols., (ed.) J.S. Sivera, et al. Els Nostres Classics, Col. Lecció B, volum 3. Barcelona, 1932, 1:269.
[88] Ibid., 1:270.

Jesuchrist perdonà a aquells quil crucificaren, lines 24–26, p. 270).
In the *Acts of Peter*, which circulated widely in the Middle Ages via
the *Golden Legend* of Jacobus of Voragine, both Peter and his dog incessantly preached the message of repentance and redemption to the
followers of Simon Magus, further contributing to favorable images
of the dog.

In an equally generous view of dogs, the late fourteenth-century
mystic Walter Hilton, made a most creative application of a canine
in his widely read *Ladder of Perfection*. He admonished in Book 1,
chapter 41, "A hound that only runs after the hare because he sees
other hounds run rests when he is tired or returns home. But if he
runs because he sees the hare, he will not stop until he has caught
it, tired though he may be. Our spiritual progress is very similar."[89]
It is fitting to finish our select view of medieval sources on this uplifting
note. Whether the Church employed dogs as types of evil or of good,
in either case the goal was always to proclaim to the reader or listener
that the grace of God is the avenue of escape from the entrapments
of the world, the flesh, and the Devil.

4. *Dogs, Bread and Simon Magus in the Middle Ages*

We have seen already the prominent place of the dog eating its own
vomit as drawn from Proverbs 16:21, but there is another image of
feeding hungry dogs, as drawn from the *Passio*, deserving our attention.

The use of bread to placate the angry disposition of the dogs has
remarkable similarities to some of the legends regarding the Greek
mythological dog Cerberus, the many-headed guardian of Hades—
three heads according to some sources and fifty or more in others.
Hesiod in the *Theogony* described Cerberus as one, "who eats raw
flesh."[90] In Virgil's *Aeneid*, however, we find Cerberus is fed with a
sop or cakes made with honey and a drug to make the dog sleepy,
"melle soporatam et medicatis frugibus offam," (6.420),[91] a scene
which Apuleius in *The Golden Ass* recalled in elaborate fashion:

---

[89] Walter Hilton, *The Ladder of Perfection*, (trans.) Leo Sherley-Price. Penguin, 1957,
pp. 46–47.
[90] Evelyn-White, *Hesiod*, pp. 100–103, at 101.
[91] Williams, *Aeneid of Virgil*, p. 138 and notes on page 484.

In this manner the high tower prophetically spake unto Psyche, and advertised her what she should do: and immediately she took two half-pence, two sops, and all things necessary and went unto Taenarus to go towards Hell . . . and filled the ravenous mouth of the dog with a sop . . . she departed, and stopped the mouth of the dog with the other sop (Book 6).[92]

Not resorting to sedatives or any such devices associated with magic, Peter in the *Passio* called upon God and blessed the bread to give it the power to vanquish the dogs.[93] Nonetheless, the story of Cerberus could have been a source of inspiration for this portion of the *Passio*. Rather than a single dog like Cerberus an unspecified number of dogs attacked Peter.[94] The only other reference external to the *Passio* in the patristic era that involves Peter, bread, and dogs is in the *Acts of Peter and the Twelve Apostles* (6.1), from the Nag Hammadi Codex, which reads, "The one who carries bread with him on the road, the black dogs kill because of the bread," an unlikely source of inspiration for the *Passio*.[95] In *Canto VI* of the *Inferno* Dante made the ever-hungry Cerberus the consummate glutton possessing an insatiable appetite for souls which, "He clutches and flays and rips and rends the souls," (6.17). While Dante borrowed directly from Virgil regarding the feeding of Cerberus, he adapted the story for his own ends. Instead of feeding drugged bread honey cakes to Cerberus, Dante's Virgil stuffs fistfuls of dirt into the mouths of the dog, which has the same sedative effect upon the beast.

At once my guide, spreading both hands wide out,
Scooped up whole fistfuls of the miry ground
And shot them swiftly into each craving throat.
And as a ravenous and barking hound
Falls dumb the moment he gets his teeth on food,
And worries and bolts with never a thought beyond.

(Lines 25–30, Sayers, p. 105)

---

[92] Adlington, *Apuleius*, pp. 276–279.

[93] For a discussion of the associations with magic and Simon Magus, see E. Peters, *The Magician, the Witch, and the Law*. University of Pennsylvania Press, 1978, pp. 7–8. V.I.J. Flint, *The Rise of Magic in Early Medieval Europe*. Princeton, 1991, pp. 338–344.

[94] Hesiod in the *Theogony* says that Cerberus had fifty heads, Evelyn-White, *Hesiod*, p. 103. Apuleius does not specify the number of heads, in fact, he speaks only of one head to feed, Adlington, *Apuleius*, pp. 276–279. The rest of our Classical sources identify Cerberus as a three-headed beast, Simpson, *Gods and Heroes (Apollodorus)*, p. 99. Miller, *Ovid*, 1:208–209 and 2:16–17 and 64–65. Williams, *Aeneid of Virgil*, p. 138 and 484. Bennett, *Horace*, pp. 162–163 and 216–219.

[95] For a translation and commentary see, H.-M. Schenke, "Die Taten des Petrus

Some scholars believe that the dirt is an allusion to Genesis, in which God creates humankind (Adam) from the soil; hence Cerberus is a devourer of human souls. But why Virgil would feed humans (dirt) to the dog is not at all clear, if indeed this is the intended meaning of this passage. Dante devoted another canto to Simon Magus to condemn simony, but there the *Passio* had no place for the great poet.[96] Nevertheless, the shared similarities between Virgil's Cerberus story and the *Passio* strongly suggests possible borrowing and adaptation by the writer of the *Passio* from the Cerberus tradition in general, and from Virgil specifically.

There is one late-medieval fifteenth-century Provençal mystery play, the *Istoria Petri et Pauli*, which creatively brought Simon Peter, Simon Magus, and Cerberus together in this lengthy work containing 6,135 lines.[97]

Although Cerberus has a minor role in the play, his appearance in this work is significant in terms of the tradition that mediated this monster from the patristic era to the end of the Middle Ages. While

---

und der zwölf Apostel. Die erste Schrift aus Nag-Hammadi-Codex VI," *Theologische Literaturzeitung* 98 (1973), 13–19. A translation into English is in, "The Acts of Peter and the Twelve Apostles (VI, I)," in *The Nag Hammadi Library in English*, (ed.) J.M. Robinson. Harper, 1977, p. 267. For a recent study see, S.J. Patterson, "Sources, redaction, and *Tendenze* in the *Acts of Peter* and the *The Twelve Apostles* (NH VI, 1)," *Vigiliae Christianae* 45 (1991), 1–17.

[96] Sayers, *Comedy of Dante Alighieri*, Canto XIX, pp. 188–193. For studies on *Canto VI* and the figure of Cerberus, see G. Padoan, "Il mito di Teseo e il cristianesimo di Stazio," *Lettere Italiane* 11 (1959), 432–457. A. Piromalli, "Il peccato di Gola e l'episodio di Ciacco," *Ausonia* 20, 4–5 (1965), 50–57. L.R. Rossi, "The devouring passion. 'Inferno' VI," *Italica* 42 (1965), 21–34. G. Padoan, "Cerbero," *Enciclopedia Dantesca*. Roma, 1970, pp. 912–913. R.S. Dombroski, "The Grain of Hell: A note on retribution in '*Inferno*' VI," *Dante Studies* 88 (1970), 103–108. C. Kleinhenz, "Infernal guardians revisited: 'Cerbero, il gran vermo' (*Inf.* VI, 22)," *Dante Studies* 93 (1975), 185–199.

[97] Cerberus makes four speeches in the *Istoria Petri et Pauli Mystère en langue Provençale du XVe siécle publié d'après le manuscript original*, (ed.) P. Guillaume. Geneva: Slatkine Reprints, 1977 at 311–318, p. 11; 3636–3641, p. 134; 5923–5926, p. 229 and 6082–6085, p. 234. For a discussion of Cerberus in medieval French sources see, M. Lazar, "Les Diables: Serviteurs et Bouffons. (Répertoire et jeu chez les comédiens de la troupe infernale)," *Trétaux* 1, 2 (1978), 51–69, at 60 and 62. Also for analysis of the *Istoria Petri et Pauli*, M. Lazar, "The Saint and the Devil: Christological and Diabological Typology in Fifteenth Century Provençal Drama," in *Essays in Early French Literature Presented to Barbara M. Craig*, (ed.) N.J. Lacy and J.C. Nash. South Carolina, 1982, pp. 81–92, at 84–88. For an inventory of references to Cerberus associated with the devil see, H. Wieck, *Die Teufel auf der mittelalterlichen Mysterienbühne Frankreichs*. Leipzig, 1887. Cerberus also appears without any reference to Simon Magus in a late medieval play, Arnoul Gréban, *Le Mystère de la Passion*, (ed.) O. Jodogne. Bruxelles, 1965, his speeches appear at, pp. 55–56, 100–101, 141–142, 202, 229, 295–296, 312, 328, 349, 351, 383–384, 442–443.

the Church Fathers virtually ignored Cerberus, the dog was somewhat more popular in the Middle Ages, and as we have noted Dante
devoted an entire canto in the *Inferno* to the dog.[98] In the *Istoria Petri
et Pauli* Cerberus is given the ability to speak, and at his first appearance he introduces himself as the guardian of Hell, (Et you, Cerberus,
per conpas Gardo la porto infernallo, lines 311–312, p. 11). A cohort
of the Devil, the dog also carries out the commands and will of the
Evil One. Cerberus is one of many demonic beings that welcomed
Simon Magus to Hell after his earthly death (lines 3636–3641, p. 134)—
the only instance in medieval literature that I am acquainted with
in which the Dog of Hades and the Magician come together and the
only source, apart from the *Acts of Peter*, in which a dog is given the
ability to speak. The tenth-century Anglo-Saxon *Prose of Solomon and
Saturn* also recalled the unique nature of a speaking dog, when it
asks, "Tell me what man was the first [to be] talking with a dog. I
tell you, Saint Peter."[99]

The bread incident in the *Passio* was remembered in the Middle
Ages, and while medieval writers made only subtle alterations, they are
nevertheless interesting.[100] In the *Passio* there is mention of the types

---

[98] For example, Arnobius, "Interea dum liber Stygem, Cerberum, Furias, atque
alias res omnes curiosa inquisitione collustrat . . .," *Adversus Gentes*, book 5, *MPL* 5:1142;
Augustine, "de Cerbero, quod sit triceps inferorum canis," *De civitate Dei*, 18.13.
MPL 41:570. For a brief analysis of Cerberus in the Middle Ages, see J.J. Savage,
"The Medieval Tradition of Cerberus," *Traditio* 7 (1949–1951), 405–410.

[99] *Istoria Petri et Pauli*, pp. 11 and 134. See, J.E. Cross and T.D. Hill, *The Prose
Solomon and Saturn and Adrian and Ritheus. Edited from the British Library Manuscripts with
commentary*. McMaster Old English Studies and Texts, 1. Toronto, 1982, pp. 30, 99–
100, and see the earlier study by, W. Wilmanns, "Ein Fragebüchlein aus dem neunten
jahrhundert," *Zeitschrift für deutsches altertum* 15 (1872), 166–180, at 176–177. I wish to
thank Professor Robert Faerber (University of Geneva) for alerting me to this source.

[100] The accounts vary on the fate of the dogs after Peter's rebuke with the bread.
"Petrus uero extendens manus in orationem, ostendit canibus eum quem benedixerat
panem; quem ut uiderunt canes subito nusquam conparuerunt," (27.8–11, p. 143).
The *Blickling Homily* is in agreement with the *Passio* concerning the "vanishing" of
the dogs, *The Blickling Homilies of the Tenth Century*, (ed.) R. Morris. Early English
Texts Society, 58. London, 1880, pp. 180–181. Orderic Vitalis likewise does not
deviate on this point, *Historia Ecclesiastica*, 2.7. *MPL* 188:132. Jacobus of Voragine
used precise language that implies that the dogs fled and did not vanish into thin
air, "ille vero panem benedictum obtulit et subito ipsos in fugam convertit," 89,
p. 372 in *Jacobi a Voragine Legenda Aurea*. (ed.) Th. Graesse, reprint of 1890 edition.
Osnabrück, 1969. See the translation in W.G. Ryan, *The Golden Legend. Readings on
the Saints*. vol. 1. Princeton, 1992, p. 343. The fifteenth-century Provençal play, *Istoria
Petri et Pauli* is in agreement with Jacobus, the text on which it very likely depended
upon, "Hic Petrus porrigat dictis demonibus de pane benedicto, et hii canes, viso
pane, vertantur in fugam, et dimitant Simonem," in *Istoria Petri et Pauli*, p. 94.

of miracles Simon Magus performed to lure followers that forms the necessary background leading up to the encounter before Nero.[101] In the tenth-century *Blickling Homilies*, homily 15, "Spel Be Petrus & Paulus," these specific miracles from the *Passio* tale are recounted faithfully, but not without some embellishments. In the *Passio* the writer explained that so many people followed Simon Magus because the magician made brazen serpents move, stone statues laugh and move, and himself fly—all of which is repeated verbatim in the *Blickling Homily*. The *Leabhar Breac*, too, reports the same information, the only omission being the laughter of the moving statues. In his homily on Peter and Paul Aelfric does not mention stone dogs, much less barking ones.[102] While these details are completely absent in Amatus of Montecassino, they are recalled by Orderic Vitalis in *Historia Ecclesiastica* 2.7, who presented a fascinating alteration to the story when he introduced stone dogs which bark at the behest of Simon's magical abilities, "et lapideos canes latrare, statuas aereas ridere et moveri," while the *Passio* reads, "et lapideas statuas et aereas ridere et mouere"[103]—a significant addendum that found a permanent place in the popular *Golden Legend* (c. 1260) of Jacobus de Voragine, who added his own peculiar twist to the barking stone dogs. Jacobus, instead, has the dogs not barking, but singing, "et canes cantare."[104] The *Istoria Petri et Pauli* does not recall this fascinating change of the *Passio* by earlier medieval writers.

Another detail in the *Passio* involving textual changes in the Middle Ages refers to the moment when Peter received the bread secretly, blessed it, broke it, and quietly stuffed the fragments up his sleeves, (Petrus enim benedixerat panem quem acceperat ordeaceum et fregerat et dextera atque sinistra in manica collegerat 26.3–4, p. 143).

Aelfric, after noting the blessing of the bread by Peter, made the specific observation that the apostle, "brake, and wrapt it in his two

---

[101] "Faciebat enim serpentem aereum mouere se, et lapideas statuas et aereas ridere et mouere, se ipsum autem currere et subito in aere uideri," 11.3–5, p. 131. On the false nature of these miracles as magic see, Peters, *The Magician*, pp. 7–8 and Flint, *Rise of Magic*, pp. 338–344.

[102] *Blickling Homilies*, pp. 172–173 and in the *Passio*, 11.3–5, p. 131. *Leabhar Breac*, p. 333. B. Thorpe, *The Homilies of the Anglo-Saxon Church. Homilies of Aelfric*. Vol. 1. London, 1844, p. 377.

[103] Lentini, *Poema di Amato*, 1:132. Orderic Vitalis, *Historia*, MPL 188:132 and *Passio*, 11.4, p. 131.

[104] Graesse, *Legenda Aurea*, 89.2, p. 370, and Ryan, *Golden Legend*, p. 341. For a treatment of Jacobus's use of the word "apocrypha", see R. Gounelle, "Sens et usage d'*apocryphus* dans la *Légende Dorée*," *Apocrypha* 5 (1994), 189–210, at 205–206.

sleeves"—the inference being that the bread was broken into two pieces. Once again the *Blickling Homily*, "Spel Be Petrus & Paulus," strays from the original *Passio* text. Rather than referring to the right hand and left hand, the *Blickling Homily* instead says that Peter took the bread after blessing it, "brake it in two, and put it up his two sleeves."[105] The redactor of the *Blickling Homily* chose to interpret the right hand and left hand as a reference to the equal partition into two parts of the bread. Aside from this departure the homily remained faithful to the original *Passio*. Aelfric and the *Leabhar Breac*, likewise, do not introduce any novelties on the hidden bread and its power to vanquish the dogs.[106] Amatus of Montecassino simply reported that Peter produced the bread that silenced and humbled the hostile dogs of Simon Magus, "Proicit his panem Petrus, statimque latrare Cessant; prostrati mites gradiuntur ut agni." In yet another slight departure from the *Passio* the text portrays Simon Magus as insecure, "Augustus Caesar, omnis proclamat et aetas: 'Est magus insanus, turpissimus, hic, sceleratus,'" and nothing is said specifically about the breaking of the bread.[107] The twelfth-century liturgical poem of Adam of St. Victor, *S.S. Petrus et Paulus*, only alludes to how Nero and Simon Magus were both humbled by Christ's truth (through Peter), "Facta Christi mentione/, Simon Magus cum Nerone/Conturbantur hoc sermone/, Nec cedunt Apostolis," perhaps a vague reference to the bread encounter.[108] A second twelfth-century liturgical hymn that celebrates the Feast day of Peter and Paul commemorates Peter's blessing of the bread and conquest of Simon Magus's dogs:

> Panem dum sanctificatum
> Contra gregum simulatum
> Canum Petrus protulit[109]

The last twelfth-century text is from Orderic Vitalis, who reverted to the original *Passio* and did not specify as to how many pieces

---

[105] *Homilies of Aelfric*, p. 377. "Petrus haefde þonne þone hláf gesegnod þe he onfeng berenne, & hine tobraec on twa, & hine gedyde on his twa slefan," *Blickling Homilies*, pp. 180–181.

[106] *Homilies of Aelfric*, p. 377 and *Leabhar Breac*, pp. 334–335.

[107] Lentini, *Poema di Amato*, 4.13.7–8. 1:132 and 4.13.9–10.

[108] Wrangham, *Liturgical Poetry*, 61–64. 2:86–87.

[109] C. Blume, *Liturgische Prosen des Mittelalters*, 5. Analecta Hymnica Medii Aevi, 37. Leipzig, 1901, p. 244. A discussion of this and other relevant hymns is in, J. Szövérffy, *Psallat Chorus Caelestium. Religious Lyrics of the Middle Ages*. Medieval Classics: Texts and Studies, 15. Berlin-Classical Folia, 1983, pp. 298–299.

the bread was broken, "Petrus panem accepit, benedixit, fregit et sub manica sua abscondit." The same holds true of the *Golden Legend* of Jacobus de Voragine and one of his principal sources, the mid-thirteenth-century *Epilogus in Gesta Sanctorum*, written by the Dominican Bartholomeu of Trent.[110]

Lastly, in the *Istoria Petri et Pauli*, the narrative appended two details to the story which are absent in our other sources: first, that Peter blessed the bread with the sign of the cross, "Petrus benedicat panem cum signo crucis et abscondat in manica,"; second, that *two* demons in the form of dogs appeared to attack the apostle, "Hic venient duo demones, in forma canum, ad devorandum Petrum."[111]

5. *Fate of Simon Magus in the* Acts of Peter

The *Acta S.S. Nerei et Achillei* (*Acta S.S.*), believed to have been written somewhere between the fifth and sixth centuries, became one of the principal sources that medieval writers used to popularize the *Acts of Peter*. In their explanation of the fate of Simon Magus Aelfric, Jacobus of Voragine, Orderic Vitalis, and the *Istoria Petri et Pauli* all reveal that they came under its sway. A near-contemporary source that influenced Jacobus is the *Abbreviato in Gestis et Miraculis Sanctorum*, a mid-thirteenth century work by the Dominican John of Mailly, that mediated the *Acta S.S.* material in the Middle Ages. Even though John of Mailly used the *Acta S.S.* in his work, his abbreviated version excludes entirely the lengthier incidents with the dog at Marcellus's house. Moreover, he specifically identified the *Acta S.S.* as his source, "vel sicut dicit macellus inpassione nerei et achillei," when recalling the story about Simon Magus's expulsion from the city (Rome) by the mob, the children, and the dog.[112]

---

[110] *Historia*, 2.7. *MPL* 188:132. Graesse, *Legenda Aurea*, 89.2, p. 372 and Ryan, *Golden Legend*, p. 343. *Epilogus in Gesta Sanctorum*, chapter 58, in *Bartolomeo da Trento, domenicano e agiografo medievale. Passionale de Sanctis, textus-index*, (ed.) D. Gobbi. Trento, 1990, p. 108. I am grateful to Professor Barbara Fleith (University of Geneva) for bringing this and other sources to my attention.

[111] *Istoria Petri et Pauli*, pp. 93–94.

[112] For the *Acta S.S.* see, the Latin text, *Acta Sanctorum*, vol. 3, pp. 4–16, the dog account is at 9–10. The Greek text has been edited by Wirth, *Acta S.S. Nerei et Achillei* and Achelis, *Acta S.S. Nerei et Achillei*. The edition of John of Mailly is in, *Jean de Mailly, Abrégé des Gestes et Miracles des Saints*, (ed. & trans.) A. Dondaine. Bibliothèque d'histoire dominicaine, 1. Paris, 1947, pp. 225–226, the *Acta S.S.* is at, 199–201. The unedited manuscript of John of Mailly is Ms. B. III 14 Universitäts-bibliothek

The *Acts of Peter* relate that Marcellus reprimanded, cursed, and drove Simon Magus out of the house with his own hands. Marcellus's slaves joined in on the eviction adding curses, hitting his face with their hands, beating him with sticks and stones, and pouring pots of "filth" (excrement and trash?) over his head (14.11–24, p. 61). Simon ran to the house of Narcissus, where Peter was staying, to denounce the apostle for bringing such hostilities upon him. Peter sent a woman with a child to meet the magician with instructions to the woman to keep silent and to allow the child to speak. By a miraculous touch the child took the voice of a man and harshly rebuked Simon Magus for spreading falsehood, even reminding him of being reprimanded by a dog, and at the end of the oracle cursed Simon Magus with dumbness. Simon instantly became mute, left Rome in disgrace until the Sabbath, and as an outcast lodged in a stable (15.30–36 and 1–19, pp. 61–62). Here ends this phase of the encounters between Simon Peter and Simon Magus.

Inspired by the *Acts of Peter* and the *Acta S.S.*, Aelfric excersized literary license in his version of the house of Marcellus story, and it is an imaginative, exciting departure from these principal sources. As Aelfric tells it Simon Magus was assaulted by a crowd of people after having been reproached and confounded by Simon Peter. Escaping from the mob, Simon went to a house in which Peter was staying and tied a huge dog (mastiff) at the gate within the dwelling to devour the apostle.[113] The *Acts of Peter* never claims that Simon Magus placed the dog in front of Marcellus's house and Peter is not initially a guest of Marcellus; he comes rather as an outsider in search of Simon Magus, who incidentally is a guest of Marcellus. Aelfric continues, Peter untied the dog, apparently having been pacified by the apostle, and he sent the dog inside to inform Simon Magus that, "he no longer with his magic deceives God's people." Having received the ability to speak, the dog not only delivered the message; it also put the magician "to flight." Peter, in the meantime, had apparently followed the dog and commanded it not to bite Simon Magus. Although it did "not hurt his body, [it] tore his garments piecemeal

---

Basel Folio 31r and 31v. See also the study by K.E. Geith, "Jacques de Voragine— auteur indépendant ou compilateur?," in *Le moyen Français*, 32. *Legenda aurea—la Légende dorée (XIIIᵉ–XVᵉ s.)* Actes du Congrès international de Perpignan (séances "Nouvelles recherches sur la *Legenda aurea*), ed. B. Dunn-Lardeau, pp. 17–31, especially at 18–23.

[113] *Homilies of Aelfric*, pp. 373–374.

from his back, and, howling like a wolf, drove him along the walls, in sight of the people."[114] Once Simon Magus escaped the attacking canine he fled naked in shame and stayed away from Rome. Clearly borrowing from the *Acta S.S.*, Aelfric has Simon Magus "howling like a wolf," (quamdiu illum cum ululatu quasi lupum extra muros civitatis ejicerent).

Jacobus of Voragine combined the material from the *Acts of Peter* with that of the *Acta S.S.*, at least the Latin version, and it is well known that Jacobus depended somewhat upon John of Mailly at certain junctures. While utilizing these sources, Jacobus in turn, introduced into his account the novel details of the *Acta S.S.* and (given the immense popularity of the thirteenth-century *Golden Legend*) they entered the broader mainstream of medieval thought.

Reproduced here are the texts of the *Acta S.S.* and the *Golden Legend*. While relying less so directly on the *Acta S.S.* but more so the thirteenth-century writer John of Mailly, Jacobus did not follow verbatim adoption of either text.

Acta Nerei et Achillei (Acta Sanctorum, pp. 9–10):

> Cum ergo evasisset Simon, venit ad me, et putans me nescire, quod factum fuisset, canem immanem, quem vix catena ferrea vinctum tenebat, hunc ligavit in ingressu dicens: Videamus si Petrus, qui solet venire ad te, poterit ingredi. Sed post unam horam venit Petrus, et facto signo Crucis solvit cane, et dixit ei: Vade obloquere Simoni. Desine ministerio dæmonum decipere populum, pro quo Christus suum sanguinem fudit. Videns autem ego tanta mirabilia, cucurri ad Petrum: et genibus ejus provolutus, excepi illum in domum meam; Simonem vero expuli cum dedecore. Canis autem omnibus blandus effectus, solum Simonem persequebatur: quem cum misisset subtus se, cucurrit Petrus clamans et dicens: Præcipio tibi in nomine Domini nostri Jesu Christi, ut non figas morsum in aliquam partem ejus corporis. Canis autem nullum ejus contingere potuit membrum, sed vestimenta ita morsibus attrectavit, ut nulla pars ejus corporis tecta remaneret. Populus autem omnis, et præcipue pueri, simul cum cane post eum tamdiu cucurrerunt, quamdiu illum cum ululatu quasi lupum extra muros civitatis ejicerent.

Golden Legend (Graesse, *Legenda Aurea*, cap. 89, p. 373):

> Tunc symon, ut ait sanctus Marcellus, ivit ad domum Marcelli discipuli ejus ligavitque maximum canem ad ostium ejus domus dicens: nunc

---

[114] Ibid., p. 375.

videbo, si Petrus, qui ad te venire consuevit, ingredi poterit. Post
paululum venit Petrus et facto signo crucis canem solvit, canis autem
omnibus aliis blandus, solum Symonem persequebatur, qui apprehen-
dens eum ad terram subter se dejecit et eum strangulare volebat; accur-
rens autem Petrus cani clamavit, ne ei noceret, et canis quidem corpus
ejus non laesit, sed vestes adeo laceravit, ut ille nudus positus remaneret, populus autem et maxime pueri cum cane tamdiu post eum
concurrerunt, donec illum quasi lupum de civitate fugarent.

John of Mailly (*Abbreviato in Gestis*, Fol. 31r):

> Cum ergo evasisset Symon ivit ad domum Macelli qui erat discipulus
> eius et ligavit maximum canem ad hostium eius dicens: nunc videris.
> Si Petrus qui solet venire ad te potest ingredi. Post paululum venit
> Petrus et facto signo crucis solum canem (solvit) Canis vero omnibus
> blandus solum Symonem persequebatur quod deiciens sub se cum vel-
> let eum strangulare cucurrit Petrus ut non noceret ei canis qui corpus
> eius lesit sed vestem eius discissit ut nudus omnino remaneret, populus
> autem omnis et maxime pueri simul cum cane tam diu post eum cucur-
> runt donec illum quasi lupum per muros civitatis eicerent. Cuius oppro-
> brii pudorem non ferens per annum nusquam comparuit. Et audiens
> Macellus tanta miracula deinceps Petro adhesit et Symonem cum de-
> decore expulsit.

In the *Golden Legend* Jacobus highlights the following details: Peter set
the dog free from its chains by using the sign of the cross; the dog
became gentle with all present, except Simon Magus whom the dog
began to chase. The dog, then, knocked Simon to the ground and
attacked him, and as the animal went for Simon's throat (et eum
strangulare volebat), Peter intervened and called off the dog. Told
by Peter not to injure the magician bodily, instead the dog tears
Simon's clothes off and leaves him completely naked (ut ille nudus
positus remaneret). The crowd that was watching, a group of children,
and the dog itself chase after the naked Simon and run him out of
the city, as one would chase a wolf.[115]

Jacobus embellished the *Acta S.S.* and relied on John of Mailly in
several ways: Once Peter released the dog with the sign of the cross,

---

[115] "Et canis quidem corpus ejus non laesit, sed vestes adeo laceravit, ut ille nudus
positus remaneret, populus autem et maxime pueri cum cane tamdiu post eum
concurrerunt, donec illum quasi lupum de civitate fugarent," 89.2, in Graesse, *Legenda
Aurea*, p. 373. Ryan, *Golden Legend*, p. 344. For a study on Jacobus's sources see,
W. Hug, "Quellengeschichtliche Studie zur Petrus- und Pauluslegende der Legenda
aurea," *Historisches Jahrbuch* 49 (1929), 604–624. Jean de Mailly, *Abrége des Gestes*,
pp. 225–226.

which is in the *Acta S.S.*, the canine set about to seize Simon by the throat, and the apostle commanded the dog not to kill him. The dog's attempt to kill Simon Magus by crushing his throat with his jaws, recorded by Jacobus (et eum strangulare volebat), is not in the *Acta S.S.* text but it is in John of Mailly. Peter's invocation of the Lord Jesus Christ to command the dog not to bring bodily harm to Simon Magus in the *Acta S.S.* is absent in the *Golden Legend* (Praecipio tibi in nomine Domini nostri Jesu Christi) and John of Mailly, but Jacobus does report from the *Acta S.S.* that the dog is given leave only to tear his clothes to shreds (*GL*, "sed vestes adeo laceravit", *Acta S.S.* "sed vestimenta ita morsibus attrectavit," Mailly, "sed vestem eius discissit."). Jacobus further notes that after the attack, Simon Magus was completely naked (ut ille nudus positus remaneret), and he is chased out of the city in the buff by the crowd, the children, and the dog. The *Acta S.S.* mentions the nudity, too, but in a slightly restrained way (ut nulla pars ejus corporis tecta remaneret). On this matter it seems that Jacobus was indeed depending heavily on John of Mailly since their texts contain identical language. Three examples are sufficient to establish our point:

1. On Simon's ejection from the city:
   J. Mailly—illum quasi lupum per muros civitatis eicerunt.
   A.S.S.—illum cum ululatu quasi lupum extra muros civitatis ejicerent.
   Jacobus—illum quasi lupum de civitate fugarent.
2. On the near strangulation of Simon:
   J. Mailly—eum strangulare cucurrit
   A.S.S.—(not in the text)
   Jacobus—et eum strangulare volebat
3. On the nudity of Simon Magus:
   J. Mailly—ut nudus omnino remaneret
   A.S.S.—ut nulla pars ejus corporis tecta remaneret
   Jacobus—ut ille nudus positus remaneret

Jacobus's account is replete with several key biblical allusions. The dog's attack on Simon is reminiscent of Ahab and Jezebel in the Old Testament and the assault of Muhammad's body by dogs in the anti-Muslim polemic. Nakedness is invariably interpreted as symbolic of spiritual unveiling of shame and falsehood before God (2 Cor. 5:3). The chastisement of Simon Magus by the children refers to infants who have pure unadulterated faith (Psalm 8:2 and Mt. 21:16). Simon's eviction out of the city (Rome) seems to be an indirect reference to the expulsion of the unrighteous (sorceress, the sexually immoral, etc.), who are likened to dogs, from the New Jerusalem in Revelation 22:15. Likening Simon Magus to a wolf needs no further elaboration; we have touched on this motif earlier. Although these creative addenda are not found in the text of the *Acts of Peter*, Jacobus did not in any way violate the spirit and message of the original tale. In Orderic Vitalis and the *Istoria Petri et Pauli*, we find further influences from the *Acta S.S.*; very likely Jacobus is the source in the case of the latter text.

Orderic Vitalis emphasizes that the dog attack did not cause Simon Magus bodily harm and he also recalled the reference to nudity. He is sure to identify the mob, the dog, and children expelling Simon Magus from the city; the use of the sign of the cross to release the dog; and the identification of the magician as a wolf. However, he does not report, as Jacobus did later on, the dog's attempt to crush the throat of Simon Magus. Orderic's reliance on the *Acta S.S.* is much more pronounced than that of Jacobus and is confirmed by the near verbatim borrowings at key junctures of the narrative. I have italicized a few examples that demonstrate the convergence of these two texts:

> Evadens itaque Simon, ad Marcellum, quem jampridem seduxerat, venit; immanemque canem, quem vix ferrea catena vinctum tenebat, in ingressu ligavit. Videamus, inquit, si Petrus, qui solitus est venire ad te, poterit ingredi. Deinde post unam horam Petrus venit, *factoque crucis signo*, canem solvens ait: Vade et loquere Simoni: Desine ministerio dæmonuni decipere populum, pro quo Christus fudit sanguinem suum. Marcellus autem, tanta mirabilia videns, ad Petrum cucurrit, et genibus ejus provolutus, in domo sua illum excepit, Simonem vero cum dedecore expulit. Canis autem blanus omnibus effectus est, solum vero Simonem persecutus est. Quem cum misisset subtus se, currente Petro et clamante: *Præcipio tibi, in nomine Domini nostri Jesu Christi, ut non figas morsum in aliquam partem corporis ejus*, nullum quidem membrum ejus contingere potuit, *sed ita morsibus vestimenta ejus attrectavit ut nulla pars corporis ejus tecta remaneret.* Omnis autem populus, et præcipue pueri post eum simul cum cane cucurrerunt, eumque *cum ululatu quasi lupum [extra] muros civitatis ejecerunt.*[116]

The *Istoria Petri et Pauli* likewise included the instructions of Peter to the dog not to bring bodily harm to Simon Magus:

---

[116] "Sed ita morsibus vestimenta ejus attrectavit ut nulla pars corporis ejus tecta remaneret. Omnis autem populus, et praecipue pueri post eum simul cum cane

A faulx chin, malvas et trist,
Te comandou, per Jesu Crist,
Que non auses tochar sa chart,
Ny lou blesar en luoc ny part.
El ha ben prou dal deshonour.

(2827–2831, p. 103)

The narrator indicated that Simon's clothes were shredded by the dog, and that he was expelled from the city, but there is no mention of the nudity, "Tunc canis laceret vestimenta Simonis et exeat eum extra civitatem." The sign of the cross is used to bless the bread in the *Passio* version of the *Istoria Petri et Pauli*; the *Acta S.S.* may be a possible source via the *Golden Legend* or even John of Mailly. The mystery play also added speeches from three children who mock and ridicule Simon Magus, "Pueri romani sequantur Simonem illudentes," as he is chased out of the city.[117] It is also evident that the three children were given some form of Trinitarian symbolism in this mystery play.

6. *Simon Magus and the* Passio *Dogs in Medieval Art*

The *Passio* dog scene is preserved only in medieval artistic examples. Although few in number, they are nevertheless illuminating. Three are Italian: one at the Cathedral at Sessa Aurunca (Fig. 14), a lost fresco from the church San Piero a Grado, and another in a Vatican Library Latin Passional manuscript.[118] (Fig. 15.) A fourth possible Italian relief is on the tomb of Pope Sixtus IV (1414–1484); even if authentic, it does not recreate very closely the scenes in either the

---

cucurrerunt, eumque cum ululatu quasi lupum [extra] muros civitatis ejecerunt," *Historia*, 2.7. *MPL* 188:130.

[117] *Istoria Petri et Pauli*, p. 103.

[118] An in-depth study on Sessa Aurunca is in, D. Glass, "The Archivolt Sculpture at Sessa Aurunca," *The Art Bulletin* 52, 2 (1970), 119–131, especially at 125–128 and for the dogs figure 16. Useful are also, C. Stornajolo, "I rilievi dell'arco sul portico della cattedrale di Sessa Aurunca," *Dissertazioni della Pontificia Accademia* 6, 2 (1896), 163–180 and A. Venturi, *Storia dell'arte Italiana, 3. L'arte romanica*. Milano, 1904, pp. 570–571, figures 532, 534, 535. An extensive study of the church S. Piero a Grado is by, P. D'Achiardi, "Gli affreschi di S. Piero a Grado presso Pisa e quelli già esistenti nel portico della basilica vaticana," *Atti del Congresso Internazionale di scienze storiche* (Roma 1–9 Aprile 1903), vol. 7. *Atti della Sezione IV: Storia dell'arte*. Roma, 1905/Kraus Reprint, 1972, pp. 193–285, especially at 212–216 and 257–258. A microfiche copy of the *Latin Passional* is in the *Princeton Index of Christian Art* under the Simon Magus file, 32R76LV+82, 10A, Roma Lib. Bibl. Vaticana, lat. 8541, *Passional*.

Passio or the *Acts of Peter*.[119] And there is one non-Italian example of a *Passio* scene in a fresco in the cloister church at Müstair, Switzerland.[120] (Fig. 16.) These are the only known medieval artistic works commemorating the dog scenes that I have been able to locate. However, as in the case of Simon Magus iconography in general, there is always the possibility that other uncatalogued material awaits rediscovery and documentation.

There does exist some vagueness in the *Passio* on the number of dogs that Simon Magus magically set on Peter. The *Passio* text relates that there were several dogs conjured up by Simon Magus, but the specific number is never specified, (Et subito apparuerunt canes mirae magnitudinis et impetum fecerunt in Petrum 27.6–7, p. 143). In the Sessa Aurunca relief, the fresco at Müstair, and even the lost fresco from San Piero a Grado—for which we have a description before its destruction—there are *two* dogs shown attacking Peter.[121] The *Latin Passional* is no exception and it also shows two dogs under the taming influence of Peter.

The most popular and widely used medieval literary texts do not concur with the artistic tradition on this specific point. The *Blickling Homily* leaves the number of dogs unspecified, "þa faeringa coman þaer hundas forþ on wundorlicre mycelnesse," although it speaks of two pieces of bread and two sleeves. Orderic Vitalis likewise lacks the exact number of dogs, "Ecce canes mirae magnitudinis protinus apparuerunt."[122] Even the immensely popular *Golden Legend* neither bends on this point nor departs from the original *Passio* text, "Et subito canes maximi apparuerunt et in Petrum impetum fecerunt."[123] The only text that specifies two dogs is the mystery play, *Istoria Petri et Pauli*, in which the narrator says, "Hic venient duo demones, in forma canum, ad devorandum Petrum."[124] There is, I believe, an explanation that bridges the apparent gap between the textual and

---

[119] A brief description is in Turcio, "San Pietro e i Cani," p. 299. The *Biblioteca Apostolica Vaticana* was unable to verify this art piece as reported by Turcio.

[120] A thorough study of the fresco at Müstair is in, B. Brenk, *Die Romanische Wandmalerei in der Schweiz*. Basler Studien zur Kunstgeschichte, 5. Bern, 1963, pp. 44–49 and figure 21.

[121] D'Achiardi reproduced the Latin text that describes the scene in the now lost fresco at S. Piero a Grado, "Erant duae aliae historiae quarum unam jam fabricatores deiecerant, in qua erat Sanctus Petrus habens panem unum et offerens canibus duobus," in "Gli affreschi di S. Piero a Grado," p. 257, note 1. See also, Turcio, "San Pietro e i Cani," p. 299.

[122] *Blickling Homilies*, pp. 180–181 and Orderic Vitalis, *Historia*, 2.7. *MPL* 188:132.

[123] Graesse, *Legenda Aurea*, 89.2, p. 372 and Ryan, *Golden Legend*, p. 343.

[124] *Istoria Petri et Pauli*, p. 94.

artistic tradition. Firstly, the Sessa Aurunca, Müstair, San Piero a Grado, and *Latin Passional* representations seem to have depended directly on the original *Passio* text. If we look carefully at the Müstair fresco, Peter is feeding the barley-loaf to the two dogs using both hands simultaneously, and at Sessa Aurunca the apostle is in a similar position. In the *Latin Passional* Peter appears to be holding bread in one hand and is offering it to the two dogs. The *Passio* specifies that after Peter received the bread from Nero, he blessed it, and broke it with his *right* and his *left* hand, and placed *both* pieces up his sleeves, (Petrus enim benedixerat panem quem acceperat ordeaceum et fregerat et dextera atque sinistra in manica collegerat 26.3–4, p. 143). The artists apparently have assumed that Peter broke the bread into *two* pieces to feed *two* dogs, which explains the exact numerical detail by the artists at Sessa Aurunca, Müstair, San Pietro a Grado, and the *Latin Passional*, and which apparently influenced the *Istoria Petri et Pauli* mystery play.

The fifteenth-century tomb of Pope Sixtus IV, carved by an anonymous artist in the Tuscan style, allegedly contains so Turcio, a relief in what is possibly the most freewheeling rendition of the Marcellus story in the *Acts of Peter*.[125] It focuses primarily on the upside-down crucifixion of Simon Peter. At the foot of the inverted cross there is a dog and two childlike looking figures in a vigil as it were. According to Genesco Turcio, an earlier interpreter of this work, the dog and children both were part of the larger throng that chased Simon Magus out of the city of Rome, the seat of Simon Peter and his successors. It is implied by Turcio that both are symbolic of the watchfulness of the Church (domini canes), the childlike nature of the faith required of its members, and a testimony that even in his own death, Peter like Christ, ultimately triumphed over his arch-enemy Simon Magus and all who follow him in spirit.[126] Given the fact that the children and the dog are found at Peter's crucifixion, an episode that follows right after the death of Simon Magus, this interpretation of the relief is not unreasonable. For certain, the relief continues to identify Simon Peter with a faithful dog (*Acts of Peter*) as the hound keeps vigil at his crucifixion.

---

[125] Turcio, "San Pietro e i Cani," p. 299.
[126] Perhaps this is an allusion to the words of Jesus as recorded in the Gospel of Mark "I tell you the truth, anyone who will not receive the kingdom of God like a little child will never enter it," 10:15, and also, "From the lips of children and infants you have ordained praise," Mt. 21:16.

Conclusion

We have ample evidence, then, that dogs held an important place in the minds and lives of people in the Early Christian and medieval eras. They are either depicted metaphorically as ravenous fearful animals or,—like Odysseus's loyal dog, who died of excitement upon his master's long-delayed return—as the most faithful of all beasts. The *Acts of Peter* in its portrayal of the faithful dog and preacher of God's Word holds a significant place in the broader patristic and medieval perpetuation of a positive image of canines and the influence of this apocryphal story ran deep and wide. The dogs in the *Passio* contributed to the metaphorical tradition of the Jew, Muslim, heretic, and unbeliever as a wild, hostile, and ravenous canine that is to be shunned and feared by the members of the Church. Perhaps the most significant message in the invocation of dogs, whether positive or negative, that the patristic and medieval Church sought to convey is that there is strength in the struggle against evil, there is help in the fight against sin, and there is grace if one chooses to shun the Evil One, embodied in these apocryphal stories of Simon Magus.

AVENGING THE BLOOD OF CHILDREN:
ANXIETY OVER CHILD VICTIMS AND THE
ORIGINS OF THE EUROPEAN WITCH TRIALS

Richard Kieckhefer

Recent trials based on recovered memory of sexual abuse have led several commentators to comparisons with the historic witch trials. Often the parallel is suggested even in the titles of books on the issue, such as Moira Johnston's *Spectral Evidence*.[1] Johnston's effort at balance and objectivity is betrayed already on her title page by the overt parallel between recovered memories and the extraordinary admission of spectral evidence in the witch trials at Salem. Typically the comparisons are limited to that notorious American episode. One might wish to pursue the analogy with greater breadth and nuance, taking into account the Basque trials of 1609–14 and the Swedish case of 1668–75, and others which may in certain ways provide closer analogues to the cases of recovered memory.[2] The analogy is most obviously appropriate when the recovered memories are specifically of Satanic ritual abuse, or sexual abuse in the context of Satanic

---

[1] Moira Johnston, *Spectral Evidence: The Ramona Case: Incest, Memory, and Truth on Trial in Napa Valley* (Boston: Houghton Mifflin, 1997). Despite her title, however, Johnston makes only passing, if recurrent, reference to the historic witch trials (pp. 1, 8, 119, 126f., 200, 229f, 282, 338, and 385). Debbie Nathan and Michael Snedeker, *Satan's Silence: Ritual Abuse and the Making of a Modern American Witch Hunt* (New York: Basic Books, 1995), develop the analogy somewhat more fully. See also Elizabeth F. Loftus and Katherine Ketcham, *The Myth of Repressed Memory: False Memories and Allegations of Sexual Abuse* (New York: St. Martin's, 1994); Richard Ofshe and Ethan Watters, *Making Monsters: False Memories, Psychotherapy, and Sexual Hysteria* (New York: Scribner's, 1994); Carl Sagan, *The Demon-Haunted World* (New York: Random House, 1995); and Lawrence Wright, *Remembering Satan: A Case of Recovered Memory and the Shattering of an American Family* (New York: Knopf, 1994). For different perspectives see Hans-Günter Heimbrock and H. Barbara Boudewijnse, eds., *Current Studies on Rituals: Perspectives for the Psychology of Religion* (Amsterdam: Rodopi, 1990), and James Randall Noblitt and Pamela Sue Perskin, *Cult and Ritual Abuse: Its History, Anthropology, and Recent Discovery in Contemporary America* (Westport, Conn.: Praeger, 1995).

[2] Gustav Henningsen, *The Witches' Advocate: Basque Witchcraft and the Spanish Inquisition, 1609–1614* (Reno: University of Nevada Press, 1980); Brian P. Levack, *The Witch-Hunt in Early Modern Europe* (London: Longman, 1987), 191–92. In both these cases what was crucial was impressionable children's testimony about *remembered* assemblies witches had taken them to, not than their present experience of being tormented (even in the courtroom) by the alleged specters of witches.

rites, and in such cases the parallel is chillingly close indeed. The mythology of witchcraft in the late Middle Ages and early modern era gained plausibility from people's awareness of real necromancers, more often than not clerical;[3] analogously, the mythology of Satanic sexual abuse is plausible in our society in part because there are actual Satanic cults in our midst, a source of concern to Evangelical Christians in particular, and pedophilia is also all too real a phenomenon. In each case, then, fantasies are grounded in distorted consciousness of realities. In both eras the specialized sciences of learned authorities ratify the exceptional forms of evidence required for conviction: theological demonology (building on more sophisticated versions of scholastic theology) in the witch trials, and psychotherapy (building on certain basic premises of psychoanalysis) in cases of repressed and recovered memories. And if the witch trials expressed a misogynist society's deepest fears of women, recent allegations of abuse have given dramatic form to anxiety about male aggression.

Most importantly, in the witch trials as in cases of recovered memory (especially for Satanic ritual abuse) the gratuitous evil of the malefactors has been underscored by their supposed attack on innocent and defenseless children. Indeed, this was clearly one of the chief horrors that witchcraft held for late medieval society: it was bad enough that neighbors could be thought of as cursing those with whom they had quarreled, but witches who attacked even children were clearly committed to evil for its own sake, or out of conspiratorial fidelity to their sect and to Satan. Anxieties grounded in apprehensions that parents recall from their own childhood are reinforced by what they have learned about dangers in the world and about their own limitations as parents and protectors. The frailty of children thus becomes a lightning rod for the apprehension of adults.

It would be surprising to find any society that does not have its mythology of inhuman or superhuman malefactors—spirits, abnormal humans, or monsters, beings in whom some people may believe while others doubt or wonder. The history of such notions is of interest in itself, but of greater relevance to the understanding of historical process are the mechanisms by which such mythology invades ordinary life. Those who believe in witches may never expect to encounter them, or may fear them in an abstract way, never identifying specific

---

[3] See Richard Kieckhefer, *Magic in the Middle Ages* (Cambridge: Cambridge University Press, 1979), 153–56.

neighbors as malefactors. Most difficult to explain, and most in need of explanation, is the incarnation of myth in the world of experience, the irruption of the mythic into the everyday, the shock of discovering that mythic figures have become flesh and dwell among us. Noelle Oxenhandler tells of a young girl in California who was kidnapped from her own house at a slumber party and carried off to an unknown place and fate, like Persephone abducted by Pluto; Oxenhandler's chief interest is in the community's spontaneous transformation of living experience into myth. To be sure, it is Oxenhandler herself who makes the mythic connection explicit, but she sees others as already doing so in subtle ways.[4] Mircea Eliade tells of a Rumanian case in which the translation of historical misfortune into myth was more obviously the work of the community: the death of a young man before his wedding, an event transformed by folklore into a tragic seduction by a mountain fairy who lured the man over a cliff. As Eliade says, the poignancy of the event inspired its telling in mythic language, which "made the real story yield a deeper and richer meaning, revealing a tragic destiny."[5] In the cases Oxenhandler and Eliade reflect on, the existential force of real tragedy is conveyed by its mythic expression. The retelling does not confuse fantasy and reality, but finds a language appropriate to the realities in question. One might argue that in the witch trials and in cases of recovered memory myth serves to create rather than to recount events, and this may indeed be so. In any case, the incarnation of myth in the witch trials and in prosecution based on recovered memory has a kind of practical implication not found in Oxenhandler's or Eliade's cases. There, the mythic telling gives resonance and coherence to a story otherwise difficult to tell; it is psychologically useful. The incarnation of myth may have this function in the witch trials and in cases of recovered memory, and may be (or seem) therapeutically helpful to the accusers, but these myths intrude more violently upon reality, requiring the identification and punishment of a villain.

What I wish to explore here is the irruption of myth into the world of experience in fifteenth-century Western Europe. Even in the early years of virulent witch-hunting, in approximately the second quarter of the fifteenth century, witches were already thought of as

---

[4] Noelle Oxenhandler, "Polly's face," *New Yorker*, 29 Nov. 1993. Later reports confirmed that the girl's kidnapper murdered her.
[5] Mircea Eliade, *The Myth of the Eternal Return* (Princeton, 1954), pp. 44–46.

engaged in gratuitous affliction, killing, and eating of innocent children. The myth of the child-afflicting witch might have retained the abstraction of a grim fairytale. Even the actual deaths of children might have been ascribed not to flesh-and-blood witches but to witch-like spirits in the tradition of Lilith; Moses Gaster has traced the long history of charms to protect children against such adversaries.[6] The fact that even in the early witch trials incarnate witches were thought to victimize children has been noted, but the centrality of the theme has perhaps too seldom been underscored, and its implications too little explored. I will examine three different contexts where witches were thought to afflict and kill young children; indeed, a major part of my argument will be precisely that in fifteenth-century accounts of child attacking witches we have not a single cultural phenomenon but a set of at least three distinguishable (if related) phenomena. Alongside widespread, perhaps universal anxieties about the vulnerability of children, other factors came into play which resulted in importantly different kinds of trial. Carlo Ginzburg, in examining much the same body of material, focuses on the continuities within late medieval culture and the elements of continuity linking this culture with archaic traditions of Europe.[7] My effort here will be to qualify this emphasis on sweeping continuities, to show that the vulnerability of children to supernatural attack is a theme with significant variations.

1. *Witch-vampires charged with killing children in their cradles*

In the 1420's Bernardino of Siena preached a series of vernacular sermons at Siena, and in one he told how he had recently instigated prosecution for witchcraft in Rome. At first he found that when he preached against the charms of witches and sorcerers he elicited no response from his hearers. Then he began to insist that those who failed to accuse the malefactors were guilty of the same offense. In response, people brought accusations against a great many of their neighbors, so many that the local guardian of Bernardino's Franciscan order expressed concern at the number of accused who were threat-

---

[6] M. Gaster, "Two thousand years of a charm against the child-stealing witch," *Folk-Lore*, 11 (1900), 129–62, reprinted in Moses Gaster, *Studies and Texts in Folklore, Magic, Mediaeval Romance, Hebrew Apocrypha and Samaritan Archaeology*, 2 (London: Maggs, 1928; repr. New York: Ktav, 1971), 1005–38.

[7] Carlo Ginzburg, *Ecstasies: Deciphering the Witches' Sabbath*, trans. Raymond Rosenthal (New York: Pantheon, 1991).

ened with burning. At last, after consultation with the pope, the women whose offenses were most serious were taken into custody:

> And there was taken among others one who had told and confessed, without being put to torture, that she had killed thirty children or thereabouts, by sucking their blood; and she said that every time she let one of them go free she must sacrifice a limb to the devil, and she used to offer the limb of an animal; and she had continued for a long time acting in this manner. And furthermore, she confessed, saying that she had killed her own little son, and had made a powder from him, which she gave people to eat in these practices of hers. And because it seemed beyond belief that any creature could have done so many wicked things, they wished to test whether this was indeed true. Finally, they asked her whom she had killed. She told who these were, and whose children they were, and in what way, and at what time she had killed them. And going thither they sought the proof from the father of those children who had been killed. "Did you ever have a little son, who at such a time began to pine away, and then died?" Finally, since he replied that this was so, and since the day and the hour and the manner in which this had come to pass all agreed, it was shown to be nor more nor less than as she said. . . .

The woman confessed further that she and her fellow witches had anointed themselves with unguents, after which they believed falsely they had been changed into cats. Convicted by her own testimony, the woman was condemned and burned at the stake.[8]

Three key themes are clear in Bernardino's account: the killing of the children by sucking their blood; the manufacture of a powder from their bodies; and the citation of actual, concrete cases of infant death as caused by such attacks. A series of trials in fifteenth-century Perugia revolved around the same fundamental notions. In 1455–56 the civil authorities condemned two women to the stake for witchcraft, Filippa da Città della Pieve and Mariana da S. Sisto.[9] Filippa was said to have apprenticed herself as early as 1434 to a well-known witch, at whose command she anointed her naked body, gave herself to the Devil, and asked him to transport her wherever she wished to go. Taken to the house of a neighbor, they sucked nearly all the blood from a child as he lay by his sleeping mother. After the boy had been buried, the witches disinterred his body, separated its members

---

[8] Saint Bernardino of Siena, *Sermons*, ed. Nazareno Orlandi, trans. Helen Josephine Robins (Siena: Tipografia Sociale, 1920), 166f. (with some adaptation).

[9] Ugolino Nicolini, "La stregoneria a Perugia e in Umbria nel Medioevo: con i testi di sette processi a Perugia e uno a Bologna," *Bollettino della Deputazione di storia patria per l'Umbria*, 84 for 1987 (1988), app. 1–5 and 1–6, pp. 52–63.

by boiling, made powder from the bones and candles from the fat, and convoked unclean spirits. In various places they killed more than a hundred children in this manner. Filippa and her mistress engaged in other misconduct when they were not attacking children: made invisible by diabolical power, they stole things from people's houses; they conjured demons, they induced lust in previously chaste young men and women, they coerced the wills of other individuals. In May of 1440 Filippa used love magic to ensnare a young tailor named Giacomo, burying a bundle of noxious substances over a spot where she knew he would pass, then tightening the knot of passion by giving him a potion made with semen, her own menstrual blood, and an herb. In 1455 she was said to have caused a man's affliction by use of a bundle with magic ingredients, but when he grew ill and began vomiting she had medicines ready to restore his health, including an herbal ointment she had prepared—evidence, perhaps, that she was primarily a healer and practitioner of the amatory arts, whose occult knowledge aroused suspicion of more sinister dealings.

The woman executed the following year, Mariana, was said to have afflicted a neighbor by use of various noxious substances, enhanced by the power of demons (invoked by a priest "whose name," the trial record says, "is better not mentioned"). She too was accused of going out with another woman, who learned from her how to bewitch people and how to suck the blood of children. Fortified with diabolical unguents and incantations, they went out and entered people's homes, bringing slow death to the children they attacked. She was taken through the streets of Perugia with her head shaved and executed by burning.

These cases are drawn from a relatively small cluster, focused in Central Italy: the earliest is from 1428 in Todi; at Perugia, after the cases of 1455 and 1456, there occurred in 1501 a case exceptional (for this cluster) in that the accused witch was male.[10] In all these instances the witches went about in small bands, were aided in their expeditions by smearing themselves with unguents that evidently had magical capacities (perhaps helping them gain access to the children), and sucked the blood of infants, whose identities are given with greater or lesser specificity. In three instances the witches were

[10] Domenico Mammoli, *The Record of the Trial and Condemnation of a Witch, Matteuccia di Francesco, at Todi, 20 march 1428* (Rome, 1972), and Nicolini, "La stregoneria a Perugia," 5–87.

also accused of engaging in other magical practices, particularly love-magic. In two cases (those of 1428 and 1455) the bodies of the infants were said to be sources of fat for the manufacture of unguents, but their dead bodies were not otherwise used or abused. In only one instance (that of 1428) was the attack on infants explicitly said to be at the behest of a demonic master, Lucifer, whom the witch encountered at nocturnal assemblies (which, however, were *not* the occasion for eating the flesh of children). A similar case at Brescia in 1480, the only one in this cluster in Italy that occurred before an ecclesiastical tribunal, is unlike the other Italian cases in that we know about it not from judicial records but from a chronicle. Not surprisingly, the details differ in some important particulars from those of the other cases: rather than being sucked, the blood was offered to the demonic master as a sacrifice; rather than specifying individual victims, the source tells that the witch killed roughly three hundred of them.[11] But this case in Brescia otherwise belongs to this cluster.

What are we to make of these reports? One might suppose that notions of infant-slaying witches were reactions to the harsh reality of sudden infant death, and one might identify these trials as grounded in what we call sudden infant death syndrome.[12] High infant mortality was the norm in medieval Europe, and mortality generally reached a high point in the fourteenth century, with its epidemics and its recurrent plague. It has been estimated that in pre-industrial Europe twenty to thirty per cent of all children died in the first year of life, and only half of all children survived to five years of age. The ubiquity of infant death led Philippe Ariès to his famous (but now largely discredited) theory that medieval people did not establish close affective bonds with their offspring, that high mortality of children bred

    [11] Paolo Guerrini, ed., *Chronache bresciane inedite dei sec. XV–XIX*, 1 (Brescia, 1922), 183–85. Cf. Giuseppe Bonomo, *Caccia alle streghe: La credenza nelle streghe dal secolo XIII al XIX, con particolare riferimento all'Italia* (Palermo, 1959), 121.

    [12] Representative of the extensive literature on this topic are the books of J. Tyson Tildon, et al., eds., *Sudden Infant Death Syndrome* (New York: Academic Press, 1983); Jean Golding, et al., *Sudden Infant Death: Patterns, Puzzles, and Problems* (Seattle: University of Washington Press, 1985); Abraham B. Bergman, *The "Discovery" of Sudden Infant Death Syndrome: Lessons in the Practice of Political Medicine* (New York: Praeger, 1986); Jan L. Culbertson, et al., eds., *Sudden Infant Death Syndrome: Medical Aspects and Psychological Management* (Baltimore: Johns Hopkins University Press, 1988); Ronald M. Harper and Howard J. Hoffman, eds., *Sudden Infant Death Syndrome: Risk Factors and Basic Mechanisms* (New York: PMA, 1988); and Peter J. Schwartz, et al., eds., *The Sudden Infant Death Syndrome: Cardiac and Respiratory Mechanisms and Interventions* (New York: New York Academy of Sciences, 1988).

callousness.[13] Whatever individuals' reactions might be, the experience of losing children was common. One man of Limousin in the
early fifteenth century had thirteen children, of whom ten died in
childhood or youth, six during times of plague and famine. Even the
dukes of late medieval England lost thirty-six per cent of their sons
and twenty-nine per cent of their daughters before age five.[14]

Yet variations in the rate of infant mortality cannot readily explain
why in particular times and places people felt it necessary to explain
in mythic terms what preceding generations and most contemporaries
seem to have accepted as a natural fact of life. The label "sudden
infant death syndrome", too, has limited explanatory value. Even in a
modern context it is not clear that it refers to a single syndrome with
uniform etiology. To use the term historically is to say little more
than that infants died for reasons we do not know—reasons that
may range from infection to traumatic handling, and reasons which
modern medicine might often be able to identify with confidence if
it had the evidence. The late medieval trial cases leave us no *corpora
delicti*. Not only the killings but even the deaths may in some cases
have been purely fictional. Even if we knew they were not, and even
if we had established that the causes would have eluded both medieval and modern diagnosis, we could not say with confidence that
the rise of the witch trials coincided with an increase in the incidence of sudden and unexplained infant mortality. If we speak at all
of sudden infant death syndrome, at least in a historical setting, this
usage does not explain a phenomenon but acknowledges the limits
of our capacity to explain.

Among the anthropological parallels, one in the Tlaxcala region
of Mexico holds particular interest. During the years 1959 to 1966,
the anthropologist Hugo G. Nutini collected evidence of roughly 300
incidents in which children were believed killed by blood-sucking
tlahuelpuchis in this region.[15] These *tlahuelpuchis* are women and men

---

[13] For one telling critique see Donald Weinstein and Rudolph M. Bell, *Saints and
Society: The Two Worlds of Western Christendom, 1000–1700* (Chicago: University of
Chicago Press, 1982), 47; see also the sources cited on pp. 292–95 nn. 1, 2, and 26.

[14] Shulamith Shahar, *Childhood in the Middle Ages* (London: Routledge, 1989), 35,
149–50; Philippe Ariès, *Centuries of Childhood: A Social History of Family Life*, trans.
Robert Baldick (New York: Knopf, 1962), 39.

[15] Hugo G. Nutini and John M. Roberts, *Blood-Sucking Witchcraft: An Epistemological
Study of Anthropomorphic Supernaturalism in Rural Tlaxcala* (Tucson: University of Arizona
Press, 1993), and Horacio Fabrega and Hugo Nutini, "Witchcraft-explained childhood
tragedies in Tlaxcala, and their medical sequelae", *Social Science and Medicine*, 36 (1993),
793–805.

who, according to local belief, require human blood to sustain their own life. They are thought to transform themselves into the forms of various animals, break into houses, and attack their victims, usually infants. Nutini himself examined forty-seven bodies of infants said to have been killed in this manner. Apart from the evidence of actual deaths, he gathered more than a hundred legends and "semilegendary" accounts of *tlahuelpuchis* said to have lived at some indeterminate time. People use various means to protect their offspring from these male-factors, but the only fully effective deterrent is garlic or onion. The *tlahuelpuchis'* evil is innate. They are independent agents, acting alone, although in some circumstances they may work on behalf of the Devil and do his bidding. People do not normally accuse specific individuals of being *tlahuelpuchis*—indeed, it is dangerous to do so, for these malefactors know what is said about them and can take swift revenge. At times, however, attacks by *tlahuelpuchis* become epidemic and a consensus emerges identifying a person as a *tlahuelpuchi*, in which case a mob will descend upon and kill the accused. Such cases of lynch justice dramatize the transformation of myth into reality, the capacity of a myth to descend from the realm of abstraction to the plane of concrete and particular lives and deaths.

Like the *tlahuelpuchis*, the Italian blood-sucking witches in many ways resemble vampires.[16] The resemblance may be especially close in the case of the solitary *tlahuelpuchis*, who take on bestial form, suck blood mainly to sustain their own lives, and are repulsed by garlic and onion. The Italian witches, at least as represented in the extant sources, are more distinctly identifiable *as witches*, subservient to demonic masters, carrying out evil at these masters' behest, and gathering in small groups if not in demonic assemblies. One might suggest that a substratum of popular vampire belief is here overlaid by ecclesiastical notions of demonic witchcraft; this is a point to which we must return. The relation between this Italian witchcraft and ideas about changelings is also suggestive: in both cases an infant is abused by a demonic force, although in the case of a changeling the human

---

[16] On the history of vampires see Paul Barber, *Vampires, Burial, and Death: Folklore and Reality* (New Haven: Yale University Press, 1988); Nina Auerbach, *Our Vampires, Ourselves* (Chicago: University of Chicago Press, 1995); and Gábor Klaniczay, *The Uses of Supernatural Power: The Transformation of Popular Religion in Medieval and Early-Modern Europe*, trans. Susan Singerman, ed. Karen Margolis (Princeton, N.J.: Princeton University Press, 1990), 168–88 ("The decline of witches and the rise of vampires under the eighteenth-century Habsburg monarchy").

child is supplanted by a demonic ersatz child.[17] Yet the concepts are by no means identical, beyond the obvious factor that in both cases concern about the well-being of infants takes the form of anxiety about their susceptibility to preternatural affliction.

While the accusations in this category are in some cases global and unspecific, in many instances the records give circumstantial detail about the children the accused witches had attacked. This does not necessarily mean that the accusations came originally from the childrens' parents, but does suggest that at some point there was a meshing of the witches' confessions with what the parents and perhaps the rest of the community knew about the deaths in question. The specificity of the charges at least made it possible to consult with the parents and confirm or disconfirm the confessions, as Bernardino claimed had occurred in the case at Rome. Furthermore, the reports of child-murder related in these trials were not echoed by the mythology emerging in the early writings on witchcraft; they were not charges that demonology had led judges to anticipate.

2. Consiratorial witches charged with killing children and taking their bodies to the sabbath

A much more substantial dossier contains cases of a second, rather different type, concentrated in and around French-speaking Switzerland. The earliest of these was 1428 in the Valais, exactly the same year as the trial at Todi. Further relevant cases occurred in 1438 in La Tour du Pin, 1448 in Vevey, 1449 in the Aosta valley, 1458 and 1461 elsewhere in the diocese of Lausanne, 1462 in Chamonix, 1464 in the diocese of Lausanne, 1477 in Villars-Chabod, 1493 in Fribourg, and 1498 in Dommartin.[18] Outside this region there was a case in

---

[17] Jean-Claude Schmitt, *The Holy Greyhound: Guinefort, Healer of Children Since the Thirteenth Century*, trans. Martin Thom (Cambridge: Cambridge University Press, 1983), pp. 74–80.

[18] Joseph Hansen, ed., *Quellen und Untersuchungen zur Geschichte des Hexenwahns und der Hexenverfolgung im Mittelalter* (Bonn: Georgi, 1901; repr. Hildesheim: Olms, 1963), 459–66, 477–84, 487–99, 590–92; Martine Ostorero, *«Folâtrer avec les démons»: Sabbat et chasse aux sorciers à Vevey (1448)* (Lausanne: Cahiers Lausannois d'Histoire Médiévale, 1995); Félicien Gamba, "Die Hexe von Saint-Vincent: Ein Ketzer- und Hexenprozess im 15. Jahrhundert," in Andreas Blauert, ed., *Ketzer, Zauberer, Hexen: Die Anfänge der europäischen Hexenverfolgungen* (Frankfurt am Main: Suhrkamp, 1990), 160–81; Maxime Reymond, La sorcellerie au pays de Vaud au XVe siècle, *Schweizerisches Archiv fhr Volkskunde*, 12 (1908), 4, 7f., 11, 86f.; Maxime Reymond, Cas de sorcellerie en pays fribourgeois au quinzième siècle, *Schweizerisches Archiv fhr Volkskunde*, 13 (1909), 81–90.

1452 at Provins (roughly forty-five miles southeast of Paris) where similar charges occurred, but in a less developed form, and it seems clear that this portion of the Provins record merely echoes concepts of witchcraft more fully articulated elsewhere.[19] The key factor in all these cases is that, rather than sucking the infants' blood in their homes as they lay by their mothers, the witches brought the infants' bodies to their assemblies (often known as a "synagogue" or a *chète*), where they were eaten. Often it is specified that the infants were killed, buried, exhumed, roasted, and then eaten. Unlike most of their contemporary Italian counterparts, the witches included men as well as women. They killed and ate their own children as well as other people's. While the identities of the children are sometimes given, at least as often we hear only in vague collective terms about infants who have been taken and eaten. The witches killed the infants by mere touch or by strangling; sometimes it was said that their hands and fingers left marks on the dead infants' bodies.[20] Occasionally the witches are said to have indicated that they had no power over baptized babies, or had to leave aside the heads of such infants because they had been marked with baptismal chrism. Sometimes candles, unguents, or powders were made from the children's flesh, but the common theme is the eating of their bodies. Whereas in the Italian trials mentioned above the sucking of infants' blood is a critical factor, often the main element in the accusations, in these Swiss cases the element of anthropophagy is often of only minor concern; it is mentioned in passing, among other activities at the witches' assembly, but it is by no means necessarily the most important act or the one receiving the bulk of the sources' attention.

While the blood-sucking witches in some ways resemble vampires, belief in these flesh-eating witches comes from a fundamentally different tradition. Andreas Blauert and others have called to our attention that the witch trials specifically in Western Switzerland and Southeastern France resemble in various ways the heresy trials that had previously been carried out in those lands: in their development into

---

[19] Hansen, *Quellen*, 556–59.

[20] David J. Hufford, *The Terror That Comes in the Night: An Experience-Centered Study of Supernatural Assault Traditions* (Philadelphia: University of Pennsylvania Press, 1982), analyzes an experience that is in some ways similar: what is called in Newfoundland the "Old Hag" experience, of awaking to find oneself immobilized by a force that causes intense fear. But Hufford's subject matter is an experience of adults, not children.

large-scale judicial hunts, in the predominance of males among the accused, and to some extent in the nature of the allegations.[21] The charge of cannibalism, and in particular eating the flesh of infants, can easily be traced back to earlier stereotypes about medieval heretics and other reprobate groups.[22] The eating of infants' flesh, more obviously than the sucking of their blood, parodically recalls a eucharistic feast: it occurs within an assembly at which those assembled establish an almost totemic solidarity among themselves and with their master.

This motif is featured prominently in early writings on witchcraft. During the 1430's, four works were penned which described in detail the activities of the conspiratorial sect of witches recently arisen within Christendom: Johannes Nider's *Formicarius*, Claude Tholosan's *Ut magorum et maleficiorum errores*, the anonymous *Errores Gazariorum*, and the Lucerne chronicle of Johannes Fründ.[23] These works defined for contemporaries and succeeding generations the complex of beliefs which justified the prosecution of witches, and at the outset a crucial element of this complex was fear of infanticide. While the accounts of the *Errores Gazariorum* and Nider are well known, they are important enough for this discussion to warrant quotation in full.

The *Errores Gazariorum* tells of seven obligations to which a member of the synagogue is sworn. The fourth of these is "that he will kill as many children [*pueros*] as he is able to strangle and kill, and will bring them to the synagogue, meaning by that children of three years

---

[21] Andreas Blauert, *Frühe Hexenverfolgungen: Ketzer-, Zauberei- und Hexenprozesse des 15. Jahrhunderts* (Hamburg: Junius, 1989); Susanna Burghartz, "Hexenverfolgung als Frauenverfolgung? Zur Gleichsetzung von Hexen und Frauen am Beispiel der Luzerner und Lausanner Hexenprozesse des 15. und 16. Jahrhunderts," in Lisa Berrisch, et al., eds., *Schweizerische Historikerinnentagung: Beiträge* (Zürich: Chronos, 1986), 86–105; Agostino Paravicini Bagliani, Kathrin Utz-Tremp, and Martine Ostorero, "Le sabbat dans les Alpes: Les prémices médiévales de la chasse aux sorcières," *Sciences: raison et déraisons* (Lausanne: Payot, 1994), 67–89; and Kathrin Utz Tremp, "Ist Glaubenssache Frauensache? Zu den Anfängen der Hexenverfolgung in Freiburg (um 1440)," *Freiburger Geschichtsblätter*, 72 (1995), 9–50.

[22] See esp. Russell, *Witchcraft in the Middle Ages*; Norman Cohn, *Europe's Inner Demons: An Enquiry Inspired by the Great Witch-Hunt* (London: Chatto, 1975); also Carlo Ginzburg, *Ecstasies: Deciphering the Witches' Sabbath*, trans. Raymond Rosenthal (New York: Pantheon, 1991), 74–75. Ginzburg insists that the precedent among heretics had been interrupted, but to support that conclusion he needs to rule that certain "Waldensians" of northern Italy were not in fact heretics; in making this judgment he is perhaps drawing too clear a line between heretics and witches.

[23] For discussion of these four sources—and for comparison of them on this and other points—see especially Michael Bailey, "The medieval concept of the witches' Sabbath," *Exemplaria*, 8 (1996), 419–39.

and under. . . ." Later in the account we are given further details about the use of the children's bodies:

> Likewise, after he is seduced [into the synagogue] he does homage to the presiding devil, [who] gives him a container filled with unguent and a staff, and everything else he needs, with which the seduced man is to go to the synagogue, and he teaches him how he should anoint the staff. For that unguent is concocted by a mystery of diabolical malignity out of the fat of children who have been roasted and distilled, with other substances, as will become clear.
>
> Likewise, an unguent is made of this fat of children, mixed with the most poisonous of animals . . ., and if a person is touched once with this unguent he will perish by an irremediably evil death, sometimes lingering for a long time in his infirmity, sometimes dying suddenly.
>
> Likewise, they make powders to kill people; these powders are made from the innards of children mixed with the aforesaid poisonous animals, all of which, reduced to powder, are dispersed in the air by a member of that society in cloudy weather, and those touched by these powders either die or suffer grave and chronic illness. . . . By diabolical mystery they make an unguent [out of certain distillations], with the fat of people hanged on the gallows, and the innards of children, and the aforementioned poisonous animals . . ., and this unguent kills all people by contact alone.

But it is only toward the end of the account that we read in detail about the process of killing:

> Likewise, when they wish to strangle children as their father and mother are sleeping, by diabolical mystery they enter the parents' house in the dead of night, they grab the child by the throat or sides, and strangle him until he expires. In the morning, when he is borne to burial, the man or woman or all those who have strangled and killed the child come up and mourn the child's death with the parents and friends. But the following night they open the grave and take the child, sometimes leaving the boy's head in the grave, and they never take hands and feet with themselves, unless they want to perform some bewitchment [sortilegium] with the child's hand. After they have removed the child and refilled the grave, they carry him to the synagogue, where he is roasted and eaten, as has been mentioned.
>
> And note that there have been some who have killed their own sons and daughters and eaten them in the synagogue, such as Jeanne Vacanda, who was burned in a place called Chambéry on the feast of Saint Laurence, and who confessed before all the people that she had eaten the son of her daughter and killed him along with another woman named in her trial. . . .[24]

---

[24] Hansen, *Quellen und Untersuchungen*, 119–22.

The account in Johannes Nider's *Formicarius* is less extensive but still touches upon both the killing of the children and the use of their bodies. Nider tells of witches (*malefici*) who cook and eat their own infant children. He learned from the Bernese judge Peter von Greyerz, that in territories subject to Bern thirteen infants were eaten within a short time by witches, provoking severe prosecution. When Peter asked one female witch how they ate the infants, she answered:

> This is how it is done. We scheme against unbaptized or even baptized infants, especially if they are not fortified with the sign of the cross and prayers. We kill them with our rites as they lie in the cradle or alongside their parents, and afterward they are assumed to have been crushed [*oppressi*] or killed in some other way. We steal them secretly from their graves and cook them in a cauldron until their bones come apart and just about all their flesh has become fluid and drinkable. From the more solid matter we make an unguent suitable for carrying out our desires, our arts and transmutations. With the more fluid humor we fill a bottle or a skin, and a person who drinks of this, along with some few rites [*additis paucis cerimoniis*] at once becomes knowing [*conscius*] and a master of our sect.[25]

Johannes Fründ's chronicle tells much the same story, with a few incidental touches added. He says the witches kill their own children, roast them, and take them to their assemblies for eating. Sometimes they are so evil that they afflict their own children or others' by rubbing evil poison, causing them to turn black or blue, linger a few days, then die. After the children's death the witches exhumed them and ate them in the company of their fellows.[26] Claude Tholosan, who tried witches in the Dauphiné over several years, gives an essentially similar account. He speak of witches who sacrifice one of their children to the devil, killing it, burying it, then exhuming it, and making a powder from its body. He does also tell a tradition related to that of blood-sucking witches: on his account they go out at night, suffocate children, and draw their blood, after which they cook and eat them. This appears to be a variation on the idea of blood-sucking witches as it occurs in the Italian trials, but modified by addition of themes drawn from the French Swiss tradition of the flesh-eating witches.[27] In short, the notion that witches eat the flesh of children

---

[25] Hansen, *Quellen und Untersuchungen*, 92–93.
[26] Hansen, *Quellen und Untersuchungen*, 535.
[27] Pierrette Paravy, "A propos de la genèse médiévale des chasses aux sorcières: le traité de Claude Tholosan, juge dauphinois (vers 1436)," *Mélanges de l'Ecole Française de Rome: Moyen Age—Temps modernes*, 91 (1979), 333–79 (para. 4 and 6).

at their assemblies was very much part of a demonological myth arising in and around French-speaking Switzerland at this time.

In all of this literature the theme of infanticide is made an element in a fuller and more elaborate tale. Both the killing and the later use of the child are essentially communal acts, motivated by the purposes of the "sect" rather than the whims or cravings of individual witches. And this is the chief contribution of the 1430's to the development of witchcraft mythology: the idea of conspiratorial witchcraft, the belief that witches' malice need not be traced to the specific etiology of village quarrels, amorous misadventures, or family grievances, because the witches are at all times already gratuitously inclined toward malicious conduct. The very purpose of their sect is to increase evil in the world, to bring about the greatest suffering for the greatest number. So long as witchcraft accusations are limited to cases in which prior tension makes malice plausible, sustained witch panics cannot occur. Only when malice is seen as internally motivated within the sect does it become reasonable for anyone to see anyone else as a potential aggressor. Only then do accusations become in large measure arbitrary, perhaps even random, especially in the later stages of a fully developed hunt, when alleged witches are compelled under torture to name their accomplices.[28] This transition is far more fully developed in this second category of cases than in the first. In the Italian trials the alleged witches may have been feared chiefly because they possessed occult knowledge, and it was only to be expected that willingness to use unorthodox means for unorthodox ends would lead to friction and eventually to denunciation. In the cases of flesh-eating witchcraft from Switzerland and Southeastern France these specific mechanisms of suspicion may still have been operative but they were almost surely less necessary, and suspicion could more easily be directed at people who would otherwise be blameless. It was in these trials, and in the related literature, that the theme of the infanticide witch as a perpetrator of gratuitous evil attained its fullest development. And it was in these contexts, not surprisingly, that prosecution for witchcraft most nearly attained the status of a hunt or panic.

It is tempting to suppose that the mythology here related, being

---

[28] On the mechanisms of prosecution see H.C. Erik Midelfort, *Witch-Hunting in Southwestern Germany, 1562–1684: The Social and Intellectual Foundations* (Stanford: Stanford University Press, 1972), and Levack, *The Witch-Hunt in Early Modern Europe*, 146–69.

closer to long established heresiological topoi, derives more from ecclesiastical than from popular sources, and that in this respect these cases differ from the Italian ones. The close parallel between the Italian vampire-like witches and the *tlahuelpuchis* might lead to the hypothesis that we have there strong evidence for authentically popular notions of witchcraft, even if they seem to some extent perhaps mingled with ecclesiastical beliefs. The connection between the Swiss witchcraft trials and earlier heresy prosecution in and near Switzerland might suggest that what we have here are more specifically ecclesiastical prejudices and stereotypes. But we must resist too sharp a distinction here. In the Italian as in the Swiss trial records the accusations of child-affliction often come late, sometimes explicitly after torture has been applied. On my reading, at least, it seems plausible to take both blood-sucking and flesh-eating witchcraft as motifs used by the judges, secular or ecclesiastical, to witches antecedently suspected or defamed, sometimes over several years, as practitioners of love-magic and sometimes directly harmful magic, perhaps even at times directed at children.[29] But to say that these motifs were used by judges is by no means to say that they could not have had roots in the popular or (more precisely) common culture of late medieval Europe, and for lack of obvious relevance to specifically ecclesiastical culture it seems more likely that the element of vampirism is taken from deeply established common culture.[30]

We may be able to trace the sources of a particular belief, as Carlo Ginzburg has done on a grand and sweeping scale for certain elements in the mythology of the sabbath. We may also be able to determine whose voice we are hearing when a belief comes to expression, as I claim to have done for the late medieval witch trials. But in some contexts answering these questions about the remote and proximate *sources* for an idea may be less vital than determining the *effects* of an allegation, the ways in which the framing of the charges influenced the course of persecution and the likelihood that one or two trials might lead to sustained large-scale prosecution. While the myths of blood-sucking and flesh-eating witches are superficially similar the latter was far more explosive, with its shift of attention away

[29] In other words, I still adhere to this central thesis of my book *European Witch Trials: Their Foundations in Popular and Learned Culture, 1300–1500* (London: Routledge, 1976).

[30] On the concept of common culture see my article, "The specific rationality of medieval magic," *American Historical Review*, 99 (1994), 832–36.

from the domestic tragedy of inexplicable infant mortality and toward the concerted action of a malevolent sect perceived as the terrifying cause of the affliction. Both could be used to play upon parents' anxieties about the vulnerability of their offspring, a factor not specific to any age or culture. But the idea of a sect of flesh-eating witches, closely linked with the notion of linkage between malevolent humans and Satan himself, was the more effective means for arousing a communite to passionate hatred of the accused.

3. Witches charged simply with causing bodily harm and death to children by their bewitchment

A third category of cases is numerically less significant yet also of interest: at Marmende in 1453 several witches were reported merely to have killed children by their sorcery, and at Metz in 1456 the male leader of a band of witches confessed to having killed an infant. In these trials we find none of the key elements from either the Italian cases (sucking of infants' blood) or the Swiss ones (eating the infants' flesh at demonic assemblies). The records may simply be incomplete. But it would be surprising if we did *not* on occasion find evidence that witches were believed simply to have killed children, as they were thought to have killed adults, without needing to eat their flesh or drink their blood. When Perrussone Gapit was tried in the diocese of Lausanne, in 1464, she eventually confessed to having eaten the flesh of an infant at a diabolical assembly—but at an earlier stage in the trial a witness named Mermette Amaudry gave very different testimony. Soon after Mermette had given birth, Perrussone approached her bed one evening. Unable to cry out, Mermette had made the sign of the cross and thus prevented Perrussone from carrying off her infant. Again the next day Perrussone was unable to claim the child, but the baby died soon afterward. When Perrussone placed her hand on the head of another of Mermette's children, the child fell ill and was afflicted with paralysis. At this stage in the trial what we find is bodily harm through maleficent magic, but again without the eating of flesh and drinking of blood.[31] Cases of this sort represent a more traditional (one might even say more conservative) form of

---

[31] Hansen, *Quellen*, 559–61 (Marmende) and 565f. (Metz); Reymond, "Cas de sorcellerie," 87–90 (diocese of Lausanne).

witch accusation than the first or second type; in these trials the specific animosities of village life remained the chief motives for the accusers and, presumably, the primary motives ascribed to the witches.

This trichotomy of blood-sucking, flesh-eating, and (more simply) infant-afflicting or infant-slaying witchcraft should not suggest three neatly defined and impermeable categories. A woman tried at Boucoiran in 1491 confessed that she and other witches had gone to the homes of people specified by name, that demons had opened doors for them, and that they had afflicted and killed the children in these homes.[32] Here we find something of a composite: a French woman who admitted entering houses and killing infants in them, in the company of other women, in the manner of Italian witches, but without sucking the infants' blood, and without taking their bodies to be eaten at demonic assemblies. On the whole, however, these three categories are remarkably distinct and overlap little.

Conclusion

History may teach few lessons clearly, but it does give dramatic evidence of vengeance against evil becoming itself a source of evil. Nel Noddings argues that projection of evil onto others, "an exteriorization of evil that leaves us blameless as we try to destroy it," is especially dangerous.[33] Much of Jeffrey Burton Russell's writing has been devoted to the exploration of such themes, in particular his studies of witchcraft and his masterful multi-volume history of the Devil.[34] He argues that the mythology of evil is grounded in reality—

---

[32] Édouard Bligny-Bondurand, "Procédure contre une sorcière de Boucoiran (Gard), 1491," *Bulletin philologique et historique*, 1907, 380–405.

[33] Nel Noddings, *Women and Evil* (Berkeley and Los Angeles: University of California Press, 1989), esp. 5–34 ("Evil and ethical terror"). She argues also against a theodicy which blames humans for bringing evil into an originally good world.

[34] Jeffrey B. Russell, *Witchcraft in the Middle Ages* (Ithaca, N.Y.: Cornell University Press, 1972); *The Devil: Perceptions of Evil from Antiquity to Primitive Christianity* (Ithaca, N.Y.: Cornell University Press, 1977); *Satan: The Early Christian Tradition* (Ithaca, N.Y.: Cornell University Press, 1981); *Lucifer: The Devil in the Middle Ages* (Ithaca, N.Y.: Cornell University Press, 1984); *Mephistopheles: The Devil in the Modern World* (Ithaca, N.Y.: Cornell University Press, 1986); and *The Prince of Darkness: Radical Evil and the Power of Good in History* (Ithaca, N.Y.: Cornell University Press, 1988). For a review written from a fundamentally different perspective see H.A. Kelly, "The Devil at large," *Journal of Religion*, 67 (1987), 518–28. But see also my own review of *Lucifer* in *The American Historical Review*, 91 (1986), 93–94.

that behind the horned figure with cloven hooves there lies an active source of evil in the universe—yet he is careful to distinguish between such metaphysical realities and the mythological expressions that give rise to abuse and at times (as in the witch trials) catastrophe. But it is precisely this *discretio spirituum* that is most vital and most difficult. Some might argue that the problem lies in the metaphysical conviction itself—that the very notion of an active force for evil in the cosmos, rather than any mythological formulation of that belief, inclines the believer to zealotry. The most basic question is whether mythic language is inherently destabilizing or whether it becomes so under specific circumstances.

What I have meant to suggest here is a nuanced answer to this question, with specific reference to the witch trials of late medieval Europe. Anxieties about the vulnerability of children may be constant, and in most cultures these apprehensions may spontaneously be given mythological expression, but the crucial factor is whether and how these fears are exploited by authorities. In the early witch trials, the mythology of the flesh-eating witch comes too close to written traditions about heretics for us to have any confidence that the voice we are hearing is that of the witches' fellow villagers; it is one element in a complex of allegations that served the purposes of social and political control, and the mythology itself serves more as justification than as cause. The mythology of the blood-sucking witch seems to have been more fully a popular concern, but here too there is at least some evidence that the effort of a firebrand such as Bernardino was crucial in precipitating a crisis and translating anxiety into accusation. The third kind of case, in which the attacks on children are least mythologized and least distinguished from those on adults, is the one in which we see least evidence of ecclesiastical or governmental manipulation. Thus, while the killing of *tlahuelpuchis* in Mexico may be an act of lynch justice, in late medieval Europe the suspected child-killing witches seem to have been in greatest danger of being mythologized and executed when popular anxieties were ratified and exploited by authorities.

TEACHING AND PREACHING CONFESSION
IN THIRTEENTH-CENTURY PARIS

Alan E. Bernstein

The purpose of this article is to examine the varieties of belief about confession in different types of sources in thirteenth-century Paris.[1] I shall attempt to distinguish, within the overall discourse concerning confession, different levels ranging from the formally dogmatic, to a theological, doctrinal level, to other, intermediate levels aimed particularly at reaching a popular audience. Pursuit of a single theme across this range of expression will show how concern for popular attitudes occasioned shifts of treatment and focus in authors capable of writing at many levels. By reviewing these sources and noting the characteristics of each genre, I hope to shed some light on the difficulties of recovering the popular component of thirteenth century ideas about confession, its nature and its function.

The meaning of "popular" and the distinctiveness of "popular religion" have occasioned much debate among historians. In my view, "popular" entails no radical opposition to more official positions. I imagine a spectrum, one extreme of which is popular. But the popular pole is reached by degrees, and different sources approach it more or less. As in a spectrum, some bands harmonize better with others, like notes in a musical scale. Popular ideas often differ enough from official ones that tacit demurral, dialogue, debate, discipline, and repression may all occur, though not necessarily. Nor do all statements on a given subject fall on a straight line. The spectrum may be very broad, though assertions about confession will necessarily refer to certain central concepts that derive from the Christian sacrament of

---

[1] It is a pleasure to acknowledge the collegial and fruitful collaboration I have long enjoyed with Jeffrey Burton Russell over the issues raised in this article and many related questions. In some ways, this paper started it all. I presented an earlier version, entitled "Theology and Popular Belief: Confession in the Later Thirteenth Century," to the joint conference of the Medieval Academy of America and the Medieval Association of the Pacific in Los Angeles, March 27, 1980.

penance (unless one wishes specifically to extend the field of vision beyond the Christian community).[2]

To be sure, church leaders shared many beliefs with their charges. The resulting community has encouraged some scholars like Peter Brown to discount the idea of popular religion severely.[3] Aaron Gurevich found the interaction between high and low religion so complete that he advanced the term "grotesque" for the rugged terrain shared by simple believers.[4] Uneducated believers had "fides implicita" says John van Engen, citing Peter Lombard, who claimed that even unlettered people unable to distinguish the articles of the creed, nonetheless "believe what they do not know."[5] At the opposite extreme is Jean-Claude Schmitt, who has dramatized medieval phenomena such as a rite performed by mothers for their infants over the grave of a dog.[6] The premise underlying Schmitt's work is that traces may still be found of repressed religious beliefs deriving from popular practices that are independent of Christianity.

What I wish to develop here is a middle ground that recognizes the religious community as one (though having porous boundaries), sharing certain core beliefs articulated variously by different members according to their levels of education, circumstances in life, and particular imagination. It is clear that many of the same ideas could be found among both educated and illiterate groups, yet some concepts were more central, given more emphasis, articulated with more clarity at one end of the educational spectrum than the other. As Jeffrey Burton Russell has put it: what was "vivid" for one group, "paled" for the other.[7] To do away with the differences in experienced religion

---

[2] As is done most fruitfully in *L'Aveu: antiquité et moyen âge*. Collection de l'école française de Rome, 88 (Rome, 1986).

[3] In *Society and the Holy in Late Antiquity* (Berkeley, 1982), 13–15, Brown deplores the "cramping dualism" that contrasts popular credulity to enlightened religion. Bishops and people alike embraced the cult of saints, he observes, as one example.

[4] *Medieval Popular Culture: Problems of Belief and Perception*, trans. János M. Bak and Paul A. Hollingsworth. Cambridge Studies in Oral and Literate Culture, 14 (Cambridge, 1988), esp. Chapter 6 "'High' and 'Low': The Medieval Grotesque," pp. 176–210, where Gurevich invokes an analysis akin to set theory in mathematics to describe how there is high culture in low and low in high: "The intimacy and interweaving of 'high' and 'low'," he says, "generate grotesque situations" (p. 207).

[5] "The Christian Middle Ages as a Historical Problem," *American Historical Review* 91 (1986), pp. 519–52 at p. 545.

[6] *The Holy Greyhound: Guinefort, Healer of Children since the Thirteenth Century* (Cambridge, 1983 [1979]).

[7] *Lucifer: The Devil in the Middle Ages* (Ithaca, 1984), p. 213.

that this spectrum permits would deny distinctions thirteenth-century religious leaders themselves recognized and used as a basis for their government and pastoral work. In what follows, I will pursue the single theme of confession through various levels of discourse to see what changes in emphasis occur and so to advocate the utility of the distinction between elite and popular religion without denying the community formed by their interaction.[8]

The basis for the principal contrast between established theology and popular belief is almost disappointingly simple, yet the sources authorize it. The indicator of popular influence in discussions of confession is the presence and activity of the devil. That is, as preachers sought to involve lay audiences, and as the teachers of preachers sought to prepare them for the pulpit, they calculated that the laity was interested in the devil and how to escape him.

The declaration that informed all discussion of confession throughout the thirteenth century was the canon *Omnis utriusque sexus*, promulgated in 1215 by the Fourth Lateran Council under the direction of Pope Innocent III. This decree linked individual confession and the performance of requisite satisfaction to the reception of the Eucharist by every Catholic before Easter of each year.[9] Over and above whatever voluntary practices they may have observed before, this regulation imposed a Lenten penitential season on the laity.[10]

Besides the disciplinary decrees, Lateran IV also promulgated an opening creed, "Firmiter Credimus," which defined the devil's identity and destiny so as to limit his activity on earth. Innocent III and the conciliar fathers were opposing the Manichaean beliefs of the Cathars, who attributed to Satan a role, not only in the subversion, but in the creation of the world and of the human race. In the passage describing God as the sole creator of heaven and earth, of all things visible and invisible, the creed affirms: "The devil and the other demons were created good in their nature by God, but they became evil by

---

[8] I have attempted this type of analysis also in "The Invocation of Hell in Thirteenth-Century Paris," in *Supplementum Festivum: Studies in Honor of Paul Oskar Kristeller*. Medieval & Renaissance Texts & Studies, 49 (Binghamton, 1987), pp. 13–54.

[9] J. Alberigo, J.A. Dossetti, P.-P. Joannou, et al., *Conciliorum Oecumenicorum Decreta*, editio tertia (Bologna, 1973) henceforth C.O.D., p. 245. Also disseminated in the *Compilatio Quarta* 5, 14, 2, ed. Friedberg, *Quinque Compilationes Antiquae* (Leipzig, 1882), p. 149 and canonized by Gregory IX as 5, 14, 12 in his *Liber Decretalium* of 1234, *Corpus Juris Canonici*, 2 vols. ed. E. Friedberg, (Leipzig, 1879), 2:887.

[10] See Alexander Murray, "Confession before 1215," *Transactions of the Royal Historical Society*, Series 6, vol. 3 (1993), pp. 51–81.

themselves (per se). Humankind, however, sinned at the suggestion of the devil."[11]

The creed does not mention the devil again until it specifies how God will dispose of the him after the Last Judgment. "And at the end of time [Christ] will come to judge the living and the dead . . . according to their merits, whether they were good or bad, so that the latter may receive perpetual punishment with the devil and the former may receive everlasting glory with Christ."[12] By skipping from Eden to the Last Judgment, Innocent III and his bishops conceded to the devil no more than the power of suggesting sin to humans (as he suggested it to Adam and Eve), which must have seemed his primary function in history. The only other role assigned to this fallen creature is to be the locus of eternal punishment in fire along with the human damned, whom he successfully tempted.[13]

Although Lateran IV is the only ecumenical council to mention the devil before Trent,[14] and consequently these allusions might appear to emphasize his significance, nonetheless *Firmiter credimus* assigns fewer and more strictly defined roles to the devil than those in other sources, both Cathar and Catholic. A rapid sketch will show how the New Testament itself allows the devil and his demons plenty of influence. Even though 2 Peter 2:4 depicts them chained in nether darkness until the Last Judgment, according to other passages they are still at work. As the Adversary (1 Peter 5:8), the devil sows evil seed, sets snares (1 Tim. 3:7, 6:9), oppresses the virtuous (Acts 10:38), recruits evil followers (1 John 3:8), and challenges Jesus directly (Matt. 4:1–9). Yet, importantly, divine forces can and do overcome the Evil One. Jesus resists Satan's temptation (Matt. 4:10) and overpowers his demons

---

[11] C.O.D., p. 230: "Diabolus enim et daemones alii a Deo quidem natura creati sunt boni, sed ipsi per se facti sunt mali. Homo vero diaboli suggestione peccavit." The Lateran Creed was also published in the first position of both the *Compilatio Quarta* and Gregory IX's *Decretals*. The Lateran Creed is discussed in the light of twentieth century interpretations by Paul M. Quay, S.J., "Angels and Demons; The Teaching of IV Lateran," *Theological Studies*, 42, no. 1 (1981), 20–45. I am indebted to the late Professor Stephan Kuttner for this reference.

[12] Ibid., ". . . venturus in fine saeculi iudicare vivos et mortuos . . . ut recipiant secundum merita sua, sive bona fuerint sive mala, illi cum diabolo penam perpetuam et isti cum Christo gloriam sempiternam."

[13] By implication, the devil is lord of hell only from the time of his fall until the end of time. His lordship ends with history. After the end of time he receives only punishment, according to this extremely terse declaration. On this theme, see: Jérôme Baschet, "Satan, prince de l'enfer: le développement de sa puissance dans l'iconographie italienne (XIIIᵉ–XVᵉ siècle)" in *L'autunno del diavolo*, a curo di E. Corsini e E. Costa (Milano, 1990), pp. 383–396.

[14] Russell, *Lucifer*, p. 95 and note 9.

(Matt. 9:33–34). The apostles exorcise them (Matt. 7:22, Mark 1:34, 39; 3:15, 3:22, 9:37, 16:17; Luke 9:1, 10:17). In the end, the demons will be condemned to the eternal fire prepared for them from the beginning of the world (Matt. 25:41). By contrast, in Catharism, the devil is creator and lord of the visible world. By his deceit, he corrupted angels whom he forced into human form, taught them sex, and made a new, accursed human race, imprisoned in bodies of clay.[15]

In the medieval Catholic tradition of saints' lives, legends, and miracles, the devil and his demons tempt the just and the wavering, record the sins of backsliders and denounce them, recruit liegemen and women to serve them in evil, apprehend the souls of dying sinners, and torment the evil dead in hell from the moment of death to the Last Judgment, and then forever.[16] The diabolical roles named in the Lateran creed are fewer and less active than those just mentioned, whether Catholic or Cathar. Thus, even as it broke new ground simply by mentioning the devil, the creed of Lateran IV implicitly prescribes a certain restraint in future portrayals of diabolical activity.

Theologians teaching about confession carried this restraint to the point of silence. The theologians I am about to cite differed on aspects of their overall theories of sacramental grace. For example, in the history of theories of penance, the late twelfth and early thirteenth centuries saw the shift from contritionism to absolutionism, so theologians interpreted the priest's role variously.[17] However, these disagreements pale before the consensual strength of the core perception that in

---

[15] These roles emerge in the Cathar legends "The Vision of Isaiah" and "The Secret Supper" (also known as the "Interrogatio Johannis") translated as no. 56A and 56B in W.L. Wakefield and A.P. Evans, *Heresies of the High Middle Ages* Records of Civilization: Sources and Studies (New York, 1969), pp. 447–65. The latter is the subject of a detailed investigation by Edina Bozóky, *Le livre secret des cathares, "Interrogatio Iohannis": Apocryphe d'origine bogomile*. Textes, Dossiers, Documents, 2 (Paris, 1980). For the Cathars in general see Jean Duvernoy, *Le catharisme: La religion des cathares* (Toulouse, 1976).

[16] A long tradition of scholarship has studied this literature. A fruitful survey is that of Arturo Graf, *Il Diavolo* (Milano, 1889). More recently, see Satan (*Etudes carmélitaines*, Paris: Desclée, 1948); Alfons Rosenberg, *Engel und Dämonen Gestaltwandel eines Urbildes* (München, 1967); and Herbert Haag, *Teufelsglaube* (Tübingen, 1974). The honoree of this volume is the modern master of the subject. See J.B. Russell, *The Devil* (Ithaca, N.Y., 1977); *Satan* (Ithaca, N.Y., 1981), *Lucifer* (Ithaca, N.Y., 1984). See also J.-C. Schmitt, "Le maschere, il diavolo, i morti nell'Occidente medievale," in *Religione, folklore e società nell'Occidente medievale* (Roma-Bari, 1988), pp. 206–238. Jérôme Baschet, "Diavolo" in *Enciclopedia dell'arte medievale* (Roma, 1994), 5:644–50.

[17] E. Amann & A. Michel, "Pénitence," *Dictionnaire de théologie catholique* (henceforth DTC) 12 (1933), cols. 722–1050. E. Vacandard, "Confession (Du Concile de Latran au Concile de Trente)," DTC 3 (1908), 894–926. Jean-Charles Payen, "La pénitence dans le contexte culturel des XIIe et XIIIe s. Des doctrines contritionnistes

the operation of grace, in the functioning of the sacraments, the fundamental action occurs between God and the sinner: a relationship that excludes the devil. Theologians explained the sacrament of penance in terms of a reconciliation between God and the sinner.[18] Whatever the role of the priest, the results of confession for the penitent were caused mediately or immediately by God or God's grace. These accounts make no mention of the devil. A brief survey will support this contention.

Early in the century, Robert of Courzon wrote: "the priest confirms what God has done earlier."[19] Raymond of Penafort: "Do not take it that contrition literally remits sin, . . . but God himself, in contrition."[20] Alexander of Hales stated: "Absolution comes from Christ, by reason of the Passion."[21] And he said: "In confession, sins are expelled by renunciation through the mouth. And this expulsion signifies the ejection that the Lord makes through the interior mouth, that is, the heart."[22] Albertus Magnus: "Only God deletes fault."[23]

Thomas Aquinas declares: The sacrament of penance operates by virtue of "the abundance of divine mercy and the efficacy of the grace of Christ."[24] Another passage dramatically illustrates how Thomas sees penance as a matter involving the relationship between the sinner and God. In penance, Thomas says, recompense for the offence is made according to the will of the sinner and the decision

---

aux pénitentiels vernaculaires." *Revue des sciences philosophiques et théologiques* 61:3 (1977), 399–428. Bernhard Poschmann, *Penance and the Anointing of the Sick* (London, 1964), 155–193. P.A. Teetaert, *La Confession aux laïques dans l'Eglise latine depuis le VIIIe jusq'au XIVe s.* (Wetteren, Bruges, Paris, 1926). Paul Anciaux, *La Théologie du sacrement de pénitence au XIIe s.* (Louvain, 1949). Idem, "Le Sacrement de pénitence chez Guillaume d'Auvergne," *Ephemerides theologicae lovanienses* 24 (1948), 98–118. An indispensable collection occurs in *L'Aveu: Antiquité et moyen âge* (as above, note 2), with pertinent articles by N. Bériou, P.-M. Gy, R. Rusconi, and J. Berlioz.

[18] Thus, Isnard Frank, "Beichte II" *Theologische Realenzyklopädie* 5 (1980): "Rekonziliation," p. 415; "Versöhnung," p. 419. Similar characterization in Reinhold Seeberg, *Lehrbuch der Dogmengeschichte*, 5te Auflage, III (Graz, 1953), pp. 531, 551–52.

[19] "[Sacerdos] approbat in suo foro et judicio, quod Deus prius fecit." Cited by Amann, DTC 12:953.

[20] *Summa de Poenitentia*, Liber III, Para. 11 (Rome, 1603), p. 446b: "Verum non intelligas quod contritio dimittat peccatum proprie loquendo, sed ipse Deus in contritione."

[21] *Glossa in Librum IV Sententiarum* 17.20; Bibliotheca Franciscana Scholastica 15 (Quaracchi, 1957), p. 298: "Absolutio est a Christo ratione passionis."

[22] Ibid., 17.9.g; p. 285: "In confessione ab ore expelluntur peccata cum detestatione: quae expulsio significat expulsionem quam facit Dominus ab ore interiori, scilicet corde." Also see the nine benefits of confession listed in 17.8.f; p. 282.

[23] *De sacramentis* VI, I q.1 a.5; in *Opera Omnia*, ed. B. Geyer (Münster in Westfalia, 1958), 26:76a: "Culpam delet solus deus."

[24] *Summa contra Gentiles* IV, 72; *Opera Omnia* XV (Romae, 1930), p. 225a: ". . . abundantia divinae misericordiae, et efficacia gratiae Christi."

of God, against whom he sinned. Thus Thomas contrasts penance, in which agreement is reached by the mutual consent of the sinner and God, to a judicial sentence, in which equity is imposed by the decision of the judge. Thomas's image of penance is that of two friends settling a quarrel. The friends are the sinner and God (although the priest acts in God's place).[25]

Bonaventure refers to a pact between God and man and, on the basis of this pact, the Lord has bound himself to give grace to one who undertakes the sacrament.[26] Even while granting a significant role in penance to the priest, Richard of Mediavilla qualifies that position by saying that the priest produces the remission of faults "insofar as the divine virtue, which remits sin, assists his ministry."[27] Duns Scotus is even more sweeping, for his statement takes in all the sacraments at once. He says: "God is the immediate cause of the effects of the sacraments through his assistance in the sacrament . . . and so [his] will is the first and principal cause of its invisible effect."[28] This survey shows that theological opinion on confession did not ascribe any role to the devil. Penance is the way one restores the right relationship between oneself and God.

The situation begins to change once one turns from the literature of the schools to the reference books compiled for preachers, from teaching to preaching.[29] For when preachers, especially mendicants,

---

[25] *Summa Theologiae*, Pars III, q.90 a.2; *Opera Omnia* XII (Romae, 1906), p. 335. "Alio modo fit recompensatio offensae in poenitentia, et in vindicativa iustitia. Nam in vindicativa iustitia fit recompensatio secundum arbitrium iudicis, non secundum voluntatem offendentis vel offensi: sed in poenitentia fit recompensatio offensae secundum voluntatem peccantis, et secundum arbitrium Dei, in quem peccatur; quia hic non quaeritur sola reintegratio aequalitatis iustitiae, sicut in iustitia vindicativa, sed magis reconciliatio amicitiae, quod fit dum offendens recompensat secundum voluntatem eius quem offendit." For a fuller study that reports a similar emphasis, see Pedro Fernández Rodríguez, "El Sacramento de la Penitencia en la Suma de Teología, de Santo Tomás de Aquino," *Ciencia Tomista* 121 (1994), pp. 145–183.

[26] *Comm. in Sent.* IV d.1 p.1 a.1 q.4; *Opera Omnia*, 10 vols. (Quaracchi, 1882–1902) 4:24: "Ex tali pactione Dominus astrinxit se quodam modo ad dandum gratiam suscipienti Sacramentum. . . ."

[27] Richard of Mediavilla, *Comm. in Sent.* IV, d.14 a.2 q.I, II, III, quoted in Amann, DTC 12, col. 1024. "Le prêtre . . . produit . . . la rémission des fautes 'in quantum suo ministerio assistit virtus divina, quae peccatum remittit.'"

[28] Johannes Duns Scotus, *Reportata Parisiensa* IV, d.2 q.1, Scholium I; ed. Luca Wadding XI (Lugduni, 1639), p. 574b. "Deus ergo est causa immediata talis effectus sacramenti per assistentiam suam sacramento, cui disponit semper assistere et gratiam conferre . . . et ita sola voluntas est prima causa et principalis huius effectus invisibilis."

[29] The most comprehensive overview of medieval preaching is by Jean Longère, *La Prédication médiévale* (Paris, 1983).

considered the prospect of addressing a lay audience, they introduced the devil.[30] The homiletic relevance of the devil stems from the clerical calculation of popular concerns.[31] Though no documents reveal the people's concerns explicitly, it is possible to reconstruct them indirectly, on the rebound. To do so, one must consider the relationship between the literary genres I shall review below: the preacher's manual, the sermon, and the exemplum.

The connection between these genres was well known to participants in that first generation of preaching reform that opened the thirteenth century, when, heeding the call of James of Vitry, preachers began to reach for a popular audience, to attempt what James called the "edification of the untutored (rudes) and the education (eruditio) of the country folk."[32] In an elaborate metaphor, which I paraphrase, Pope Gregory IX saw a similar process at work when he compared the university to a workshop, where the professors turn the raw ore of untutored minds into refined metal, from which are shaped breast-plates of the faith and trumpets for sounding the praise of Christ.[33] In other words, Gregory distinguished different implements for the different functions of teaching and preaching. In a letter of 1292, Nicholas IV plays on the word "erudire." "By the study of letters," he says, "men are made learned in the sciences" (viri efficiuntur scientiis eruditi) and "the uneducated are educated" (erudiuntur rudes).[34] Contemporaries used their distinction between the *rudes* and the *eruditi* to develop the rhetorical strategy of their pastoral office. Thus, James of Vitry advised: "One should present easy and simple doctrine to the weaker audience and the bread of a more solid doctrine to more advanced hearers."[35] To the *rudes*, he urged preachers to

---

[30] For mendicant preaching and its dissemination see D.L. d'Avray, *The Preaching of the Friars: Sermons Diffused from Paris Before 1300* (Oxford, 1985). Though focused on Italy, see Katherine L. Jansen, "Mary Magdalen and the mendicants: The Preaching of penance in the late Middle Ages," *Journal of Medieval History* 21 (1995), 1–25.

[31] See Jacques Berlioz, "L'auditoire des prédicateurs dans la littérature des exempla (XIIIe–XIVe siècles)," *Medioevo e Rinascimento* 3 (1989), pp. 125–158; Zelina Zafarana, "La predicazione ai laici dal secolo XIII al XIV," *Studi medievali* Ser. 3, 24 (1983), pp. 265–75.

[32] Jacques de Vitry, Sermones de Temporibus, Prologus, ed. J.B. Pitra *Analecta Novissima Spicilegii Solesmensis, altera continuatio* (Paris, 1888), 2:188–93, at p. 192: "ad aedificationem rudium et agrestium eruditionem."

[33] *Chartularium Universitatis Parisiensis*, ed. H. Denifle & E. Châtelain, 4 vols. (Paris, 1889–97) Vol. 1, no. 79, p. 137: "Ibi ferrum de terra tollitur, . . . lorica fidei . . . fit. . . . Et lapis . . . in es vertitur . . . et fiunt predicatione sonora preconantia laudes Christi."

[34] Ibid., vol. 2, no. 578, p. 55.

[35] James in Pitra, p. 189: "Occurrere debeat cum facili et simplici doctrina, quantum ad juniores, et cum panibus solidioris doctrinae instruendo majores."

offer "the almost corporeal, palpable and such-like things that they know by experience."[36] To accommodate this shift in levels, preachers dropped the academic discussions of penance, which were focused on the relationship of the sinner and God. Instead, for the *rudes*, the popular audience implied by preachers' manuals and explicitly addressed in sermons, they focused on the devil and advocated confession as an escape from his snares.

One place where this progression of ideas is very clear is in the treatise *On Different Preachable Matters* (De Diversis Materiis Predicabilibus), written between 1250 and 1261 by the Dominican alumnus of the University of Paris, teacher at the Dominican Studium at Lyons, and Inquisitor, Stephen of Bourbon. Lecoy de la Marche published excerpts from his treatise in his *Anecdotes Historiques*. Stephen's treatise is a compilation of related biblical passages and glosses, theological and philosophical synopses, and finally, moral illustrations or exempla arranged according to subject.[37]

Stephen's theology is completely expository. He does not discuss problems and resolve them. Instead, he simply presents the conclusions of theology so that they may be reported in sermons. In the chain of doctrinal communication, beginning with papal pronouncements and descending through theological argumentation, Stephen's treatment of confession represents the first appearance of the devil. He states, for example, that confession presents twelve obstacles to the devil.[38]

---

[36] James in Pitra, p. 192: ". . . corporalia et palpabilia et talia quae per experientiam norunt."

[37] Etienne de Bourbon, *Anecdotes historiques*, ed. A. Lecoy de La Marche (Paris: Renouard, 1877) (henceforth EdeB). To rectify the misleading impression given by Lecoy de la Marche's selections, it is necessary to consult the manuscript, Paris, B.N. lat. 15970, fols. 137–686, now in the process of being edited under the direction of M. Jacques Berlioz. The manuscript was bequeathed to the Sorbonne by Peter of Limoges, a former master of that house who died in 1304. At fol. 686v it states: "Iste liber est pauperum magistrorum de Sorbona ex legato M. Petri de Limovacens. quondam socii domus huius. Cathenata 162 inter sermones." It was chained in the library's reference room. L. Delisle, *Le Cabinet des manuscrits*, 4 vols. (Paris, 1868–81), 3:74. For Peter of Limoges and his bequest, see ibid., 2:167–69. Though somewhat later, the St. Victor manuscripts containing Stephen's work (Paris, B.N. lat. 14598–14600) are considerably more legible.

[38] Each of the following "inconveniences" that confession imposes on the devil serves as the heading of a sub-section in Stephen's discussion of confession (taken from Paris, B.N. lat. 15970):

Primum incommodum est quia per confessionem ab homine [dyabolus] expellitur et fugatur quod signatur (258rb–va).
Secundum incommodum eius est quia mediante confessione castrum suum fortis armatus quod muniverat perdit et predam quam diu captam tenuerat solutis eius vinculis amittit (258va).

It hurts his demons, undermines his fortress, confuses him, reveals his secrets, dissolves his pacts, and exposes his filth. It obstructs his mouth so that he cannot accuse sinners of what they have confessed, it erases what he has written, it blinds him so that he cannot recognize sinners, it permits him no rest, it torments and afflicts his demons, and it overturns and annihilates projects that he has been developing for 30 or 100 years or more. Under another heading, Stephen states that confession liberates humans in many ways, but primarily from the devil: it liberates sinners from the oppression of the devil, from servitude to the devil and to sin, from the bonds and chains of the devil, from the mouth of the devil, and the pit of hell.[39]

This selection of rubrics is not fully representative. Stephen does not exclude God from the picture. Some discussions fit the model of the theologians, such as the paragraph devoted to the way the sinner ought to be moved to confession by God's glory and grace, which is conferred in it and through it.[40] Other passages pit God directly against the "strong man" of Mark 3:27, who is Satan: "In confession and absolution God ties the strong man up tight, wastes his house, and destroys the deadly weapons of the sinners."[41] Thus Stephen's compilation occupies a middle band in the spectrum between a divine and a diabolical focus in explaining confession. It introduces references to the devil that were omitted from theology, but also allows room

---

Tercium incommodum est quia in confessione et absolutione Deus fortem [scil. Sathanam] alligat et domum eius evacuat, destruens vasa mortis peccatorum. (Quarto) Dyabolum confundit confessio.
(Quinto) Secretum dyaboli confessio aperit et fedus eius dissolvit (258vb).
(Sexto) Turpitudinem dyaboli aperit et ostendit quam turpis sit ille.
(Septimo) Os dyaboli obstruit ut non possit hominem accusare de eo de quo accusavit se in confessione.
(Octavo) Scripta delet dyaboli (259ra).
(Nono) Dyabolum quasi excecat ut peccatorem non cognoscat (259va).
(Decimo) Dyabolum quiescere non sinit.
(Undecimo) Demones torquet et affligit.
(Duodecimo) Virtutem Sathane destruit et adnichilat quod laboravit multis annis Sathanas, scil. 30 vel 100 vel amplius, confessio irritat et adnichilat una hora (259vb).

[39] "Hominem liberat, primo ab oppressione dyaboli. . . . Item liberat a servitute dyaboli et peccati. . . . Item liberat a vinculis et cathenis dyaboli. . . . Item liberat de ore dyaboli et de puteo inferni" (260rb).

[40] Stephen lists twelve factors which ought to move sinners to confession. Among them: "debet ad hanc movere gratia et gloria que in hac et per hanc a deo conferuntur" (258rb).

[41] This is the third "inconvenience" that confession presents to the devil. See note 38, above.

for God, his glory, and his grace to operate either within the penitent or against the devil directly. The pivotal position of Stephen's compilation may best be represented by this statement, which juxtaposes both elements: "God remits the sin of one who confesses humbly, and the devil loses the control he had over that person's heart; for whenever sin is dismissed from a person's heart, the devil, too, is doubtless ejected."[42] In the exposition of confession that prefaces the relevant sermon exempla, therefore, Stephen builds on the theological tradition, in which desire for a correct relationship with God suffices to induce confession, by introducing the devil, a negative force, and a clearer, less abstract, more familiar incentive to confess, these preachers calculate, in the minds of the common people, the *rudes*.

By contrast, in the exempla collected by Stephen, the balance tilts dramatically in the devil's favor, and mention of God becomes minimal. Before proceeding to an analysis of selected exempla, however, it is necessary to define and describe them briefly. As they relate to sermons in the thirteenth century, exempla are moral illustrations of precepts advanced in sermons. The moral of the story (that is, of the exemplum) should theoretically coincide with the counsel the preacher is offering. In earlier discussions of the exemplum as a rhetorical device, Alan of Lille and James of Vitry regard exempla as the most appropriate means of reaching the unlettered, as milk is the most appropriate food for infants. Unlettered country folk need to have their lessons presented through reference to objects and events of which they have direct knowledge, and James of Vitry and Alan of Lille praised exempla as "familiar" to the people. Exempla were collected and chosen for their expected appeal to a popular audience, for the common people, for "rusticis et rudibus." They were intended to edify and amuse them, to keep them awake and retrieve their attention.[43]

---

[42] "Humiliter confitenti remittit deus peccatum, et dyabolus eum quod in corde hominis habebat amittit principatum; ubi enim peccatum remittitur de corde peccatoris, procul dubio dyabolus eicitur" (260rb).

[43] For James of Vitry see Thomas F. Crane, *The Exempla... of Jacques de Vitry* (London, 1890), intro. p. xli, note. For Alan of Lille, *De Arte Praedicatoria*, PL 210: 114c: "Debet uti exemplis... quia familiaris est doctrina exemplaria." The classic treatment of exempla is J-Th. Welter, *L'Exemplum dans la littérature religieuse et didactique du moyen âge* (Paris-Toulouse, 1927). His discussions of James and Alan are on pp. 66–9 and 118–124. Jean Longère discusses exempla in *Oeuvres oratoires des maîtres parisiens au XIIᵉ s.*, 2 vols. (Paris, 1975) 1:58–63. Now the standard work is C. Bremond,

This intention, made clear in the prologues to the exempla collections, helps to define the term "popular" as I mean it in this paper. It does not mean "originating from the people,"[44] but it does mean "aimed at the people and recognizing their experience." By considering each exemplum separately and remembering the intentions expressed by the compilers themselves in the prefaces of their works, it is possible to approximate the religion of the people as it was understood by the clergy, particularly the mendicants. Moreover, since Lateran IV, the clergy had to encourage the laity in the obligation to confess at least once a year. Thus it is possible to reconstruct the religious concerns of the popular audience by studying how the clergy presented confession. We cannot hear tales as told by the mouth of the people, but we can identify what the clergy prepared for their ears.[45]

A few exempla from Stephen's collection will show how they portray the consequences of confession.

1. Confession cleanses the soul (a). A rich man who suddenly became poor, in desperation, pledged himself to the devil. The hand with which he did homage turned black. He was unable to clean it. After a long time, he confessed. "But when, weeping, he confessed, that black hand suddenly became white and returned to its pristine color."[46]

2. Confession cleanses the soul (b). A woman led a dance in the square in front of a church in Anjou and distracted people from the sermon. Demons possessed her and she broke out in boils. Relics

---

J. Le Goff, & J.-C. Schmitt, "L'Exemplum." Typologie des Sources du Moyen Age Occidental, 40 (Turnhout, Belgium, 1982). I have examined some specifically religious functions of the exemplum in "The Exemplum as 'Incorporation' of Abstract Truth in the Thought of Humbert of Romans and Stephen of Bourbon," in *The Two Laws: Studies in Medieval Legal History Dedicated to Stephan Kuttner*, L. Mayali and S.A.J. Tibbetts, Studies in Medieval and Early Modern Canon Law 1 (Washington, D.C., 1990), pp. 82–96. See also L.-J. Bataillon, "Similitudines et exempla dans les sermons du XIIIe siècle," in *The Bible in the Medieval World: Essays in Memory of Beryl Smalley* (Oxford, 1985), pp. 191–205.

[44] The phrase is Jean-Claude Schmitt's. See "'Religion populaire' et culture folklorique. A propos d'une réédition: 'La piété populaire au Moyen Age,'" *Annales E.S.C.* 31:5 (1976), p. 942.

[45] Guides for priests in administering confession also fit this genre. J. Goering and P.J. Payer have published a Dominican manual from the 1220s, in which the priest is to combine threats and assurances during confession. Whereas concealing sin would scorn God, there is no sin that cannot be dissolved. "[C]ave <tibi> quia Deus non irridetur. . . . [S]i celares ex industria tua unum peccatum, de aliis ueniam consequi non posses. . . . [Q]uia quamuis peccata magna sint, tamen Dei misericordia in confessione lauantur." "The Summa Penitentie Fratrum Predicatorum" *Mediaeval Studies* 55 (1993), pp. 1–50 at 26–27, lines 25–38.

[46] EdeB, no. 182, pp. 159–60.

provided no help. She apologized to the preacher she interrupted and, when the friars prayed for her, the demons went away, but the boils remained. Then she confessed and was cleansed.[47]

3. Confession empties the devil's sack. A sacristan saw the devil with a large sack. The devil told him it contained all the shortcomings of the brothers, but the devil lamented the brothers' chapter meetings because, on those occasions, the brothers accuse each other, confess, and do penances, which empty his sack and make him lose all he has worked for.[48]

4. Confession erases the devil's memory. (This is one version of the exemplum of the Roman Matron, or of the Incestuous Widow, to be examined further.) A certain widow was very well known to her bishop because of the religious way of life he observed in her. But, at the instigation of the devil, she sinned with her own son and had a child from that union. This same devil, wishing to confound her, assumed human form and went to the bishop, saying that, on a certain day, he would prove that that woman was a horrible sinner. For her part, the woman, seeing the day approach, confessed her sin. When she appeared before the bishop on the assigned day, the devil opened his papers and found that all he had written about her had been erased, and he could not even recognize her.[49]

5. Confession blinds the devil. A knight was travelling with a certain companion to an appointed place to meet a demon who was to answer the knight's suspicions about his wife. As they approached the place, the friend knew where they were going and grew conscious of his sin. He withdrew as if to relieve himself and, calling a squire, confessed his sin to him, because he could not have a priest. When the knight asked the demon about his wife, he said she was an adulteress, but he could not say with whom, because shortly before the adulterer had been removed from his records. And when the knight showed him the colleague, the demon said he did not know him.[50]

6. Confession delivers from maritime perils. During a sea voyage, a certain very beautiful woman so attracted those who were on her

---

[47] Ibid., no. 185, pp. 161–2.
[48] Ibid., no. 179, p. 157.
[49] Ibid., no. 178, pp. 156–7.
[50] Paris, B.N. lat. 15970, fol. 259va–b. This very famous exemplum appears in virtually all the standard collections, including that of James of Vitry, whom Stephen acknowledges as his source. For other versions see Frederic C. Tubach, *Index Exemplorum. A Handbook of Medieval Religious Tales*. FF Communications, 204 (Helsinki, 1969), nos. 1200 and 1508. On Tubach's work, see *Les "Exempla" médiévaux*, eds. J. Berlioz & M.A. Polo de Beaulieu (Carcassonne, 1992).

ship that nearly all who were there sinned with her either in deed or in thought. She avoided neither father nor son, but shamed herself, although in secret, with all. When a storm arose and the ship was placed in danger, she began to call out all her sins to everyone and to confess them, believing that others would be put in danger because of them. Then, with each confessing to the others, the sea relented from its fury. With calm restored, no one was able to know which woman it was.[51]

These exempla are sufficient to allow some statements about the theology or cosmology implicit in them. It is clear that there is no mention of divine mercy or of grace. Confession erases the devil's memory or his notes and so prevents him from prosecuting the sinners, and therefore it is implied that they may now be saved. God's own omniscience is seemingly of no account in these tales. It is as if God needed the devil as a prosecutor in order to damn a sinner. The conclusion one would draw from these exempla is that it is more important to escape the devil than to placate the divine judge. In the exempla, the central relationship is that between the sinner and the devil.

To this analysis one might object that the escape from the devil recounted in these tales is through the power of God, that it is God who erases the devil's notes, removes the boils, calms the sea. Yet these tales offer no explicit mention of grace, mercy, or even God himself. There is only the sudden reversal of circumstances following confession. And even then, as in the exemplum of the near shipwreck, the action has an impersonal, almost magical role. Other exempla attribute the same efficacy to the sign of the cross, to invocations of the Virgin, or uttering the name of Jesus.[52] It is also noteworthy that

---

[51] EdeB, no. 183, p. 160.

[52] For the name of Jesus, see Tubach, nos. 345 and 3448. The sign of the cross banishes a devil come to remove a soul from a deathbed in no. 1346. Cf. no. 840. Invocation of the Lord is efficacious in nos. 1594 and 5133. In EdB, no. 114, p. 99, invocation of the Virgin brings her to the aid of a woman suddenly experiencing labor pains and trapped before the incoming tide at Mont-Saint-Michel. Sometimes the Virgin and confession work together as in Tubach, no. 2737 or, as in no. 1587, she may defend the sincerity of contrition against the devil, who claims a woman's soul. Perhaps the most widespread example of the Virgin's action is in the legend of Theophilus, to which an introduction may be found in Moshe Lazar, "Theophilus: Servant of Two Masters. The Pre-Faustian theme of Despair and Revolt," *Modern Language Notes* 87:6 (1972), 31–50. I have excluded examples (such as EdB, no. 135, pp. 114–15), in which a particular devotion to the intercessor exists prior to the crisis and might seem to "merit" supernatural intervention.

many of the penitents in these stories seem to reserve recourse to confession for moments of emergency or despair. Then, confession at the last minute provides the way out.

Lateran IV had emphasized Satan's role as a tempter. In these exempla, however, the devil goes beyond this function. He is able not only to instigate sin, but, further, he enslaves those who have followed his suggestions. In the stories involving pacts with himself or his demons, he seems clearly to be more versatile than foreseen in the Lateran Creed. The freedom of action granted the devil in the plots of these sermon tales establishes a source of energy or a pole contrary to the divine grace that is the focus of the theological accounts of confession. This diabolical activity begins to approximate the role for evil associated with Manichaeism and Catharism. Yet these tales form part of a body of beliefs that clerics knew were held by the people. Preachers judged that, if they wanted their sermons to be effective, they should take these ideas of their audience into account. Thus preachers, in their desire to reach the popular audience, catered to popular ideas that attributed to the devil greater activity than had been specified in Lateran IV or conceded by theologians.

The result of the preachers' accommodation of the popular acceptance of the devil's versatility was a shift in the center of gravity of the fundamental drama that underlies confession. In contrast to the Lateran Creed, therefore, because of the exempla used in preaching confession, the drama must include three protagonists: God, the penitent, the devil. The integrity of the drama will not be affected by changes in the protagonists' roles, as long as the protagonists themselves remain the same and as long as the action concerns the final disposition of the penitent's soul.

These, then, are two variants of the same drama. In the theological variant, center stage presents the penitent and God, who seek to compose their differences. The devil, although offstage, is nonetheless a party to the drama, because it is understood that he is waiting to receive the sinner's soul, should negotiations between God and the sinner fail. In the variant espoused by the exempla, center stage presents the sinner and the devil, with God offstage. If the sinner effects his escape, God will receive his soul. In either version (and this is what assures its unity), the drama revolves around the sinner's choice.

Although the sinner's decision remains central, there is considerable tension between devil-focused and God-focused accounts of confession.

In either version, however, the sacrament of penance is made the way to God and it is that fact which allowed the preachers to match their sermon messages to popular anxieties. This point becomes clearer in the analysis of a particular sermon, which will show how one of the exempla in Stephen of Bourbon's collection was actually used.

The sermon comes from a Paris manuscript (B.N. lat 16481) containing 218 sermons from the liturgical year 1272–73.[53] The preacher is the Dominican Lambert of Liège, about whom virtually nothing is known other than his contribution of three sermons to this collection.[54] The sermon in question was delivered at St-Germain l'Auxerrois, the most popular and perhaps the wealthiest parish in Paris, right in front of the Louvre, on February 26, the first Sunday of Lent, 1273.[55] Recalling Innocent III's legislation to the effect that the faithful must confess annually before Easter, this sermon has an important function in launching the penitential season. Lambert's theme comes from 2 Cor. 6:1: "We urge you not to receive God's grace in vain." I shall paraphrase the sermon in order to show how Lambert mixes the conclusions of theology with popular sayings and the exemplum of the incestuous widow to communicate the message that confession is the means of escaping the devil.

Christ's greatest gift, Lambert begins, is the sacrament of the altar at Easter. Seven weeks are given for preparation to receive it and it is dangerous for the unworthy to do so. The way to become worthy is to cure the spirit. Lambert develops at length a parallel between the physician's cure of the body and the priest's cure of the soul. Three steps emerge: first you must know that you are sick, then you must tell a doctor, and finally, you must do what he tells you. The same is true of spiritual disease. Lambert considers these three points

---

[53] See the detailed study of this manuscript by Nicole Bériou, "La prédication au béguinage de Paris pendant l'année liturgique 1272–1273," *Recherches Augustiniennes* 13 (1978), 105–229. This volume was also bequeathed to the Sorbonne by Peter of Limoges and shelved as number 179 among the manuscripts concerned with sermons. The cycle can be assigned to 1272–73 by collating the coincidence of fixed and movable feasts and verifying this result by the biographical data available on the preachers named in the volume. The manuscript is unique for the thirteenth century in that it provides the author, feast day, and site for nearly every sermon recorded.

[54] Quetif-Echard, *Scriptores Ordinis Praedicatorum*, 2 vols. (1719–1723), 1:268. J.B. Schneyer lists a fourth sermon that he attributes to Lambert, Rouen, A560, fol. 6ra, "Species caeli gloria stellarum" in his *Repertorium der lateinischen Sermones des Mittelalters*, 11 vols. (1969–90), 4:1.

[55] Raymond Cazelles, *Nouvelle histoire de Paris de la fin du règne de Philippe Auguste à la mort de Charles V, 1223–1380* (Paris, 1972), pp. 113–15, 150–51, et passim.

individually and gives examples of what he means. On the first point he exhorts his audience: "Know that you are sick. Don't take water to your neighbor's house when yours is aflame. When you take stock of your spiritual health, don't exaggerate your good deeds, for which God owes you nothing except through his generosity. Concentrate instead on your evil deeds, for which, through his justice, he owes you eternal punishment.

On the second point, he counsels that this accounting alone is not enough. The soul must also reveal the faults it discovers to a superior. Just as a wife should acknowledge and reveal her faults to her husband and lord and come humbly before him, acknowledging that she has done wrong, seeking mercy, and promising to improve, and so earn his gratitude and indulgence; so should the soul acknowledge its transgression against Christ its spouse, and immediately he will enfold the soul with mercy and be completely pleased and happy. In more prosaic terms, Lambert put the lesson like this: "Don't just sweep up all the dust and, like the lazy housewife, leave it in a corner to be scattered through the house again. Throw it out!" It is the same with sins. If you hide them in a corner of your conscience, demons will scatter them about. You must express them, because confession cleanses the soul and erases sins from the devil's book.

To show how this happens, Lambert says, I will tell you the story of the Roman matron, whose husband died leaving her with a very young son, whom she loved so much that she let him sleep in her bed every night. And the devil so arranged it that she continued to do this until the boy was fully grown. Then it happened that she became pregnant by her son. When the child was born, she threw the infant in a well. Then she knew that if she had been in great sin before, now she was in even greater. And the devil had arranged all this. So when he saw that it was done, he went, disguised as a lawyer, and denounced her at the court of the emperor. The emperor sent for the woman who came and pleaded for a delay in her case. Then she came to herself and, although the sin was serious and gross and ugly, she hastened to the pope and confessed the whole story to him. And while she was confessing, she was so contrite and wept so abundantly and with such great grief that the pope cried too, out of compassion. In the end, he gave her the penance of saying one Pater Noster. Then the woman asked him for advice about appearing in the emperor's court. The pope said that she could go there boldly, because no one would ever be able to harm her thereafter. On the assigned day, she appeared before the emperor, who called on the lawyer to press the charges he had made against the woman. But when the lawyer stepped forward, he could not remember ever having seen her before. Looking at her more closely, he said that she was a holy woman. He then vanished from before the eyes of the emperor and was never seen in that court again. Now therefore you may see how great is the power of confession. And so, my dear ones, if the devil deceives you into some sin, confess it by Christian confession and thus you will return to your Redeemer. But let no one delay, because no one knows how much time remains.

The third point is that you must do what your priest orders, just as you would follow the diet imposed by the physician. Do penance, meditate, fast. Do not flee God's grace. Do not fear fasting and discipline in this life, because if you do, you will have great poverty and shame in the next world. Therefore let us do penance while we are able and while we have time. And so it comes to this, that anyone in a single day of penance may receive grace, if he is able to accept what God gives freely in a thousand ways. That is Lambert's sermon.[56]

This sermon contains several references to grace and God's desire to forgive sins. It ends with a plea that Lambert's hearers not spurn the opportunity provided by the Lenten season. The soul is called the spouse of Christ, thus stressing divine concern for the individual. Despite the devil-focused exemplum of the incestuous widow, the sermon itself cannot be regarded as devil-focused in its portrayal of confession. Nonetheless, the use of this version of this exemplum reveals much about how the sermon was put together and about the use of exempla in general. For the exemplum of the incestuous widow was known in other versions, like that recounted by James of Vitry in which the woman's eventual safety derived from her devotion to the Virgin.[57] In Gautier de Coincy's poem *De une noble fame de rome*, one of his *Miracles de Nostre Dame*, the Virgin personally represents the widow at the emperor's court.[58] But Lambert would clearly not select a version that would detract from his emphasis on confession.

---

[56] Paris, B.N. lat. 16481, fols. 132rb–134ra.

[57] Jacques de Vitry, ed. Crane, no. CCLXIII, pp. 110–111, and notes, pp. 246–49.

[58] Cited in Crane's detailed note on this story, ibid., pp. 247–49. See also the related exemplum edited by Th. Kaeppeli, "Un recueil de sermons, préchés à Paris et en Angleterre," AFP 26 (1956), pp. 161–191 at 181, in which a widow sleeps with her husband's brother, kills all the illegitimate children, and tries to kill herself. In agony, she thinks of hell and decides to call on the Virgin, who saves her life.

And it is the fact of selection, of calculation, that is primary. For just as a compiler or preacher chooses from many versions of exempla, he also chooses among listeners' beliefs as he knows them. Thus Lambert, like Stephen before him, knew that, whatever theology had taught him about grace, the lay audience was more concerned about the devil. And his selection of a devil-focused exemplum, whose climax comes in the act of confession, reveals his assessment of the populace.

In conclusion, Lambert's sermon allows a possible resolution of the difficulty concerning the "Manichaeizing" tendencies of the sermon exempla. It would be wrong to imply that popular Christianity in the thirteenth century was really Manichaeism in disguise. Nonetheless, there is a spectrum in Christian discourse that ranges from God to the devil, from good to evil, and which I have characterized here as "God-focused" and "devil-focused." The anomaly that this terminology implies for thirteenth-century Christian experience needs to be made explicit.

In the dualism of which Manichaeism is the most relevant variant for Christian history as a whole and Catharism for the twelfth and thirteenth centuries, good and evil are two opposed forces that contest control of the cosmos.[59] Although in theologically refined Christianity, the supreme goodness of God reduces evil to nothingness, it is clear even in the writings of St. Paul, St. Augustine, and numerous others, that, except for a limited number of technical questions, the independence and power of evil remained a problem.[60] Thus, even though Christ procured ultimate victory over evil by his resurrection, and the eventual containment of evil is assured after the general resurrection, nonetheless, between these two cosmic events, evil enjoys a certain liberty about which individual writers varied considerably. In practical terms, therefore, evil—as personified by the devil—retains a presence in the ethical life of the individual. The exempla dramatize this presence (as James of Vitry said the exempla should), though, at the same time, the exempla always include the possibility of liberation through confession in particular and the sacraments in general.

---

[59] See especially Wakefield and Evans, *Heresies* (as in note 15, above), No. 59, "The Book of Two Principles," pp. 511–91, where Good has the ability to win territory, and hence souls, from Evil.

[60] Russell's remarks on this subject are extremely important. "Orthodox Christianity is itself a quasi-dualist religion" (*Lucifer*, 185); "An odd convergence of Catholic and Cathar views lies beneath the surface" (ibid., 190).

There exists in the exempla, therefore, a certain functional dualism, which is employed didactically to explain ethical life in the present. It is a *functional* dualism, rather than a "dualism in principle," because it introduces a polarity that was absent in the technical, theological accounts of confession.[61] Whereas the theologians explain confession with reference only to God, the exempla introduce an opposed, albeit weaker, figure, the devil. Lambert of Liège illustrates how preachers resolved this tension between the two poles by urging their hearers to move from evil to good and by indicating, in confession, the means of doing so. Yet his use of the exemplum of the Roman matron shows that Lambert could not disclose the calm without the storm, the peak without the abyss, the divine without the diabolical. Thus the polarity between God-focused and devil-focused tales may be dualizing or Manichaeizing, because the second pole (however inferior its mode of existence) was needed as a frame of reference. (And it is the ontological inferiority of the second pole that makes it dualizing or Manichaeizing rather than outright dualism or Manichaeism.) Only the specialized, erudite theologian could explain confession in terms of grace alone and so reduce, somewhat, the fear of evil.

The existence of functional dualism only emerges from examining the spectrum that runs from official and learned to popular religion, from supplementing theological explanations with an array of sources progressively aimed at a popular audience. The rhetorical needs of the exempla and the sermons that transmitted them to the people reveal much about popular religion, though it must be inferred indirectly, as the clerics read the people. Although this second pole does not have the force or ontological standing of the evil principle in Catharism, it nonetheless indicates the use of a certain functional dualism by means of which preachers could encourage their audience to flee evil by seeking good in the person and office of the confessor.

---

[61] Adolph Harnack saw a similar tension in the early Christian communities. On the one hand, he says, they sensed the presence of evil keenly, but still trusted in the integrity of God's creation. On the other hand, he observed, they conceded to "the uncultured" an "impression of the wickedness of the course of this world, and the vulgarity of all things material" that would pass away at the end of time. He contrasted the latter "theoretic dualism" that they tolerated to a "dualism in principle" that they rejected. *History of Dogma*, 3rd ed. trans. Neil Buchanan, 7 volumes bound as 4 (New York, 1961 [c. 1900]), 1:182–83.

DESTRUCTION OF THE FLESH – SALVATION OF THE SPIRIT: THE PARADOXES OF TORTURE IN MEDIEVAL CHRISTIAN SOCIETY*

Edward Peters

I

The use of coercion in matters of ecclesiastical discipline troubled many European thinkers, none of whom expressed their difficulties more eloquently than the great humanist, Juan Luis Vives:

> I am surprised that Christians hang on religiously, with the utmost attachment, to so many pagan practices, which are not only contrary to Christian charity and meekness, but also against humanity (as Lactantius [*Divinae Institutiones* V.20, VI.10] and Nicholas [Nicholas I, *Ep.* 99 to the Bulgars] argue). Augustine [*De civ. Dei* 19.6] says that torture is in use for the sake of human society: but who could fail to note that he is speaking to and about pagans? But what in fact is this necessity—so intolerable and deplorable that it should be purged if possible in floods of tears—if it is not useful and if it can be abolished without detriment to the public good? How is it that there are so many people ... who allow a man whose criminality is in doubt to be submitted to the severest torture? We men, endowed with every humanitarian sense, torture men in order that they may not die innocent, although we are more sorry for them than if they were to die: often enough the torments are far worse than death.... It has become a commonplace among rhetoricians to speak for and against it. But while what they have to say against it is very powerful, the arguments in favor are weak and useless.[1]

* Earlier versions of material in this essay were presented at the Rutgers University Medieval Workshop on "Religion and Torture," New Brunswick, New Jersey, on April 20, 1996 and at The Shelby Cullom Davis Center for Historical Studies Colloquium, "Reason, Coercion, and the Law: Reassessing Evidence," Princeton University, November, 1995. I am grateful to Karl F. Morrison and Natalie Zemon Davis for the invitations to Rutgers and Princeton and for their hospitality, and to Richard Helmholz and James A. Brundage for their helpful comments, as well as to my colleague Alan Kors. The subject seems appropriate in a volume of essays dedicated to Jeffrey Burton Russell, whose own concerns with this and related problems have produced an impressive and enduring scholarly oeuvre.
[1] Cited in Francesco Compagnoni, "Capital Punishment and Torture in the Tradition of the Roman Catholic Church," in *The Death Penalty and Torture*, ed. Franz

Vives' text is not only a powerful indictment of torture inflicted by Christians, but a historical commentary on the oldest arguments in favor of and against forensic torture generally—originally those of the Greek and Roman forensic rhetoricians—and of the earliest Christian attitudes toward it—from the Latin apologists to the ninth century of Nicholas I.

Not only did the earliest Christian communities and individual Christians like Paul himself (Acts 22:22–30) and Tertullian either evade torture when they could or condemn its use by Christians, but they also expressed considerable reluctance to litigate in Roman courts and to judge fellow Christians at all or to invoke any but the most mild disciplinary practices, except for exclusion as a last resort.[2] But these standards were also exercised in growing communities with more and more complex affairs to manage, and the late-third-century

---

Böckle and Jacques Pohier, Concilium: Religion in the seventies, Vol. CXX (1979), 39–53 at 43. Compagnoni cites Vives from the commentary on *De civitate Dei* XIX.6 in the Froben edition of Basel, 1551. The new edition of the commentary on *De civitate Dei* in Vives, *Opera Omnia*. Edicions Alfons el Magnànim: Valencia, 1992–, three vols. to date, has not yet reached the comment on XIX.6. Further discussion in my *Torture*. Blackwell: Oxford-New York, 1985; expanded edition, University of Pennsylvania Press: Philadelphia, 1996, and in Kenneth Pennington, *The Prince and the Law, 1200–1600*. University of California Press; Berkeley-Los Angeles-Oxford, 1993, 132–164. The question has been most recently posed by Johannes Fried, "Wille, Freiwilligkeit und Geständnis um 1300. Zur Beurteilung des letzten Templergrossmeisters Jacques de Molay," *Historisches Jahrbuch* 105 (1985), 388–425; Mario Sbricoli, "'Tormentum idest torquere mentem': Processo inquisitorio e interrogatorio per tortura nell'Italia comunale," *La Parola all'Accusato*, ed. Jean-Claude Maire Viguer and Agostino Paravicini Bagliani. Sellerio editore: Palermo, 1991, 17–32; Winfried Trusen, "Das verbot der Gottesurteile und der Inquisitionpozess. Zum Wandel des Strafverfahrens unter dem Einfluss des gelehrten Rechts im Spätmittelalter," *Sozialer Wandel im Mittelalter. Wahrnehmungsformen, Erklärungsmuster, Regelungsmechanismen*, ed. Jürgen Miethke and Klaus Schreiner, Jan Thorbecke Verlag: Sigmaringen, 1994, 235–247.

[2] On the reluctance to judge, Luke 6:37; Romans 2; 1 Corinthians 5; 1–13. On forbearance, Romans 2:1; with a spirit of gentleness, Galatians 6:1; to exercise fraternal admonition, Matthew 18:15 and forgiveness of personal offenses, Matthew 18:21–35; On the *haereticus homo*, the "factious man," Titus 3:10–11, he is to be corrected twice and then, if unrepentant, avoided in 2 Thessalonians 3:14–15. The community indeed had authority to bind and loose, Matthew 18:15–35, but it was to do so in a spirit of fraternity/sorority, using persuasion and resorting to expulsion as a last resort. There is a good brief discussion in Elizabeth Vodola, *Excommunication in the Middle Ages*. University of California Press: Berkeley-Los Angeles-London, 1986, 4–12, and a more detailed account of the development of active ecclesiastical discipline in Jean Gaudemet, *L'Église dans l'empire romain (IVᵉ et Vᵉ siècles)*, 2nd ed. Sirey: Paris, 1989, 213–287, Elizabeth Schüssler-Fiorenza, "Judging and Judgment in the New Testament Communities," *Judgment in the Church*, ed. William Bassett and Peter Huizing. Seabury: New York, 1970, 1–8, and Goran Forkman, *The Limits of the Religious Community: Expulsion from the Religious Community in the Qumran Sect, within Rabbinic Judaism, and within Primitive Christianity* (Lund, 1972).

Didascalia and the slightly earlier work of Cyprian reveal a more elaborate pattern of ecclesiastical discipline and judgment. The pattern grew more elaborate yet with the enormous growth of the Church in the fourth and fifth centuries and the appearance of those new and troublesome figures, the Christian soldier, judge, and emperor, whose roles so greatly vexed Augustine and others and helped subsequently to create much medieval and early modern legal and political thought. One can trace in Augustine's own career a transformation of thought about coercion that moved him further away from the idealized Christian past so praised by Vives.

It is in this context that we find Augustine's bleak meditation on the dutiful (and, *pace* Vives, in the first quarter of the fifth century probably Christian) judge in *The City of God*, XIX.6:

> What of those judgments passed by men on their fellow men, which cannot be dispensed with in cities, however much peace they enjoy? . . . For indeed those who pronounce judgment cannot see into the consciences of those on whom they pronounce it. . . . [The witness or defendant who is tortured] suffers, for a doubtful crime, a punishment about which there is not the shadow of a doubt, and not because he is discovered to have committed it, but because it is not certain that he did not commit it. . . . In view of this darkness that attends the life of human society, will our wise man take his seat on the judge's bench? . . . Obviously he will sit, for the claims of human society constrain him and draw him to this duty; and it is unthinkable to him that he should shirk it. . . . For the wise man does not act in this way through a will to do harm, but because ignorance is unavoidable—and yet the exigencies of human society make judgment also unavoidable. Here we have what I call the wretchedness of man's situation, at any rate . . . in his judicial capacity.[3]

Although some of this passage echoes a commonplace in Roman forensic rhetoric, we must remember that Augustine himself was a judge, and his letters to secular judges and others (*Epp.* 133, 138, 153, and esp. 93 and 185) reflect similar ideas.

But even before the fourth century there existed a language of spiritual offense and divine judgment and punishment that often stood in sharp contrast to the outward community restraint that scripture urged. Paul himself had recorded his own divinely forced conversion, and *Acts* records his escape from torture without expressing disapproval

---

[3] Augustine, *Concerning the City of God against the Pagans*, trans. Henry Bettenson. Penguin: Harmondsworth, 1972, XIX.6, 859–860, here condensed.

of the practice iself. If Paul urged the community to strive for internal peace, Pauline—and later Augustinian—anthropology was all too clear about the weakness of fallen human nature (Galatians 5:19–21), those evils in the heart that made men unclean (Mark 7:21–23). And if they were not purged, sinful humans would not only fail to inherit God's kingdom (Galatians 5:19–21), but would also suffer great and unending torments. As sins came to be classified in various ways (including differing degrees of gravity), the kind of purgation required for them became more extensive, and the kind of punishment that purgation was designed to avert became both more severe and more graphic. From *The Apocalypse of Paul* through the vision-literature of the Middle Ages down to Dante, a spiritual universe of judgment, fear, and torment grew up side by side with the terrestrial practices condemned by Tertullian, Lactantius, Augustine, and Nicholas I.[4]

Those terrestrial practices had become terrible in the Roman courts and arenas of the third and fourth centuries.[5] The criminal jurisprudence of the classical period of Roman law, deficient in any case, was of little immediate use in the face of what Fritz Schultz has characterized as an imperial criminal procedure "so undefined, arbitrary, and authoritarian, that any juristic construction of concepts and principles would have been devoid of significance."[6] Augustine's bleak meditation in *De civitate Dei* 19.6 was not un-à propos; it addressed a pressing and apparently insoluble dilemma, and not merely a residue of pagan practice, as Vives later suggested. With Augustine's doctrine of spiritually therapeutic *disciplina*, reflected in his exegesis of Luke 14:23, and by later exegetes of Canticles 2:15, and Judges 15:4, the image of the little foxes, it constituted a long and influential legal anthropology in the Western world.[7] As Robert Markus has

---

[4] One of the most useful studies of the process is Alison Morgan, *Dante and the Medieval Other World*. Cambridge University Press; Cambridge, 1990, a work whose title belies its extensive coverage and intellectual achievement.

[5] There is a large and growing literature. I cite here only the essays by Denise Grodzynski and Jean-Pierre Callu in the volume *Du châtiment dans la cité. Supplices corporels et peine de mort dans le monde antique*, Collection de l'École française de Rome 79, 1984.

[6] There is a useful discussion—and the remark of Schultz—in Richard Fraher, "The Theoretical Justification for the New Criminal Law of the High Middle Ages: 'Rei publicae interest, ne crimina remaneant impunita'," *University of Illinois Law Review* (1984), 577–595, at 592.

[7] There is a large literature. For our purposes, see Maisonneuve (below, n. 9), 37–40; Peter Brown, "St. Augustine's Attitude to Religious Coercion," in Brown, *Religion and Society in the Age of Saint Augustine*. Northwestern University Press: New

shown, many of the earlier optimistic certainties of Augustine's world were becoming much less certain as the fourth century turned into the fifth.[8]

Moreover, the new imperial protectors of Christianity had taken up a number of offenses against the Church and the faith and incorporated them into imperial criminal law, and they incorporated some of them, like heresy, into the stiffest parts of that law, the *crimina publica*.[9] Aside from the authoritarian and largely administrative character of fourth-century imperial criminal jurisprudence and the ferocious punishments exacted, criminal legal procedure itself, consisting largely of the *cognitio extraordinaria*, the ancestor of the *inquisitio* procedure, routinely employed torture as a legal incident (as well as part of the aggravated death sentences of the third and fourth centuries), and it employed torture on wider and wider classes of persons. The old class-restraints that had long limited the application of torture had fallen into neglect, and torture was virtually universally employed. The Christianization of the emperors after Constantine resulted in the amelioration of some of the most terrible forms of torment and execution, but they also preserved the jurisprudence, such as it was, upon which they had originally been based. Not for nothing did Justinian refer to *Digest* 48 and *Code* 9 as the *libri terribiles*.

II

Nicholas I could dismiss torture because he was looking back from the ninth century to a world that had long since discarded, ignored, or forgotten most Roman imperial criminal jurisprudence and procedures and substituted for them the complex processes of public and private penance, dispute-settlement, the *accusatio* procedure, the

---

York-Evanston, 1972, 260–278; R.A. Markus, *Saeculum: History and Society in the Theology of St. Augustine*. Cambridge University Press: Cambridge, 1970, 133–153 (and the work of Markus cited in the next note); Klaus Schreiner, "'Duldsamkeit' (tolerantia) oder 'Schrecken' (terror)," in *Religiöse Devianz*, ed. Dieter Simon. Vittorio Klostermann: Frankfurt, 1990, 159–210, at 161–175.

[8] Markus, "Saint Augustine's Views on the 'Just War'," *Studies in Church History* 29 (1983), 1–13, and most recently in *The End of Ancient Christianity*. Cambridge University Press: Cambridge, 1990.

[9] Henri Maisonneuve, *Études sur les origines de l'inquisition*. J. Vrin: Paris, 1960; David Hunt, "Christianising the Roman Empire: the evidence of the Code," in *The Theodosian Code*, ed. Jill Harries and Ian Wood. Cornell University Press: Ithaca, 1993, 143–158.

ordeal in instances of great uncertainty and great importance, and very limited royal authority or public authority of any kind.[10] That world had indeed maintained and elaborated a Christian penitential system, and it continued to produce visions of the terrible state of the damned in the afterlife.[11] But it emphasized purgation and concerned itself with the *salus animarum* of people who, from a largely monastic and hence world-rejecting perspective, were in any case living in a temptation-filled and dangerous world. It also inflicted severe and often savage punishments on the unfree and on aliens and offenders of low social status convicted of particularly offensive crimes, but it reserved such procedures for the powerless (and occasionally for political enemies); they could only with great difficulty be inflicted on free people. Nicholas I spoke not only theoretically, but accurately. Torture and the most savage forms of punishment had indeed virtually disappeared from his world. And so he could prescribe that they must now disappear from that of the Bulgars as well.

But the world of Nicholas and the Bulgars also had a time-bomb— or rather several related time-bombs—ticking away in them. First, Christianity itself was the fundamental bond of society, but it posed a number of problems when translated into public activity. For all of their violence, many of the eleventh- and twelfth-century nobility shared an anxiety over salvation and experienced the apparent disjunction between the demands of a Christian life and the necessities of exercising authority in this world. The First Crusade had gone some way toward reconciling this disjunction, and more ways were developed in the course of the twelfth century.[12] We can see some of these effects in Ralph of Caen's rephrasing of the dilemma of the Augustinian judge in his description of Tancred:

---

[10] Robert Bartlett, *Trial by Fire and Water: The Medieval Judicial Ordeal.* Oxford University Press: Oxford, 1986, and the remarks of Pennington, *The Prince and the Law*, 132–135; cf. Trusen, "Das Verbot der Gottesurteil," and Klaus Schreiner, "Rechtgläubigkeit als 'Band der Gesellschaft' und 'Grundlage des Staates'. Zur eidlichen Verpflichtung von Staats- und Kirchendienern auf die 'Formula Concordiae' und das 'Konkordienbuch'," *Bekenntnis und Einheit der Kirche. Studien zum Konkordienbuch*, ed. Martin Brecht and Reinhard Schwarz. Anton Hiersemann: Stuttgart, 1980, 352–377.

[11] Cyrille Vogel, *En rémission des péchés. Recherches sur les systèmes pénitentiels dans l'Église latine.* Variorum: Aldershot-Brookfield, 1994, and Morgan.

[12] There is a large literature. See, e.g., Marcus Bull, *Knightly Piety and the Lay Response to the First Crusade.* Oxford University Press: Oxford, 1993, and Ernst-Dieter Hehl, cited below, n. 14.

Day after day his prudent mind was in turmoil, and he burned with anxiety all the more because he saw that the warfare which flowed from his position of authority obstructed the Lord's commands. For the Lord enjoins that the struck cheek and the other one be offered to the striker, whereas secular authority requires that not even relatives' blood be spared. The Lord warns that one's tunic, and one's cloak too, must be given to the man intending to take them away; but the imperatives of authority demand that a man who has been deprived of both should have whatever else remains taken from him. Thus, the incompatability dampened the courage of the wise man whenever he was allowed an opportunity for quiet reflection. But after the judgment of Pope Urban granted a remission of sins to every Christian setting out to overcome the Gentiles, then at last the man's energies were aroused, as though he had earlier been asleep; his strength was renewed, his eyes opened, and his courage was redoubled. For until then . . . his mind was torn two ways, uncertain which path to follow, that of the Gospel, or that of the world.[13]

Others, too, especially canon lawyers like Anselm of Lucca, Ivo of Chartres (neither jurist particularly interested in the expeditions against Muslims but rather on the inner workings of Christian society), and later Master Gratian, dealt with the same problem and came to a similar conclusion: "Moses did nothing cruel when he put several people to death at the command of God."[14] The crusade was not the only instance that offered layfolk justification in using force that was not morally repellent.

Second, the texts of earlier Roman law—the *Codex Theodosianus*—had circulated throughout Carolingian Europe along with some forms of investigatory procedure—the visitations of bishops and the Carolingian *Rügeverfahren*—but the *Digest* had not, until its rediscovery and circulation at the turn of the twelfth century. The recovery of the *libri terribiles*, among other *libri*, and their inviting jurisprudence was one more such time-bomb.

---

[13] Cited by Bull, 3–4.

[14] Anselm of Lucca drew the phrase from Augustine's *Contra Faustum* (22.79). The occurrence is cited and briefly discussed in Ernst-Dieter Hehl "Was ist eigentlich ein Kreuzzug?" *Historische Zeitschrift* 259 (1994), 297–336, at 306–308, with useful references. The use of the phrase by jurists and theologians needs more research. It appeared in the pseudo-Augustinian *De vera et falsa penitentia* in the eleventh century and in the *summa* of the pseudo-Stephen Langton in the early thirteenth. Gratian stated that *militare non est delictum . . . nec rempublicam gerere criminosum est* (C.23 q.1 c.5; cf. C.23 q.4 d.g.a. c.37; C.23 q.5 d.g.p. c.48). Cf. Stanley Chodorow, *Christian Political Theory and Church Politics in the Mid-Twelfth Century: The Ecclesiology of Gratian's Decretum.* University of California Press; Berkeley-Los Angeles-London, 1972, 54–63, 223–246.

Another was the transformation of penance itself. The new focus on intention and will in twelfth-century theology was a boon to palaeopsychology, but it also transformed the sinner, and later the criminal, into a more deliberative actor, one more precisely responsible for his actions.[15] It also opened up the category of criminal sins and formalized the Augustinian distinction between venial and mortal sins as a function of the gravity of the act and the participation of the will in it. Elizabeth Vodola and Johannes Fried have raised the related and equally important question that the new concern with reason and will in the context of baptismal promises and confession—and the psychology that the new confession presupposed—had other consequences: long before the reappearance of torture and the active juridical prosecution of heresy, Fried argues, the relations among sin, guilt, confession, free will, and ethics became one of the central themes of scholastic thought. The freedom of the will became a fundamental doctrine, as did the immovability of the will by force or necessity. As Vodola pointed out, the canonist Huguccio of Pisa "distinguished between conditional and total coercion"; Innocent III spelled out the doctrine more explicitly in his decretal *Maiores* (X. 3.42.3); as the jurists later succinctly said, *coacta voluntas voluntas est.*[16] General discus-

---

[15] Stephan Kuttner, *Kanonistische Schuldlehre von Gratian bis auf die Dekretalen Gregors IX*, Studi e Testi 64 (Vatican City, 1935).

[16] Fried, 420. Cf. Elizabeth Vodola, "*Fides et culpa*: The Use of Roman Law in Ecclesiastical Ideology," in *Authority and Power: Studies on Medieval Law and Government Presented to Walter Ullmann on His Seventieth Birthday*, ed. Brian Tierney and Peter Linehan. Cambridge University Press: Cambridge, 1980, 83–97, at 86–87, regarding forced baptism and the doctrine *voluntas coacta voluntas est*. See also the work of Yerushalmi and Schatzmiller, cited below, n. 36.

It is worth pointing out that this doctrine appears to have varied across the broad spectrum of juristic problems that required its invocation. In an unpublished paper, James Brundage has indicated that coercion appears to have been treated somewhat differently in cases of marriage: "Coerced Consent and the 'Constant Man' Standard in Medieval Canon Law," delivered at the Shelby Cullom Davis Center for Historical Studies Colloquium, Reason, Coercion, and the Law: Reassessing Evidence, Princeton University, November, 1995. I am grateful to Professor Brundage for permission to cite his paper in this essay. Johannes Fried also deals briefly with the problem of coercion in the marriage literature in his "Über den Universalismus der Freiheit im Mittelalter," *Historische Zeitschrift* 240 (1985), 313–361, at 354–355.

One of the standards for estimating the nature of coercion was, as Brundage and Fried point out, that of the *vir constans*, "the constant man," invented apparently by Gaius (*Digest* 4.2.6) and invoked by Romanists and canonists (Gratian, Decretum C.15 q.6 cc.1–2; Alexander III in X. 4.1.15) alike from the twelfth century on. Romanists (Accursius) categorized force as compulsive, disquieting, expulsive, and ablative; canonists as in the compulsive, expulsive, tributive, and disquieting. The kind of force considered in this essay is compulsive. But there seems to be a sharp difference in the canonists' treatment of force in cases of coerced marriage and in torture.

sions of baptism and marriage contained legal observations and doctrines concerning problems of coercion and will that could be applied elsewhere in canon and secular law with more deadly results. Torture itself, for example, could not break the will or even move it. Used with the proper procedures, it was possible to formulate the principle that "no torture can violate an individual's free will (*Keine Folter kann den freien Willen eines Menschen vergewaltigen*).[17] Since torture seeks only the truth, it can move the taciturn will to speak, but not to lie.[18]

The great movement of reform beginning in the mid-eleventh century succeeded in removing the Church from the control of the laity, but it also opened up new possibilities for reconstructing that relationship on a new basis, including the clerical recognition of the laity as a legitimate law-enforcing power—and the laity's acceptance of that role as it had accepted the crusading role. Finally, outside of learned law and theology proper, there occurred both the great population explosion of the eleventh and later centuries and the growth of governance that fought to cope with and control new and larger (and more tumultuous) societies.

Exactly how governments—both ecclesiastical and secular—attempted to do this is the subject of many histories. Most recently four scholars have approached the problem from persuasive and influential angles. R.I. Moore has posited the creation of a "persecuting society" as a result of some of the changes described above. James Given has analyzed the "technologies of power" that spiritual and temporal authorities developed and used. Kenneth Pennington has argued that the use of law by rulers was a critical component, not only in developing theories of rights but in developing forms of coercion. Richard Fraher has surveyed the new criminal law that resulted, first within the church as a means of disciplining otherwise

---

In an electronic communication, James Brundage has suggested that jurists regarded coercion in the criminal sphere in an entirely different context from marriage and other civil obligations. In the instance of criminal law, they accepted the results of torture as a single further *indicium* that was necessarily corroborated by other *indicia*, including the subsequent confession made without torture. But the doctrine of the *vir constans* seems to have played a very small role.

Most recently on the problem of will see Risto Saarinen, *Weakness of the Will in Medieval Thought from Augustine to Buridan*, Studien und Texte zur Geistesgeschichte des Mittelalters, Bd. XLIV. E.J. Brill: Leiden-New York-Cologne, 1994, and Bonnie Kent, *Virtues of the Will: The Transformation of Ethics in the Late Thirteenth Century*. Catholic University of America Press: Washington, D.C., 1995, 150–198.

[17] Fried, 423.
[18] Ibid., 424.

unreachable criminous clerks and later as a means of dealing with criminals in general and the emergence of the principle that justified punishment in this world, *ne crimina remaneant impunita.*[19]

Our focus has narrowed. When we address the question of ecclesiastical coercion and the use of torture and other forms of deliberately inflicted suffering outside the sphere of disciplining criminous clergy, we must speak of a preparatory period dating from around 1050 and a period of development after 1150. Our problem has become a specifically historical one, and we must look at late twelfth- and thirteenth-century western Europe and the character of Latin Christianity for our answers.

III

Although the Church Fathers had used the Roman terms of criminal law—*crimen, maleficium, delictum, peccatum*—they used them in the sense of sins, thereby requiring for them purgation and reconciliation.[20] In the late eleventh and twelfth centuries, however, the language of sin and crime took on new meanings and relationships. In the pseudo-Augustinian *De vera et falsa poenitentia* of the mid-eleventh century, for example, the doctrine of temporal penitence for sin in this world is called punishment, as it is in the mid-twelfth-century "archaic" (but not entirely) Norman confessor's manual, *Homo quidam* in MS Avranches 136.[21] The author of *De vera et falsa poenitentia*, as well as Anselm of Lucca after him, argued that divine justice required pun-

---

[19] R.I. Moore, *The Formation of a Perscuting Society*. Blackwell: Oxford-New York, 1987; James B. Given, "The Inquisitors of Languedoc and the Medieval Technology of Power," *American Historical Review* 94 (1986), 336–359 and Given's *The Inquisitors of Languedoc and Medieval Penal Practice*. Cornell University Press; Ithaca, 1997; Pennington, *The Prince and the Law*; Fraher, "The Theoretical Justification," and most recently "Conviction According to Conscience: The Medieval Jurists' Debate Concerning Judicial Discretion and the Law of Proof," *Law and History Review* 7 (1989), 23–88, as well as Sbricoli, "*Tormentum id est torquere mentem,*" 19–21.

[20] Fraher, "Conviction," 8. See also Alexander Murray, "Confession before 1215," *Transactions of the Royal Historical Society* 6th ser. 3 (1993), 51–81.

[21] The first is considered at some length in Berman, 172–3, 179–185, and in Johannes Gründel, *Die Lehre von den Umständen der Menschlichen Handlung im Mittelalter.* Münster, 1963, 121–125, 218–219, and more recently in a Crusade context by Ernst-Dieter Hehl, "Was ist eigentlich ein Kreuzzug?" at 313; the latter in Morgan, 119–120. See Pierre Michaud-Quantin, "Un manuel de confesion archaïque dans le manuscrit Avranches 136," *Sacris Erudiri* 17 (1966), 5–54. Michaud-Quantin designates the work *Homo quidam*.

ishment for the guilt of sin, and that such punishment might be inflicted in this world as well as the next.[22] The work of Burchard of Worms, Peter Abelard, and later twelfth-century canonists and theologians continued this line of reassessment of both sin and sinner. Such punishment was required because sin was an offence against divine law. Some sins began to look more and more like crimes; some crimes began to look more and more like sins, and both began to look different from the way they had looked earlier. They were also separated. Crimes themselves were reserved to secular justice because of its God-given responsibility for maintaining public order; sins were reserved to the clergy because they were responsible for the *salus animarum*. But sins were triable according to two distinct principles: the internal forum dealt with sins that were within the competence of the priest to forgive, confession was required and sealed, and penance imposed according to the complexities of the new confessional science. The external forum dealt with sins that were beyond the priest's competence and required trial before an ecclesiastical judge, either by denunciation or inquisition, and confession was to be sought and made openly—they came to be called criminal sins. As Berman has put it, "Criminal sins were different from other sins in that their sinfullness, that is their offensiveness to God, was measured by standards of ecclesiastical law applied by ecclesiastical judges acting under authority of their jurisdiction—rather than by standards of divine law applied by God himself through priests acting under authority of their orders."[23]

Twelfth-century theologians could thus argue that criminal sins had to be grave offenses; i.e., mortal sins of a particular character, that the sin be manifested in an external act, and that the sin as act be capable of causing *scandalum*. The work of canon lawyers complemented that of the theologians. Along with the three conditions of the theologians they also emphasized the doctrine of intent—that is, the sinner, in wilfully committing an act that was grave, externally manifest, and clearly scandalous, was contumacious toward God and the Church. These changes in the notion of and jurisdiction over sin did not remain the exclusive preserve of theologians and canon lawyers.

---

[22] Kuttner's theme has been recently elaborated by Fried, "Wille, Freiwilligkeit," 418–425, and by Harold Berman, *Law and Revolution*. Harvard University Press: Cambridge, Mass., 1983, 164–198.

[23] Berman, 187.

They offered a new way of reading Roman criminal law, of conceiving crime as an offense against public authority, and justifying the actions of legitimate authorities, including interrogatory torture and the infliction of punishment, on that basis. Although canon and civil lawyers were aware of the differences in their disciplines, they thought along similar lines, particularly in the matter of secular crimes and criminal sins and in the texts of manuals of confession. Thus, the vague remarks on criminal psychology scattered throughout Roman law—Ulpian's *metus poenarum* (Dig. 1.1.1), Paulus' *voluntas perniciosae libidinis* (Dig. 47.11.1), and the commonplaces *dolus malus* and *mens rea*—took on a new character in the developing psychology of sin and crime in the twelfth and thirteenth centuries. And punishments and penances also came to resemble each other more. Alison Morgan has argued that in the twelfth century particularly harsh forms of punishment used in secular law were represented as the punishments in the afterlife described in the visionary literature.[24]

But with punishments—and torture—I have gotten ahead of myself. One of the most striking points in the legal literature of the late twelfth and early thirteenth centuries is the interest that writers then and later took in exceptional crimes. This point has not, I think, received the full attention it deserves. Much of the history of criminal law from second century Rome to the nineteenth century (with some occasional echoes in the twentieth) is the history, not of a comprehensive theory of criminal law, but of great attention paid to exceptional offenses, with the results of this attention then applied to criminal legal theory generally. These became the *crimina excepta, crimina maiora*, that had started out in the Theodosian Code in the fifth century, added simony and nicolaitism in the moral revolution of the late eleventh and early twelfth centuries, usury and heresy in the twelfth century, and eventually came to include sins against nature, homicide, treason, sacrilege, incest, conspiracy, adultery, and perjury.[25] It was

---

[24] The point is made by Morgan, 119–121. On the difference in the uses of the *ordo iudiciarius*, for example, see Linda Fowler-Magerl, *Ordines Iudiciarii and Libelli De Ordine Iudiciorum*, Typologie des sources du moyen âge, Fasc. 63. Brepols: Turnhout, 1994, 23.
[25] There is a brief discussion in Richard Fraher, "Preventing Crime in the High Middle Ages: The Medieval Lawyers' Search for Deterrence," in *Popes, Teachers, and Canon Law in the Middle Ages*, ed. James Ross Sweeney and Stanley Chodorow. Cornell University Press: Ithaca-London, 1989, 213–233 at 218. See also Vodola, 78.
I am inclined to see the origins of the category in the "five crimes customarily excepted" in the Sirmondian Constitutions, 7 and 8. On the collection, see Mark

these great offenses that tested the capacity of all legal systems—the requirement of the notoriety of the offense, the *fama* of the accused, legal safeguards, rules of procedure (including problems of summary procedure and the use of torture), and the law of evidence, as well as the form of punishment. There is a large literature on each of these topics, and it need not be rehearsed here.[26]

IV

What does need to be rehearsed here is the problem of coercion in the light of twelfth- and early thirteenth-century developments in the notions of sin, crime, and the legitimate use of force.

For all of their new early thirteenth-century concern with criminality, both ecclesiastical and secular courts acknowledged that their primary obligations were to divine and human justice, both in regard to the individual offender and the community, and that that justice required strenuous efforts to achieve the restoration and the salvation of even the worst criminals, even of those sent to torture or condemned to death, either by secular authorities or by the Church in its internal discipine or in the process of relaxation to the secular arm. The canonist Huguccio quoted Augustine, whose concept of spiritually therapeutic *disciplina* underlay much of the new criminal law of the late twelfth century and later, to the effect that "we must not cease in the disciplining of the wicked, and by all those means according to which we are able to compel them so that they return to the Church, even though they may not wish to and refuse to."[27]

Vesey, "The Origins of the *Collectio Sirmondiana*: A New Look at the Evidence," in Harries and Wood, *The Theodosian Code*, 178–199. Cf. *Theodosian Code* IX. 38, a series of constitutions dealing with imperial pardons for crimes in which a number of different excepted crimes are discussed. I am working on an essay called "*Crimen Exceptum*" that deals with the phenomenon at greater length. A preliminary version was delivered at the X International Congress for Medieval Canon Law at Syracuse University in August, 1996.

[26] Much of it is discussed in Fraher, "Conviction According to Conscience" and by Fowler-Magerl. On infamy, see my "Wounded Names: The Medieval Doctrine of Infamy," in *Law in Medieval Life and Thought*, ed. Edward B. King and Susan J. Ridyard, Sewanee Medieval Studies 5 (1990), 43–89. There is very little useful literature on the development of both legally permitted techniques of torture and forms of physical punishment. On prisons, see my chapter, "Prisons Before the Prison," in *The Oxford History of the Prison*, ed. Norval Morris and David Rothman. Oxford University Press: New York, 1995, 3–47.

[27] *Ad* C.23 q.4 c.25, cited by René Pahud de Mortanges, "Strafzwecke bei Gratian

Such an assumption, based on the *amor correctionis*, prohibited any court's acting out of greed, revenge, hatred, or personal animosity, but it did not prohibit the use of any legitimated means. Those means had been worked out in the practice of criminal jurisdiction by lay powers and scholars from the late twelfth century on, and by canon lawyers from Gratian through Innocent IV. They were intended to achieve correction and deterrence as well as retributive justice.

But it is also important to note the extent to which learned jurists and law-makers emphasized the necessity of following due process, and the extent to which even Innocent III drew back just when it seemed that he was in a logical position to justify abrupt procedures or impose new punishments.[28] Especially in the case of torture, jurists of both laws worked out meticulous and detailed rules of procedure that required, among other things, restrictions on the kinds and frequency of torture that could be employed, and a voluntary repetition of a confession originally made under torture, but the repetition was to be made later, and away from the scene of the torture.[29] One of the dangers of the new criminal jurisprudence was the great difference between the obsessive procedural rules of the learned lawyers and the actual practices of unlearned or semi-learned courts. Bartolus was particularly contemptuous of judges who rushed to torture. Huguccio of Pisa permitted ecclesiastical judges to use only moderate forms of torture, and it is interesting to see Johannes Andreae just over a century later make the similar argument that ecclesiastical torture should be done using switches, rods, or whips rather than the standard secular procedures of the rack, the strappado, or the other harsher

und den Dekretisten," *ZRG, KA* 109 (1992), 121–158, at 127 n. 24. See in general, Klaus Schreiner, "'Duldsamkeit' (tolerantia) oder 'Schrecken' (terror)."

[28] See Winfried Trusen, "Der Inquisitionsprozess. Seine historischen Grundlagen und frühen Formen," *ZRG, KA* 74 (1988), 168–230, and idem, "Von den Anfängen des Inquisitionsprozess zum Verfahren bei der *inquisitio haereticae pravitatis*," in *Die Anfänge der Inquisition im Mittelalter*, Peter Segl, ed., Bayreuther Historische Kolloquien, Bd. 7. Bohlau: Cologne-Weimar-Vienna, 1993, 39–76. Trusen, like Fraher, sees Innocent's first mobilizing of the inquisitorial procedure, not against heretics, but against criminous clergy. I would argue that the paralels between ecclesiastical inquisitorial procedure and criminal justice in the secular world need further exploration. See my essay, "The Prosecution of Heresy and Theories of Crimnal Justice in the Twelfth and Thirteenth Centuries," in *Vorträge zur Justizforschung. Geschichte und Theorie*, Bd. 2, Heinz Mohnhaupt and Dieter Simon, eds. Vittorio Klostermann: Frankfurt, 1993, 24–42. There is a slightly different reading of Trusen and Innocent in J.M.M.H. Thijssen, "Master Amalric and the Amalricians: Inquisitorial Procedure and the Suppression of Heresy at the University of Paris," *Speculum* 71 (1996), 43–65.

[29] Edward Peters, *Torture*; Fried, "Wille, Freiwilligkeit," 395–396.

forms of legally sanctioned interrogatory torture.[30] Bartolus spoke of
a "light" form of torture that he himself had used *pro forma* in order
not to be accused of having failed to employ torture when legally
obliged to do so, and this may have been similar to that described
by Johannes Andreae.[31] In both kinds of courts, torture could only
be applied after the gravity of the charge was determined to be
sufficient, the accumulation of sufficient *indicia*, the procedure of close
questioning, sometimes that of prolonged confinement and physical
debilitation, and an initial and formalized display of the instruments
of torture. Initially, at least, there was widespread reluctance to use
the incident on restricted classes of defendants, particularly those with
good, or at least unblemished reputations.

In this context, such well-worn subjects as the inquisition-process,
with its requirements of confession and its incidence of torture, were
in place (the latter, I think, by the last quarter of the twelfth century
in some secular courts, although not everywhere in Europe) and may
have been applied in secular courts and in ecclesiastical courts against
clergy well before they were applied to heretics, although no thorough
survey of the beginnings of the use of torture in the twelfth century
has been done for either kind of court system.[32] I have waited a long
time to get to heretics, because these procedures and the attitudes
that underlay the prosecution of heretics from the late twelfth century
on—including the use of torture and the stake—were not invented
and adopted originally or primarily for cases of heresy. Heresy is the

---

[30] The point has been made often, e.g., H.A. Kelly, "Inquisition and the Prosecution of Heresy: Misconceptions and Abuses," *Church History* 58 (1989), 439–451, at
445. Huguccio, however, knew what he was talking about, and I am inclined to
take him at his word that church courts did employ this form of torture in the case
of criminous clergy by the late twelfth century.

[31] On Bartolus, see Fraher, "Preventing Crime," 231, an important discussion in
the context of Albertus Gandinus' much broader allowance of the use of torture "as
social theater". On one instance in the lay courts in which the bare threat of torture
produced a confession, see *The "Coutumes de Beauvaisis" of Philippe de Beaumanoir*, trans.
F.R.P. Akehurst. University of Pennsylvania Press: Philadelphia, 1992, C. 69, 1956,
pp. 715–716.

[32] See, for example, the brief discussion of the use of torture by eleventh-century
castellans as a means of extortion in Richard Landes, *Relics, Apocalypse, and the Deceits
of History: Ademar of Chabannes, 989–1034*. Harvard University Press: Cambridge, Mass.,
1995, 27. These early instances suggest the informal adoption of the practice without the framework of learned law, and hence are problematic in the history of
judicial torture. The discussion of the cult of St. Leonard of Noblat in Bull, *Knightly
Piety and the Lay Response to the First Crusade*, 235–249, deals rather with prisoners and
the aggravated confinement practiced by their castellan-captors in order to extort
money than with torture.

best-known, but far from the only offense that the new criminal law came to treat. The secular world defined crime and dealt with criminals in the course of the twelfth century, the ecclesiastical world in the wake of Gratian, later conciliar and papal laws, and the jurisprudence of canon law scholarship. This was a system into which heresy was construed to fit—as a crime—because it was understood to violate the majesty of both the ecclesiastical and the secular spheres—and the contract of Baptism.[33] And the means of punishing convicted heretics changed as the secular law changed, for it was the secular law that did the punishing. The steps in the process have been traced by Gründmann, Hageneder, Walther, Trusen, Fraher, and Johannes Fried. They have yet to be fully assimilated into Anglophone scholarship.

The new uses of coercion by ecclesiastical authorities between 1150 and 1250 indeed had enduring consequences. But they were the product of a particular time and place, of a particular theory of anthropology (every ideology presupposes a particular anthropology—*Menschenbild*), the nature of secular society, of justice and a new science of law, and of the Church itself.[34] And they were dangerously subject to the twin prospects of interested passion (e.g., Philip the Fair's furious attacks on the alleged sins of the Templars, the danger to all of France that they posed, and the absolute duty of a Christian king—indeed, *un roi très chrétien*—to correct them) and a failure of professionalism, prospects that jurists themselves—Bartolus, for example, and Lucas de Penna—fully recognized and warned against. One need only consider the case of the Templars in order to perceive this subjection at its most compelling and grotesque.[35] Torture was, and remained, a *res fragilis*.

But simultaneously with the case of the Templars, as Dante's *Commedia*, especially the *Inferno* and *Purgatorio*, makes abundantly clear,

---

[33] Othmar Hageneder, "Die Häresie des Ungehorsams und das Entstehen des hierokratischen Papsttums," *Römische historische Mitteilungen* 20 (1978), 29–47. The heretic was not only pertinacious and contumacious, but also disobedient. See also Helmut G. Walther, "Ziele und Mittel päpstlicher Ketzerpolitik der Lombardei und im Kirchenstaat 1184–1252," in *Die Anfänge der Inquisition im Mittelalter*, ed. Peter Segl. Bohlau: Cologne-Weimar-Vienna, 1993, 103–130.

[34] On the law, most recently, see Manlio Bellomo, *The Common Legal Past of Europe, 1000–1800*. Catholic University of America Press: Washington, D.C., 1995.

[35] Johannes Fried, "Wille, Freiwilligkeit". See also Malcolm Barber, *The Trial of the Templars*. Cambridge Univesity Press: Cambridge, 1978, esp. 56–57, 80–84, 89–97, 114–117, 126–127; Joseph R. Strayer, *The Reign of Philip the Fair*. Princeton University Press: Princeton, 1980, 285–295; Peter Partner, *The Murdered Magicians: The Templars and Their Myth*. Oxford University Press: Oxford-New York, 1982.

the punishments in the afterworld become more graphic as well. Dante wrote of punishments and purgation in a world that knew very well how powerful they could be, a world that saw them in person and also painted in churches and in the *pitture infamanti*. By 1300 the principle of destroying the flesh in order to save the spirit had become joined to that of preserving the Christian community and the public good—either as the Church or as any Christian principality—from attacks that seemed more threatening and less resistable than they once had.

The doctrine of the destruction of the flesh in order to save the spirit also ran a great risk, in spite of all the safeguards and precautions that jurists and popes reiterated. It ran the risk of being wrong about the nature and freedom of the will. Fried's argument might be supported by considering the history of the stringent contemporary doctrines concerning the forced baptism of Jews, according to which even the remotest indication of the exercise of free will was assumed to indicate the complete and committed freedom of the will.[36] But was the will immoveable? Not everyone thought so. Some thinkers argued that torture and prolonged confinement and questioning could and did deprive the will of its freedom, although such arguments were not effectively widespread before the seventeenth century.

Fried concludes his essay with the words of Pierre de Bologna, one of the most articulate of the Templars' defenders. Pierre de Bologna argued eloquently that the methods of the assault on the Order by Philip the Fair and others deprived the knights of "freedom of mind, which is what every good man ought to have," since once a man is deprived of his free will through imprisonment, confiscation of his property, the exercise of power against him, and torture, he is deprived of all good things, "knowledge, memory, and understanding."[37] Absunt *scientia, memoria*, and *intellectus*, how is the will to be directed? When—and if—one is reduced to such circumstances, how could any court accurately judge him? Here is the return of

---

[36] Joseph Schatzmiller, "Converts and Judaizers in the Early Fourteenth Century," *Harvard Theological Review* 74 (1981), 63–77, and especially Yosef Hayim Yerushalmi, "The Inquisition and the Jews of France in the Time of Bernard Gui," *Harvard Theological Review* 63 (1970), 317–376. Cf. Schreiner, "'Duldsamkeit...'," an essay that focuses on forced conversion of infidels.

[37] Quoted, with paraphrase, by Barber, 148, and Fried, 425. There is a similar criticism of the use of torture against the Templars in a text edited by Christopher Cheney, "The Downfall of the Templars and a Letter in their Defence," in Cheney, *Medieval Texts and Studies*. Oxford University Press: Oxford, 1973, 314–327.

Augustine's dilemma, but now it is shored up by a forensic anthropology considerably more elaborate and dangerous. It is an anthropology that neglected another Augustinian text, one taken up by Gratian (C.24 q.1 c.29): *ubi caritas non est, non potest esse justitia*.[38] But *justitia*, like *caritas*, was a personal virtue, it was said to be served by judges if they acted *rationabiliter*, were motivated solely by *amor correctionis* in the hope of *liberatio afflictorum*, and unmoved by either *odium* or *zelum ultionis*. In this sense *caritas* could not be invoked readily against a judge who used torture or sentenced the convicted to the death penalty. But did these definitions address Pierre de Bologna's question? If Pierre de Bologna and those jurists like Bartolus who complained about *iudices saevi* were right, if will could indeed be moved in such a way, as it often was then and later, one must ask whether the spirit could be saved at all.

---

[38] Helmut Walther uses this phrase to frame the discussion in his article, "Häresie und päpstliche Politik: Ketzerbegriff und Ketzergesetzgebung in der Übergangsphase von der Dekretistik zur Dekretalistik," in *The Concept of Heresy in the Middle Ages (11th–13th C.)*, W. Lourdaux and D. Verhelst, eds., Mediaevalia Lovaniensia, Series I/Studia IV. Leuven University Press: Leuven, 1983, 104–143.

PROPHECY AND ORDER:
MYSTICISM AND MEDIEVAL COSMOLOGIES
IN THE TWELFTH AND THIRTEENTH CENTURIES[1]

Cheryl A. Riggs

In 1968 Jeffrey Burton Russell wrote an influential little book titled *A History of Medieval Christianity: Prophecy and Order*. In it he developed the concept that a tension existed between the prophetic spirit and the spirit of order within Christian tradition. Russell explained, "both prophecy and order seek the Kingdom of God; but prophecy seeks the end of the world and uncompromisingly hopes for immediate confrontation with God, while order works more patiently within the world and with the imperfect materials at hand."[2] In the Middle Ages, the polemic on Christian cosmogony pitted the spirit of prophecy against that of order. Some charismatic leaders promoted creation constructs antithetical to Christian tradition, which resulted in accusations of and condemnations for heresy. As a result, those who wrote speculative treatises on creation theology found their ideas being questioned, due in part to theological compatibility with certain heretical constructs. Even long standing interpretations came under closer scrutiny in the wake of heretical challenges to the spirit of order.

Philosophy in the Middle Ages often had been concerned with theological issues that juxtaposed the cosmogony of ancient philosophers with that of *doctrina sacra* and Patristic tradition.[3] There was an

---

[1] This essay is, in part, based on an unpublished manuscript, Cheryl A. Riggs, *A Short History of Christian Cosmology*, which originated from research in the unpublished doctoral dissertation, Cheryl A. Riggs, "The concept of Creation in Four Fourteenth Century English Mystics: A contextual study in the history of Christian cosmology," (University of California, Santa Barbara, 1989).

[2] Jeffrey Russell, *A History of Medieval Christianity: Prophecy and Order* (Arlington Heights, Illinois, 1968), p. 1.

[3] Literature on medieval cosmogony is numerous. Several good general reviews of the dialectics of the period are: Marie Dominique Chenu, *La théologie au douzième siècle* (Paris, 1959); Lawrence Roberts, ed. *Approaches to Nature in the Middle Ages*, v. 16 of Medieval and Renaissance Texts and Studies (Binghamton, 1982), David Lindberg, *Science in the Middle Ages* (Chicago, 1978), Richard Dales, *The Scientific Achievement of the Middle Ages* (Philadelphia, 1973), and Pierre Duhem, *Le Système du monde: histoire des doctrines cosmologiques de Platon a Copernic*, 10 v. (Paris, 1906–1916).

attempt to reconcile the role of Nature and emerging theories of science with that of the Genesis accounts and the God of history. Theories on the origins of the world, the eternity of the world, universals, pantheism, and attempts to reconcile Aristotelian hylomorphism and Neoplatonism increasingly were scrutinized. The influx of Greek and Arabic science encouraged a reorientation from the historical cosmology of Augustine toward the hierarchical cosmology of the new view of the cosmos through natural philosophy.[4]

From the early Patristic period, commentaries on Genesis, *hexamerons*, and cosmological treatises discussed the origins of the world in light of Greek antecedents from Platonism, Neoplatonism, and Aristotelian (or peripatetic) metaphysics. These antecedents were adopted to help explain the origins of the universe and human culpability. Greek cosmology, however, was not entirely compatible with Christian doctrines, and often adaptation of the Greek constructs presented inconsistencies between creation theories and other theologies. No clearly defined doctrinal statement on creation had emerged from the early Christian centuries, and, consequently, a diversity of interpretation persisted in cosmological debates. In the twelfth and thirteenth centuries, when heretics espoused such theories as an evil creator and pantheism, a crisis finally materialized. The diversity of opinion that before had been accepted in an atmosphere of toleration now became problematic. The spirit of order, working to preserve and protect Christian belief from damaging disparity, was hard pressed to clarify a cosmogony that preserved orthodoxy. This was accomplished but at the expense of speculative theology.

Some mystics joined the cosmological polemic by advocating certain creation constructs while espousing their mystical experiences. For the sake of brevity only a selection of their writings can be reviewed here. The selection is narrowed to include early writers whose works influenced mystics' cosmology and several mystics whose writings touched on the twelfth and thirteenth century debates on creation. By examining the opinions expressed in these treatises, we can observe why their ideas challenged the spirit of order in the thirteenth century. The essence of the controversy lay in the attempt to define a single

---

[4] Marie Dominique Chenu observed that hexameral literature espoused cosmological theories that were highly influenced by natural philosophy. Marie Dominique Chenu, *La théologie au douzième siècle* (Paris, 1957). Trans. by Jerome Taylor and Lester Little. *Nature, Man, and Society in the Twelfth Century* (Chicago, 1968), p. 17. See also Edward Grant, "Cosmology," in Lindberg's *Science in the Middle Ages*, p. 267.

orthodox cosmogony out of the complex cosmological traditions in Christian theology. Christians had inherited two concepts: *creatio ex nihilo* and Neoplatonic emanationism.

A complete historical analysis of creation theology is too complex for this essay, but a short review is requisite in order to reveal the dichotomies that placed the mystical prophetic spirit in contention with ecclesiastical authority. The Greek idea of *hyle* (eternal primordial matter) was rejected by early Christians, who saw that it threatened the immutable, omnipotent power of the monotheistic Godhead as the single eternal being. As a consequence, the idea of *"creatio ex nihilo"* had been generally adopted. All things were made out of nothing or from non-existence (*ex ouk ontos, ek tou me ontos*). By the early third century, theologians were using the phrases *ex nihilo* or *de nihilo* in conjunction with the verbs *facere, creare*, and *condere* in relation to the origin of the cosmos.

The construct of *creatio ex nihilo* allowed an interpretation of creation that identified the Trinity as wholly other from the cosmos. The three persons of the Trinity shared the same *substantia*, which was wholly different than the *substantia* of the created ontological order. It was necessary for Christians to distinguish between that which is created and that which is uncreated.[5]

The actual meaning of "nothingness" in the *creatio ex nihilo* construct, however, was unclear; its ambiguity led to various interpretations in both the patristic and medieval periods. Three main positions dominated, 1) that *nihil* is actually *aliquid*, 2) that *nihil* is somehow *Deus*, 3) that *nihil* literally is *non aliquid*. The basic statement of *creatio ex nihilo* was generally accepted to mean that nothing other than God existed eternally; God, being omnipotent, created without benefit or necessity of pre-existent material from which to fashion the cosmos. Speculation concerning in what manner and by what method God created, however, filled myriad medieval manuscripts.

St. Augustine, the most influential late Patristic theologian in western medieval thought, proposed that the material "out of which God has created all things is what possesses neither species nor form, and this

---

[5] *Agenoskein*, uncreated, was used for the Trinity, and *genoskein* was used for that which was created. *Agennein*, unbegotten, was used for the Father, and *gennein*, begotten, was used for the Son. With this special vocabulary, distinctions were made that clarified the relationship within the Divine hypostasis and the relationship of the creator to the created. The cosmos is created but not begotten; the Son is "begotten, not made"—Nicene Creed.

is nothing other than nothing."[6] If an unformed matter exists, he argued, then it must be created by God, "even if the universe was created out of some formless matter, this very matter was created from something which was wholly nothing."[7] If formless matter has a capacity to receive forms, then it cannot be called the "nothing" from which God creates. Augustine also argued that God did not create from Himself, because then creation would be equal to the begotten Son and, therefore, also to the Father.[8]

Creatio ex nihilo was further analyzed by others, including John Scotus Eriugena, the ninth century philosopher whose works also heavily influenced medieval theologians.[9] Eriugena argued that God is the first cause, who brings creatures into being out of nothing, and nothing is not pre-existent matter.[10]

Bernard of Clairvaux (1090–1153) was an influential theologian and mystic who defended the *creatio ex nihilo* concept and the spirit of order during the theologically tumultuous twelfth century.[11] Bernard's cosmology is reflected throughout the corpus of his works.[12] Bernard argued, "in frustration the philosophers seek material. . . . He made all things through Himself. From what? From nothing."[13] For Bernard,

---

[6] Augustine, *De vera religione*, 18.35–36 in J.P. Migne, ed. *Patrologiae Latina* (Paris, 1844–1864), v. 34. (Hereafter cited as PL.) All references for Augustine are from PL, vols. 32–47. See also *De natura boni contra Manichaeos*, 18: 26–27; *Confessiones*, 11.5; 12.1–8; 13; *De libero arbitrio*, 3.15.42; and *De Genesi ad litteram*.

[7] Augustine, *De vera religione*, PL 18.35–36.

[8] "*Fecisti enim coelum et terram; non de te: nam essent aequale Unigenito tuo, ac per hoc et tibi; et nullo modo justum esset, ut aequale tibi esset, quod de te non esset. Et aliud praeter te non erat unde faceres ea, Deus una Trinitas, et trina Unitas: et ideo de nihilo fecisti coelum et terram . . .*" in *Confessiones*, 12.7.

[9] Eriugena divided all being into four primary categories. For this study the two significant categories are God and created being: *natura quae creat et non creatur* and *natura quae creatur et non creat*. See Eriugena, *De divisione naturae*, 1.1; 2.1; 3.23 in PL, v. 122.

[10] Eriugena, *De divisione naturae*, 1.12; 2.24; 3.5f. Many theologians argued that God created from nothingness: for examples, Anselm and Thomas Aquinas both argued that primal material must be created by God from nothing. Anselm, *Monologium*, 5–8 and 9–12, in PL, v. 158; Thomas Aquinas, *Summa Theologiae*, 1.44, Petri Caramell, ed. 6 v. (Marietti, Rome, 1952).

[11] In fact, a prior had written to him regarding Bogomils and had pleaded to Bernard to "catch us the little foxes that destroy the vines." See *De consideratione*, PL, v. 182.

[12] But Bernard's fullest explanation of creation is found in his *Tractatus de gratia et libero arbitrio*, in PL, v. 192.

[13] Bernard of Clairvaux, *De consideratione*, Book 5.6.14 in PL, v. 182. "*Frustra philosophi materiam quaerunt: non eguit materia Deus. Non enim officiam quaesivit, non artificem. Ipse per se omnia fecit. Unde? De nihilo: nam si ex aliquo fecit, illud non fecit, ac per hoc nec omnia. absit ut de sua incorrupta incorruptibilique substantia tam multa fecerit; etsi bona, corruptibilia tamen.*"

creation does not come into being through God as the material cause
but by God from nothing. God is the efficient cause and the created
cosmos is wholly other.

> What is God? Out of whom all things, through whom all things, in
> whom all things. Out of whom all things by creation, not generation.
> Through whom all things, so that you do not decide that there is any
> other author and maker. In whom all things, not as in space, but as
> in virtue [power]. Out of whom all things, as the one principle and
> author of everything. Through whom all things, so that an area of
> space is not brought forward. Out of whom all things, not from whom,
> because God is not material: he is the efficient, not the material cause.[14]

For Bernard of Clairvaux, there could be no wavering on the omnipotence of God. God is the efficient cause of all being.

St. Bonaventure (1217–1274), another influential theologian and
mystic who defended the *creatio ex nihilo* construct, wrote many treatises
on theology that touched on issues. His cosmology is chiefly found
in book two, distinctions 1–11 of his commentary on the Sentences
of Peter Lombard, a short section on creation in part two of the
Breviloquium, in the sermons on the *Hexaemeron*, and in the mystical
treatise *Itinerarium mentis in Deum*.

The collation or sermons on the *Hexaemeron* were delivered in 1273
and were Bonaventure's reaction to the Aristotelian influences of the
day. Such issues as the eternity of the world were refuted, and a
warning against straying from scripture and patristic precedent was
given. Bonaventure vehemently opposed the concept of the eternity
of the world.[15] Bonaventure also argued that the world was created
from nothing, it had a definite beginning, and it came into being
after not-being, *esse post non-esse*.[16]

Bonaventure did embrace the concept of *hylomorphism*, albeit altered
somewhat. The created cosmos was a multiplicity of being that entailed
both matter and form juxtaposed to the simplicity and unity of the
incorporeal Creator. But Bonaventure altered the concept by accept-
ing the existence of immaterial angels as spirit—theirs is not matter
in the ordinary sense; theirs is a "spiritual" matter. In addition, Bonaventure's concept of a *materia prima* is matter inherently infused with

---

[14] *De consideratione*, Book 5.6.14. See also *De consideratione*, Book 5.12 and *Sermones
in cantica canticorum* (hereafter cited as Sermon), sermon 4.4 in PL, v. 183.

[15] *Commentum*, 2.1.1.2 *conclusion*, v. 2, part 1 (1885) in *Doctoris Seraphici S. Bonaventurae
opera omnia*, 10 v. (Quarachhi: Collegium S. Bonaventurae, 1881–1902).

[16] *Commentum*, 2.1.1.1.2.1–6; *Breviloquium*, 2.1 in v. 5, part 1 of *opera omnia; Hexaemeron*,
6.4; 5.36, in v. 5, part 2 of *opera omnia*.

form at the moment of creation. There is no "time" when unformed matter exists; time is created with matter. But, within matter there are the forms of *rationes seminales* that emerge at the appropriate time. The *seminalis* activates a being from *esse in potentia* to *esse in actu*.[17] In this sense Bonaventure differs from Aquinas and many earlier medieval Aristotelians who saw matter and form as a final unity in created particulars. Bonaventure called this an insane idea, and instead argued that matter was infused with the potency of many forms or properties.

Bonaventure's concept of nothingness is also in the tradition of Augustine, Anselm, and eventually Aquinas: that nothing is not "something." The creation is *factio non de aliquo*. God is not the material cause of creation but the originator. There is no co-eternal material principle from which God creates. Bonaventure cautioned his readers to avoid the error of suggesting an eternal co-existing principle.[18] For Bonaventure, where before there was nothing, God created existence from non-existence.

The *creatio ex nihilo* construct was the generally accepted cosmogony of Christian tradition yet how God created remained the topic of speculative theology, primarily because of the construct's lack of a coherent philosophical definition. Although *creatio ex nihilo* was well established, it was not the only creation concept examined by Christian intellectuals. Platonic and Neoplatonic cosmology contributed the construct of emanation to Christian creation theology. Plato's *Timaeaus* and particularly Plotinus' *Enneads* germinated a different interpretation of the cosmos' origin. Neoplatonism argued that the Ineffable One emanated an ontological scale of being out of necessity of its nature; the first result was the *Nous*, or mind, where the eternal Ideas resided. Emanation then continued into the World Soul, which in turn emanated into individual souls that also emanated into material being. The creation, therefore, was a product of continued emanation into a hierarchical scale until finally reduced to unformed matter. Many Christians adopted the imagery of the emanation of the One, inserting the Trinity into the Neoplatonic structure: the Father was the Ineffable One, the Son (*logos*) was the *Nous*, and the Holy Spirit, the World Soul.

The main obstacle to complete synthesis with Christian philosophy, however, was the idea that emanation, although it did not diminish the Ineffable One, somehow was the diffusion of the essence of the

---

[17] *Commentum*, II.18.1.3.
[18] *Breviloquium*, 2.1: "*de nihilo excluditur error ponentium aeternitatem circa principium materiale.*"

Ineffable into corporeal reality. On the surface, the employment of the construct merely suggested an image of *bonam diffusivum sui*, the emanation of God's goodness or love into creation—an image that enjoyed great popularity during the Middle Ages when describing the nature of God. When adopted literally as a cosmology, however, this emanationist construct could lead to pantheism.

A second difficulty lay in the relationship of sin and evil to the concept of the diffusion of the good. If goodness diffuses, emanating an ontological scale, then participation in goodness is also hierarchical; the more corporeal the entity (denoted by location on the scale of being) the less good. Consequently, unformed matter at the base of the scale was the least good, and to some extent, equated with evil. Dualism between spiritual and material being was directly equated with the hierarchy of goodness diffused.

The diffusion of the good into emanated reality had consequence in Christian redemptive theology. Since corporeal nature itself was sometimes viewed as weighing the spirit down, its very nature could turn the spirit toward the depths of sin and despair. The incorporeal spirit, however, being akin to the One, struggled to re-ascend the ontological scale toward the ultimate goodness and perfection of the pure, immaterial oneness of the Creator. Christian rhetoric, however, usually tried to minimize this aspect of Neoplatonic cosmology with admonitions that sin is always a product of human will, and not just a circumstance of ontological placement.[19] Through rhetorical gymnastics, theologians accepted the idea of the diffusion of the good and used its imagery when discussing sin but, at the same time, qualified it with statements that reminded the reader that matter is not intrinsically evil.[20]

---

[19] Emanationism suggested *apocatastasis*, which is the concept that, just as all creation emanated from God, all creation would return to God. This suggested that sinners, demons, and even the devil would return to God in an involuntary retrograde of the ontological diffusion. This concept had been condemned at the Council of Constantinople in 543. Prior to condemnation it had been supported by Clement of Alexandria, Origen, Gregory of Nyssa, but later was implied by Pseudo-Dionysius the Aereopagite, from whom many medieval mystics adopted it. Bernard of Clairvaux argued against this concept in a sermon (Sermon 54, in PL, v. 183) in which he emphatically stated that demons would not be redeemed by God without turning their will.

[20] One example is Augustine, *De moribus ecclesiae catholicae et de moribus manichaeorum*, 2.2.2 in PL, v. 32. See also: *Enchiridion*, 11–23, in PL 40 and *De libero arbitrio*, 1.16.35 in PL, v. 32. Augustine insists in certain passages that evil is actually privation, having no being itself, and that God does not create evil, therefore, matter is not evil.

Interestingly, the same mystics who adhered to the *creatio ex nihilo* tradition adopted and adapted emanationist imagery through the mystical tradition. The concept of *via negativa*, which suggested the pattern of ontology of being and a dualistic attitude toward spirit and matter, was particularly influential. While Augustine did not use the term emanation, he certainly used emanationist imagery as well as the Platonic construct of the presence of ideas in the mind of God. Augustine explained that the farther one is from God, who is absolute being, the less participation there is in being (which is familiar Neoplatonic ontology).[21] This affects his theology of goodness as he explains that the soul holds both rational and irrational attributes; the irrational identifies with emotion, which causes the soul to turn toward corporeality and sin. Rational attributes lead the soul back to God. This is what separates humans from animals on the ontological scale. Since Augustine also equates non-being with nothingness, then irrational behavior pulls the soul toward nothingness and *minus esse*. Moral behavior, then, mirrors the ontological scale of being found in Neoplatonism.[22] In Augustinian mysticism, the soul is drawn toward its source, desiring unification in sublime ecstacy in the same way that the soul in Neoplatonism is drawn toward union in the Ineffable One.[23]

Medieval mystical theology inherited Neoplatonic ideas primarily through the sixth century mystic, Pseudo-Dionysius the Areopagite, whose works enjoyed a resurgence in the twelfth century. Inherent in this *via negativa* tradition are certain theological precepts concerning the act of creation and the relationship of the created to the creator and the soul to the body. God in Himself is a unity, undifferentiated and Ineffable; He is essentially the Neoplatonic One, who is beyond being and the origin of all things. God created an ontology of being through self-manifestation or theophany, while remaining inviolate.[24] In addition, God is the universal cause of all being, "everything in

---

[21] Augustine, *Confessiones*, 12.7.

[22] Augustine, *De beata vita*, 2.8, 2.30; see also *De libero arbitrio*, 3.7.21f. and *De civitate*, 11.23.

[23] For this idea see *De beata vita* generally, and also see *De diversis quaestionibus ad simplicianum liber primo*, q.2.21 on the role of grace. Augustine also draws the idea of *rationes seminales* from Plato's discussion of the existence of potentialities. These *rationes seminales* unfold in the proper time and are patterned after the Ideal Forms of the diversity of being. See *De Genesi ad Litteram*, 6.5.8, and 5.4.7–9 regarding vegetation being created before it actually grows on earth.

[24] Pseudo-Dionysius, *Mystical Theology*, in *The Complete Works*, translator, Com Luibheid. (New York, 1987) ch. 3, pp. 138–140 and ch. 5, p. 141. See also *Divine Names* in *The Complete Works*, chs. 1–2, pp. 49–67.

some way partakes of the providence flowing out of this transcendent Deity which is the originator of all that is. Indeed nothing
could exist without some share in the being and source of everything."[25] Those who misunderstood the inviolability of God tended to
adopt pantheism instead of the panentheism actually suggested in
this Pseudo-Dionysian construct.[26] Much of Dionysian theology found
its way into medieval theologians' and mystics' writings during the
Middle Ages.

Bernard of Clairvaux's cosmology was centered on the *creatio ex
nihilo* construct as he understood it. Yet, Bernard also used emanationist
language and imagery. In one of his sermons he describes God as a
reservoir, a fountain of life that is so full of Himself (which does not
translate very eloquently into English) that he gushes forth and dances
into all places to fill them with his favors.[27] In one description, Bernard
explains that the variety of forms and species in creation emanate or
flow from God like the sun's rays (a typical emanation image). Yet,
he immediately cautions that what is seen is from God, not God
Himself.[28]

Hildegard of Bingen (1098–1179) was a contemporary of Bernard,
and wrote several influential treatises. Her *De operatione Dei*, which is
her most mature work, has a cosmological theme.[29] Most of Hildegard's emphasis is metaphorical exposition, such as the world being

---

[25] *Celestial Hierarchy*, ch. 4.1, in *The Complete Works*, p. 156. See also *Divine Names*,
chs. 5.4–10.1 in *The Complete Works*, pp. 98–119. Dionysius' cosmogony suggests that
God generates all things from out of Himself, which is similar to that of Origen's
theology.

[26] John Scotus Eriugena had translated the writings of Pseudo Dionysius the
Areopagite into Latin. Neoplatonic emanationist ideas are strongly present in his
Periphyseon or *De Divisione Naturae*, and some later readers interpreted his ideas as
pantheism. For this, the work was condemned at the Council of Paris in 1210 and
at Sens in 1225. See *De divisione naturae* in PL, v. 122. Some pertinent passages are:
1.7, 2.22–23, 2.36, 3.19, 3.23, 5.15.

[27] Sermon 18.4 in PL, v. 183.

[28] *Itaque de ipso vides, seb non ipsum*, in Sermon 31.3 in PL v. 183. These sermons
are mystical in content, which is exactly the context one would expect to see
emanationist imagery.

[29] *The Book of Divine Works* is the more common title of this work, which can be
found in PL, v. 197, cols. 739–1038. All references will be to vision numbers for
ease of reference to the various editions of her work. See the critical German text
by Heinrich Schipperges, *Welt und Mensch* (Salzburg, Austria, 1965) and the English
text edited by Matthew Fox, *Hildegard of Bingen, Book of Divine Works, with Letters and
Songs* (Santa Fe, New Mexico, 1987), the translation used here. For an overview of
Hildegard's theology see Sabina Flanagan, *Hildegard of Bingen, A Visionary Life* (London
and New York, 1989).

a garden. Hildegard does not analyze the construct of *creatio ex nihilo* but does employ language from the Genesis tradition, i.e. humanity is fashioned from the earth in God's image. Also, in her *Causae et curae*, she shows influences from Greek cosmology—that of the four primal elements of which the world is composed. This, of course, relates to her exposition on medicine. "For man has the heavens and the earth and other created things in him. He is one and all things are hidden within him.[30] She sees creation in the *via positiva* tradition, juxtaposed to the more common *via negativa* tradition of most mystical theology.

Hildegard sometimes employs emanationist language that suggests pantheism. She explains that the Holy Spirit is the fire of life in which all things partake. Hildegard explains that God, having made everything, lives in every created thing.[31] Yet, this is not a categorical statement of pantheist cosmogony; it is closer to metaphorical imagery because she clarifies her statement through three levels: the literal, the allegorical, and the moral.[32] At various points in Hildegard's cosmology, however, the Neoplatonic themes of emanationism and the dichotomy of soul and matter do appear. Hildegard uses the common emanationist imagery of the rays of the sun being the created order. In addition, she states that all created things exist in the Godhead as ideas before they exist in creation as formed things.[33] She also discusses the ontological opposition between soul and body when she points out that humanity is created from the "vile" earth.[34] The soul and body are locked in a struggle as long as they are united.[35] Yet, Hildegard's interest lies in salvation history rather than in the theological debates on the two inherited constructs.

There were several twelfth and thirteenth century German mystics, particularly women, who followed a mysticism of union-of-natures that brought their ideas close to pantheism.[36] The Béguines, practicing

---

[30] *Causae et curae*, Book I.4 in P. Kaiser (Leipzig, 1903).

[31] Vision 4.105.

[32] Vision 5.

[33] Vision 1.7.

[34] Vision 4.14. Vile here does not necessarily mean disgusting but is more closely associated with being degraded, suggesting a hierarchy between spirit and matter.

[35] Vision 4.16, 4.20, 4.21.

[36] Wesenmystik, meaning the union of essences or natures of soul and God through the mystical experience. This also seemed to challenge the necessity of the institutional church and its clergy and sacraments, which was at the bottom of most condemnations of such groups and part of the reason why the spirit of order was skeptical of mystical experiences.

a revered pietism and focusing on essential mystical union as brides of Christ, influenced many lay followers. Mechthilde of Magdeburg (1207–?1282), for example, suggested that the *via negativa* union was the co-mingling of natures: "then the beloved goes into the Lover, into the secret hiding place of the sinless Godhead. . . . And there, the soul being fashioned in the very nature of God, no hindrance can come between it and God. . . . Thou [the soul] art by nature [literally en-natured] already mine. Nothing can come between Me and thee."[37]

St. Gertrude (1256–1302) echoed Mechthilde's essential union in her *Revelations*. Gertrude uses imagery suggestive of pantheism when explaining the love of God: "God will be all in all. . . . O most noble balsam of the Divinity, pouring Thyself out like an ocean of charity, shooting forth and budding eternally, diffusing Thyself until the end of time."[38] Women mystics were held to a particular standard of orthodoxy; many of their writings quickly came under close examination. There were two results: if they were questionable they were most often suppressed and the women condemned, or the women carefully crafted revisions that avoided the questionable ideas.[39]

Bonaventure also used Neoplatonist imagery, which he inherited from predecessors such as Augustine and Anselm. Ideas reside eternally in the mind of God and are part of Him—the Ideas are the Word, the second person of the Trinity. The Ideas are the exemplars for creation.[40] If there were no Ideas in the mind of God, there would be no creation. He incorporated the term *emanare*, a word Thomas Aquinas also adopted. Bonaventure said that the metaphysics of Christianity is emanation, exemplarity, and consummation.[41] Like Hildegard, his imagery took the metaphor of light or illumination, as in the metaphor of the sun's rays shining on creation.[42]

---

[37] Lucy Menzies, *The Flowing Light of the Godhead* (London, 1953), pp. 24–25. For further information on Mechthild, see Caroline Walker Bynum, *Jesus as Mother* (Berkeley and Los Angeles: University of California Press, 1982), pp. 228–247 and John Howard, "The German Mystic, Mechthild of Magdeburg," in Katharina Wilson, *Medieval Women Writers* (Athens, GA.: University of Georgia Press, 1984), pp. 153–185, and see Elizabeth Alvilda Petroff, ed. *Medieval Women's Visionary Literature* (New York and Oxford, 1986) for insight into the Béguine movement.

[38] St. Gertrude, *The Revelations of St. Gertrude*, Part II.6 in Elizabeth Alvilda Petroff's *Medieval Women's Visionary Literature*, p. 227.

[39] Julian of Norwich, for example, worked on her visions for twenty years, expanding and clarifying her experience. Heretofore there has not been a complete comparative analysis of women's mystical experience with that of men's nor a thorough review of whether the gender of the mystic effected different ecclesiastical response.

[40] *Hexaemeron*, 1.12–17.

[41] *Hexaemeron*, 1.17.

[42] *Hexaemeron*, 12.14.

Bonaventure's mystical treatise includes more Neoplatonist and emanationist imagery than his other writings. His conceptualization throughout his *Itinerarium mentis in Deum* is that of *bonum est diffusivum sui*. Bonaventure's terminology actually implies a pantheistic creation; he states that the triune God exists uncircumscribed in all things, through his power, presence, and even essence.[43] His strongest emanationist imagery is in the sixth chapter, where he discusses the diffusion and emanation of the Trinity and the *hypostasis*. He quotes Pseudo-Dionysius in saying that the good diffuses itself, and the highest good, the Trinity, must be the most self-diffusive. He explains that self-diffusion cannot exist unless it is "actual and intrinsic, substantial and hypostatic, natural and voluntary, free and necessary, lacking nothing and perfect."[44] He seems to imply more than mere metaphor; diffusion into creation is compared with the diffusion within the Trinity. Diffusion into creation, he explains, is merely a point within the enormity of the Divine triune diffusion, which includes the sharing of *substantia*. In comparison, the diffusions of the Trinity and the creation are quantitatively different but not qualitatively different in Bonaventure's treatise. Here he is trying to describe the immanence of God, but his terminology threatens God's transcendency.[45]

Much of the polemic on creation theology in the twelfth and thirteenth centuries came from the mouths of heretical leaders, whose piety had gained them a loyal following. R.I. Moore suggests that the return to introspection and contemplation in the eleventh century brought with it the stimulus for dynamic spiritual personalities to become potential antagonists to the institutional church.[46] Those living austere lives demonstrated a renewal of spirit sorely lacking in what many perceived as a corrupted church hierarchy.

The "immediate confrontation with God" (as Russell described the prophetic spirit) is the essence of the mystical experience; the mystical union is a direct, intuitive knowledge of God, and is by its very

---

[43] *Itinerarium mentis in Deum*, 1.14; 2.1, in v. 5, part 2 of *opera omnia*. What Bonaventure means by God's essence is unclear; he seems to be saying God's essence is found in creation, a clear statement of pantheism if taken literally.

[44] *Intinerarum*, 6.2. of *opera omnia*: "*Summa autem diffusio non potest esse, nisi sit actualis et intrinseca, substantialis et hypostatica, naturalis et voluntaria, liberalis et necessaria, indeficiens et perfecta.*"

[45] At this point in Christian theology there is no term for transcendent immanence; the term panentheism was not introduced until the eighteenth century.

[46] R.I. Moore, *The Origins of European Dissent*. (London, 1977), pp. 47ff. and pp. 83ff. Piety lent authenticity to their beliefs.

nature unique and inexplicable. Mysticism has been described as the flight of the alone to the alone, and as such remains a singular experience of God juxtaposed to the normative corporate experience of the ekklesia. Because of their distinctive encounter with the Divine, mystics are seemingly independent of formal ecclesiastical intermediation. They frequently tried to communicate the meaning of the unitive experience with the Godhead to others, and, in so doing, spoke with certitude and authority. It was, therefore, the singularity of the mystical experience and the mystics' piety that made them suspect to the spirit of order.

Many individuals in positions of authority reacted to heresy with a bunker mentality, which led them to design defensive mechanisms that addressed both real and perceived attacks on church structure and tradition. In Christian history, previous inspirational leaders had become catalysts for heretical theologies, many of which had cosmological issues at their core.[47] Those in authority believed they were under siege by antagonists who espoused heterodox cosmogonies; mystics whose writings suggested error, therefore, were especially worrisome to those entrusted with doctrinal preservation. In a sense it was guilt by intellectual and spiritual association.

Out of this cacophony of cosmological structures and inconsistent theologies confusion arose, and confusion is always antithetic to the spirit of order. As a consequence, a series of councils dealt with cosmological controversies from the eleventh to the thirteenth centuries in an attempt to clearly establish a Christian cosmogony. Like the early Christian conciliar reaction to Greek cosmogonies and the heresies of the first centuries, these councils reacted to perceived heretical promulgation of misinterpreted cosmological ideas. Many who promoted emanationist imagery (which sometimes included pantheism) faced conciliar condemnation.

The Fourth Lateran Council of 1215 finally established the concept of *creatio ex nihilo* as a doctrine.[48] The Council listed points essential to cosmological issues in response to heretical challenges. The main tenets were: 1) both spiritual and corporeal natures were made *ex nihilo* [not emanated], 2) creation is temporal [it does not emanate],

---

[47] Such as the Manicheans, Paulicians, Messalians, and Bogomils.

[48] "... *qui sua omnipotenti virtute simul ab initio temporis utramque, de nihilo condidit creaturam, spiritualem et corporalem....*" lines 10–12 *Conciliam Lateranense IV 1215, Constitutiones, 1. De fide catholica* in Josepho Alberigo, et al., eds., *Conciliorum Oecumenicorum Decreta*, 3rd ed. (Bologna, 1973), p. 230.

3) humanity is a unity of soul and matter [the body is not less good than soul], 4) creation is good, and 5) sin is the result of the devil's temptation [evil is not privation of good and the devil will not be saved without a change in will—anti-*apocatastasis*].

The concept of *creatio ex nihilo* does not lend itself so easily to the contemplative schema. It preserved the nature of the Trinity and the complete dependence of the created on the Creator but it did not inspire contemplative prayer. The *via negativa* mystical tradition, akin to Neoplatonic ideas, kindled the fire of love deep in the soul, leading it toward its creator and loving union.

The late thirteenth and fourteenth centuries were a crisis for spiritualism.[49] The theological climate of the fourteenth century was volatile; ecclesiastical authority was defensive and cosmological debate was all but silenced. More people with less education were reading and interpreting what they read literally. The century was fraught with catastrophic events, which often leads to conservatism on the part of authorities.[50]

The prophetic spirit was challenged with multiple investigations into speculative theology. Marguerite Porete, for example, was burned at the stake in 1310 because her heretical views, in part, suggested that individuals could achieve a sinless state through mysticism, thereby negating the role of the institutional church.[51] Meister Eckhart, who was extremely popular, discovered that ideas that previously had been accepted within the diversity of cosmological debate no longer would be tolerated.[52] For some, the personal certitude gained in the ecstatic experience was replaced with nominalist resignation through the *via moderna*.

---

[49] This is particularly true for groups like the Beghards and Béguines, the Brothers of the Free Spirit, the Friends of God, and similar quietist movements. In addition there was the tension between Friars Preachers and Friars Minor.

[50] Disease, war, economic catastrophe, and social upheaval created an atmosphere of distrust and disillusionment. These religious issues cannot be taken out of this historical context.

[51] The bull *Ad Nostrum* specified several errors in the heresy of the Free Spirit, for which Beguines and Beghards were condemned. Among them were: 1) that humans could achieve a sinless state, 2) that in the "spirit of liberty" individuals are not subject to human obedience [the church], and 8) that the perfect need not rise at the elevation of the Host because thinking on the Eucharist or the Passion is a sign of imperfection. See E. Friedberg, *Corpus iuris canonici*, v. 2, col. 1183.

[52] In 1326, Eckhart embarked on a perilous defense of his ideas, particularly a defense of his concept of *intellectus* and the ground of the soul's equality with God. His Trinitarian idea that God is above being (which was certainly Neoplatonic tradition and had been inherited from several important medieval theologians) was also

Yet for others, the search for the Ineffable did continue, and, although some mystics' writings were condemned, most (like those of the fourteenth century English mystics Julian of Norwich or the anonymous author of the Cloud of Unknowing) carefully navigated the theological mine fields laid in the previous centuries. Christian cosmology also continued to be discussed, albeit with greater care toward orthodoxy. In this atmosphere of beatific visions and skepticism, the symmetry between the spirit of prophesy and the spirit of order continued to give balance to Christian tradition.

---

condemned. Most of his difficulty lay in the piety of the day—his sermons were transcribed by individuals not equipped to understand the nuances of his theology but took him literally, which was exactly the kind of blind adoption of ideas that the institutional church feared most. When Eckhart died in 1327, he was in route to an inquisition. His ideas for the most part were not new and were preserved and put forward again by followers, such as John Tauler. For a good translation of Eckhart, see Raymond B. Blakney, *Meister Eckhart* (New York, 1941).

MEDIEVAL HERETICS OR FORERUNNERS OF THE REFORMATION: THE PROTESTANT REWRITING OF THE HISTORY OF MEDIEVAL HERESY

Abraham Friesen

In his *Essay on the Development of Christian Doctrine* first published in 1845—the year he joined the Roman Catholic Church—John Henry (later Cardinal) Newman wrote: "The School of [Bishop Richard] Hurd and [Sir Isaac] Newton hold, as the only true view of history, that Christianity slept for centuries upon centuries, except among those whom historians called heretics." Was Newman complaining? Had he not held similar views prior to his conversion to Catholicism? Only a few lines prior to the above statement Newman had himself asserted that "some hypothesis, this or that, all parties, all controversialists, all historians must adopt, if they would treat of Christianity at all."[1] Had Newman's "hypothesis" changed with his conversion? And had that change resulted in a different interpretation of the "development of Christian Doctrine"?[2]

The interpretation of medieval church history Newman identified as that of Hurd and Newton may have had its roots in the writings of the medieval heretics themselves,[3] but its Reformation formulation was the product of another conversion, one much more famous than his own—that of Martin Luther. The reformer expressed that interpretation with some clarity already in his response to Leo X's bull, *Exsurge Domine*, threatening him with excommunication. There, arguing that Luther's "errors, as expected, were not *Catholic* articles but are opposed to the *teachings or beliefs of the Catholic Church*,"[4] Leo placed the would-be reformer at the end of a long line of medieval heretics. But Luther rejected this judgment based on the "hypothesis" that the Church's teachings were the ruling criteria, and, from his new hypothesis of *scriptura sola*, reversed Leo's judgment, asserting:

---

[1] John Henry Cardinal Newman, *An Essay on the Development of Christian Doctrine* (New York: Longmans, Green & Co., 1949), 84.

[2] Ibid.

[3] See especially Gordon Leff, "The Making of the Myth of a True Church in the Later Middle Ages," *Journal of Medieval and Renaissance Studies* 1, no. 1 (1971), 1–15,

[4] Johann Walch, *Luthers Saemmtliche Schriften*, XV (St. Louis, 1905), 1442.

> These heretics have done nothing wrong against God, indeed, they committed a much more serious crime: they desired to possess the holy Scriptures and God's Word, and—poor sinners that they were—insisted that the pope live a moral life and preach the Word of God honestly and forthrightly, not threaten [innocent] persons with papal bulls with the gay abandon of a drunken sailor.[5]

Within a year he followed this up with an even more explicit statement in a letter to Albrecht Duke of Mansfeld, prophesying: "The Gospel will come to the front and will prove that the wise are fools, and the fools are the wise, and that those who are called heretics are Christians, and that those that call themselves Christians, heretics."[6]

Luther's conversion was based on the Pauline doctrine of the "righteousness of God" and had the Bible—not the Church's current teachings—as its authority. Indeed, in his search for a gracious God, the Church's teachings had become Luther's problem. He had therefore turned from them to the Bible; eventually it became the ultimate source of authority for him. Because she had placed her authority above that of the Bible, the reformer charged that the Church had been misled into believing that her teachings constituted orthodoxy and those of her opponents, heresy. No wonder Church authorities were now "burning the true saints [while they were] themselves heretics."[7]

Luther had arrived at the conclusion that the Church's teachings—by which she determined heresy—were at odds with the teachings of the Bible only gradually and reluctantly.[8] When he "posted" his Ninety-Five Theses on 31 October 1517, he had not yet begun to question the Church's right or power to determine orthodox teaching; nor did he as yet deem those teachings to be at odds with the Bible. But in the aftermath of the official reaction to his attack on indulgences, Luther did begin to argue that, in the case of a disagreement over theological issues not yet definitively determined, it would not be heretical to appeal to a future council against the arbitrary decision of an ill-informed pope. On 29 November 1518, he appealed to just such a future council, reiterating that appeal with increasing frequency in the years to come.

---

[5] Ibid.

[6] John Nicholas Lenker, ed. & trans., *Sermons of Martin Luther*, I (Grand Rapids: Baker Book House, 1983), 15.

[7] Lenker, *Sermons*, II, 102.

[8] See especially Theodor Kolde, *Luther's Stellung zu Concil und Kirche bis zum Wormser Reichstag, 1521* (Guetersloh, C. Bertelsmann, 1876).

Having decided in favor of a conciliarist solution to his quarrel with the pope, it must have been just a little disconcerting to Luther to be forced, by John Eck at the Leipzig Disputation in the summer of 1519, to choose between the "biblical" teachings of a John Hus and the Council of Constance's condemnation of those teachings. But he did choose—in favor of *sola scriptura* and the conclusion that Church councils in general, and Constance in particular, had erred. Thus, by 1520, when he was threatened with excommunication, Luther had already reversed the criteria—the hypothesis—by means of which he judged who was a Christian and who a heretic. A year later he could even declare in his *Grund und Ursach*: "It is therefore true that all heresies have either arisen, or been reinforced by bishops and the scholars [of the Church]."[9]

If the Council of Constance had erred and the Roman Church was the source of all heresies, then John Hus—burned at the stake by the fathers gathered in council at Constance—must have been the true Christian. Early in his monastic career Luther had happened upon a volume of Hus' writings but had turned from it in horror because of the latter's notoriety as a condemned heretic. Eck's argument at Leipzig, however, forced him to take a second look at those writings. He now found them, in many respects, fully Christian. And so he defended Hus against the condemnation of the council. Later he was given a copy of Hus' *De ecclesia* by some Hussites who had attended the disputation. Upon reading it he wrote to his friend George Spalatin on 14 February 1520:

> I have taught and held all the teachings of John Hus, but thus far did not know it. John Staupitz has taught it in the same unintentional way. In short we are all Hussites and did not know it. Even Paul and Augustine are in reality Hussites. See the monstrous things into which we fall, I ask you, even without the Bohemian leader and teacher. I am so shocked that I do not know what to think when I see such terrible judgments of God over mankind, namely, that the most evangelical truth was burned in public and was already considered condemned more than two hundred years ago. Yet one is not allowed to avow this.[10]

---

[9] Martin Luther, "Grund und Ursach aller Artikel D. Martin Luthers, so durch roemische Bulle unrechtlich verdammt sind," *D. Martin Luthers Werke*, VII (Weimar: Hermann Boehlaus Nachfolger, 1966), 313. Hereafter cited as *WA*.

[10] Gottfried G. Krodel, ed. & trans., *Luther's Works*, vol. 48, *Letters I* (Philadelphia: Fortress Press, 1963), 153.

No longer was there any doubt: the great heretic had been the true Christian, and the "official" Christians on the council who had condemned Hus, the heretics.

To this juncture, Luther had not placed the Church's confusion of heretic with Christian and Christian with heretic into an apocalyptic context; he did so, however, in February of 1520 upon reading Ulrich von Hutten's edition of Lorenzo Valla's treatise on the Donation of Constantine. That treatise demonstrated, beyond any reasonable doubt, that the Donation—repeatedly employed by the Church to support its argument in favor of temporal power—was a papal forgery. Already convinced that he was living in the last days,[11] Luther could no longer suppress the conviction that the pope was the Antichrist—the "Abomination of Desolation" residing at the very heart of the Church—and that the Roman Church was the "Babylonian Whore." Revelation 17:6 described her as "drunken with the blood of the saints, and with the blood of the martyrs of Jesus." Such an apocalyptic understanding of the church at Rome could only confirm Luther's conviction that the heretics were now persecuting the true Christians. It was an understanding that so permeated Protestant thinking in the age of the Reformation that it became the common currency of virtually every branch of Protestantism, magisterial as well as radical. The only issue these two groups disagreed on in this latter regard was the definition of the "true" church and at what point the Roman Church had begun down its heretical path. The two were interrelated and important issues, for how one defined the true church and where one drew the line of demarcation between the latter and the false church determined who was, and who was not, to be considered a heretic.[12]

Luther developed his historical perspective on the medieval church

---

[11] See Luther's sermon on Luke 21, 25–36, printed as early as 1522: *Sermons, I,* 59–86.

[12] Luther developed the above view of the Roman Church in opposition to the "true"—or "his"—church in a much more comprehensive manner in his 1541 "Against Hanswurst," *Luther's Works,* 41 (Philadelphia: Fortress Press, 1966), 185–256, especially 190–230. The former radical, Gerhard Westerburg, wrote of this piece—and the Lutheran interpretation generally—in his *Der Allerheiligster Vater der Papst / vnnd die Heilige Mutter die Roemische Kirch ... inn sachen des Glaubens nich Ihren koennen* (Cologne, 1545), 16: "Nun von der Pabstlichen Kirchen / dz die selbige nit die ware Christliche Kirch sey / haben gnug bezeugt Doctor Martinus Luther / vnnd Philippus Melanchthon / vnder anderen Gelehrten zu vnseren zeiten / Man lese den Lutherum in seinem buch wider Hans Worst gemacht / da saget er / das die Paepstliche Kirche nicht die Christliche Kirche ist / auch nicht vonn der Christ-

in the midst of the rapidly changing conditions of the first five years of the Reformation. These changes convinced him that he was living in the last days.[13] But as time passed and events continued to unfold, it began to dawn on Luther—and many others with him—that he had misread the times.[14] Eventually, therefore, he was forced to face the reality that his revolt against the papacy, rather than signaling the imminent fall of Antichrist, had merely resulted in the diminution of the Roman Church and the establishment of a rival church which he had somehow to legitimate historically. This he attempted to do at considerable length in his 1541 "Against Hanswurst," some five years before his own death.

At the heart of Luther's interpretation in this document stood his conviction that the visibility of the true church stood in direct relationship to the clarity and purity with which the Word of God was taught and preached. According to this criteria, therefore, the turning point in the Church's development had to be placed at the point where she had begun to mix the divine with human teachings. Introduced most noticeably under the Scholastics—Luther repeatedly charged that the Bible had lain hidden "under a bench" for some three to four hundred years—these human teachings had increasingly supplanted the teachings of Christ and his apostles.[15] At other times, and using other criteria such as the subversion of the sacraments—as he did in "Against Hanswurst"—Luther could place the turning point considerably earlier, into the ninth century. But wherever he placed the point of no return, Luther still assumed—given his emphasis on *sola scriptura*—that the true church had an unbroken existence here on earth even though it had, during the time when the Word had lain hidden "under a bench," been barely visible. He supplemented this belief with his argument that the two sacraments instituted by Christ—baptism and the eucharist, though improperly interpreted by the Roman Church and overladen with human additions and innovations opposed to the teachings of Christ and the

---

licher Kirch herkomme / sonder wol drinnen ist als das vnkraut in den weizen / vnnd der Entchrist in den Tempel Gottes sitzet. . . ."

[13] See especially Martin Greschat, "Luthers Haltung im Bauernkrieg," *Archiv fuer Reformationsgeschichte*, LVI (1965), 31–47.

[14] Heiko Obermann has even argued that Luther's changing attitude toward the Jews also stands under the sign of the last days.

[15] See Abraham Friesen, *Thomas Muentzer, A Destroyer of the Godless* (Berkeley, Los Angeles, Oxford: The University of California Press, 1990), 33–36.

practice of the primitive church in the last six hundred years—had nonetheless remained essentially undefiled in the Church.[16] In a somewhat similar manner, a remnant of true believers had also always been present in the Church.[17]

Luther's interpretation of medieval heresy bore fruit especially in the great martyrologies of the sixteenth century. Like Luther, these writers felt compelled to justify their claim that they—not the Catholic Church—constituted the true church; that they were the legitimate heirs to the apostolic church. To do so, they employed—as had Luther in "Against Hanswurst"—another ancient criteria of the true church: that of suffering persecution.[18] At the point where she began to persecute others, therefore, the Roman Church could no longer be considered a true church. Sebastian Franck made this case as early as his *Chronica* of 1531.[19] John Foxe also made the case in his *Acts and Monuments*. When he arrived at what he termed "papal persecutions" in his study, he observed:

> We come now to a period when persecution, under the guise of Christianity, committed more enormities than ever disgraced the annals of paganism. Disregarding the maxims and the spirit of the Gospel, the papal Church, arming herself with the power of the sword, vexed the Church of God and wasted it for several centuries, a period most appropriately termed in history, the "dark ages."[20]

---

[16] Martin Luther, "Against Hanswurst," *Luther's Works*, 41 (Philadelphia: Fortress Press, 1966), 207. "You [Catholics] were indeed baptized in the true baptism of the ancient church, just as we were, especially as children. Now if a baptized child lives and then dies in his seventh or eighth year, before he understands the whorelike church of the pope, he has in truth been saved and will be saved—of that we have no doubt. But when he grows up, and hears, believes, and obeys your preaching with its lies and devilish innovations, then he becomes a whore of the devil like you and falls away from his baptism and bridegroom—as happened to me and others— building and relying on his own works, which is what you whoremongers preach."

[17] Ibid., 210.

[18] "Ninth, nobody can deny that we experience the same suffering (as St. Peter says [I Pet. 5:9]) as our brethren in the world. We are persecuted in every place, strangled, drowned, hanged, and tormented in every way for the sake of the word. Our lot is like that of the ancient church, and in this we are beyond measure like it, so that we may well say we are the true ancient church." Ibid., 197. Luther protested too much, for when Ludwig Rabus came to write his Lutheran martyrology in 1552, he found a dearth of actual martyrs. See Robert Kolb, *For all the Saints. Changing Perceptions of Martyrdom and Sainthood in the Lutheran Reformation* (Macon, GA: Mercer University Press, 1987), 89.

[19] ". . . das die warhafftig kirch niemandt verfolge / sunder alleyn verfolgung leide." *Chronica Zeitbuch vnnd Geschichtbibell* (Darmstadt: Wissenschaftliche Buchgesellschaft, 1969), cxxxvii.

[20] William Byron Forbush, ed., *Foxe's Book of Martyrs* (Philadelphia & Chicago: The John C. Winston Co., 1926), 43.

From this point onward, Foxe regarded the opponents of the Roman Catholic Church to be the true Christians, saying:

> Popery having brought various innovations into the Church, and over-spread the Christian world with darkness and superstition, some few, who plainly perceived the pernicious tendency of such errors, deter-mined to show the light of the Gospel in its real purity, and to dis-perse those clouds which artful priests had raised about it, in order to blind people, and obscure its real brightness.[21]

Whereas Luther had not named names in 1520 when he spoke of those condemned by the Church of heresy, Foxe did, arguing that men like Berenger, Henry of Toulouse, Peter Waldo, the Albigenses, Wycliffe and the Lollards had all "determined to show the light of the Gospel." This "light of the Gospel" was the touchstone for him as it had also been for Luther. Because he deemed them defenders of the Gospel, these persons became for him the forerunners of the Reformation and the carriers of the true church during the "dark ages"—a term that took on a religious rather than cultural conno-tation in Foxe's hands. In spite of his allusions to the above, how-ever, the 1559 first English edition of his work began with the story of John Wycliffe; and throughout all the subsequent editions, the great English Scholastic remained the essential Christian hero of the Middle Ages.[22]

Though Foxe, like Luther, judged the medieval church by the extent to which "the light of the Gospel" had then been visible, he also accepted infant baptism as a mark of the true church. Furthermore, since he called on Elizabeth to restore Protestantism in all its glory to England, he lauded Constantine, the first "Christian" emperor, as the ruler who had ended the persecution of the primitive church by the pagans. He called him a "second Moses" who had "so established the peace of the Church, that for the space of a thousand years we read of no set persecution against Christians until the time of John

---

[21] Ibid.

[22] William Haller, *The Elect Nation. The Meaning and Relevance of Foxe's Book of Martyrs* (New York: Harper and Row, 1963), 121. "Although it be manifest that there were diverse before Wickliff's time, who have wrestled and laboured in the same cause and quarrel that our countryman Wickliff hath done, whom the Holy Ghost hath from time to time raised and stirred up in the Church of God, something to work against the bishop of Rome, to weaken the pernicious superstition of the friars, and to vanquish and overthrow the great errors which daily grow and prevail in the world, yet nothwithstanding, forsomuch as they are not many in number, neither very famous or notable, we will begin with the story of John Wickliff." W. Grinton Berry, ed., *Foxe's Book of Martyrs* (Grand Rapids: Baker Book House, 1988), 49.

Wickliff."[23] Hoping that Elizabeth, like Constantine, would bring
"peace to the Church of England after an era of hatred and persecution," Foxe dedicated the 1563 edition to his queen.[24] These two
criteria, then—infant baptism and the union of Church and State—
could play no role in determining the point at which the true church
had ceased to exist, as they were to do for the radicals later on.

Both Foxe, and Jean Crespin the martyrologist of the Reformed
Church in France,[25] could point to an indigenous crop of sixteenth-
century martyrs; the German Ludwig Rabus, however, had difficulty
finding Lutherans who had actually given their life for the cause
because of the early support of the movement by territorial princes
and some of the free imperial cities. But neither Crespin nor Rabus
could, like Foxe, point to a great indigenous national martyr, like
Wycliffe, who had suffered under the Roman Church. Crespin therefore also began his study with Wycliffe, William Thorpe, John Hus
and Jerome of Prague, and he too dismissed the earlier "martyrs"
with the words:

> Here and there a few pious persons are to be found before the time of
> Wycliffe who, in their hearts, cursed the temporal and spiritual tyranny
> of the popes. Some even opposed them verbally and in writing, as
> did those pious persons who have been disparagingly called Waldenses
> and Albigenses.[26]

The latter, however, along with Foxe's Berenger and Henry of
Toulouse, remained names only; Crespin, like the others, had little
interest in what they had actually stood for. They served these martyrologists simply as evidence of opposition to the papal tyranny. Yet
by the very mention of their names, Luther and the martyrologists
had opened the door to the re-reassessment of these medieval heretics. Though they focused on Wycliffe, Hus and Jerome of Prague,
the martyrologists—like Luther before them—assumed that all of
them, like the great reformer himself, had only "desired to possess the
holy Scriptures and God's Word."[27]

---

[23] Ibid., 42 & 47.
[24] Haller, *Elect Nation*, 124.
[25] I was able only to see a 1590 German translation of Crespin's martyrology,
entitled: *Martyrbuch, darinnen merckliche, denkwurdige Reden und Thaten viler heiliger Martyrer
beschriben werden* (Herborn, 1590).
[26] Crespin, *Martyrbuch*, 94.
[27] In his "Against Hanswurst," Luther was at some pains to explain away the
second part of his 1520 statement—that the pope live a moral life—saying repeat-

Luther had hardly pried open the door to the reconsideration of medieval heresy, however, when it was thrown wide open and the entire issue placed in doubt by Sebastian Franck with his assertion that if "a single error makes one a heretic, then God help us all!"[28] Though Franck sought to level the medieval heretical playing field, he nonetheless continued to regard the Catholic Church as the great heretic to be opposed; his impartiality—based on his contention that it was only human to err—applied to all others. In any case, everyone judged heresy from the vantage point of his own convictions. Were the Bohemians to judge, he asserted, John Hus would be the most orthodox of theologians and the pope and his minions the most perverse of heretics. The same held for all other groups.[29] Because he regarded the Catholic Church to be the greatest heretic, however, Franck, the impartial historian, gave all those who had, and continued, to oppose the Roman Church the place of honor—without distinction—in his book. Or did he?

Not even Franck was as impartial as thought himself to be. From time to time in his massive tomb he indicated his own preferences, and these were thoroughly mystical. He regarded the Word of God, placed on such a high pedestal by Luther and the martyrologists, a "dead letter" if unenlightened by the Holy Spirit. Indeed, it was the experience of the "baptism of the Holy Spirit" in the "abyss of one's soul"[30] that was the key to a correct understanding of the Word of God. Faith, therefore, did not come from hearing alone; it came from the experience of such a baptism.[31] Like other mystics, Franck then also denigrated the externals of the Christian religion—ceremonies, sacraments, institutions, etc.—and defined the true church in purely spiritual terms.[32] According to him, therefore, heresy derived

---

edly: "This we say about doctrine, which must be pure and clean, namely, the dear, blessed, holy, and one word of God, without any addition. But life, which should daily direct, purify, and sanctify itself according to doctrine, is not yet entirely pure or holy [Luther was being optimistic!], so long as this maggoty body of flesh and blood is alive." *LW*, 41, 218.

In his assumption that these medieval heretics wished only to possess the Word of God, Luther was essentially correct. But this says as yet nothing about how they interpreted it! See especially Margaret Deansley, *The Lollard Bible and other Medieval Versions* (Cambridge: The University Press, 1966).

[28] Franck, *Chronica*, iv.

[29] Franck, *Chronica*, lxxxj.

[30] On the mystical understanding of this term, see Friesen, *Muentzer*, 10–32.

[31] Franck, *Chronica*, iv–v.

[32] See especially his letter to John Campanus in George Hunston Williams and Angel Mergal, eds., *Spiritual and Anabaptist Writers*.

from a "pharisaical" reliance upon the dead letter of the Word unenlightened by the Holy Spirit. As a result, every heretic had his peculiar passage of Scripture to prove his particular perspective. Only if everyone became a mystic like Franck and possessed the presence of the Holy Spirit could unity of understanding and interpretation be achieved.[33]

Franck's religious convictions brought him into sympathy with the great German mystics of the later Middle Ages and their followers in the sixteenth century: Hans Denck, Ludwig Haetzer and even Thomas Muentzer, though he rejected the latter's revolutionary activity. Had he not left the medieval mystics largely unmentioned, they would surely have become his forerunners. These mystics, however, did not come into their own until they had passed through the second of these great defenders of mysticism, Gottfried Arnold (1666–1715), and had emerged, somewhat disguised, in the work of the third, the nineteenth century Ludwig Keller.

Like Franck, Gottfried Arnold too argued that those accused of heresy by the thoroughly corrupted church of the Middle Ages were in fact witnesses to the truth. In the West, he argued, the Waldenses constituted the largest group of such witnesses.[34] In spite of this assertion, however, his discussion of medieval mysticism—especially of the *German Theology*—and the sixteenth-century Anabaptists, made it apparent that his heart lay with the mystics whom he regarded as the most important dissenters.

Arnold introduced the *German Theology* by quoting Luther's own preface to his 1518 edition of the work where the reformer had associated, in terms of its importance, the *German Theology* with the Bible and the writings of St. Augustine. He followed this up with the later endorsements of Johann Arndt and others.[35] No wonder, then, that he selected a mystic as his hero in the age of the Reformation, thereby indicating what he considered to be the true line of apostolic succession. But his selection of David Joris, the Dutch archheretic of the sixteenth century, was nonetheless unique if not iconoclastic.[36] Calling him a "theosophus mysticus" and an ardent student of the Bible, Tauler and Thomas Kempis, Arnold proceeded to attempt to

---

[33] Franck, *Chronica*, ccj.
[34] Gottfried Arnold, *Kirchen und Ketzergeschichte* (I use the Dutch translation of 1701 which is in my possession)—the *Historie der Kerken en Ketteren* (Amsterdam: Sebastian Petzold, 1701), I, 636.
[35] Arnold, *Historie*, 862–863.
[36] Ibid., II, 533–559.

vindicate the man who later died incognito in Basel as George of Bruges in 1554, quoting in full Joris' defence of himself sent to Anna, Duchess of Oldenburg, in 1540.

It was in the work of Ludwig Keller—in his 1882 biography of Hans Denck and his 1885 *The Reformation and the Older Reform Parties*—that these medieval mystics, and especially the anonymous author of the fifteenth-century *German Theology*, came to be regarded as the medieval exponents of true Christianity. For even though Keller adopted the Waldenses as the carriers of the true church through the Middle Ages—calling them "old evangelical parties"— he filled their thought with mystical content.

Well before Keller, however, the Waldenses, only mentioned in passing by the mainline Protestant martyrologists of the sixteenth-century, had come to figure prominently as the forerunners of the generally despised sixteenth-century Anabaptists. The latter, although slaughtered in greater numbers than any other Protestant group— and that even by fellow Protestants!—were not to be considered true martyrs according to Rabus and Crespin. Indeed, the latter, although he asserted that persecution was a sign of the true church,[37] denied that Anabaptists met the criteria of true martyrdom, arguing:

> These three characteristics [suffering for the sake of righteousness, for the sake of Christ, and for having done good] have to be taken into consideration. For that miserable Satan always seeks to emulate our Lord God in order to harden people, as he did that godless Pharao in Egypt, by duplicating the miracles of Moses through his magicians. Therefore, (because he sees that our Lord God has such a great host of witnesses to his truth today), he is at pains to attest and beautify his own heresies and lies by means of his own sanctimonious and false martyrs; in our day these are the Anabaptists.[38]

But when it came to their own persecution of these, or similar, "heretics"—Feliz Mantz in Zurich as early as 1527, in Electoral Saxony in the early 1530s and, perhaps most notoriously, Michael Servetus in Geneva in 1553—they studiously avoided raising the argument they had themselves used against the Roman Catholic Church: that persecuting others was a certain sign of the apostate church.

These pariahs of the sixteenth century, employing the Waldenses, now sought to construct an actual Protestant apostolic succession from

---

[37] "Dieselbigen [signs of a true church] kennzeichen werden angezeiget Matth. 5:10. Selig seyn die / so da verfolgung leiden um der gerechtigkeit willen / dann solcher ist der himmelreich." Crespin, *Martyrbuch*, 3.

[38] Crespin, *Martyrbuch*, 4.

the early church to the sixteenth century Anabaptists; neither the
magisterial reformers and their martyrologists, nor the mystical historians of heresy had sought to do this before Keller. But neither of
these latter groups had rejected as much of the Catholic Church as
the Anabaptists did either. The latter, for example, placed the de-
mise of the church at a much earlier point in time than either the
reformers or the mystics; most placed it with the union of Church
and State under Constantine.[39] Some, like Thomas Muentzer, even
placed it in the period just after the death of the disciples.[40] The
Anabaptists also rejected infant baptism, also placing its introduction
in the years before Constantine. For that reason alone, they had to
rejected the magisterial argument that continuity could rest on the
sacraments; as far as they were concerned, the first baptisms in the
early church had all been adult or believers' baptisms. The introduction of infant baptism therefore constituted a clear break with that
apostolic church and its theology. The same was true of the union of
Church and State: Constantine marked a radical, and not welcome
departure from the Believers' Church of the age of the apostles.
Indeed, without Constantine there would never have been a persecuting church. The cooperation of the magisterial reformers with what
they called "godly rulers" was merely an excuse to grasp power and
lord it over those who disagreed with them; inevitably it led to their
becoming persecuting, and therefore also apostate churches.

Because the magisterial reformers and their martyrologists rested
their assumption for the continuity of the true church either on the
sacraments or the clarity with which the Word of God had been
taught and preached (the Anabaptists argued that neither infant
baptism nor the union of Church and State could be proven on the
basis of this Word of God),[41] they sought their forerunners in the
heretics of the late Middle Ages: Wycliffe, Hus and the like. The Anabaptists, because they rejected infant baptism and the Constantinian
transformation and therefore placed the fall of the Church much
earlier, chose differently, at first, however, not for reasons of continuity. The argument for direct linkages and continuity were only
made later and then not by all Anabaptists; only by the Dutch—

---

[39] See especially Walter Klaassen, "The Anabaptist Critique of Constantinian
Christendom," *The Mennonite Quarterly Review*, LV (July 1981), 3:218–230.

[40] See Friesen, *Muentzer*, 33–52.

[41] Stanislaus Hosius, *A Most Excellent Treatise of the begynnyng of heresyes in our tyme.*
(Reprint: Yorkshire, Scolar Press, 1970).

especially Tileman J. van Braght, the great Anabaptist martyrologist—
and then only in the early seventeenth century. This argument can
be said to have transformed the study of medieval heresy, however.

The similarities between certain groups of Waldenses and Anabaptists were apparently first noted by Sebastian Franck. In his 1536
Chronica he wrote:

> But they [the Waldenses] are divided into two / or as some would
> have it / into three groups / into the large / small / and very small /
> [the latter] hold many things in common with the Anabaptists / [they]
> have all things common / baptize no children / do not believe in the
> physical presence in the eucharist.[42]

But similarities did not yet constitute continuity; nor did Franck or
even the *Hutterite Chronicle*, written in the latter part of the sixteenth
century, posit one. And this in spite of the fact that the *Chronicle* did
argue in favor of a continuity of the true church through the ages.[43]
With reference to Peter Waldo, the *Chronicle* said only:

> Waldo, a powerful citizen of Lyon in France at the time of Pope John
> XXII, was of the same opinion [as the other dissenters]. He divided
> his goods among the poor; it was from him that the Waldenses have
> come. They lived in Bohemia under great hardship and suffered much
> at the hands of the Roman Christians.[44]

Even the early Anabaptists, immediately after the first believers' baptisms in Zurich on 21 January 1525, did not call on the Waldenses
as their forerunners, much less refer to them as their spiritual pro-
genitors. Rather, when questioned in prison by Ulrich Zwingli as to
the justification for the action they had taken, the rebaptized cited
St. Paul's *rebaptism* of the twelve Ephesian disciples of John the Baptist
as recorded in the first few verses of Acts 19.[45] Had there been any
early continuity, or even contacts, between the first Anabaptists and

---

[42] Franck, *Chronica*, ccxxxj.
[43] Rudolf Wolkan, ed., *Geschicht-Buch der Hutterischen Brueder* (Vienna: Carl Fromme
G.m.b.H., 1920), 29–29.
[44] Ibid., 29.
[45] This early Anabaptist citation of Acts 19 as justification even led to a massive
reinterpretation of the passage in question by the magisterial reformers, all of them
contending that Paul had not in fact rebaptized with water. Yet every Church Father
and Scholastic theologian—even Melanchthon in his *Loci Communes* of 1521—had
earlier argued that St. Paul had indeed baptized. See my forthcoming *Erasmus, the
Anabaptists and the Great Commission* (Grands Rapids, Eerdmans Publishing Co., 1998),
Appendix I.

the Waldenses, the former must surely, at some point, have objected to the accusation of being rebaptizers. This they never did, later on even citing the monastic argument that entry into a monastery constituted a second baptism to justify their actions.[46] And the *Hutterite Chronicle*, which mentioned the Waldenses as those who had opposed the Roman Church in the Middle Ages, saw the origin of the movement in Zwingli's Zurich Reformation.[47]

It was in the Netherlands that it first became advantageous for the Dutch Doopsgezinde to argue in favor of a direct continuity between Anabaptists and medieval Waldenses—and the reasons had nothing to do with any evidence for such a continuity. They had rather everything to do with polemical strategy. For from virtually the moment of his own rebaptism in January of 1536, Menno Simons, the restorer of Dutch Anabaptism, had been accused of being a Muensterite—that terrible term that haunts the German psyche to this very day. Throughout his life, Menno sought to refute the charge; his Dutch followers, haunted by the possibility of such a connection well into the nineteenth century, sought to do so as well. To accomplish this, the great Dutch martyrologist—taking a page out of the work of his fellow martyrologists with their "Lutheran" view of the history of medieval heresy—argued for a direct connection between the Waldenses and Menno Simons. He did not do it because he was interested in that continuity *per se*, he did it rather because he wished to free Menno from any Muensterite contamination by connecting him to a highly regarded group of medieval heretics who happened to have much in common with the Anabaptists. This is made apparent by the following passage:

> For more than a century up to the present day, people have been made to believe that the Anabaptists contemptuously so-called, have been but recently sprung from some erring spirit—some say, from the Muensterites, etc.: whose fabulous faith, life and conduct, the true Anabaptists have never recognized.[48]

---

[46] See Abraham Friesen, "Anabaptism and Monasticism: A Study in the Development of Parallel Historical Patterns," *Journal of Mennonite Studies*, vol. 6 (1988), 174–197.

[47] "Es begab sich, dasz Ulrich Zwingel und Konrad Grebei, einer vom Adel, und Felix Mantz, alle drei fast erfahrene und gelehrte Maenner in deutscher, lateinischer, griechischer und auch hebraeischer Sprach zusamen kamen, anfingen sich mit einander zu ersprechen in Glaubenssachen, und haben erkennt, dasz der Kindstauf unnoetig sei, auch denselben fuer kein Tauf erkennt." *Hutterite Chronicle*, 34.

[48] Thieleman J. Van Braght, *The Bloody Theater of Martyrs Mirror*, translated by Joseph F. Sohm, 5th ed. (Scottdale, PA: Mennonite Publishing House, 1950), 17.

And in a footnote to the term "Muensterites," van Braght wrote:

> Aside from the fact, that the Anabaptists did not spring from the Muensterites, but have existed through all the times of the Gospel, as has been sufficiently shown, we should, moreover, state that the pernicious and evil proceedings which took place at Muenster about the year 1534 . . . must be placed at the account of some Lutheran preachers [Bernard Rothmann], to whom a certain "Jan of Leyden" had recommended and taught Anabaptism.[49]

Somewhat later, citing Jacob Mehring's *History of Baptism* as authority, van Braght put names to this lineage in the sixteenth century by establishing the connection between Waldenses and Anabaptists.[50] That this "apostolic succession" is established with specific reference to the charge of Muensterite origins, of which Menno already repeatedly complained, leads to the supposition that van Braght developed the thesis to disarm the charge that Menno had been tarnished with Muensterite connections. Gerhard Roosen used the argument in the same sense in his 1753 *Unschuld und Gegen-Bericht der Evangelischen Tauffgesinnten Christen, so Mennoniten genannt werden, ueber die unverschuldete Beschuldigung, als ob sie von der aufruerischen Muensterschen Rotte entsprossen, und derselben Grund und Lehre fuehreten* [A Counterattack and Declaration of Innocence of the Evangelical Anabaptist Christians, called Mennonites, against the undeserved Accusation that they derive from the Revolutionary Muensterites and adhere to their Principles and Teachings].[51] Johannes Deknatel, in his *Auszug der merkwuerdigsten Abhandlungen aus den Werken Menno Simons* [An Excerpt from the most Remarkable Discussions from the Writings of Menno Simons],[52] went so far as to assert:

> There were Anabaptists even before Menno's time, and it is clear that many improvements had already been made before the great Reformation, among the Waldenses, under Wycliffe, under Hus and their followers by means of which God prepared the work [of the Reformation]. In the same way there were, as Menno observes, groups of Waldenses who had been gathered into congregations under the cross, etc. But because of the severe persecutions they were scattered, many of whom settled in the Netherlands; it was probably these, according to Menno's own testimony in his Departure from the Papacy, who asked Menno to be their chief overseer.[53]

---

[49] Ibid.
[50] Ibid., 364–365.
[51] (Hamburg, 1753), 20–22.
[52] Translated from the Dutch (Koenigsberg, 1765), 21.
[53] Ibid.

As late as 1872 Christian Sepp could still write that his Doopsgezinde forebears had been all but paranoid about accusations of a close relationship between Menno and Muenster. This kept the issue alive and it was addressed anew by J.H. Halbertsma in his 1843 *De Doopsgezinde en hunne Herkomst* [The Anabaptists and their Origins].[54] He attempted to prove the connection by a comparison of their respective teachings.[55] Halbertsma was answered in 1844 by A.M. Cramer and S. Blaupot ten Cate. As late as 1836, in his *Het leven en de Verrigtingen van Menno Simons* [The Life and Deed of Menno Simons], A.M. Cramer had still referred to Menno as the "Waldensian Menno."[56] In his 1844 study, however, Cramer was more cautious, suggesting there were two problems with Halbertsma's theory specifically and the theory in general: first, the similarity in the teachings of the Waldenses and Anabaptists could simply derive from a similar reading of the Bible; second, Menno and the early Dutch Anabaptists knew absolutely nothing about the Waldenses and never spoke of them.[57] Blaupot ten Cate, while sketching the Waldenses in Europe in the late Middle Ages and the Reformation on a broad canvas, and arguing that they were indeed older than Waldo—being a continuation of the ancient apostolic faith[58]—nevertheless had to concede that there was no direct link from the Waldenses to either Swiss Anabaptist leaders or those of the Netherlands, and that the similarity of views could easily be explained by a similar reading of the Bible.[59] The missing link, the "smoking gun," had not yet been discovered.

Some forty years later, Ludwig Keller retrieved the thesis and developed it in his 1885 *The Reformation and the older Reform Parties* in a manner that had not been attempted before. Most interpreters of Keller's *The Reformation* have taken the study to be an attempt to revive and refurbish the old defense of Anabaptism, as did Elias Dosker when he wrote in 1909:

---

[54] (Deventer: J. de Lange, 1843).

[55] Ibid., 225–409.

[56] (Amsterdam: Johannes Mueller, 1836), 1–41.

[57] J. Boeke and A.M. Cramer, *Twee Brieven ter Toelichting en Toetsing der Schets van J.H. Halbertsma, "De Doopsgezinde en hunne herkomst"* (Amsterdam: J.D. Sijbrandi, 1844), 70–80.

[58] This aspect of Waldensianism, of course, was very important to the Anabaptists with their argument that the true church died, at the latest, with Constantine.

[59] Blaupot ten Cate, *Gedachten over de Getals-Vermindering bij de Doopsgezinde in Nederland* (Amsterdam: Frederick Muller, 1844), 119–125.

Since 1885 when Ludwig Keller published his *Reformation und die aelteren Reformparteien. In ihrem Zusammenhang dargestellt* [Leipzig], the question of the true origin of the Anabaptists has been a matter of debate. With considerable ingenuity and show of reason, Keller argues for the historical genesis of the sect from the well-known medieval movements of the Petrobrusians, the Apostolic Brothers, the Arnoldists, the Moravian Brethren, and the German Mystics.[60]

Dosker refused to accept this theory, arguing that "sober historians," among whom he undoubtedly numbered himself, saw "'a fanatical ultra reformatory movement'" in Anabaptism "which revealed itself first in Germany in the so-called 'Wittenberg fanaticism' of 1521–1522 . . . [and] later associated itself with the atrocious Peasant War."[61] Like other earlier historians and theologians, Dosker was not about to allow Mennonites an easy escape from their revolutionary past. Mennonites and Baptists, however, saw in Keller— the outsider, indeed a member of the German state church—an impartial vindicator of their position.

But there was more to Keller's thesis than met the eye. There was, already in the introduction, a direct attack on the "orthodox" state churches for their long-standing attempt to cover up the real history of these "old evangelical brotherhoods" by vilifying them as heretics and sectaries. Furthermore, Keller linked these brotherhoods closely to the guilds of mason in fourteenth-century Germany and suggested that they belonged to a tradition that went as far back as the apostolic church.[62] What was this tradition?

In his explication Keller clearly pitted Paul against Christ. The old evangelical tradition, he argued adhered to Christ's teachings and had accepted those of Paul only insofar as they agreed with the Master's.[63] It was this tradition the Waldenses had tenaciously adhered to; yet they were, for the sake of unity, liberal in their toleration of differing viewpoints.[64] The ethical principles of the Sermon on the Mount,[65] discipleship,[66] freedom of the will,[67] a limited

---

[60] Henry Elias Dosker, "Early Dutch Anabaptists," *Papers of the American Society of Church History*, 2nd Series, vol. II (New York, 1910), 189, ed. by Samuel Macauley Jackson.

[61] Ibid.

[62] Keller, *Die Reformation*, 209–238.

[63] Ibid., 45.

[64] Ibid., 41.

[65] Ibid., 40.

[66] Ibid., 43.

[67] Ibid., 58.

pacifism,[68] the acceptance of believer's as well as infant baptism, these had been their central beliefs. But their ideology had been the ideology of the medieval mystics. He called Meister Eckhart a Waldensian[69] and the exponent of a specifically "German theology,"[70] a mystical theology, and his followers "friends of God."[71] One of these had been John Tauler,[72] and, Keller continued,

> it was not unlikely that that famous fourteenth-century treatise, the *Deutsche Theologie*, belonged to the reworked products of Waldensian literature which exercised such an extraordinary influence in sixteenth-century Germany, a tract earlier attributed to John Tauler and which Luther had published under the title: *A German Theology*.[73]

Having already placed Hans Denck into this mystical tradition in his 1882 biography, Keller now also established Denck's Waldensian credentials, as well as his connections to the guilds of masons, asserting:

> Denck's family, whether Wolfgang Denck was Hans Denck's father or uncle, was most intimately associated with the brotherhood of German stone masons. Here the idea of the older "congregations" had been most faithfully preserved and now Providence determined that the faith stored in that place should come out of the guilds and be transplanted back into the life of the church. The mediator of this process was Hans Denck who therefore deserves our special interest.[74]

At this juncture, however, an even more important person entered the picture. In his letters, especially in those to John Horsch, Keller had drawn this mystical lineage from Tauler, the *German Theology*, by way of Hans Denck to Johann Arndt, Jacob Boehme, and others. He now also inserted Johann von Staupitz, the head of Luther's Augustinian order who had, according to Keller, mediated the Bible, Augustine, and the "mystics" to Luther.[75] It was a decisive insertion, for it allowed Keller to assert that

> the literature of the old evangelical churches had gained [in Luther] another champion besides Staupitz who was far superior to the latter

---

[68] Ibid., 52.
[69] Ibid., 158.
[70] Ibid., 162.
[71] Ibid., 163.
[72] Ibid., 166.
[73] Ibid., 171.
[74] Ibid., 333–334.
[75] Ibid., 340–341.

in energy and action. It was Luther who contributed most, between 1517 and 1520, to the renewal of the old evangelical theology.[76]

Unlike Staupitz, however, Luther had not remained true to this theology.[77]

In the same year Keller published his *The Reformation* [1885], he also published a shorter piece entitled "Johann von Staupitz und das Waldensertum" [John Staupitz and the Waldensians],[78] where he developed the "Waldensian Staupitz" thesis more fully, focusing on Nuremberg as center of the Waldensian influence that had determined the religious outlook of Staupitz as well as of Denck. The monograph on Staupitz followed in 1888.[79]

Having anchored Denck firmly in the Waldensian and mystical tradition, Keller proceeded, on the authority of van Braght's *Martyrs Mirror*, to establish the Waldensian antecedents of the Anabaptists. Referring to the latter as "old evangelical Anabaptists [Taufgesinnte],"[80] he sought to establish Conrad Grebel's and Ludwig Haetzer's Waldensian credentials.[81] Keller faced less serious obstacles when he came to Dutch Anabaptism, for from van Braght on to contemporary scholars like Galenus Abrahams, Gerhard Roosen, J.H. Halbertsma, Blaupot ten Cate, and A.M. Cramer, all agreed as to their "old evangelical" and Waldensian roots.[82] But Dutch Anabaptism—and especially Menno Simons—was far too dogmàtic for Keller; he needed Hans Denck to establish the mystical theological content of the entire movement. Thus he had, on the one hand, to dismiss Menno and, on the other, to resurrect the Waldensian thesis that had already been rejected by the Dutch Doopsgezinde themselves. In this fashion Keller made use of the interpretation of the medieval church emanating from Luther, the Waldensian theory emanating from van Braght, and filled it all with the mystical content emanating from Franck, Arnold and the *German Theology*.

Keller's study had hardly seen the light of day than an essay appeared in the prestigious *Zeitschrift fuer Kirchengeschichte* [The Journal

---

[76] Ibid., 342.

[77] Ibid., 346–347.

[78] Kudwig Keller, "Johann v. Staupitz und das Waldensertum," *Historisches Taschenbuch*, 6te Folge, IV (Leipzig, 1885), 117–167.

[79] Ludwig Keller, *Johann v. Staupitz und die Reformation* (Leipzig: S. Hirzel, 1888).

[80] Keller, *Die Reformation*, 372ff.

[81] Ibid., 381–382.

[82] Ibid., 396–397.

of Church History] by the Lutheran church historian, Theodor
Kolde,[83] entitled: "Johann von Staupitz, a Waldensian and Anabaptist: a Church Historical Discovery." Calling Keller an "enthusiastic
apostle of the Anabaptists," Kolde baldly accused him of being a propagandist for Waldenses and Anabaptists. In a frontal attack on his
interpretation, Kolde proceeded to "unmask" Keller's "Waldensian"
Staupitz, refuting virtually every one of Keller's assertions. He recognized clearly enough that Hans Denck was the linchpin of Keller's
great "old evangelical" chain of being and proceeded to demonstrate
that Nuremberg had had no Waldensian community that might have
drawn both Staupitz and Denck into its intellectual orbit.[84] Kolde
concluded that only a man who had allowed himself to become ensnared in a kind of *idee fixe*, which made him incapable of historical
judgment, could write such history.[85] Other attacks followed: some *en
passant*, others more directly, as Hermann Luedemann's 1896 *Reformation und Taeufertum in ihrem Verhaeltnis zum christlichen Prinzip* [Reformation and Anabaptism in its Relationship to Christian Principles].[86] The
attacks became so severe that Keller was forced to defend himself in
writing. He did so in 1897 in his *Grundfragen der Reformationsgeschichte.
Eine Auseinandersetzung mit literarischen Gegnern* [Fundamental Questions
of Reformation History. A Debate with Literary Opponents].[87] We
cannot enter into a discussion of this protracted debate here, except
to say that it ushered in a new era in the study of medieval heresy,
for no reputable mainline church historian was prepared to accept
Keller's speculations. But in order to refute Keller, their own scholarship had to be based on hard evidence and reasoned arguments.

The response to Keller's *The Reformation* was much more positive
from Baptists than from Mennonites, as Keller himself noted on
occasion.[88] The latter had themselves given up the theory some years
before Keller's 1885 book, and they all read the devastating critique
it garnered in German scholarly journals. Even S. Cramer, the Dutch
Mennonite scholar, very sympathetic with Keller's goals, wrote on

---

[83] On Kolde, see D. Hermann Jordan, *Theodor Kolde. Ein deutscher Kirchenhistoriker*
(Leipzig: A. Deichert, 1914).
[84] Theodor Kolde, "Johann v. Staupitz, ein Waldenser und Wiedertaeufer. Eine
kirchenhistorische Entdeckung," *Zeitschrift fuer Kirchengeschichte*, VII (1885), 426–447.
[85] Ibid., 446–447.
[86] (Bern: W. Kaiser, 1896).
[87] (Berlin: Hermann Heyfelder, 1897).
[88] Keller to H. van der Smissen, 21 July 1886. *Keller Correspondence*, Mennonite
Library and Archives, Bethel College, North Newton, Kansas, MLA.MS.64. Hereafter cited simply as *Keller Correspondence*.

13 June 1885: "I have read Kolde's article: I feel very badly for you and for the cause. But did you not attempt to prove too much?"[89] And H. van der Smissen, the Hamburg editor of the *Mennonitische Blaetter*, wrote on 29 June 1885: "I have already heard that Kolde treated you very severely; may I ask for a reference to the journal and the number in which the attack occurred?"[90] Small consolation from those whom Keller was ostensibly serving.[91]

Baptist church historians have treated Keller much more generously. The reason for this is that the theory that Keller appeared to be propounding had already been appropriated by Baptist historians well before Keller appeared on the scene. As early as 1846, J. Newton Brown, in *The Life and Times of Menno, the Celebrated Dutch Reformer*,[92] spoke of "Waldensian Baptists" finding refuge in Frisia four centuries before Menno's birth,[93] though Menno had not been aware of their existence until the rebaptism of Sicke Snyder in 1531.[94] With this established, Brown could assert that the Muensterites "had nothing in common with the Baptists, except the denial of infant baptism— for they held to a worldly, not a spiritual kingdom."[95] Quoting from Cardinal Hosius with reference to heresy in the Church prior to the Reformation, Brown proclaimed: "Such are the concessions of illustrious Romanists to the long unbroken line of our martyr witnesses."[96]

An excellent example of the similar, but broader, theory, can be found in J.M. Cramp's *Baptist History from the Foundations of the Christian Church to the Close of the Eighteenth Century*, first published without date by the American Baptist Publication Society of Philadelphia. A second edition appeared in 1865, and a third in 1868. An English edition was produced in London in 1868 and another in 1871. Even a German translation was published by the J.G. Oncken Verlag in 1870.[97] Obviously, the book traveled well in Baptist circles. Cramp,

---

[89] S. Cramer to Keller, 13 June 1885. *Keller Correspondence.*

[90] H. van der Smissen to Keller, 29 June 1885. *Keller Correspondence.*

[91] For the real reasons for Keller's scholarship in this field, see Abraham Friesen, *History and Renewal in the Anabaptist/Mennonite Tradition* (North Newton, KS: Bethel College, 1994), the 1992 Menno Simons Lectures.

[92] Brown's essay was first published in the *Baptist Memorial* in 1846 and was later published in book form by the American Baptist Publication Society of Philadelphia in 1853.

[93] Ibid., 15.

[94] Ibid., 16.

[95] Ibid., 21.

[96] Ibid., 26.

[97] The first in this line of succession may well have been Thomas Crosby, *The History of the English Baptists from the Reformation to the Beginning of the Reign of*

a professor of church history at Acadia College in Nova Scotia, voiced his Baptist orientation early in the study:

> Unquestionably the progress of religion in the community, which was emphatically designated "The Church," was altogether downward during the "Transition Period" [from Constantine to the close of the "Dark Ages"]. It is an interesting inquiry, how far the spirit of the gospel was preserved, and its essential truths maintained, by those whom ecclesiastical historians have denominated "heretics" and "schismatics." I shall pursue this inquiry in succeeding chapters. In order to find the true church, we must look out of the "Church" commonly so called.[98]

Cramp traced this "decline" of the Church, especially in regard to baptism, from its inception to the rise of Scholasticism. It was in the wake of the latter movement that groups of dissenters, who sowed the seed of the later Baptist harvest, had arisen. Not yet the authentic product, they "had [nevertheless] imbibed the right principle." Cramp observed, "One cannot help thinking that they must have been Baptists, so entirely does the position they maintained harmonize with our own."[99] Having all but declared these "heretics" Baptists, Cramp proceeded to trace the fate of men like Henry of Lausanne, Arnold of Brescia, Berenger, Wycliffe, the Bohemians. From this context he then asserted:

> When Luther blew the trumpet of religious freedom, the sound was heard far and wide, and the Baptists came out of their hiding places, to share in the general gladness and to take part in the conflict. For years they had lived in concealment, worshipped God by stealth, and practiced the social duties of Christianity in the best manner they could, under the most unfavorable circumstances, and fondly expected to enjoy the co-operation of the reformers in carrying into effect those changes which they knew were required in order to restore Christian churches to primitive purity. They were doomed to bitter disappointment. The Reformers had no sympathy for Baptist principles, but strove to suppress them.[100]

The Baptist interpretation of Church history may well also have had its origin in van Bracht's *Martyrs Mirror*, though its wider source seems to have been the Protestant martyrologies in general. When Keller's

---

King George I, 2 vols. (London: By the Author, 1738–1740). See Robert G. Torbert, *A History of the Baptists*, 5th ed. (Valley Forge: Judson Press, 1963), 18.
   [98] Cramp, *Baptist History*, 54.
   [99] Ibid., 117.
   [100] Ibid., 151–152.

writings then appeared in the 1880s, they were welcome corroboration from what at first appeared to be an impartial outsider. But whereas Mennonites quickly gave up the theory once the attacks shredded Keller's scholarship, Baptist church historians did no such thing. Hence Elias Dosker's attack on them in 1909. That attack—and others—notwithstanding, E.H. Broadbent proclaimed in his *The Pilgrim Church*, first published in 1931 and repeatedly thereafter:

> Perhaps the largest use has been made of the works of Dr. Ludwig Keller, especially for the history and teaching of the Waldenses. His position as Keeper of the State Archives, giving access as it does to most important documents, has been used by him to investigate the histories of those known as "heretics," and his publications are an invaluable contribution to the understanding of these much misunderstood people. Dr. Keller's book, "Die Reformation und die aelteren Reformparteien" is a mine of information and all who can do so should read it. Use has also been made of his book "Ein Apostel der Wiedertaeufer" and of a number of others written by him.[101]

Like many other Baptist historians who adopted Keller's reversal of the established churches' claim to sole legitimacy, Broadbent asserted that the apostolic faith had passed down through the centuries, not by the dominant Roman Catholic Church, or even by its reformed Reformation counterparts, but by the persecuted, dissenting minority groups of Christians who had rejected the Constantinian compromise from late Antiquity to the Reformation and beyond. Such a thesis had of necessity not only to be challenged but also condemned by the apologists of the established Protestant churches. It was one thing for them to enlist Hus, Wycliffe, and even the Waldenses in their cause; quite another for the despised Anabaptists and the less fearful Baptists to do so. One can see this reaction even in the great German Church historian, Johann Lorenz von Mosheim, who wrote in his great history of Christianity:

> The modern Mennonites not only consider themselves as the descendants of the Waldenses, who were so grievously oppressed and persecuted by the despotic heads of the Roman Church, but *pretend*, moreover, to be the purest offspring of these respectable sufferers, being equally averse to all principles of rebellion, on the one hand, and all suggestions of fanaticism on the other.[102]

---

[101] E.H. Broadbent, *The Pilgrim Church* (London: Pickering & Inglis, 1955), viii.

[102] John Lawrence Mosheim, *An Ecclesiastical History*, 6 vols., trans. Archibald Maclain (Charlestown, Mass.: Samuel Etheridge, 1810), 4:427–428.

That minorities, non-conformists, dissenters, "outsiders" all, should
be considered the transmitters of the authentic "deposit of apostolic
faith and practice" posed a threat to even these Protestant churches
not even a Dosker could ignore. How could the Anabaptists, whom
even the Protestants regarded as heretics, suddenly become orthodox
disciples? How could such a dramatic reversal of established ecclesiastical norms even be contemplated? But this was the product of
Luther's pen; he had begun it all. Just now he had been done one
better by the very radicals he had despised and eventually persecuted. But this was precisely both Keller's and Broadbent's intent.
Thus the latter wrote in the concluding paragraph of his introduction:

> The tragedy and the glory of "The Pilgrim Church" can only be faintly
> indicated as yet, nor can they be fully known until the time comes
> when the Word of the Lord is fulfilled: "there is nothing covered, that
> shall not be revealed; and hid, that shall not be known" (Matt. 10:26).
> At present, albeit through mists of our ignorance and misunderstand-
> ing, we see her warring against the powers of darkness, witnessing for
> her Lord in the world, suffering as she follows in His footsteps. Her
> people are ever pilgrims, establishing no heavenly city. In their like-
> ness to their Master they might be called Stones which the Builders
> Rejected (Luke 20:17), and they are sustained in the confident hope
> that, when His kingdom is revealed, they will be sharers in it with
> Him.[103]

Broadbent's version of the Keller thesis is held in some Baptist circles
to this day. Jack Hoad, in *The Baptist* (1986), cites an extensive Baptist bibliography to confirm such a position. He observes that "many
American Baptists claim John, the Forerunner of Jesus Christ, as the
first 'baptist' and trace their beginnings from him."[104] In so doing,
Hoad continues, "they advance a continuity which claims to trace
their churches' history through various separatist movements, such
as the Montanists, Novationists, Donatists, Cathari, Paulicians, Petrobrusians, Waldenses and Anabaptists, down to the baptist churches
of today."[105]

When Herbert Grundmann first wrote his now classic *Religioese
Bewegungen im Mittelalter* he observed:

---

[103] Broadbent, *Pilgrim Church*, xi.
[104] Jack Hoad, *The Baptist: An Historical and Theological Study of the Baptist Identity*
(London: Grace Publications Trust, 1986), 19.
[105] Ibid.

it is the Protestant historical research that has most forcefully concerned itself with the history of these [medieval] sects and heresies, because Protestants saw themselves as the heirs and defenders of the religious goals these sects sought to achieve. The other history of heresy, emanating from the history of the monastic orders and carried out by the orders themselves, together with this Protestant history of heresy are undoubtedly responsible for many extraordinarily worthwhile studies because, in them, the impartial interest of the historian is combined with the existential empathy of those who were concerned about their "own cause."[106]

The truth would appear somewhat more complex.

I believe it can be said that all of those who, in one fashion or another, saw themselves as heirs to the medieval heretics were not really interested in what the latter stood for—with the possible exception of Foxe's interests in Wycliffe. Beginning with Luther and the martyrologists, they were primarily interested in legitimating themselves against the attacks of the Catholics, and they sought to use the medieval heretics to accomplish this. Little was done by Protestant scholars in terms of actual research on these heretics until the Anabaptists and Ludwig Keller tried to enlist them—especially the Waldenses—in their own defense. Keller's attempt to establish the mystical theology of the *German Theology* and Hans Denck as orthodoxy in his 1885 *The Reformation* in particular alienated established Protestant opinion. It was in order to undermine these two interpretations that mainline Protestant scholars began their own in-depth studies of medieval heresy. In the process, Keller's theories were destroyed and the Anabaptist connection to the Waldenses—already under internal attack—definitively given up. The only group that has continued to claim an "heretical" apostolic succession from Constantine to the sixteenth-century Anabaptists is the Baptist Church. But even they may, upon closer—and critical—less dogmatic inspection, come to realize that the medieval heretics have little in common with them other than the appeal to the Gospel in order to oppose the claim to absolute authority of the Roman Catholic Church.[107]

---

[106] Herbert Grundmann, *Religioese Bewegungen im Mittelalter* (Hildesheim: Georg Olms Verlagsbuchhandlung, 1961), 6.

[107] For a fuller discussion of the topics addressed in the last section of this essay, see Friesen, *History and Renewal*, and "The Baptist Interpretation of Anabaptist History," Paul Toews, ed., *Mennonites and Baptists: A Continuing Conversation* (Winnipeg, MB: Kindred Press, 1993), 39–71.

COSMIC AND SEXUAL LOVE IN RENAISSANCE THOUGHT: REFLECTIONS ON MARSILIO FICINO, GIOVANNI PICO DELLA MIRANDOLA, AND LEONE EBREO

Bernard McGinn

Eros/amor occupied a special role in Renaissance thought, both in philosophy and in literature. Rarely in the history of European culture has so much yearning gushed forth so recklessly onto the printed page. To restrict ourselves to the more philosophical treatments, between Marsilio Ficino's *De amore* in 1484 and Benedetto Varchi's *Sopra alcune quistioni d'amore* (1554) major "trattati d'amore" were produced by Giovanni Pico della Mirandola (1486), Pietro Bembo (1505), Francesco da Diacceto (1508), Mario Equicola (1525), Agostino Ninfo (1529), Sperone Speroni (1542), Giuseppe Betussi (1544), and Tullia d'Aragona (1547). Other works that were central to Renaissance culture, especially Baldassare Castiglione's *Cortigiano* of 1528, also deal extensively with the nature of *amor*.[1] Among these many treatises one that stands out for its originality is Leone Ebreo's *Dialoghi d'amore* written about 1501, but not published until 1535 when its author was already deceased.

The literature that deals with the *Dialoghi* has mostly been concerned with the influence of its conception of *eros* as a human emotion on the treatment of love in European literature.[2] But for Renaissance

---

[1] For English introductions to this literature, see Nesca A. Robb, *Neoplatonism of the Italian Renaissance* (London: Allen and Unwin, 1935), ch. VI; and John Charles Nelson, *The Renaissance Theory of Love* (New York: Columbia University Press, 1958).

[2] See the most recent English monograph, T. Anthony Perry, *Erotic Spirituality. The Integrative Tradition from Leone Ebreo to John Donne* (University of Alabama, 1980). Two older studies give more attention to the cosmic dimensions, but from a different perspective than that adopted here. See Heinz Pflaum, *Die Idee der Liebe. Leone Ebreo* (Tübingen: Mohr, 1926); and Suzanne Damiens, *Amour et intellect chez Léon l'Hébreu* (Toulouse: Privat, 1971. For an important survey of Leone's sources, see S. Pines, "Medieval Doctrines in Renaissance Garb? Some Jewish and Arabic Sources of Leone Ebreo's Doctrines," *Jewish Thought in the Sixteenth Century*, ed. Bernard Dov Cooperman (Cambridge: Harvard, 1983), 365–98. On placing Leone within the context of Italian Renaissance Judaism, see Arthur M. Lesley, "The Place of the *Dialoghi d'amore* in Contemporaneous Jewish Thought," *Ficino and the Renaissance*,

thinkers human sexual love was only a part of the wider picture of
a universe suffused by love, a world in which *eros/amor* was a transcendental and cosmic term that could be predicated both of God
and the entire universe. If we compare Leone's view of this universal love with how his major Christian predecessors, Marsilio Ficino
and Giovanni Pico della Mirandola,[3] treated these issues, we may dis-
cern how this Renaissance philosophical ecumenism was not only
an important chapter in the history of the relations of Christianity
and Judaism, but also might provide inspiration for contemporary ecumenical dialogue.

I. *The Evolution of* Eros

In order to grasp the main issues under discussion in Renaissance
theories of love, some background is needed on the evolution of
understandings of *eros* in western thought from the time of Plato,
however inadequate any brief sketch must be.[4]

Plato held that *eros* was acquisitive desire or longing for something not possessed. This longing begins on the physical level in the
"shock of beauty" at the sight of a beautiful boy. Plato generally dis-
approved of having such love find physical satisfaction; rather, he
insisted that sexual longing needs to be transformed into longing for
spiritual beauty if the soul is to experience the true heights of *eros*.
We *must* begin on the physical level; we *should* end on the spiritual.
However, it is wrong to think that for Plato erotic love is mere pos-

---

edd. K. Eisenbichler and O.Z. Pugliese, *University of Toronto Italian Studies* 1 (1986),
69–86.
    [3] Leone was acquainted with Pico's nephew, Gianfrancesco, and seems to have
had access to Pico's writings through him. While in Naples Leone frequented the
humanist circle of Pantormo, Mario Equicola and Cardinal Egidio da Viterbo in
which Ficino's works circulated. It is difficult to think that he did not know the *De
Amore*; indeed, S. Pines, "Medieval doctrine in renaissance Garb?", 387–91, argues
that it was his main Christian source. On Leone's relation to Ficino, see Jean
Festugière, *La philosophie de l'amour de Marsile Ficin* (Paris: Vrin, 1941), 53–58, who
stresses the connection with Pico. Among the later authors of "trattati d'amore,"
Leone is mentioned by G. Betussi, Tullia d'Aragona and Benedetto Varchi.
    [4] For what follows, see Bernard McGinn, "God as Eros: Metaphysical Founda-
tions of Christian Mysticism," *New Perspectives on Historical Theology: Essays in Memory
of John Meyendorff*, edited by Bradley Nassif (Grand Rapids: Eerdmans, 1996), 189–
209. For a rather different view, concentrating on poetic accounts, see Peter Dronke,
"L'amor che move il sole e l'altre stelle," *Studi Medievali*, 3rd series, 6 (1965),
389–422.

sessiveness; it is also the creative desire to produce, that is, to bring forth beauty in and from the beloved (see *Symposium* 206E).

Since *eros* is fundamentally a need or lack, Plato held that it could not be found on the divine level. *Eros* is not a god, but a "great daimon," an intermediary reality which makes possible the soul's ascent to the world of ideal Beauty. Still, if the gods do not love what is beneath them, they are not indifferent either (in the manner of Aristotle's Unmoved Mover). In the *Timaeus* Plato said that the Demiurge's goodness and lack of envy lead him to "wish all things to be as like him as possible" (*Timaeus* 29E). When later Platonists recognized that not all eros need be conceived of as "need," this goodness without envy might itself be seen as archetypal *eros* in the Maker of all things.

The first Christians were convinced that the God and Father of Jesus was "Love," but they never used the term *eros* for God, preferring the neutral term *agape* upon which they could construct a new theology of divine love. The new Testament teaching on the God who is love reaches a climax in 1 John where God not only gives love, but where we read "God is love" (1 Jn. 4:8).

Origen was the first to argue that *agape* and *eros* are really one and the same thing—"You must take whatever scripture says about *caritas* [*agape*] as if it had been said with reference to *amor* [*eros*], taking no notice of the difference of terms, for the same meaning is conveyed by both."[5] Although Origen carefully distinguished various forms of love according to the worthiness of objects toward which they are directed (unseemly ones of sensual delight, indifferent ones of human arts, and saving ones of the spiritual world), he insisted that the power that motivates all love comes from above. Origen went a step further, if only in tentative fashion. If human passionate *eros* has its source in God, can God be thought of as in some way erotic? Such a conception would seem to conflict with the notion that God's perfection demands immutability. How can a yearning God not be a changing and imperfect God? The main intent of Origen's theology was to protect divine perfection and immutability; but a measure of how seriously he took his view that God is *Eros-Agape* is found in a few texts where he hints at a God whose love makes him capable of suffering for his creation. In the most noted of these he asserts: "The

---

[5] Origen, *Commentarium in Canticum Canticorum*, Prologus, in *Origenes Werke*, Vol. 8, ed. W.A. Baehrens (Leipzig: Hinrich, 1925), 70–71.

Father himself is not without suffering. If he is asked, he has mercy and takes pity, feeling some love. He undergoes change in the things in which he cannot exist due to the greatness of his nature. He undergoes sufferings [*passiones*] for us."[6] Thus, there are hints of a passionate God in Origen, as well as a fully-developed doctrine of the passionate soul. What Origen lacks is a sense of the universe filled with *eros*. For this we must turn to his successors, both pagan and Christian.

Plotinus made two important changes in the Greek philosophical understanding of *eros*. First, if only in ambiguous fashion, he created a place for *eros* in the downward way, i.e., the path of emanation or creation. For Plotinus the *eros* by which the soul loves the Good originates in the Good itself. "The soul loves him, moved by him to love from the beginning," as he put it in *Ennead* 6.7.31. This led Plotinus to a second innovation. If *eros* is placed in the soul by the ultimate source, must not that Source be *Eros* in some way? This is exactly what he says in *Ennead* 6.7.22: the Good "is at once lovable and love and love of himself." Plotinus appears to be the first pagan thinker to make this identification. For him the First Principle not only causes *eros* as the goal or end that all things desire, but also in some way *is* Eros.

Proclus, the last great pagan Neoplatonist, never said that the hidden One, or Source of all, is *Eros*, and thus from this perspective he is less daring than Plotinus. But from another point of view he goes further, for Proclus was the first to provide a full cosmic interpretation of *eros* as the central dynamic principle of the universe. *Eros* is "moderately" transcendental for Proclus, being found on the level of the intelligible gods (Goodness, Wisdom and Beauty) that are placed below the One. Corresponding to this triad are three essential powers—faith, truth and love—that proceed downward to all the orders of the cosmos. "From above, then, love ranges from the intelligibles to the intra-mundane, making everything revert to divine Beauty."[7] The circular chain of love that binds the universe together involves both the downward love (*eros pronoetikos*) by which superiors love inferiors providentially and the upward love (*eros epistreptikos*) by which inferiors love superiors reflexively. Finally, for Proclus *eros* was fundamentally not passive, that is, something received in the soul through the vision

---

[6] Origen, *Homilia in Ezechielem* 6.6, in *Origenes Werke*, Vol. 8, 384–85.

[7] *Proclus: Alcibiades I. A Translation and Commentary*, by William O'Neill (The Hague: Nijhoff, 1965), 32–33 (#51).

of the beautiful, but was rather an activity on the part of higher causes. "We must observe that divine love is an activity, wanton love a passivity; the one coordinates with intellect and divine beauty, the other with bodies."[8]

Dionysius the Areopagite, who used both Origen and Proclus, brought this evolution to a conclusion, especially in the fourth chapter of *The Divine Names*.[9] Chapter 4 is devoted to Goodness as the predominate positive or cataphatic name of God, but since Goodness is identical with Beauty, and the longing for Beauty both brings all things into being and is their goal (DN 4.7), it is precisely God as Eros which is the inner meaning of Goodness and thus forms the main topic of the discussion (DN 4.10–17).

For Dionysius, as for Proclus, the whole universe is governed by the circle of love. "All things must desire, must yearn for, must love, the Beautiful and the Good. Because of it and for its sake, subordinate is returned to superior [*eros epistreptikos*], equal keeps company with equal, superior turns providentially to subordinate" [*eros pronoetikos*] (DN 4.10). But Dionysius goes beyond Proclus by developing Origen's discussion of God as *Eros*. Because *eros* and *agape* signify the same reality (4.11), real *eros* [*to ontos eros*] is not the distant image we experience in physical attraction, but is the "simplicity of the one Divine *Eros*" (4.12), which Dionysius pregnantly defines as "the Good of the Good for the sake of the Good" (4.10). Dionysius's most important innovation comes in his insistence that Divine *Eros*, like its human counterpart, must be ecstatic, that is, it must produce a situation in which "the lover belongs not to self but to the beloved" (4.13). But how can God become ecstatic, or go out of himself without changing and losing his absolute perfection? Dionysius's answer penetrates to the root of his dialectical Christian Neoplatonism:

> It must be said that the very cause of the universe in the beautiful, good superabundance of his benign *eros* for all is carried outside of himself in the loving care he has for everything. He is, as it were, beguiled by goodness, by love (*agape*) and by yearning (*eros*) and is enticed away from his dwelling place and comes to abide within all things, and he does so by virtue of his supernatural and ecstatic capacity to remain, nevertheless, within himself (DN 4.13).

---

[8] O'Neill, *Proclus: Alcibiades I*, 37 (#56).

[9] The *Divine Names* has been edited by Beate Regina Suchla, *Corpus Dionysiacum I. De Divinis Nominibus* (Berlin: De Gruyter, 1990); DN 4 can be found on 143–80. I will use the translation of Colm Luibhead found in *Pseudo-Dionysius. The Complete Works* (New York: Paulist Press, 1987).

In other words, God is the only lover who can go totally out of himself in a complete ecstasy of self-giving because he alone has the supreme ecstatic power to remain absolutely within himself, utterly transcendent to all things. He loves himself in all things from the same ground and for the same reason that he loves himself apart from all things. In Dionysius's thought God is doubly ecstatic (transcendentally and providentially), while the universe becomes ecstatic only reflexively, that is, in the erotism of *epistrophe*, or return.[10]

Dionysius, it should be noted, made no attempt to relate his objective cosmic *eros* to the subjective forms of human love, though the implications of his thought tend to match those discernable in Origen—human *eros*, though it may partake of the divine source, is a shadow so distant that it can only be disruptive of true erotic pursuits. A more positive evaluation of human yearning love is found in another Christian Platonist of late antiquity, Boethius.

The beautiful poem found in *Consolation of Philosophy* 2.8 provides a powerful, if less complex view, of how the God who is Love rules the universe governed by love. The first part hymns the harmony based on *amor*,[11] while the second part reverses this picture to present a sketch of the chaos that would result if Love let slip the reins. The final third returns to the theme of unity, this time on the human level. *Amor* is described as the source of all social conjunction, including the "chaste loves" of holy matrimony. Boethius concludes with the hope that human loves will reflect cosmic Love:

O felix hominum genus,	O blessed humankind,
Si vestros animos amor	If the Love that rules heaven
Quo caelum regitur regat.	Could rule your souls too.[12]

By the early sixth century C.E., then, a distinctive Christian view of God as *Eros* had emerged, one which owed much to Plato and the Greeks, but more to the attempt to think through the implications of a God who was Love in all senses. Space does not permit a survey of analogous developments in Judaism and Islam, through many of

---

[10] On God's ecstasy in himself, see also *Letter* 9.5, and *Celestial Hierarchy* 13.4 in the Dionysian corpus.

[11] E.g., Boethius, *Consolation of Philosophy* 2.8 (ed. Loeb Classical Library, 222):

> Hanc rerum seriem ligat
> Terras ac pelagus regens
> Et caelo imperitans amor.

[12] Boethius, ibid.

these, such as Ibn Sina's *Treatise on Love*,[13] had influence on Leone Ebreo. In order to frame the Renaissance discussion, however, it will be helpful to mention two thirteenth-century authors whose views of cosmic *eros* were never far from the minds of Renaissance thinkers.

Thomas Aquinas agreed with Dionysius that *amor* (not just *caritas*) was one of the names of God. In q.20 of the Prima Pars of the *Summa theologiae*, he insisted that even though love is generally thought of as a passion (i.e., something undergone or "suffered") it must be ascribed to God. God is will (Ia, q.19, a.1), and the "first movement of the will and of any appetitive power is love," because while the will and any appetitive power tend to good or evil as objects, good always has the priority (q.20, a.1). In the sensitive appetite love is always something that the body undergoes, but in acts of the intellective appetite we must distinguish between the desire for a good not possessed (which implies imperfection) and the loving joy in a present good, which does not. Love in the latter sense can be predicated of God as a truly transcendental term.

In the same *quaestio* Thomas demonstrated the universality of God's love (q.2) and the general principles governing the modes of expression of universal love (aa.3–4). Thus far Thomas was in basic agreement with Dionysius, but it is interesting to see how he interpreted the fourth chapter of *The Divine Names* in his commentary on that work. In discussing the issue of God's ecstasy, Thomas made use of a distinction between *amor concupiscentiae* (the love of desire by which we love things as means to an end) and *amor amicitiae* (the love of friendship whereby we tend towards another for himself). He argued that only the latter can be truly ecstatic, that is, lead the lover outside the self. Therefore, of the three types of love mentioned by Dionysius (love of inferiors for superiors, love of equals toward equals, love of superiors toward inferiors) Thomas held that only the first kind was truly ecstatic.[14] Therefore, Thomas's God (who loves only in the third way) is truly *Amor*, but not ecstatic *Amor*: he does not go out of himself.

We should also recall how Dante closed his *Divina Commedia* with an echo of Boethius's hymn to Love's universal power—"l'amor che

---

[13] See the translation and study of Emil Fackenheim, "A Treatise on Love by Ibn Sina," *Mediaeval Studies* 7 (1945), 208–28.

[14] See *Expositio de Divinis Nominibus*, ed. Ceslaus Pera (Rome: Marietti, 1950), 142–43 (Lect. X, 431–32).

move il sole e l'altre stelle" (Paradiso XXXIII, 145).[15] Love was not
only the overarching theme of the *Commedia* (see especially the central cantos containing Vergil's speeches on love in Purgatorio XVII–
XVIII), but was also the subject of the *Convivio*, which can be described as a philosophical treatise on cosmic love. Dante's treatment
of this now well-established theme in western thought is both an
interesting summation of inherited wisdom, and in some ways a new
departure, at least to the extent that Beatrice, who served as the
manifestation of both visible beauty and the beauty of philosophy
(*Convivio* 2.2), played an essential role in the poet's trajectory of *eros*
from the world of sense to that of spirit and what lay beyond. In
giving the human experience of *eros* a role in the transformative ascent,
Dante both reappropriated a possibility largely dormant since Plato
and also served as an important predecessor for the discussions of
the role of sexual love in the Renaissance.

II. *Cosmic and Sexual Love in the Renaissance*

The extent of the originality of Renaissance thought, especially of
Renaissance Platonism, has been and will continue to be debated.
Thinkers like Marsilio Ficino and Giovanni Pico della Mirandola,
and even more Leone Ebreo, had direct access to a wider range of
sources than most of their medieval predecessors, but did this broader
knowledge bear fruit in terms of real philosophical creativity? Here
I will argue that in attempting to incorporate human erotic experience into philosophical and theological views of cosmic love worked
out in the previous millennium Renaissance thinkers did make an
important new contribution.[16]

Marsilio Ficino's *De amore* can be seen as attempting to enrich the
standard Christian view of cosmic love by a return to Plato which

---

[15] On the relation between the two, see Peter Dronke, "L'amor che move," 389–
91. See also Kenelm Foster, "Dante and Eros," in *The Two Dantes and Other Studies*
(Berkeley: University of California, 1977), 37–55.

[16] Positions on the originality of Renaissance theories of love have varied. Anders
Nygren in *Eros and Agape* (Philadelphia: Westminster, 1953), 667–80, saw Ficino's
reassertion of Platonic *eros* as destroying Augustine's *caritas* synthesis and thus making possible Luther's rediscovery of biblical *agape*. Irving Singer in *The Nature of Love*
(Chicago: University of Chicago, 1984), 2:165–208, noted the importance of new
elements in Renaissance views of love, but failed to show their integration into the
cosmic pattern.

tried to incorporate a new valuation of human erotic experience (largely homosexual). Nevertheless, the deep tensions and ambivalences in his account rendered Ficino's argument less than successful. The clever and learned (but not always deep) Giovanni Pico della Mirandola, in his *Commento sopra una Canzona d'amore di Girolamo Benivieni*, mounted an attack on Ficino for not being platonic enough and in so doing undercut the main premises of the Christian view of cosmic love to return to a purely Platonic position that mingled elements of Plotinus and Proclus. Pico's view of human erotic experience's role was also more limited than Ficino's. Finally, Jehudah Abravenel, or Leone Ebreo as he was known to his Christian readers, presented a position whose main lines were close to Ficino, but which actually went beyond the Florentine. Leone's notion of *amor* not only surpassed Ficino's in the complexity and range of the sources he used,[17] but it also seems to be more consistent, especially in its integration of sexual love into the cosmic circle.

In a brief article it will not be possible to give a full analysis of each of these three treatments of love.[18] Instead, I will highlight major features of their theories by addressing each with a common set of questions—(1) What is the nature of love? (2) Is God love? (3) What role can human sexual love play in the return of God?

In defining love, all three authors agree that in some sense love is the desire for beauty, though they do not understand desire and beauty in the same way. Ficino puts it the most straightforwardly: "When we say love [*amor*] understand the desire for beauty" (*De Amore* 1.4, cf. 2.9). Pico begins from a broad definition similar to Thomas Aquinas, where *amor* is any attraction to what has the appearance of

---

[17] See, e.g., William Melczer, "Platonisme et aristotelisme dans la pensèe de Lèon l'Hébreu," *XVIᵉ Colloque Internationale de Tours. Platon et Aristote à la Renaissance* (Paris: Vrin, 1976), 293–306.

[18] For the three treatises I have made use of the standard editions: (1) *Marsile Ficin: Commentaire sur le Banquet de Platon*, edited and translated by Raymond Marcel (Paris: Les Belles Lettres, 1956); (2) *Giovanni Pico della Mirandola. De Hominis Dignitate, Heptaplus, De Ente et Uno e Scritti Vari*, edited by Eugenio Garin (Florence: Vallecchi, 1942); (3) *Leone Ebreo (Giuda Abarbanel). Dialoghi d'amore*, edited by Santino Caramella (Bari: Laterza, 1929). Sears Jayne has annotated translations of the first two treatises, which I will use unless otherwise noted: *Marcilio Ficino. Commentary on Plato's Symposium on Love* (Dallas: Spring Publications, 1985); and *Commentary on a Canzone of Benivieni* (New York: Peter Lang, 1984). There is one complete translation of Leone's *Dialoghi, The Philosophy of Love (Dialoghi d'Amore) by Leone Ebreo*, translated by F. Friedberg-Seeley and Jean H. Barnes (London: Soncino Press, 1937), as well as a translation of Book 1 in *Renaissance Philosophy*, edited by Arturo B. Fallico and Herman Shapiro (New York: Modern Library, 1967), 172–228.

good, but he says that he will use the term more restrictedly "to mean only that love which is a desire to possess what is, or seems to us, beautiful."[19] The discussion of Books 1 and 3 of Leone's *Dialoghi* is more intricate, involving an analysis of the relation of love and desire to different kinds of goods, as well as to knowledge. Love and desire (which are always based on prior knowledge) initially seem to be different because we love what we possess and desire what we do not; but a discrimination of the various kinds of goods based on Aristotle's distinction of the useful, the pleasurable, and the good or virtuous (see *Ethica Nichomachea* 8.2) demonstrates that while love and desire have different modalities in the case of what is merely useful (e.g., wealth) and are coterminous and finite in the case of what is pleasurable (e.g., wine), in the love of what is good (*onesto*) love is always found together with desire. Leone summarizes thus:

> The good differs from profit and pleasure in that it is always an object of love—both when it is desired and lacked, and when it is possessed and no longer desired. It differs, moreover, in another outstanding property: while virtue, in respect to the other two, consists in a mean between love and desire . . ., so far as the good is concerned, the more uncontrolled our love and desire, the more meritorious and virtuous it is.[20]

Book 3 contains a further discussion of the relation of love and desire, arguing for the identity of the two, "although in a manner of speaking one species of love is more properly called desire, and another, love."[21] The change here involves the recognition (against the views of "some modern theologians" who want to make desire entirely distinct from love) that even when something good is possessed and enjoyed we continue to desire its possession.

The fact that Ficino and Pico concentrate immediately on love as desire for *beauty* (though they conceive of it in different ways),[22] while Leone emphasizes desire for various kinds of *goods*, demonstrates an important difference, but not an absolute distinction. Leone too insists

---

[19] Giovanni Pico della Mirandola, *Commento* 2.4. In 2.9 love is described as the desire to behold the beautiful, either corporeally or incorporeally.

[20] *Dialoghi* 1 (ed. 23; translation of Shapiro, 191). This confirms the preliminary definition of love, "Love is an affect of the will to enjoy, through union, the thing we judge to be good [*buona*]" (ed. 13; Shapiro, 181).

[21] See the lengthy discussion in *Dialoghi* 3 (ed. 207–15; the passage cited is on 211.

[22] One of the fundamental ambiguities of Ficino's work is that it contains at least

on a connection between love and beauty, at least with regard to all love below Divine Love. In discussing the relation between goodness and beauty, he affirms that "Beauty is a grace which delights the soul with its knowledge and moves it to love" (*Dialoghi* 3, ed. 226). Beauty is a species or an aspect of the good—it is the subjective good, the good as the object of personal desire.[23] Book 3 affirms that *insofar as* love is conceived of as the desire for beauty, love cannot be predicated of God, because he lacks no beauty. But because love is *essentially* the desire for the good, and the good is something that can be desired for other beings (i.e., objectively), we can ascribe it properly to God. By broadening his treatment through a consideration of the other transcendental terms, especially goodness and existence (something can only be loved if it exists), Leone comes closer to the treatments of Dionysius and Thomas Aquinas (both of whom emphasized goodness in defining love) than to those of Ficino or Pico.

All three authors give love a cosmic role in the universe, though in different ways. Here too, Leone is closer to Ficino than to Pico. Ficino's *De amore* contains three extended descriptions of the cosmic role of *amor*. The treatments in Speeches 2 and 3 are dependent on Dionysius's *Divine Names* 4 and to a lesser extent on Plotinus (especially *Enneads* 5.5 and 5.8). Speech 2 stresses the circle of love by which "divine *beauty* has generated *love*, that is, a desire for itself, in all things," a desire that returns creation to God in supreme *enjoyment* (Speech 2.2). Speech 3 discusses the three modes of love (descending, reciprocal and ascending) first found in Proclus and made classical in Christianity by Dionysius (3.1–4). Here, Ficino's emanational understanding of divine production (i.e., from the Father as Absolute Perfection through the Son as Intellect, to the Spirit as Will) undercuts the dialectical and ecstatic view of the God-world relation found in

---

three different views of beauty which are never really integrated: (1) beauty as a "grace consisting in the harmony of various things" (1.4); (2) beauty as the "external blossom" of internal goodness (5.1); and (3) beauty as the grace of the Divine Face reflected in created mirrors (5.4). Pico's *Commento* 2.8–9 says that beauty is harmony in every composite thing, especially in visible things (cf. 3.st.6, where beauty is both harmony and grace).

[23] *Dialoghi* 3 (ed. 315–58) contains an important treatise on beauty in which love is defined as the desire to be joined to and to reproduce the image of the beauty that is loved. On Leone's view of beauty, see Nelson, *Renaissance Theory*, 98–101. In seeing beauty as a formal or spiritual principle rather than harmony of parts, Leone is closer to Ficino and Plotinus than to Pico. See N. Ivanoff, "La beauté dans la philosophie de Marsile Ficin et de Léon Hébreux," *Bibliothèque de humanisme et renaissance* 3 (1936), 12–21.

Dionysius. God's desire to share his perfection is the source for all propagation within the universe, but there is no hint that *producing* the other means *being in* the other ecstatically. Ficino's third treatment of universal love (Speech 7.13–14) is close to Proclus's *Commentary on 1 Alcibiades.*

Giovanni Pico della Mirandola, like Ficino, adapted an emanational view of the God-world relation, one so close to Plotinus that it created significant problems for Christian belief. (This may well have been one of the reasons that Bienivieni and others held the *Commento* back from publication.) In Pico's view God first produces the Angelic Mind, a creation that is necessary in order to explain how multiplicity comes from unity (*Commento* 1.3–5). As a consequence, Pico broke with long-standing Christian teaching by asserting that the Ideas are not found in God himself, but only in this first angelic creation (*Commento* 1.6 and 13). He also held that the third transcendental principle was the created Rational Soul, a version of the Platonic *anima mundi* (*Commento* 1.7 and 12–13). Pico did not deny that love has a cosmic role, but he restricted it to the forms of production and return *below* the level of the Angelic Mind (*Commento* 2.11–14, 21a; 3. chs. 1–2 and st. 2, 4–7).

For Leone Ebreo "love is a lifegiving spirit which penetrates the whole world and a single bond which unites the whole universe" (*Dialoghi* 2, ed. 165). Given the extensive and eclectic nature of his sources, Leone's discussions of the modalities of this cosmic love are varied. The whole of Book 2 of the *Dialoghi* is an extended treatment of how seven modes of loving pervade all the levels of creation—the elements, the celestial bodies, and the heavenly intelligences. From the evidence of a number of passages, it is possible to construct a picture of Leone's divisions of love, descending and ascending—one that has no identifiable prototype, though it borrows from many sources.[24]

Analyzing how these three authors describe the nature and cosmic functions of love introduces our second basic question: to what extent

---

[24] Leone's Map of Love:

$$
\text{I. Descending:} \begin{cases} \text{A. Divine Love} \begin{cases} \text{intrinsic} \\ \\ \text{extrinsic} \end{cases} \\ \\ \text{B. Share of Heavenly Intelligences in} \\ \quad \text{Providential Love} \end{cases}
$$

do these authors claim that God himself is love? Pico della Mirandola sets himself off from the others by returning to what might be called a pure Platonic view. Since he defines beauty in terms of harmony of parts, the absolutely simple God cannot really be beautiful, even analogously (*Commento* 2.8). Nor, as we have seen, are the Ideas present in God, but only in the Angelic Mind (*Commento* 1.13), the only reality directly created by God (*Commento* 1.4). Therefore, while it is true to say that all things desire and love God, either naturally or cognitionally, God himself does not love anything in the sense of desiring or having some reciprocal relation with it. God is not love![25]

Ficino and Leone Ebreo, on the other hand, make considerable effort to describe how God himself can be said to be *Eros/Amor*. Ficino claims that it is God (not something below him) who is the source of all beauty and therefore of all love (*De amore* 6.17). Although he does not share Dionysius's dialectical view of how God goes out of himself in love to create a universe whose purpose is to go out of itself in returning to him, Ficino does agree with the Areopagite, Aquinas, Dante, and the majority Christian view since the time of Origen that love in the sense of *eros* is pre-eminently in God:

> The desire to propagate one's own perfection is a certain type of love. Absolute perfection is in the supreme power of God. The perfection of the divine Intellect contemplates. And from there the divine Will desires to propagate the same perfection outside itself. Out of this love of propagation, all things are created by him.[26]

In Book 3 of the *Dialoghi*, after arguing for the identity of love and needful desire, Leone Ebreo was confronted with the problem of how God can be said to be love if he lacks nothing. The Jewish philosopher argued that Plato was wrong in saying that because the gods lack nothing they do not love. Both scripture and reason show that God

---

		Heavenly Intelligence
II. Ascending:	A. Non-Human	Celestial Bodies
		Elements
		love of God
	B. Human	spiritual love
		sensual love

[25] In *Commento* 2.2 Pico does indeed, speak of a "love with which God loves his creatures," but he cannot tell us what it is because his theory really has no place for such love.

[26] Ficino, *De amore* 3.2. See also the related passage in 5.4.

has produced all things and therefore loves them as a Father does his children.[27] In this passage, and in a later one considering the first of the five questions that provide much of the structure for Book 3 (Whether love was born?), Leone emphasized that while love always involves some lack, in the case of God's love the lack is in the creature not in the Creator. Thus, Divine Love can be defined as "the will to benefit his creatures and the whole universe and to increase their perfection as far as nature will allow."[28] Since love in the universal sense is desire for some good (and not just desire for beauty which is a particular subjective good for created things), God is love in the sense that he wills the good of created things, which good always involves a lack since these things are less than God.

Later, in discussing his second question (When was love born?), Leone distinguishes between God's intrinsic and extrinsic love. Intrinsic love (God's love for himself) is the relation of the First Lover, or Divine Intellect, who is produced (not born) from the First Beloved (Divine Beauty) and the Love or bond that unites them.[29] This "trina natura," while not really the Christian Trinity, was close enough to some trinitarian theologies based on the analysis of love to have facilitated the story of Leone's conversion. In a manner not unlike Plato's Demiurge, the Divine Intellect in loving the Divine Beauty "desires to produce a child in its likeness," and thus becomes the cause of the first extrinsic love, the primary couple constituted of Adam (the First Intellect reflecting the Ideas) and Eve (the chaos of Prime Matter containing the Essences).[30]

Leone Ebreo speaks of the circle of love as embracing both "productive love" (*l'amor producttivo*), that is, God's desire as effective and formal cause of the production and maintenance of Divine Beauty

---

[27] Leone Ebreo, *Dialoghi* 3 (ed. 215–19). Later Leone qualifies his attack on Plato by saying that he was speaking only of human love, not love in general.

[28] *Dialoghi* 3 (ed. 234). See the discussion in Bk 2 concerning how superiors love inferiors (ed. 155–58).

[29] *Dialoghi* 3 (ed. 253–58). See also the related passage in 3 (ed. 371).

[30] *Dialoghi* 3 (ed. 258–59). Leone's view of this First Intellect may reflect Averroistic aspects of his thought, for despite his avowed allegiance to Plato, in the words of Alfred Ivry, "Ebreo is, however, more of an Aristotelian, and more of an Averroist, than he would care to admit" ("Remnants of Jewish Averroism in the Renaissance," *Jewish Thought in the Sixteenth Century*, 247). On the complex question of the relation of Leone's understanding of the emanation of the universe and the views of Neoplatonism and medieval Arab Aristotelians, especially Avicenna and Averroes, see Herbert Davidson, "Medieval Jewish Philosophy in the Sixteenth Century," *Jewish Thought in the Sixteenth Century*, 125–30.

in the world, and "reductive love," which is God's desire as final cause leading all things back to union with himself (*Dialoghi* 3, ed. 369–80). In the end, for Leone, as for Dionysius, Thomas Aquinas, and Dante, the love by which we love God is not different from the love with which he loves us—"God, moreover, is one and the same as the pleasure which is his and the object which inspires it" (*Dialoghi* 3, ed. 382).

The higher stages of the return of love for Leone, as for Ficino and Pico, must be realized through the activation of the spiritual powers of the knowing subject. Mystics since Plato had agreed that love and knowledge need to be transformed in order to ascend to the higher world and to achieve union with God, either in this life or in the next. Leone put it this way: "The end of the loves of the universe is through the final act that unites with the Creator," because "the lover's delight [*dilettazione*] is his union with the beauty he loves" (*Dialoghi* 3, ed. 379–80). While it would be interesting to investigate these three Renaissance thinkers on their understanding of union and the roles of love and intellect in achieving it, these complex issues cannot be taken up here. Rather, we must turn to our third and final question: How far does subjective erotic experience, that is, human sexual love, enter into the soul's return to God?

Christian mystics and theologians, such as Origen, Dionysius, and Thomas Aquinas, always admitted that human sexual love was a part of the downward cycle of the great circle of love, a creation of Divine Goodness. But they gave erotic experience no real place in the return cycle, usually seeing it after Adam's Fall as something to be avoided lest it distract from the necessary transformations of the material to the spiritual. The poets, like Boethius, and even more so, the twelfth-century Platonist Bernardus Silvestris in his *Cosmographia*, gave sexual love a greater role, though in a more objective rather than in a subjective sense. The late medieval philosophical poets, especially Dante, Boccaccio, and Chaucer, were more prepared to think about the integration of sexual experience, especially of the courtly variety, into the reductive cycle of cosmic love.[31] But it is not until the Renaissance theorists that we find considerable speculative discussion of the role of sexual love in the ascent to God.

The ways in which Ficino, Pico, and Leone Ebreo strove to integrate

---

[31] On Bernardus, Boccaccio, and Chaucer, see Dronke, "L'amor che move," 415–22.

human erotic experience into the soul's return to God hinged on their respective definitions of love and beauty. Because Ficino and Pico understood love primarily in terms of the desire to enjoy beauty rather than the desire for the good the way that Leone did, they had greater problems effecting an integration.

Ficino's primary definition of beauty, as we have seen, was "a certain grace which most often originates above all in a harmony of several things" (*De amore* 1.4). This grace is threefold: of souls known through intellect; of bodies through sight; and of sounds through hearing. "I ove, therefore, is limited to these three; an appetite which follows the other senses is not called love, but lust or madness" (ibid.). Hence, Ficino asserts that the desire for coitus, since it involves the sense of touch, is not love but its opposite. This was the reason for his numerous attacks on the lustful desire that impels souls to copulation (e.g., 2.9, 6.1, 6.8, 6.10, 7.1, 7.12, 7.15, etc.). Of course, as a good Platonist, Ficino still gave the *sight* of a beautiful body, especially a beautiful young male body, an important place in the soul's ascent. Through their mutual perception of beauty, both physical and intellectual, man and boy cultivate a love for higher beauty (see 2.9, 7.1). Speech 6.14 in the *De amore* argues that those more suited to heavenly rather than vulgar love naturally love young males rather than women or children, "since in them sharpness of intellect flourishes more completely, which, on account of its more excellent beauty, is most suitable for receiving the learning which they wish to procreate."

There is, however, another line of thought in Ficino found in several of his discussions of the two Venuses—the Heavenly and the Earthly or Vulgar. These twin Venuses that signify the desire to contemplate and the desire to procreate originate in the Angelic Mind and the World Soul and from them are spread through the universe (see 6.5, 6.7–8). Hence, the desire to procreate, though much abused, is essentially good, "since the procreation of offspring is considered to be as necessary and virtuous as the pursuit of truth" (6.8). Indeed, as divine gifts, both kinds of love seek to procreate—intellectual love through teaching and writing, bodily love, "in order to make eternal life available to mortal things," seeks "to procreate handsome offspring by a beautiful woman" (see 6.11 and 2.7). From this perspective, Ficino roundly condemns homosexual intercourse (6.14). Thus, the Florentine thinker affirms the basic goodness of procreative *heterosexual* love as an expression of the downward path of cosmic *eros*, but his understanding of beauty's role in the upward way emphasizes

sublimated *homosexual* attachment. The most he will say is that procreative love is good as long as it does not go beyond its measure or
interfere with contemplative love (2.7).

In his desire to be more platonic than Ficino, Pico della Mirandola
has even less of a role for heterosexual *eros*. He too makes much use
of the two Loves that proceed from the two Venuses, the Earthly
Venus, which is desire for corporeal beauty, and the Heavenly Venus,
which is "the intellectual desire of ideal beauty."[32] Earthly love has
two varieties: the love of corporeal beauty *in itself*, which arouses the
desire for coitus; and the love of corporeal beauty that has been
abstracted from its physical form and made into intelligible beauty
(*Commento* 3.2). The former is bestial or irrational love and contributes
nothing to the soul's ascent (3.4; as well as 3.st.1). The latter is the
first, or imperfect, stage of human love that prepares the way for the
transition to the two divisions of heavenly love: perfect human love
(the memory of the vision of perfect beauty before the soul was put
in the body); and angelic love, which is achieved when the soul is
united to its intellect and "flies up to the intelligible heaven where
he happily rests in the arms of the First Father" (3.2). Like Ficino,
Pico admits that bestial love "is less unseemly with the feminine sex";
but as far as the ascension of love is concerned, "most men who
have been affected by heavenly love have loved some young man of
virtuous character, the more beautiful his body, the more attractive
his virtue . . ." (3.st.1). Thus, there is no positive role for heterosexual
eros in the soul's upward path. Indeed, Pico's insistence that the ultimate contact with the Heavenly Venus, or Angelic Mind, is effected
by the kiss of death (*binsica*) rather than by anything suggesting sexual union conforms to the general suspicion of heterosexuality in his
deeply Platonic *Commento*.[33]

Leone Ebreo took a more positive, though not wholly unambiv-
alent, view of the role of heterosexual love, not only in the downward
sweep of *eros*, but also in its ascent. As befitted his Jewish perspective on the commandment to procreate, love between man and woman
played a key role in the transformation of *eros*, though Leone restricted its mystical potential more than many of his Kabbalistic
sources had. From the theoretical point of view, what enabled Leone
to achieve this more positive evaluation was his understanding of love

---

[32] See *Commento* 2.11–14 (the quotation is from 2.13), as well as 3.1–4.
[33] See especially *Commento* 3.st.4 (ed. 556–58; translation, 150–51).

primarily in terms of goodness rather than of beauty alone. Thus, he agreed with Ficino that only sight and hearing have beauty as their object; but he went on to say that the other senses—taste, smell and even touch—still have *good* objects, and therefore their use can form a part of love's return to its source.[34] For Leone the twin loves born of Venus, love of corporeal things and love of spiritual things, are both good (*onesto*), although the former must be used in moderation and in the service of the latter (*Dialoghi* 3, ed. 289). Much of the humor of the *Dialoghi* rests in the tension between the female Sophia's desire for increased spiritual knowledge and the frustrated male Philo's amorous advances based on his immoderate desire for physical satisfaction. But the *Dialoghi* insist throughout on the positive role that sexuality can have in the soul's trajectory of love. For Leone, the satiety of copulation need not eliminate the heart's love, but rather should enhance and integrate true spiritual love between man and woman whose definition he gives as "the conversion of the lover into the beloved together with a desire for the conversion of the beloved into the lover."[35] This love, which is engendered by reason but not limited by it, was planted by God in humanity from the beginning, as Moses teaches (see *Dialoghi* 3, ed. 299–308).

Yehudah Abravenel was one of those Jewish philosophers, like Solomon ibn Gabirol, whom fate cast in a more Christian light than is historically accurate. Both thinkers were even at times thought to have become Christian, just as Philo had been baptized by some of the Church Fathers. It is far more accurate to see Leone's intention, as Riccardo Scrivano puts it, as expressing "an important aspect of the question of Jewish culture by proclaiming the superiority (that is the continuity and influence) of the Hebrew tradition over the classical, the mediaeval, and modern ones."[36] Though masked by the general eirenicism of the *Dialoghi* with their diverting interchanges between Sofia and Philo, Leone gives a hint of his real program

---

[34] See *Dialoghi* 3 (ed. 226–27). *Dialoghi* 1 (ed. 48–49) explains that touch and taste are given primarily for the good of the species and are therefore more limited, involving a satiety and cessation of desire that the more spiritual senses do not.

[35] *Dialoghi* 1 (ed. 50; using the translation of Friedberg-Seeley, 55). See the whole section in *Dial.* 1 (ed. 47–58, as well as *Dial.* 3, 365–67).

[36] Riccardo Scrivano, "Platonic and Cabalistic Elements in the Hebrew Culture of Renaissance Italy: Leone Ebreo and his *Dialoghi d'amore*," *Ficino and Renaissance Neoplatonism*, 137. See also Lesley, "The Place of the *Dialoghi d'amore*," 82, on how Leone makes Plato and Kabbalah (traditions appropriated by Christians) serve Judaism.

when Sofia tells Philo, "I am pleased to see you make Plato a follower of Moses and numbered among the Kabbalists" (*Dialoghi* 3, ed. 251). Leone did not merely assert the superiority of the Jewish version of the *prisca theologia*, he argued for it by showing the convergence of the best thinkers of the past and present with Judaism, especially with the wisdom of the Kabbalah. In so doing he created a theory of cosmic love whose scope bears comparison with the most ambitious Christian theologians and poets and whose view of the role of heterosexual *eros* was to have a powerful impact on Christian thinkers during the next two centuries—an impressive achievement, and one which may still have ecumenical possibilities.

THE ALFONSINE TABLES AND THE END OF THE WORLD: ASTROLOGY AND APOCALYPTIC CALCULATION IN THE LATER MIDDLE AGES[1]

Laura Smoller

Beginning in the fourteenth century, medieval European astronomers and astrologers based their calculations on a series of Latin astronomical tables attributed to Alfonso X ("the Wise") of Castile (r. 1252–82). Known now to have been the product of scholars working in Paris in the 1320s, the so-called Alfonsine tables incorporated a number of innovations over thirteenth-century astronomical tables. Amongst these changes was the adoption of a double motion of the fixed stars and planetary apogees (*auges*), combining two competing theories about their motion. While this innovation had the apparent goal of reconciling the two sides of thirteenth-century debates about the motion of the eighth sphere, it also provided astrologers who were so inclined with a new set of theories with which to predict the end of the world. To these astrologers, the Alfonsine tables suggested that the world might end some time between the years A.D. 1750 and 1801.

We can trace the path of this idea in several fourteenth- through sixteenth-century authors. Because the Alfonsine figure in effect postponed the apocalypse by some centuries from the present, it could appeal to those who wished to suggest that some present crisis was an opportunity for reform and not the work of Antichrist and his agents. Thus, for example, Pierre d'Ailly seized upon the data from the Alfonsine tables to downplay the apocalyptic significance of the Great Schism in 1414, on the eve of the Council of Constance. But the outlook need not be so rosy. D'Ailly's work was copied in 1444 by the physician and astrologer Jean de Bruges, writing in the crisis atmosphere surrounding the Council of Basel and Flemish involvement in the Hundred Years' War. Both authors' works, in turn, formed the basis of a 1531 prediction by Dijon astrologer Pierre Turrel,

---

[1] In memoriam Wilbur Knorr, who did not live to share our long-postponed conversation about the Alfonsine tables.

contemplating the rise of Lutheranism in Germany. These two last works demonstrate a less optimistic interpretation of the delayed apocalypse. Both Jean de Bruges and Pierre Turrel predicted the End for some time near the year 1800, as had d'Ailly. But they insisted that events from their own times signalled just so many preambles to Antichrist, not a crisis after which reform was to follow.

The Latin compilation known as the Alfonsine tables was most likely a product of Parisian astronomers (probably John of Murs and/ or John of Lignères) working in the 1320s. It had taken definite form by 1327, the date in which John of Saxony composed a set of "canons" explaining the tables' use and which invariably accompanied the tables in their manuscript and printed forms.[2] They differed from previous astronomical tables in a number of respects, among the most important of which were the adoption of a double motion for the fixed stars and planetary apogees and the expression of mean coordinates in tropical rather than sidereal time (that is, coordinates are expressed in the ninth sphere, rather than the eighth sphere, which contains the fixed stars and planetary apogees).

Previously, the slow apparent drift of the eighth sphere (stars and apogees) had been understood either by regular precession or by trepidation, that is, via a motion called access and recess. The former theory posited a slow eastward motion of the fixed stars, whether at the rate of 1° per one hundred years (Hipparchus's and Ptolemy's figure) or 1° every sixty-six years (al-Battani's calculation). The latter theory, associated with the name of the ninth-century Arab astronomer Thabit ibn Qurra, postulated moving vernal and autumnal equinoctial points that actually described small circles around those fixed points demarking the vernal and autumnal equinox along the ecliptic. This so-called motion of access and recess had the effect of creating a movable ecliptic with which moved the fixed stars and planetary apogees.[3] In the thirteenth century, debate had raged about which

---

[2] For a discussion of the tables' Parisian origins and their major innovations, see Emmanuel Poulle, "The Alfonsine Tables and Alfonso X of Castile," *Journal for the History of Astronomy* 19 (1988), 97–113. The Latin tables contain a number of innovations over Castilian canons supposedly corresponding to the original version of the "Alfonsine tables." The Latin tables and John of Saxony's canons are edited in Emmanuel Poulle, ed. and trans., *Les tables alphonsines avec les canons de Jean de Saxe. Edition, traduction et commentaire* (Paris: C.N.R.S., 1984).

[3] O. Neugebauer, "Thâbit ben Qurra 'On the Solar Year' and 'On the Motion of the Eighth Sphere': Translation and Commentary," *Proceedings of the American Philosophical Society* 106 (1962), 264–99.

explanation was to be preferred, both of which had the support of important authorities.

The Alfonsine tables solved this debate by adopting both sorts of motion: a precessional motion with a period of 49,000 years and a trepidational motion with a 7000-year period for access and recess. It is not clear whence these numbers arose. The 49,000-year period posits a rate of precession much slower than either of the most usual medieval figures. Thabit's description of access and recess proposed a roughly 4077-year period, whereas the ninth-century astrologer Albumasar implied that the period was 640 years.[4] Modern authors have suggested that the figures may have been chosen because of the resonances of the number seven. The period of access and recess seems to suggest a cosmic week of seven thousand years, while the precessional period points to a week of such weeks (7 × 7000 = 49,000).[5] Whether unwittingly or not, the double motion of the eighth sphere posited in the Alfonsine tables yielded a numerologically satisfying *magnus annus* (Great Year).

Material within the tables themselves pointed to further subdivisions of this Great Year. Table 12 of the Alfonsine tables gives figures for the equation of the eighth sphere's movement of access and recess for only 0° through 90° of the small circles described by the movable equinoctial points. There is good reason for this incompleteness. As John of Saxony explains, the same figures apply, in reverse, for 90° through 180° and can be used in like manner for 180° through 360°.[6] In effect, however, the tables' economy of presentation divides the 7000-year period for access and recess into four sub-periods of 1750 years each (0° to 90°, 90° to 180°, 180° to 270°, and 270° to 360°). But there is another more practical reason for this choice as well. According to Table 9.1, which lists "root" positions

    [4] For Thabit, see Neugebauer, p. 297. Albumasar (Abu Ma'shar), *De magnis coniunctionibus, annorum revolutionibus, ac eorum profectionibus, octo continens tractatus* (Augsburg: Erhard Ratdolt, 1489), tr. 2, diff. 8, fol. [D6v]: "Et iam fiet similiter mutatio communis maior cum compleverit motus orbis iste .9. [8] gradus accedendo vel recedendo: et illud contingit in omnibus .664. [640] annis." (That is, 8 degrees of longitudinal movement multiplied by 80 years per degree.)

    [5] Poulle, "The Alfonsine Tables," p. 106; and John D. North, *Richard of Wallingford: An Edition of His Writings with Introductions, English Translation and Commentary*, 3 vols. (Oxford: Clarendon Press, 1976), 3:197–99: "It looks almost as though we have found two respects in which the Alfonsine astronomers gave God advice on the ordering of the universe."

    [6] Poulle, ed., *Les tables alphonsines*, pp. 131 (Table 12), 62 (John of Saxony).

for the eighth sphere's motion of access and recess, the movement of access and recess was at 0° at roughly the time of the Incarnation.[7] By interpolation, that would mean the movement of access and recess would attain 90° only in 1766.[8] As John of Saxony wisely notes, "we do not need that retrograde calculation [for 90° through 360°] in our lifetime because there will be many years before 90 degrees shall be attained."[9] And, as some later astrologers would postulate, there might be no need to calculate after that period anyway.

Although this is never made explicit in the Alfonsine tables, the tables offered two possible methods for would-be calculators of the End. This first is based on the 7000-year period of access and recess. From the time of the Epistle of Barnabus (ca. A.D. 120), Christian commentators had assumed that the history of the world would in some way parallel the account of its creation in Genesis, substituting one millennium for each of the seven days of Creation week.[10] In the early Middle Ages, the assumption was that the world would end in its six thousandth year, with the eternal repose of the blessed corresponding to the seventh day of rest in Genesis. By the later Middle Ages, when the world had long surpassed this age by most calculations, the theory was revised. Some authors began to argue that the End would come any time before the world's 6500th year; others, that the world would endure to the age of 7000.[11] The 7000-year period of access and recess, then, could seem perhaps irresistibly consonant with the week of millennia suggested by Genesis. With a major sub-period beginning around the time of the Incarnation, the

---

[7] Poulle, ed., *Les tables alphonsines*, p. 124.

[8] By Poulle's calculation; see ibid., p. 199.

[9] "Sed illa computatione retrograda non indigemus in vita nostra quia erunt multi anni antequam veniant 90 gradus." Ibid., p. 62. And p. 102: "Sed quia multi anni erunt antequam 90 gradus veniant, ideo non curo declarare quid post sit faciendum, sed videant illi qui tunc temporis vitam ducent."

[10] For the history of this tradition in the early Middle Ages—and its vital link to calculations of the world's age—see Richard Landes, "Lest the Millennium Be Fulfilled: Apocalyptic Expectations and the Pattern of Western Chronography 100–800 C.E.," in Werner Verbeke, Daniel Verhelst, and Andries Weldenhuysen, eds., *The Use and Abuse of Eschatology in the Middle Ages* (Louvain: Leuven University Press, 1988), pp. 137–211.

[11] For example, John of Paris (world would end before its 6500th year); Felix Hemmerlin (world would end in its 7000th year, 36 years from the current year of 1456); see Laura Ackerman Smoller, *History, Prophecy, and the Stars: The Christian Astrology of Pierre d'Ailly, 1350–1420* (Princeton, NJ: Princeton University Press, 1994), p. 88. The world had long since surpassed its 6000th year according to the standard Eusebian chronology (5228 years from Creation to the start of Christ's ministry), but not by the Hebrew (Vulgate) dating (Creation at 3952 B.C.).

eighth sphere's trepidational movement could appear to be in sync with the broad plan of salvation history.

The second possibility for apocalyptic calculation implicit within the Alfonsine tables lay in the 49,000-year period for the complete precession of the fixed stars and planetary apogees. This proved to be an eschatological dead end, however. True, the tables' eschewing of earlier figures for the rate of precession yielded here, too, a numerologically satisfying result, although the 49,000-year cycle did put a completion of that revolution in an unimaginably distant future. Unfortunately, however, speculations arising from the eighth sphere's period of precession were decidedly problematic by the time the Alfonsine tables were compiled in Paris in the 1320s. The Hipparchan/Ptolemaic calculation of precession at 1° per century had yielded an assumption that the world would complete some sort of Great Year in its 36,000th year (100 years × 360°). In its most extreme form, this theory implied a dangerous fatalism: when the stars returned to their original positions, the same series of events would recur on earth, and history would repeat itself. A statement to this effect was one of the two hundred and nineteen propositions Bishop Stephen Tempier condemned in Paris in 1277: "That when all the heavenly bodies have returned to the same point, which is accomplished in 36,000 years, the same effects will recur as are in existence now."[12] A less extreme interpretation suggested that the world would end upon the stars' completion of the 36,000-year cycle of precession. Authors in Paris around the year 1300, however, had attacked even this theory with the counter-argument that God could speed up the movement of the orbs as he pleased, thereby completing the circle of precession in a much shorter time.[13] Given the difficult implica-

---

[12] The condemnations are edited in Heinrich Denifle and Emile Chatelain, eds., *Chartularium Universitatis Parisiensis*, 4 vols. (Paris: Delalain, 1889–97), 1:543ff.; and Pierre Mandonnet, *Siger de Brabant et l'averroïsme latin au XIIIme siècle*, 2nd ed., 2 vols. in 1 (Louvain: Institut Supérieur de Philosophie, 1908 and 1911), pt. 2, pp. 175–91. The relevant proposition is number 6 in Denifle and Chatelain's and number 92 in Mandonnet's edition: "Quod redeuntibus corporibus coelestibus omnibus in idem punctum, quod fit in XXX sex milibus annorum, redibunt idem effectus, qui sunt modo." It is not at all clear that anyone in Paris believed this proposition. It smacks of fatalism, of the eternity of the world, of everything Tempier distrusted about Greek philosophy; but it is also patently bad astrology. The rate of the eighth sphere's precession is independent of the periodicity of planetary configurations. When stars *and* planets might be expected to return to their original positions at Creation (even if that was known) was a much more complex calculation. Furthermore, no medieval astrologer argued for the kind of fatalism Tempier's condemnation implies.

[13] This argument appears in Arnold of Villanova's *De tempore adventus Antichristi*,

tions arising from specifying a period of precession, it is perhaps understandable that neither the Alfonsine tables themselves nor the canons of John of Saxony explicitly state the number of years for a complete precessional period.[14] While later eschatological calculators could find material of interest contained within the tables, their Parisian compilers left that information deeply buried.

Parisian interest in the world's end was intense in the years just prior to the compilation of the Alfonsine tables. The final decades of the thirteenth century had witnessed a flurry of apocalyptic concern, fueled to no small measure by the writings (real and spurious) of Joachim of Fiore and their appropriation by the Spiritual wing of the Franciscan Order.[15] For the Franciscan Spirituals, the events of the year 1294 had raised the stakes enormously. The elevation of the hermit-pope Celestine V—and his subsequent resignation and replacement by Boniface VIII—convinced many Spirituals that Antichrist himself was on the throne of St. Peter. Increasing radicalism, heresy convictions, burnings, and the ultimate condemnation of the Spirituals followed in the first decades of the fourteenth century. In this charged atmosphere, several scholars in Paris around the year 1300 wrote treatises investigating the time of Antichrist's advent. Interestingly,

---

of which lengthy excerpts are edited in Heinrich Finke, *Aus den Tagen Bonifaz VIII: Funde und Forschungen*, Vorreformationsgeschichtliche Forschungen, 2 (Münster: Aschendorff, 1902), pp. CXXIX–CLIX. The pertinent passage appears at p. CXXXIV: "Astrologi vero, qui probant, quod motus retardationis octave sphere compleri ne quit in paucioribus annis quam in XXXVI milibus, debent scire, quod suam potentiam et sapientiam Deus non alligavit naturalibus causis.... Et si totius retardationis revolutio necessaria foret, ut asserunt, ad universalem perfectionem, nichilominus Deus est potens motum orbium velocitare, quantum placuerit, et revolutionem complere brevissimo tempore, ita ut revolutiones L vel centum annorum compleantur in uno anno vel dimidio." This passage of Arnold's was cited with approval in John of Paris's *Tractatus de Antichristo*. See Sara Beth Peters Clark, "*The Tractatus de Antichristo* of John of Paris: a Critical Edition, Translation, and Commentary," Ph.D. diss., Cornell University, 1981, p. 62.

[14] Nor is the 7000-year access and recess period immediately obvious from tables or text, but already in John of Ashenden's 1347 astrological *Summa* these periods are associated with the Alfonsine tables. Johannes Eschuid [John of Ashenden], *Summa astrologiae iudicialis de accidentibus mundi quae anglicana vulgo nuncupatur* (Venice: Iohannes Lucilius Santritter, 1489), fol. 14v: "Ad verificandum tamen tabulas Alfonsii motus ille trepidationis in .7000. annis non citius completur. Motusque stellarum fixarum secundum longitudinem non citius quam in 49,000 annis completis perficietur quod est rectius anni magni tempus."

[15] See, in general, Bernard McGinn, "Angel Pope and Papal Antichrist," *Church History* 47 (1978): 161–69; Marjorie Reeves, *The Influence of Prophecy in the Later Middle Ages: A Study in Joachimism* (Oxford: Clarendon Press, 1969), pp. 135–70, 194–224; David Burr, *Olivi's Peaceable Kingdom: A Reading of the Apocalypse Commentary* (Philadelphia: University of Pennsylvania Press, 1993).

they brought astrological calculations into their works—despite the stern warnings of Stephen Tempier in 1277.[16] One of these authors, the physician Arnold of Villanova, eventually found a welcoming patron in Boniface VIII, despite the fact that the Parisian theologians had condemned his bald prediction that Antichrist would arrive in 1378 and despite his decidedly pro-Spiritual Franciscan sentiments.[17] Another, Henry of Harkley, denied flatly that anyone could know with certainty the time of the world's end.[18]

Amongst these authors was the Dominican theologian and political philosopher John of Paris, who in 1300 penned a treatise on Antichrist. John wrote in response to the recent prediction by Arnold of Villanova.[19] Arnold's prognostication of Antichrist's advent, based upon numbers in Daniel 12, was roundly condemned by the faculty of theology in Paris, both for his flat assertion that one could have certain knowledge of the time of Antichrist's arrival and for his audacity, as a lay person, in attempting to speak authoritatively on such subjects. To counter Arnold's claims, John denied that anyone could have certain knowledge of the time of Antichrist's advent, whether based on Scripture, prophecy, or astrology. On a more moderate note, however, John admitted that, by probable conjecture, one could surmise that the world would endure only another two hundred years.

What is most interesting here is that John based his prediction on

---

[16] The real thirteenth-century champion of astrological calculations of the apocalypse was Roger Bacon. [See his *Opus maius*, part 4, as in The *"Opus maius" of Roger Bacon*, ed. John Henry Bridges, 2 vols. (Oxford: Clarendon Press, 1897), vol. 1, pars 4, pp. 253–69.] It has recently been argued that Bacon's condemnation by the Franciscan order in 1277 was due to the excessive claims he made for astrology's ability to predict religious change. [Paul Sidelko, "The Condemnation of Roger Bacon," *Journal of Medieval History* 22 (1996), 69–81.] There is no contemporary evidence indicating what in Bacon's work was deemed offensive, however; Sidelko argues simply on the basis of Bacon's assertions about the stars' effects on religion.

[17] See the description of the controversy surrounding Arnold's treatise in Clark, "The *Tractatus de Antichristo*," pp. 7–12; and in Franz Pelster, "Die Quaestio Heinrichs von Harclay über die zweite Ankunft Christi und die Erwartung des baldigen Weltendes zu Anfang des XIV Jahrhunderts." *Archivio italiano per la storia della pietà* 1 (1951), 32–46.

[18] See the commentary and edition of his text in Pelster, "Die Quaestio."

[19] John's treatise is edited in Clark, "The *Tractatus de Antichristo*"; Arnold's appears in lengthy excerpt in Finke, *Aus den Tagen Bonifaz VIII*. Arnold's prediction is at p. CXXXII: "Quod nobis hic sufficit, istud est, scilicet quod completis mille CC.X.C. annis a tempore, quo populus Judaicus amisit possessionem terre illus [sk], stabit, ut ait dominus, abhominatio desolationis, scilicet Antichristus in loco sancto, quod erit circa septuagesimum octavum annum centenarii sequentis videlicat [sk] quarti decimi a salvatoris adventu."

two foundations: first, the notion that the world would last only 6000 years (which he attributed to the third-century bishop Methodius) and, second, a calculation of the world's age based on the rate of precession of the planetary apogees.[20] In other words, he sought to find a way to predict the world's end from the eighth sphere's movement that avoided both the 36,000-year Great Year and the condemned fatalism that period implied. As John noted, Arnold of Villanova had rightly scorned the notion that the world would not end until the completion of the 36,000-year cycle of the fixed stars' movement. What John suggested instead was a calculation of the world's age based on the position of the sun's apogee. (There was to be no chronological certainty from scrutinizing Scripture or authorities, for those following the Septuagint came up with a considerably greater figure for the world's age than did those following the Hebrew numbering contained in the Vulgate.) First, John assumed that the planets were created "in their most optimal disposition" and that the sun therefore was created in Aries 15°, in which the sun has its dominion, exaltation, and strength. This made sense to John as well because the earthly paradise "as we hypothesize, is beneath Aries to the east."[21] Second, John assumed that the sun's apogee was also at Aries 15° at creation, so that the earth might be rendered more temperate by the sun's being at its most distant point from earth. Third, John assumed a rate of precession of one degree per hundred years (Ptolemy's figure) for the fixed stars and planetary apogees. Fourth, John accepted Ptolemy's calculation that the sun's apogee was at Gemini 6° in his own days. From these assumptions it was a matter of simple arithmetic to calculate that 5100 years had elapsed between

---

[20] John has in mind the pseudo-Methodius *Revelationes*, originally composed in seventh-century Syria, but widely circulated in Latin translation in the medieval west. Much of John's chronological information comes from Roger Bacon's *Opus maius* (see Bridges ed., vol. 1, pars 4, pp. 190–93). Ptolemy had maintained that the solar apogee did not share the precessional movement of the fixed stars, but later medieval astronomers demonstrated that it did.

[21] John of Paris, in Clark, "The *Tractatus de Antichristo*," p. 46: "Supponimus stellas creatas in optima sui dispositione in principio mundi, et ideo cum secundum Astrologos per se regnum, exaltatio, et fortitudo solis sit in Ariete (precipue secundum maiores in XV gradu), supponamus solem ibi creatum. Non enim videtur conveniencius alibi solem primitus collocari quam in medio tocius celi per equidistanciam ab utroque polo; cum paradisius terestrix, ut supponimus, sit sub Ariete ad orientem." (John is referring to the "dignities" astrologers assigned to planets in horoscopes. The "exaltation," for example, was a specific degree of the zodiac that was different for each planet. If a planet was in its exaltation in a given astrological chart, astrologers assigned it a certain number of "dignities," which were computed for each planet in order to determine the strongest influence on the chart.)

Creation and Ptolemy's era (A.D. 130) because the solar apogee had moved 51°. This meant that precisely 5000 years had elapsed between the time of Adam and Jesus's baptism, satisfying in itself because it confirmed Methodius's dating (based on divine revelation).[22] Thus, John in A.D. 1300 was living somewhere near the 6300th year of the world.

That the world had therefore surpassed the six millennia it was supposed to endure did not bother John; nor did it lead him to discredit Methodius's theory. Rather, John insisted that the figure 6000 should be taken to stand for any number up to 6500.[23] For that reason, he opined, "for the next two hundred years the time is suspect."[24] Based as it was on a largely outdated understanding of planetary precession,[25] John's calculation nonetheless pointed out a safe way in which the slow motion of the eighth sphere might be applied to the study of the world's end by, quite simply, sidestepping the issue of the Great Year. Evidently, it was safe enough. When, in 1313, Henry of Harkley penned a scathing treatise denouncing the ability of astrologers or any calculators to know the time of the advent of Antichrist, he deliberately avoided mention of John's prediction of when the 6500th year would come based on the solar apogee. Rather, he took John to task for the "most vain" theory that the heavens would speed up in order to complete their 36,000-year cycle in a shorter time.[26] But this was not the calculation on which John hung his hat, and we can perhaps assume that Henry could poke no holes in John's "safer" prediction.

---

[22] Ibid., pp. 46–47.

[23] Ibid., p. 44: "Et quia ultra V^C annos est maior pars millenarii (cum secundum syndocem computando, maior pars tocius pro toto computetur in Scriptura), si ultra VI millia annorum iam completa restarent plus quam V^C anni, quorum III^C iam completi sunt, magis deberet vocari VII millenarius mundi quam fragmenta sive minucie VI millenarii. . . . Et ideo cum ultra VI^M annorum iam III^C annos compleverimus tanquam fragmenta quedam verisimiliter, coniecturari potest secundum prophetiam quod de toto cursu mundi non plus remanent quam II^C annos usque ad finem mundi."

[24] Ibid., p. 47: "Et ita ex eius prophetia [pseudo-Methodius] verisimiliter teneri potest sine tamen temeritate assertionis tempus esse suspectum usque ad II^C annos, ultra quorum spacium non durabit cursus huius mundi communis."

[25] As John himself understood; see his discussion of alternative figures for the rate of precession and of the trepidation theory at ibid., pp. 59–61.

[26] Pelster, "Die Quaestio Heinrichs von Harclay," pp. 81–82 ("Ista sunt vanissimi." p. 82) Henry of Harkley copied John of Paris's computation of the world's age based on the motion of the solar apogee, but followed up by deriding those who believed that the heavens would move faster and faster toward the end so that the 36,000-year Great Year could be completed in 7000 years. (p. 81) This is a subtle shift from John's argument and indicates either a misreading or deliberate misunderstanding of John's text.

The double motion of the eighth sphere presented in the Alfonsine
tables and John of Saxony's canons seemed to dis-invite calculations
of a Great Year based on precession. Within two decades of the
appearance of the *Canons*, however, the English astrologer John of
Ashenden (Johannes Eschuid) used the Alfonsine tables to correct a
number of opinions about the length of a Great Year based either
on precession or on trepidation.[27] According to Ashenden, the Alfonsine tables' 49,000-year period of precession was "more correctly"
the time of the Great Year than any of these previous figures. Ashenden did not make either motion of the eighth sphere a basis for astrological calculations. Nor did he evince any interest in forecasting
the time of the world's end, although he did devote a number of
pages to figuring out the time of its beginning. Rather, Ashenden
set forth a number of theories for predicting large-scale changes in
the world from planetary conjunctions, the completion of ten orbits
by the planet Saturn, and changes in a purely hypothetical coupling
of planets and signs that he dubbed the "magnus orbis."[28] All of
these theories derive ultimately from Albumasar, and the first two
at least had been disseminated beyond merely astrological circles in
the thirteenth century in the writings of Roger Bacon and the pseudo-
Ovidian poem *De vetula*.[29] Albumasar's thirteenth-century followers
had picked up as well on theories that could help calculate the time
of the End, and Bacon had exultantly written, "I know that if the
Church should be willing to consider the sacred text and prophecies ... and should order a study of the paths of astronomy, it
would gain some idea of greater certainty regarding the time of Antichrist."[30] Ashenden himself quoted passages from Albumasar pre-

---

[27] Johannes Eschuid, *Summa astrologiae iudicialis*, quoted in n. 14, above.

[28] Johannes Eschuid, *Summa astrologiae iudicialis*, tr. 1, diff. 1, chap. 3. A new *magnus
orbis* commences every 360 years, under the rulership of one planet and one sign.
See Smoller, *History, Prophecy, and the Stars*, pp. 71–72.

[29] I.e., in Albumasar's *De magnis coniunctionibus* and Bacon's *Opus maius*. A period
similar to the *magnus orbis* appears in Albumasar's lost *Book of the Thousands*. See
David Pingree, *The Thousands of Abu Ma'shar*, Studies of the Warburg Institute, 30
(London: Warburg Institute, 1968). The *De vetula* appears in two modern editions:
Dorothy M. Robathan, *The Pseudo-Ovidian De Vetula: Text, Introduction, and Notes*
(Amsterdam: Adolf M. Hakkert, 1968), and Paul Klopsch, ed., *Pseudo-Ovidius De vetula:
Untersuchungen und Text*, Mittellateinische Studien und Texte, 2 (Leiden: Brill, 1967).
The astrological material appears in Book 3.

[30] I quote the translation in R.B. Burke, trans., *The Opus Majus of Roger Bacon*,
2 vols. (Philadelphia: University of Pennsylvania Press, 1928), 1: 290. [Latin in Bridges
ed., *Opus maius*, vol. 1, p. 269.]

dicting "mutations in kingdoms and sects" with the completion of the eighth sphere's motion of access and recess.[31] Neither Bacon's promises nor the information imbedded in the Alfonsine tables appear to have moved John of Ashenden in the middle of the fourteenth century. Perhaps he was cowed by the Parisian theologians; perhaps he was too interested in trying to establish a place for astrology at the English court.[32] Perhaps the context was not right. When the Black Death struck, Ashenden was much more concerned with attempting to show that his astrological calculations had accurately forecast the disaster than he was with trying to fit the event into an eschatological framework. Whatever the reasons, another half century would pass before we can find an astrologer calculating the end of the world based on the figures in the Alfonsine tables.

On May 10, 1414, the French cardinal Pierre d'Ailly completed a treatise entitled *De concordantia astronomie cum hystorica narratione* (The concordance of astrology with historical narration). This was the third of d'Ailly's major treatises dealing with the stars written in the years after 1410, in a series of writings that displayed an increasing knowledge of astrology, but a continued debt to the writings of Roger Bacon (and his source, Albumasar).[33] In this work, d'Ailly set out to demonstrate the relationship between astrological events and major changes on earth throughout history. The work's culmination was d'Ailly's prediction that Antichrist would arrive in the year 1789, a prediction set within the context of a discussion of the Great Schism, its possible apocalyptic significance, and d'Ailly's hopes for the upcoming Council of Constance.

D'Ailly based his prediction upon several astrological phenomena. First, he relied upon the significance of planetary conjunctions, particularly those of the two "superiors," Saturn and Jupiter. Albumasar and other Arab astrologers had noticed that successive mean conjunctions of Saturn and Jupiter tended fall in a regular pattern. That is, a series of approximately twelve conjunctions would all fall within the three signs of one triplicity, or group of similar astrological signs,

---

[31] Johannes Eschuid, *Summa astrologiae iudicialis*, f. 14, quoting Albumasar, *De magnis coniunctionibus*, tr. 2, diff. 8.

[32] As Hilary Carey suggests in *Courting Disaster: Astrology at the English Court and University in the Later Middle Ages* (New York: St. Martin's Press, 1992), pp. 85–91.

[33] I will refer to the following incunabular edition: Pierre d'Ailly, *Concordantia astronomie cum theologia. Concordantia astronomie cum hystorica narratione. Et elucidarium duarum precedentium* (Augsburg: Erhard Ratdolt, 1489). See the fuller discussion in Smoller, *History, Prophecy, and the Stars*, esp. chs. 3, 4, and 6.

before moving on to the next group of three, and so on round the circle. (There are four triplicities: the fiery, earthy, airy, and watery. The signs are assigned in succession to one of the four triplicities, so that a planet traversing the zodiac would pass first through a fiery sign, then through earthy, airy, and watery signs before entering another fiery sign.) Since the time between any two successive conjunctions will be approximately twenty years, this dictates a period of 240 years during which the planets are joined within a given triplicity. The shift in triplicity after 240 years (great conjunction) and particularly the return to the original triplicity after 960 years (greatest conjunction) were thought to signify great changes on earth. According to d'Ailly, just such a conjunction was to occur around the year 1692.[34]

Second, and again following theories outlined by Albumasar and Roger Bacon, d'Ailly noted that the planet Saturn would complete a 300-year cycle of ten revolutions in the year 1789. As with Saturn-Jupiter conjunctions, Saturn's completion of ten circuits of the zodiac was supposed to portend great changes in mores, religions, and dynasties.[35] D'Ailly (following Albumasar) had correlated with this astrological phenomenon the appearance of such earthly leaders as Alexander the Great, Jesus, Mani, and Muhammad.[36] He had used decades of Saturn's orbits to periodize world history.[37] It was fitting that such an astrological sign might also herald the advent of Antichrist.

Third, d'Ailly noted that between the conjunction and the completion of Saturn's ten orbits there would be a "status" or "statio" (standing still) of the eighth sphere from the years 1764 to 1789. He equates this phenomenon with the completion of the eighth sphere's access and recess in A.D. 1765, that is, the moment when the movable

[34] *Concordantia astronomie cum hystorica narratione*, ch. 60, fol. [d7v]: "Iam vero de octava maxima coniunctione loquamur quam futuram esse diximus si deus voluerit anno ab inicio mundi .7040. a diluvio .4798. vel circiter et post illam erit complementum .10. revolutionum saturnalium anno christi 1789. Et hoc erit post dictam coniunctionem per anos. 97. vel prope." It was not unusal for such infrequently occurring astrological events to have effects which occurred many years after the fact. See, e.g., d'Ailly's remarks in *De figura inceptionis mundi et coniunctionibus mediis sequentibus*, Vienna, Österreichische Nationalbibliothek, MS 5266, fol. 48r: "Sciendum est quod constellationes celestes secundum quod fiunt ex coniunctionibus tardioribus etiam principales suos effectus tardius producunt."
[35] *Concordantia astronomie cum hystorica narratione*, chs. 47–48, citing Albumasar, *De magnis coniunctionibus*, tr. 2, diff. 8.
[36] *Concordantia astronomie cum hystorica narratione*, ch. 47.
[37] Ibid., chs. 47–51.

equinoctial point attained a position of 90° on its small circle (putting the movable vernal equinox at a longitude of Aries 0°). D'Ailly's figure is thus quite close to Poulle's calculation based on the Alfonsine tables (attaining 90° on May 16, 1766).[38] D'Ailly's use of the term station indicates that he thinks of the eighth sphere's access and recess as in some way analogous to the planets' movement along their epicycles, where the shift from direct to retrograde motion (or vice versa) marks a station. That the completion of the movement of access or recess was of great significance d'Ailly knew from his reading of Albumasar's *De magnis coniunctionibus*. There he read that the completion of even one degree of access or recess, particularly when coupled with Saturn's movement from one sign to another (as certainly would happen at the completion of ten revolutions), signifies changes in the world and celestial and terrestrial signs, the revolution of sects, the permutation of kingship from one people to another, wars, diseases, and earthquakes. There would be a greater general change when the eighth sphere completed the entire motion of access or recess (which would happen every 640 years, according to Albumasar).[39] D'Ailly must have been doubly confident of this theory when he applied Albumasar's reasoning to the Alfonsine tables' figures for access and recess. If the completion of ten revolutions of Saturn, a greatest conjunction of Saturn and Jupiter, and a station of the eighth sphere all occurred around the time of the Incarnation, then surely their clustering in the eighteenth century must have great significance as well.[40]

---

[38] *Concordantia astronomie cum hystorica narratione*, ch. 60, fols. [d7v]–[d8r]: "Inter dictam coniunctionem et illud complementum dictarum .10. revolutionum erit status octave spere circiter per annos .25. quod sic patet quia status octave spere erit anno .444. post situm augium qui secundum tabulas astronomicas sunt adequate ad annum christi 1320 perfectum. Et ideo anno Christi 1764 quibus si addas .25. fiunt anni .1789. quos prediximus. . . . Anno Christi 1765 diebus. 136. completis erit statio motus accessus et recessus et habebimus pro motu eius .30. [90] gradus." Poulle's figure is in *Les tables alphonsines*, p. 199.

[39] Albumasar, *De magnis coniunctionibus*, tr. 2, diff. 8, fol. [D6v]: "Et iam dixerunt imaginum domini quod orbis habet motum 8 graduum in quibus accedit et quod accessio eius in omni gradu et recessio eius in eis erit omnibus .80. annis et quando completur in accessione aut recessione est gradus. 1. si illud contingit cum permutatur etc. Et illud est cum permutatur Saturnus de signo ad signum significat esse accidentium in mundo et signa celestia et terrestria et revolutionem sectarum et permutationem regni de gente ad gentem: et casum bellorum infirmitatum et esse terre motuum in climatibus. . . . Et iam fiet similiter mutatio communis maior cum compleverit motus orbis iste .9. [8] gradus accedendo vel recedendo: et illud contingit in omnibus .664. [640] annis."

[40] There is a conjunction shortly before the Incarnation in d'Ailly's *Elucidarium* and in Bacon's *Opus maius*, but not in the *Concordantia astronomie cum hystorica narratione*

That this great change might indeed mark the advent of Antichrist
d'Ailly gathered from another astrological theory found in Albumasar
and Roger Bacon. According to this line of reasoning, there were to
be only six great religions (called laws or sects) in all human history,
signified by the six possible planets that could come into conjunction
with the planet Jupiter.[41] The first five of these had already appeared;
only the sect signified by Jupiter's conjunction with the moon had
not yet materialized. That this last sect was to be characterized by
magic and lying pointed to its identification with Antichrist and his
followers. It was a simple deduction to see the triple shift around
1789 as signifying the fiend's advent.

As I have argued elsewhere, d'Ailly's prediction of Antichrist's arrival
for 1789 must be seen within the context of his changing views of
the eschatological meaning of the Great Schism (1378–1414). When
he made this prediction, d'Ailly had abandoned his earlier notion
that the division in the church marked the imminent advent of
Antichrist. Instead, on the eve of the Council of Constance, he now
argued that this turmoil could be forestalled by swift human action
(with divine assistance) to heal the Schism and to reform the church
"in head and members." Although the astrological forecast for 1414
was dismal, d'Ailly's prediction of the time of Antichrist in the safely-
distant future gave him hope that the Council would indeed succeed
in its mission.[42] The periodization suggested by the Alfonsine tables
was central to d'Ailly's postponement of the End.

A quarter century after Pierre d'Ailly's death in 1420, his theories
caught the eye of a physician and astrologer working in Louvain
named Jean de Bruges.[43] In 1444, Jean composed a lengthy prognos-

---

(the closest corresponding conjunction there is in ca. 225 B.C.). See Smoller, *History,
Prophecy, and the Stars*, ch. 4.

[41] The other religions or sects are Judaism (Jupiter with Saturn), the Chaldean
religion (Jupiter with Mars), the Egyptian religion (Jupiter with the Sun), Islam
(Jupiter with Venus), and Christianity (Jupiter with Mercury). See Smoller, *History,
Prophecy, and the Stars*, p. 62.

[42] Smoller, *History, Prophecy, and the Stars*, esp. ch. 6.

[43] About Jean we know next to nothing. There is a brief mention of Jean in the
late fifteenth-century compilation of Simon de Phares, in Ernest Wickersheimer, ed.,
*Recueil des plus celebres astrologues et quelques hommes doctes faict par Symon de Phares du temps
de Charles VIIIe* (Paris: Champion, 1929), p. 255. (Simon writes that Jean composed
astrological treatises and that some say he predicted the ruin of France by the deaths
of the dukes of Orleans and Burgundy.) See also Lynn Thorndike, *A History of Magic
and Experimental Science*, 8 vols. (New York: Columbia University Press, 1923–58),
4:146–47; Jean-Patrice Boudet, *Lire dans le ciel: La bibliothèque de Simon de Phares, astrologue
du XVe siècle* (Brussels: Centre d'Étude des Manuscrits, 1994), pp. 80–83.

tication about the end of the world.[44] In this treatise, he used astrology as a way to interpret a number of contemporary disasters including the current schism pitting Pope Eugenius IV against the Council of Basel and its appointed antipope. As with Pierre d'Ailly, Jean's work rested upon theories about Saturn-Jupiter conjunctions and the influence of the eighth sphere's trepidational movements. As a practicing astrologer, Jean gave his readers much fuller descriptions of planetary conjunctions and their interpretations than did theologian d'Ailly. He also considerably expanded upon d'Ailly's use of the movement of the eighth sphere for astrological forecasting.

Throughout the first nine of his treatise's twelve chapters, Jean explained earthly events by the pattern of Saturn-Jupiter conjunctions, and he maintained that each roughly 240-year era of history took its character from that of the triplicity in which the two superior planets were then conjoined. Jean attributed a string of current disasters, ranging from papal schism to war in Flanders, to contemporary conjunctions of Saturn and Jupiter in Scorpio and the reigning aquatic triplicity. No conjunction is more injurious to Christendom, asserts Jean, for several reasons. First, Scorpio is a fixed sign and therefore will signify more durable effects.[45] Second, there were many shifts of triplicity happening around his time.[46] Third, one could expect disasters

---

[44] Paris, Bibliothèque Mazarine, MS 3893, fol. 65–99 (the sole Latin MS). There is a Latin incunable edition: *Pronosticum, sive tractatus qui intitulatur de veritate astronomie, a principio mundi usque in ejus finem* (Anvers: T. Martens, before 1503). There is also a French version, existing in two MSS: Paris, Bibliothèque Nationale, MS lat. 7335, fols. 115ra–131ra; Paris, Bibliothèque Ste. Geneviève, MS 2521, fols. 37–57v. See Boudet, *Lire dans le ciel*, pp. 80–81.

[45] Bibliothèque Mazarine, MS 3893, ch. 1, fol. 67v: "Citra famosum enim tocius orbis diluvium singulas coniunctiones magnas saturni videlicet et Jovis cum permutatione triplicitatis volvens et revolvens nullam repperi durabiliorem nullamque maiorem nullam ecclesie catholice magis divisivam nullamque vere religioni nocitivam magis nullam christiani sanguinis magis effusivam nullamque humane compagnie magis corruptivam quam coniunctionem illam magnam quam in presenti triplicitate ad signum scorpionis ter novimus permutata. Primum patet propter signi stabilitatem quia scorpio est signum fixum quare licet tarde inceperit diu durabit eius effectus. . . ." (The effects would be slow to start but would last long, Jean says.) There was a long tradition of negative associations surrounding the sign Scorpio. See Luigi Aurigemma, *Le signe zodiacal du Scorpion dans les traditions occidentales de l'Antiquité gréco-latine à la Renaissance* (Paris: La Haye, 1976).

[46] Bibliothèque Mazarine, MS 3893, ch. 1, fol. 68: "Secundum vero ponitur propter multiplicitatem triplicitatis permutationum nam mirabili modo et quasi miraculoso triplicitas aerea ter ad signum scorpionis fuit permutata quod citra diluvium nequa-quam scitur accidisse . . . quanto coniunctio [cum] permutatio[ne] triplicitatis infortu-nata fuerit pluralior tanto influentia maior et effectus perniciosior quare novitates causabit pessimas et a seculo non auditas." (Jean refers to true, not mean, conjunctions).

because of the nefarious qualities of the sign Scorpio, under which Muhammad was born, and which imparts its malign character to the entire aquatic triplicity.[47] Fourth, when Saturn and Jupiter are joined in Scorpio, benevolent Jupiter has less influence than malevolent Saturn.[48] Astrologically speaking, times were not good in the fifteenth century, according to Jean.

According to Jean, the earthy and watery triplicities, composed of opposite signs, signaled opposite effects for God's people. The earthy triplicity held sway at the times of Abraham; David and the prophets, Christ; and the doctors of the Church and its greatest union and prosperity. (What Jean means by this last period is far from clear; assuming 960 years between successive returns to the earthy triplicity, this would put his fourth period of prosperity anywhere from the tenth through the twelfth centuries. Perhaps he refers to the Gregorian Reform.) Corresponding in mirror fashion to the good times under the earthy triplicity were the events under the sway of the watery signs: the enslavement of Israel in Egypt; the false prophet Nimrod and the Babylonian captivity of the Jews; the rise of Muhammad and the Saracens; and schism in the late medieval church.[49] Since the earthy triplicity had seen the birth of Christ, Jean reasoned, it was only logical to expect the arrival of Antichrist to come under the watery triplicity, and particularly when the conjunction of Saturn and Jupiter was in Pisces, the sign in direct opposition to Virgo, the sign in which Saturn and Jupiter were conjoined (in Jean's reckoning) at the time of Christ's birth.[50] Further, Jean suggested, following Albumasar, that Christianity might not endure beyond 1460 years, the so-called maximum years of the sun (here standing for the Christian religion). If one could find a Saturn-Jupiter conjunction in Pisces around the year 1460, one might reasonably expect to see then the

---

[47] Ibid, fol. 68–68v: "Tertium patet propter nepharium signum stellarum qualitatem. . . . Et Abraham Avenesre in libro coniunctionum dicit quod hec coniunctio cum permutatione triplicitatis in signo scorpionis falsum et [68v] mendacem nasciturum de vilibus gentibus annunciavit machometum." In chapter 2, Jean describes how those stars causing effusions of blood have their influence augmented in Scorpio. The Flood took place under a Saturn-Jupiter conjunction in Scorpio (fol. 72).

[48] Ibid., ch. 3, fol. 70: "Quia ergo in hac coniunctione Saturnus est fortior Jove, effectus eius in mundo magis apperebit."

[49] Ibid., ch. 9, fols. 87–87v.

[50] Ibid., ch. 9, fol. 88: "Et est ratio quia constellationes oppositorum signorum ut dictum est contrariorum sunt effectuum. Si triplicitas ista est 7a inclusive post nativitate christi dum coniunctio pervenerit ad signum piscium erit directe in opposito nativitatis christi que fuit precedente coniunctione saturni et jovis in permutatione triplicitatis in signo Virginis."

preambles to Antichrist's advent.[51] Jean had described just such a conjunction for 1464 in the sixth chapter of his treatise, but had also in the following chapter carried forth his description of conjunctions—all portending bad—to 1544.[52]

From Jean's discussion of Saturn-Jupiter conjunctions, then, it is not clear how long Christians must be tormented waiting for the advent of Antichrist and the end of the world. Like Pierre d'Ailly, Jean found an answer to that question in the Alfonsine tables' description of the eighth sphere's access and recess. Superimposed upon the pattern provided by planetary conjunctions, Jean also periodized history according to the motion of the eighth sphere. That is, he expanded upon Pierre d'Ailly's interpretation of the "standing still" to occur in 1765 by insisting that previous stations of the eighth sphere had also accompanied major shifts in human events. Following the Alfonsine tables, Jean described four stations of the eighth sphere at 1740 years intervals: one at the Creation of the world, another at its renewal by Flood (A.M. 1740), a third at the Exodus (A.M. 3500), and a fourth around the birth of Christ (A.D. 14). This fourth station also signified the destruction of the Jews' kingdom under Titus. Jean noted as well the triplicity in which Saturn and Jupiter conjunctions fell during each of these stations: Creation under the fiery triplicity, the Flood under the aquatic signs, Exodus under the airy triplicity, and the Nativity under the earthy triplicity.[53]

A fifth station would occur, Jean said, in 1765, bringing the world to its 7000th year in completion of the cycle of access and recess,

---

[51] Ch. 9, fol. 88–88v: "Sed quia secta antichristi religioni christiane maxime contraria erit et adversa merito in triplicitate opposita benedicti Christi incarnationis est [88v] antichristi nativitas exspectanda. Si enim a nativitate Chrsiti computetur 1460 anni qui sunt anni sol maiores de quibus loquitur Albumasar numerus ille annorum circa dictam oppositionem in primo piscium ut in precedentibus patuit directe fineretur [?]. Non quod facto numero annorum predictorum circa dictam oppositionem Antichristus statim debeat apparere."

[52] The conjunction for 1464 is described in ch. 6, fol. 80v: "Postea anno [14]64 erit coniunctio Saturni et Jovis in principio piscium et quia.... Jupiter sit ... inferior saturno quare magis videbitur effectus Saturninus, et erit coniunctio ista in summo mercurii dolore et in oppositione ymaginis virginee benedictam incarnationem significantis ut postea dicetur quare [81r] non est spes magna de prosperitate christiane politie quantum ad influentiam celestem tunc temporis exspectanda." Jean discusses conjunctions up to the year 1475 in ch. 6 and those from 1484 to 1544 in ch. 7.

[53] Ibid., ch. 10, fol. 90r: "Et fecit iste circulus in qualibet revolutione quattor stationes equales: duas videlicet longitudinales in quibus longitudo maxima est, latitudo vero nulla; et alias duas latitudinales in quibus latitudo maxima est longitudo vero nulla." The four stations are described at fols. 90v–91r. Although he knows that he is dealing with four periods that should add up to 7000 years, Jean consistently

and accompanied by a return to the fiery triplicity in which the world
was created.[54] The return to the original positions signified to Jean
the greatest of all possible changes, for if each station marked some
great renovation in the world, how much more was to be expected
when the entire circle was completed. And if each change of triplicity
signified great alterations in the world, the return to the original
triplicity—that is, Saturn and Jupiter's conjunction in the first of
Aries—must herald the greatest of changes: either the world's total
renovation or its complete destruction.[55] As had d'Ailly, Jean supplemented his view of the eighteenth century by reference to Saturn-
Jupiter conjunctions. In particular, he noted that the two planets were
to be conjoined in the first of Aries in 1702.[56] Like other late medieval
astrologers, Jean assumed that the greatest of effects on earth would
follow just this so-called greatest conjunction, which served as the
starting point for the cycle of Saturn-Jupiter conjunctions through the
four triplicities. Further, Jean noted that Jupiter's influence would
be weakened by a number of celestial phenomena in the eighteenth
century, increasing the strength of Saturn's baleful influence. Finally,
he reasoned that since a station of the eighth sphere under the watery
triplicity had signalled the world's renovation by the Flood, the coming station under the fiery triplicity would herald a deluge of fire,
which would mean the world's end.[57] Jean was pleased to present

---

gives 1740 years as the period between stations, even when the number is spelled
out. E.g., fol 90v: "In prima statione sequente qui fuit transactis mille septigentis
quadraginta annis. . . ." It would seem that Jean is fudging some here. Since he
follows those authors who place Creation at 5200 years before the birth of Christ,
and he wishes to have three periods precede the station at A.D. 14, he can come
closer to having a station at Creation by making those periods 1740 years than
by the 1750 year-period that would result from an accurate division of 7000 by 4.
(3 × 1740 = 5220)

[54] Ibid., fol. 91r: "Finaliter vero completo septimo millenario ab origine mundi
quod erit anno Christo 1765 erit iterum octave sphere statio et in eadem triplicitate
ignea a qua planete hora creationis mundi moveri primitus increpeantur et faciet
octavus circulus unam revolutionem completam et significabit statio illa renovationem
mundi universalem aut finem eius simpliciter [?] exspectandam."

[55] Ibid.: "Nam si quelibet octave sphere statio et in qualibet triplicitate tantam ut
dictum est alterationem et quasi totalem renovationem fecerit in hac inferiora quanto
magis ergo in statione revolutionale et triplicitate originale mutationes maxime fient
in hoc mundo."

[56] Ibid., ch. 11, fol. 92v: "Insuper coniunctio famosissima Saturni et Jovis in
principio arietis que erit [illegible] anno christi 1702 generales et maiores mundi
alterationes ostendit in terra."

[57] Ibid., fol. 94v: "Videtur ergo probabile cum naturali lumine per presentem
triplicitatem aquatica antichristum et per futuram igneam diluvium per ignem natu-
raliter exspectandum."

astrological speculations in conformity with Christian truth, which expected the world's end in its 7000th year, to be preceded by a series of adversities and turmoils.[58]

Like d'Ailly, however, Jean was not interested simply in the end of the world. He was also concerned to link this vision of the end to his own troubled times, and this he accomplished by analyzing Saturn-Jupiter conjunctions from 1346 down to 1544. Jean held no rosy view of his own or future days. Although the conjunction for 1544 would mark a shift away from the watery triplicity, Jean noted that Jupiter was falling and Saturn rising in that conjunction and that furthermore the conjunctions would then would shift back to the watery triplicity, and then to the "infortunatissima" conjunction in the first of Aries. In short, Jean added, "I see no hope for the prosperity of the whole human polity as regards the celestial infuences to come."[59] Pierre d'Ailly, by contrast, had envisioned a period of reform after the horrors of the Schism in his own days and before the advent of Antichrist in 1789, a view of the End ultimately derived from Joachim of Fiore's interpretation of the apocalypse.[60] In this common late medieval schema, a period of turmoil under a first Antichrist would be followed by a period of peace and consolation for the church on earth. Jean de Bruges offers a far more pessimistic vision of the future from his astrological calculations. There is no upcoming reformation in which to place our hopes, he surmises. On the other hand, he does not abandon his readers to despair entirely. He ends his treatise by urging princes, magnates, prelates and doctors of divine and human science to work for the peace and reformation of the church and Christendom in order not prematurely to bring on that schism that would precede Antichrist's arrival and the church's desolation.[61] Without asserting that the stars necessitate human actions, he reminds his readers that the heavens' influence on

---

[58] Ibid., fol. 94v–95r, citing Daniel on the world's 7000 years; and Matthew 24 on earthquakes, famines, and other turmoils.

[59] Ibid., ch. 7, fol. 84r: "Non video spem ullam de prosperitate tocius humane policie quantum ad influenciam celestem in posterum exspectandam."

[60] Smoller, *History, Prophecy, and the Stars*, pp. 103–112.

[61] Bibliothèque Mazarine, MS 3893, ch. 12, fol. 95v: "Eya, ergo vos principes et magnates videte quomodo justus judex deus gloriosus nos terret . . . diversis miseriis ut propinquum eius iudicium timeamus. . . . Rogate, queso, que ad pacem sunt Ihrusalem et ecclesiam. Iam dolentem comfortate; iam errantem reformate; iam divisam reintegrate naufragantem ad portum reducite. Ne fiat illud magnum scisma quod preambulum erit antichristo. In cuius adventu de ecclesia verificabitur illud Jheramie prophete: Omnes porte eius destructe. . . ."

the passions is so great that the better part of Christendom will be in danger of falling to Antichrist—unless God provides a remedy.[62]

As did Pierre d'Ailly, Jean de Bruges found in the Alfonsine tables' description of the eighth sphere's access and recess an acceptable way to conjecture about the world's end. Because they both relied on the Alfonsine figures, both authors predicted that the last days were some centuries distant from their own times. Both men lived in a time of crisis in which apocalyptic expectations ran deep, yet neither foresaw the reign of Antichrist in their own lifetimes. For d'Ailly, writing in the months before the Council of Constance, his astrological prediction of Antichrist's advent offered hope that the Council might indeed heal the Schism and reform the church (although he warned that, should the Council fail, surely Antichrist would arrive soon).[63] Jean de Bruges offered no such hope to his readers, but rather assumed that for some time Christians had suffered under a set of astrologically-driven preambles to Antichrist's advent. A better theologian, though less competent astrologer, than Jean, d'Ailly avoided setting the world's duration at 6000, 6500, or even 7000 years. As venerable an authority as Augustine had reproved the notion that the world's six ages were to be understood as literal millennia.[64] On the other hand, the astrologer Jean offered a much more complex and sophisticated reading of Saturn-Jupiter conjunctions than did d'Ailly. Nonetheless, in expanding upon d'Ailly's use of the Alfonsine figures for the eighth sphere, Jean ended up presenting a simplistic and suspiciously symmetrical periodization of world history in which the twin patterns of Saturn-Jupiter conjunctions and stations of the eighth sphere showed a remarkable synchronicity. If he was aware that the Alfonsine tables also described a slower precessional motion for the fixed stars and apogees, Jean kept silent about that fact. In sum, Jean's treatise demonstrated what could happen when one alert

---

[62] Ibid., fol. 98: "Alioquin dormite iam et requiescite. Ecce appropinquabit qui vos tradet in manus peccatorum, alter pharoa vel machometus filius perditionis perfidissimus antichristus. Nam si virtus influentialis astrorum tantam in passionibus observaverit dispositionem et obedientiam, procul dubio magna pars christianitatis erit in periculo subversionis et obprobrium sempiterni, nisi ille solus sapiens providere [remedium] velit qui vere dominatur astris deus gloriosus in secula benedictus." This is an oblique reference to Pierre d'Ailly's *Concordantia astronomie cum hystorica narratione*, ch. 59 {"Sed deus est ille vere sapiens qui solus dominatur astris, cuius singulari auxilio huic malo conveniens poterit adhiberi remedium." (fol. [d7v])}.

[63] See Smoller, *History, Prophecy, and the Stars*, pp. 102–08, 110.

[64] In the *City of God*, 20:7–9.

to apocalyptic speculations encountered the numerologically charged periods embedded in the Alfonsine tables' descriptions of the eighth sphere. Now fully detached from the tainted doctrine of the Great Year, the eighth sphere's period of access and recess showed willing astrologers how God's plans for the world's end were carefully written in the stars.

Nearly a century later, in 1531, the Dijon astrologer Pierre Turrel took up the ideas of Pierre d'Ailly and Jean de Bruges in a treatise entitled *Le Periode, cest a dire, la fin du monde.*[65] Turrel, a native of Autun, had won the praise of contemporaries not just for his astrological skill, but for his learning in a number of areas. In 1517 his talents earned him the position of principal of the municipal school in Dijon. In the 1520s he had published an edition, with commentaries, of the introductory textbook on astrology by Alchabitius, a *Computus*, and a number of astrological prognostications and almanacs. His astrological and eschatological pursuits seem to have gotten him into trouble with the Dijon town council, however, for they expressed concern that he was neglecting his pupils, dabbling in diabolical arts, and speaking publicly about theological matters on which he was not qualified to pronounce. Turrel nonetheless kept his job, perhaps until the end of his life, which may have come in 1531.[66]

Turrel's 1531 treatise reflects not so much his personal difficulties in the previous years as his sense that he was living in a time of severe crisis.[67] Stunned by the advance of Lutherans in Germany

---

[65] Pierre Turrel, *Le Periode, cest a dire, la fin du monde, Concernant la disposition des chouses terrestres, par la vertu et influence des corps celestes, Compose par feu Maitre Pierre Turrel, Philosophe et Astrologue, Recteur des escoles de Dijon* (Lyon?: s.n., ca. 1550). According to the author's note on fol. XXXI, the French text is a translation of a Latin treatise composed in the monastery "des Trois Valées." Whether that Latin work was Turrel's or another's is not clear. Thorndike thinks a MS of the Latin version of Turrel's treatise exists, but gives no specific reference to that MS (*History of Magic and Experimental Science*, 5:310).

[66] Following Thorndike, *History of Magic and Experimental Science*, 5:307–12, and Joseph Garnier, *Chartes de communes et d'affranchissements en bourgogne*, 4 vols. (Dijon: Darantière et Jobard, 1908), 4:698–702 (Thorndike's source).

[67] He may have replied obliquely to the attacks on his studies, however. In the prologue, after defending astrology (as conjecture and not as infallible predictions), and noting that Pierre d'Ailly had called it a "natural theology," Turrel made mention of "Plutonic dogs" who sought to denigrate the science. (fol. Vv): "Parquoi ceste science Dastronomie plus que aultres sciences naturelles, doibt estre bien admirable, exaltee, et de louange à toutes proferee. Laquelle ledict Cardinal de Cambray [Pierre d'Ailly] theologien appelle theologie naturelle. Toutes fois plusieurs cheins plutoniques solicitez et stimulez des diables envieulx de nature humaine, la diffament, la mettent en pieces et de toute leur puissance la denigrent, pource que point ne saroient

and Turks abroad, he calculated the time of the world's end using
the 7000-year period of access and recess of the eighth sphere, 354
year and 4 month cycles of planetary rule taken from the Jewish
astrologer Abraham ibn Ezra, the schema of triplicities indicated by
the pattern of Saturn-Jupiter conjunctions, and the completion of
ten revolutions of Saturn every 300 years.[68] Turrel's stations of the
eighth sphere, derived from a creation date of 5199 B.C., pointed to
the completion of the 7000-year cycle in A.D. 1801, or as he put it,
in 270 years from the present.[69] Like Jean de Bruges (on whom he
relied, as well as on d'Ailly, Albumasar, and Abraham ibn Ezra),
Turrel associated the stations of the eighth sphere with the reigning
triplicities generated by Saturn-Jupiter conjunctions. As did Jean, he
placed stations at the Flood, Exodus, and around the time of Christ,
and Turrel also associated this latter station with the Jews' losses
under Vespasian and Titus.[70] Like Jean de Bruges, he noted that the
subsequent station would complete the circle of access and recess
and would be accompanied by a return to the fiery triplicity in which
Saturn-Jupiter conjunctions fell at Creation. Whether that would signal
a total renewal of the world or its complete destruction was not clear
from that evidence alone, although Turrel followed Jean de Bruges
in noting that near the world's end the heavens would produce many
constellations with destructive, ruinous effects.[71] And in the treatise's

---

lentendre ni acquerir honneur." Turrel's first chapter, however, opens with an extended tirade against the Jews, then against "cy Lutheriens, et malheureux Taborites
qui prophanes les écclises et temples de Iesuchrist." (fol. IX).

[68] In his first, second, third, and fourth chapters, respectively. The fifth chapter
explores a number of eclipses to take place in the years 1485–1539.

[69] Turrel, *La Periode*, fol. XIIIv.

[70] Ibid., fol. IIII: ". . . environ la fin de la primiere [station], vint le deluge universel.
A la secunde la perdition des Egiptiens en la mer erithree quon appelle Rouge. A
la troisieme la perdition des Iuifz faicte par Vaspasien et Titus son filz empereur des
Romains." The stations are discussed more fully at fol. XII–XIII, where Turrel
links the station in the world's 5250th year with the birth of Christ. Turrel explicitly
states (fol. XII) that there are 1550 years between stations: "En suivant la doctrine
des Theorists qui le mouvement du firmament ont excogoter et entendu lequel se
fict en sept mil ans quil ya quatre stations esgalles dont chascune des quatre le
mesurent par lespace de mil cinq cens cinquante ans." But the dates he gives for
these stations make it clear that he is working with a figure of 1750 years between
stations. Again, like Jean de Bruges and Pierre d'Ailly, Turrel ignored the Alfonsine
tables' description of the eighth sphere's slower precessional motion.

[71] Ibid., fol. XIII: "[O]u le monde renouvellera ou du tout sera terminez. Ce que
nous monstre et enseigne experience, la mere de toutes sciences. Car tout ainsi que
au commancement du monde les constellations ont estez multiplicatives et augmen-
tatives de nature et humaine propagation ainsi en sa declination et pres de sa der-
niere fin sera des constellations destructives et ruineuse en toutes facon." Turrel is
following the line of reasoning in Jean de Bruges, ch. 10, fol. 91v.

prologue, he stated without qualification that the final station would signal "the perdition of the entire world."[72]

To add more certainty to his conjecture, Turrel corroborated his prediction by considering other theories, presumably looking for signs of those malign conjunctions that would herald the world's end. First, he looked to the cycles generated by the rule of each planet, with an accompanying angel, for 354 years and 4 months (a theory he reports he had taken from Abraham ibn Ezra). Here, too, the heavens pointed to important periods in world history and—another of Turrel's preoccupations—the history of the Burgundians. After the first cycle of seven planets' rule, according to Turrel, the Flood occurred. After the second, Jesus was born. (And, he notes, the Burgundians were converted to Christianity under the same rulership of Saturn and Caphiel.)[73] The completion of a third cycle would take place in the 7440th year of the world, and Turrel hinted that the world would not endure to see that cycle's end.[74] As he wrote, Turrel insisted, there were only three years and four months remaining to Mars's rule before the Moon would begin its turn.[75] Whether the upcoming reign of the Moon would signify a time of justice and peace or a period of inconstancy and monsters, Turrel left to "more learned" astrologers.[76] He did predict, with evident pleasure, that the end of Mars's reign meant bad news for the Germans, whom Turrel associated with both Mars and malign Scorpio, Mars's domicile. That

---

[72] Ibid., fol. IIII: "A la quatriesme [station], la pardition de tout le monde."

[73] Ibid., fol. XVIv: "Saturne meine le premier, pource que la premiere heure du iour ou cessa Dieu à discipliner, et endoctriner Adam, regna Saturne, apers [sic] Saturne, mena Venus autant de ans et de mois, apres Iupiter, puis mercure, puis Mars, apres la Lune, puis le Soleil. Apres lequel retourna Saturne et lors environ ce gouvernment vint le grand deluge." And fol. XVIII [XVII]v: "Apres de rechief regna Saturne, seul cinq mille trois cens quinze ans seullement [i.e., until the 5315th year of the world]. Et soubz ceste menee nostre seigneur Iesuchrist fut naez."

[74] Ibid., fol. XVIII: "Le Soleil sept mille quatre cens [quarante] ans seulement [i.e., until the world's 7440th year]. De rechief pour la quatriesme foys regnera Saturne, se le monde ne prent sa fin et sa derriere Periode."

[75] Ibid., fol. XVIII: "Par les chouses devant dictes appart clerement que ceste annee icy mil cinq cens trente et ung selon laquel de bergoignes et aultres ne restent de la menee de Mars que trois ans quatre moys."

[76] Ibid., fol. XVIII [bis] v ("Puis que le regne de la Lune sera tantost venu, comme ia est dict ce seroit à entendre en ce temps viendra habundance de paix, iusques au royaulme dela Lune [i.e., the Roman empire] exclusivement, mais cela ie laisse discuter aux plus doctes.") and XIXv ("Mais venons à laduction et gouvernement de la Lune, quest bien prouchaine soubz laquelle viendront chouses de grande merveilles inaudites et non accoustumees, car elle avec le signe de Libra . . . signifiera aussi entre les hommes merveilleuse, malheur et inconstance diversite, instabilite, fraction de foy, violence, diffamete. Car il naistra moult de monstres.")

heresies had arisen in Germany was only one sign that the end of its ascendancy was near.[77] And although he discounted the theory, Turrel devoted considerable space to the theory that a final sect of Antichrist would be signified by the conjunction of Jupiter and the Moon.[78] To determine whether Antichrist would come under the Moon's upcoming reign, one would have to look to other astrological signs.

To that end, Turrel also looked to the periods defined by Saturn-Jupiter conjunctions, and, like Jean de Bruges, he saw little reason for hope from the current aquatic triplicity. The watery signs signified victories for southern regions, and Turrel anticipated that the Turks would prosper under the current triplicity, but would not keep their gains thereafter.[79] He noted that some maintained that Antichrist would be born under the watery signs and, again like Jean, drew his readers' attention to the malign conjunction of Saturn and Jupiter in Scorpio in 1544.[80] When, in 111 years, the conjunctions should shift to the fiery triplicity, Turrel was equally pessimistic: malign Saturn would be at the height of its influence, and Jupiter at the nadir.[81] Further, under that triplicity would occur that most significant conjunction, the joining of Saturn and Jupiter in the beginning of Aries in 1702. Because other inauspicious astrological phenomena of the same year served to strengthen Mars's malign power and because this important conjunction would occur around the same time as the eighth sphere's completion of its 7000-year cycle, Turrel concluded that this conjunction would have to point to the world's destruction, and not its renewal. "It is not likely," he wrote, "that the world will be renewed afresh, either by celestial influences or by

---

[77] Ibid., fol. XVIII–XIX.

[78] Ibid., fol. XIXv–XXv.

[79] Ibid., fol. XXI: "Item comme afferme Albumasar soubz la triplicite aquatique fut le Roiaulme de Ethiope et de Pharaon en grand vigueur et bruyt en renommee. Pource quilz sont meridionaulx. Dictes en autant du present Turc tyrant de Asie et Grece qui nous est meridional lan mil cinq cent trente et ung. Et croies que se quil à acquis du couste de midy, il ne le gardera pas."

[80] Ibid., fol. XXI and XXIv: "Helas environs les ans nostre Seigneur mil cinq cens quarante quatre de rechief se applicqueront aux maulxditz signe du faulx Escorpion les superierues planettes de quoy apres parlerons. . . . Finabelment veullent dire aulcuns que lantechrist naistra soubz la triplicite Aquatique qui signifie tant vrais que faulx prophetes." See also fol. XXII [XXVI].

[81] Ibid., fol. XXIII: "Car ceste presente triplicite aquatique termine de quoy nous reste mil cinq cens trante un encoires cent et unze viendra la triplicite du feu, et lors se conjoindront Saturne et Iupiter au Sagittaire signe de feu, et lors le pere de courruption Saturne au signe de feu sera en son auge hause et exalte et Iupiter cheut en son detriment."

God's power, but rather brought to an end and destroyed."[82] Following Jean de Bruges, Turrel predicted that the world's destruction would come in a rain of fire, presided over by the fiery triplicity. Antichrist would arrive either then, or under the current watery triplicity.[83]

To cap his predictions, Turrel noted the importance of Saturn's completion of ten revolutions, following, with either confusion or deliberate changes, Pierre d'Ailly's prediction for 1789.[84] For good measure he recited a variety of theological opinions about Antichrist (including a list of eight preambles to Antichrist according to pseudo-Methodius, which he also drew from d'Ailly's treatise). Turrel equated the Ottoman Turks with pseudo-Methodius's Ishmaelite enemies of the final days, but followed pseudo-Methodius in describing their defeat at the hands of a last Roman emperor.[85] This is the only glimmer

---

[82] Ibid., fol. XXIIIv–XXIIII: "Il me semble advis que faille conceder la ruine totalle du monde, veu que lors nature sera totallement debissee et debilitee.... Il nest vraysemblable, ne par coelestes influences, ne par la puissance de Dieu: que le monde de rechief soit renouvvelle, mais termine, et destruict." Turrel asserts that God implanted signs of the world's destruction in the heavenly movements. Fol. XXIIII: "Ainsi que dict Albert: car [Dieu] à voullu signer par les corps coelestes que le monde durera iusques au terme qui luy à impose: car ainsi par son commandement le mouvement du monde a commance."

[83] Ibid., fol. XXIIIIv: "Item, si la maxime coniunction au signe aquatique infortune à deluge, signifie comme tesmoingnent tous Astrologues quand plustost la maxime coniunction au signe de feu tres infortunee avec la revolution accomplie de laltitude firmament ne sera accomplie en amenant le deluge de feu de ceste Cremation du monde universelle." And fol. XXI [XXV]: "Nest vraysemblable de pouvoir à icelle divine providence repugner, ny resister, il semble doncques probable en lumiere naturelle, que y fault attendre Lantechrist si ia nest venu par linfluence de la triplicite aquatique et naturellement le deluge de feu par la triplicite ignique: et cecy semble affermer et conceder le Cardinal de Aliaco...."

[84] Ibid., fol. XXVv: "Parlons de la huitiesme maxime, et merveilleuse coniunction que les Astrologues disent estre faicte environ les ans de nostre Seigneur mil sept cens octante et neuf, avec dix revolutions Saturnelles: et oultre environ vingtcinq ans apres, sera la quatriesme, et dernier station de laltitudinaire firmmament, toutes ses chouses considerees et calculees concluent les Astrologues que si le monde iusques la dure, quest à Dieu tant cougneu des tresgrandes et admirables mutations, et altercations seront au monde...." He misreads d'Ailly in placing the Saturn-Jupiter conjunction in 1789 and then in placing the eighth sphere's station around 25 years later, i.e., ca. 1814. The misreading may be deliberate in order to put d'Ailly's station closer to Turrel's final station in 1801, rather than d'Ailly's 1765. The rest of the passage follows closely d'Ailly's *Concordantia astronomie cum hystorica narratione*, chs. 60 and 61.

[85] This treatise is the earliest surviving witness to the Last World Emperor legend that became such a potent part of medieval eschatology. The text is edited in Ernst Sackur, *Sibyllinische Texte und Forschungen. Pseudomethodius, Adso und die Tiburtinische Sibylle* (Halle: Niemeyer, 1898). Turrel follows the summary in d'Ailly, *Concordantia astronomie cum hystorie narratione*, ch. 63.

of hope in a treatise full of gloom and dire warnings, and Turrel simply records this prediction without comment. How it squares with the information he gathered from the stars is not clear, unless in the Turks' defeat under a Last World Emperor we are to read the possible Turkish losses Turrel foresaw with the passing of the aquatic triplicity.

Like the works of Pierre d'Ailly and Jean de Bruges, Pierre Turrel's treatise bears ample evidence of an attempt to relate his own times to a larger, more cosmic history. His pages are peppered with angry outbursts against Taborites, Lutherans (whom he dubs "German Scorpionists"), and Jews. To add to the sense of seige he predicts victories to the Turks. That false prophets have arisen in his days and will continue in strength Turrel attributes to the current aquatic triplicity and to the upcoming conjunction of Saturn and Jupiter in Scorpio in 1544. With obvious influence of the contemporary witch fascination, he attributes the birth of false prophets to the work of incubi and succubi released under Saturn-Jupiter conjunctions in Cancer or Capricorn. Muhammad's birth is so explained, as will be the birth of Antichrist.[86] Such a conjunction had occurred, according to Turrel, in 1504, and one could anticipate the appearance on the scene of its monstrous offspring around 1533.[87] Turrel's final chapter afforded a closer look at the several years ahead, examining eclipses to take place from 1532 through 1539. For the most part his predictions were grim: wars, plagues, and heresies. Like Jean de Bruges, he ended his treatise with an exhortation to princes to protect their mother church and God from the attacks of heretics.[88]

Through the works of Pierre d'Ailly, Jean de Bruges, and Pierre Turrel, we can trace the development of one tradition of astrological

---

[86] Turrel, fol. XXII: "Disent apres les Philosophes que soubz la coleure du tropiq quand il si faict une grande coniunction de Saturne, et Iupiter, de Cancer, ou Capricorne, il ya des maulvais esperits nommes succubes et incubes et president aux songes des hommes: et pourtent les semences humaines gettes par pollutions, aux ventres des femmes, au moien de quoi se engendrent de merueilleux hommes changeans les loix et controuvant nouvelles sectes: Ainsi fut engendre mahommet, merlin. Aussi sera lantechrist."

[87] Ibid, fol. XXIIv: "Il est à suspitionner quil en fut engendre lan mil cinq cens et quatre: car les planettes furent ioinctes soubz le solstice Estival au signe de Cancer montant sur lorison du signe de Libra, quest signe daer signifiant les prophetes. Et ce doibt monstrer ledict engendre environ son eage de trante ans que sera deans deux ou trois ans dicy."

[88] Ibid., fol. XXXI: "Donc, O princes et princesses, seigneurs, et dames, secoures à vostre mere tresdolente abiecte, et desolee, et ne souffres point que ses abhominables heretiques, et infideles, soillent, et broyllent celluy qui vous a faict à sa semblance."

calculation of the apocalypse. These calculators took as one of their bases the Alfonsine tables' description of the eighth sphere's movement. Their writings demonstrate how vital astrological predictions had become to apocalyptic speculations in the later Middle Ages. By the mid-sixteenth century and on through the seventeenth century, such prognostications—widely circulated in cheap printed forms—would bolster and fuel religious warfare and political revolution as partisans saw themselves engaged in a war of God's saints against the forces of Antichrist.[89] But before their predictions could be taken seriously, astrologers had to address the lingering charges of fatalism embodied in Bishop Stephen Tempier's condemnations of astrological propositions in 1277. That fatalism was epitomized by the doctrine of the Great Year, after which all the stars would return to the same places and all the same events would recur on earth. To rescue the Great Year by suggesting that the 36,000-year period instead pointed to the world's end left a ludicrously long span of years after Jesus's birth and the inauguration of the world's sixth and final age. What eventually attracted astrologically-minded apocalyptic thinkers to the Alfonsine tables was the possibility of reading the end of the world in a celestial period that was consonant with Christian tradition: the 7000-year period of the fixed stars' access and recess.

The practice began cautiosly enough. Pierre d'Ailly mentioned only one station of the eighth sphere, that in 1765. He did not even tell his readers that the previous station had coincided roughly with the birth of Christ. To d'Ailly, any station signified great change; to suggest that this one pointed to Antichrist's birth he had to underscore its near coincidence with a greatest conjunction of Saturn and Jupiter and the completion of ten of Saturn's orbits. Only the theory that there was but one sect left to appear in the world convinced

---

[89] See, especially, Denis Crouzet, *Les guerriers de Dieu: La violence au temps des troubles de religion, vers 1525–vers 1610*, 2 vols. (Seyssel: Champ Vallon, 1990), 1:103–53; Patrick Curry, *Prophecy and Power: Astrology in Early Modern England* (Cambridge: Polity Press, 1989); and Bernard Capp, *English Almanacs, 1500–1800: Astrology and the Popular Press* (Ithaca, NY: Cornell University Press, 1979). Cf. Robin Bruce Barnes, *Prophecy and Gnosis: Apocalypticism in the Wake of the Lutheran Reformation* (Stanford, CA: Stanford University Press, 1988), pp. 141–81 (Lutheran astrological apocalypticism encouraged Stoic perseverance and calls to repentance); and Ottavia Niccoli, *Prophecy and People in Renaissance Italy*, trans. Lydia G. Cochrane (Princeton, NJ: Princeton University Press, 1990) (astrological predictions for a flood in 1524 were linked to fears of Lutherans and the dismantling of the Church, but popular culture was suspicious of astrology).

d'Ailly that this series of celestial phenomena might indeed point to Antichrist's advent. D'Ailly was a theologian by training. He had spent pages justifying astrology against its critics, and his prognostication for 1789 demonstrated a prudent restraint and cautiousness. For astrologers (and amateur apocalypticists) Jean de Bruges and Pierre Turrel writing in d'Ailly's wake, the station in the eighteenth century was no longer just a station of the eighth sphere; it marked the completion of the entire 7000-year cycle. And that 7000-year cycle, as both authors claimed, had begun at Creation. For these two astrologers, the question was not so much what major change to expect in the eighteenth century, but rather whether after 7000 years the world would be renewed or destroyed. To answer that question they, like d'Ailly, turned to a number of other astrological theories. They predicted thereby the end of the world at the eighth sphere's station—and not Antichrist's arrival, as had d'Ailly. It was a subtle, but important, shift. By postponing Antichrist's advent until the eighteenth century, Pierre d'Ailly could offer some hope that the church would weather the crisis of Schism and go on to see a period of reform and peace. By tying the eighth sphere's station to the End, rather than to Antichrist's appearance, Jean de Bruges and Pierre Turrel left open the possibility that the fiend could arrive even centuries earlier: in their own times. Hence, their more pessimistic visions. It was precisely this possibility that Antichrist could be among us at any moment that fueled apocalyptic fervor and religious strife in the sixteenth century.

The irony in the story of these apocalyptic calculations is that in popularizing the Alfonsine figure, they distorted the Alfonsine tables' careful consideration of the fixed stars' and apogees' movement. The tables' innovation, after all, had been to resolve the competition between theories of precession and trepidation by adopting both movements for the eighth sphere. In so doing, the tables' compilers had endowed those two motions with periods that were deeply numerologically satisfying (49,000 and 7000 years). And when apocalyptic calculators like Jean de Bruges and Pierre Turrel did seize upon the smaller of these periods as the basis for their work, they did so precisely because the 7000-year period of trepidation, with its four sub-periods, could mesh so perfectly with a Christian tradition that saw all of history unfolding in a week of millennia. But their embrace of the Alfonsine tables' 7000-year period for access and recess and their bold assertions that its completion marked a return of all the heavenly bodies to their original positions meant that they had to ignore the inconvenient fact of the slower precessional movement. To consider this second motion of the eighth sphere would mean admitting that after 7000 years the stars did not, in fact, come back to their original configuration at Creation. It was as if God had neglected to close an important loop. Hence Pierre d'Ailly, Jean de Bruges, and Pierre Turrel all passed over the 49,000-year Alfonsine period for precession in silence, as if the tables allowed only for a single trepidational movement of the eighth sphere. Thus, the Alfonsine tables' great triumph among astrological predictions of the apocalypse signalled a studied forgetting of one of the tables' most important innovations.

SATAN: MAKING A HEAVEN OF HELL,
A HELL OF HEAVEN

Neil Forsyth

The eminent biologist, Richard Lewontin, writes in a recent *New York Review of Books* that however important Aristotelian rhetorical analysis may be for the history of science, it will not tell us why we accept, simply because it is well put, what we otherwise would not believe. His example is Milton's Satan:

> Although every moral and political conviction I have speaks against it, I am nearly driven by Milton's insidious poetry to believe that it is 'Better to reign in Hell than serve in Heaven.' For a pedagogical Aristotle this would be a particularly fine example of an 'antithesis' in the 'periodic' mode dissected in Book III, Part 9: the parallel but opposing structure, 'Better to . . ., than to . . .' the contrast of functionally linked 'reign' and 'serve,' the final antitheses of 'Heaven' and 'Hell,' two words beginning with the same sound but with different endings. For me however it is an almost irresistibly seductive flight of English speech, a Siren music that can be withstood only by lashing myself to the mast of my convictions. Many times more dangerous than 'mere' rhetoric, artful language creates its own logic.[1]

What Lewontin refers to here is one of the oldest and most famous issues among readers of English poetry—the attractiveness of Satan. To this subject Jeffrey Burton Russell has devoted much of his generous and literate attention. For me his work was an important discovery. Because his first book on *The Devil* announced so clearly its theme of "the history of a concept" and continued it so methodically in subsequent volumes, I saw how I could focus my own book, *The Old Enemy*, in a way that did not simply repeat Russell's findings. I could make my Satan, as it were, not so much the embodiment of evil as a character in a narrative, a subject to be approached not so much with the tools of philosophy or theology, or even of the historian of concepts, but with those of literature. I developed my view of Satan through analysis of ancient myths and of theology, which I put in parallel with each other: the key to the analysis was the

---

[1] *New York Review of Books*, March 6, 1997, p. 51.

system of narrative structure adapted from Vladimir Propp's work on *The Morphology of Folktales*.[2] What I want to do here, however, is not to pursue that formalist approach but to take us inside the literary Satan, chiefly Milton's, to show by reading the language carefully what has really been at stake. In that mode, then, we should insist in the example above not on the power of evil, but on the power of literature to make us feel it: thus what we analyze is not the concept contained somehow in the speech but, as Lewontin sees, the speech itself, "almost irresistibly seductive."

We should also recall that this is not evil speaking, but Satan, and that Satan is not *a priori* evil. Indeed in Milton's *Paradise Lost*, Satan is initially simply the Enemy, he who opposes and rebels against the divine decree: he chooses evil later just to be different, since (or rather *if*) God is good:

> If then his Providence
> Out of our evil seek to bring forth good,
> Our labour must be to pervert that end,
> And out of good still to find means of evil. (I.162–5)[3]

Later, when Satan has arrived on Earth and seen the newly created physical world, the sun included, this initial choice of his becomes the famous cry, "Evil be thou my Good" (IV.110). The place to begin then in trying to understand the Miltonic Satan is with the character, not the philosophical abstraction. And the way to investigate the character is through his language, that Siren music.

On this principle let us explore a little more fully the language in which Satan expresses these choices. The second passage quoted just

---

[2] Neil Forsyth, *The Old Enemy: Satan and the Combat Myth* (Princeton, 1987): I showed that it was mainly the ancient figure of the satan, the enemy, who gave Christianity (though not Judaism) that mythological cast which has been so much at issue in recent theology. I was thinking especially of the "demythologizing" tradition initiated by the German theologian Rudolf Bultmann, an associate of Heidegger's, but also of a book that a few years ago disturbed the much quieter waters of English theology, *The Myth of God Incarnate*, ed. John Hick (London: SCM Press, 1977). And if it is Satan who most obviously shows Christianity as myth—not in any pejorative sense, but simply because myths are the kinds of stories in which we believe, then it is also Satan who makes the link to literature, since myths, from Aristotle to the present, have been seen as a category of literature. Myths are narratives, and Christianity, particularly when seen from the satanic perspective, was seen to be narrative too. Milton, I suggest, was an accurate reader of the Christian tradition when he put Satan and his war with Christ so close to the center of the major Christian poem of our culture: this follows from the role of Satan in the New Testament.

[3] Here and in subsequent quotations, *Paradise Lost* is cited from the edition by Roy Flannagan (New York: Macmillan, 1993).

now, "Evil be thou my Good,"[4] is part of the great speech of self-exploration and self-accusation that Satan makes on Mt. Niphates, once he has landed on the new Earth. He recognizes that it was Pride and worse Ambition which threw him down, that he had no good reason to rebel, he acknowledges that he fell of his own free will, and discovers that Hell is not the place he just left behind but his own state of mind.

> Me miserable! which way shall I fly
> Infinite wrath, and infinite despaire?
> Which way I flie is Hell; myself am Hell;
> And in the lowest deep a lower deep
> Still threatning to devour me opens wide,
> To which the Hell I suffer seems a Heav'n.
> O then at last relent: is there no place
> Left for Repentance, none for Pardon left?
> None left but by submission; and that word
> Disdain forbids me, and my dread of shame. (IV.73–82)

Again there is that play with the words that "begin with the same sound" but have such "different endings"—and we realize this rhetorical fact is not "merely rhetorical": the ending is not only in the sound, and we begin to suspect that Milton is exploiting the shape of these sounds for the shape of his narrative. What is it then, that accounts for the different endings, in Hell or in Heaven? We shall return to this question.

Satan now urges himself to relent, only to discover how true is what he just said, "myself am Hell," for in addressing himself in this dialogue of one, he is addressing Hell, and Hell is defined by damnation, by the inability to repent. This speech registers what it would feel like to be damned. "For never can true reconcilement grow Where wounds of deadly hate have pierced so deep," and the word "deep" again picks up what was initially a physical measure of distance from God's Heaven and turns it into an inner state.

But can this be right? Is this what Milton does, to equate the inner depth of the modern self with Hell? It seems so. Before the Fall (which draws Adam and Eve also into his way of being), Satan is the only character in the poem who soliloquizes, and who thus

---

[4] "Good" here shifts around between "righteousness" and "benefit" at least, and is defined only by its opposite. These supposedly Platonic absolutes were already reduced in a famous passage in Milton's *Areopagitica* to "twins" that come into the world "cleaving together" and are only with great difficulty, like mixed beans, sorted asunder.

has that depth we have come to expect in literature, at least since
Faustus, or since Hamlet claimed to have "that within which passeth
show."[5] Certainly it was this, more even than his heroic defiance of
God, which led eighteenth century critics like Addison to declare
themselves for his "high superior nature." They thus came into conflict
with those like Johnson who insisted that Satan's speeches were "big
with absurdity."[6] Milton's Satan is also the ancestor of all those
characters in Romantic literature, from Byron's Cains or Manfreds
and Mary Shelley's nameless monster to Dostoevsky's underground
man who articulate this negative state and make it their *raison d'être*.[7]

The Romantic poets admired Milton's Satan because he is so
resolute in his determination to explore this dangerous consciousness,
but also perhaps because he is the perfect image, extended and expanded from Marlowe, of what is genuinely Faustian about the risk
the Renaissance tried to take within its Christian humanist context.
"Alone and without guide, half-lost" (II.975), Satan nonetheless

> Springs upward like a Pyramid of fire
> Into the wilde expanse, and through the shock
> Of fighting Elements, on all sides round
> Environ'd wins his way; harder beset
> And more endanger'd, then when Argo pass'd
> Through Bosporus betwixt the jostling Rocks:
> Or when Ulysses on the Larbord shunned
> Charybdis, and by th'other whirlpool steard. (II.1013–20)

---

[5] The fullest case for the tragic hero (Faustus, Macbeth, Beatrice-Joanna, Ferdinand)
as a precursor of Satan is made in Dame Helen Gardner, "Milton's Satan and the
Theme of Damnation in Elizabethan Tragedy," *English Studies*, N.S. I, 1948, 46–66,
reprinted in her *A Reading of Paradise Lost* (Oxford: Clarendon Press, 1965), pp. 99–
120. See also O.B. Hardison, Jr. "In Medias Res in Paradise Lost," *Milton Studies*
XVII, ed. James D. Simmonds (Pittsburgh: University of Pittsburgh Press, 1983),
27–41. Closer to the point made here are John Carey, "Milton's Satan" in Dennis
Danielson, ed. *The Cambridge Companion to Milton* (Cambridge University Press, 1989),
pp. 131–46, and Catherine Belsey, *John Milton: Language, Gender, Power* (Oxford: Basil
Blackwell, 1988), pp. 85–91.
[6] Joseph Addison, *Critical Essays from the Spectator*, ed. Donald F. Bond (Oxford:
Oxford University Press, 1970), pp. 110–11; Arthur E. Barker, "'And On His Crest
Sat Horror': Eighteenth-Century Interpretations of Milton's Sublime and his Satan,"
University of Toronto Quarterly 11 (1942), 421–36. The idea that Satan is the true hero
of the epic goes back to Dryden (though he was using "hero" in the non-heroic
sense) and was commonplace in France as well as England during the period: see
Roger Sharrock, "Godwin on Milton's Satan," *Notes and Queries*, New Series 9 (1962),
pp. 463–5.
[7] Reviewed by J.B. Russell in *Mephistopheles* (Ethic: Corneal University Press, 1986),
pp. 168–250.

He strikes out into new areas of space and time, into a sea that no-one has ever crossed before (like Jason or Odysseus, but also like Vasco da Gama or Columbus), into studies of depth perspective in art and in scientific drawing (Leonardo), into a new church without the sanctions of Rome and priesthood and tradition (Luther), into the strange world revealed within the telescopic mirrors (Galileo), into the unknown region of the dreaming and reflecting self (Descartes), into the politics of a republic beyond the supposedly divine right of kings (Macchiavelli, Winstanley), into poetic freedom and indeterminacy (Milton on his "flying steed unrein'd", VII.17)[8]—all beyond the point where he has any secure place to anchor, and where the space may be endless, the depth bottomless. It is the association of all this with Hell (and here with Chaos), with what is Godless or forbidden or beyond redemption, that made the Miltonic images exemplary of a period and a whole cultural shift.[9]

Milton makes his Satan discover/invent this modern state of subjectivity through becoming a subject. He is a "subject" in our contemporary theoretical sense (the "humanist subject"), and certainly his troubled "I" is prominent in the poem. But he is a "subject" also in the more literal, root sense of the term (*sub iectus*, thrown under): he discovers at the moment of his rebellion just what it means to be subject to God. Subjection is the origin of his subjectivity. And he doesn't like it at all. The result is that he is thrown out and down and under, into Hell, and it is as he emerges from there that he also emerges into full subjectivity in the Niphates speech, a dramatic soliloquy in the tragic Shakespearean mode.[10] He explores himself, and finds he is exploring what it means to be in Hell, down and under. God and Heaven are what is high and unitary, while "depth"

---

[8] Stevie Davis, *Milton* (Hemel Hempstead: Harvester Wheatsheaf, 1991) p. 98, well takes this as the image of "a power not susceptible of perfect conscious control; the instability of language available to the aberrant fallen consciousness, with its rich capacity for fabrication and fanciful invention, makes every act of writing potentially fallacious."

[9] Milton, for example, uses early in the poem the widespread folktale or seamen's yarn of the Sinbad-like figure who drops anchor on what he thinks is an island, only to find it is "that Sea-beast Leviathan." This is a simile for Satan "chain'd on the burning lake" at I.200–210, but we do not find out what happened to the sailor.

[10] According to Milton's nephew, Edward Phillips, this passage was written "several years before the poem was begun," when Milton was still intending to write a tragedy called "Adam Unparadised." These lines were "designed for the very beginning of the said tragedy," Helen Darbishire, ed. *The Early Lives of Milton* (Oxford: Oxford University Press, 1932), pp. 72–3.

is that "profoundest Hell," and himself. The oppositional war with God continues in these new terms, and this depth is now not only his refuge but the site of the battle: he appeals to Eve's own inner image of herself, and when he succeeds, Adam and Eve join him in this newly invented and Hellish interiority.

The doubleness of this Satan character should now be obvious: at this very moment in the poem, when he is from the theological point of view admitting that God was right, he shows himself to embody that subjectivity, those hidden depths, that are the source of his appeal to the reader, and that God lacks. God may be right, and Satan seems to say so, but the reader has, or believes himself to have, an inner self like Satan's, and experiences the split self as Satan does. God may be right, but it is Satan with whom we sympathize. Never mind that the moral hierarchy of the poem is thereby seriously distorted.

Consider further a wonderful and famous moment later in the poem where Satan is looking for Eve, hoping to find her separate from her husband, and suddenly comes upon her, alone. The moment can be read from both pro- and anti-Satan points of view, and is charged with the ambivalence of the poem. So smitten is he with Eve's beauty that

> That space the Evil one abstracted stood
> From his own evil, and for the time remain
> Stupidly good, of enmity disarm'd,
> Of guile, of hate, of envie, of revenge. (IX.464–6)

The apparent implication is that Satan's nature is still drawn to love but that his will is what drives him to revenge. For a brief moment his evil separates off, is no longer a quality of himself.[11] As he stands there, he "recollects" himself, and launches on yet another self-directed soliloquy, this time addressing his thoughts:

> Thoughts, whither have ye led me, with what sweet
> Compulsion thus transported to forget
> What hither brought us, hate, not love, nor hope
> Of Paradise for Hell. (IX.473–6)

---

[11] For this comment, see Alastair Fowler, in his 1971 Longman edition, ad loc., p. 466. "Stupidly good" is a resonant phrase that has been much commented on, and which reproduces the Satanic ambivalence: what kind of word is "stupidly" here, is it primarily Latin or English, does it qualify mainly Satan, or good, and whose evaluation is it?

Hatred then is what his will tells him to practice, but his other, better, more unreflective self would allow him to love, even to hope he might somehow be admitted to this Paradise, not forced to spy on it like a lonely voyeur. Which way should we read this? His response to Eve is, I think, what we should have had ourselves, male or female: she is "the fairest of her daughters" (see IV.324), and gives delight. Yet Satan, momentarily smitten, does not take the chance to give up his revenge, but insists on it the more in spite of his better nature.[12] The moment is characteristic in evoking both sides of the problem, and not resolving them. Of all the characters in modern literature, it is Milton's Satan who shows us what undecidability or indeterminacy is really like.

Earlier in the poem, Satan has faced a similar moment. As he sees Adam and Eve for the first time, at the close of one of the greatest and most moving descriptions in all literature, he responds instantly and with wonderful immediacy, no hidden smirk or hypocrisy here:

> O Hell! what doe mine eyes with grief behold,
> Into our room of bliss thus high advanc't
> Creatures of other mould, earth-born perhaps,
> Not Spirits, yet to heav'nly Spirits bright
> Little inferior; whom my thoughts pursue
> With wonder, and could love, so lively shines
> In them Divine resemblance, and such grace
> The hand that formd them on thir shape hath pourd. (IV.359–65)

The exclamation is entirely and characteristically modern: "O Hell!", a casual curse—yet this is Satan himself swearing by Hell, addressing it even, and so, once again, addressing himself. But what is most surprising, perhaps, is that he says he could love the human pair.[13] And why? because of their likeness to God, he whom we thought we knew he hated. Not only in the subjectivity, but even in the surprises, the twists of consciousness, Satan is like us.

What prompted Milton to offer us this remarkable image of ourselves, of modernity? Is it that he gives us all this, and then knows he can take it away? We get this gloriously and inescapably sympathetic figure set within the discourse of a narrator who is often warning us off:

---

[12] See Carey, "Milton's Satan," p. 139.

[13] Is there perhaps, as my colleague Margaret Tudeau suggests, an echo of Miranda's response to Ferdinand in *The Tempest* 1.2, or perhaps 5.1.183 ('O brave new world')? If so, the overlapping of the innocent virgin and Satan sets up interesting resonances.

> So spake the Apostate Angel, though in pain,
> Vaunting aloud, but rackt with deep despair. (I.125–6)

is the first of many such warnings. This discrepancy has been thoroughly and even brilliantly analyzed by Stanley Fish,[14] who has disposed of at least the older kinds of objections to the double or contradictory narration by showing how the image of Satan requires it. The reader is constantly invited to notice his own Satanic urges, as Lewontin, fine reader, does in the piece I quoted at the beginning, and, if one is to be a fit reader of Milton's Christian and Puritan epic, one is required to correct these urges. Go back and read that again, says the warning voice, and you'll see how much you too were tempted by the language of Satan in your self. The text becomes a test. It is only in yourself that this undecidability rests.

Many modern Miltonists have accepted at least some version of this way of reading the poem. The reader becomes, as it were, the true hero, proving in himself the basic system of Christian belief and in so doing contrasting himself with Satan. The redemptive structure of the poem is repeated in the reader, constantly, with each Satanic occasion, but Satan himself is excluded (he excludes himself) from this redemptive possibility. His exclusion is a measure, finally, of the reader's salvation. Yet, rich and important as this way of reading the poem has been since it was first expounded thirty years back in *Surprised by Sin*, I have a small reservation. Not because it assumes we are all fallen creatures and need the constant prodding of a didactic narrator to discover just what that fall has meant for us—in a way that is obvious about any didactic literature, though not about its constant need to remind us—, but because it becomes, in those silken words of the master, all a little too easy. Reading *Paradise Lost* becomes a fairground roller coaster ride. Here we go again, a scream of excitement as we plunge down and then those gasps of relief as the ride restores us to equilibrium and two-footed verticality. What confidence we all show in the maker of the ride, that it will hold us up, and take us through to the end!

If we return to Milton's language we will notice that he does not make it at all easy to recover from these vertiginous plunges into the abyss of Satanic selfhood. (Indeed how could he, since this is where our own thoughts always lead us?) No more than he makes it always

---

[14] Stanley Fish, *Surprised By Sin* (London: Macmillan, 1967).

easy to distinguish between what it is that constitutes Satan and God. It is partly, as Lewontin noted, a matter of sound. The alliterative relation between Heaven and Hell is something the poem has special fondness for, and it invites the ear to hear further similarity. In this respect, Milton was clearly learning from Marlowe. Marlowe's Mephistopheles is behind the language of the Niphates speech, he who had said

> Why this is Hell nor am I out of it,
> Thinkst thou that I, who saw the face of God,
> And tasted the eternal joys of Heaven,
> Am not tormented with ten thousand hells?[15]

The second version of this topos is even more terrifying:

> Hell hath no limits, nor is circumscribed
> In one self place; but where we are is Hell
> And where Hell is, there must we ever be.
> And to be short, when all the world dissolves,
> And every creature shall be purified,
> All places shall be Hell that is not Heaven. (2.1.122–26)

Milton's Satan on Niphates' top has (and this the narrator insists on before he speaks)

> . . . troubl'd thoughts, and from the bottom stir[s]
> The Hell within him, for within him Hell
> He brings, and round about him, nor from Hell
> One step no more than from himself can fly
> By change of place. (IV.19–23)

In *Dr. Faustus* Marlowe exploits the sounds, and so makes Hell a language game. Faustus "confounds Hell in Elysium" (1.3.59), not simply mixing classical and Christian afterlife, but allowing the sound of Hell to spill into the first syllable of Elysium. This word in turn was Elizium in Marlowe's spelling, suggesting another wordplay with a female name that would be highly evocative for a contemporary audience. No wonder Marlowe's contemporary and rival, Thomas Nashe, complained of those writers who thrust Elysium into Hell. Marlowe may not have known the origin of the English word Hell in the Norse goddess "Hel," though if he did, it would give further point to another overlapping sound:

---

[15] *Dr. Faustus* 1.3.78–81, in Christopher Marlowe, *The Complete Plays*, ed. J.B. Steane (Harmondsworth: Penguin, 1969).

> Was this the face that launched a thousand ships
> And burned the topless towers of Ilium?
> Sweet Helen, make me immortal with a kiss.

But when this Hellish Helen does kiss him, he immediately loses his soul and has to beg for it back:

> Her lips suck forth my soul: see where it flies!
> Come, Helen, come, give me my soul again.
> Here will I dwell, for Heaven is in these lips,
> And all is dross that is not Helena. (5.1.85–94)

Faustus' desire even now is scholarly as well as sexual: he wants to abolish the gap that separates him from the classical past and from the beauty of Homer's Helen. What appears on stage, though, is actually at two removes from the beautiful woman of legend: she is technically a succubus (as the language shows with its talk of sucking forth the soul), therefore merely a devilish lookalike, and behind the costume she is a boy, since the roles of women on the Elizabethan stage were played by boys.[16] Marlowe makes this frustration a source of almost gloating uncertainty, as we wait for the inevitable summons of Faustus to Hell. It is so terrifying on stage partly because it is so well imagined by Marlowe and partly because, so far as we know, he didn't believe any of it. Like the Hellmouth prop that, as in medieval drama, would remain on stage throughout the action, this Hellfire idea was a convention, a Christian fiction, and Marlowe was well beyond it, though clearly not beyond the knowledge of that Renaissance self that had become the image of Hell. Milton learned this idea and its language from him.

In Milton, however, it goes a step further. Unlike Marlowe Milton had not entirely renounced the Christian worldview that spawned the images of Hell. Paradoxically he saw its problems more thoroughly. Milton complicates the image of Satan and his hell in two ways. One is that he makes his own poetic persona, the narrator of *Paradise Lost*, unmistakably like Satan: they both aspire beyond the bounds of what has been done before, they both take courageous flight, the narrator has also fallen on dark days,[17] and Satan is himself a bit of a poet and story-teller: dressed as a serpent, he makes up a splendid

---

[16] See further Neil Forsyth, "Heavenly Helen: Hell in *Dr. Faustus*," *Etudes de Lettres*, octobre–décembre, 1987, pp. 11–23.

[17] William Riggs, *The Christian Poet in Paradise Lost* (Berkeley: University of California Press, 1972), has a fine account of these parallels, pp. 15–45.

tale for Eve of how he came to taste the fruit and how much good it did him, and he also inspires a troubling but powerful dream in Eve's subconscious.

Milton's other way of complicating things is that the speech of Satan contains some rhetorical oddities that establish curious connections with or likenesses to God. Just before he proclaims "Evil be thou my Good," he considers the possibility of escaping from this prison of the self. Go back and read again the speech quoted above in which he calls upon himself to repent. Notice what happens. Did you not first think, as you read the speech, that it was not himself to whom Satan was appealing, but God?

> Oh then at last relent: is there no place
> Left for Repentance, none for Pardon left?

He is begging God to ease up, in fact to allow him to repent, to return him, as he is to say in a moment "By Act of Grace" to "my former state." The speech has already made it rather difficult to tell who is being addressed at any moment. It began, of course, as an address to the sun ("how I hate thy beams"), but even there, the language is slippery. Sun sounds like "son," a common pun. In Satan's case it is especially appropriate, since it was the Son's promotion, his "Begetting" or Exaltation that started the trouble in the first place and led to the rebellion: from the beginning Son and Satan are opposed. Satan then moves into meditation about himself and God, using the third person "he" for god, and first person for himself. This continues for many lines of reflection until suddenly he starts addressing . . . well, whom? It quickly becomes clear it is himself. Follow it through for a few lines:

> O had his powerful Destiny ordaind
> Me some inferiour Angel, I had stood
> Then happie; no unbounded hope had rais'd
> Ambition. Yet why not? som other Power
> As great might have aspir'd, and me though mean
> Drawn to his part; but other Powers as great
> Fell not, but stand unshaken, from within
> Or from without, to all temptations arm'd.
> Hadst thou the same free Will and Power to stand?
> Thou hadst: whom hast thou then or what to accuse,
> But Heav'ns free Love dealt equally to all?
> Be then his Love accurst, since love or hate,
> To me alike, it deals eternal woe.
> Nay curs'd be thou; (IV.58–71)

And we wonder again who is being addressed. As this inner meditation continues, then, the divided self splits and produces two voices, then two selves, one of which accuses the other—and then curses it, and so himself. This is another and even more powerful image of damnation. Not only can he not repent, he cannot even, when he tries, address God. The stage convention of the soliloquy has become a prison of solipsism, as clearly delineated as any in literature. He tries to say to God "o then at last relent" but he is the only one who replies, and the reply is negative. No relenting, no repentance, and again the sound of the words conveys more of the meaning: God will not relent, because you cannot repent.

Is this right, though? Is this what the text implies? Certainly, yet it leaves us with an unpleasant taste. What happened for the reader was that he could imagine Satan addressing God, since as he (I) uses those words, I would hope to be able to speak to God if I chose. But Satan appears so to choose, he wants to, and yet he can't. God becomes present to the reader, if not to Satan, as we hear Satan addressing God, and so we realize the enormity of this situation. How fearful it is, and it is God who set it up, God who damned him, so that he cannot, even when he tries, relent/repent. How different, then, is that God addressed from the Satan who hears? He did it himself, we say, yet who is He? It is God doing it, as the poem says elsewhere: "Man therefore shall find grace, The other none" (III.131–2). The rhetoric of Satan has brought God into the text and equated him with the self of Satan.

Such is the terror of this idea of God that Origen, the greatest and most intelligent of the early fathers, tried to save Christianity from it. He propounded a doctrine of *apokatastasis*, that even the devil would be saved. For this he was attacked by Augustine and posthumously condemned in 543.[18] And Milton learned from this: he agreed with God.[19]

One way to read this text then is to take ourselves out of it and say it is merely Satan condemning himself. But another is to experience the absent God in the text as he is appealed to, even if it is only a misreading quickly canceled by the reader, and see how,

---

[18] J.B. Russell, *Satan: the Early Christian Tradition* (Ithaca: Cornell, 1981), pp. 144–48.

[19] Harry F. Robins, *If This Be Heresy: a Study of Milton and Origen*, Illinois Studies in Language and Literature 51 (Urban, Ill., 1963).

momentarily, in the reader's consciousness at least, Satan and God have replaced each other.[20] Ultimately, as most sensitive readers of the poem recognize, the problem of Satan leads beyond itself to the problem of God. An omniscient and omnipotent God is merely toying with these defiant devils, yet Satan's function within the narrative, and within Christian doctrine, is simply to be the one who opposes omnipotence: he is the enemy. In this speech, though, the problem becomes personal and inward to the reader, and so reproduces the

---

[20] A similar moment occurs at the climax of *Paradise Regained*, when Satan and Christ are perched together on the pinnacle of the temple in Jerusalem. Christ's enigmatic response to Satan's final challenge, "Tempt not the Lord thy God," makes Satan fall, smitten with amazement. The difference between the two seems finally clear, and yet just at this moment the two become one, in a pronoun.

> So Satan fell; and straight a fiery Globe
> Of Angels on full sail of wing flew nigh,
> Who on their plumy vans received him soft
> From his uneasy station. (*PR* IV.581–584)

Generations of readers have had to go back at that point to realize that Christ rather than Satan must be the referent of the pronoun *him*, as the rest of the narrative continues to describe how these angels set him down in "a flowery valley on a green bank" and serve him a meal of celestial food divine. But just for a moment, the dark secret was out, that hero and enemy are one and the same, good and bad father, good and bad son. In *Paradise Lost* Adam and Eve listen

> With admiration and deep Muse to heare
> Of things so high and strange, things to thir thought
> So unimaginable as hate in Heav'n,
> And War so neer the seat of God in bliss
> With such confusion. (VII.52–56)

Our reaction to the momentary identification of Satan with Christ at the end of *Paradise Regained* is likely to be similar—and certainly that difficult pronoun *him*, inhabited by both Christ and Satan, is a measure of how far Milton's language was capable of going to find out what was threatening and subversive in his devil.

Did Milton know that according to an ancient Gnostic tradition, Christ, not Satan, was the serpent of Genesis, the bringer of Gnosis or spiritual knowledge? Or did he simply exploit the ambiguities of the traditional equations? The Gnostics were, in many ways, the most sophisticated readers of scripture in the ancient world, steadily finding the hidden meaning beneath the surface text, and Milton was certainly capable of taking the same route to his beliefs. Christ as the "general serpent" (one form of the Gnostic belief) could be reinforced by the recommendation Christ makes in the gospel saying: "Be ye wise as serpents, and gentle as doves" (Matthew 10:16). If Milton knew the Gnostic tradition, he also knew, as a reader of Irenaeus on heresies, that the church had repressed it. Indeed Irenaeus, writing to combat the rival Gnostic readings of scripture, even gives his own version of the gospel saying, carefully separating the serpent from the dove: "Then was the sin of the first-formed man healed by the virtue of the First-Begotten (Christ), the wisdom of the serpent was conquered by the simplicity of the dove, and the chains were broken by which we were in bondage to death." Thus did the struggle with rival interpretations produce the sharp oppositions of orthodoxy. See *The Old Enemy*, pp. 345–6.

way in which it had presumably become so for Satan, and so led to
his initial rebellion. His intelligence though fine could never have
been perfect, since he had never been more than a high archangel[21]:
God's announcement about the Son's exaltation is thus capable of
provoking his jealousy, as it does, and as God knows it will.

If God and Satan can at times seem so alike as to replace each
other, so can Heaven and Hell. It may even be true for Satan that
it is better to reign in Hell than serve in Heaven, since he tries to
ignore, perhaps is already beginning to forget, the difference. As
he greets the new place, he welcomes it as his new Heaven, but if
we listen to what it says, and to the structure of its saying, we hear
something else:

> Farewel happy Fields
> Where Joy forever dwells: Hail horrours, hail
> Infernal world, and thou profoundest Hell
> Receive thy new Possessor: One who brings
> A mind not to be changed by Place or Time.
> The mind is its own place, and in itself
> Can make a Heav'n of Hell, a Hell of Heav'n.
> What matter where, if I be still the same. (I.249–56)

The alliteration on the h-words begins with the Hail and Horrors
and Hell, "profoundest" as in the "deep" associations noted above.
And if the mind can indeed make either heaven or hell in itself,
what the mind who says these words has made is not a heaven of
hell but a hell of heaven. That, we may note, is exactly what he has
just done. Yet this is in fact a magnificent heresy, based on Stoic
doctrine, that the inwardness is all, that there is no place called
Tartarus, and that hell and heaven are indeed to be found only
within the mind. Satan seems here to invent it, and immediately to
believe it, but it was a common though subterranean version of
Christian doctrine, that "the kingdom of god is within you" and
therefore we have heaven and hell within ourselves.[22] We should not
then differentiate too readily between what Satan says and the truth.
Nor should we prejudge the structure that is to dominate the poem:

---

[21] On the archangel's imperfect knowledge, see Milton's *De Doctrina Christiana*, in
the Yale edition of the *Complete Prose*, ed. Don M. Wolfe et al. (New Haven, 1953–
82), Vol. 6:227—full knowledge was the Father's alone.

[22] See the note by Merritt Y. Hughes in his edition of *The Complete Poetry and
Major Prose* (New York: Odyssey Press, 1957), ad loc. He refers to Jacob Boehme,
The Threefold Life of Man, xiv, 72.

within the antithesis of this line, it is true, the making a hell of heaven comes last, and may be thought to cancel the reverse possibility, but viewed from another point of view, the chiastic structure of the line encloses hell within heaven. As the narrator comments when Satan comes back to his senses after being briefly touched by Eve's graceful innocence, "the hot hell that always in him burns, Though in mid-heaven, soon ended his delight, and tortures him now more."

Hell within heaven! The closeness of those mighty opposites is the key to what Milton does with them, and to what they are felt to be like. I think Milton knew this, and felt the need from time to time to insist on the proper distinction. So in this case he continues the speech beyond the famous line. It does not end with "Better to reign in Hell than serve in Heaven" but with a variant slightly less grand, and perhaps this time genuinely despairing. Satan suggests to his companion Beelzebub that they call their "associates and copartners of our loss," the other fallen angels, off the "oblivious Pool" where they still lie astonished by their fall, and decide whether

> once more
> With rallied Arms to try what maybe yet
> Regaind in Heav'n, or what more lost in Hell? (I.268–70)

The speech ends there, and the emphasis corrects that earlier balance and shifts us, not to the self, but towards loss and hell as what is truly Satanic.

Perhaps the most important distinction of this kind is between Satan's exploration of these interior depths and Adam's after the Fall. The parallels are very close: at his moment of extreme despair, Adam talking to himself in soliloquy sees himself as Satanic as he panics about death:

> Thus what thou desir'st
> And what thou fearst, alike destroyes all hope
> Of refuge, and concludes thee miserable
> Beyond all past example and future,
> To Satan only like both crime and doom.
> O Conscience, into what Abyss of fears
> And horrors hast thou driv'n me; out of which
> I find no way, from deep to deeper plung'd! (X.837–43)

Eventually, though it takes a long stretch of marvellous narrative, through a bitter and then finally loving dialogue with Eve, Adam does emerge from this state and discovers a way to salvation. He recalls the promise made in the garden, that "thy Seed shall bruise The serpent's head" (X.1031–32).[23] This text, Milton's version of the *protevangelion*, is a key to the Christian version of the combat myth,[24] and reminds us that the battle between these cosmic enemies is now to continue on the earthly plane: one immediate result is that true repentance like Adam's (and conspicuously unlike Satan's) can bring pardon. This pair, like those other more verbally balanced pairs, Dante's Dis/Dio,[25] and Milton's Devil/Deity,[26] Hell/Heaven, indeed begin the same, as do Adversary and Adam for that matter, but the endings differ: the satan remains storm-tossed but Adam/Eve (the pairing in crucial, it is now only Satan who is impaired)[27] can move on to a place of rest or a safe haven. A person may plunge through meditation into that interior Hell discovered by the late Renaissance, and nonetheless be granted a way out and back to light.

Literary studies have usually been divided off, either historically or institutionally, from religious studies. But Milton's Satan bridges the gap: he corresponds partly to the figure of religious belief, although he is primarily a character in an epic narrative. Of course, like all characters in literature, Satan is not really "there"—he is absent and only conjured into imagined presence by the reader's activity. I choose these words carefully, for this fascinating but rather risky parallel between literature and magic allows us to see the importance of the historical moment for Milton's work. An example will help us: several stories circulated during the period about performances of Marlowe's *Dr. Faustus*. In one especially interesting case, "as Faustus was busy with his magical invocations," the cast of the play suddenly felt as if a mysterious other had joined them: "there was one devil too many."[28] Everyone was so frightened that they called off the performance, went home quietly and spent the night in prayer—unusual behavior for

---

[23] Georgia Christopher, *Milton and the Science of the Saints* (Princeton University Press, 1982), pp. 163–72, and see *Milton Quarterly*, 30, Oct. 96, p. 141; 31, Dec. 97, pp. 124–30.

[24] See Forsyth, *The Old Enemy*, 266–72, 346–7 and Russell, *Satan*, p. 72.

[25] Forsyth, "Of Man's First Dis," in *Milton in Italy*, ed. Mario Di Cesare (Binghamton: MRTS, 1991), 345–69.

[26] PL I.373; see Stanley Fish in *The London Review of Books*, 10 June 1993.

[27] R.A. Shoaf, *Milton, Poet of Duality* (New Haven: Yale 1985/1990?), pp. 15–16 for a wonderfully suggestive exploration of this (and many other) puns in *Paradise Lost*. On the importance of the pairing, see Diane McColley, *Milton's Eve* (Urban: University of Illinois Press, 1983).

[28] See E.K. Chambers, *The Elizabethan Stage* (Oxford University Press, 1923), vol. 3, p. 424.

actors. This story suggests that secular theatre and religious ritual were still not entirely differentiated, at least in the popular mind. In fact, the right to conjure, to control the mystery by which literary and dramatic inventions can seem to be really present, was an important issue in the political struggles among church, court and parliament,[29] just as the question of Christ's "real presence" during the Mass was a major point of disagreement. From the time of James I, the monarch exerted more and more direct control over the theater, and when parliament took power from the king in 1642, beginning the Civil War, it closed the theatres. The interiority that had been so important an invention of the stage passed now into "literature," and even when the theatres were reopened after the Restoration, there is nothing comparable to what Milton was doing in this private and circumscribed world of poetry, for which he hoped he might "a fit audience find, though few" (VII.25).

So it was during Milton's lifetime that these issues were fought over and the modern view began to emerge of literature as a separate, secular practice, detached from social institutions and designed for aesthetic or reflective rather than moral or religious satisfaction: it is to this emerging view that Satan's interior hell appeals. But this view was still contemporary with another, more traditional notion—the one that required as normal the censorship of literature because of its power to shape and challenge social consciousness. Milton's Satan clearly partakes of both worldviews—indeed this confrontation of ideologies is an important reason for the ambivalence I have tried to illustrate in this essay. Milton treats Satan as an object of traditional religious belief—yet partly as a result of *Paradise Lost*, Satan became henceforward a literary character, to reappear in some of the best known plays, novels or romantic poems of the European cultural heritage. The Satan Blake found in Milton, for example, is not a figure of religious belief but a source of poetic energy and imagination, indeed the one real source, and his opponents represent the repressive world that was coming to be with the industrial revolution—which forces the arts into that separate, marginalized status they have since taken on. Or, to take a more general example, so compelling is the character of Satan in *Paradise Lost* that generations of English

---

[29] See Stephen Greenbelt's argument in "Shakespeare and the Exorcists," incorporated into his book *Shakespearean Negotiations: The Circulation of Social Energy in Renaissance England* (Oxford University Press, 1988).

speakers, knowing their Milton better than their Bible, have assumed that Christianity teaches an elaborate story about the fall of the angels after a war in heaven, and have been surprised to find no mention of Satan in the biblical Book of Genesis.

One can say, then, that Milton's Satan was invented at the last possible moment, at the very time when belief in the devil was in decline, undermined by the new forms of rationalism or liberal religion—or the excesses of the great witch-persecutions of the sixteenth and seventeenth centuries.[30] Indeed in Milton's theological treatise, *De Doctrina Christiana*, written probably at the same time as *Paradise Lost*, Satan rarely appears. There Milton is more interested in the symbolic and interior aspect signaled by George Herbert when he wrote: "devils are our sins in perspective." If we compare the treatise and the poem, we become aware that Milton's own view of Satan shares the same ambivalence as the experience he offers the reader of his great poem. Satan is both sympathetic and repulsive, in the various ways I have tried to demonstrate; Heaven and Hell are and are not different; there is hate, and there is Heaven, and there is hate in Heaven.

---

[30] Eve's dream is the main locus of witch-lore in Milton, though there are other references: see my "The Devil in Milton," *Etudes de Lettres* (Lausanne, 1989), pp. 79–96. On this subject, since Jeffrey Russell has written so extensively and with such force about medieval witchcraft, I wish to call our readers' attention to new material from the Vaudois cantonal archives for the early years of the fifteenth century currently being researched and published by Lausanne students under the direction of Professor Baldassare Paravicini. Many complete trial transcripts are now available, with analyses in the form of "mémoires de licence". The chief interest is in how early the material is, its completeness, the variety of types of character brought to trial, the differing results of the trials, and the evidence for churchly imposition of the diabolical interpretation of witchcraft, complete with Sabbat.

HOLINESS AND OBEDIENCE: DENOUNCEMENT OF TWELFTH-CENTURY WALDENSIAN LAY PREACHING[1]

Beverly Mayne Kienzle

In 1199 Innocent III summoned the abbots of Cîteaux, Morimondo and La Crête to investigate events in the diocese of Metz where lay men and women reportedly were meeting in secret to read the scriptures and other texts in translation, to discuss them and to preach to one another.[2] These lay people were followers of Waldes, whose 1173 conversion drew adherents to a lay movement grounded in imitation of the apostolic life. Expelled from Lyon in the early 1180s and condemned by the Council of Verona in 1184, the Waldensians dispersed, taking with them a commitment to voluntary poverty and a conviction that the gospel should be proclaimed by all.[3] The reaction of the ecclesiastical hierarchy against the Waldensians' evangelizing

[1] An earlier version of this paper was delivered May 4, 1995 at the conference, "Models of Holiness in Medieval Sermons," organized by the International Medieval Sermon Studies Society and held in conjunction with the 30th International Congress on Medieval Studies, May 4–5, 1995, The Medieval Institute, Kalamazoo, Michigan. I am grateful to Kay Shanahan, Harvard Divinity School, for her careful retyping and proofreading of this article.

[2] The letters are contained in PL 214:695–699, Epis. II.141 and 142; PL 214:794, Epis. II.235. They are discussed by Leonard E. Boyle, "Innocent III and Vernacular Versions of Scripture," in *The Bible in the Medieval World: Essays in Memory of Beryl Smalley*, ed. Katherine Walsh and Diana Wood, SCH Subsidia 4 (Oxford, 1985), pp. 97–107. See also *Die Register Innocenz' III*, II: Pontifikatjahr 1199–1200, eds. O. Hageneder, W. Maleczek, A.A. Strnad (Rome-Vienna, 1979), pp. 271–76, doc. 132 (141) and 133 (142), pp. 432–34, doc. 226 (235). The episode is discussed by Grado Merlo, "Sulle 'misere donniccuiole' che predicavano", in G. Merlo, *Valdesi e valdismi medievali, II. Identità Valdesi nella storia e nella storiografia* (Turin, 1991), p. 107; Kurt Victor Selge, *Die ersten Waldenser, I: Untersuchung und Darstellung* (Berlin, 1967), pp. 290–93, and H. Grundmann, *Movimenti religiosi nel medioevo* (trans. of Munich, 1970; 1st edition, Berlin, 1935), (Bologna, 1980), pp. 98–100. K.V. Selge points out a passage in Caesarius of Heisterbach where the bishop of Metz spotted two "servants of the devil" in his audience, presumably Waldensians [I, p. 290; *Dialogus Miraculorum* 5.20, (Cologne, 1872), pp. 299–300]. PL 214:695–96: "tam in dioecesi quam urbe Metensi laicorum et mulierum multitudo non modica tracta quodammodo desiderio Scripturarum, Evangelia, Epistolas Pauli, Psalterium, moralia Job et plures alios libros sibi fecit in Gallico sermone transferri, translationi hujusmodi adeo libenter, utinam autem et prudenter intendens, ut secretis conventionibus talia inter se laici et mulieres eructare praesumant, et sibi invicem praedicare...."

[3] The movement's history is reviewed in detail by Giovanni Gonnet in "Le cheminement des vaudois vers le schisme et l'hérésie (1174–1218)," *Cahiers de Civilisation*

is part of a larger twelfth-century context that involved economic change, the growth of cities and literacy, and an upsurge in popular religious movements parallel to the burgeoning of monasteries and schools and the increased production of sermons in those environments.[4] Here we focus on a point where the popular and the elite intersected and conflicted: the reaction against dissent that constitutes an important chapter in the history of persecution.[5] This twelfth-century persecution followed the solidification of social and political structures in the eleventh century, when, in Jeffrey Burton Russell's view, the concept of a hierarchical church had been articulated and firmly established by the Gregorian reforms.[6]

In the conflict between Waldensian and orthodox practices, the opposing views of the two sides hinged on differing views of holiness and, in particular, of its relationship to obedience. Both sides argued from the authority of scripture and of patristic writings. While the Waldensians emphasized the responsibility to obey God alone and the obligation of all believers to spread the good news, the orthodox polemicists constructed a code of holiness rooted in obedience to the hierarchy and denounced lay preachers who did not conform to it. In condemning unauthorized lay preaching, the clerical writers move from the accusation of disobedience to mount a campaign of propaganda and demonization employing the language of pollution, social reversal and apocalypse—language that links the rhetoric of twelfth-century persecutors to that of both earlier and later periods of persecution.[7]

Médiévale (Paris, 1976), 309–345. Recent scholarship is discussed in *Les vaudois des origines à leur fin (xiie–xvie siècles)*, ed. Gabriel Audisio (Turin, 1990), which summarizes the international colloquium of that title, Aix-en-Provence, 8–10 April 1988. Especially helpful is the article by Grado G. Merlo, "Le mouvement vaudois des origines à la fin du xiiie siècle," pp. 15–35. Other sources include: R.I. Moore, *The Origins of European Dissent* (Oxford: Blackwell, 1985), esp. pp. 228–31; and Malcolm Lambert, *Medieval Heresy: Popular Movements from the Gregorian Reform to the Reformation*, 2nd edition (Oxford: Blackwell, 1992), pp. 62–94.

[4] Jean Longère's article, "Le pouvoir de prêcher et le contenu de la prédication dans l'Occident chrétien," in *Preaching and Propaganda in the Middle Ages: Islam, Byzantium, Latin West*. Penn-Paris-Dumbarton Oaks Colloquia III, Session of October 20–25, 1980, ed. George Makdisi, Dominique Sourdel, Janine Sourdel-Thoumine (Paris, 1980), situates this concern with preaching in a broad context from the second to the thirteenth century. See especially p. 69.

[5] For this aspect of my work, I am indebted to R.I. Moore's *The Formation of a Persecuting Society* (Oxford: Blackwell, 1987), here esp. p. 5.

[6] Jeffrey Burton Russell, *Dissent and Order in the Middle Ages: The Search for Legitimate Authority* (New York, 1992), pp. 3–4, 11.

[7] R.I. Moore, *Formation*, pp. 4–5, deals very briefly with the place of the twelfth

This study examines some of the literature directed against the Waldensians with a view to analyzing the arguments articulated in those writings. How the Waldensians saw themselves and their adversaries is another topic, one that Anne Brenon has treated in her work on fifteenth-century Waldensian texts.[8] Here we look only at the orthodox side, at late twelfth-century polemical writings by Geoffroy of Auxerre, Bernard of Fontcaude, Alain of Lille and also at the three letters of Innocent III concerning the events in Metz. Our focus is the process of argumentation and the language associated with it. The analysis is structured first around the major points of the arguments and then around the type of language used against the dissenters.

The works of several other scholars have been instrumental in shaping our analysis: various historians of the medieval Waldensians, such as Peter Biller, Anne Brenon, Giovanni Gonnet, and Grado Merlo; R.I. Moore's *The Formation of a Persecuting Society*, Chaim Perelman and L. Olbrechts-Tyteca *The New Rhetoric*,[9] and of course the works of Jeffrey Burton Russell who has written extensively on the Devil, the associations medieval people envisioned with the Devil and demons, and the relationship of that phenomenon to social structures.[10] Russell has also pointed out the importance of the sermon as a bridge between elite and popular culture,[11] and the controversy viewed here revolves tightly around preaching and its authorization. Moreover, the sources that our study examines also shed light on how the denunciation and demonization of certain groups was propagated, because these writings provided reference material for preachers

century in the history of persecution, and on p. 133, he argues that since the political message of heretical leaders was considered more dangerous than their religious message, "obedience was the test of the heretic."

[8] Anne Brenon, "Christianisme et tolérance dans les textes cathares et vaudois du bas Moyen Age," in *Ketzerei und Ketzerbekämpfung in Wort und Text*, ed. Peter Blumenthal and Johannes Kramer (Stuttgart, 1989), pp. 65–77.

[9] R.I. Moore, *Formation*; Chaim Perelman and L. Olbrechts-Tyteca, *The New Rhetoric: A Treatise on Argumentation* (Notre Dame: Univ. of Notre Dame Press, 1969). Antoinette Clark Wire's *The Corinthian Women Prophets: A Reconstruction through Paul's Rhetoric* (Minneapolis: Fortress Press, 1990), and her application of the "New Rhetoric" has also provided a useful model.

[10] See especially Jeffrey Burton Russell, *Lucifer: The Devil in the Middle Ages* (Ithaca, 1984). Russell points out in *Dissent and Order in the Middle Ages*, p. 6, that the church's opponents have been labeled as the Devil's followers since as early as the second century; and Elaine Pagels has explored that same tendency in New Testament texts and early Christianity. *The Origins of Satan* (New York, 1995).

[11] J.B. Russell, *Dissent and Order in the Middle Ages* (see note 6 above).

involved in the campaign to denounce those whom the church feared and wished to discredit.[12]

The Sources

The appearance of diverse dissenting religious movements in the twelfth century spurred the production of polemical literature aimed primarily at the Cathars but with some attention directed towards the Waldensians.[13] The three earliest polemical sources we have from the late twelfth century are two sermons forming part of an Apocalypse commentary by Geoffroy of Auxerre[14] and two treatises:[15] first, the *Adversus Waldensium sectam liber* by Bernard, Premonstratensian abbot of Fontcaude, who composed it around 1191 after witnessing a dispute where the Poor of Lyon were pronounced heretics;[16] and second, the *Summa quadripartita* written around 1190–1194 by Alain of Lille, a university master who joined the Cistercian order towards the end of his life.[17] The 1199 letters from Innocent III (*Epistolae*

---

[12] Preaching, frequently studied as an instrument of propaganda, was enhanced by the practiced rhetorical skills of monks. Concerning the related genre of the letter, Giles Constable examines the persuasive power of the monastic letter in "Papal, Imperial and Monastic Propaganda in the Eleventh and Twelfth Centuries," in *Preaching and Propaganda in the Middle Ages*, pp. 181–82.

[13] As some historians have pointed out, both groups were seen to have a higher level of coherence and sophistication than they possessed. See R.I. Moore, *Formation*, p. 151; and G. Merlo, *Valdesi e valdismi medievali* (Turin, 1984), pp. 8–25.

[14] Geoffroy of Auxerre, *Super Apocalypsim*, ed. Ferruccio Gastaldelli with an introduction by Jean Leclercq, Temi e Testi 17 (Rome, 1970), Sermo XIV and XVIII, pp. 175–82, 210–11.

[15] G. Gonnet, "Le cheminement", p. 321, points out that these treatises inaugurated the genre: "dans le but expressément formulé de combattre d'une façon systématique les hérétiques de leur temps ils ont inauguré par là-même la grande littérature polémique des xiie et xiiie s."

[16] *Adversus Waldensium sectam liber*, PL 204:793–840. According to Christine Thouzellier, the dispute took place around 1185–1187. Bernard Gaucelin, archbishop of Narbonne called it together; Raymond de Daventrie arbitrated and the Poor of Lyon were pronounced heretics. C. Thouzellier, *Catharisme et Valdéisme en Languedoc à la fin du xiie et au début du xiiie siècle* (Paris, 1966), pp. 50–51. W.L. Wakefield and A.P. Evans date the debate around 1190 and Bernard's death by 1193. Walter L. Wakefield and Austin P. Evans, *Heresies of the High Middle Ages: Selected Sources Translated and Annotated* (New York, 1969), p. 211. See also Libert Verrees, "Le traité de l'abbé Bernard de Fontcaude contre les Vaudois et les Ariens," *Analecta Praemonstratensia* 31 (1955), 5–35.

[17] *Liber secundus: contra Waldenses* is published in PL 210:377–400. Some additions to the PL version are made by C. Thouzellier, *Catharisme et Valdéisme*, p. 82, who discusses the text and its probable date.

141, 142, 235) concerning the events in Metz constitute our fourth source from this period.

Obedience

Taken together the sources make arguments for what constitutes lawful and holy preaching based on six areas, all violated somehow by the dissidents: 1. obedience, 2. commission, 3. education, 4. language of authorities used, 5. gender and marital status, 6. setting. These six points of argumentation rest somehow on the first, however: the assumption that obedience is owed to the Roman Church, its bishops and priests.[18] This is set forth most explicitly by Bernard of Fontcaude who explains in his first chapters that to disobey the Church is tantamount to disobeying Christ and the apostles. Furthermore, to disobey and thus be excommunicated is to be delivered into the hands of Satan (I.i–iv, PL 204:795–96).

Commission

Central to Bernard of Fontcaude and Alain of Lille's thinking is the idea that the preacher must be sent, that is commissioned by a higher authority. Their principal proof text is Romans 10:15a ("And how can men preach unless they are sent?"), later used in Canon Three of the decrees issued by the Fourth Lateran Council (1215).[19] Bernard allows that God or authorized human beings may send preachers, but the preachers may not send themselves (V.vii–viii, PL 204:845). Alain of Lille echoes this and adds that commissioning is done by God, proven by good works and confirmed by miracles. He describes a sort of chain of commissioning with God as the ultimate authority. Even Jesus, who constitutes what rhetoricians call the perfect model

---

[18] R.I. Moore, *Formation*, p. 133, asserts that since the political message of heretical leaders was considered more dangerous than their religious message, "obedience was the test of the heretic."

[19] *Enchiridion Fontium Valdensium*, ed. Giovanni Gonnet, I (Torre Pellice, 1958), p. 163 cites the canon: "Quia vero nonnulli sub specie pietatis virtutem eius, iuxta quod Apostolus ait, abnegantes, auctoritatem sibi vendicant praedicandi, quum idem Apostolus dicat: 'Quomodo praedicabunt, nisi mittantur?' Omnes qui prohibiti, vel non missi, praeter auctoritatem ab apostolica sede vel catholico episcopo loci susceptam, publice vel privatim praedicationis officium usurpare praesumpserint, excommunicationis vinculo innodentur, et nisi quam citius resipuerint, alia competenti poena plectentur."

for the purposes of argumentation,[20] was subordinate: sent by God
to preach, he in turn sent the apostles. Alain adds other models,
asserting that the prophets too were sent by God, and he lists Jonah,
Jeremiah, Amos, Isaiah and Malachy (PL 210:378–379C). Ideas similar
to Alain's are found in Innocent III's Epistle 141 where he includes
the example of John the Baptist's commission (Jn. 1:6). He remarks
that even an inward and invisible commission must be attested by
the witness of scripture or by the working of miracles.[21]

Education

The second requirement for a valid preacher is education, an exi-
gency doubtless related to the persistent attitude that the heretic was
an illiterate.[22] Bernard of Fontcaude's discussion of education focuses
on the enlightenment of the Holy Spirit. The apostles, he says, were
unlettered before their calling, as stated in Acts 4:13—a text cited by
the Waldensians to justify their claim to the right to evangelize. The
abbot explains, nonetheless, that the Lord opened his understanding
to the apostles so that they might comprehend the Scriptures (Luke
24:45) and he sent them the Holy Spirit. Heretics, the abbot contends,
lack faith and therefore, like the vain teachers of 1 Timothy 1:6,
they do not understand the scriptures. (V.xvi, PL 204:809–810). Alain
of Lille, author of an *ars praedicandi*, takes a more academic point of
view. If it is dangerous for the wise and holy to preach, he asserts,
then preaching is extremely dangerous for the uneducated who do
not know what should be preached, nor to whom, how, when and
where preaching should be done (PL 210: 379CD).[23] He also observes that even very holy men who understand the scriptures, as do

---

[20] See C. Perelman and T. Olbrechts-Tyteca, *New Rhetoric*, p. 371.

[21] PL 214:697BC: "Quod si forte quis argute respondeat quia tales invisibiliter
mittuntur a Deo, et si non visibiliter mittantur ab homine, cum invisibilis missio
multo sit dignior quam visibilis, et divina longe melior quam humana . . . potest et
debet utique ratione praevia responderi quod cum interior illa missio sit occulta,
non sufficit cuiquam nude tantum asserere quod ipse sit missus a Deo, cum hoc
quilibet haereticus asseveret: sed oportet ut astruat illam invisibilem missionem per
operationem miraculi vel per scripturae testimonium speciale."

[22] R.I. Moore, *Formation*, esp. pp. 135–140, deals with the hostility of the twelfth-
century literate elite towards those they considered unlettered. Peter Biller deals
with this persistent topos in "Heresy and literacy: earlier history of the theme," in
Heresy and Literacy, 1000–1530, Cambridge Studies in Medieval Literature, 23 (Cambridge, 1994), pp. 1–9.

[23] PL 210:379CD: "Quomodo etiam praedicabunt illitterati qui scripturas non
intelligunt? . . . Si sapientibus et sanctis periculosum est praedicare, periculosissimum

many Cistercians, are nonetheless not commissioned as preachers.[24] Innocent III also addresses the issue of education, asserting in Epistle 141 that no simple and unlearned person should presume to attain the sublimity of the scriptures nor to preach it to others, when even the prudent and learned have insufficient understanding of its depths.[25]

Language

Closely tied to the issue of education is that of language. Vernacular translations of the scriptures and the Church Fathers, the foundational sources for sermon material, were met with suspicion. Innocent III's 1199 letters did not condemn the Waldensians' translations, as Leonard Boyle has demonstrated carefully,[26] but he was certainly wary of them. The pope specified that the lay people in Metz had translations of the Gospels in a language of Gaul, as well as of Paul's Epistles, the Psalter, the *Moralia in Job* and many other books (Epist. 141, PL 214:696C). In letters 142 to the Bishop and Chapter at Metz and 235 to the Cistercian abbots, he states the questions he wants answered about the translations, which he says should not be done nor be used without education (Epist. 142, PL 214:699B). The bishop and the chapter are ordered to find out the following: who did the translations; with what intent; what is the faith of those using them; what is the cause for their teaching; whether they venerate the Holy See and the catholic church (PL 214:699C). The Cistercian abbots receive the same list with additional comments, among them that a refusal to accept correction should be punished under canon law (PL 214: 794CD). Alberic of Trois Fontaines' chronicle recounts that the abbots were sent to Metz to preach and that they burned the translated books and wiped out the sect. Nonetheless, Romance and German translations were mentioned again in Liège in 1202.[27]

---

est idiotis, qui nesciunt quo praedicandum, quibus praedicandum, quomodo praedicandum, quando praedicandum, ubi praedicandum."

[24] PL 210:379D: "Videmus etiam sanctiores iis non praedicare, qui intellectum sacrae Scripturae habent, ut multos Cistercienses, quia nimirum missi non sunt."

[25] PL 214:696D: "Tanta est enim divina Scripturae profunditas, ut non solum simplices et illitterati, sed etiam prudentes et docti non plene sufficiant ad ipsius intelligentiam indagandam. Propter quod dicit Scriptura: 'Quia multi defecerunt scrutantes scrutinio (Ps. 63:7). Unde recte olim in lege divina statutum ut bestia, quae montem tetigerit, lapidetur; ne videlicet simplex aliquis et indoctus praesumat ad sublimitatem Scripturae sacrae pertingere, vel eam aliis praedicare.'"

[26] See the article by L. Boyle cited in n. 2 above.

[27] The chronicle of Alberic de Trois Frontaines reports: "Item in urbe Metensi pullulante secta, que dicitur Valdensium, directi sunt ad predicandum quidam abbates,

Gender and Marital Status

The three orthodox polemicists deal with the question of gender. If a lay person's preaching is unauthorized and dangerous, then all the more so is a woman's, for her nature—viewed as subordinate, sinful and seductive—is not suited for proclaiming the word of God.[28] A battery of biblical texts, mostly from the Pauline corpus, supplies fuel for the polemicists. All cite 1 Corinthians 14:34–35[29] and 2 Timothy 3:6.[30] Alain adds 1 Timothy 2:1 to illustrate that no woman should be permitted to teach because Eve was created second and deceived

qui quosdam libros de latino in romanum versos combusserunt et predictam sectam extirpaverunt" (MGH SS 23, 878). K.V. Selge, *Die ersten Waldenser*, I, pp. 292–93, points out the translations cited in Liège in 1202.

[28] On the denunciation of Waldensian women preachers, see B.M. Kienzle, "The Prostitute Preacher: Patterns of Polemic against Medieval Waldensian Women Preachers," in *Women Preachers and Prophets through Two Millennia of Christianity*, ed. B.M. Kienzle and P.J. Walker (Berkeley and Los Angeles, pp. 99–113, 1998). On the continued preaching by Waldensian women, see Peter Biller, "The preaching of the Waldensian sisters," in *La prédication sur un mode dissident: laïcs, femmes, hérétiques . . . (XIe–XIVe)*. Actes de la 9e Session d'Histoire Médiévale de Couiza organisée par le C.N.E.C./René Nelli, 26–30 août (forthcoming, Carcassonne, 1998); and "What did happen to the Waldensian sisters? The Strasbourg Testimony, . . ." in *Mélanges Giovanni Gonnet*, ed. F. Giacone (forthcoming, 1998).

[29] *Super Apocalypsim*, p. 179: "Bene Paulus mulieres in ecclesiis loqui prohibens, ait: 'Domi viros suos interrogent'. 'Domi', non foris; 'interrogent', non docere praesumant; nec se invicem, sed 'viros'; non quoscumque, sed 'suos'". Bernard of Fontcaude, VII.i; PL 204:825D: "Praeter errores jam dictos, graviter errant; quia feminas, quas suo consortio admittunt, docere permittunt, cum hoc sit apostolicae doctrinae contrarium. Scriptum est enim: 'Mulieres in ecclesiis taceant . . .' ecce Apostolus jubet, ut mulieres taceant in ecclesiis materialibus, vel in congregationibus fidelium, non quidem ab oratione vel laude Dei, sed a doctrina; et ne quae in ecclesia aliquid interrogent sub occasione docendi, sed domi viros suos." Alain of Lille, PL 210:379D: "Ipsi etiam obviant Apostolo, in hoc quod mulierculas secum ducunt, et eas in conventu fidelium praedicare faciunt, cum Apostolous dicat in Epistola prima ad Corinthios: 'Mulieres in ecclesias. . . .'"

[30] *Super Apocalypsim*, p. 179, ll. 150–51: "In quibus non desunt miserae etiam mulierculae oneratae peccatis, quae domos penetrant alienas. . . ." Bernard of Fontcaude, VII.ii, PL 204C: "Hinc Apostolus de pseudochristis et haereticis ait Timotheo: 'Habentes quidem speciem pietatis, virtutem autem ejus abnegantes; et hos devita. Ex his enim sunt, qui penetrant domos; et mulierculas ducunt captivas, oneratas peccatis, quae ducuntur variis desideriis.'" (2 Tim. 3:6). Alain of Lille, PL 210:379–80: "Ipsi etiam obviant Apostolo, in hoc quod mulierculas secum ducunt, et eas in conventu fidelium praedicare faciunt, cum Apostolus dicat in Epistola prima ad Corinthios. . . ." It should be noted that these texts were born in controversy. For a summary of scholarship on the Pastoral Letters, see Ralph P. Martin, "1, 2 Timothy and Titus," in *Harper's Bible Commentary*, ed. James I. Mays, San Francisco, 1988), pp. 1237–44; and Robert A. Wild, "The Pastoral Letters," in *The New Jerome Biblical Commentary*, ed. Raymond E. Brown, Joseph A. Fitzmyer, Roland E. Murphy (Englewood Cliffs, NJ, 1990), pp. 891–902. G. Merlo, "Sulle 'misere donnicciuole',"

Adam.[31] Bernard of Fontcaude calls on several other texts, along with the examples of Eve, Job's wife and Pilate's wife.[32]

Geoffroy of Auxerre uses Jezebel as an anti-model[33] and as the central figure for his attack on women preaching, a topic I have examined in depth elsewhere.[34] Geoffroy combines the identities of Jezebel, the prophet of Revelation 2:20,[35] with that of the wicked queen of Israel (1 Kings 18:4, 21:23; 2 Kings 9:7–37), explaining that her name signifies iniquity and impurity. It is Jezebel with this double identity who, according to Geoffroy, is brought back to life in the activities of the women Waldensians, whom he targets with accusations of promiscuity.[36]

Only Bernard of Fontcaude treats the question of marital status, citing 1 Corinthians 7:3 and asserting that those who have wives and are oppressed with the weight of earthly care, are not suitable for disseminating the word of God (V.xi, PL 204:816C). Bernard does allow for preaching by a lay man who is not married, if he is authorized by the church. There was an intense debate in the late twelfth century over lay preaching, and the figures of Raymond of

---

p. 104, rightly points out that a distorted mirror is used when the Waldensian women are associated with the *mulierculae* of 2 Timothy, but he does not refer to the Greek text or the passage in the New Testament *Sitzenleben*.

[31] PL 210:380A: "Item Apostolus in Epistola prima ad Timotheum: 'Mulier in silentio. . . .'"

[32] VII.ii, PL 204:821BC: "Seducunt mulieres prius, per eas viros; ut diabolus prius Evam, et per eam Adam. Sic et Job per ejus uxorem subvertere voluit dicentem: 'Adhuc permanes in simplicitate tua? Benedic Deo, et morere' (Job 2:9). Sic et per uxorem Pilati dicentem ei: 'Nil tibi et justo illi: multa enim passa sum hodie per visum propter illum' (Mt. 27:19). Mysterium passionis Domini voluit impedire, ne per ejus mortem, amitteret imperium." The statement by Job's wife is repeated in PL 240:826AB.

[33] See C. Perelman and T. Olbrechts-Tyteca, *New Rhetoric*, p. 367, on the use of the anti-model in argumentation. Elsewhere I discuss Alain of Lille's similar use of the female jackal. See "La prédication: pierre de touche de la dissidence et de l'orthodoxie," in *La prédication sur un mode dissident* (forthcoming, Carcassonne, 1998). J. Longère, *Oeuvres oratoires des maîtres parisiens au XIIᵉ siècle*, 2 vols. (Paris, 1975), I, p. 421, remarks that both Alain of Lille and Jacques de Vitry use this image for heretics.

[34] See note 28 above.

[35] Elisabeth Schüssler Fiorenza remarks that the woman prophet in the book of Revelation must have had a great influence, for her city, Thyatira, became a center of Montanism. *In Memory of Her: A Feminist Theological Reconstruction of Christian Origins* (New York, 1983), p. 33.

[36] *Super Apocalypsim*, p. 180, ll. 164–166: "Quid ergo dicimus, fratres, quis illam Iezabel post annos mille iuvenculam suscitavit, ut per vicos et plateas meretricula praedicatrix occurrat?" R.I. Moore points out that some male leaders of popular movements were also accused of promiscuity. *Formation*, p. 100.

Toulouse and Rainier of Pisa stand out as pious lay men whose preaching was allowed, although preaching was generally denied to all lay people.[37]

Setting

Finally, the proper setting for preaching receives some attention in our sources.[38] The authors agree that preaching should be done in public space, not in private. For women, a distinction is made specifically between preaching and teaching: the former less tolerated than that of men, the latter permitted in private.

Innocent III specifies that preaching is a public act, not to be performed in secret, for Jesus instructed his disciples to speak in the light and to proclaim over the rooftops (Mt. 10:27). The gospel should not be preached in secret conventicles, as the heretics do, but expounded publicly in churches, since Jesus responded to the high priest that he had said nothing in secret (John 18:20) (Epist. 241, PL 214:695–696). Bernard, Geoffroy and Alain also criticize the secret meetings of the Waldensians. The three use 2 Timothy 3:6 to attack Waldensians who enter the houses of other people,[39] and Geoffroy singles out the women for this, changing the Vulgate text, "qui domos penetrant," to read: "quae domos penetrant."[40]

Bernard of Fontcaude opposes public teaching by women when he criticizes the boldness of women who teach the words of God publicly when Paul forbade them from even praying or prophesying unless they were veiled (VII.iii, PL 204:826C). He sees Titus 2:3, which

---

[37] For a recent study on lay preaching, see Philippe Buc, "'Vox clamantis in deserto'? Pierre le Chantre et la prédication laïque," in *Revue Mabillon* n.s. 4 (= v. 65), (1993), 5–47; and on Raymond of Toulouse and Rainier of Pisa, see *Mouvements dissidents et novateurs*. Actes de la 2e Session d'Histoire Médiévale de Carcassonne organisée par le C.N.E.C./Centre René Nelli, 28 août–1er septembre 1989 sous la présidence du Professeur André Vauchez, *Heresis* 13–14 (1990), p. 343. Innocent III granted permission to preach to the third orders of the Humiliati (1201) and of the Poor of Lyon (1208), enlisting them in his fight against heresy. See John M. Trout, "Preaching by the Laity in the Twelfth Century," *Studies in Medieval Culture* 4.1, ed. John R. Sommerfeldt, Larry Synergaard, and E. Rozanne Elder (Kalamazoo, 1975), p. 95.

[38] Conflicts of this period led to the establishment of guidelines for preaching, such as the 1204 Statutes of Paris that were concerned with the setting for and the control over orthodox teaching. See J. Longère, "Le pouvoir," pp. 169–70.

[39] *Super Apocalypsim*, p. 179; PL 204:821C; PL 210:380CD.

[40] *Super Apocalypsim*, p. 179, line 150: "In quibus non desunt miserae etiam mulierculae oneratae peccatis, quae domos penetrant alienas. . . ."

recommends that older women teach young girls, as applying only to old women and young girls and only to private teaching, not public. Given the abbot's objections, the Waldensians apparently used this text to justify female evangelizing in public (VIII.v, PL 204:826D).[41]

Language of Opposition

Such were the major requirements for holy preaching in the view of the orthodox writers. We now turn to the language the three polemicists used to discredit the opposition by denouncing what they perceived as a threatening disobedience, seen in the violation of the necessary grounds for valid preaching. As R.I. Moore has pointed out, the unauthorized preacher "represented unlicensed, uncontrolled power."[42] The polemicists' charges of unholiness are grounded in a conceptual framework that views disobedience as heresy, and heresy as the work of the Devil. They employ language of pollution,[43] reversal of the social order, and apocalypsis as they use biblical texts to create an atmosphere of fear and danger. We begin with a general discussion of the process of demonization at work in these texts, and we then analyze the orthodox writers' rhetoric in the three categories of pollution, reversal of the social order and apocalypsis.

Throughout the polemical texts, the dissidents are associated in various ways with Satan,[44] the anti-model par excellence. For example,

---

[41] VIII.v, PL 204:826D–827B: "Ad quod notandum est, Apostolum non dicere, ut publice viros anus doceant, sed private adolescentulas, ita tamen ut eas prudentiam illam doceant quam consequenter subdit. . . . Repellunt igitur, ne doceant mulieres haeresim sapientes, secundum praedicta autem verba, ne doceant, nisi sint anus moribus et aetate, et ne doceant, nisi adolescentulas: imo, omnino interdicitur eis, ne doceant; ideo scilicet quia non sunt sanae in fide, sine qua esse convincitur, quisquis obediens non est, ut superius monstratum est." Robert Wild places this verse in the context of duties of the members of a Christian household, while the author of the Pastoral Epistles generally "did not want women teaching men in a worship context." "Commentary on Titus," in *New Jerome*, p. 895.

[42] R.I. Moore, *Formation*, p. 104.

[43] Moore, *Formation*, pp. 100–101, discusses fear of sexual pollution and fear of social change, relying on the analysis of Mary Douglas, *Purity and Danger* (London, 1966), esp. pp. 140–58.

[44] "'Quisquis autem,' inquit Apostolus, 'non habet spiritum Christi, hic non est ejus (Rom. 8).' Item illud de verbis Apostoli: 'Omnis Christianus, dilectissimi, qui a sacerdotibus excommunicatur, Satanae tradi dicitur. Quomodo? scilicet, quia extra ecclesiam est diabolus; sicut in ecclesia Christus. Ac per hoc quasi diabolo traditur, qui ab ecclesiastica communione removetur. Unde illos, quos tunc Apostolus Satanae

in Bernard of Fontcaude's first chapters, where he places his general discussion of obedience and disobedience, we saw that he launches the attack against the disobedient and excommunicated, immediately demonizing them (I.i–ii, PL 204:795–796). They deserve to dwell with Satan, Bernard says, because disobedience is a mortal sin (I.vi, PL 204:797) that merits eternal death or damnation. He cites the example of Korah, struck by fire from heaven because of his revolt against Moses and Aaron (Numbers 16:31–35; I.vi.).[45]

Accusations made against the dissidents, while divisible into the three categories of pollution, reversal of the social order, and apocalypticism, share a common perception that links fear of one to fear of the other: fear of pollution to fear of threat against the social order, fear of threat to the social order to fear of the end of time; and in addition, associations made in one category transfer to the others. As J.B. Russell has emphasized, heretics were viewed as agents of Satan, and this notion intensified during the twelfth century, fueled by exaggerated ideas about Cathar dualism but applied to all tendencies considered heretical.[46]

Pollution

The language of pollution includes implications of disease, infection, impurity and insanity. The papal epistles do not use language as highly charged as that of the other writers we examine. Still in Innocent III's Epistle 235 to the Cistercian abbots, the dissidents are

---

traditos esse praedicat, excommunicatos a se esse demonstrat.'" Bernards adds 2 Thess. 3:14 to support his point: "Hinc est etiam, quod idem Apostolus ait ad Thessalonicenses: 'Si quis non obedierit verbo nostro per epistolam, hunc notate; et ne commisceamini cum illo, ut confundatur (2 Thess. 3:14).' Ecce Apostolus mandat inobedientem sibi reprehendi, et a caeterorum communione vel convictu abjici, ut sic abjectus erubescat."

[45] PL 204:797: "Core quippe, et ejus complices insurrexerunt contra Moysen et Aaron sacerdotes Domini; et confestim igne coelitus misso, combusti sunt. Contradictione ergo Core pereunt, qui sacerdotum imperio contradicunt, et ideo ignis aeterni incendio concremantur. Unde 'vae,' id est, aeterna damnatio est illis." The figure of Korah appears in Jewish preaching to characterize the rebel against the community. See Carmi Horowitz, *Models of Holiness in Medieval Sermons*. Proceedings of the International Symposium (Kalamazoo, May 4–7, 1995), organized by the International Medieval Sermon Studies Society, ed. Beverly Mayne Kienzle, Edith Dolnikowski, Rosemary Drage Hale, Darleen Pryds, Anne T. Thayer (Louvain-la-Neuve, 1996), FIDEM, Textes et Etudes du moyen âge, 5, pp. 175–92.

[46] J.B. Russell, *Lucifer*, pp. 185–190. Although Russell's analysis of Catharism needs to be updated, as does most work currently available in English on Catharism, his point remains valid.

identified as weeds to be uprooted and as diseased elements of the church when the prelates are charged to uproot vices and to cut and cure carefully the bodies of the sick.[47]

The polemicists' language of pollution targets both the words and the beliefs of the Waldensians. 2 Timothy 2:17, describing the words of false teachers as gangrenous is cited by Bernard of Fontcaude.[48] Geoffroy of Auxerre uses it in his Sermon XVIII.[49] Bernard of Fontcaude warns that the heretics will corrupt the healthy like a cancer; he combines the element of disease with the image of yeast that pervades the dough and swells it with pride.[50]

The common association of heresy and leprosy also appears in these texts.[51] For Alain of Lille, Azariah (2 K 15:5 and 2 Par. 26:21), struck by leprosy, is a type for the dissidents, who by their usurpation of the preaching office, are struck with the spiritual leprosy of mortal sin.[52] The Premonstratensian abbot asserts with an extended weak analogy that the disobedient heretic should be shunned because his beliefs are like the disease of leprosy. Bernard explains that the varied skin color of a leper represents the falsehood that the heretic confuses

---

[47] PL 214:793D: "Ea est in fovendis virtutibus et vitiis exstirpandis a praelatis Ecclesiarum servanda discretio et circumspectio adhibenda, ne vel internascentium densitate spinarum enormiter frumenta laedantur, vel insuper seminatorum zizaniorum evulsione triticum evellatur. In abscidendis etiam et curandis corporibus infirmorum sic oculi diligentia praecedere debet manus officium et ferrum digitus praevenire, ne si cauterium adhibeatur incaute, non tam partes infirmas non sanet quam sanas infirmet; quod tanto diligentius in mentis languoribus est servandum, quanto animam novimus corpore digniorem et spiritualia carnalibus praeponenda."

[48] PL 204:813BC: "Apostolus enim ait ad Timotheum: 'Profana,' id est haereses, 'inaniloquia devita' (2 Tim. 2:17), id est [quae sunt] sine fructu, etsi non ita mala, ut profana. 'Multum enim proficiunt ad impietatem,' id est contra cultum Dei; 'et sermo eorum, ut cancer serpit,' paulatim, quae sana sunt corrumpendo."

[49] *Super Apocalypsim*, p. 210: "Denique super modernis eorum vulpeculis, quae non cessant vineam Domini et eius sponsae nequiter demoliri, inveteratos in eadem malitia et quorum sermo serpens ut cancer ad impietatem nimis profecerat...." Here Geoffroy is referring to the Waldensians' public hearing in Toulouse in 1180. See M. Lambert, *Medieval Heresy*, pp. 64–65; C. Thouzellier, *Catharisme et Valdéisme*, pp. 25–36; K.V. Selge, *Die ersten Waldenser*, I, pp. 27–35. The accusation Geoffroy makes later in the sermon seems to represent views attributed to the Cathars and to demonstrate that the two groups are confused in his perception.

[50] PL 204:820C: "Trahunt nempe ad impietatem more cancri, paulatim sana membra, id est fideles, corrumpunt, atque quasi fermentum eos, qui sibi participant, quasi massam similae, amissa naturali dulcedine catholicae unitatis inflant ad superbiam, et acidos reddunt...."

[51] On heresy and leprosy, see R.I. Moore, *Formation*, esp. 63–65.

[52] PL 210:379BC: "Legitur etiam in libro quarto Regum, quod Ozias rex quia sacrificandi officium sibi usurpavit, lepra percussus est. ... Similiter, lepra spirituali, id est peccato mortali pecutitur, qui praedicatoris officium sibi usurpat."

with truth (II.i, PL 204:798C). He argues for the necessity of clerical authority to judge heresy when he reasons that Jesus sent the leper he cured to the priests (Lk. 5:14), so that a priest must judge whether a heretic is pure or not.[53]

In Geoffroy of Auxerre's commentary sermon, we have seen that Jezebel appears as a type for the heretical preacher. Since Jezebel's name is interpreted as flowing blood and excrement, the associations of iniquity and impurity are transferred from her figure to the Waldensians.[54] We recall the related accusations of sexual promiscuity, when the two women of Clermont are cast as a resuscitated Jezebel running through the streets like a prostitute-preacher.[55]

Finally, Geoffroy also accuses the Waldensians of madness, saying that they should use hellebore juice,[56] considered a remedy for insanity.

Threat to the Social Order

The presentation of the dissidents as threats to the social order entails accusations of deceit, destruction, theft and refusal to work, which is a type of theft. These accusations are often based on comparisons to animals and insects,[57] and they frequently entail language of pollution and apocalypticism.

---

[53] "Ut vero clarius pateat, quantum sacerdotes excellant caeteris, et quod eis sit deferendum et obediendum, ex verbis Salvatoris potest perpendi, qui curato a lepra ait: 'Vade, ostende te sacerdoti, et offer munus, quod praecepit Moyses in testimonium illis' (Luc. 5). Sacerdotum quippe est discernere et judicare, qui sint catholici, quive haeretica contagione respersi. Inde est, quod cum multos languentes Dominus sanaverit, leprosos tantum ad sacerdotes misit. In leprosi quippe corpore varius color, designat in haeretico homine veritatem falsitati permistam. Plane Dominus nolui leprosum, licet mundatum, hominum coetibus agregari, sine judiciio sacerdotis, ut aperte ostenderet eum, qui ab unitate catholica erraverit, licet forte resipuerit, sine sacerdotali judicio, conventibus fidelium minime aggregandum."

[54] Geoffroy cites Jerome's interpretation of Jezebel's name (*Liber interpretationis hebraicorum nominum* 80.20, CC 72:160): "In eo quoque quod Iezabel fluens sanguinem vel sterquilinium interpretatur, de abundantia iniquitatis et immunditiae eadem appellatione notatur . . .", *Super Apocalypsim*, p. 178. Jerome states: "Iezabel fluxus sanguinis vel fluens sanguine. Sed melius ubi est sterquilinium." A clear association between women, heresy and sexual immorality is made in Tertullian, *De praescriptione haereticorum* XXX; Eusebius, *Historia Ecclesiastica* V.18.3; and Timothy of Constantinople, *De iis qui ad ecclesiam accedunt*, PG 86:20. I am grateful to Karen King for these references.

[55] See above, n. 36.

[56] *Super Apocalypsim*, p. 179: "Elleborum unde suorum pigmenta acuant, immo figmenta verborum, vituperatio est et derogatio clericorum."

[57] J.B. Russell observes that New Testament texts associate various creatures with demons and only the serpent and the lion with the Devil. *The Devil: Perceptions of Evil*

Deceit threatens when Bernard of Fontcaude likens the heretics' tongues of those of serpents (Ps. 139/140:4) who deceive the hearts of the innocent.[58] Again he compares the poisonous words of the dissenters to the the arrows in Psalm 10:3 (11:2), shot in the dark at the hearts of the upright. Bernard interprets the darkness as the darkened moon or the church, clouded by blasphemers and by the deaths of the martyrs.[59] In another place, he says that the heretics have a poisoned spirit.[60] Geoffroy of Auxerre also compares the dissidents to parrots.[61] Both Bernard of Fontcaude and Alain of Lille describe the heretics as false prophets who hide their identity like wolves in sheep's clothing (Mt. 7:15) or who prey on the Lord's flock.[62]

The threat of destruction is conveyed when the Premonstratensian abbot compares the heretics to locusts (Rev. 9:3–7),[63] and to the little foxes destroying the vineyard,[64] an interpretation of Song of Songs 2:15, found in Geoffroy of Auxerre and his predecessor at Clairvaux, Bernard.[65] Bernard of Fontcaude also compares the dissidents to the

---

from Antiquity to Primitive Christianity (Ithaca and London, 1977), p. 245. He lists the more numerous animals identified with the Devil in medieval folklore in *Lucifer*, p. 67.

[58] PL 204:824B: "Ore vero nocent; quia, sicut scriptum est: 'Acuerunt linguas suas sicut serpentes, venenum aspidum sub labiis eorum' (Ps. 139:4). Acuerunt linguas suas sicut serpentes, ut per dulces sermones et benedictiones seducant corda innocentium. Et ideo venenum aspidum est eis, non in labiis, sed sub labiis; quia non aperte, sed occulte laedunt et more serpentium per linguam morsu venenum erroris insanabile immittunt."

[59] PL 204:822BC: "Vel, in obscura luna, id est ecclesia, quae obscurata fuit in exordio fidei, vel quae obscurata fuit in exordio fidei, vel quae obscuratur nebulis blasphemorum; vel, cum caedibus martyrum cruentatur. In hac obscuritate sagittant haeretici."

[60] PL 204:821A: "habentes animum venenatum. . . ."

[61] *Super Apocalypsim*, p. 179: "Verbis compositis et exquisitis acuunt linguas suas, novos exhibent psittacos, ignorantes de quibus loquuntur, de quibus affirmant."

[62] PL 204:807C: "De non catholicis vero, id est haereticis, dicitur: 'Attendite a falsis prophetis . . .';" PL 204:821A: ". . . et quasi lupos spirituales, qui rapiunt et dispergunt gregem Domini, sicut scriptum est: 'Intrinsecus sunt lupi rapaces';" PL 210:377CD: "Sunt quidam haeretici qui se justos esse fingunt, cum sint lupi veste ovina induti. De quibus Dominus in Evangelio dicit: 'Attendite. . . .'"

[63] PL 204:823–24: "Meritor vero per locustas instabiles, saltantes, ore nocentes frugibus, plus quam caetera minuta animalia, haeretici designantur. Quia 'in veritate non steterunt, sed exierunt ex nobis; quia non erant ex nobis. Si enim fuisset ex nobis, mansissent utique nobiscum.'"

[64] *Super Apocalypsim*, pp. 179, 210: "Ad demoliendam vineam Domini vulpeculae prodierunt, personae contemptibiles et prorsus indignae, praedicationis officium usurpantes . . .;" "Denique super modernis eorum vulpeculis, quae non cessant vineam Domini et eius sponsae nequiter demoliri. . . ."

[65] Sup. Cant. 64.3, *Sancti Bernardi Opera* 2 (Rome, 1957), p. 170.

bulls of Psalm 67(68):31(30) which for him represent proud and undaunted heretics who deceive men of womanly weakness.[66]

Alain of Lille, who entered the Cistercian order late in life, died
at Cîteaux in 1203, and thus probably had a Cistercian audience in
mind,[67] is especially angered at the Waldensians' rejection of all work
but preaching. He charges that the Waldensians boldly preach in
order to fill their bellies rather than their minds and that, unwilling
to work for food with their own hands, they prefer to live leisurely
and to preach falsehood in their pursuit of food. He asserts that,
according to 2 Thessalonians 3:10, anyone who doesn't work should
not eat.[68]

A final category of language implying threat to the social order
centers around accusations that the heretics are thieves and usurpers
of the preaching office. For example, Korah, struck by fire because
he rebelled against Moses and Aaron (Numbers 16:31–35) deserves
mention again here as the type of the usurper or rebel against priestly
authority in both Bernard of Fontcaude and Alain of Lille.[69] Bernard
makes other references to the heretics as thieves, citing John 10:1
and 10:8 for his purposes: ". . . he who does not enter the sheep-
fold by the door but climbs in by another way, that man is a thief
and a robber . . ."; and: "All who came before me are thieves and
robbers."[70]

Apocalypticism

For these late twelfth-century writers, threats to order are often viewed
in the context of apocalyptic biblical passages, where the destruction
or reversal of the social structure precedes the end of time. Hence

---

[66] PL 204:821C: "Seducunt et viros femineae debilitatis, sicut scriptum est: 'Congre-
gatio taurorum in vaccis populorum.' Tauros vocat haereticos; qui sunt superbi et in-
domiti cum vitiis; qui congregantur in vaccis populorum, hoc est in illis, qui facile
possunt seduci."

[67] Jean Longère, *Oeuvres oratoires*, I, pp. 25–27; II, pp. 25–26.

[68] PL 210:378C: "Qui potius ut satient ventrem quam mentem, praedicare prae-
sumunt, et cum non velint laborare propriis manibus ut acquirant victum, malunt
otiose vivere et falsa praedicare, ut venentur cibum (1 Cor. 4) cum Paulus dicat:
'Qui non laborat, non manducet' (2 Thess. 3)."

[69] PL 204:797D; PL 210:379BC.

[70] PL 204:814C, 815D: "Et iste est, qui 'non intrat per ostium, sed ascendit aliunde,
et est fur et latro. Fur autem non venit, nisi ut furetur, mactet et perdat' (Jn. 10:1);"
"De quibus Salvator in Evangelio Joannis loquitur: 'Omnes qui ante me venerunt,
fures sunt et latrones' (Jn. 10:8)."

language directed against the Waldensians likens them to forerunners of the apocalypse: false prophets, antichrists, and agents of Satan.

In a string of insults aimed at the dissident preachers said to ravage God's vineyard in France, Geoffroy of Auxerre alludes to Jude 19, asserting that, among other things, the heretics are "animal-like and lacking the spirit."[71] As we have seen, he evokes the figure of Jezebel in Revelation 2:20 with the power her figure possesses as both the wicked queen of Israel and the false prophet at the end of time.[72] As the type for the heretical preacher, she incarnates all the categories of demonizing rhetoric: pollution, threat to the social order, and apocalypticism. All these converge in the figure of a woman, termed a prostitute-preacher, who reappears after 1,000 years,[73] clearly signaling the threat that Geoffroy of Auxerre thought unauthorized women preachers posed to society.

Bernard of Fontcaude draws on Matthew 7:15 at least three times to link the heretics to the false prophets, describing them as "spiritual wolves" who prey on and disperse the Lord's flock.[74] He also cites Matthew 24:24, 11: "Pseudo-christs and pseudo-prophets will rise up . . ." to claim that the heretics should be rejected as pseudo-prophets.[75] Jeremiah's warning in Lamentations 2:14 concerning prophesying false things supports the same contention.[76] Alain of Lille also evokes Matthew 7:15, directly identifying the false prophets as the Waldensians.[77] Alain also calls on 2 Corinthians 11:13 where, he says,

---

[71] *Super Apocalypsim*, p. 179: ". . . sed potius sine spiritu, iuxta illud: 'Animales, Spiritum non habentes.'"

[72] *Super Apocalypsim*, p. 178: "'Permittis', ait, 'mulierem Iezabel, quae se dicit prophetam, docere et seducere servos meos.' Non mihi videtur eiusmodi pseudo-prophetissam Iezabel nuncupatam, sed ob imitationem malitiae nomen illius quondam impiissimae reginae Israel meruisse. Illa prophetas Domini corporali nece multaverat, haec ad seducendos servos eius exemplis et suasionibus perniciosis . . . insistebat."

[73] Moore, p. 95, cites L.L. Otis, *Prostitution in Medieval Society: The History of an Urban Institution in the Languedoc* (Chicago, 1985), p. 16 on use of the word "meretrix" which was employed so commonly that in the twelfth century it was necessary to qualify it with "publica" in order to differentiate a prostitute from a woman whose behavior was considered scandalous. Geoffroy's use of the word clearly includes an accusation of promiscuity if not actual prostitution.

[74] PL 204:807C, 809; 821A. See note 62 above.

[75] PL 204:809C: "Merito igitur repelluntur quasi pseudoprophetae. Et certe Dominus ait: 'Surgent pseudochristi. . . .'"

[76] PL 204:809BC: "Et de hujusmodi Jeremias populo Israelitico: 'Prophetae tui videbunt tibi falsa, non aperiebant iniquitatem tibi, ut te ad poenitentiam provocarent.' Tales sunt isti, qui populo Christiano viderunt, et praedicant falsa."

[77] PL 210:377C: "Sunt quidam haeretici qui se justos esse fingunt, cum sint lupi veste ovina induti. . . . Hi Waldenses dicuntur, a suo haeresiarcha, qui vocabatur Waldus, qui suo spiritu ductus, non a Deo missus."

Paul reproaches pseudo-preachers because they were preaching without having been sent.[78] The Pauline text refers to pseudo-apostles transforming themselves into apostles of Christ (verse 13) as Satan transformed himself into an angel of light (verse 14).[79] The apocalyptic context and content of the references used by the polemicists sharpens the demonization of the disobedient preacher.

All three writers use 2 Timothy 3:1 describing the intrusion and deceit of the wicked who will come in times of stress in the last days. Geoffroy feminizes the intrusive deceivers to associate them with the female followers of Waldes when he berates their activities in Clermont.[80] Bernard explains that the Apostle's words apply to pseudochrists and heretics; he includes 2 Timothy 3:5 and 6 when he discusses those whom the heretics deceive and do not deceive (BF VII.ii, 821C).[81] Alain exegetes verses 1 to 6, applying the words phrase by phrase to the Waldensians, whom he says the biblical verses suit *maxime*.[82]

Bernard of Fontcaude likens the dissidents to antichrists and calls for their exclusion from society. He explains that there should be no association with the perfidious heretics. They should be treated just like the excommunicated, that is, not heard; like the lost and obviously incorrigible, that is, avoided; like the disobedient, that is, not mingled with; and like antichrists, that is, not greeted nor taken in, but shunned like the profane and vain talking. Finally he characterizes their speech, alluding to 2 Timothy 2:16—the godless chatter that will lead people astray, which is likened to gangrene in the next verse.[83]

---

[78] PL 210:379C: "Item, in Epistola secunda ad Corinthios, pseudopraedicatores arguit, quia missi non erant, sed sua auctoritate praedicabant."

[79] 2 Cor. 11:13–14: "Nam eiusmodi pseudoapostoli operarii subdoli transfigurantes se in apostolos Christi. Et non mirum ipse enim Satanas transfigurant se in angelum lucis."

[80] *Super Apocalypsim*, p. 179, ll. 151ff. See also B.M. Kienzle, "The Prostitute-Preacher," cited above in n. 28.

[81] PL 204:821C: "Hinc Apostolus de pseudochristis et haereticis ait Timotheo: 'Habentes quidem speciem pietatis . . . quae ducuntur variis desideriis.'"

[82] PL 210:380B–D: "Haec omnia maxime conveniunt Waldensibus, qui 'elati' sunt, praelatis Ecclesiae detrahentes; 'superbi', propria opera jactantes; 'blasphemi' in Deum per haereses, 'parentibus' carnalibus et spiritualibus 'inobedientes', quia negant obedientiam praelatis suis. . . ."

[83] PL 204:820C: "Haec sacrarum Scripturarum verba, quasi commonitoria salutis fidelibus Christi cogitanda, memoriterque retinenda excerpsimus; ut aperte sciant, non esse participationem, seu societatem habendam cum perfidis haereticis, nec audiendos, quasi anathematizatos, sed vitandos quasi perditos et manifeste incor-

Conclusion

In summary, late twelfth-century orthodox authors writing about the Waldensians condemn them for disobedience and disqualify them from being valid preachers on that grounds as well as on five other criteria: commission, education, language, gender and marital status, and setting, all of which relate back to the question of obedience to the church's authority. All the writers do not deal with every issue. Marital status, for example, is discussed only by Bernard of Fontcaude while Innocent III's letters concerning the Waldensians in Metz are not concerned with the problem of gender.

The language that the three polemicists employ against the dissidents is set within a frame of demonization and colors them with three sorts of associations: pollution, threat to the social order and apocalypticism. The authors argue from the authority of biblical texts and the church fathers, constructing their case with various rhetorical techniques: images, comparisons, associations and weak analogies. They use their source texts to construct a new reality. In so doing, they both make the events of their own day fit the mold of the authoritative texts and stretch the authoritative texts to make them conform to contemporary events. The ecclesiastical writers rely on practiced methods. As Giles Constable has pointed out in another context, monastic writers were skilled at writing literature of persuasion.[84] Furthermore, we see them adapting methods of exegesis familiar to them: typology where a biblical model or anti-model is a figure for the twelfth-century person or group;[85] allegory where symbols are interpreted to make associations that discredit twelfth-century dissidents. To a great extent, the polemical writers recycle, if you will, the arguments, techniques and language of their sources: books of the Bible reflecting controversies in the early church and patristic writings on heresy and on the role of women in the church. Some studies

---

rigibiles, nec eis commiscendum esse, quasi inobedientibus, nec salutandos, aut in domum recipiendos, quasi antichristos, sed quasi profanos et inaniloquos devitandos. Trahunt nempe ad impietatem et more cancri, paulatim sana membra, id est fideles, corrumpunt. . . ."

[84] See note 12 above.

[85] Beryl Smalley pointed out that the use of familiar types in biblical exegesis could have an influence that was "beneficent or sinister." *The Study of the Bible in the Middle Ages* (Notre Dame, Ind., 1964), pp. 25–26.

have been done on this process of recycling arguments and images, but certainly more work remains to be done.[86]

J.B. Russell discusses three major viewpoints on heresy in the Middle Ages, all involving an element of feared permanence, whether it was an unchanging "Platonic reality," an essential evil like the Devil "changing its form and appearance in time and place," or "a heretical 'apostolic succession'" mirroring the orthodox one.[87] These beliefs in the permanence and evilness of heresy help us to understand why the recycling of sources occurred, why their argumentation is so closed, and why their language is so virulent. Whichever of the three attitudes (or a combination thereof) a twelfth-century orthodox writer adopted, he saw himself challenging an evil threat, what in describing this twelfth-century view, Russell has called "a monolithic threat" whose source was Satan and whose purpose was "to block the kingdom of God."[88]

While the analysis of these twelfth-century texts written against heresy relates closely to the way medieval writers remembered, used and interpreted their sources, it also has a bearing on the wider context of debates over authority in diffusing the faith, particularly with regard to preaching. That the Waldensians' stand on preaching by all believers provoked such a strong reaction underscores how powerful a tool of propaganda preaching was in the Middle Ages. Finally, the study of these twelfth-century polemical texts contributes to the history of persecution in the Middle Ages and to the study of rhetoric as a tool to demonize adversaries, to construct models of holiness and holy preaching that served to exclude and to justify the persecution of those labeled as disobedient, who dissented or differed from definitions of orthodoxy.

---

[86] J.B. Russell, *Lucifer*, p. 184, n. 58, points out how fourteenth-century writers used Augustine's description of fourth-century Luciferans to apply to Waldensians of their day. See also R. Lerner, *The Heresy of the Free Spirit in the Later Middle Ages* (Berkeley, 1972).

[87] J.B. Russell, *Dissent and Order*, p. 4.

[88] J.B. Russell, *Dissent and Order*, p. 62.

LOLLARD INQUISITIONS:
DUE AND UNDUE PROCESS

Henry Ansgar Kelly

Inquisition, or inquisitorial procedure, was a new form of criminal trial developed by Pope Innocent III at the turn of the thirteenth century; he established it in its definitive form at the Fourth Lateran Council in 1215.[1] It enjoyed an immediate success, and it became the basis of procedure not only in all of the ecclesiastical courts of the Western world, but also in all of the secular courts, with the exception of England. I am particularly interested in studying the rights of defendants in the inquisitorial system as practiced in the English ecclesiastical courts, in comparison with defenses permitted in secular courts at the same time. In this paper I will concentrate on one aspect of this subject, namely, church actions taken against the dissidents known as Lollards in the last decades of the fourteenth century and the first half of the fifteenth century.

The early campaign against John Wyclif and his Oxford followers culminated in 1382 in an unusual form of proceeding that deviated from the normal format of trials "in matters of faith," in that, instead of responding to formal charges of having preached or taught erroneous doctrine, the defendants were required to comment on a series of twenty-four propositions condemned as heretical or erroneous by a council of bishops, theologians, and canon lawyers. I have shown elsewhere the details of this procedure and of a similar procedure employed against John Hus at the Council of Constance in 1415.[2] Here I wish to detail other kinds of trials that were used during the same time.

---

[1] *Qualiter et quando* no. 2, *Decretales Gregorii IX* 5.1.24: Innocent III, canon 8 of the Fourth Lateran Council, A.D. 1215, ed. Emil Friedberg, *Corpus iuris canonici*, 2 vols. (Leipzig, 1879–81; repr. Graz, 1959), 2:745–47; for the relevant text, see my "Inquisitorial Due Process and the Status of Secret Crimes," *Proceedings of the Eighth International Congress of Medieval Canon Law*, ed. Stanley Chodorow, Monumenta iuris canonici, Series C: Subsidia, vol. 9 (Vatican City, 1992), pp. 407–27, esp. 410 n. 7.

[2] H.A. Kelly, "Trial Procedures Against Wyclif and Wycliffites in England and at the Council of Constance," forthcoming in the *Huntington Library Quarterly* 61 (1998).

In a normal inquisition (one that followed the *ordo juris*), the defendant would either confess or deny the charges; if he denied them, the judge would attempt to prove them by documents or by the written testimony of witnesses; and if he lacked sufficient evidence of actual guilt, but could establish only the *fama* of guilt that triggered the charges—that is, testimony of trustworthy persons who believed him guilty—the judge could order purgation. This meant that the defendant was required to declare his innocence of the charges under oath, and also to find a stipulated number of neighbors or associates who would swear to his credibility and good reputation. A trial of this sort is set forth in the formal summary by John Buckingham, bishop of Lincoln, of the process he conducted against William Swinderby, concluded on July 11, 1382. Swinderby, suspect of preaching heresy and delated by public fame, was cited to appear before the bishop's commissaries, who leveled charges against him and gave him a term to respond; his response was to deny all wrongdoing. Because of the vehement fame against him, the commissaries fixed a date for canonical purgation and also to allow opponents of the purgation to prosecute the charges. Three friars appeared as denouncers to prove the charges; they produced witnesses whose testimony was published by the bishop and his commissaries, whereupon the bishop convicted him of five errors and six heresies, which he abjured.[3]

We should note that the denouncers in the above case do not function according to the mode of *denuntiatio* set up by Innocent III, according to which a denouncer brings a fault to the judge's attention for the purpose of fraternal correction.[4] Rather, their function seems to be a combination of the earlier *promovens*, or interested aggrieved party who initiates the action, and the *promotor officii judicis*, or judge's assistant.[5] But rather than being appointed by the judge, in this case volunteers for the position were solicited and accepted by the judge.

---

[3] *Fasciculi zizaniorum magistri Johannis Wyclif cum tritico*, ed. Walter Waddington Shirley, Rolls Series 5 (London, 1858), pp. 334–37; the text of the bishop's letter was doubtless taken by the compiler from Bishop Trefnant's register, where it appears, in a transmittal letter from Buckingham dated 10 February 1390, at the beginning of the 1391 process against Swinderby. See *Registrum Johannis Trefnant, episcopi Herefordensis, A.D. 1389–1404*, ed. William W. Capes (London, 1916), p. 231.

[4] *Decretales Gregorii IX* 2.1.13; 5.1.16; 5.3.31 (Friedberg, 2:242–44, 737–38, 760).

[5] Both of these functions are to be distinguished from the independent prosecutor, or *promotor fiscalis*, that was soon to develop in France. See my "Inquisition and the Prosecution of Heresy: Misconceptions and Abuses," *Church History* 58 (1989), 439–51, p. 446 n. 34.

Or at least this is the way Bishop Buckingham presents the matter in his summary. But in his own register it is recorded that the same three friars had presented the original charges, to the number of sixteen, against Swinderby.[6] Furthermore, since the bishop instructed the clergy of the archdeaconry of Leicester "to cause all and sundry who were willing to speak against Swinderby at the time of his purgation to come forward and to denounce him,"[7] are we to conclude that no other denouncers appeared and that the three promotors were obliged to step in again? In his later trial, held in 1391, Swynderby asserted that more than three opponents did come forward: as he was about to make his purgation, "there stooden forth five friars or more, that some of them never saw me before nor heard me, and three lecherous priests." But his account is compatible with there being only three denouncers, with the others functioning as witnesses: "Some of these they cleppeden denunciators, and some were clepped comprobators, that were there falsely forsworn, pursuing busily and crying, with many another friar, with great instance, to give the doom upon me, to burn me," and so on.[8]

On May 14, 1391, the archbishop of Canterbury, William Courteney, notified his province, especially the dioceses of St. David's and Llandaff, that in his recent metropolitan visitation of the Lincoln diocese, he had established by the testimony of witnesses as well as by public fame and the notoriety of the fact itself that, after his abjuration, Swinderby had relapsed, or at least "prolapsed," from bad to worse ("de malo in pejus prolapsus") by preaching the same and other doctrines repugnant to the Faith, and he forbade anyone, under pain of major excommunication, to allow or attend the preaching of one thus convicted of heretical depravity.[9]

---

[6] See Anne Hudson, *The Premature Reformation: Wycliffite Texts and Lollard History* (Oxford 1988), p. 74, citing Lincoln Archives Office, Episcopal Register XII, fols. 242–44, and see also K.B. McFarlane, *John Wycliffe and the Beginnings of English Nonconformity* (London, 1952), p. 122. I assume that the friars were the same: in the bishop's letter they are identified as the Franciscan Roger Frysby, the Augustinian John Hunchay, and the Dominican Thomas Blakstone. McFarlane says that they were masters of theology from these three orders.

[7] McFarlane, p. 123.

[8] *Registrum Trefnant*, pp. 238–39 (spelling modernized).

[9] David Wilkins, *Concilia Magnae Britanniae* (London, 1737; repr. Brussels, 1964), 3:215. His statement of proof is: "prout nuper coram nobis in visitatione nostra metropolitica prefate Lincolniensis diocesis ex plurimorum fide dignorum attestatione, ac alias fama publica et facti notorietate, que nulla poterant tergiversatione celari, referente, informationem accepimus evidentem" (in my citations of Latin, I remedievalize *ae* to *e*).

Before this time, however, action was being contemplated against Swinderby elsewhere, namely, in the diocese of Hereford, for on November 10, 1388, the sheriff had been ordered to hand Swinderby over to the bishop, John Gilbert.[10] No action seems to have been taken at that time, and he only came to trial later in 1391, under Gilbert's successor, John Trefnant, with no notice being taken of the archbishop's pronouncement that he was already re-convicted. However, the trial record is preceded by a letter of Bishop Buckingham, dated February 10, transmitting his 1382 "sentence," or account of Swinderby's conviction and abjuration,[11] which presumably Trefnant solicited in preparation for a trial of relapse.

In his official account of the trial, Trefnant says that Swinderby appeared before him on June 14, 1391, having been summoned as vehemently defamed of schismatic heresy and of perverse doctrines, both public and occult, to answer charges formulated by *nonnulli Christifideles fideique catholice zelatores*, which had been presented to the bishop for the purpose of informing his office ("ad informandum officium nostrum"). The articles as administered to Swinderby are still addressed to Trefnant and speak of the defendant in the third person. The formulators promise (in the passive voice) that if he should deny the articles, they will be proved by trustworthy witnesses and legitimate documents.[12] When Swynderby submitted an elaborate denial of the articles, after he failed to answer further citations, the anonymous *nonnulli* continued to prosecute the case by bringing in witnesses, awkwardly referred to as *testes pro parte nonnullorum Christifidelium*.[13] Some time after Swynderby's final appearance in court on October 3 (the bishop's account does not give a date), Trefnant declared him a heretic, schismatic, and false informer and seducer of the people, to be shunned by all until he deserved to be reconciled to the Church.[14] There is no explanation of why he was not convicted as relapsed into heresy. Perhaps the bishop and his assessors accepted Swinderby's argument that his abjuration in Lincoln had been forced. At any rate, his sentence ends, in effect, with a mere invitation to

---

[10] McFarlane, p. 129.

[11] See n. 2 above.

[12] Ibid., p. 233. See the translation by John Foxe, *Acts and Monuments*, ed. 4, ed. Josiah Pratt (London, 1877), 3:111. Foxe refers to the charges as "articles by the promoters laid against him" (p. 112).

[13] *Registrum Trefnant*, p. 255.

[14] Ibid., p. 271.

abjure, whereas Swinderby himself, in his subsequent appeal to the king's justices and to the knights of Parliament, pointed out that a heresy conviction entailed the death penalty,[15] and, as we saw above, he claimed to have been threatened by death in the 1382 trial. The archbishop's letter of May 4, cited above, alludes to the death penalty when it says he wishes to prevent Swinderby from infecting other people, lest their blood be required at his hands in an extreme judgment ("ne ipsorum sanguis in extremo judicio, quod absit, de nostris manibus requiratur"), but it pronounced no penalty against Swinderby himself. It may be that the authorities were as yet reluctant to impose the ultimate sanction demanded by Church law.[16]

Trefnant also reports on the trial of Walter Brute, which began soon after Swynderby trial. According to the rubric, the process was promoted from the bishop's own office and also at the instance of certain Christian faithful ("ex officio promotus ac eciam ad instanciam quorundam Christifidelium").[17] This terminology is in contrast to the later common formula, according to which it was the judge's office that was promoted, not the trial.[18] This time we are shown the *quidam Christifideles* presenting the charges to the bishop and taking an active-voice role: "We give and exhibit and intend to prove" first of all that Brute, being gravely defamed, was cited to appear several times before Trefnant's predecessor, Bishop Gilbert, and so on.[19]

Trefnant then reveals the chief of the *quidam* as Walter Pryde, penitentiary of the Hereford Cathedral, when he recounts that Pryde and his colleagues presented to him, formally sitting in judgment, two public instruments against Brute: one was a witnessed statement made by him on October 14, 1391, that Swynderby had been wrongly convicted on the preceeding October 3; the second was a notarized

---

[15] Ibid., p. 272. McFarlane, p. 133, says that there is no record of any reaction to this appeal. But the *Fasciculi* reports that Swinderby made an appeal to Richard II and to the audience of the duke of Lancaster (John of Gaunt) during his 1382 trial; as a result, the trial was recessed and the matter committed to Parliament, which decreed that it should be sent back to the bishop (p. 340).

[16] On the theoretical availability of the death penalty for heresy before the 1401 legislation, see Alison McHardy, "*De heretico comburendo*, 1401," *Lollardy and the Gentry in the Later Middle Ages*, ed. Margaret Aston and Colin Richmond (1997, forthcoming).

[17] *Registrum Trefnant*, p. 278.

[18] I discuss these matters in *The Matrimonial Trials of Henry VIII* (Stanford, 1976), p. 266, where I cite the commission given to the vicar-general of the bishop of Winchester in 1535: he is authorized to proceed "ad alicujus partis procurationem, promotionem, sive instantiam, etiam ex officio mero, mixto, vel promoto."

[19] *Registrum Trefnant*, p. 279.

statement of Brute's assertions to the bishop on January 19, 1392 against tithes and the taking of oaths, and his admission that earlier in the month he had eaten and communicated with Swynderby. The bishop then ordered the two conclusions to be put in writing and given to Brute.[20] The second document seems to be an official report of a session of the trial not otherwise recorded. In fact nothing else of the trial is recorded until the end. We are not told how Brute was originally summoned and charged with the articles formulated by the *quidam*, nor how he responded. But it is clear from the report of the January 19 session that at least in part of his response he stated his present belief rather than answering charges of past actions or statements (which was all that was required by the *ordo juris*).

We do not know whether he was forced to speak his mind on his beliefs, rather than addressing the previously listed charges of committed offenses. The bishop simply says that Brute presented to him, partly in person and partly through messengers, various papers written in his own hand in reply to the conclusions and articles which Trefnant had assigned to him at various times and places for his response.[21] The resulting prolix treatise does not refer directly to any objected article but simply details his views on various points, enveloped in clouds of personal philosophy.[22]

The final days of the trial are not recounted as part of letters patent from the bishop, like the first part, but rather are described in a third-person narrative. By the time that Brute finished his response, the trial had gone on for almost two years, to the latter half of 1393. The bishop set October 3 and the days following for his sentence, but no sentence is recorded. Rather, we are told that, in the presence of seventeen theologians (including Nicholas Hereford, who had been tried for heresy in 1382 and excommunicated as a fugitive from justice, and who finally abjured in 1390) and two canonists, three days were spent in showing Brute the heresies and errors in his writings. On October 6 he read a simple statement submitting himself to the Gospel, the Church, the four Latin Fathers, and Bishop Trefnant, whereupon a theologian preached on St. Paul's text, "Noli altum sapere, sed time" ("Be not high-minded, but fear," Rom. 11:20).[23] There follows a list of the "conclusions, heresies and errors condemned

---

[20] Ibid., pp. 283–85.
[21] Ibid., p. 285.
[22] Ibid., pp. 285–358.
[23] Ibid., pp. 395–60.

by Bishop John and his assessors on October 6,"[24] but Brute himself
does not seem to have been convicted of heresy, and his submission
to the bishop's correction does not look like an abjuration. In his
opening statement, Brute had said that he would willingly accept
correction from anyone who would show him his errors by scriptural
reasons,[25] so that perhaps he was exonerated of formal heresy. Heresy is defined later in the register, at the end of the "sentences" of
the chancellor of Cambridge and other Cambridge scholars against
Swinderby's doctrines, thus: "Heresy is a false dogma contrary to
the Catholic faith and the determination of the Church, which is
pertinaciously defended," and a heretic is defined as one who in-
vents such a new doctrine or who follows and pertinaciously defends
one invented by others.[26] The crucial element of pertinacity must
have been judged lacking in Brute.

A promoted trial, reported by the Carmelite John Langton in
Fasciculi zizaniorum, was conducted by Archbishop Courteney in 1392
against the Irish Cistercian Henry Crump. Crump was examined by
the archbishop on ten questionable conclusions that he had allegedly
defended at Oxford, which he denied. But on three of the conclusions
he was accused by way of denunciation ("per modum denuntiationis
accusatus") by a Dominican friar named John Paris, acting on the
occasion as promotor for the archbishop ("tanquam per promotorem
officii domini Cantuariensis in hac parte"), and he was convicted by
the depositions of nine witnesses and compelled to abjure.[27]

Courteney's successor, Archbishop Arundel, used his chancellor,
Robert Hallum, to serve in effect as his promotor in the trial of the
Lollard William Sawtrey in 1401, calling him the "organ of his voice,"
and employing him to read the articles and the sentence.[28] In the
same year Hallum served as promotor in the trial of a London parish

---

[24] Ibid., pp. 360–65.

[25] Ibid., pp. 285–86.

[26] Ibid., p. 393. The Cambridge sentences are given immediately after the list of
Brute's condemned views, on pp. 365–93. On p. 394, *error*, *blasphemia*, and *scisma* are
defined.

[27] *Fasciculi*, pp. 343–48. Langton identifies himself on p. 348; he adds that a little
later there was discovered a letter from the bishop of Meath to the University of
Oxford, dated 1 April 1385, recounting the trial in which he had found Crump
guilty as an impenitent and obstinate heretic on 18 March of the same year; the
letter follows on pp. 349–56; then he appends a letter from Richard II to Oxford,
dated 30 March 1393, suspending Crump from teaching and summoning him to
his council to respond to charges of spreading heresy—but with no mention of his
previous convictions (pp. 358–59).

[28] Wilkins, 3:256. For a chronology of Sawtrey's trial, see McHardy, "*De heretico*."

priest, Robert Bowelond, who was delated to Arundel during his visitation of the diocese of Coventry and Lichfield, for "incest" and grave incontinence with a nun from a priory in the diocese. Bowelond may have been the man of this name identified by William Thorpe as an early follower of Wyclif;[29] he chose for his judge Philip Repingdon, one of the Oxford Wycliffites convicted and rehabilitated in 1382, now the abbot of his monastery of canons regular at Leicester. He denied the charge, and proofs of witnesses and other evidences sufficient for conviction were produced at the promotion of Hallum and in the presence of the archbishop's commissary and other clerics deputed by the archbishop for the purpose.[30]

We have seen that Archbishop Courteney considered Swynderby convicted a second time by notoriety in 1391. When Courteney conducted a visitation of the Lincoln diocese in 1391, he established by the testimony of witnesses as well as by public fame and the notoriety of the fact itself that Swinderby had relapsed.[31] In 1389 he had used visitation witnesses not only to establish the initial public fame of alleged heretics at Leicester, but also to convict them by notoriety. However, when they subsequently appeared before him to be tried in person, he clearly did not consider them to have been convicted and then relapsed; rather, he received their confession of heresies and errors as a first conviction.[32] On the same day that he convicted the Lollards of Leicester as notorious heretics, Courteney also dealt with an anchorite named Matilda (Maud) who had been reported as infected with Lollard doctrines. She was first examined (at her hermitage, according to Wilkins's interpretation) on the same questionable conclusions that the others had been accused of,[33] and, because her

---

[29] William Thorpe, *The Testimony of William Thorpe*, ed. Anne Hudson, *Two Wycliffite Texts* (Oxford, 1993), p. 93; see notes, p. 111.

[30] Wilkins, 3:262–63.

[31] Wilkins, 3:215: "prout nuper coram nobis in visitatione nostra metropolitica prefate Lincolniensis diocesis ex plurimorum fide dignorum attestatione, ac alias fama publica et facti notorietate, que nulla poterant tergiversatione celari, referente, informationem accepimus evidentem."

[32] Ibid., pp. 208–12; see the more recent edition by Joseph Henry Dahmus, *The Metropolitan Visitations of William Courteney, Arbishop of Canterbury, 1381–1396* (Urbana, 1950), pp. 164–72; see esp. p. 171 (Wilkins, p. 211 col. 1): "de heresibus et erroribus per viam notoriam convictos, excommunicatos denunciavimus, a Christi fidelibus evitandos." Their subsequent appearance in court, confession, abjuration, and reception of penance follow.

[33] Wilkins, p. 209: "Dominus archiepiscopus ad eandem Matildem sic reclusam *misit, et* ipsam super conclusionibus heresibus, et erroribus predictis diligenter examinavit"; Dahmus, *Metropolitan*, p. 166, omits the italicized words, and assumes that

answers to the *interrogata* were not clear but rather sophistical, the archbishop assigned a day and time for her to appear before him and respond "concerning certain articles and interrogatories about the aforesaid heresies and errors to be objected to her for the correction and salvation of her soul."[34] In other words, an informal interrogation preceded a formal presentation of charges and interrogations in an inquisitory trial. She confessed her errors, and asked for and received pardon.[35]

After the condemnations of 1382, there was still concern in England with identifying and condemning Wycliffian errors, but there is no clear example of their being used *en bloc* in court in the way in which they were administered to Repingdon and others. However, Archbishop Arundel did seem to have some such list of errors ready to apply to the priest William Thorpe when he confronted him in 1407. According to Thorpe's autobiographical account, Arundel considered his reputation as a Lollard well established, and he urged a streamlined process: "I will, shortly, that thou swear now here to me that thou shalt forsake all the opinions which the sect of Lollers holdeth and is slandered with, so that after this time, neither privily nor apertly, thou hold none opinion which I shall, after that thou hast sworn, rehearse here to thee."[36] When Thorpe declined this invitation to abjure, the archbishop produced certified testimony from Shrewsbury that Thorpe had preached five specific errors there, which Thorpe denied. Then, at the suggestion of one of his assistants, Arundel asked him to explain then and there what he held about each of the five alleged errors. At another clerk's urging, Thorpe was asked to explicate a dubious-sounding assertion ("It is a sin to swear well") from a sermon of St. John Chrysostom, which was found in the possession of one of Thorpe's associates. Thorpe reports, "I was some deal aghast to answer hereto, for I had not busied me to study about the wit thereof," but he says that the archbishop was satisfied with his impromptu explanation.[37]

Courteney summoned the recluse to him (p. 49); but something is clearly missing from the text as he gives it.

[34] "Super articulis et interrogatoriis predictas hereses et errores concernentibus sibi ad anime sue correctionem et salutem objiciendis."

[35] Dahmus, *Metropolitan*, p. 49.

[36] Thorpe, *Testimony*, p. 34 (I modernize the spelling); see H.A. Kelly, "The Right to Remain Silent: Before and After Joan of Arc," *Speculum* 68 (1993), 992–1026, esp. p. 1008 n. 74.

[37] Thorpe, pp. 76–77.

In the Canterbury Convocation of 1407, held at Oxford, Archbishop Arundel prohibited the reading (teaching) of any work by Wyclif or anyone else since his time without first being officially approved, and no translation of the Scriptures made in the time of Wyclif or later was to be read without episcopal or provincial license.[38] The constitutions were officially published in 1409, and in the same year Arundel set about compiling a new list of Wycliffian heresies and errors. His Oxford committee emerged with 267 propositions, which were condemned in a Canterbury synod in 1411. The list was for-

---

[38] See Joseph H. Dahmus, *The Prosecution of John Wyclyf* (New Haven, 1952), p. 152; but Dahmus errs in saying that the archbishop's constitutions dealt only with Wyclif's translations of the Bible; rather, they dealt with all translations of the Bible. For the text, see Wilkins, 3:317, and also William Lyndwood, *Provinciale* 5.4.3 (1432; Oxford, 1679; repr. Farnborough, 1968), p. 286, and in the final appendix, p. 66: "nec legatur aliquis hujusmodi liber, libellus, aut tractatus [containing translations] jam noviter, tempore dicti Johannis Wickliff, sive citra, compositus, sive componendus in posterum," etc. Nicholas Watson, "Censorship and Cultural Change in Late-Medieval England: Vernacular Theology, the Oxford Translation Debate, and Arundel's Constitutions of 1409," *Speculum* 70 (1995) 822–64, p. 825, cites C.R. Cheney, "William Lyndwood's *Provinciale*," *Medieval Texts and Studies* (Oxford, 1973), pp. 158–84 at 172 n. 7, as saying that the constitutions were issued in 1409, two years after their "first drafting"; but what Cheney says is that they were first *issued* in 1407 and finally published in 1409. Watson's characterization of the constitutions on pp. 827–28 contains a number of errors, some induced by reliance on John Foxe's paraphrase. The constitutions do not "impose limits on the discussion of theological questions in the schools," as long as articles determined by the Church are not called into question (no. 9); they do not require a monthly inquiry "into the views of every student at the university" but only an inquiry as to whether any student is holding suspect doctrines (no. 11); they do not prohibit the study of Wyclif's works altogether, but only such as are not approved by a panel of twelve censors; the panel is not to be appointed by the archbishop but by one or both universities, as the archbishop thinks best (no. 6); not all authorized preachers are required to present themselves for examination by the ordinary, for the parochial clergy are exempt (no. 1); preachers are forbidden to discuss the sins of the clergy only when no clergy are in the audience, and similarly they are not to discuss lay sins before an entirely clerical audience (no. 3); there is no prohibition against preaching the sacraments, as long as orthodox doctrine is followed (no. 4); only temporary parochial clergy are ordered to restrict themselves to preaching what is expressly contained in Peckham's *Ignorantia sacerdotum* (no. 1); no ban of subject matter is extended to schoolmasters—except, of course, anything contrary to the determinations of the Church! (no. 5)—and there is no prohibition of "all argument over matters of faith outside universities"; there is a prohibition against the unauthorized reading, not ownership, of new translations of Scripture (no. 7). Finally, Watson's assertion (p. 892 n. 16) that *translatio* in medieval texts "routinely refers to acts of interpretation or exegesis or to 'the exposition of meaning in another language'" is dubious, and is supported only by reference to a twelfth-century Italian dictionary; no such usage has been recorded in England: see R.E. Latham, *Revised Medieval Latin Word-List from British and Irish Sources, with Supplement* (Oxford, 1980).

warded to Rome for further condemnation.[39] But in two high-profile
cases dealt with by Arundel, those of the tailor John Badby in 1410
and the knight John Oldcastle in 1413, the defendants were interrogated only on the specific charges against them. In both cases, however, the questions were aimed not at establishing the truth of the
charges, that they had propagated heretical ideas, but at determining
whether they currently endorsed those ideas. In Badby's case, he
had already been convicted in the previous year, after being delated
to Bishop Peverel of Worcester for having held, taught, and publicly
maintained a heretical view of the Eucharist. In that original trial
also, instead of requiring him to confess or deny his guilt of the
charged crime, the bishop simply asked him what he believed on the
subject. Under Peverel's interrogation, Badby readily acknowledged
that he firmly held the implicated doctrine, and his response served
as the basis of Arundel's review in Convocation. Arundel urged Badby
to revoke his assertion of belief, and, when he refused, his previous
conviction was ratified.[40]

Oldcastle was delated directly to Archbishop Arundel, who summoned him to trial on five charges. After being excommunicated for
defying the summons, he was arrested and brought before the archbishop, who recited the charges and offered to absolve him of the
excommunication. Oldcastle responded by reading a prepared statement of his beliefs. Upon consultation with assessors, Arundel said
that he must respond to the articles. But rather than asking him
whether he had committed the specified crimes, he said that Oldcastle
must say whether he believed that material bread remained after
consecration and whether it was necessary to confess to a priest. When
Oldcastle refused to respond (as was his right), Arundel said that if
he did not make a clear response he could declare him a heretic.
Then, "taking pity on him," the archbishop gave him a set of four
articles in English, all concerning present belief: "How believe ye
this article?" or "How feel ye this article?" After hearing his responses,
Arundel declared him a heretic, saying that he was unwilling to confess his error or purge himself of it or to renounce it ("errorem suum
noluerit confiteri, aut se purgare de eodem, nec etiam detestari").[41]
We note that Oldcastle was not put under oath, perhaps because

---

[39] Wilkins, 3:322, 339–51; Dahmus, *Prosecution*, pp. 152–53.
[40] Wilkins, 3:325–28.
[41] Ibid., 3:353–56.

he refused to be absolved of excommunication, and, in spite of
the archbishop's implied claim in the sentence, he was not offered
compurgation.

A group of eight suspected heretics from Bristol, some of whom
had connections with Oldcastle, were treated differently. The record
is rather complicated and needs an overview. The suspects were
indicted before royal commissioners in 1413 or 1414 on charges of
Lollardy and turned over to the local ordinary, Nicholas Bubwith,
bishop of Bath and Wells, for ecclesiastical trial. They successfully
purged themselves in mid-1414 and early 1415, but it was only on
June 18, 1417, that the king requested verification of the suspects'
claim of purgation; presumably the suspects had been kept in prison
in the meantime. On October 4, the bishop's office replied with an
account of seven of the defendants. The king inquired again on
November 28 about the other suspect, Christina More, and reply
was made on January 10, 1418.[42]

Four of the suspects were delivered on June 28, 1414, to Bubwith's
commissioners. On July 5, they were brought before the bishop himself to "respond upon matter of Lollardy and to other articles concerning the Catholic faith and the determination of Holy Church."
They took an oath to tell the truth to all interrogations ("ad omnia
interroganda"). Bishop Bubwith first interrogated Edmund Brown
on the fourteen articles of faith, the ten commandments, the seven
sacraments, the seven works of mercy, and the "seven cardinal virtues," asking him how he thought ("interrogavit qualiter sentiit") about
each. Brown responded that he thought well and as a Catholic about
them, and that he had never thought or held the contrary and never
would do so. Similarly, when asked about the seven mortal sins, he
replied that they were all to be avoided. The other three defendants
responded in the same way.[43] We note that they were not required
to expound upon any of the articles and risk making damaging mis-
statements of doctrine.

Then the bishop objected to them *ex officio* and interrogated them,
under their oath, asking them to say whether they were Lollards, or
had read any books of Lollards, and so on, and whether the articles

---

[42] *The Register of Nicholas Bubwith, Bishop of Bath and Wells, 1417–1424*, ed. Thomas
Scott Holmes, 2 vols. (London, 1914), 1:283–90 (no. 716), 298 (no. 745). See John
A.F. Thomson, *The Later Lollards, 1414–1520* (Oxford, 1965), pp. 22–24.

[43] *Register of Bubwith*, pp. 284–86.

upon which they had been indicted (before the royal commissioners) were true, and whether the fame about them in Bristol, that they were Lollards, was true or false. They all declared their innocence, and offered to purge themselves. Purgation with twelve compurgators each was ordered on July 23, and a call was put out for volunteers to come forth and speak against the defendants and impede the compurgation. But no such opponents appeared, and the purgation was successfully performed before the bishop's official, John Welles. However, in spite of the fact that they succeeded in clearing themselves, they "abjured in the form of law" (that is, no doubt, they were forced to abjure) all heresy and all Lollardy, declaring that from then on ("decetero") they would abstain from all suspect gatherings. Those present included the mayor and one of the sheriffs of Bristol.[44] On the same day, July 23, Christina More's trial took place, with the same result. She made her purgation on October 23 before John Storthwayt, the bishop's commissary general.[45]

The other three suspects were delivered from the king's prison in Bristol by the mayor and a sheriff, acting on a royal writ, on January 30, 1415, to Storthwayt, and he held their trial on the same day (Bishop Bubwith was by now at the Council of Constance).[46] Concerning the articles of faith, virtues, and so on they made responses similar to those of the the first four. Then the commissary, acting "*ex officio* and in the forum of mere correction of soul," objected to them the crime of heresy and error, in general and in particular, and especially concerning the chapters and articles of Lollardy on which they had been indicted and defamed; all objections met with constant denials.[47] When asked about the fame of the crime of Lollardy that labored against them, they responded with a strong declaration that it was true, *penitus animis* ("to the depths of minds"?), and they earnestly and humbly asked to clear themselves by purgation or any other reasonable and legal means. Purgation was set for February 25 in the same way as before, except that this time fifteen compurgators

---

[44] Ibid., pp. 286–88.

[45] Ibid., p. 298.

[46] A.B. Emden, *Biographical Register of the University of Oxford to A.D. 1500* (Oxford, 1957, repr. with additions, 1989), 1:295.

[47] *Register Bubwith*, 1:288–89: "Crimen heresis et erroris, tam in genere quam in specie, ac presertim capitula et articulos Lollardie super quibus, ut premittitur, fuerunt indictati et publice diffamati, eis et eorum cuilibet ex officio in foro mere correccionis anime per dictum commissarium objectum et objecta, constanter negarunt et negavit quilibet eorundem."

were required of each. The suspects were all cleared, and after making their abjuration, they were restored to good fame.[48]

We see, then, that the trials of the Bristol suspects did not follow the inquisitorial procedure of summoning defamed persons, listing and explaining the charges on which they were defamed, proving that the bad fame against them really existed, and then, when the truth of the charges could not be proved by confessions or documents or witnesses, subjecting them to purgation. Instead, they were inter-rogated under oath about their beliefs, then required to respond to the truth of the charges on which they had been indicted in the secular court, and finally required to say whether the fame against them was true. If they had denied the truth of the fame, then the bishop and his delegates would haved been obliged by law to prove the existence of the fame before receiving witnesses to the truth of the charges or ordering purgation. But since the defendants admitted that they were defamed, but groundlessly, and they themselves re-quested purgation, the ordering of purgation could be considered pro-cedurally regular. But what about the abjuration?

William Lyndwood, writing between 1423 and 1430,[49] sets forth the law on abjuration in his commentary on the 1407/07 legislation of Archbishop Arundel: "You should know that everyone who is gravely suspect of heresy and wishes to return to the unity of the Church can be compelled to abjure heresy."[50] But Lyndwood is speak-ing of convicted suspects, of those who, by means of witnesses or other lawful proofs, are convicted of having said or done something suggestive of heresy (in this case, holding that the Church cannot make laws restricting preaching) and formally pronounced by the judge to be, not heretics, but suspected of heresy. Then, unless these suspects repudiate the proved opinion or action, they are to be de-clared heretics.[51] But in addition to such repudiation, Arundel also

---

[48] Ibid., p. 289.

[49] C.R. Cheney, "William Lyndwood's *Provinciale*," *Medieval Texts and Studies* (Oxford 1973), pp. 158–84, at 160.

[50] William Lyndwood, *Provinciale* (1432; Oxford, 1679; repr. Farnborough, 1968), 5.5.1, p. 292, v. *abjuraverint* (note *h*): "Scire enim debes quod omnis qui est graviter suspectus de heresi, volens redire ad unitatem ecclesie, potest compelli heresim abjurare," citing Alexander IV, *Accusatus*, *Sext* 5.2.8 (Friedberg, 2:1071–72).

[51] Lyndwood, loc. cit., v *convicti* (note *f*): "Per testes vel alias probationes legitimas, et in hac convictione requiritur pronunciatio, ut dixi supra, *De simonia*, c. *Nulli*, v. *convictus* [p. 281 note *o*], et debet hec pronunciatio esse, non scilicet ut pronuncietur hereticus, sed ut pronuncietur sic dixisse verbo, actuve fecisse, per quod satis apparet

requires them to make an abjuration in due form, and it is here that Lyndwood makes the above statement.[52]

According to the law, then, since the Bristol defendants were not convicted, they were wrongly required to make an abjuration, and it should follow that if they were later convicted of falling into heresy it ought not be considered a relapse but rather a first conviction. There is a good chance that this would have been the judgment if the case had arisen in Convocation, because Lyndwood was now effectively in charge of defining Church law in the province of Canterbury. Three months or so before the first of the Bristol suspects were delivered for trial, Henry Chichele had taken over as archbishop of Canterbury, and on August 1, 1414, he appointed Lyndwood his chancellor and auditor of causes. By 1417 he was the official of Canterbury, the chief judge of the province under the archbishop. His views on relapse can be seen in the 1421 trial of William Taylor in convocation. The archbishop turned towards the jurists present and asked them to consult their books on what was to be done in a case of relapse. Lyndwood replied immediately (*incontinenti*) with a written response: 1) A suspect of heresy, cited and absent through contumacy, becomes vehemently suspect, but this is not sufficient for a criminal conviction. 2) Deliberate continuance such contumacy changes the vehement presumption of guilt to violent presumption, which suffices for automatic conviction. 3) If such a person returns before condemnation and is ready to abjure, he should be allowed to do so. 4) A person who abjures heresy in a general way and later falls into a species of heresy is considered relapsed. 5) A relapsed heretic is to be left to the secular court without hope of remission.[53] He does not make it clear in this statement, as he does in his later gloss, that before such a defendant is required to make an abjuration he much be formally sentenced as vehemently suspect (in this case,

---

eum sentire quod ecclesia non posset sic statuere, et sic per consequens de heresi suspectum esse: et nisi resipiscat, pro heretico damnandum fore."

[52] Further on, 5.5.2, p. 296, v. *simpliciter* (note *d*), Lyndwood asks whether a person who abjured one form of heresy and later fell into another form of heresy should be considered relapsed. He cites John Andrew as saying no, Archdeacon Guy of Baysio as saying yes; he finds an argument to support Andrew, and then notes that Andrew himself in another gloss supports the positive response, which is also that of Geminianus (Dominic of San Gimignano), an exact contemporary of Lyndwood's (he died before 1436). Geminianus says that a person who abjures one form of heresy can be seen to abjure all forms because they are all connected.

[53] *The Register of Henry Chichele, Archbishop of Canterbury, 1414–1443*, ed. E.F. Jacob, 4 vols. (Oxford, 1983–47), 3:168.

for contemputously refusing to appear in court). In his commentary, he defines relapse as the repetition of the same fault (*iteratio ejusdem delicti*).[54] He goes on to distinguish between true relapse (one conviction of heresy followed abjuration and then by another conviction of heresy) from fictitious relapse, drawing on the decretal *Accusatus* of Alexander IV, according to which one of the convictions, before or after abjuration, is not of heresy but of vehement suspicion of heresy (like proven association with heretics).[55]

An early case of relapse held before the archbishop in which Lyndwood served as examiner and assessor was the trial of John Claydon on August 17, 1415. The form of the trial is not entirely clear. Only one item is objected to him, namely, that he had been and still was notoriously defamed of heresy and also vehemently and notoriously suspect. He responded by publicly and judicially confessing that for twenty years he had been reputed in the view of the common people to be vehemently suspect of Lollardy and heretical depravity, and notoriously defamed of the same, such that in the time of Bishop Braybrook of London (1381–1404) he was kept in prison for five years, until in the time of Henry IV he made an abjuration before the king's chancellor John Scarle (in office until March 9, 1401). The rest of the trial seems to consist of interrogations. Chichele asked him if he had ever abjured heresy before anyone else, and he publicly and judically confessed that he had made a solemn abjuration before Archbishop Arundel about two years later ("circa biennium elapsum") in a Convocation of the clergy at St. Paul's, when, because of the aforesaid vehement suspicion and infamy he was charged with articles allegedly savoring of heresy and error and contrary to the determination of the Church. Included in the abjuration was a promise to abstain from all communication with men defamed and suspect of these opinions.[56] This was apparently not considered a second conviction, perhaps because his earlier abjuration was not preceded by a trial or because Chancellor Scarle had no ecclesiastical jurisdiction over him.

Archbishop Chichele then asked Claydon if he possessed any books written in English. He responded that he could not deny that he had possessed several English books, for it was because of these books that

---

[54] Lyndwood, loc. cit., v. *relapsus* (p. 296 note *l*).
[55] Ibid., v. *relapso* (note *n*); see n. 28 above for *Accusatus*.
[56] *Register of Chichele*, 4:132–33.

he was arrested by the mayor of London, and he believed that the mayor had the books in his custody. The mayor, who was present, testified that this was so, and in his opinion they were the worst books he had every read. Regarding one of the books, Claydon confessed that he had had it copied and had heard about a fourth of it read. On being questioned whether he thought the content of the book was good and Catholic, he answered that much of what he had heard was very salutary, and that he particularly liked a sermon that was copied there. Finally, Claydon was questioned about Richard Baker, and he confessed that he had had frequent communication with him, even though he knew that he was suspected or defamed of heresy.[57]

After these confessions, Chichele committed the books to Robert Gilbert, master of theology, to Lyndwood, doctor of both laws, and to other clerics for examination, and he ordered the admission of three witnesses. The first, David Berde, a twenty-three-year-old servant of Claydon's, illiterate, like his master, was asked three questions: Did he know the book exhibited to him by the examiner, which certain persons vehemently suspect of heresy called *The Lantern of Light*? Did he know that Claydon read this book or had it read to him? Did he know if Claydon approved, held, or taught the contents of the book as good and Catholic? Berde responded that he did know the book and knew that it contained the ten commandments in English and other matters which he could not remember. He said that Claydon listened to it and commended it and never rejected anything he heard in it as suspect. But Berde could remember nothing more than the first commandment being read from the book. The second witness, another illiterate servant, Saundre Phelip, aged fifteen, on being asked the same three questions, testified that the book was copied and corrected in Claydon's house and in his presence, and that Richard Baker and a person named Montfort, who were held to be vehemently suspect of Lollardy, on several days came and discussed the book with Claydon. The third witness, Baltazar Mero, aged thirty, concorded with Berde, except that he could not remember anything of the content of the book. He added that he had seen Claydon often communicate on articles of Sacred Scripture with Baker and Montfort, who he said were held to be suspect of Lollardy.[58]

Then a committee consisting neither of Gilbert nor Lyndwood but

---

[57] Ibid., p. 133.
[58] Ibid., pp. 133–36.

of four friars, all masters of theology, reported on the books: they all contained many heresies and errors, and fifteen in the *Lantern* were singled out. Finally, after consulting with Lyndwood and other assessors, Chichele decreed that the books were to be burned, and, because the assessors believed Claydon to have relapsed into abjured heresy, because of what had been confessed and testified to and proved by the evidence of facts and deeds, he read the definitive sentence against him, delivering him to the secular judge.[59]

Apart from the severity of the conclusion, the procedure in this case seems regular enough. Claydon was not quizzed about his present beliefs, except in an attempt to discover whether he had knowingly supported heresy in the past, but it would seem that the results were inconclusive, since he did not admit to supporting any specific doctrine, either then or in the past. The evidence presented about his possession of suspect books and consorting with a suspected Lollard should have led only to a conviction of vehement suspicion of heresy, and, according to Lyndwood's later explication of Alexander IV's decretal, this would not have been sufficient even for a fictitious conclusion of relapse, if his first conviction under Arundel was also for no more than suspicion.

The finding of heresies and errors in Claydon's books is not said to have contributed to his condemnation, but only to the decision to have them burned. The possession of suspect English books was not covered in the constitutions of 1407/09, but it was incorporated into the constitution that Chichele issued in the year following the Claydon trial.[60]

Meanwhile, at Constance, the posthumous trial of John Wyclif took place in 1415, as did the trials and condemnations of two of his Bohemian admirers, John Hus and Jerome of Prague. The proceedings against Hus were notable above all in his first being required to write his opinion of propositions ascribed to Wyclif.[61] But though Hus's examination on Wycliffite doctrines does not seem to have played a part in his formal trial, it may have influenced the procedure set forth in the bull of Martin V, *Inter cunctas pastoralis cure solicitudines,*

---

[59] Ibid., pp. 136–38.

[60] Ibid., 3:18–19, *Statutum editum contra hereticos*, 1 July 1416: archeacons and episcopal judges are to make inquisition not only into those holding heresies and errors but also "those possessing suspect books written in the common English tongue." For the procedures called for in this statute, see Jacob's introduction, 1:cxxxii, but see also my correction of his account, in my "English Kings and the Fear of Sorcery," *Mediaeval Studies* 39 (1977), 206–38, pp. 222–23 n. 64.

[61] For details, see my "Trial Procedures."

issued on February 22, 1418, and addressed to all archbishops, bishops, and inquisitors of heretical depravity, especially those in Bohemia and Moravia, where, the pope says, the errors of Wyclif, Hus, and Jerome are still flourishing. The prelates of those regions are like silent watchdogs, unable bark, not being ready, with the Apostle, "to revenge all disobedience" (2 Cor. 10:6).[62] The remedies that he first enjoins are entirely standard and in accord with the established *ordo juris.* All persons who are found by a competent ecclesiastical judge to be "suspect by suspicion alone," specifically of favoring the doctrine or any article of the above-named heresiarchs, are to undergo canonical purgation, and, if they fail, to be condemned as heretics. It should go without saying, though in fact the pope goes ahead and says it, that if anyone is actually found guilty of such an offense, he is to be canonically punished.[63] But then Pope Martin orders a method of dealing with suspects that goes beyond previously approved inquisitorial procedure. Lest prejudice and scandal should befall the orthodox faith on the pretext of ignorance, he says, he rehearses the forty-five articles of Wyclif originally condemned at the council, together with the thirty condemned articles of Hus, and orders them transmitted to the kingdom of Bohemia and to other places where this doctrine has festered; he requires bishops and inquisitors to compel all persons defamed or suspected of such pestiferous taint to respond under oath to the individual articles according to interrogatories, given below, that are suitable to each article, under pain of *confessatum crimen,* excommunication, suspension, interdict, or other formidable canonical or legal penalties, when and however they see fit and the nature of the circumstances requires.[64] The thirty-seven questions that follow

---

[62] Martin V, *Inter cunctas,* ed. Hermann von der Hardt, *Magnum oecumenicum constantiense concilium,* 6 vols. (Frankfurt, 1697–1700, 1742) 4:1518–31, and John Dominic Mansi, *Sacrorum conciliorum nova et amplissima collectio,* 27 (Venice, 1784) 1204–15; I follow the text and numbered sections of the *Bullarium romanum,* 26 vols. (Turin, 1857–67), 4:665–67, here citing the salutation, introduction, and §1, p. 665 (Hardt, 1518–20, Mansi, 1204).

[63] Ibid., §9, pp. 667–68 (Hardt, 1522, Mansi, 1206).

[64] Ibid., §11, pp. 668–69 (Hardt, 1522–23, Mansi, 1207). The last part of the text reads: "Precipimus et mandamus ut quilibet eorum . . . omnes infamatos seu suspectos de tam pestifera labe sub confessati criminis, excommunicationis, suspensionis, interdicti, aut alia formidabili pena canonica vel legali, prout, quando et quemadmodum eis videatur expedire et facti requireret qualitas, ad singulos hujusmodi articulos per juramentum corporaliter prestitum, . . . juxta infrascripta interrogatoria ad quemlibet articulum convenientia, respondere compellant." Wyclif's articles are given in §12, pp. 669–71 (Hardt, 1523–25, Mansi, 1207–09), and Hus's in §13, pp. 671–73 (Hardt, 1525–27, Mansi, 1209–11), condemned at the council on 4 May

the articles are headed by the instruction: "Upon the aforesaid articles, each person suspected of them or arrested for asserting them is to be interrogated according to the following method" ("Super premissis autem articulis, quilibet de eis suspectus seu in eorum assertione deprehensus juxta modum interrogetur"). The first questions concern the suspect's personal knowledge of the three heresiarchs (1–2), whether he honored them after their death (3–4), and whether he believes in the authority of the Council of Constance and its condemnations (5–8). Does he possess their books? (9–10). Especially if he is literate, he is to be asked if he believes (that is, approves and considers valid) the sentence of the council on the 45 articles of Wyclif and the 30 of Hus (11). The next questions concern the lawfulness of swearing, and the sinfulness of perjury (12–14). The remaining questions concern matters of faith connected with the heresiarchs' errors, but phrased positively, so that a "yes" answer would be an assertion of orthodoxy: for instance, "Whether he believes that a Christian who contemns the reception of the sacraments of confirmation or extreme unction or the solemnization of matrimony commits a mortal sin" (19).[65]

The pope continues: If anyone is found defamed or suspect by secret information or otherwise of the doctrine of these heresiarchs, he is to be cited to appear before the bishop or other ecclesiastical judge with jurisdiction over him, with no proctor or advocate, to respond on oath concerning the aforesaid articles or on other appropriate ones. This letter is to be published, minus the articles and interrogatories (!), and all such heretics are to be denounced as excommunicated.[66] All bishops and other inquisitors are to diligently search out all offenders, and those whom they find to be defamed of such heresy and error, or whom they find, by their own confession or factual evidence, or by other means, to be infected by such taint, they are to punish by excommunication, suspension, interdict, or other appropriate penalties ("eos quos per inquisitionem hujusmodi diffamatos, vel per confessionem eorum seu per facti evidentiam, vel alias, hujusmodi heresis et erroris labe respersos reperietis, auctoritate

---

1215 (Hardt, 4:153–55; Mansi, 27:632–34) and 6 July 1415 (Hardt, 4:407–12; Mansi, 27:754–55), respectively.

[65] Ibid., §14, pp. 673–75 (Hardt, 1527–29, Mansi, 1211–13). The *Bullarium* skips one of the questions, which we can label 28a: "Item, utrum credat religiones ab ecclesia approbatas a sanctis patribus rite et rationabiliter introductas" (last item on p. 1528 of Hardt, 3rd from bottom of col. 1212 of Mansi).

[66] Ibid., §§15–16, pp. 675–76 (Hardt, 1529–30, Mansi, 1213).

predicta etiam per excommunicationis, suspensionis, et interdicti . . . [penas] et per alias penas . . . corrigatis et puniatis"). This sounds as if the merely defamed are to be punished in the same way as those found guilty; but the pope goes on to specify that persons who are defamed of the articles are bound to purge themselves, while those who are convicted of the articles by witnesses or their own confession or other legitimate proofs are to be forced to abjure and undergo fitting punishment, and if they refuse to comply, the judges are to proceed against them *ex officio*, all appeals ceasing, as against heretics, and punish them, even consigning them to the secular court.[67]

At first glance, it might seem that the pope has gone beyond traditional procedure, in allowing defamed defendants who refuse to answer questions to be convicted as if they had confessed the crime. However, though he does not quite say so, he seems to consider the interrogation as part of the purgation process, as incorporated into inquisitorial procedure. According to standard due process, the judge should cite a suspect and charge him with, say, having preached the doctrine of Wyclif and Hus, on the basis of public fame to that effect. If the judge can prove no more than the existence of the fame, then he can require the defendant to purge himself by affirming his innocence under oath. Pope Martin has added the requirement, in order to make the charge and the purgatory assertion perfectly clear, of having the defendant respond to clear questions of heterodoxy and orthodoxy, which require only positive or negative answers to establish the defendant's orthodoxy. It would seem to be a reasonable procedure. What was wrong with it, and why shouldn't the pope impose it? After all, he was in charge!

The answer to what was wrong with the procedure is that it violated the principle that the Church does not judge secret matters,[68] since

---

[67] Ibid., §17, p. 676 (Hardt, 1530, Mansi, 1213–14).

[68] Enunciated, for example, in the Ordinary Gloss to Gratian, D. 32 c. 11, *Erubescant*, where Urban II says, "de manifestis quidem loquimur; secretorum autem cognitor et judex est Deus" ("We are speaking of manifest thing, whereas of secret things God is the one who know and judges") (Friedberg, 1:120). The Gloss says, "Ex hoc patet quod ecclesia non judicat de occultis" ("From this it is clear that the Church does not judge concerning hidden things"); see *Corpus juris canonici*, 3 vols. (Rome, 1582; repr. Lyons, 1606), 1:131, v. *secretorum*. Innocent III, writing in two decretals on simony, dated 1199 and 1207, states the principle thus: "Si excessus eorum esset ecclesie manifestus, que non judicat de occultis, pena essent canonica feriendi" ("If their excess were manifest to the Church, which does not judge concerning hidden things, they would deserve canonical punishment"), *Decretales* 5.3.33 (Friedberg, 2:763); "Nobis datum est de manifestis tantummodo judicare. . . . Sine

the questions go beyond the effort to establish specific past crimes to force statements of present belief. This is the sort of thing that only a confessor should be able to ask a penitent within the secrecy of the confessional.

There is extant a copy of *Inter cunctas* addressed to all of the bishops of England,[69] and the whole text was copied into the *Fasciculi zizaniorum*. The bull may have been influential in formulating a somewhat similar system of interrogation of Lollards, which was approved at the Canterbury Convocation of 1428.[70] However, Lyndwood, who participated in the convocation and who vetted at least the *Modus et forma procedendi et processus faciendi contra hereticos* formulated there,[71] did not draw on *Inter cunctas* in when commenting on such matters in the *Provinciale* (in his glosses on the constitutions of 1407/09). He did, however, draw on Continental Imperial law to justify some aspects of the stipulated procedure, namely the extravagant *Ad reprimendum* of Henry VII, Holy Roman Emperor from 1308 to 1313. When Arundell says that "indications" are sufficient for conviction ("sufficit convincere per indicia"), Lyndwood explains *indicia* as slight—though sufficient—demonstrations of guilt, and adds that the word can also be understood as sanctioning procedure not only by accusation and inquisition but also by denunciation, as in the extravagant.[72] When Arundell decrees that the

---

dubio . . . isti apud districtum judicem qui scrutator est cordium et cognitor secretorum culpabiles judicantur" ("It is given to us to judge only concerning manifest things. . . . Without doubt those [who acted with simoniacal intention] are judged guilty by that strict judge who is the scrutinizer of hearts and the knower of secrets"), ibid., 5.3.34.

[69] Hardt, 4:1518–19.

[70] *The Register of Henry Chichele, Archbishop of Canterbury, 1414–1443*, ed. E.F. Jacob, 4 vols. (Oxford, 1983–47), 3:191–92. See Anne Hudson, "The Examination of Lollards," *Bulletin of the Institute of Historical Research* 46 (1973), 145–59, repr. with an appendix in *Lollards and Their Books* (London, 1985), pp. 125–40, at 128–30. *Inter cunctas* is not given in the printed excerpts of the *Fasciculi* manuscript, Oxford, Bodleian MS E. Musaeo 86; it is contained on ff. 138rb–145ra, as Professor Hudson informs me. In her article she deals only with the interrogatories, §14.

[71] *Register of Chichele*, 3:191–92. I accept the identification of the *Modus* with the *Informacio ad procedendum contra hereticos* edited by Hudson, "Examination," pp. 136–39; see Thomson, *Later Lollards*, pp. 224–25, and Hudson, p. 128. The rules of procedure are correct, as far as they go, except that the suspect is wrongly called *hereticus*, as if already convicted, and no memtion is made of the need to establish *fama* (which could be omitted by ordinaries, unless the defendant insisted on it).

[72] Lyndwood 5.5.4, p. 302 note *x*: "i.e., per demonstrationes leves, sufficientes tamen. . . . Et potes intelligere *indicia*, ut scilicet non solum procedat contra tales per accusationem vel inquisitionem, sed etiam per denunciationem, sic quod aliqua via data possit constare de commisso crimine, ut patet in extravagante que incipit *Ad reprimendum*, Collatione 11." See *Corpus juris civilis*, ed. John Fehius, 6 vols. (Lyons

trial can proceed even in the defendant's absence, without the case being contested (*lite non contestata*), Lyndwood says that this is founded on *Ad reprimendum*.[73]

A form of abjuration was also approved with the *Modus et forma procedendi*, and in two of the three extant copies of the two documents, including a collection from Lichfield, two lists of articles "upon which heretics or Lollards should be examined" precede the abjuration. Since the articles are in the form of questions rather than propositions, they could only be employed to ascertain present belief, not past teaching, and the only procedurally orthodox use for them (taking the procedure of *Inter cunctas* to be unorthodox) would be to examine suspects who have agreed to abjure all errors previously held, taught, and affirmed, in order to add articles to the formula of abjuration. As the text of the abjuration is given, only two examples are given, followed by an *et cetera*.[74] However, in the register of Thomas Polton, Bishop of Worcester (1426–33), the lists appear in the middle of the manual, after defendants have denied the charges and witnesses have been deposed. There is no procedural justification for interrogating defendants on their beliefs at this stage, and Lyndwood would hardly have sanctioned it on the basis of formal law. Its placement here therefore probably signals an abuse of due process, possibly inspired by *Inter cunctas*.[75] But even the Lichfield sequence would have been a ready

1627, repr. Osnabrück 1966), 5:2:141–67 at 145–46. Bartolus in his gloss to *inquisitio* (col. 145) calls inquisition a *jus novum* not permitted in common law (*de jure communi*) but allowed in canon law when there is *publica fama*. But here he says it is allowed even when there is no fame, referring to Henry VII's second extravagant, *Quoniam nuper*, ad v. *publice vel occulte* (col. 171).

[73] Lyndwood, loc. cit., note *c*: "Istud fundatur in dicta extravagante *Ad reprimendum*."

[74] Hudson, "Examination," p. 136: "ante hanc horam nonnullos articulos et opiniones fidei catholice et determinacioni sancte romane ecclesie repugnantes tenui, docui, et affirmavi, videlicet, quod venerabiles ymagines non sunt venerande seu adorande, ac eciam quod peregrinaciones ad gloriosum Thomam martirem et alia loca pia non sunt licite, etc." These examples correspond roughly to nos. 26 and 28 of the jurist's list (p. 134). The lists appear before the abjuration in the Harley MS (from Lichfield) and the Balliol MS (see pp. 132, 140).

[75] In "Right to Remain Silent," p. 1011 n. 91, I suggested that the Polton sequence was the original placement, but I now agree with Hudson that the Lichfield order makes more sense. In the Polton register, the lists come after section VIII (p. 138), just before the guideline on the use of torture for half-proved crimes. On this latter point, Lyndwood in his *Provinciale* (5.5.4 ad v. *non obstante*, p. 305 note *f*) cites the same laws as the manual, namely, the Clementine *Multorum* (n. 87 above) and Gratian's *Imprimis* (C.2 q.1 c.7, Friedberg, 1:442); see Kelly, "English Kings," p. 213 (cf. pp. 231, 237). Thomson's objection that *Multorum* was not relevant to England because "the inquisition" had not been introduced there (p. 230 n. 3) is not to the point,

invitation to abuse suspects' rights, by quizzing them on their beliefs before charging them with public crimes, or in lieu of charging them.

The 1382 policy of requiring suspects to give opinions on Wycliffite views was used to examine university-trained scholars, and though it could be compared to the Continental abuse of grilling suspects *de se et aliis*, especially when the inquisitors were armed with lists of heresies to guide their questions, it was more likely inspired by scholastic practices in the universities.[76] The final examination of Walter Brute in 1393 also seems to resemble a scholastic discussion. In contrast, the lists of questions attached to the abjuration formula of 1428 may have been primarily devised for the examination of the unlearned. This is John Thomson's assumption: "As many of the Lollards were ignorant and illiterate it would *a priori* seem the only effective way of eliciting their views."[77] If this was indeed their purpose, we can easily see how they could be used to circumvent and not assist due process. In the only case we know of in which one of the lists was used, in the diocese of Bath and Wells in 1448, the articles were put to a very old and blind chaplain named John Yonge, and his responses were later made the basis of accusation before the bishop, who declared him a heretic.[78] It does not appear to have been a fair trial, but the result may have been regarded as educative rather than punitive, for the "mere correction of soul," as Commissary Storthwayt put it in Bristol in 1415. We can perhaps see something of the sort in the 1389 case of Matilda, the recluse of Leicester, treated above, where an informal interrogation gave rise to formal charges along with accompanying questions: *certi articuli et interrogatoria*. But though the outcome might seem benign in these cases, where the suspects were willing to comply, in others they proved not so harmless, for

---

since the decretal sets forth the rights and limitations of bishops as well as papal delegates in conducting heresy inquisitions. Moreover, torture was available to ecclesiastical judges in other kinds of cases, including civil suits; see especially John Teutonicus, Ordinary Gloss to Gratian, C.15 q.6 dictum ante c.1 ad v. *Quod vero* (*Corpus juris canonici*, 3 vols., Lyons, 1606, 1:1080), and see my *Canon Law and the Archpriest of Hita* (Binghamton, 1984), pp. 110–11, 184–85.

[76] See my "Trial Procedures." The decretal *Accusatus* of Alexander IV mentioned above, when it refers to an oath that witnesses take to tell the truth *tam de se quam de aliis* (Friedberg, 2:1072, §3 of the decretal), reflects a stage in the self-incriminatory interrogation of defendants, as practiced on the Continent. See "Right to Remain Silent," p. 1000.

[77] Thomson, p. 226.

[78] *The Register of Thomas Bekynton, Bishop of Bath and Wells, 1443–1465*, ed. H.C. Maxwell-Lyte and M.C.B. Dawes (London, 1934–35), 1:120–27.

instance, in Bishop Alnwick's trials in Norwich.[79] The fact remains that these methods were used to force persons to expose themselves to criminal charges, and to create punishable crimes where none existed before. As Thomson points out, "Examination by questioning could serve to systematize beliefs into a more rigid form than that in which they were in the mind of the accused."[80] To be legal, examinations of this sort should have been confined to the realm of the internal forum in the sacrament of confession. To use such procedures in the external forum was fundamentally contrary to the "Magna Carta of ecclesiastical civil rights" established at the Fourth Lateran Council, which allowed inquisitorial prosecution only for previously committed public crimes. The only concession made later to heresy inquisitors, duly noted in the *Modus et forma procedendi*, was that the identity of endangered witnesses might be concealed.[81]

But it was inevitable that defenders of the faith would find the defense safeguards too confining and would seek ways of bending or ignoring them, with or without the realization that they were going counter to the law. The most ingenious solution to the problem that I know of in England is that encountered in the reign of Queen Mary, where Cranmer, Ridley, and Latimer seem to have been ordered to engage in a formal debate on disputed questions of the nature of the Eucharist before they were tried.[82] Since they acquiesced, all the incriminating evidence that was needed was obtained without violating the canons of due process—except in spirit! But that story remains to be researched and told.

---

[79] N.P. Tanner, ed., *Heresy Trials in the Diocese of Norwich, 1428–1431* (London, 1977); see my "Inquisitorial Due Process," pp. 425–26.

[80] Thomson, p. 229.

[81] Hudson, p. 138, section VIII; Kelly, "Inquisition," pp. 443–44. The text in Hudson should read, "si *tamen* viderit quod ex donacione copie *imineret* periculum," etc. The defendant is allowed to name persons who he suspects may be biased for some reason, say enmity ("puta *inimicicie*").

[82] Foxe, *Acts and Monuments*, 6:439, 767.

"ENGLYSCH LATEN" AND "FRANCH": LANGUAGE AS SIGN OF EVIL IN MEDIEVAL ENGLISH DRAMA

Richard K. Emmerson

"Hell is certainly a noisy place," Richard Rastall states, as he describes the various sounds that playwrights employed to characterize the diabolic locus in medieval drama.[1] These sounds range from playing out-of-tune music and farting to banging pots and pans and cursing. Stage Hells, in other words, were a figural as well as literal "pandemonium" long before Milton invented the term to name the capital of Lucifer's new kingdom (*Paradise Lost*, 1.756). The noise became a stage sign of the chaos and disharmony of evil, an aural signifier of the theological concept of sin, just as elsewhere the heavenly songs sung by angels figured on stage the harmony characterizing virtue. But what of the representation of evil on earth, that temporal battleground between the eternal forces of good and evil? Once again, evil is usually characterized by blasphemous, often foul, language spoken by those who are allied to the forces of Hell, such as Cain in the *Towneley Cycle*, whom Abel accuses of "vayn carpyng" (2:99).[2] In the Wakefield Master's "Murder of Abel" Cain repeatedly requests the devil's aid ("The dwill me spede," 2:137, 2:236), blasphemes God ("he myght wipe his ars withall," 2:240), and curses Abel ("kys the dwills ars behynde," 2:268). Within just a few lines the brothers come to represent the two cosmic forces of good and evil, and their antagonistic allegiances are precisely juxtaposed for the play's audience when

---

[1] Richard Rastall, "The Sounds of Hell," in *The Iconography of Hell*, ed. Clifford Davidson and Thomas H. Seiler, Early Drama, Art, and Music Monograph Series 17 (Kalamazoo: Medieval Institute Publications, 1992), 102–31, esp. 111.

[2] Martin Stevens and A.C. Cawley, eds., *The Towneley Plays*, vol. 1, Early English Text Society (henceforth EETS) supplementary series (henceforth ss) 13 (London: Oxford University Press, 1994); all references to plays in this cycle will be cited in text by play and line numbers. The provenance and date of the cycle, often called the "Wakefield Cycle" after the Yorkshire city with which it has been traditionally associated, remains a matter of scholarly dispute; see the introduction to Stevens and Cawley, *Towneley Plays*, 1:xix–xxii; and Peter Meredith, "The Towneley Cycle," in *The Cambridge Companion to Medieval English Theatre*, ed. Richard Beadle (Cambridge: Cambridge University Press, 1994), 134–37.

to Abel's "com furth, in Godys name" (2:146), Caym immediately responds "ryn on, in the dwills nayme" (2:149).

Such language enlivens dialogue and is a regular feature of the comic action in much popular vernacular drama during the Middle Ages. It continues, furthermore, to be one of the most memorable features in twentieth-century revivals of these plays. Because modern audiences respond straightaway to such language at a primal level, we are likely to understand it primarily as a comic device and to miss a more serious dimension of its sign value for medieval audiences. For such language not only dramatically enriched these popular plays but also thematically signified that the ultimate and genuine foolishness of evil was to be mocked by "religious laughter," a laughter that finds its roots in "a *fully* Christian point of view," as V.A. Kolve explains:

> God is in control, the evil and the demonic behave stupidly because that is their nature, and the proper reaction to this example of the rightness of things is laughter. In the Corpus Christi drama, as in the sources it drew upon, the severance from God is chiefly a result of man's stupidity, of his failure to be intelligent. Lucifer falls from heaven as a fool who has attempted the impossible and who could have known (had he but considered) its fundamental impossibility. Cain thinks God can be cheated in offering. Satan makes a fatal mistake in setting under way the plot to kill Christ, and hell is harrowed as a result. Anti-Christ is likewise a buffoon, a confidence man. Stupidity, even in social terms, is funny, but when it willfully expresses itself in opposition to God's plan—a plan not only intelligible but known—it becomes more than merely laughable. It is also, in some outrageous sense, perverse, and the laughter it attracts is correspondingly unrestrained and unsympathetic.[3]

To understand the comic representation of evil in the popular drama of late medieval England, therefore, it is necessary to consider the serious implications that underlie its blatant language and funny stage business. This essay will begin to examine these implications by focusing on the use of language as sign in late fifteenth-century English drama, specifically in the plays that comprise the *Towneley Cycle* and in *Mankind*. It will particularly investigate the ways in which these plays draw upon and invert the established ideology of Latin and Anglo-French to characterize evil.

"The Second Shepherds' Play," the best-known English mystery

---

[3] V.A. Kolve, *The Play Called Corpus Christi* (Stanford: Stanford University Press, 1966), 140; for a full discussion of "religious laughter," see 124–44.

play, represents the Wakefield Master's fascination with the comic potential of language and with the serious consequences of its abuse by figures of evil.[4] It is particularly effective in using contemporary ideologies of language to characterize its central comic antagonist, Mak. For example, when Mak approaches the three shepherds who have been complaining about the times while freezing on the Yorkshire moors, he rather inconsistently tries to put on a southern dialect to claim, "ich be a yoman,/ I tell you, of the kyng" (13:291–92).[5] The First Shepherd responds, "Why make ye it so qwaynt?" (13:300), and when Mak continues his inept attempt to be highfalutin, he tells him what to do with his pseudo-dialect: "Now take outt that Sothren tothe,/ And sett in a torde" (13:311–12). Mak is hereby shown to be an ineffective, if comic, impostor who is rightly put in his place, but his attempt to adopt "that Sothren tothe" also signifies his "otherness." It links him to "thise gentlery-men" (13:26) about whom the First Shepherd complains in his opening dialogue, the representatives of the absentee landowners who enclose the fields and oppress the peasantry with taxes (13:24).

Later in a crucial scene Mak briefly adopts Latin as he utters his night-spell:

> Fro my top to my too,
> *Manus tuas commendo,*
> *Poncio Pilato.* (13:383–85)

To ensure that the audience registers this comic twisting of Christ's words on the Cross (Luke 24:46), Mak continues: "Cryst-crosse me spede!" (13:386). What at first seems to be simply another example of inept language, however, is quite effective as part of a spell that ensures the shepherds sleep while Mak steals their sheep. This parody of divine speech is another way that the Wakefield Master characterizes Mak as an evil "other" set in opposition to the three shepherds. If the shepherds become the "local" representatives of the Yorkshire audience in this pageant staged in the here and now but set in

---

[4] The Wakefield Master, the comic genius of the medieval English stage, composed five complete plays in the *Towneley Cycle* and revised another nine plays. See Stevens and Cawley, *Towneley Plays*, 1:xxviii–xxxi. On the Wakefield Master's language see Martin Stevens, *Four Middle English Mystery Cycles* (Princeton: Princeton University Press, 1987), esp. 156–63. Although this essay focuses on the work of the Wakefield Master, it considers the use of Latin and Anglo-French in the entire *Towneley Cycle*.

[5] Mak here first uses the southern form, "ich," then revealingly slips into the northern form, "I." On Mak's use of this and other southern forms see the notes by Stevens and Cawley, *Towneley Plays*, vol. 2, EETS ss 14 (1994), 501.

Palestine during the past of salvation history, then Mak, through his language, is linked both to the present oppressive worldly powers that the northern audience associated with southern England in the fifteenth century and to past figures from salvation history who will soon follow Mak on stage in the cycle's forthcoming Passion sequence: Pilate, whom Mak invokes, and Jesus, whom Mak parodies.

To understand fully the dramatic effect of Mak's language, we must recognize that language "means" on stage not only by *what it says* (its semantic level) but also by *how it signifies* (its semiotic level). It isn't just that Mak commends his spirit to Pontius Pilate instead of to God the Father (the semantic level); it is equally significant that he does so in Latin (the semiotic level). As the language of the Church—of its sacred books, liturgy, and canon law—Latin is a signifier carrying meaning in its own right as a spiritual language beyond the signified denoted by the individual words of Mak's spell. That spiritual language should be the conduit of truth, not deception, as when in "The Second Shepherds' Play" the angel later announces the birth of Jesus, singing *Gloria in excelsis* (13:919f.) before giving directions in English to the three shepherds to go to "Bedlem" (13:929). Latin should be the language of sacred, not false, prophecy, as when the Second Shepherd, on his way to meet the Christ child, cites Isaiah 7:14 in Latin:

> For Isay sayd so:
> *Ecce virgo*
> *Concipiet* a chylde that is nakyd. (13:982–84)

During the fifteenth century England remained culturally a trilingual nation in which Anglo-Norman, Latin, and Middle English each carried its own ideological thrust and was each associated with one of the three traditional estates: the aristocracy and landed gentry, associated with the Court; the clergy, associated with the Church; and the vast third estate, comprising those who worked the land in the country and produced and traded goods in the city. English was the everyday language of virtually all the nation's citizens, was widely used in a growing body of popular literature, and was increasingly accepted as a cultural language, but many patrons still preferred their romances in French and their books of hours in Latin, suggesting that, for serious reading associated with aristocratic and religious pursuits, English continued to lack the prestige of its textually more established competitors. The persistent privileged position of Latin, associated with religion in general and the clergy in particular, is evident, for example, in the legal authority of the so-called "neck verse," a benefit of clergy by which an accused criminal could escape hanging by reciting a verse of Psalm 50 in Latin. By putting Latin in the mouths of Mak and the Second Shepherd, however, the playwright suggests that it isn't the estate of the person who speaks Latin that matters but for what ends that language is spoken. Although divine intervention may propel the Second Shepherd to quote sacred scripture in Latin, demonic power may also manipulate Latin for its own evil, if comically foolish, attempt to deceive and to parody Christ.[6]

We have seen that in a trilingual culture a dramatist's choice of Latin to portray a figure of evil is significant. It is therefore worth examining in more detail, on the one hand, Mak's thematic and linguistic connections with the tyrant to whom he commends his spirit, Pontius Pilate, and, on the other hand, the ways in which these plays contrast his language with the language spoken by Jesus, the cycle's primary figure of good. Pilate opens the twentieth play in the cycle, "Conspiracy and Capture," by boasting:

> For I am he that may
> Make or mar a man,
> Myself if I it say,
> As men of cowrte now can:
> Supporte a man today,
> To-morn agans hym than. (20:27–32)

Like Mak, Pilate here associates himself with the Court, which the northern perspective of this cycle repeatedly satirizes. If Mak only briefly dabbled in Latin, however, Pilate is amazingly grandiloquent. He opens the "Play of the Dice"—which follows the "Crucifixion" and portrays the soldiers gaming for Jesus' cloak—with a five-stanza rant. The first stanza is delivered completely in Latin, and the next four mix Latin and English, cleverly rhyming the two languages:

> Stynt, I say! gyf, men, place
> *Quia sum dominus dominorum*;
> He that agans me says,
> *Rapietur lux oculorum.*

---

[6] Mak's parody of Christ's last words on the Cross and the parodic "nativity" that Mak and Gill enact on stage—in which Gill "gives birth" to a lamb-child that, in a grisly allusion to the Eucharist, she swears she will eat (13:775)—suggest that Mak may be a comic "type" of Antichrist. On the play's parody see Linda E. Marshall, "'Sacral Parody' in the *Secunda Pastorum*," *Speculum* 47 (1972), 720–36.

> Therfor gyf ye me space
> *Ne tendam vim brachiorum,*
> And then get ye no grace,
> *Contestor iura polorum.*
> *Caueatis!*
> Rewle I the Iuré
> *Maxime pure;*
> Towne *quoque rure,*
> *Me paueatis!* (24:14–26)

Such macaronic boasts serve practical as well as thematic purposes. Pilate, probably coming on stage by moving through the audience, twice commands the audience to make room, a practical injunction given in English because the audience must understand if it is to move aside to allow him to pass. An important feature of his function as chief villain in the *Towneley Cycle*, his rulership over the Jewry (which amusingly rhymes with "*pure*"), is also given in English. But what is the audience to make of the Latin? They may comprehend *Caveatis*, and if so, this word supports Pilate's English commands. And they may recognize *dominus dominorum* as biblical words applied to God and Christ (cf. Apoc. 17:14), and if so, this Latin phrase helps characterize Pilate as an ambitious and haughty, if foolish, lord. It is less likely that the vast majority of the audience would understand the remainder of the Latin. But if such is the case, it doesn't necessarily follow that the remainder of the Latin is without meaning to the audience. It would still signify thematically, for it underscores the cycle's characterization of "Syr Pilate, prynce" (24:180) as a ranting tyrant, an evil manipulator of privileged language for his political ends.

In contrast, in the passion sequence the language spoken by Jesus is humble and gentle, his stage presence being largely marked throughout by a profound silence. This characterization is in part due to the fact that a dignified silence characterizes Jesus in the gospel accounts of these scenes, but his dramatic silence is also a very effective stage sign that is remarked on by the cycle's figures of evil. In the Wakefield Master's "Buffeting," for example, Jesus' silence provokes a long diatribe from Cayphas:

> Illa-hayll was thou borne!
> Harke, says he oght agane?
> Thou shall onys or to-morne
> To speke be full fayne.
> This is a great skorne
> And a fals trane;

> Now wols-hede and outhorne
> On the be tane,
> Vile fature!
> Oone worde myght thou speke ethe,
> Yit myght it do the som letht;
> *Et omnis qui tacet*
> *Hic consentire videtur.* (21:196–208)

It is no coincidence that Jesus' silence is condemned by a Latin proverb.[7] Cayphas uses the authoritative language to "put words in the mouth" of Jesus, to justify his punishment and to assert his acquiescence. A few lines later Anna twice cites more Latin, both times with legalistic connotations: "*Et hoc nos volumus,/ Quod de iure possumus*" (21:310–11), and "*Sed nobis non licet / Interficere quemquam*" (21:389–90). Both cases resemble the Latin of Cayphas in that the prestigious language is cited to authorize injustice and to mask wicked actions under the veneer of law.

Thus the contrast between Jesus and his evil accusers is energized by their use of Latin in the face of his silence. What perhaps is even more significant is that when Jesus does speak in the *Towneley Cycle*, he rarely speaks Latin. He never speaks Latin, for example, in "John the Baptist," "Crucifixion," "Resurrection," "Ascension," and "Judgment," where the theological matter and biblical context would envision it. Particularly revealing is the language of the young Jesus in "Christ and the Doctors." When the *N-Town Play* stages this episode, Jesus responds to the doctor in a learned Latin: "Omnis sciencia a Domino Deo est."[8] In contrast, in *Towneley* he speaks totally in English and limits his teachings to simple Christian doctrine, establishing his eternal authority in a brief English two-line response to the Second Master:

> 2 *Magister.*   Whenseuer this barne may be
>   That shewys thise novels new?
> *Iesus*   Certan, syrs, I was or ye,
>   And shall be after you. (18:81–84)

---

[7] In their note on this proverb Stevens and Cawley quote from Cotgrave's *Dictionarie of the French and English Tongues*, published in 1611: "'Many, who know not much more Latine, can say, *Qui tacet consentire videtur*'" (*Towneley Plays*, 2:558).

[8] Stephen Spector, ed., *The N-Town Play*, EETS ss 11 (Oxford: Oxford University Press, 1991), play 21, line 33. On the differing effect of the *N-Town* "Christ and the Doctors" in comparison with the *Towneley* play, as well as with the versions in *York* and *Chester*, see Gail McMurray Gibson, *The Theater of Devotion: East Anglian Drama and Society in the Late Middle Ages* (Chicago: University of Chicago Press, 1989), 131–32.

The two sets of rhymes here are particularly effective. The "be"/ "ye" rhyme suggests that the young child ("barne") lived before the old Master, and the "new"/"you" rhyme suggests that, despite appearances, it is the Master's, not the eternal doctrine of Jesus, that really is "new." Even when in the "Crucifixion" Jesus gives up the ghost, he does so in English:

> Now is my passyon broght tyll ende!
> Fader of heuen, into thyn hende
> I betake my saull. (23:648–50)

The contrast to Mak's earlier Latin parody of Jesus' words on the Cross could not be more explicit. Throughout the *Towneley Cycle*, in fact, the words of Jesus exemplify a characteristic noted by Martin Stevens: "The essential premise of the Towneley cycle as a whole about language is that simplicity and artlessness mark the speech of the virtuous,"[9]

Jesus does speak Latin on three occasions. The first is in the "Conspiracy and Capture," after Peter cuts off the ear of the high priest's servant, whom medieval tradition named Malcus. Malcus cries, "Helpe, alas, I blede to dede!" (20:711), and Jesus immediately restores the ear, stating "*In nomine patris*, hole thou be!" (20:715). It is significant that these words are not recorded in the scriptural account of this story (Matt. 26:51–52; Mark 14:47; Luke 22:50–51); instead, Jesus' Latin ritualistically draws on the supernatural "magic" of the language to accomplish his miracle. Similarly, in the "Harrowing of Hell" Jesus twice chants his ritualistic challenge to the devils in Latin: "*Attollite portas, principes, vestras et eleuamini porte eternales, et introibit rex glorie*" (25:120f.; 25:188f.). These words (cf. Psalm 23:7, 9), traditionally associated with the Harrowing of Hell and regularly sung as part of the liturgy of Holy Saturday, have a similarly powerful supernatural effect, leading to the destruction of the gates of Hell, which occurs, interestingly enough, after the Latin is paraphrased in English:

> Ye prynces of hell, open youre yate
> And let my folk furth gone!
> A prynce of peasse shall enter therat,
> Wheder ye will or none. (25:197–200)

In "Thomas of India," the only other play in which Jesus briefly speaks Latin, the language is similarly evoked in an enchanted situ-

---

[9] Stevens, *Four Middle English Cycles*, 158.

ation. Twice Jesus mesmerizes his followers who have assembled after the Resurrection, and both times he sings *Pax vobis et non tardabit; hec est dies quam fecit Dominus* (28:104ff.; 28:120ff.).[10] First Jesus mystically appears, then immediately vanishes, but after suddenly appearing and singing the second time, he identifies himself, speaking in English.

These three instances are the only Latin spoken by Jesus in the entire cycle. Otherwise the Latin of good characters in the cycle's thirty-one plays is restricted to a few lines spoken during five highly delimited situations, the first two involving divine figures, the second three situations involving human characters. First, Deus twice speaks a few lines of Latin to establish divine decorum. He opens the cycle's first pageant, "Creation," with one line of Latin, which he immediately paraphrases in English:

Ego sum alpha et o,
I am the first, the last also,
Oone God in magesté. (1:1–3)

Similarly, when Moses in "Pharaoh" asks God's name, Deus responds: "I say thus: *Ego sum qui sum*" (8:185). The second situation involves four angelic songs sung in Latin (13:919f.; 17:132f.; 26:229f.; 29:289f.), all well-known liturgical songs. Otherwise, the angels always speak in English. Even during the "Annunciation" Gabriel greets Mary with "Hayll, Mary, gracyouse!" (10:77), rather than with the expected *Ave Maria*. The angels, therefore—as well as Deus and Jesus—are associated primarily with English.

The other three situations where Latin is spoken on stage by figures of good involve human characters either quoting biblical prophecies, singing liturgical songs, or performing at moments of supernatural intervention. A few scraps of prophecy are delivered in Latin by Moses at the beginning of the "Play of the Prophets," and then in the same play by David (7:91f., 150f.), the Sibyl (7:162f.), and Daniel (7:216f.). Other short Latin prophecies are spoken by two of the shepherds on their way to Bethlehem in the "First Shepherds' Play" (12:502–3; 12:559ff.) and by David in the "Harrowing of Hell" (25:402–3). Good

---

[10] JoAnna Dutka, *Music in the English Mystery Plays*, Early Drama, Art, and Music Reference Series 2 (Kalamazoo: Medieval Institute Publications, 1980), 73, was unable to find a source for this song, either in the liturgy or another play. Stevens and Cawley suggest that "the words were part of a lost song which combines several biblical allusions as follows: *Pax vobis* from Luke xxiv.36 or John xx.19, 21, 26; *et non tardabit* from Hab. ii.3; *hec . . . Dominus* from Ps. cxvii.24" (*Towneley Plays*, 2:620). They also note that the Psalm verse was sung during Easter Sunday Mass.

characters also sing liturgical songs in Latin on four occasions. The *Te Deum laudamus*, for example, is sung twice, once by Ysaias at the conclusion of the "Harrowing of Hell" (25:416), and once by a saved soul at the conclusion of "Judgment" (30:830). The placement of this song of praise at the conclusion of the two plays in which the power of God is most explicitly made evident on stage is appropriate. Since the *Te Deum* often concluded the earliest liturgical plays, when it introduced congregational singing, and since it was well-known as the hymn that concludes Matins, it is possible that the audience was invited to sing the song at these points in the *Towneley* play as well. Ysaias also invites the souls awaiting Christ in the "Harrowing of Hell" to sing the first verse of *Saluator mundi* (25:44f.), and in the "Salutation" Mary sings *Magnificat anima mea dominum* (11:48f.).[11]

Finally, four good characters speak the kind of ritualistic Latin that Jesus speaks in the cycle. In two of these cases, both involving biblical characters, their Latin is closely linked to divine intervention in human affairs. In the Wakefield Master's staging of the Flood, Noah prepares to build the ark with a prayer that recalls the words of Jesus when he restores the ear of Malcus:

> Now assay will I
> How I can of wrightry,
> *In nomine patris, et filij,*
> *Et spiritus sancti. Amen.* (3:361–64)

And John the Baptist recites a similar ritual Latin when he baptizes Jesus (19:185–90). The other two cases, both from the Wakefield Master's two shepherds' plays, are more complicated. They involve the kind of twisted Latin used by Mak when he commended his spirit to Pilate. The Third Shepherd in the "First Shepherds' Play," for example, uses Latin in a night-spell:[12]

> For ferde we be fryght,
> A crosse lett vs kest—
> Cryst-crosse, benedyght
> Eest and west—
> For drede.

---

[11] Stevens and Cawley note that the entire *Magnificat* is sung in the other three Middle English cycles and suggest that, although only the first line of the *Magnificat* is given here in the manuscript, the entire song was probably sung at this point (*Towneley Plays*, 2:480).

[12] On the night-spells see William Munson, "The Layman's Prayer Contest of the Crossing Charms in the Towneley Shepherds' Plays," *Mediaevalia* 11 (1989), 187–201.

> *Iesus onazorus*
> *Crucyefixus,*
> *Morcus, Andreus,*
> God be oure spede! (12:417–25)

Although the Latin is garbled, its function is meritorious, and it is immediately followed in the play by the divine intervention of the angel who announces the birth of Jesus. More disturbing are the words of the First Shepherd in the "Second Shepherds' Play," spoken after he awakes from Mak's spell:

> *Resurrex a mortruus!*
> Haue hold my hand.
> *Iudas carnas dominus!*
> I may not well stand. (13:504–7)

This garbled Latin is difficult to interpret.[13] Like Mak's night-spell it may point to characters in later pageants that will stage scenes related to the passion of Christ. The allusion to Judas, furthermore, may be an appropriate response to Mak's theft of the parodic "lamb of God." In determining whether or not this Mak-like use of Latin makes the First Shepherd a confederate of Mak (or, worse, of Judas), however, it is important to realize that, like the garbled night-spell spoken by the Third Shepherd in the "First Shepherds' Play," it is uttered before the angel announces the birth of Jesus. The First Shepherd's response to the annunciation becomes crucial, therefore. He now ceases his endless complaints about the times and recalls prophecies of the Nativity. Unlike Mak, the First Shepherd undergoes a conversion, which is symbolized when the search for the lamb stolen by Mak is replaced by the discovery of the true Lamb of God.[14]

In contrast to these five brief and highly specialized situations in which figures of good speak Latin, evil figures speak Latin much more extensively in the *Towneley Cycle*. In addition to the legalistic Latin of Cayphas and Anna in the "Buffeting," Latin is spoken by the Torturer in the "Scourging" (22:163) and by the First Counselor in "Herod the Great":

---

[13] For possible interpretations of these lines see Stevens and Cawley, *Towneley Plays*, 2:503.

[14] The "Second Shepherds' Play" leaves Mak's status ambiguous; whether or not he is "converted" in part depends on how the conclusion of the play is staged. See, for example, Míčeál F. Vaughan, "Tossing Mak Around," in *Approaches to Teaching Medieval English Drama*, ed. Richard Emmerson (New York: Modern Language Association, 1990), 146–50.

> Truly, syr, prophecy
> It is not blynd.
> We rede thus by Isay:
> He shal be so kynde
> That a madyn, sothely,
> Which neuer synde,
> Shall hym bere:
> *Virgo concipiet,*
> *Natumque pariet,*
> *Emanuell* is hete,
> His name for to lere. (16:302–12)

These words, which echo the prophecy spoken by the Second Shepherd in response to the angel, here only serve to stoke Herod's rage concerning the birth of a new "King of the Jews." It reveals that evil characters—in this case, one of the counselors who recommends the massacre of the innocents—can also quote prophecy in Latin. Similarly, although the First Master in "Christ and the Doctors" also can quote prophecy in Latin, "*Ex ore infancium et lactencium perfecisti laudem*" (18:90f.; cf. Ps. 8:3, Matt. 21:16), he basically denies the prophecy with a strong "Neuertheles, son" (18:93), explaining that children are not to be heeded by masters:

> For certyrs, if thou wold neuer so fayn
> Gyf all thi lyst to lere the law,
> Thou art nawther of myght ne mayn
> To know it as a clerk may knaw. (18:97–100)

He here claims the cleric's greater authority to interpret scripture in Latin. Although the moral condition of the First Master is not comparable to that of the First Counselor or Torturer, he does represent how the clerical language is used in the cycle to oppose Jesus.

Devils, of course, are evil by definition, yet even they know Latin. The mischievous Titiuillus, whom the Wakefield Master added to the cycle's Doomsday play,[15] speaks Latin on four occasions, sometimes even speaking the truth:

> *Diabolus est mendax*
> *Et pater eius.* (30:415–16)

---

[15] At least five of the *Towneley Cycle* pageants were borrowed from the *York Cycle*, and of these "Judgment" was significantly revised by the Wakefield Master. See Stevens and Cawley, ed., *Towneley Cycle*, 1:xxvii–xxviii; and Richard Beadle, ed., *The York Plays* (London: Edward Arnold, 1982).

Such Latin poses a dilemma, because it is a "true" statement spoken by the self-acknowledged Father of Lies. Titiuillus also speaks the kind of nonsense Latin we associate with Mak, and it is significant that his boisterous use of language fragments is part of his self-definition. When the First Demon asks his name shortly after he comes on stage, Titiuillus responds:

> *Fragmina verborum,*
> *Titiuillus colligit horum;*
> *Belzabub algorum,*
> *Belial belium doliorum.* (30:363–64)

Latin is also spoken by the First Demon against those whom Jesus later identifies as "Kames kyn" (30:648):

> *Qui vero mala,*
> *In ignem eternum.* (30:558–59)

This Latin, in part a biblical citation (cf. Matt. 25:41), is a hellish prophecy that directly precedes the appearance of Jesus in judgment. Interestingly, the saved are directed to Heaven not by a parallel use of Latin, but in English.

As the great villain of the cycle Pilate is particularly associated with the sanctioned language of authority. His opening thirteen-line stanza in the "Play of the Dice" is an impressive Latin tour-de-force using a mere three rhymes:

> Cernite qui statis
> Quod mire sim probitatis;
> Hec cognoscatis,
> Vos cedam ni taceatis.
> Cuncti discatis
> Quasi sistam vir deitatis
> Et maiestatis;
> Michi fando ne noceatis,
> Hoc modo mando.
> Neue loquaces
> Siue dicaces,
> Poscite paces
> Dum fero fando. (24:1–13)[16]

---

[16] Stevens and Cawley translate the passage as follows: "Notice, you who stand [by]/ that I am of wondrous valour;/ know this,/ I will slay you unless you keep quiet./ Learn, all of you,/ that I am a man of god-like nature/ and majesty;/ do not harm me by speaking,/ thus I command./ [Be] neither talkative/ nor garrulous,/ demand peace/ while I speak" (*Towneley Plays*, 2:584).

It is hard to imagine what these lines could mean to the vast majority of the audience who would not be literate in Latin. Pilate's diction is quite unlike the simple Latin spoken by Jesus and other figures of good in the cycle, which might potentially be known to the audience, since it cites traditional prophecies and liturgical songs. It is, furthermore, often immediately paraphrased in English. But Pilate's fast-paced rhymes are no more likely to have been understood by most members of his fifteenth-century audience than by most members of a twentieth-century audience, even in the university settings in which most medieval plays are revived nowadays. Clearly the semantic value of Latin is not primary here; instead, it must be understood as a sign of authority gone mad. In fact, in these central plays Latin is so extensively associated with Pilate that it becomes his signature and a sign of his treachery. At the conclusion of the first stanza of the Wakefield Master's "Scourging," for example, Pilate states:

> I am full of sotelty,
> Falshed, gyll and trechery;
> Therfor am I namyd by clergy
> As *mali actoris*. (22:10–13)

It is significant that his Latin "name" is conferred by clergy.

The thirty-seven words of Latin spoken by Pilate in just the *first* stanza of the "Play of the Dice" is more Latin than Jesus speaks in the entire cycle. This notable differentiation between the extensive use of Latin by powerful, yet evil, figures and its rare use in highly delimited situations by figures of good challenges the established ideology of language that typifies fifteenth-century England. Latin in the *Towneley Cycle* continues to be associated with power, but not in the hands of the good. Similarly, the choice of English for most of the words spoken by Jesus is also thematically significant. It is a linguistic analogue for the incarnation, in which the spiritual language of Jesus becomes flesh in the earthly language of his people. By putting English in the mouth of Jesus, the playwright elevates the everyday language of northern England spoken by the vast majority of the play's audience, while at the same time contrasting it to the privileged languages of the first and second estates, the aristocracy and clergy whose allegiances are to the authorities centered in the south.

Although Anglo-French is not as common in the *Towneley Cycle*, this privileged language of high culture and government authority is treated in a fashion that resembles the cycle's handling of Latin.

Anglo-French is associated with the Court and the upper class, so it should not be surprising that at the end of the "Play of the Dice," which began with Pilate's extensive Latin, the tyrant concludes his ranting by invoking Anglo-French: "Dew vows [garde], monsenyours!" (24:435). Herod the Great is also associated with Anglo-French. The Wakefield Master on three occasions puts scraps of anglicized French in his mouth. The first time emphasizes Herod's crazed wrath upon learning that the Magi have avoided his trap:

> Fyrst vengeance
> Shall I se on thare bonys;
> If ye byde in these wonys,
> I shall dyng you with stonys—
> Yei, ditizance doutance! (16:243–47)

As Stevens and Cawley point out, "ditizance doutance," "a corruption of 'dites sans doutance,'" typifies the language of those with "great pretensions" but with little knowledge of French.[17] The phrase functions linguistically, in other words, like Mak's "Sothren tothe," to suggest that the king is putting on airs.

The difference here, however, is that, unlike Mak, Herod really is the Court and has genuine power to do evil. If Mak's evil is limited to a stolen sheep that is ultimately recovered and replaced on stage by the innocent Christ child, Herod's includes ordering the massacre of innocent children. His frenchified ranting, therefore, is another way that the cycle uses a linguistic sign to link corrupt power to evil. The ranting continues throughout "Herod the Great," which concludes with an eighty-line diatribe of the kind that must have given rise to Shakespeare's transformation of Herod's name into a verb meaning to rant: "it out-herods Herod" (*Hamlet* III.ii.1f.). The last two lines allude to two features that characterize "Herode the ryall" (16:726):

> Bot adew!—to the deuyll!
> I can no more Franch. (16:740–41)

Herod's links to the devil and to French suggest how the northern perspective of the *Towneley Cycle* once again inverts commonplace linguistic ideology to couple worldly power and evil. For, although Stevens and Cawley may be right that the French Herod alludes to

---

[17] Ibid., 2:525.

here is the word "adew" in the previous line,[18] it also seems likely
that his entire invective, in fact, that all his raging throughout the play,
is metaphorically identified as "Franch," since it is clearly associated
with mad political power. Herod's "I can [i.e., know] no more Franch"
may be the medieval equivalent of the contemporary American saying,
"Pardon my French," which usually follows a particularly foul curse.

Another use of Anglo-French in *Towneley* parodies the opening of
a court proclamation when Cain instructs Garcio, his quick-witted
boy, to cry out "'oyes, oyes, oy!'" (2:419). That this official language
is put in the mouth of the first murderer is certainly suggestive. A
similar proclamation associating Anglo-French with political and legal
authority is also parodied in *Mankind* (ca. 1465–70), one of the best
and certainly the liveliest English morality play.[19] Here the central
vice, Mischief, orders his three associates, New Guise, Nowadays,
and Nought, to conduct a comic manor-court session to try Mankind:

> MYSCHEFF.   I wyll not so; I wyll sett a corte.
> Nowadays, mak proclamacyon,
> And do yt sub forma jurys, dasarde!
> NOWADAYS.   Oyyt! Oy3yt! Oyet! All manere of men and comun
> women
> To þe cort of Myschyff othere cum or sen!
> Mankynde xall retorn; he ys on of owr men. (664–69)

The hilarious "trial" that follows primarily parodies Latin "sub forma
jurys," and includes an "Englysch Laten" that typifies this play's sharp
wit and irreverent treatment of the language of both governmental
and religious authority.[20] Mischief's response to Nought's legal record
is particularly amusing:

---

[18] Ibid., 2:530.

[19] Mark Eccles, ed., *The Macro Plays*, EETS 262 (Oxford: Oxford University Press,
1969), 153–84, notes 216–27. All references to the play will be cited in text by line
numbers; references to the notes will be cited by page numbers. *Mankind* is one of
three morality plays included in the Macro manuscript, Folger Library MS V.a.354.
Place names in the play establish its East Anglian origin, and Gibson (*Theater of
Devotion*, 108–13) has linked it to Bury St. Edmunds. For the moral plays in general
see Pamela M. King, "Morality Plays," in *Cambridge Companion to Medieval English
Theatre*, ed. Beadle, 240–64.

[20] Although *Mankind* clearly is a product of popular theatrical traditions and has
usually been understood as a play designed for a traveling troupe, the linguistic
sophistication of the text has led some critics to suggest that the play's audience
must have been quite sophisticated. See Lawrence M. Clopper, "Mankind and Its
Audience," *Comparative Drama* 8 (1974–75), 347–55. On its staging and its connections
with popular theatre see David Bevington, *From Mankind to Marlowe* (Cambridge,
Mass.: Harvard University Press, 1962).

> Here ys blottybus in blottis,
> Blottorum blottibus istis.
> I beschrew yowr erys, a fayer hande! (680–82)

Mischief continues the parody by linking the court to an ale house while cancelling two cultural centers the later Middle Ages still identified with Latin, the Crown and classical antiquity:

> Carici tenta generalis
> In a place þer goode ale ys
> Anno regni regitalis
> Edwardi nullateni
> On 3estern day in Feuerere—þe 3ere passyth fully,
> As Nought hath wrytyn; here ys owr Tulli,
> Anno regni regis nulli! (687–93)

The king in this proclamation becomes Edward the Nothingth,[21] and Cicero is elided as nought.

Such burlesque of Latin typifies the language of the vices as well as of the play's devil, whose name by now will be familiar: "Ego sum dominancium dominus and my name ys Titivillus" (475). The devil's Latin resembles Pilate's arrogant language, but in this play it is not left unanswered. Everything is subject to mockery, including the vices' chief comrade in wickedness. When Titivillus asks Nought for the money he and the other vices have just collected from the audience to lure the devil on stage, Nought responds by punning on Titivillus's self-definition, rhyming the name of the French patron saint with "peny," and concluding with a lewd comment:

> Non nobis, domine, non nobis, by Sent Deny!
> þe Deull may daunce in my purse for ony peny;
> Yt ys as clen as a byrdys ars. (587–89)

Titivillus is brought on stage by the vices after Mankind beats them with his spade, the sign of his estate and his duty to work as the play's representative of sinful human nature.[22] The goal is to direct

---

[21] Eccles notes that "Edward IV reigned from 1461 to October 1470, and from April 1471 to 1483" (*Macro Plays*, 225), so *regis nulli* may allude to the six-month break in Edward's reign. I think it is more likely a nonsense allusion to the Crown in general, however, perhaps reflecting provincial disgust with the intrigues of Court associated with the War of the Roses.

[22] The spade also links Mankind to the first digger of the earth, Adam. See Steven May, "A Medieval Stage Property: The Spade," *Mediaeval English Theatre* 4 (1982), 77–92; and Gibson, *Theatre of Devotion*, 159–61.

Mankind away from Mercy, whose speeches open and close the play and who represents the chief means of Mankind's salvation. Titivillus accomplishes this task in quick succession by placing a board under the earth to thwart Mankind's digging, stealing Mankind's grain and then his spade, and sending Mankind to relieve himself. When Mankind returns, he falls asleep and Titivillus, like Mak in the "Second Shepherds' Play," sets about his final deception. He whispers into his victim's ear that Mercy stole a horse, broke his neck while riding in France, and will now be hanged, leaving Mankind despairing of Mercy.

Burlesque Latin is crucial to these scenes and to others during which Mankind is tempted, at first remains steadfast, but then yields to the attractions of the contemporary world, which are symbolized by his donning of a newly tailored coat cut so ridiculously short that it is useless. The vices, who speak even more Latin than does Pilate in the *Towneley Cycle*, adopt the sacred language for a string of clerical abuse, linking the friars to the devil (325–26), for example. They consistently transform the spiritual into the material, applying the sacred language to the body. When Mischief threatens castration, Nought responds in panic, "In nomine patris, choppe!" (440). These carnal allusions are also mustered to curse, the profane Latin sometimes evoking a much more bawdy English response:

NOWADAYS. Who spake to þe, foll? þou art not wyse!
Go and do þat longyth to þin offyce:
Osculare fundamentum!
NOUGHT.   Lo, master, lo, here ys a pardon bely-mett.
Yt is grawntyde of Pope Pokett,
Yf ȝe wyll putt yowr nose in hys wyffys sokett,
ȝe xall haue forty days of pardon. (140–46)

What the Latin and English share here, of course, is a sacrilegious mockery of the Church, its clerics, offices, and even its sacraments.

But Latin is not always the tool of ridicule. Mankind, for example, quotes it "To defende me from all superstycyus charmys:/ 'Memento, homo, quod cinis es et in cinerem reuerteris.'" (320–21). This basic theological truth, which sets forth the play's understanding of human nature and is central to the moral lesson ultimately dramatized on stage, is spoken in a moment of high seriousness. Mankind also cites Latin to sustain himself after beating the vices with his spade (397), and to pray: "Pater noster qui es in celis" (554). This prayer is spoken during a poignant, dramatic moment, when Mankind falls to his knees on his plot of land, which he significantly consecrates as his "kerke"

(553). Mercy also repeatedly uses Latin in a serious vein near the conclusion of the play, in the closing comments which are clearly directed at the moral regeneration of the audience as well as of Mankind. There is no sense in these final speeches that the language is used to mock or deceive. The speeches are crucial in recasting the play from exuberant comedy to sober didacticism and to teaching its serious moral lesson.

How, then, does Latin signify in this play? An answer is suggested by the depiction of the morality's central figure of good, Mercy. His character is complex because it functions dramatically as both symbol and personification. On the one hand, Mercy acts as a symbol of the institutional Church in its capacity as the established means of salvation, and as such he is a clerical figure. His clerical status is underscored by the fact that in *Mankind* Mercy is gendered male and is called "goode fader" (86), whereas traditionally Mercy is female and one of the allegorical Four Daughters of God, as in *The Castle of Perseverance*, a companion morality in the Macro manuscript.[23] On the other hand, Mercy is a personification of a divine attribute, and although in this play Mercy does not become one of the Four Daughters, his affinity to this personified attribute is signaled near the end of the play when he specifically recalls the other three "daughters," Justyce, Equite, and Trowthe (840–41). In these closing scenes the Latin Mercy speaks is serious and not the object of burlesque laughter. When he advises Mankind to declare, "Miserere mei, Deus!" (830), for example, Mankind finally pronounces the words that lead to his salvation: þan mercy, good Mercy! What ys a man wythowte mercy?" (835).

When, however, Mercy earlier speaks as a cleric, he is almost always mimicked, and his overblown language is regularly deflated. When he first meets the three jocular vices who enthusiastically entertain the audience, he designates himself as a clerical spoilsport by scorning their fun and refusing to dance. Then, when asked his name, he responds: "Mercy ys my name by denomynacyon./ I conseyue ȝe haue but a lytyll fauour in my communicacyon" (122–23). His heavy

---

[23] *The Castle of Perseverance*, scene 22, ed. Eccles, *The Macro Plays*, 95–98; for the Four Daughters see Eccle's note on 200. For a semiotic analysis of this, one of the earliest and by far the most complex morality play, see Richard K. Emmerson, "The Morality Character as Sign: A Semiotic Approach to *The Castle of Perseverance*," in *Medieaval and Early Renaissance Drama: Reconsiderations*, ed. Martin Stevens and Milla Riggio, *Mediaevalia* 18 (1995, for 1992), 191–220.

latinate diction is the linguistic equivalent of his heavy-footed refusal
to dance, and it elicits a response both witty and vulgar from the
vices:

NEW GYSE.   Ey, ey! yowr body ys full of Englysch Laten.
             I am aferde yt wyll brest.
             "Prauo te," quod þe bocher onto me
                When I stale a leg a motun.
             ȝe are a stronge cunnyng clerke.
NOWADAYS.   I prey yow hertyly, worschyppull clerke,
                To haue þis Englysch mad in Laten:
             "I haue etun a dyschfull of curdys,
             And I haue schetun yowr mowth full of turdys."
             Now opyn yowr sachell wyth Laten wordys
             And sey me þis in clerycall manere! (124–34)

This passage reveals how Latin signifies clerical status in these opening scenes and, in fact, throughout much of the play. For the vices,
and presumably for the audience, "Laten wordys" are the articulate
signifiers of the signified "clerycall manere."

It is not surprising that the play humorously links clerical Latin to
Mercy or that it satirizes his "Englysch Laten." But does this imply
that the unrestrained "religious laughter" that Kolve identified as a
characteristic of popular drama is now directed not at evil characters
but at Mercy, the morality's central figure of good? An answer is
suggested by two scenes in which clerical Latin is shown to be a
sham, a cover for evil, and a kind of false learning, scenes that suggest
the moral ambiguity of clerical status and the reason why "Laten
wordys" are equated to a "mouth full of turdys." In the first, the
three vices—preparing to raise havoc in the neighborhood—are urged
by New Guise to memorize "owr neke-verse" (520) in case they are
caught. This obvious social comment on the use of Latin by clerics
to avoid criminal responsibility in secular courts presumably reflects
the audience's lay point of view. In the second scene Mercy searches
for the fallen Mankind who has gone off with the vices to drink and
play football, ending up drunk in a ditch. Mercy gives a long clerical
disquisition in which he mixes real Latin with his "Englysch Laten,"
identifies himself as Mankind's "father gostly" (765), and finally cries
out: "Mankynde, vbi es?" (771). New Guise answers this question,
"Hic hyc, hic hic, hic hic, hic hic!" (775). The drunken hiccups of
the vice here serve as a brilliant response to Mercy's Latin "where
are you?" since the latinate hiccups are translated, "here, here, here!"

(775). This scene, during which Nowadays and Nought have been relieving themselves in the background, is a masterpiece of bawdy stage business. Nevertheless, it has serious implications as well, for it suggests that the "spirit" infusing Latin is not holy and that what it takes to speak the language of the cleric is not divine but alcoholic inspiration.

The ambiguous treatment of Latin in *Mankind* is thus clarified. When, on the one hand, Latin is used by the faithful Mankind or when it denotes the word or attribute of God, it is treated seriously and with respect, leading ultimately to the salvation of Mankind. In this sense, Latin retains its traditional spiritual authority, but because of its association with God and the devout, not because of its association with the institutional Church. When it is associated with clerical authority and learning, on the other hand, it is treated comically and with contempt, leading Mankind to despair and perilously close to damnation.[24] The great masters of this Latin are the vices, who repeatedly out-cleric the cleric. Yet ultimately Mercy shifts from symbolizing the institutional cleric and comes to personify God's mercy. The morality play concludes by suggesting the proper role of Latin, but not before dangerously satirizing its use and abuse at length. This doubleness in the play's treatment of Laltin suggests that, as in the *Towneley Cycle*, the privileged spiritual language is a complex sign in *Mankind*. If Anglo-French seems consistently the object of satire aimed at a powerful, yet corrupt, Court, the status of Latin is more ambiguous. It can be both used for good and abused for evil, which suggests that what matters is not so much the person who uses the language but the purpose for which it is used.

This essay's analysis of language as stage sign has been limited to some comic masterpieces of medieval English drama. A study of other vernacular plays, including those that minimize comic action, would reveal other ways in which the two privileged languages of late medieval England signify on stage. In the *Chester Cycle*, for example, Octavius and the Magi speak Anglo-French, which once again signifies royalty, but Octavius is later "converted" by the Sibyl's prophecies, and the three kings worship the Christ child, so this courtly

---

[24] Paula Neuss, "Active and Idle Language: Dramatic Images in *Mankind*," in *Medieval Drama*, ed. Neville Denny, Stratford-upon-Avon Studies 16 (London: Edward Arnold, 1973), emphasizes how "the 'idle' language of the Vices (though it may be entertaining to the audience) is a dangerous form of temptation to Mankind" (51).

language is used in a positive sense. The status of Latin, however, is more ambiguous. Jesus in the pageant staging his miracles speaks a series of brief Latin sentences, which he immediately paraphrases in English: "Ego et Pater unum sumus: my Father and I are all on" (13:8).[25] This Latin, as well as that of Deus in the cycle's opening lines (1:1–2), is majestic and spiritual. In the "Coming of Antichrist," however, the deceiving pseudo-Christ also uses Latin very effectively, not for comic effect, but to beguile the faithful in the last days.[26] This deceptive use of Latin in a learned cycle that treats the language with serious respect makes Antichrist's dramatic control of the spiritual and authoritative language genuinely frightening. It is not possible here to pursue these and other linguistic sings in *Chester*, the other two Middle English cycles, or other moralities. It is, though, worth extending such analysis to the full range of popular vernacular plays in order to examine the extent to which they adopt, modify, or challenge the commonplace ideology of language during this crucial transition period in English history, and the ways in which language becomes a sign of the duplicity of evil on stage.

---

[25] R.M. Lumiansky and David Mills, eds., *The Chester Mystery Cycle*, vol. 1, EETS ss 3 (Oxford: Oxford University Press, 1974), cited by play and line numbers.

[26] Lumiansky and Mills, *Chester Mystery Cycle*, 23:1–8. On "The Coming of Antichrist" see Richard K. Emmerson, *Antichrist in the Middle Ages: A Study of Medieval Apocalypticism, Art, and Literature* (Seattle: University of Washington Press, 1981), 180–87; and Richard K. Emmerson, "'Nowe Ys Common this Daye': Enoch and Elias, Antichrist, and the Structure of the Chester Cycle," in *Homo, Memento Finis: The Iconography of Just Judgment in Medieval Art and Drama*, ed. David Bevington, Early Drama, Art, and Music Monograph Series 6 (Kalamazoo: Medieval Institute Publications, 1985), 89–120.

HEAVEN AND FALLEN ANGELS IN OLD ENGLISH

Catherine Brown Tkacz

While the Director of the Medieval Institute at the University of Notre Dame, Jeffrey Burton Russell expanded his already considerable linguistic skills by learning Old English, partly at the urging of Carl T. Berkhout with whom he collaborated on *Medieval Heresies: A Bibliography, 1969–1970*.[1] Thus the Old English primary sources Jeffrey draws on in his five-volume history of the Devil (1977–1988) he knows first hand. Among the Old English passages he cites is the Fall of the angels in the poem *Genesis A*.[2] This passage can be shown to be the focal instance of a larger pattern in Old English poetics. In this pattern the Fall of the angels is both an inversion of a literary formula used in saint's passions and also a logical, psychologically compelling consequence of the decreative act of rejecting God. This essay will explore the Old English commonplace of God's shoving the Devil out of Heaven and will then, as Jeffrey himself has done in his research, shift from the Devil to Heaven. For Heaven was the focus of "Glory in Time," his presentation as the 1991 Faculty Research Lecturer for the University of California at Santa Barbara, and his new book, *A History of Heaven: The Singing Silence*, appearing simultaneously in Italian and English, is deservedly gaining immediate approbation, with three book clubs making it their choice or alternate of the month.[3] This essay will follow suit and, imitating Jeffrey and the Lord, first shove Satan out of Heaven and then concentrate on Paradise.

---

[1] By Carl T. Berkhout and Jeffrey Burton Russell, Subsidia Mediaevalia, 11 (Toronto: The Pontifical Institute for Mediaeval Studies, 1981).

[2] Jeffrey Burton Russell, *Lucifer: The Devil in the Middle Ages* (Ithaca: Cornell University Press, 1984), 133–34, 138–41, 319.

[3] *Storia del Paradiso celeste* (Rome and Bari: Laterza, 1996) and *A History of Heaven: The Singing Silence* (Princeton: Princeton University Press, 1997). So far it has been the selection of these book clubs: Book of the Month Club (alternate), History Book Club, Catholic Book Club.

Shoving Satan out of Heaven

The shoving of Satan out of Heaven is a clever variation of an Old English poetic formula, recently recovered. In 1993 it was shown for the first time that Old English poets created Christian formulas de novo.[4] It had long been known that they had adapted pagan formulas to the new Christian context,[5] but now it is known that they also invented new, explicitly Christian ones. Specifically, Old English poets drew on the biblical account of the Three Young Men in the fiery furnace to devise this Daniel material: 1) the verb *scufan* 'shove' used in conjunction with fiery torment; 2) the juxtaposition of *wlite* 'brightness, beauty' and *ungewemmed* 'immaculate', often in a formula; and 3) anaphora on the negatives *næs* and *ne* linking the formula with a series of details referring to the unharmed state of the saint's body, hair, and garments. This constellation of terms and syntactic details recurs in Old English Christian literature in differing contexts: where it is essential, e.g., in *Daniel*; where the comparison with the Three Young Men is a traditional enhancement of a hagiographic account, e.g., in Cynewulf's *Juliana*; where it is appropriate mainly because of the typology of the Three Young Men, that is, in the *Andreas*; and— the context focal here—where its associations lend irony and resonance to a narrative, as in the account of the fallen angels in *Genesis A*.

Exhaustive word studies of key terms in this formula revealed specifically Christian connotations: *wlite* 'brightness, beauty,' is a consistently Christian term implying the perfect heavenly state of God, the angels, unfallen creation especially man, and the soul restored by baptism and maintained by virtue and grace;[6] *ungewemmed* 'immaculate,' has all the implications of the Latin *immaculatus*;[7] and the mundane verb *scufan* 'to shove' turns out to have explicitly Christian patterns of use that the Old English poets deploy to contrast

---

[4] Catherine Brown Tkacz, "Christian Formulas in Old English Literature: *Næs hyre wlite gewemmed* and Its Implications," *Traditio* 48 (1993), 31–61.

[5] Anita R. Riedinger focuses on Christian adaptation of Germanic materials on both the level of the concept, showing the presentation of "a new Christian hero" in the *Andreas*, and in smaller scope of the formula, identifying Christian formulas evidently devised by adapting a pre-existing formula system; for instance, presenting *blissum hremig* and the pair *sorgum hremig* and *gehþum hremig* as, in effect, new Christian productions from the Germanic system *x hremig*; "The Old English Formula in Context," *Speculum* 60 (1985), 294–317.

[6] For the full word study, see Tkacz, "Christian Formulas," 39–44.

[7] Tkacz, "Christian Formulas," 46–48.

Heaven and Hell actively. Repeatedly saints are *shoved* unjustly into torment, and sinners, especially the disobedient angels, are *shoved* out of bliss.[8]

The normative role of the verb *scufan* in hagiographic accounts, used with a new twist in narrating the Fall of the angels, is modeled evidently on diction of the Book of Daniel, where Nebuchadnezzar has Daniel cast into the lions' den.[9] Sts. Agnes, Eugenia, Juliana and the apostle John are among those described in Old English texts as *bescofene* into fire or fire-heated torments; an Anglo-Saxon hymn commemorates the martyrdom of saints "bescofene on fyre."[10] Some texts juxtapose this unjust shoving with mention of Hell. Vividly, one homilist speaks in the voice of Christ, who affirms himself slain for man's deeds and "on hellewite bescofen."[11] But Christ alone endured the harrowing; for the martyrs, Ælfric states, their betrayors "scufon hi forð to heofonrice. and ferdon him sylfe to helle wite."[12]

Saints are, by martyrdom, shoved into Heaven, but the sinful are by their own disobedience shoved out of bliss. At Judgment Day, a dozen Old English texts assert, sinners will be shoved into Hell, in contrast with the blessed who will enter bliss.[13] Adam and Eve are described in a dozen different texts as shoved from mirth into heavy toil.[14] And, first in the series of the disobedient, the disloyal angels are shoved out of Heaven.

The Fall of the disobedient angels is recounted in several Old English texts, ten describing Lucifer and his cohorts as "shoved" (*bescofene*) out of Heaven.[15] The poetic description of God's actively

---

[8] For the full word study, see Tkacz, "Christian Formulas," 48–51.

[9] Tkacz, "Christian Formulas," 49.

[10] ÆLS (Agnes) 216; ÆLS (Eugenia) 396; Jul 582; ÆHom I, 4 58.24; HyGl 2 (Stevenson) 117.4.

[11] HomM 14.2 (Healey) 19.

[12] ÆCHom II, 42 313.101.

[13] HomS 6 (Ass 14) 133; ÆCHom II, 21 189.288; cf. ÆCHom II, 37 277.160 and ChrodR 1 60.25. Related are HomU 12.2 (Willard) 36 and Ch 1208 (Rob 22) 11. See also WCan 1.2 (Torkar) 35 (*scyfð*). Texts which contrast the blessed to the damned are Sat 598–635; Eluc I (Warn 45) 23; ÆCHom II, 42 313.101. Cf. ÆCHom II, 38 283.128 and ÆCHom I, 7 112.5.

[14] GuthB 852; ÆCHom I, 10 154.10; HomM 9 18; HomM 11 (PetersonVercHom 14) 23; HomS 2 (PetersonVercHom 16) 218; HomS 3 (VercHom 8) 56; HomS 8 (BlHom 2) 46; HomS 9 46; HomU 57 (Warn 44) 15; WHom 6 46; WHom 14 44; HomS 9 52.

[15] Also useful on this topic may be an article unavailable to me: Maria Vittoria Molinari, "La caduta degli angeli ribelli: considerazioni sulla *Genesi B*," *Filologia germanica* 28–29 (1985–86), 517–40.

shoving out the disobedient angels derives from a vivid passage in *Genesis A*, and the simple verb "shove" proves to be as neatly nuanced as T.D. Hill has shown *utableow* to be in Vercelli Homily XIX.[16] In *Genesis A* in the account of the Fall of the angels the poet cleverly inverts the formulaic material used in hagiography to express the preservation of saints from harm: instead of showing persecutors who unjustly shove innocent saints into fiery tortures, the poet uniquely has God himself shove the disobedient angels into hellfire, a point the poet emphasizes with alliteration and emphasis by first position:

Sceof þa and scyrede   Scyppend ure
oferhydig cyn   engla of heofnum,
wærleas werod.   Waldend sende
laþwendne here   on langne sið
geomre gastas;   wæs him gylp forod,
beot forborsten,   and forbiged þrym,
wlite gewemmed.

Gen 65–71a

(Our Shaper shoved then and cleaved the proud band of angels out of Heaven, the untrustworthy troop. The Wielder sent the hating horde on a long journey, the wretched spirits; their boast was void, their threat demolished, and degraded their might, their radiance ruined.)[17]

This is a deliberate, ironic reversal of the Daniel material used in the Old English poems *Daniel, Azarias, Juliana,* and *Andreas* and elsewhere. As in the normative passages, God is present and active, and fiery torment is at hand (although here not detailed until a later passage). But, whereas the usual account tells of a saint shoved into fiery torture but miraculously preserved, here, for the only time in Old English literature, the phrase *wlite gewemman* occurs without a negative particle or prefix, and concludes a list of the degradations of the fallen angels. In every other occurrence of the formulaic phrase in Old English, *wlite gewemmed* is preceded by a negative particle and heads a catalogue of details of the divinely arranged physical preservation of a saint.[18] The poet of *Genesis A* has emphasized the self-destruction of the angels by placing the key phrase in final position

---

[16] "When God Blew Satan out of Heaven: The Motif of Exsufflation in *Vercelli Homily XIX* and Later English Literature," in *Sources and Relations: Studies in Honour of J.E. Cross*, ed. Marie Collins et al. (Leeds: The University of Leeds School of English, 1985), 132–141.

[17] Author's translation.

[18] See also the description of the Devil as "wann and *wlite*leas," And 1168.

in the sentence. The Daniel material is used fittingly here, for the angels, who know of God's power, act against their knowledge, whereas saints such as Juliana, who lack the perfection of absolute angelic knowledge, act more wisely out of faith; and God, preserver of his faithful saints' beauty unspotted, though they be shoved into persecutors' fires, is here the one who himself shoves the faithless angels out of Heaven and into hellfire.

The striking image of God in this active role appealed to Cynewulf and the poet of *Christ and Satan* as well. In the poem *Elene*, Cynewulf narrates the conversation of Judas, a Jew who has become a Christian, with a Devil. In response to the Devil's threats, Judas recalls the angel's Fall:

Ne þearft ðu swa swiþe,   synna gemyndig,
sar niwigan   ond sæce ræran,
morðres manfrea,   þæt þe se mihtiga cyning
in neolnesse   nyðer *bescufeð*,
synwyrcende,   in susla grund
domes leasne,   se ðe deadra feala
worde awehte.

(El 939–945a)

(You've no need, intent on sins, so swiftly to renew pain and raise up strife, evil ruler of crime, because the mighty King—he who raised up so many of the dead with a word—shoved you, sin-working, into the abyss below, into torture's world, without honor.)[19]

In *Christ and Satan*, the Fall of the angels is recounted directly:

   Let þa up faran   ece drihten;
wuldre hæfde   wites clomma
feondum oðfæsted,   and heo furþor *sceaf*
in þæt neowle genip,   nearwe gebeged,
þær nu Satanus   swearte þingað,
earm aglæca,   and þa atolan mid him,
witum werige.

(Sat 441–447a)

(Then the eternal Lord acted: gloriously he inflicted torment's bonds upon the fiends and shoved them further into that deep obscurity, narrowly abased, where now Satan miserably holds counsel, poor wretch, and the repellant ones with him, weary with torments.)

---

[19] Author's translation.

These passages in *Elene* and *Christ and Satan* have similarities: both describe Satan as an *æglæca* in an a-verse (Sat 446a, El 901a) and recount that God shoved him into *neowle genip* (deep obscurity, Sat 444a) or *neolnesse* (the deep, the abyss; El 942a). More focal is the constant among all three passages in that they present God—our Shaper, the mighty King, the eternal Lord—as shoving Satan out of Heaven.

In contrast, all but one of six homilies using this diction identify no agent for the action, using the past participle to report that the fallen angels "wurdon . . . bescofene" or "wurdon . . . ascofene."[20] This homiletic syntax is also in the poem *Guthlac A*: "scofene wurdon / fore oferhygdum in ece fyr" (633b–634). Further, in the numerous other texts using *scufan* to describe either the expulsion of Adam and Eve from Paradise or the Last Judgment, as a rule the past participle is used.[21] Only an anonymous homily for Ash Wednesday recounts the Fall as an exchange of actions between Adam and the Lord: Adam transgressed his Lord's law when he ate from the forbidden tree and therefore "drihten hine *sceaf* ut of neorxnawange on wræcaið þisses lifes. . . ."[22] In only two texts describing Judgment Day is the active predicate used. In the Old English translation of the *Elucidarium* of Honorius of Autun, as in the anonymous Ash Wednesday sermon just cited, parallelism is involved and seems to provide the main reason for the active predicate. The dyer who loves all colors and applies them as is fitting is likened to God in his actions toward individual men. The concluding parallel clauses refer to Judgment using alliterating predicates:

    & for þan man sæigð þæt
    he lufeþ þa þa he bringð into his rice
    and hataþ þa þa he *bescufð* into helle.[23]

Generally, with just these three exceptions, dozens of prose texts recount the Fall of the angels, the Fall of man, and Judgment using a past participle derived from *scufan*.[24]

---

[20] ÆCHom I, 24 342.17; ÆCHom I, 36, 538.30; HomM 13 (Peterson VercHom 21) 167; HomS 34 (Peterson VercHom 19) 23; HomU 27 (Nap 30) 76.

[21] Tkacz, "Christian Formulas," 50–51.

[22] HomS 9 52.

[23] Eluc 1 (Warn 45) 23. The other text is HomS 6 (Ass 14) 133.

[24] In a different context, not just the idea but even the alliterating predicates from *Genesis A* are also found, in a charter's concluding malediction upon whoever might violate the charter: "beo he ascyred and gesceofen into helle grunde, a a buten ende"; Ch 1208 (Rob 22) 11.

Pastoral reasons evidently prompted Ælfric and the preachers of the Vercelli homilies to use agentless past participles. By avoiding an emphasis on God's action in shoving the sinful out, the preachers more effectively remind their listeners of the sinner's own role in his end. Even the sole sermon using an active predicate, Ælfric's homily for Epiphany, does so in a way that makes this point. He observes that God did not force (*bescufe*) the angels to disobey: they transformed themselves voluntarily.[25] (Consistently both homilists and poets cite the Devil's sin of *[ofer]modignes* or *oferhygednes*.) Interestingly, *scyfe* 'shove', the noun cognate with *scufan*, can mean the inclination or "impulse" to sin, either at the Devil's instigation or from "inner stirrings."[26] The homilists who use the past participle evidently did not want to emphasize God's shoving the disobedient angels into Hell, lest the listening congregations miss the reminder about personal responsibility.

Now, having shoved Satan out—or rather, allowed him in his overweening pride to oust himself—we are free to concentrate on that from which the Devil has exiled himself, Heaven.

Heaven in Old English[27]

The point of departure for this study of descriptions of Heaven in Old English was the set of word studies leading to the discovery of the formulaic Daniel material. That research showed that Old English poets created new Christian poetic formulas, drawing on the diction of the Bible, especially as emphasized in the liturgy.[28] The present

---

[25] ÆCHom I, 7 112.5.

[26] *Inpulsu*: PrudGl 4.2 (Page) 37. "Deofles scyfe": Conf 4 (Fowler) 283 and 308; HomU 48 (Nap59) 28; LawICn 23; WHom 14 33; WPol 2.2.2 (Jost) 10. Inner stirrings: CP 33.215.11 and 15; CP (Cotton) 33.214.12 and 17.

[27] A preliminary version of this section of the essay was presented at the 29th International Congress on Medieval Studies, Western Michigan University, May 7, 1994, in a session sponsored by the Sources for Anglo-Saxon Culture.

[28] For details of the liturgy, see Milton McC. Gatch, "The Office in Late Anglo-Saxon Monasticism," in *Learning and Literature in Anglo-Saxon England: Studies Presented to Peter Clemoes on the Occasion of His Sixty-Fifth Birthday*, ed. Michael Lapidge and Helmut Gneuss (Cambridge: Cambridge University Press, 1985), 341–62; Gatch, "Old English Literature and the Liturgy: Problems and Potential," *Anglo-Saxon England* 6 (1977), 237–48; and *The Liturgical Books of Anglo-Saxon England*, ed. Richard W. Pfaff, Old English Newsletter, Subsidia 23 (Kalamazoo: The Medieval Institute, Western Michigan University, 1995). For lists of Greek, Latin, and Gallo-Roman Christian loanwords in Old English, etc., see Hugh Swinton MacGillivray, *The Influence of Christianity on the Vocabulary of Old English*, Studien zur Englischen Philologie, 8

study of Old English descriptions of Heaven[29] reveals additional poetic formulas, and again the Bible and liturgy influenced the dictional groupings. Moreover, the new research shows that a useful source of information is the body of biblical glosses and translations, especially of the Psalter, and that important, frequently repeated prayers such as the Lord's Prayer and the Gloria seem to be particularly influential. While this phenomenon should come as no surprise, documenting it confirms what common sense suggests and opens the way for new work. It is well to attend to the influence of spoken and sung Christian texts such as the psalms, canticles, and daily prayers, upon the vocabulary and formulas of a poetry which was at first entirely oral. Consider the case of the Three Young Men. The song of the three boys, the canticle known by its opening word, Benedicite, was a regular part of the liturgy of the hours, and those who sang this canticle were, like the three in the fire, standing while they sang. In short, the repetition of this canticle in the liturgy could impress it in the imagination, while in addition it would be possible for the participant in the liturgy to be aware of his actions of standing and singing as a recreation of the biblical experience. Quite naturally, this canticle is influential in Christian compositions: Greek, Latin, and Old English literature all have a formulaic reference to the Three Young Men, based on biblical diction.[30] In the case of Old English poetry, which was initially entirely oral, we should consider all the more seriously the possibility that orally performed Christian materials such as prayers and canticles influenced imagery, vocabulary, grouping of words, and syntax.[31]

The initial research on the Daniel formulas in Old English revealed, in addition to the Daniel pattern itself, two other dictional pairs involving the noun *wlite* and two additional Christian formulas using these pairs. At least seven times the phrase '*wlitig* and wynsum' occurs as an a-verse.[32] It is also found in homilies and, reversed as 'wynsum

---

(Halle an der Saale: Max Niemeyer, 1902; repr. Tübingen: Max Niemeyer, 1973), 148–58.

[29] See also Ann Marie Bohara, "More than Words Can Reckon: The Rhetoric of Afterlife Descriptions in Anglo-Saxon Poetry and Prose," Ph.D. diss., University of Pennsylvania, 1985.

[30] Tkacz, "Christian Formulas," 32.

[31] This idea was first suggested by the author during Paul E. Szarmach's NEH Summer Seminar, "Old and New Approaches to *Beowulf* and Old English Literature," Western Michigan University, 1995. On orality and literacy, see Katherine O'Brien O'Keeffe, *Visible Song: Transitional Literacy in Old English Verse*, Cambridge Studies in Anglo-Saxon England, 4 (Cambridge: Cambridge University Press, 1990).

[32] "*Wlitig* ond *wynsum*": DEdg 3a; OrW 63a; Pan 65a; Phoen 203a and 318a

and *wlitig*,' in Psalm glosses.[33] Sometimes *wlite* is combined with *wuldor* to form a Christian formula.[34] The phrase *wuldre gewlitegad* 'gloriously beautified' constitutes the a-verse of five lines of Old English poetry.[35] The alliterating pair *wlitig* and *wuldor* (sometimes in a compound) also recurs, in, for instance, *Phoenix* 117.[36] Also, *wuldres wlite* means Heaven as when Andreas' soul goes *in wuldres wlite* (Jul 311a).[37]

All of this raised the question of the full story of the terms paired with *wlite*: *wynsum* 'delightful' and *wuldor* 'glory.' Since the original

---

(with "wuldre" in 318b); Rid 84 20a; and Sat 213a. See also "ond wlitigra ond wynsumra," Phoen 131a.

[33] *Wlitig and wynsum*: HomU 17.1 (KlugeE) 16 and 92, and HomU 17.2 (KlugeG) 15 and 81. See also St. Agnes's praise of Christ as better than men: "his ansyn is *wlitigre* and his lufu *wynsumre*"; ÆLS (Agnes) 42. *Wynsum & wlitig* is in three glosses on Ps. 146:1: PsGlF (Kimmens), PsGlG (Rosier), PsGlJ (Oess). See also HyGl (Oliphant) 3903.

"Wlitig" is not in all glosses on this verse, because the Latin differs. The Latin in the glossed Psalters is Jerome's revision of the Septuagint. There are two traditions for this particular verse, one with "iucunda" alone, the other with "iucunda decoraque"; see WV 1:950. Half of the Old English glossed Psalters represent one tradition, half the other. It is the full phrase which is three times glossed "wynsum & wlitig" and once "wynsum and aarweorðlic"; PsGlI (Lindeloef) 146.1.

[34] Similar pairings are frequent, e.g., "*wlite* and *wuldre*" (GenA 36a), "*wuldorfæstne wlite*" (GenA 2193a), "*wuldorlicne wlite*" (MSol 56). For "*wuldres wlite*," see n. 37 below. See also the recurring phrase "to *wlite* and to *wuldre*"—ÆCHom II, 33 252.106, CP 4.39.13, HomU 2 (Belf 11) 72; cf. "fram *wlite* and fram *wuldre* heofena rices" and "on *wlite* and on *wuldre*"; HomU 32 (Nap40) 56 and 136. See also HomU 37 (Nap46) 171 on the saints at judgment seeing "heora *wuldor* and heora *wlite*." The alliterating pair is also found in the Psalms, e.g. PsGlF (Kimmens) 20.6. Cf. "*wlite* þæs *wuldorlecan* lichoman," the Old English translation of Bede's "species corporis gloriosi" in his account of a heavenly vision (Bede 4 11.288.14 and *Bædae opera* 2:288). See also ChristC 1587; Phoen 609; Rid 84 24; and Sat 222b–23b. V.V. Bushtueva discusses *wuldor* and its adjectival suffixes in "Odnoosnovnye edinitsy nominatsii iusloviia ikh realizatsii v iazyke (na materiale drevneangliiskikh prilagatel'nykh)," *Vestnik Leningradskogo Universiteta* 23 (1985), 70–74.

[35] *Wuldre gewlitegad*: in *Andreas* it occurs in a blessing (543a) and in a description of the temple in Jerusalem (669a); in *Solomon and Saturn* 398a, it occurs in a reference to baptism; and in Metrical Charm 11, invoking protection, verse 30a uses the formula in a description of the seraphim, while in *Azarias* it describes the Three Young Men as they emerge unharmed from the furnace (187a). In four other texts *wuldor* and *gewlitegad* are in close proximity: Glor I 2a and 5a, El 1310b and 1321a, and esp. LPr III 12b–13a and Phoen 117. See also "wuldorbeagas . . . gewlitegod"; HyGl3 (Gneuss) 42.3.

[36] *Wlitig* and *wuldor* are also paired twice in *Andreas*, in the disciples' vision of heaven and in Andrew's prayer concluding the narrative (870, 1721). See also "þæsne wlite, & þis wuldor"; HomU 2 (Belf 11)107. In *Daniel* and *Azarias*, God is described as *wlitig and wuldorfæst* and the Three Young Men pray, "*wlitiga . . . þin wuldor* on us!" (Dan 285, 326; Az 6b–7, 42–43).

[37] *Wuldres wlite*: also HomU 15 (Robinson) 48, Part 16a, PPs 56.13, and Sat 231a. The words are reversed, *wlite wuldres*, in PPs 95.6. Other expressions also occur, as "hiofena rices *wlite*," HomS (FörstVercHom 9) 190.

research on the Daniel material entailed examining every Old English passage containing the word *wlite*, this had included every passage where it alliterates with *wynsum* or *wuldor*, but the question remained, do these two terms pair up without *wlite*? *Wuldor* and *wynn* have long been known to be associated with Heaven, but the focus of Halvorson, for instance, has been on their general meaning, not their rhetorical and poetic roles.[38] A logical sequel to the earlier research, then, is to examine all occurrences of these alliterating terms, *wuldor* 'glory' and *wynsum* 'delightful.' Other scholars such as Halvorson, Keiser, MacGillivray, Bohara, and Roberts have treated the wealth and range of terms in Old English descriptions of Heaven; this study focuses simply on a trio of alliterating terms in order to identify more Christian poetic formulas.[39]

The body of evidence for the *Traditio* article was not scanty, involving over 1200 occurrences of *wlite*, *gewemman*, and *scufan*, but the present study involves nearly five times as much data.[40] The 611 occurrences of *wlite* and its cognates are again pertinent. The bulk of the evidence to be sifted involved *wuldor* and its cognates (four adjectives, two verbs, and one other noun form), for they occur 2622 times,[41] and in addition there are 168 occurrences of the 26 com-

---

[38] Nelius O. Halvorson treats *wuldor* and *wynn* within his discussion of "Salvation and Heaven," 80–87; *Doctrinal Terms in Ælfric's Homilies*, University of Iowa Humanistic Studies, n.s. 228 = 5.1 (Iowa City: The University of Iowa, 1932), see index.

[39] Halvorson, *Doctrinal Terms*; Albert Keiser, *The Influence of Christianity on the Vocabulary of Old English Poetry*, Part I, University of Illinois Studies in Language and Literature 5.1 (Urbana: University of Illinois Press, 1919), with *wuldor* on p. 126; MacGillivray, "[Christian Vocabulary]"; Bohara, "Afterlife Descriptions"; and Jane Roberts, "A Preliminary 'Heaven' Index for Old English," in *Sources and Relations: Studies in Honour of J.E. Cross*, ed. Marie Collins et al., Leeds Studies in Old English, n.s. 16 (Leeds: The University of Leeds, 1985), 208–19.

[40] *Wlite* and cognates, 611 occurrences; *Gewemman* 449; *Scufan* and prefixed forms, 195; Tkacz, "Christian Formulas," and Tkacz, "Unlocking the Word Hoard: Conducting Word Studies Using the Microfiche Concordance to Old English," *Old English Newsletter* 29.1 (1995): 32–39, esp. 38, nn. 12 and 21.

[41] The noun *wuldor* occurs 2010 times, 918 of them with gloss. Fully 1990 occurrences begin with (three consist of) the letters *wuld*. Excluded from this total are two occurrences of *wulde* which are from the verb *woldan*, one occurrence of *wuldes* which means "woods," one occurrence of *wuldra* which is a form of the cognate verb *wuldrian* and is counted with it, and one occurrence of *wuldrum* which means "wild animals." The other instances of *wuldor* are sixteen beginning with *uuld*, the unique form *woldor*, and the two occurrences of *wylder*, as well as the unique occurrence of the compound *heofonwuldre*.

The four cognate adjectives are *wuldorfæst* (43 occurrences/14 of them glossed), *wuldorful* (124/52), *wuldorlic* (57/21), and *wuldrig* (18/17). The two cognate verbs are *wuldorfullian* and *wuldrian*, which occur 367 times, glossed 201 times. The other noun form is rare: *wuldrung*, occurring three times, always glossed.

pounds beginning with *wuldor*.[42] Crosschecking by Latin evidence for *wuldor* entailed reviewing the 1410 occurrences of *glori** in the electronic corpus of Old English.[43] *Wynn* and its cognates (four adjectives, one verb, and two other noun forms) occur 896 times,[44] and there are 42 occurrences of compounds beginning with *wynn*.[45] Further reviewing these 5749 occurrences[46] indicates that other alliterating terms are—no surprise—important in this context, and the present essay touches on some key ones.

It appears that biblical texts and glosses, prayers, and homilies popularized, and probably in some cases introduced, diction and alliterative groupings found in poetry. Seven new formulaic patterns, including five which yield a full line of verse, are presented here. All are rooted in the diction of the Bible and popular prayers.

For instance, *wuldor* translates *gloria* in at least 89 verses in the Psalms, and *wuldrian* translates *gloriare* or *glorificare* in another 20. Moreover, *wuldor* figures in focal biblical passages. The angel's announciation to the shepherds, "Gloria in excelsis Deo . . ." is rendered with *wuldor*: "Sy *wuldor* gode on heannyssum, and on eorðan sib mannum þam ðe beoð godes willan."[47] Recounted in Luke 2:14 and echoed in the account of the Transfiguration (Lk. 19:38), this announcement figures in the West Saxon Gospels, glosses on Luke, and at least seven homilies.[48] The phrase "king of glory" (*rex gloriae*)

---

[42] Most occur just one to five times. *Wuldorcyning* occurs 47 times. *Wuldorbeag* occurs 40 times and its verbal form *wuldorbeagian* 27 times; they are the only glossed compounds, with 19 and 21 glosses respectively, usually *corona[re]*.

[43] I am grateful to Antonette diPaolo Healey and her staff of the Dictionary of Old English at the University of Toronto for allowing me to search the electronic corpus for *glori** in July, 1995, before it was available on-line. This visit was part of Paul E. Szarmach's NEH Summer Seminar, mentioned above. On *glori**, see also Tkacz, "Word Hoard," 36–37.

[44] Excluded are the numerous occurrences of forms of *win* 'wine,' *wine* 'friend,' and *gewinnan* 'to fight.' *Wynn* is found 148 times, only six times with a gloss. Its adjectives are rare and unglossed: *wynfæst* (unique), *wynleas* (3 times), and *wynlic* (16 times). *Wynsum* and its related verb and noun forms are much more frequent: {*[ge][un]*}*w[i/y]ns***[m/n]*{*lic*}* (426/179); the verb {*ge*}*wynsumian* (104/85), and the noun {*[ge][un]*}*wynsumnes* (198/118). The noun *wynsummunga* occurs once. For the conventions of reporting the parameters of the word search, see Tkacz, "Word Hoard," p. 34.

[45] *Wyndream* occurs 23 times, always glossed. A dozen other compounds occur one to five times each, never glossed. Not considered here are the sixteen proper nouns—personal names and toponyms—beginning *W[y/i]n-*.

[46] The number of occurrences of the individual terms is greater than the total number of passages involved, because some passages contain one or more term (or one or more occurrence of the same term).

[47] ÆCHom I, 2 30.24.

[48] Lk (WSCp) 2.13 + 19.38, LkGl (Li) 2.14 + 19.38, and LkGl (Ru) 2.14 +

of Ps. 23/24:7–10 appears as the *cyning wuldres* in several glosses on the Psalter and on the canticles.[49] The Paris Psalter even interpolates the epithet *wuldres cyning*.[50] The phrase, as will be seen, recurs in other contexts.

While the noun *wynn* occurs only once in the Psalms (PPs 119.5), its cognates recur in the Psalter itself as well as in translations and glosses. The adjective *wynsum* is in 36 verses, the verb *wynsumian* in 30, and the derived noun *wynsumnes* in 23. *Wynsum* usually renders *suavis* (75 times) or *jocundus* (62 times). The verb *wynsumian* conveys *exultare* (44), *jubilare* (30), or *exaltare* (6). *Wynsumnes* translates the related nouns *exultatio* (60), *suavitas* (18), *jubilatio* (17) or *jocunditas* (17).

Moreover, glosses create pairs of these three alliterating terms. *Wynsumian* and *wuldrian* occur together occasionally in the Old English version of Psalms, in the Paris Psalter, and in glosses on the Psalms.[51] The Paris Psalter joins *wlite* and *wuldor* (PPs 95.7) and opens rich alliteration on *w*- with *wuldor* in a verse rendered so as to recall the *Gloria*:

> *Wuldor* si *w*ide   *w*eruda drihtne
> and on *w*orulda *w*oruld   *w*unie syððan,
> blissie on his weorcum   bealde drihten.

> (PPs 103.29 [v. 31])

Even though one would expect prayers to draw on the diction and pairing of the scriptures and of glosses, some of their emphases are beyond what one would assume. Naturally *wuldor* is in all Old English versions of the *Gloria*. The prose gloss of the Gloria is the most direct and complete:

19.38. Homilies: ÆCHom I, 2 30.24 + 36.35 + 38.10, ÆCHom I, 3 56.33, ÆCHom I, 14.1 206.12 (uses Mt. 21), ÆCHom I, 38 582.32; HomS 1 (VercHom 5) 186, HomU 10 (VercHom 6) 62, and LS 19 (PurifMary) 149.

[49] *Cyning wuldres*: Glosses on Psalm 23.7–10 = PsGlA (Kuhn), PsGlB (Brenner), PsGlD (Roeder), PsGlF (Kimmens), PsGlG (Rosier), PsGlH (Campbell), PsGlI (Lindeloef), PsGlJ (Oess), and PsGlK (Sisam). Canticles = PsCa A 2 (Kuhn) 2.14, PsCa E (Liles) 14.14, and PsCa F (Rosier) 14.14. On *cyning*, see also the studies of Marie B. Murtagh, "Some Words for 'Lord' in Old English Poetry: An Investigation of Word Meaning and Use," Ph.D. diss., Boston University, 1985, and Henry Paul Schweitzer, "The Idea of the King in Old English Literature," Ph.D. diss., Fordham University, 1941.

[50] PPs 70.18–21.

[51] *Wynsumian* and *wuldrian*: Ps. 31.7 (modern v. 11). *Wynsumiað* and *wuldur*: PsGlC (Wildhagen) 65.2. *Wuldor* and *wyn*: PPs 61.7.

Sy *wulder* god fæder & his anum sunu mid þam
frofergaste & nu ða & on ecnysse sy hit swa.

Sit gloria deo patri eiusque soli filio cum paraclito
spiritu et nunc et in perpetuum.

The short verse setting emphasizes *wulder* with alliteration:

Wuldor sy ðe ane *wurð*mynt,   *w*ereda drihten,
fæder on foldan,   fægere gemæne,
mid sylfan sunu   and soðum gaste. Amen.

(Glor II)

In the long setting (Glor I), a 57-line meditation on the text, *wuldor*
and *gewlitegod* occur in the opening, a seven-line response to the word
"Gloria." *Wlite* recurs twice (15b, 44a), the second time alliterating
with *wuldorgife* (44b) in a passage describing the rule of the "cyning
innan *wuldre*" (42a).

In the Old English settings of the Lord's Prayer, one finds that
again glory holds a larger place than one might expect. In even the
brief version (11 lines) of the Exeter Book, probably the earliest of
the three,[52] although the poet skipped the petition concerning forgiveness, he added an opening reference to glory (*wuldres dream*, 2a).
The longest setting (123 lines), more a meditation on the prayer than
a translation of it, mentions glory in the same place as the short
setting, the second a-verse, this time in the phrase "cyninc on *wuldre*."
Compare this to the recurring "cyning *wuldres*" of the psalms and
canticles and to the phrase "cyning innan *wuldre*" brought to the Old
English Gloria (Glor I 42a). In the longest Old English Lord's Prayer,
a later a-verse also honors God with glory (59a). The third setting
of the prayer is notable in that it uses the three alliterating terms all
in a row:

swa hluttor is   in heofon*wuldre*
wynnum gewlitegod   a to *w*orlde forð.

(12–13)

Wuldor recurs again, without alliteration, in 33b.

Obviously the *cyning wuldres* of Ps. 23/24:7–10 led to "cyning on/
in[nan] wuldre" in the verse Glorias and in the Lord's Prayer. The

---

[52] E.V.K. Dobbie, ed., *The Anglo-Saxon Poetic Records*, vol. 3: *The Exeter Book* (New York: Columbia University Press, 1936), lxiii–iv.

popular phrase "king of glory" and the compound "glory-king" have four formulaic roles. The phrase *wuldres cyning* is found five times as a b-verse.[53] It is also used in thirteen homilies.[54] *Cyninga wuldor* occurs as a half-verse ten times.[55] As a b-verse, it is three times matched with an a-verse consisting of "acenned" with a one-syllable verb beginning with w- and, once, the word "Crist":

acenned wearð   cyninga wuldor
        (El 5b = 178b)
Crist wæs acennyd,   cyninga wuldor
        (Men 1b)

The compound *wuldorcyning*, found twice in prose, constitutes an a-verse five times in poetry, twice with a b-verse of "to widan feore."[56] The phrase "wuldor cyning" constitutes a b-verse in *Seasons of Fasting* (74b). Four other poems expand the b-verse, prefacing "wuldor cyning" with two or three syllables beginning with s-:

siþþan wuldor cyning
        (Christ A,B,C 565b, Fates 27b)
sohton him wuldor cyning
        (Dream 133b)
swa swa wuldor cining
        (Met 26.45b)

As for the Gloria itself, variations on it serve to conclude scores of homilies. (The question of which variations are taken over from Latin sources is too complex to be addressed here.[57]) Here is a typical example, from Ælfric:

Sy him. a. wuldor mid his heofonlican fæder. and ðam halgan gaste. on anre godcundnysse. on ecere worulde;[58]

---

[53] *Wuldres cyning* (five times, b-verse): Christ 565b, Dream 133b, Fates 27b, Met 26.45b, Seasons 74b.

[54] *Wuldres cyning*: ÆCHom II, 4 40.320, ÆCHom II, 5 51.274 (with Latin), ÆLS (Sebastian) 468, ÆLS (Denis) 175, HomS 1 (VercHom 5) 1, HomS 21 (BlHom 6) 17, HomS 27 85, HomS 28 264 + 269, HomS 33 (Foerst) 208, identical to HomS 44 206, HomS 45 (Tristr 3) 234; Nic (A) 573 + 600 + 606 + 655 + 658, and Nic (C) 303.

[55] *Cyninga wuldor* in poems, 7 b-verses, 3 a-verses: And 171b, 555b, 854b, 1410a; El 5b = 178b; ChristA,B,C 508a; Jud 155a; Jul 279b; Men 1b; and Res 21a. See also WPol 2.1.1 (Jost) 2.

[56] *Wuldorcyning*: ChristA,B,C 161a, Dan 308a, El 1321ab, Ex 548ab, and Met 20.162a. Prose: Instr 193 and LS 16 (MargaretHerbst) 355.

[57] For basic comments, see Tkacz, "Word Hoard," 36–37.

[58] ÆCHom II, 14.1 149.351. See also ÆHom 2 290, ÆHom 10 207, and ÆLS (Edmund) 275.

Sometimes this homiletic closing is shorn of its trinitarian reference.[59] Usually the closing is expanded to include *lof* 'praise' or *wurðmynt* 'honor.' Through the influence of the Gloria, *wuldor* generally comes first: only ten times does one find "lof and *wuldor*,"[60] but thirty-seven times Ælfric uses the phrase "*wuldor* and lof," sometimes without referring to the Trinity,[61] elsewhere with extended references to one or more Persons of God.[62] Perhaps partly influenced by the pairing of "*wuldor* and wurðmynt" in the Old English Ps 28.2, Ælfric sometimes uses that pair in the closing, again with *wuldor* generally first.[63] Once he uses all three terms: "*wuldor* & lof & wyrðmynt."[64]

The Gloria and the derivative homiletic closings are clearly the context for such poetic lines as *Elene* 892b–93, which concludes a numbered section (x) of the poem: "Sie him *wuldor* and þanc / a butan ende eallra gesceafta." This passage from *Christ* is similar: "Si him lof symle / þurh woruld worulda, *wuldor* on heofnum" (ChristA,B,C 777).

---

[59] ÆCHom II, 37 274.78, ÆCHom II, 39.1 297.331, ÆCHom II (Prayers) 345.7, ÆHom 17 293, ÆHom 221, ÆHomM 4 (Ass) 5 180, ÆLS (Agatha) 236, ÆLS (Ash Wed) 293, ÆLS (Julian & Basilissa) 434, ÆLS (Book of Kings) 473, and ÆLet 5 (Sigefyrth) 225.

[60] *Lof* preceding *wuldor*, as in "Him sy lif & *wuldor* aa butan ende, amen," WHom 2 69; see also WHom 7a 12 + 46, WHom 8c 177, WHom 377, ÆCHom I, 17 (App) 189.2, ÆCHom I, 28 414.34, ÆCHom II, 13 136.290, and ÆCHom II, 16 164.96; cf. WHom 20.1 128.

[61] *Wuldor and lof* without reference to Trinity: ÆCHom I, 6 102.34, ÆCHom I, 26 384.17, ÆCHom I, 31 476.21, ÆCHom I, 39 606.26, ÆCHom II, 12.2 126.582, ÆCHom II, 15 160.336, ÆCHom II, 218.214, ÆCHom II, 28 229.252, ÆCHom II, 30 240.151, ÆHom 3 182, ÆHom 5 290, ÆHom 6 367, ÆHom 14 235, ÆHom 21 427, ÆHom 22 672, ÆHomM 15 (Ass 9) 452, ÆLS (Mark) 97, ÆLS (Auguries) 271, and ÆLS (Chrysanthus) 356.

[62] *Wuldor and lof*: ÆCHom I, 2 44.4, ÆCHom I, 25 364.5 (regular reference to Trinity), ÆCHom I, 33 500.26 (full clause for each Person), ÆCHom I, 36 556.22 (with elaboration on Christ), ÆCHom I, 38 (App) 205.R.11, ÆCHom II, 10 91.339, ÆCHom II, 11 109.587, ÆCHom II, 23 203.136, ÆCHom II, 30 240.151, ÆHomM 5 (Ass 6) 186, ÆHomM 14 (Ass 8) 329, ÆLS (Exalt of Cross) 218, ÆLS (Oswald) 287, ÆLS (Maur) 368, ÆLS (Eugenia) 427, ÆLS (Swithun) 496, ÆLS (Maccabees) 810, and ÆLS (Martin) 1493.

[63] *Wurðmynt and wuldor* (5 times): ÆCHom I, 4 76.22, ÆCHom I, 31 470.14, ÆHom 8 252, ÆHom 13 233, and ÆLS (Æthelthryth) 131.

Wuldor and wurðmynt (14 times in Ælfric): ÆCHom II, 8 71.127, ÆCHom II, 27 220.197, ÆCHom II, 31–32 247.176, ÆCHom II, 35 267.238 (with alliteration on *w-* throughout), ÆCHom II, 36.1 271.106, ÆCHom II, 42 316.202, ÆHom 8 252, ÆHom 15 228, ÆHom 16 230, ÆHomM 7 (Bel 4) 154, ÆLS (Maurice) 178, ÆLS (Peter's Chair) 292, ÆLS (Forty Soldiers) 274, ÆLet 1 (Wulfsige CCCC 190) 116; see also HomU 15 (Robinson) 79 and HomU 35.2 (Nap44) 349.

[64] ÆHom 1 470.

Moving from *wuldor* to *wynsumnes*, from "glory" to "delight," one finds that *wynsum*, like *wlitig*, implies heavenly and unfallen perfection. For instance, God is "wynsumlican scyppend."[65] Jesus is the Father's "wynsuman sunu."[66] Mary, too, is described using *wynsum*.[67] Alleluia is "wynsum lof heofonlicum weorodum."[68] A vision of Heaven is "wynsuman slæpe."[69] Correspondingly, the Fall, which made the Devil *wliteleas*, is also the loss of *wynn*; Satan, newly fallen, bitterly contrasts his *wite* 'torment' to the still-innocent Adam's *wynn*.[70] Like *wlite*, so too *wynne* can mean Heaven.[71]

In Old English poetry, three full-line formulaic patterns emerge, combining *wynn* and *wuldor* and, not surprisingly, alliterating on w-. The following supplies a full line in *Christ*, *Guthlac*, and *Juliana*: an a-verse including the genitive plural of a noun beginning with w- and meaning "people," and *wynn*, and a b-verse consisting of an unaccented one-syllable word and the phrase "*wuldres* þrym." Note that the word *þrym* 'majesty,' also recurs with *wuldor* in the Psalms and canticles.[72]

Eala *wifa wynn*	geond *wuldres* þrym
	(ChristA,B,C 71)
winemæga wyn,	in *wuldres* þrym
	(GuthA,B 1357)
Gemunað *wigena wyn*	ond *wuldres* þrym
	(Jul 638)

A second full-line pattern is related. In it the optional b-verse consists of a genitive plural of *wiga* 'man' followed by "þrym." The a-verse, found seven times in *Andreas*, *Elene*, *Guthlac*, *Vainglory*, and *Christ and Satan*, consists of the phrase *wuldres wynn*, sometimes prefaced by one or two unstressed syllables.[73] The full line exists in *Elene* and *Andreas*:

---

[65] HomS 32 72.

[66] ÆLS (Agnes) 223.

[67] LS 18.1 (NatMaryAss 10N) 297 = LS 18.2 (NatMaryAss 10J) 300.

[68] HyGl 3 (Gneuss) 48.1.

[69] ÆLS (Swithun) 251.

[70] GenA,B 918–919a + 945 = Eden's *wynn*; Sat 40a–43 = Heaven's *wynn*. Satan's contrast: GenA 364. For the idea that the Devil rejoices (*wynsumiað*) at people's sin and damnation, see the parallel passages HomS 40.1 (Nap49) 70 and HomS 40.3 (McCabeVercHom 10) 81.

[71] Sat 197; cf. Hell 50.

[72] *þrym*: "Pleni sunt cæli et terra maiestatis gloriae tuae," Ps. 14.6; "Fulle syndon heovenas & eorþe mæinþrymmes wulde þines"; PsCaK (Sisam) 14.6. See also PsCaC (Wildhagen) 19.6, PPs 70.18–21, PPs 144.11.

[73] The a-verse pattern alone: El 843 + 1038, GuthA,B 1345, Sat 174, Vain 65.

on *wuldres wyn.*	Bide *wigena* þrym
	(El 1089)
þæs *wuldres wynn,*	*wigendra* þrim
	(And 887)

Another full-line pattern adds a third alliterating term frequently found with *wuldor* and/or *wynn* in biblical glosses and homilies: *wunian* 'to dwell.'[74]

| a-verse: | [inflected form of *wunian*] in/on *wynnum* |
| b-verse: | [verb/verbal phrase] *wuldres* blæd/sweg |

wunodon on *wynnum,*	geherdon *wuldres* sweg,
	(Sat 235)
wuniað in *wynnum,*	habbað *wuldres* blæd
	(Sat 506)
wunað in *wynnum,*	þæt is *wuldres* bled
	(Sat 592)[75]

The complete trio of terms found adjacently in the Lord's Prayer—*wuldor, wynn, wlite*—is also used in homilies, as in the rhythmic phrase "on *wlite* and on *wuldre* and on *wynsumnesse*"[76] and in Agnes's praise of Christ: "His *wlites wuldriað* þa *wynsumum* tunglan, sunne and mona þe middangeard onlihtað."[77] In poetry, also, these three words evocative of Heaven occur together. They are found within three lines in *Christ and Satan* (648–50), within two lines in *Guthlac* (817–18) and Riddle 84 (25–26), and within a single line of *Phoenix*, capping a description of that heavenly bird: "*wlitig ond wynsum, wuldre* gemearcad" (Phoen 318).

Gauging whether formulaic material is a Christian adaptation of a pre-Christian formula system, or the product of a newly devised Christian formula system can be difficult. The system yielding "þæt wæs god cyning," "þæt wæs grim cyning," and "he wæs riht cyning," could also yield explicitly Christian references to God, as in Juliana's assertion, "þæt is soð cyning!"[78] Regarding the formulas identified in this essay, the various forms of "King of Glory" as a half verse could probably be understood as Christian formulas produced on

---

[74] Halvorson mentions *wunung* in heaven; *Doctrinal Terms*, 86. See also "wensæm wunyincge," HeptNotes 3. Ælfric teaches that almsdeeds earn "æt Gode þa heofonlican *wununge* and þæt ece *wuldor*"; ÆHom 11 365.

[75] Cf. Sat. 554–56 and 650.

[76] HomU 32 (Nap40) 136.

[77] ÆLS (Agnes) 51.

[78] God: Beo 11, 862, 2390. Grim: Deor 23. Riht: El 13. Soð: Jul 224.

pre-Christian models, but the five full-verse patterns appear to be essentially Christian in both composition and diction.

The present essay, in delineating the roles of *wlite, wuldor,* and *wynn* in descriptions of Heaven in Old English, adduces further evidence that the Bible and liturgy influenced homilists and poets in their choice of alliterating terms. There is still much to be done in exploring the role of the orally performed texts of Christian worship in influencing the diction, imagery, and ideas of Old English Christian poetry. As for Satan's dramatic ousting from Heaven, it is fitting that here too all the Devil can manage is to be derivative, for the topos of shoving Satan out of Heaven is a clever variation, by the poet of *Genesis A,* of the Daniel material. Thus the Devil is defined by his loss and his lack, "wann and wliteleas," and "wlite gewemmed," while the plenitude of Heaven's *wlite, wuldor,* and *wynn* abides and flourishes.

PETER THE VENERABLE ON THE "DIABOLICAL HERESY OF THE SARACENS"[1]

John Tolan

Peter the Venerable, Abbot of Cluny, travelled to Spain in 1142–43. There he assembled a team of translators whom he enticed to produce a full, annotated Latin version of the Koran, along with translations of other Muslim texts and of an Arab-Christian polemical work, the *Risālat al-Kindī*. Using this collection of texts (often referred to as the *Collectio Toletana*), Peter himself composed two anti-Islamic tracts: the first, his *Summa totius haeresis Saracenorum*, describes and vilifies Islam to a Christian readership, the second, the *Contra sectam siue haeresim Saracenorum*, attempts to refute Islam on its own terms and enjoins its Muslim readers to convert to Christianity.[2]

Why did Peter the Venerable undertake, at great cost and considerable effort, this ambitious venture? James Kritzeck rightly emphasizes

[1] An earlier version of this article was presented to the seminar "Savoirs et Pouvoirs: Histoire Culturelle de l'Espagne Médiévale," at the Collège d'Espagne in Paris, February, 1997; thanks to the participants of that seminar for their helpful comments, in particular to the organizer, Adeline Rucquoi, and to Gabriel Martinez-Gros. Thanks also to Robert Bartlett and Thomas Burman for their comments and corrections, and to Bernard McGinn for bibliographical advice.

[2] On Peter the Venerable and his polemics against Islam, see James Kritzeck and Giles Constable, eds., *Petrus Venerabilis, 1156–1956: Studies and Texts Commemorating the Eighth Centenary of his Death*, Studia Anselmiana 40 (1956) [hereafter abbreviated PV]; *Pierre Abélard, Pierre le Vénérable: Les courants philosophiques, littéraires et artistiques en occident au milieu du XIIᵉ siècle*, Colloques internationaux du Centre National de la Recherche Scientifique 546 (Paris, 1975) [hereafter abbreviated PAPV]; D'Alverny, Marie-Thérèse, "Deux traductions latines du Coran au Moyen-Age," *Archives d'histoire doctrinale et littéraire du Moyen Age* 16 (1947–48): 69–131 (reprinted in D'Alverny, *Connaissance de l'Islam dans l'Occident médiéval* (Aldershot, 1994)); eadem, "Pierre le Venerable et la légende de Mahomet," *Congrès international des sciences historiques à Cluny* (Dijon, 1950), 161–70 (reprinted in D'Alverny, *Connaissance*); Kritzeck, *Peter the Venerable and Islam* (Princeton, 1964); idem, "De l'influence de Pierre Abélard sur Pierre le Vénérable dans ses oeuvres sur l'Islam," in PAPV, 205–14; Jean-Pierre Torrell, "La notion de prophétie et la méthode apologétique dans le *Contra Saracenos* de Pierre le Vénérable," *Studia Monastica* 18 (1975): 257–82; Richard Lemay, "L'apologétique contre l'Islam chez Pierre le Vénérable et Dante," *Mélanges offerts à René Crozer* 2 (Poitiers, 1966), 755–64; Jean Jolivet, "L'Islam et la raison, d'après quelques auteurs latins des IXᵉ [*sic*: should be XIᵉ] et XIIᵉ siècles," in A. Cazenave and J. Lyotard, eds., *L'art des confins: Mélanges offerts à Maurice Gandillac* (Paris, 1985), 153–64.

the uniqueness of this endeavor, and the zeal with which Peter and his associates brought it to completion. Yet if Kritzeck characterizes it as "project to study, comprehensively and from original sources, the religion of Islam,"[3] these are not the terms that Peter the Venerable himself employs. For Peter, the point is not to "study" a "religion" but to refute a particularly vile form of heresy. Previous scholars have shown that Kritzeck's vision of Peter as a tolerant, irenic student of Islam is wide of the mark; yet these same scholars, seeming to accept Peter's own claim that no-one before him had refuted the "heretic" Muḥammad, ignore Peter's use of earlier anti-Muslim polemic.[4]

This article is an attempt to rectify this picture, to place Peter the Venerable's important initiative in context, or rather in two contexts: first, Peter's selective use of an earlier, Christian Arabic tradition of anti-Muslim polemic; and, second, Peter's own very particular concerns and outlook which shape his views of Islam. Peter (like other twelfth-century authors on Islam) understood and portrayed this "Saracen heresy" according to the fears and hopes of twelfth-century Europe. Peter uses previous polemical works: the *Risālat al-Kindī* (by a ninth-century Arab Christian author) and the *Dialogi contra Iudeos* of Andalusian Petrus Alfonsi. He nevertheless portrays Islam in a very different light, reflecting the preoccupation with heretics close to home, the ambivalence toward philosophical and scientific study, and a need to intellectually justify Christianity in face of a wave of texts and ideas flowing in from the Arab world. He strove to explain Islam in ways that would account for the wisdom and opulence of its adherents while reassuring the Christian reader that he is right to remain true to his ancestral faith.

Peter the Venerable was poised at the confluence of various winds of change sweeping over Europe: monastic reform, new heretical movements, new applications of logic to theology (including attempts to prove the fundamental doctrines of Christianity by rational arguments). Peter wrote to condemn the heretic Peter of Bruys, he mediated between Abelard and Bernard of Clairvaux, welcoming Abelard as one of his monks, he read Petrus Alfonsi's *Dialogi contra Iudeos*,

---

[3] Kritzeck, *Peter the Venerable and Islam*, 15.

[4] For criticisms of this image of Peter as a tolerant student of Islam, see M. Brolis, "La crociata di Pietro il Venerabile: guerra di arma o guerra di idee?" *Aevum* 61 (1987): 327–54; Benjamin Z. Kedar, *Crusade and Mission: European Approaches toward the Muslims* (Princeton, 1984), 101. Indeed, in order to form this image of a tolerant Peter opposed to crusading, Kritzeck had to wilfully overlook the evidenced

reusing its anti-Talmudic arguments in his own *Adversus Iudeorum inveteratam duritiem*, and he traveled to Spain where he hired translators—taking them away from their study of philosophy and astronomy—to translate the *Collectio Toletana*. Throughout Peter's polemics, we see hopes and worries of the abbot, fighter of heresies and interested spectator of the new developments in knowledge.

What intellectual baggage did Peter bring along on his encounter with Islam? He did not confront it *tabula rasa*; how then did his previous experiences and ideas affect the way he read and reacted to the Koran and the other works of the Toledan Corpus? My aim is not to narrate Peter's biography; that has been amply done.[5] Rather, I want to highlight the elements in his life that will shape his understanding of Islam, the intellectual frame of reference that was constructed before he confronted the law of Muḥammad and through which he read the Koran and other texts on Islam.

The first and broadest influence is his monastic education and his experience as a monk and abbot. As a child oblate virtually weaned on the bible and Church fathers, he is bound to find the Koranic stories of (say) Potiphar's wife and Joseph, or of Abraham and his son Ishmael, to be strange and deviant. Even more shocking, of course, would be the Koranic Jesus: born of the virgin Mary, yet uncrucified and undivine. Yet this would not have been completely unfamiliar to a reader of the Church Fathers—Augustine and others—who often wielded their pens against deviant Christologies. Peter will place himself proudly in their tradition as he writes to combat what he can only see as the latest and most virulent Christological heresy.

As abbot, Peter piloted Cluny through what Lester Little has called "the critical phase of the crisis of monasticism."[6] Cluny found itself under increasing criticism from advocates of reform, notably the

---

amassed by Virginia Berry, "Peter the Venerable and the Crusades," in PV 141–62. See also two review's of Kritzeck's book: Richard Lemay in *Middle East Forum* 41 (1965): 41–44; S.M. Stern in *Medium Aevum* 35 (1966): 248–52.

Kritzeck has also been criticized for errors in his editing and translating of Peter's Latin texts; Stern, Lemay, and Torrell each give corrected readings of several passages. I have unfortunately been unable to consult a new edition of Peter's texts with German translation: Petrus Venerabilis, *Schriften zur Islam*, R. Glei, ed. (Altenberge, 1985).

[5] Jean Leclercq, *Pierre le Vénérable* (Abbaye Saint-Wandrille, 1946); Torrell and Bouthillier, *Pierre le Vénérable et sa vision du monde*, 3–104; Constable, 2:257–69 ("Chronology and itinerary of Peter the Venerable").

[6] Lester Little, "Intellectual Training and Attitudes towards Reform," in PV, 235–49, p. 236.

Cistercians. Much has been written about the "feud" between Cluny and Cîteaux and about the friendly if at times strained exchanges of letters between Peter and Bernard of Clairvaux.[7] At the heart of the issue, perhaps, was the Cistercian accusation that the Cluniacs slavishly followed the *letter* of the Benedictine Rule, while the Cistercians followed the Rule in *spirit*. Intentionality, or inward purity, is what matters, according to many twelfth century thinkers, rather than slavish obedience to ritual; this formed the basis for Abelard's (and Heloise's) critique of monastic formalism.[8] It may thus have struck a chord in Peter to read in Petrus Alfonsi's *Dialogi* and in the *Risālat al-Kindī* that Muslims clung to formal, ritualistic purity (e.g., in ablution before prayer) rather than true purity (sinlessness and contrition).[9]

In the twelfth century the line was often thin between reform and heresy—or, to use the terminology of Lester Little, between "moderate" and "radical" reform.[10] If the role of faith and intentionality in monastic discipline could be a source of friendly debate between Peter and Bernard, it could also be incendiary, as was shown several

---

[7] A.H. Bredero, "The Controversy between Peter the Venerable and Saint Bernard of Clairvaux," in PV, 53–71; idem, *Cluny et Cîteaux au douzième siècle: l'histoire d'une controverse monastique* (Amsterdam, 1985); Torrell and Bouthillier, *Pierre le Vénérable et sa vision du monde*, 92–101 (who give full bibliographical references to other studies on the subject).

[8] Heloise, *Epistola* 1, in Abelard, *Historia calamitatum*, Jacques Monfrin, ed. (Paris, 1967), appendix, p. 116; Little, "Intellectual Training and Attitudes towards Reform," 238.

[9] Petrus Alfonsi, *Dialogi contra Iudeos*, Klaus-Peter Mieth, ed., with Spanish translation by Esperanza Ducay (as Pedro Alfonso de Huesca, *Diálogo contra los Judíos* [Zaragoza, 1996]) §V, p. 98; "Apología del Cristianismo de Al-Kindi," José Muñoz Sendino, ed. in *Miscelánea Comillas* 11–12 (1949): 339–460—passage cited at p. 421.

The text cited above as "Apología del Cristianismo de Al-Kindi," is a non-critical edition of the Latin translation of the *Risālat al-Kindī* commissioned by Peter the Venerable. The Arabic text is edited as *Risālat 'Abd Allâh Ibn Ismâ'îl al-Hâshimî ilâ 'Abd al-Masîh Ibn Ishaq al-Kindî wa-Risâlat al-Kindî ilâ al-Hâshimî* (*The Apology of El-Kindi: A work of the Ninth Century, Written in Defence of Christianity by an Arab*), A. Tien, ed. (London, 1885); for a French translation of the Arabic text, see P.G. Tartar, trans., *Dialogue islamo-chrétien sous le Calife al-Ma'mûn (813–834): Les épîtres d'al-Hashimî et d'al-Kindî* (Paris, 1985). On the *Risālat al-Kindī* and its importance to later works of medieval anti-Islamic polemic, see Armand Abel, "L'Apologie d'Al-Kindi et sa place dans la polémique islamo-chrétien," *Atti del covegno internazionale sul tema: L'oriente cristiano nella storia della civiltà* (Rome, 1964), pp. 501–523; P. Sjoerd van Koningsveld, "La Apología de Al-Kindî en la España del siglo XII: Huellas toledanas de un 'animal disputax'" in *Estudios sobre Alfonso VI y la reconquista de Toledo. Actas del II congreso Internacional de Estudios Mozárabes* 1 (Toledo, 1986), 107–29.

On Petrus Alfonsi's *Dialogi*, see John Tolan, *Petrus Alfonsi and his Medieval Readers* (Gainesville, 1993).

[10] Little, "Intellectual Training."

times during the twelfth century—quite literally so for Peter of Bruys, who in order to burn crucifixes built a bonfire at Saint Gilles les Boucheries, only to end up immolated on his own fire by the angry inhabitants. Almost all of the little known about this heresy comes from the *Contra Petrobrusianos*, in which Peter the Venerable enumerates five principal heretical doctrines of Peter of Bruys: the heresiarch was against infant baptism, against the building and use of churches (since all places are equally holy to God), against the veneration of crucifixes (which should be destroyed rather than revered), against the sacrament of the Eucharist, and against the prayers and offerings for the souls of the dead. Why write a tract against a man who already has been burned for his errors? Because, Peter says, these errors are now spreading to Gascony: "that stupid and impious heresy is killing many, like some pestilence."[11] He addresses his tract as a letter to the bishops of Die, Embrun, and Gap, whom he enjoins to extirpate the heresy through preaching, resorting if necessary to the arms of laymen:

> Your task is to drive them out them of those places, in which their dens are found, by preaching and also—if it should prove necessary— by the armed force of laymen. But because it is a greater service to convert them than to exterminate them, it is proper to employ Christian charity. Let authority be proffered to them and let reason be employed, so that if they wish to remain Christians they may be compelled to desist by authority and if they wish to remain humans, they may be compelled by reason. [*Contra Petrobrusianos*, 3]

This is the same attitude that he will show towards Islam: it is best to convert the infidels by preaching to them in the spirit of Christian love, but failing that, the force of arms should be used.[12] Christians can be brought back to the fold through arguments based on authority (*auctoritas*); non-Christians, since they are human and ergo rational, can be brought to Christian truth through reason (*ratio*). This strategy underlies not only his polemics against the Petrobrusians, but those against Judaism and Islam: while he bitterly condemns Jews who refuse to listen to Christian "reason," he hopes that rational argumentation might convince Muslims to embrace Christianity.

---

[11] Petrus Venerabilis, *Contra Petrobrusianos hereticos*, James Fearns, ed., *Corpus Christianorum Continuatio Medieualis* 10 (Turnholt, 1968), 3.
[12] Peter the Venerable, *Contra Sectam*, 232; on Kritzeck's (mis)interpretation of this passage, see Brolis and Kedar (works cited above, note 4).

Parallel to his anti-Islamic strategy, too, are the two purposes he ascribes to his *Contra Petrobrusianos*: first, to try to convince the heretics to abandon their stupidity (*stulticia*); failing that, he hopes he may at least warn his Christian readers away from the errors of the heretics [*Contra Petrobrusianos*, 6]. Moreover, he says that he should not pass over any heresy in silence, but—in the tradition of the Church fathers—fight them with the twin weapons of reason (*ratio*) and authority (*auctoritas*). To this end, he organizes his tract into five parts (one for each of the principal errors of Peter of Bruys); he marshals a large array of scriptural citations to refute each point. While Robert I. Moore is certainly right to characterize the *Contra Petrobrusianos* as "by far the most powerful and sophisticated rebuttal of popular heresy in this period," Jean Châtillon has noted the cultural and social gap between such learned, exegetically-based polemics and the popular heresy it was meant to combat.[13] It is doubtful that this strategy would have had much impact on the practice of heresy, but Peter was writing the kind of polemics he knew how to write, in the tradition of such learned rebuttals of heresy. It is the same tradition he will perpetuate in his polemics against Islam, with the same results. Peter was aware that some of Peter of Bruys' errors were shared by Catholics: the questioning of the efficacy of prayers and masses for the dead, for example. Such doubts would have seemed especially troubling to the abbot of Cluny, whose monks continually said masses for the souls of dead lay benefactors: he specifically addresses such "secret thoughts of certain Catholics."[14]

The enthusiastic embrace of *ratio* as a means to spiritual truth characterizes Peter's polemics against Jews, Petrobrusians, and Muslims, and marks him off from contemporaries such as Bernard of Clairvaux. Learned study and speculation, far from leading one into dangerous error, lead toward Christian truth. This attitude may have induced Peter to welcome to Cluny Peter Abelard, recently condemned as a heretic, and to help orchestrate his reconciliation with Bernard, the

---

[13] Robert I. Moore, *The Origins of European Dissent* (Oxford, 1985): 102; Jean Châtillon, "Pierre le Vénérable et les Pétrobrusiens," in PAPV, 165–76; see also James Fearns, "Peter von Bruis und die religiöse Bewegung des 12 Jahrhunderts," *Archiv für Kulturgeschichte* 48 (1966): 313–17; Torrell and Bouthillier, *Pierre le Vénérable et sa vision du monde*, 162–71.

[14] Petrus Venerabilis, *Contra Petrobrusianos*, 4 & 165; Torrell and Bouthillier note that the same purpose underlies many of the stories in Peter's *De Miraculis* of visits from ghosts of those who have benefitted from the prayers of Cluny's monks (*Pierre le Vénérable et sa vision du monde*, 170–71).

repeal of his excommunication, and his acceptance as a monk at Cluny. The episode is well-known enough to need no re-telling here.[15]

Several scholars have speculated on the influence Abelard may have had on Peter the Venerable's anti-Jewish and anti-Islamic polemics, in particular through his *Dialogue between a Philosopher, a Jew, and a Christian*.[16] While Peter did not directly use Abelard's *Dialogue*, it, like Peter's own apologetical work, reflects the same spirit of rationalistic debate, the same hope of proving Christian truth to Jews through exegetical argument based on the Old Testament and to "Pagans" (a term which probably embraces both ancient paganism and Islam) using only rational argumentation. It is also clear that Abelard is continuing Anselm's tradition of *fides quaerens intellectum*: the Christian seeking rational confirmation of his faith. Even if the exercise serves no missionary purpose, it can be useful in dispelling the doubts of the Christian reader.

Peter's own anti-Jewish polemic is a far cry from Abelard's irenic tract. He composed his *Against the Inveterate Stubbornness of the Jews* in 1144, revising and expanding it in 1146–47.[17] The first four chapters of his work include the standard *topoi* of anti-Jewish polemic since Augustine; they comprise an attack based on a Christian exegesis of the Old Testament. Peter's fifth chapter, however, is a direct assault on the Talmud. Here he makes use of Petrus Alfonsi's *Dialogi Contra Iudeos* and the *Alphabet of Ben Sira*,[18] although he claims that Christ

---

[15] Peter the Venerable, *Letters* §98 (pp. 258–59), §115 (303–08), §167 (400–01), §168 (401–02); Torrell and Bouthillier, *Pierre le Vénérable et sa vision du monde*, 89–92; Piero Zerbi, "San Bernardo di Chiaravalle e il concilio de Sens," in *Studi su S. Bernardo di Chiaravalle* (Rome, 1975), 49–73; idem, "Remarques sur l'*Epistola* 98 de Pierre le Vénérable," in PAPV, 215–34; Rudolf Thomas, "Die Persönlichkeit Peter Abaelards im *Dialogus inter Philosophum, Iudaeum et Christianum* und in den *Epistulae* des Petrus Venerabilis: Widerspruch oder Übereinstimmung?," in PAPV, 255–69.

[16] Kritzeck, "De l'influence de Pierre Abélard sur Pierre le Vénérable dans ses oeuvres sur l'Islam," in PAPV, 205–14; Jolivet, "L'Islam et la raison"; Petrus Abaelardus, *Dialogus inter Philosophum, Iudaeum et Christianum*, Rudolf Thomas, ed. (Stuttgart, 1970) (English translation by Pierre Payer as *Dialogue of a Philosopher with a Jew and a Christian* [Toronto, 1979]).

[17] For the dates of composition, see Friedman's introduction to her edition of Petrus Venerabilis, *Adversus Iudeorum inveteratam duritiem*, LVII–LXX; Torrell and Bouthillier, *Pierre le Vénérable et sa vision du monde*, 172–74; M. Kniewasser, "Die antijüdische Polemik," 59.

[18] See Tolan, *Petrus Alfonsi*, 116–17; Friedman's introduction to Peter's *Adversus Iudeorum inveteratam duritiem*, pp. xvii–xviii; J. Kritzeck, *Peter the Venerable and Islam* (Princeton, 1964), 27, n. 83; Gilbert Dahan, *Les Intellectuels chrétiens et les Juifs au moyen âge*, (Paris, 1990), 458–59.

alone gave him knowledge of the Talmud.[19] But where Petrus Alfonsi's repudiation of Talmudic legends is replete with rational and scientific counter-arguments, Peter merely responds to these Talmudic legends with this invective, addressed, significantly, to his Christian reader:

> What do you hope for, reader? What do you expect? Do you think that I will take some action against the Jews about these things? Nay, let me not act against them in these things, let me not respond to impudent dogs and vile pigs as if they were capable of reason and hence show them to be worthy of any response in these matters.[20]

If Peter needs to refute Judaism, he expresses little hope that his refutation will result in the conversion of Jews. Aware that they have withstood centuries of such argumentation, he prefers to impute this to their lack of human reason, to their "bovine intellect," than to any lack of rational basis for Christian truth.[21] He will approach the Muslims with more confidence that his rationalistic apologetics may win converts.

Peter the Venerable seems to have decided upon his polemical enterprise against Islam during a trip to Castile-León in 1142–43.[22] He went to visit Cluniac houses in Spain and to receive a donation from King Alfonso VII. At Najera he assembled his team of translators, whose efforts were apparently to be coordinated by his personal secretary, Peter of Poitiers.

One of Peter the Venerable's letters has largely escaped the attention of earlier scholars. It is the *Letter to Peter of Poitiers against those who claim that Christ never openly called himself God in the Gospels*.[23] The issue addressed evokes the Muslim claim that Jesus was a mere human

---

[19] *Adversus Iudeorum inveteratam duritiem*, V, 126.

[20] *Adversus Iudeorum inveteratam duritiem*, V, 151.

[21] "bouinus intellectus," (Peter the Venerable, *Aduersus Iudaeorum inveteratam duritiem*, 43). Yvonne Friedman, in her introduction, cites eleven places where Peter refers to the Jews as animals (p. viii, note 5).

[22] On this trip, see Constable 2:257–69; C.J. Bishko, "Peter the Venerable's Journey to Spain," 163–75; Torrell and Bouthillier, *Pierre le Vénérable et sa vision du monde*, 59–67; Manfred Kniewasser, "Die antijüdische Polemik des Petrus Alphonsi (getauft 1106) und des Petrus Venerabilis von Cluny (+1156)," *Kairos* new series 2 (1980): 34–76; Kritzeck, *Peter the Venerable and Islam*, 3–14.

[23] *Epistola ad Petrum de Joanne contra eos qui dicunt Christum nunquam se in Evangeliis aperte Deum dixisse*, PL 189:487–508. Constable (2:331–43) shows that Petrus de Joanne and Peter of Poitiers are indeed one and the same: Peter the Venerable himself in *De Miraculis* describes how he met the other Peter at the monastery of St. Jean d'Anselmy (hence the *de Joanne*); Petrus Venerabilis, *De Miraculis* §I: 4, D. Bouthillier, ed., *Corpus Christianorum continuatio mediaevalia*, 83 (1988): 14–15.

prophet and that the Gospel that he revealed said nothing of his divinity. Yet here Peter is addressing a community of Christians, apparently clerics, for he recalls to Peter of Poitiers that the latter had told him of a conversation with "certain brothers" who asserted that nowhere in the Gospel did the Savior clearly say that he was God. Although Peter of Poitiers had not mentioned the names of these brothers, Peter the Venerable says that he believes he knows who they are, and that he believed that their question sprung "not from weakness of faith, but from love and zeal to know things of which they were ignorant before." [PL 189:487] He describes them as learned, erudite, religious men. Peter says that he will respond to them and show them that Christ did indeed claim to be God, lest doubt should rise up in the hearts of such men.

Who are these learned Christian brothers who voice a very Muslim-sounding objection to one of the most basic principles of Christian biblical exegesis? It is tempting to identify them with some of the translators working on Toledo corpus: perhaps the exposure to the Muslim view of Christianity led these Christians to question their own exegetical traditions. Perhaps the doubts were in fact those of Peter of Poitiers, who attributed them to nameless "brothers." Yet these doubts could have been expressed by other philosophically-inclined Christians of the twelfth-century, and the text is undated. Abelard's trinitarian speculations got him into trouble without any help from the Muslims; certainly a thoughtful student of the bible could raise these objections.

If Peter the Venerable does not specifically say that Muslim views inspired these learned brothers, he certainly implies it. He describes how after the Church's victory over paganism, Satan created heretical errors to lead the faithful astray: Manicheism and Arianism both deny the true divinity of Christ. But worse, for Peter, is Satan's deception of the Saracens:

> Since Satan has occupied almost half the earth with his Saracens, he teaches them to preach that Christ is better than all men and the best, so that they nevertheless deny he is God. . . . For there is no doubt that it would not be religious, but rather sacrilegious to place any hope of salvation in him who, not divine, could neither be called saviour nor would be able to save anyone. The Corruptor of human nature with this poison has tainted and infected those whom I mentioned, the Saracens of modern times. He has taught them to preach that Christ was born from the Virgin, and sent by God, and that He is the Word of God and the Spirit of God (as he understood it); but he has persuaded

them that He was not God and had not died. In this way the Infidel
showed them that it was useless to believe anything, useless to preach
anything, since (with the faith in the divinity and death of Christ ex-
tinguished in human hearts) there would be no salvation for humans
who could neither be saved by Christ's divinity nor redeemed through
his incarnation. [PL 189:489–90]

Peter goes on at some length to show that Jesus did indeed claim to
be God, explaining why he usually did so indirectly. He is not in
lack of grist to bring to this mill: he provides abundant scriptural
citation to back up his quite standard exegesis. What is interesting in
this text for our purposes is that he has clearly defined Islam as a
heresy devised by Satan, a heresy centered around the denial of
Christ's divinity. Moreover, this heretical "poison" can apparently
corrupt the mind of learned Christians, and perhaps not only the
"brothers" mentioned in Peter of Poitiers' letter. Peter may have
in mind philosophically-inclined theologians or perhaps translators of
Arabic texts into Latin, who would be more directly exposed to this
Muslim source of "infection"; indeed, the two groups overlapped.
His little tract makes no pretensions of trying to convince Muslims
or other unbelievers of the divinity of Christ; he merely hopes to
prevent the same error from taking root in the hearts of good
Christians.

This fear of contamination imbued a sense of urgency to his translation project; he needed to make Muslim texts available to learned
Christians and needed to show them the errors of their "perverse
heresy." If the Arabic studies of such scholars were dangerous, the
way to combat the danger was through more study: full knowledge
of the "Saracen errors," he thought, would encourage the Christian
to remain steadfast in his faith. This sense of purpose pervades not
only the two polemical tracts of Peter the Venerable, but also the
work of the translators of the collection.

The translation of the Koran was the centerpiece of the collection,
and Peter is quite aware of its importance. Robert of Ketton produced
not a literal rendering of the Muslim sacred text but a Latin adaptation
in which difficult and obscure passages are explained; it is generally
impossible for the reader to distinguish between the actual text of the
Koran and the explicative material inserted by Robert. While scholars
have long criticized Robert for this, current scholarship on medieval
translation has shown that this was a common practice. Moreover,
as Thomas Burman has recently shown, Robert scrupulously studied

Muslim Koranic commentaries in order to understand the standard Muslim interpretations of difficult and important passages; indeed, much of his interpolated material is adapted from such Muslim commentaries.[24] Robert has gone to great lengths to provide an accurate and comprehensible Latin version of the Koran.

Yet Peter the Venerable's copy of Robert's translation was heavily annotated; these annotations certainly guided Peter's reading of the text.[25] Much has been written about these annotations, which seem to date from the twelfth century and to have been made soon after the different works in the codex were bound together; they appear in different parts of the codex, and the reader is at times referred to another work in the collection.[26] It is unclear who wrote these annotations, although nominees include Robert himself, Peter of Toledo, and Peter of Poitiers. The annotations seem in fact to have been the result of at least two people: some of them show a basic ignorance of key Muslim beliefs and practices while others show good knowledge of Islam.[27]

Whoever and however many their authors, the annotations clearly show the polemical intent of the translation. They guide the reader of the "diabolical Koran" [83r] by pointing out (through innumerable "Nota") passages that would seem particularly shocking to the Christian (and especially monastic) reader. The reader is constantly told to note the "insanity," "impiety," "ridiculousness," "stupidity," "superstition," "lying," and "blasphemy" of what he is reading. The very rubrics added at the opening of many Suras make this clear: "A stupid, vain, and impious Sura" [119v]; "Sura of stupidity and lies, like the previous ones" [128v]; "Vain and impious Sura [128v]; "Diabolical

---

[24] Thomas E. Burman, "*Tafsīr* and Translation: Robert of Ketton, Mark of Toledo, and Traditional Arabic Qur'ān Exegesis," (forthcoming); thanks to Tom Burman for letting me see this article before publication.

[25] The original manuscript of the *Collectio Toletana*, used by Peter the Venerable as he composed his own anti-Islamic works is conserved in the Bibliothèque de l'Arsenal (MS n° 1162); see D'Alverny, "Deux traductions."

[26] See, for example, 57r, in the Koran translation, the reader is referred to the translation of the *Risālat al-Kindī* ("bonus et doctus Christianus cuius liber in isto codice continetur").

[27] For the debate on the identity of the annotator and examples of the variety of the annotations, see Thomas Burman, *Religious Polemic and the Intellectual History of the Mozarabs* (Leiden: Brill, 1994), 85–89. An example of a basic misunderstanding of Muslim practice is one annotation's assertion that Muḥammad was buried in Mecca (MS A, 21v).

Sura, like the previous ones" [129r]; "Repeating the habitual ditties endlessly and ineptly" [72r].

Wherever Koranic stories differ from their Biblical counterparts, the annotator brands them as heretical or ridiculous: the Koranic version of the Cain and Abel story is a "stupid fable" [46r]; the story of Joseph and Potiphar's wife is "insane lies and lying insanity" [69v]. When the Koran describes prophets not mentioned in the Bible, the comments of the annotator are no less caustic: "Note the unheard of names of prophets. Who ever heard of such prophets other than this diabolical one [meaning Muḥammad]. . . . I think that these were not men but demons: they possessed this Satan, and in this way he concocted his ravings [presumably the Koran]" [67v].

Especially ridiculed is the Muslim christology, dubbed "stupid and heretical sayings about Christ" [32v]. The annotations qualify Muslim traditions on Jesus and the Virgin as "monstrous and unheard-of fables" [33v]. The origins of this Christology are diabolical: "Note how inconsistent! how changeable! What vain and contradictory things are brought together in this diabolical spirit!" [32v]. "Note how he everywhere says that Christ is the son of Mary, but against the Christians and the faith says that the son of Mary is not the son of God—which is the sum of all this diabolical heresy" [35r].

For the annotators, the devil and his follower Muḥammad are the authors of this heresy. Numerous annotations accuse Muḥammad of being too fond of women, and of playing on the Saracens' lust by promising them houris in heaven [33v, 92r, 92v, 110r, 126r, 127v]. He threatens his followers with hellfire in order to get them to follow his law and to conquer Christian lands [29v]. All of this is in line with earlier heresies: "Note that he everywhere promises such a paradise of carnal delights, as other heresies had done before"[26r].

At several places the annotators reveal a penchant for rationalistic argument against the Koran. One annotation remarks that knowledge of the form of human and animal uteruses may have been given to Muḥammad by a physician [112r]. Another opposes the Koranic notion of miracle with a twelfth-century Christian definition: if the Koran ascribes to God the "miracle" of holding up the birds that fly in the air and the fish that swim in the sea, the annotator retorts that this is not miraculous, but part of the natural order that God instituted at creation. This misunderstanding of natural phenomena shows "the ignorance of an insane man" [77r]. Such attacks on the "irrationality" of the Koran are the stock and trade of Spanish

Christian polemics against Islam in the twelfth century, seen for example in Petrus Alfonsi's *Dialogi*.

When Peter the Venerable opened the Arsenal manuscript of Robert of Ketton's Koran, he found a text whose rubrics and marginal annotations guided his understanding of what he was reading. He was told where to be shocked, what to find ridiculous, irrational, etc. The annotations initiated him into a Mozarabic polemical view of Islam.

Yet while his reading of *Risālat al-Kindī*, Petrus Alfonsi, and the annotations will teach him to see Islam through Mozarabic eyes, the polemical strategy that he produces in his two apologetical works is different: it reflects his own peculiar concerns. In his *Summa totius haeresis ac diabolicae sectae Saracenorum siue Hismahelitarum*, Peter will try to explain Islam to the readers of the Toledan corpus: to Christian readers who wish to understand the nature of the "heresy of the Saracens." In his *Contra Sectam siue haeresim Saracenorum*, on the other hand, he will try to refute Islam on its own terms, creating his own polemical strategy.

The continuity of Peter's approach with that of Mozarabic Christians as well as the novelty of Peter's approach become apparent when we compare Peter's two polemical works with two works that he used: the Latin translation of the *Risālat al-Kindī* and Petrus Alfonsi's *Dialogi*. His use of the former has already been noted by Kritzeck, whose detailed analysis of the *Summa* I intend neither to replicate nor replace.[28] Peter addresses his *Summa totius haeresis ac diabolicae sectae Saracenorum siue Hismahelitarum* to a Christian audience, as a preface to the translations of the Toledan corpus; he probably composed it shortly after his return from Spain. Peter describes the purpose of his brief tract:

> It ought to be told what sort of a bird Muḥammad was, and what he taught, so that those who will read that book [the Koran] may better understand what they read and know how detestable were his life and his teachings.[29]

Peter wants to dispel the false opinions that many hold about the Saracens and Muḥammad, whom some wrongly identify with the heresiarch Nicholas, whose followers are condemned in Revelations

---

[28] Kritzeck, *Peter the Venerable and Islam*, 115–52.

[29] Peter the Venerable, *Summa totius haeresis Saracenorum*, in Kritzeck, *Peter the Venerable and Islam*, 205.

(2:6 & 15). The only source of information that he explicitly cites on Muḥammad's life is Anastasius Bibliothecarius' Latin translation of Theophanes' *Chronographia* (of which Cluny possessed a manuscript in the twelfth century).[30] That he should use Anastasius (and cite him) is natural: none of the texts translated in the Toledan collection provides a straightforward biography of Muḥammad for the uninitiated reader. Peter will fill in Anastasius' account with information gleaned from *Risālat al-Kindī* and Petrus Alfonsi's *Dialogi* (it is not always clear which, since Petrus Alfonsi himself relies heavily on the Arabic text of the *Risāla*). Peter's account of Muḥammad's life and teachings is much briefer than those of either of these sources, but he adds a clear sense of where the prophet and his followers fit in the history of error: the devil works behind and through Muḥammad, leading a third of the world's population into error. Historically, Peter places Muḥammad in the history of heresy, as a particularly loathsome and dangerous heresiarch.

Peter describes Muḥammad as a poor, vile, unlettered Arab who achieved wealth and power through bloodshed, thievery, and intrigue. Finally realizing that a feigned religious vocation would serve his ambitions, he claimed that he was a prophet and usurped the authority of king. Then, at the bidding of Satan, a heretical Nestorian monk named Sergius came and joined Muḥammad: together, along with several Jews, they forged a new heretical doctrine.

> Muḥammad, schooled in this way by the finest teachers—Jews and heretics—composed his Koran. He wove together, in his barbarous fashion, nefarious scripture from the fables of the Jews and the ditties of the heretics.

All of this corresponds closely to Petrus Alfonsi's description.[31] Peter goes on to describe what the Koran says about Moses and Jesus, about the torments of hell and the carnal pleasures of paradise. This mixture of truth and error inextricably woven together shows Muḥammad to be the consummate heresiarch; here Peter compares

---

[30] Benjamin Kedar, *Crusade and Mission*, 90n.

[31] Petrus Alfonsi, *Dialogi* §V, pp. 94–95; the same material is in the Latin translation of the *Risālat al-Kindī* ("Apologia del Cristianismo," 401–02 & 413–14). Peter seems to be following Alfonsi's narration of these events rather than that of the *Risālat*, though he does correct Alfonsi, who identified Sergius as a Jacobite monk [*Dialogi*, p. 95]; Peter, (following the *Risālat* ["Apologia del Cristianismo," 413]) identifies Sergius as a Nestorian (Peter the Venerable, *Summa*, p. 206).

Muḥammad to earlier heresiarchs (not something done by either of his sources):

> Vomiting forth almost all of the excrement of the old heresies (which he had drunk up as the devil poured it out), he denies the trinity with Sabellius, with his Nestorius he rejects the divinity of Christ, with Mani he disavows the death of the Lord, though does not deny that He returned to heaven. [*Summa*, p. 208]

Peter holds Muḥammad's life—in particular his polygamy—up to opprobrium. Mixing good and evil, sublime and ridiculous, Muḥammad created a monstrous cult, similar to the animal described by Horace as having a human head, a horse's neck, and feathers.[32]

The intention of this diabolic heresy, Peter continues, is to present Christ as a holy man, loved by God, a great prophet—but wholly human and in no way son of God.

> Indeed [this heresy], long ago conceived by the plotting of the devil, first spread by Arius, then promoted by this Satan, namely Muḥammad, will be completed by Antichrist, in complete accordance with the intentions of the devil. [*Summa*, p. 208]

Peter sees three great adversaries whom the devil uses to lead Christians astray: Arius, Muḥammad, and Antichrist. Each manages to trick his followers into denying Christ's divinity. In order to better elucidate this anti-Christian doctrine, Peter also compares Muḥammad to the philosopher Porphyry, who (Peter erroneously claims) was an apostate from Christianity.[33] Having asked the oracles of his gods about Christ, Porphyry was told by the demon Hecate that Jesus had been a virtuous man, but that his followers sinned gravely in attributing divinity to him; Porphyry's views are repudiated, Peter tells us, by Augustine. Indeed, in *De ciuitate Dei* xix.23, Augustine describes an utterance of the oracle Hecate, reported by Porphyry in his ἐκ λογίων φιλοσοφίας; for Augustine, this shows the clever hostility of the demons, who, wishing to appear objective, praise Jesus at the same time that they condemn the central truth of Christianity. Yet Muḥammad is worse than the apostate philosopher, says Peter, for

---

[32] Peter the Venerable, *Summa*, 208; Horace, *Ars poetica* 1:1–2.

[33] The idea that Porphyry was an apostate Christian is common in Christian texts since the fifth century. See Robert M. Grant, "Porphyry among the Early Christians," in W. der Boer et al., eds., *Romanitas et Christianitas: Studia Iano Henrico Waszink* (Amsterdam: North Holland, 1973), 181–87; John J. O'Meara, *Porphyry's Philosophy from Oracles in Augustine* (Paris: Études Augustiniennes, 1959), esp. 52ff. Thanks to Bernard McGinn for bringing these works to my attention.

whereas God did not permit Porphyry to seduce Christians with his errors, Muḥammad has led countless people into eternal perdition. It is for this reason, Peter tells us, that he composed his *Summa*, and that he had the entire Toledan corpus translated: "I translated from Arabic into Latin the whole of this sect, along with the execrable life of its evil inventor, and exposed it to the scrutiny of our people, so that it be known what a filthy and frivolous heresy it is." [*Summa*, 210–11]

While Peter uses the works of earlier anti-Islamic polemicists, he clearly felt that they were inadequate. He sets aside much of their material, apparently deeming it useless: for example the names of Muḥammad's associates or the polemical descriptions of 'Ali's teachings and the birth of Shi'ism (Peter did not know enough about Islam to appreciate the importance of the latter). On the other hand, Peter finds that these earlier polemics lack a proper taxonomy of error, a lack of the sense of Islam's place in the divine plan. The devil inspired heresiarchs to lead the faithful into error; only through careful comparison with the teachings of other heresiarchs and the perusal of anti-heretical works of the Church fathers could this new and dangerous heresy be combatted.[34]

Peter is aware that his *Summa* is merely an introduction to the "Saracen heresy" for the Christian reader, not a refutation of it. The man whom he deemed most appropriate to refute Islam was Bernard of Clairvaux, to whom he sent a letter along with the Latin translation of the *Risālat al-Kindī* in 1144. He tells Bernard that he is aware that the *Risāla* has not proved useful to the Saracens in their own language and will not become more useful to them by virtue of being translated into Latin. "Yet perhaps it will be useful to some Latins, to whom it will teach things of which they were ignorant and will show what a damnable heresy it is. It will show them that they must defend themselves against it and attack it, should they ever come across it."[35] This characterization of the defensive purpose of the translation of the *Risālat al-Kindī* indeed could characterize the whole of the *Collectio*

---

[34] One can only be dismayed by Kritzeck's assertion that one Peter's great achievements was "the dissociation of Mohammed from other heresiarchs" (*Peter the Venerable and Islam*, 27–30); clearly, he is doing precisely the opposite.

[35] Peter the Venerable, *Letter* §111, p. 295. Another version of this letter is edited by Kritzeck (pp. 212–14); the latter version does not contain Peter's criticisms of the *Risālat al-Kindī*. Several passages of the text are also common to the *Summa*. For the relationship between these three texts, see Constable 2:275–84, D'Alverny, "Deux traductions," 72–76; Kritzeck, *Peter the Venerable and Islam*, 27–30.

Toletana, including Peter's own *Summa*. For an offensive tract against Islam, a real rational refutation of the Saracen heresy, the *Risālat al-Kindī* apparently would not do; who better to compose such a refutation than Bernard: theologian, fighter of heresies, and preacher of crusade?

Bernard, however, failed to respond to that summons, and Peter himself undertook the task of refuting Islam, probably in 1155–56.[36] The work as it survives is composed of a long prologue and two books; it may be that Peter wrote more that was subsequently lost or that he left it incomplete at his death on Christmas day, 1156.[37]

Both the structure and the strategy of the *Contra Sectam siue haeresim Saracenorum* are quite different from those of the *Summa*. In the *Summa* he lambasted Muḥammad from a Christian perspective; in the *Contra sectam* (after a prologue in which he justifies his polemics to Christian readers) he (in book one) enjoins his Muslim readers to listen impartially to his arguments and tries to convince them that according to the Koran they should accept Christian scripture. In book two he tries to prove that Muḥammad is not a prophet, by contrasting his life with those of Old Testament prophets.

In the long prologue to the *Contra Sectam*, Peter justifies his enterprise by placing himself in the company of the church fathers who refuted earlier heretical doctrines, following the rule that "every error should be refuted" (p. 225). He lists the names of ancient heresiarchs, "names monstrous to Christians," and then those of the holy men who rebutted their heresies. The need to refute Muḥammad's sect is particularly urgent; its acolytes are the "worst adversaries" of the Church (220), for they dominate Asia and Africa and are present even in Europe (in Spain).

Peter then gives a rhetorical objection to this line of argument: one could say that the Saracens were pagans (*ethnici* or *pagani*) rather

---

[36] Peter of Poitiers wrote a letter to Peter the Venerable in summer or autumn of 1155 in which refers to Peter's polemics against Jews and Petrobrusians and rejoices at the fact that he will now undertake to refute the errors of the Saracens. The letter is edited by Kritzeck (*Peter the Venerable and Islam*, 215–16). On Peter of Poitiers, see Constable 2:331–43; Torrell and Bouthillier, *Pierre le Vénérable et sa vision du monde*, 180–83. Torrell and Bouthillier have misunderstood the relationship between the *Summa* and the *Contra sectam*; they refer to the *Summa* as "placée en Préface du *Contra Sarracenos*" (ibid., 336). In fact the two texts are completely independent.

[37] For Kritzeck, the text is complete as is (*Peter the Venerable and Islam*, 155–56) Torrell and Bouthillier think that he had planned on writing more (*Pierre le Vénérable et sa vision du monde*, 182).

than heretics. For did not John define the "many Antichrists" (which, for Peter, means heresiarchs) as those who "went out from us, but they were not of us" (I John 2:19), in other words as those who had been part of the Church and had broken away from it? Peter notes that, like heretics, the followers of Muḥammad adopt parts of the Christian faith and reject other parts, while they also follow some rites which seem to Peter "pagan." Like certain heretics, Peter says, Muḥammad "wrote in his impious Koran" that Christ was born of the Virgin Mary, lived without sin, and performed miracles; like the Manicheans, the Saracens deny His death. Like the pagans, on the other hand, they reject baptism, the mass, and the other sacraments. Heretics or pagans, "choose whichever you like." [*Contra sectam*, 227] He asserts that pagans should also be opposed by written polemic; here, too, he lists the names of illustrious church fathers who attacked paganism in their writings. Peter himself generally prefers to consider the "Mahometan error" as a heresy.

Peter addresses one final rhetorical objection to his tract: why compose for Muḥammad's followers a treatise in Latin, a language they do not understand? Here Peter has two responses. First of all, he hopes that someone may undertake to translate his tract into Arabic; after all, the fathers frequently translated works useful to the church from Hebrew to Greek, Greek to Latin, Latin to Greek, etc. Secondly, Peter says that his tract may prove useful to Christian readers, even if it stays untranslated (which it did). If there are any Christians who have the slightest tendency to respect or admire Islam, Peter hopes his work will quickly dissuade them.

> Perhaps this tract will cure the hidden cogitations of some of our people, thoughts by which they could be led into evil if they think that there is some piety in those impious people and think that some truth is to be found with the ministers of lies. [*Contra sectam*, 230]

Who are these Latin Christians who in their "hidden cogitations" might think that the Saracens were pious? Peter does not say, but certainly the most likely candidates were the translators and students of Arabic science and philosophy. One such scholar, Adelard of Bath, proclaimed "I learnt from my masters, the Arabs, to follow the light of reason, while you are led by the bridle of authority; for what other word than 'bridle' can I use to describe authority?"[38] Might

---

[38] Adelard, *Questiones naturales, Beiträge zur Geschichte der Philosophie der Theologie des*

such preference for "Arabic reason" over "Latin Authority" lead such Christian scholars into doubt, even apostasy? As he had shown in his *Epistola ad Petrum Ioannem* and his *Contra Petrobrusianos*, Peter is concerned about the doubts that the devil may sow in the minds of Christians in order to lead them into heretical error. In this light his polemics look more like a defense of Christianity than an offensive missionary effort.

While the prologue to the *Contra Sectam* is a defense of his tract to possible Christian detractors, the text itself is addressed to "The Arabs, sons of Ishmael, who serve the law of him who is called Muḥammad." [*Contra sectam*, 231] He tells his readers that it is love that bids him write to them, love that Christian law enjoins on him. "I love you; loving you, I write to you; writing, I invite you to salvation." [*Contra sectam*, 232] Peter realizes, he says, that the first reaction of his Arab readers will be that they would never abandon the law given them by their prophet. He also is aware that the Koran enjoins death on those who dispute the Muslim law.[39] This, he says, astounds him, because his Arab readers are "not only rational (*rationales*) by nature, but logical in temperament and training (*ingenio et arte rationabiles*)" they are, moreover "learned in worldly knowledge (*scientiam secularem*)." [*Contra sectam*, 233] The injunction against debating religion flies in the face of the Arabs' propensity for learning: no rational man should accept something as true without first verifying its truth for himself.

These Arab philosophers use their reason to comprehend nature; do they not know that this nature, the highest object of the search for truth, asks Peter, the uncreated creator, the ultimate substance or essence, is God?[40] Should they not use their reason to investigate the truth concerning God? The law prohibiting religious dispute is an "infernal counsel," a law fit for irrational sheep, not rational men. Instead of reaching for your swords or stones when a Christian comes

---

Mittelalters 31, pt. 2, 11. See Charles Burnett, "Adelard of Bath and the Arabs," *Rencontres de cultures dans la philosophie médiévale: traductions et traducteurs de l'antiquité tardive au XIVe siècle* (Leuven, 1990), 89–107.

[39] Peter the Venerable, *Contra Sectam*, 233; he quotes the Koranic injunctions at p. 237. On this, see Kedar, *Crusade and Mission*, 99–104.

[40] "Quae uero est natura haec, que substantia, uel essentia? None illa, quae communi uniuersarum gentium more, iuxta proprietatem uniuscuiusque linguae Deus creditur, Deus dicitur? Est igitur natura illa, Deus ille, qui solus increatus est, qui solus creator est, . . ." [*Contra sectam*, 235]. Peter may have taken the identification of *substantia* with God the creator from Petrus Alfonsi, who identifies the creator with God the Father and with *substantia*. Petrus Alfonsi, *Dialogi contra Iudaeos* §6, pp. 104–05; see Tolan, *Petrus Alfonsi*, 36–37.

to preach the gospel, Peter says, follow rather the example of Christians who dispute with Jews, listening patiently to their arguments and responding wisely. (This hardly characterizes the rancor of Peter's own anti-Jewish tract.) Or follow the example of King Ethelbert of Kent, who received Christian missionaries with honor and heard them out.

Peter has emphasized the rationality and learning of his Muslim audience; this is all the more striking when contrasted with his descriptions of the enemies of his *Aduersus Iudaeorum inveteratam duritiem*, whom he brands as beasts without reason. There he contents himself with lambasting irrational Jewish beliefs for a Christian audience, showing no hope of converting Jews. Here, on the contrary, he pleads with his learned Muslim readers to hear him out, invoking the pagan king Ethelbert. Muslims, it seems, should be predisposed to recognize Christian reason; in order to prevent this, Muḥammad had forbidden them under pain of death from debating matters of the faith.

Having crossed this first theoretical hurdle to gain a hearing from his rational, philosophical Muslim readership, his first and fundamental argument in favor of Christianity is not rationalistic or scientific but scriptural. While earlier polemics (including both the *Risālat al-Kindī* and Petrus Alfonsi's *Dialogi*) often tried to prove the Trinity using various triads of philosophical concepts, Peter makes no such attempt.[41] Such argumentation is foreign to him; since exegetical argumentation is his forte, his most pressing need is to establish the validity of the Bible to his Muslim audience so he can then comfortably deploy the scriptural weapons he handles so well.

In order to prove the validity of the Jewish and Christian scriptures, Peter starts from the normal Christian viewpoint that Koranic stories of, say, Abraham or Noah are corrupted versions of their Biblical counterparts; we have seen that the marginal notations in Robert's translation of the Koran reflected this notion. Peter says that he was amazed to find that Muḥammad, in the Koran, had mixed elements from Christian and Jewish scriptures and moreover had praised those scriptures. Assuming, rather than arguing for, the primacy of Judeo-Christian scripture, he argues that if these scriptures are divine, they should be accepted wholly, not in part; if they are not divine, they should be rejected wholly, not in part. [*Contra sectam*, 248]

---

[41] "Apología del Cristianismo," 395–96; Petrus Alfonsi, *Dialogi* §VI, pp. 105–06 (see Tolan, *Petrus Alfonsi*, 36–39). For other examples of this common ploy, see Burman, *Religious Polemic*, 72–73, 81–82, 163ff.; Daniel, *Islam and the West*, 200–09.

He knows what the Muslim objection to this argument will be: the charge that the God-given scriptures of Jews and Christians have been corrupted and that only the Koran represents the uncorrupted word of God. Here he refers to Muslim stories—gleaned from a marginal annotation to the Koran[42]—according to which the Jews lost the Torah on their way back to Israel after the Babylonian captivity. Here Peter is quite capable of ridiculing this story using his scriptural arsenal. In particular, he employs the logical arguments gleaned from the *Risālat al-Kīndī* showing how difficult it would be for Jews and Christians, dispersed over half the world, to connive together to corrupt the Torah.[43] He argues similarly against charges that Christians have corrupted the Gospel. He then concludes book one with the assertion that he has proved that the Bible is divine, that it is superior to the Koran, and that its authority should be accepted by all Muslims. [*Contra sectam*, 262]

In book two, Peter attempts to prove that Muḥammad is not a prophet, for a prophet by definition foresees the future, wheras Muḥammad did not. Here Peter is unaware that the Muslim concept of *rasul* is quite different from the Christian notion of *propheta*. In showing that Muḥammad does not correspond to Peter's notion of prophethood, he is scoring a point that would carry little weight with a Muslim audience.[44] Peter uses material from the *Risālat al-Kīndī*, reshaping it to fit into his more coherent, theologically-based structure. Peter narrates only the details of Muḥammad's life that are necessary to show that he is not a prophet: in particular his inability to foresee his military defeats and his failure to produce miracles.[45]

Peter asserts that the last of the Prophets was John the Baptist. Yet Paul foretold of the errors of false prophets: "For the time will come when they will not endure sound doctrine . . . and they shall turn away their ears from the truth, and shall be turned unto fables."[46] Just so, says Peter, were the Saracens converted to the fables of Muḥammad and Jews to the fables of the Talmud. He describes the prophecies and virtuous lives of various of the Hebrew prophets and challenges his readers to produce anything analogous in order to

---

[42] MS A, 28v; Peter the Venerable, *Contra Sectam*, 251; see Kritzeck, *Peter the Venerable and Islam*, 177–78.

[43] Peter the Venerable, *Contra Sectam*, 252–53; "Apología del Cristianismo," 443–45.

[44] Peter the Venerable, *Contra Sectam*, 266ff.; the same point is made more briefly in the "Apología del Cristianismo," 406.

[45] "Apología del Cristianismo," 400–06; Peter the Venerable, *Contra Sectam*, 276ff.

[46] II Timothy 4:3–4; Peter the Venerable, *Contra Sectam*, 285.

prove that Muḥammad is a prophet. This brings him back to his
initial argument on the Koran; the Saracens should accept Christian
scripture, reject Muḥammad, and convert to Christianity. [*Contra sectam*,
288–91]

Whether Peter considered his polemical work complete or whether
he intended to write further,[47] his polemical strategy, while indebted
to that of his Arab and Spanish predecessors, is clearly distinct from
it. While effusively expressing his admiration and respect for philosophy
and *ratio*, Peter is clearly not adept in the scientific-rational forms of
argumentation common in the *Risālat al-Kindī*, Petrus Alfonsi's *Dialogi*
and other such works. He is much more at home when he can marshal
his formidable knowledge of scripture to refute Saracen errors.

This difference is clearly seen in the organization of the *Contra
sectam*. The *Risālat al-Kindī* opens with a defense of the Trinity based
on a triad of divine attributes, an argument which apparently failed
to impress Peter, since he does not reproduce it. Petrus Alfonsi opens
his attack on Islam by vilifying Muḥammad; since his anti-Islamic
chapter is part of a debate between a Christian and a Jew, this is an
understandable ploy to discredit Islam in the eyes of his Jewish inter-
locutor (indeed, this is the same strategy that Peter adapts in his
Summa). Peter realized that to open the *Contra Sectam* by directly attacking Muḥammad would only provoke the hostility of his Muslim audience. Instead, Peter uses a few well-chosen Koranic citations to try
to prove that Muslims should accept Christian scriptures; once he
has done that, he can return to the exegetically-based polemical
method that he had employed in the *Contra Petrobrusianos* and the
Aduersus Iudaeorum inveteratam duritiem.

In this enterprise, as we have seen, Peter saw himself as continuing
the tradition of the Church fathers, of scripturally-based explication
and refutation of heresy, just as he saw his *De miraculis* as a continuation
of the traditions embodied in the writings of Gregory the Great.[48]
His dissatisfaction with the earlier works of polemic that he used
seems to stem from the fact that they do not resemble the works of
the fathers with which Peter was so familiar. This, perhaps, explained
why these had failed to convert the Muslims: they were not proper
theological tracts.

---

[47] See above, note 37.
[48] Torrell and Bouthillier, *Pierre le Vénérable et sa vision du monde*, passim (see index,
p. 441, "Grégoire le Grand").

If Peter thought that his polemics would be more likely to convert Muslims, he was of course badly mistaken. Peter had only a superficial bookish knowledge of Islam, nothing to compare with the more direct knowledge of Petrus Alfonsi or (especially) of the author of the *Risālat al-Kindī*. We might offer Peter's anti-Muslim polemics the same reproach that Châtillon leveled against his *Contra Petrobrusianos*: Peter's elaborate, scripturally based arguments seem ill-equipped to convert his readers.

Yet in both works, Peter attempted to offer a defensive campaign against diabolical error: such polemics could quash the doubts of catholic readers. Torrell and Bouthillier have shown how, for Peter, Cluny was God's citadel constantly besieged by demons.[49] As Cluny's spiritual head, Peter was particularly well-placed to repulse demonic incursions: through pastoral care of his monks, through doctrinal works such as his *De miraculis*, and through his trilogy of theological polemics against Jews, Petrobrusians, and Saracens. If Muslim, Jews, and heretics could not be brought into the fold, at least their satanically-inspired errors could be dispelled from the minds of Christians.

---

[49] Torrell and Bouthillier, *Pierre le Vénérable et sa vision du monde*, 308–14 & passim.

NICOLAS EYMERIC AND THE CONDEMNATION OF ORTHODOXY[1]

Gary Macy

One of the most frequent mistakes that the ordinary person makes in thinking about the medieval church consists in imagining that it was somehow a monolithic institution, united in thought and action by a united hierarchy. The reasons for such a perception are easily identifiable. The post-Reformation propaganda of both Romans and Protestants made precisely this claim. For Romans, the one true church had always and everywhere agreed in the fundamental dogmas proclaimed at Trent, although some periods might have a better understanding than others, thus preserving a unified voice down through the centuries. For Protestants, that medieval invention, the Roman curia, used its totalitarian powers to ruthlessly enforce its heretical will. This mythology suited equally well the anti-clerical agendas of the Enlightenment. In this scenario, religion, especially institutional religion, presented a unified opposition to science, education and any form of liberation. According to the Disney version of this lie, "It was the Dark Ages and men's minds were dark." All three of these misperceptions of the medieval church are alive and well, propagated up to the present day practically without change since the time of the Reformation.[2]

Now, it doesn't take much reflection to begin to seriously doubt the possibility of such a church. The European Middle Ages covered a period of roughly eight hundred to a thousand years and everywhere from Skibberren to Palermo and Tashkent to Iceland, and it would be stunning if any institution could remain unchanged over such an expanse of both time and space.

---

[1] An earlier version of this paper was presented at the symposium, "Tradition and Ecstasy: The Agony of the Fourteenth Century" at the Claremont Graduate Schools on November 20, 1992.

[2] For a more complete discussion of the politics involved in defining the medieval church, see Gary Macy, "Demythologizing 'the Church' in the Middle Ages," *Journal of Hispanic/Latino Theology*, 3 (1995), 23–41 and idem, "Was there a 'the Church' in the Middle Ages?" *Unity and Diversity in the Church*, edited by Robert Swanson, Studies in Church History, vol. 52, Blackwell: Oxford, 1996, 107–116.

The language of the Middle Ages fools us. They spoke in absolutes, as befit a society shaped by Roman law, by the forms of Plato, and by the logic of Aristotle, but this does not mean that these absolutes mirrored reality. After all, all sides of a dispute used equally absolutist language, and medieval political rhetoric contains far more invective (and of a nastier sort) than even modern campaign managers could devise.

There is a sense in which all politics in the Middle Ages really was local politics. Nowhere is this truer than in that cornerstone of the myth of the totalitarian Middle Ages, the Inquisition. Thanks to the work of modern historians, summarized in Edward Peters, *Inquisition*,[3] most scholars now accept that there was no "Inquisition" (with capital "I") in the Middle Ages, but rather a series of local inquisitions (with a small "i"). Sometimes these were sponsored and supported by Rome, but they were always fundamentally local inquests, or hearings. Most often, of course, the word conjures up for us inquisitions for heresy; but inquisitions, "inquests," could be held to gather the facts of any crime or even just to take a census. Inquisitions for heresy, as all other "inquisitions," had a very local flavor and much depended on both the support of local politicians and on the character of the person in charge of the inquisition, the Inquisitor.

Although handbooks for inquisitors did exist, there was no established body of doctrine to which Inquisitors could turn. Hard cases were sometimes referred to councils of learned professionals, especially of course, theologians. The most important cases were directed to blue-ribbon panels of theologians from Paris, who, true to the best of academic traditions, often disagreed with one another. Inquisitors, then, were free to some extent to make it up as they went along, which meant that standards of orthodoxy could differ from place to place and from time to time.

This paper will examine two extreme cases in which people were accused and convicted of heresy by a local inquisitor for teaching perfectly orthodox doctrine. Both cases took place in a region infamous for its persecution of both Jews and Moslems, the kingdom of Aragon in the fourteenth century. The Catalan Dominican, Nicolas Eymeric, was democratic in his dislikes, however, and as Inquisitor of Aragon, attacked Christians as readily as non-Christians. He had a special hatred for his fellow Catalan, the theologian Ramon Lull and for

---

[3] University of California Press: Berkeley, 1989.

the physician and scientist, Arnold of Villanova. He wasn't fussy, however, and was quite willing to try to condemn beghards and beguines, spiritual Franciscans, Cathars and Waldensians.

Nicolas was born in Gérone in Catalonia, entering the Dominicans in his home town while in his early teens. He did well in the order, becoming Master of Studies in Barcelona in 1351 and sublector there the following year. Ten years later, he was appointed Vicar of the province of Aragon, after having attained the degree of Master in Theology. From 1357 until 1360, he served his first stint as Inquisitor General of Aragon. He was removed from office by his own order during the General Chapter of the Dominicans held in Perpignan in 1360. When he was elected provincial prior of Aragon in 1362, the appointment was squashed by Pope Urban IV. Appointed Inquisitor General again in 1365, he served in this post until he was banned from the realm of Aragon by King Pedro IV in March of 1375. Nicolas fled to the papal court in Avignon where he continued a pamphlet war against his many enemies. He was finally able to return to his position as Inquisitor upon the accession of a new king, Juan I, in 1387. Nicolas fared no better with King Juan, who deposed Nicolas in 1392. Once again Nicolas returned to Avignon to rail against his opponents. Nicolas finally retired to his home town in 1397 and died two years later. As his career makes abundantly clear, Nicolas was not an easy man with which to get along.[4]

Although Nicolas produced extensive writings including scripture commentaries, theological tracts and occasional works against Ramon Lull, Arnold of Villanova and other assorted "heretics," Nicolas is best known for his *Directorium inquisitorum*, written in 1376. A comprehensive manual for Inquisitors as well as a self-aggrandizing and spiteful account of his own tenure as Inquisitor, Nicolas' work was often reprinted throughout the early modern period and became the handbook for the Spanish Inquisition.

In the section of the *Directorium* that gives examples of heresies or errors condemned by the inquisitors of Aragon outside the papal curia, but with the approval of the Pope, Nicolas told of his own appeal to Rome concerning heretics preaching in parts of Aragon

---

[4] On Nicolas' life and works see Emilio Grahit y Papell, *El Inquisidor Fray Nicolás Eymerich, Catalanes Ilustres*, Manueal Llach: Gerona, 1878; Johannes Vincke, *Zur Vorgeschichte der Spanishchen Inquisition*, Beiträge zur Kirchen-und Rechtsgeschichte, 2, Peter Hanstein Verlandbuchhandlung: Bonn, 1941, 32–45 and Thomas Kaeppeli, O.P., *Scriptores Ordinis Praedicatorum Medii Aevi*, 3, ad Sabinae: Rome, 1980, s.v.

and Catalonia. According to the Inquisitor, Gregory XI sent a letter back forbidding the preaching of these doctrines under pain of excommunication.[5] Nicolas then listed five doctrines as condemned. Three treat of the Eucharist, and two speak of the Blessed Virgin. The first holds that the body of Christ ceases to be present and that the substance of the bread returns to the species whenever the host falls into any inappropriate place. The second asserts that the same thing happens when the host is eaten by a mouse or some other animal, and the third claims that the substance of bread replaces the body of Christ even when chewed and digested by recipients.[6] The fourth article argued that Mary was filled with grace during the conception of Jesus and thus from that moment on, could not receive any further graces. The final teaching follows logically. Since Mary was already full of grace, the Holy Spirit conferred no further grace to Mary at Pentecost.[7]

During this discussion, Nicolas mentioned that he had included a copy of the papal letter he received in this case in an earlier section of his work. The transcription of the letter dated 1371 was indeed included among other papal decrees, but does not quite fit the description given by Nicolas. First, and most obviously, although the letter mentions teachings on the Eucharist, the teachings on the Virgin

---

[5] Decima questio est hereses seu errores condemnati extra curiam romanam per inquisitores Aragonie heretice pravitatis auctoritate apostolica et de expresso mandato domini nostri pape. . . . Postmodum vero tempore Gregorii xi. frater nicholaus Eymerici ordinis predicatorum inquisitor heretice pravitatis in partibus aragonie et Cathalonie ante dictis sucessor immediatus prefati fratris nicholai roselli ad cardinalatum apicemas sumpti informavit eundem dominum gregorium quod in dictis partibus infrascipti articuli de sacramento altaris et beata virgine publice predicabuntur: qui dominus gregorius prehabito multorum concilio magistrorum mandavit dicto inquisitori et prelatis ominibus paritum predictarum per suas litteras de quibus agitur in prima parte huius operis quatenus illos articulos interdicerent per sententiam excommunicationis in ecclesiis cathedralibus partium predictarum quod et fecit." *Directorium inquisititorum, pars* 2, *questio* 10, Barcelona, 1503, n.p.

[6] "Primus quod si ostia consecrata cadat seu proiiciatur in cloacam lutum seu alium turpum locum quod speciebus remanentibus sub eis desinit corpus christi et reddit substantia panis. Secundus quod si ostia consecrata a mure corrodatur seu a bruto sumatur quod remanentibus dictis speciebus sub eis desinit esse corpus christi et redit substantia panis. Tertius quod si ostia consecrata a iusto vel peccatore sumatur quod dum species dentibus teritur christus ad celum rapitur et in ventris hominis non trahicitur." Ibid.

[7] "Quartus, quod beata maria mater christi in conceptione filli sui sic fuit gratia plena, quod ex tunc in gratia non prodecit nec proficere potuit. Quintus: quod Spiritus Sanctus in die Pentecostes veniens in beatam virginem mariam et Apostolos, gratiam nullam contulit beatae Mariae, sed apostolis; quia sic erat gratia plena, quod in gratia proficere non valebat." Ibid.

are not included. Secondly, the letter is actually by two cardinals, although under the express orders of the Pope. Thirdly, the teachings were banned only in the areas under Nicolas' control, but not generally condemned, and the preacher of these doctrines, the Franciscan Johannes de Latone, was sent a letter and asked to stop preaching these things only in Aragon and Catalonia.[8]

In other words, Nicolas' description of the events was not quite accurate. Judging by the actual curial letter, it would seem that the Franciscan, Johannes de Latone, was condemned by Nicolas for his preaching on the Eucharist, and that when the case was appealed to Rome (presumably by Johannes or the Franciscans on his behalf), the Pope merely wrote to Johannes asking him to stop teaching in the areas under Nicolas's control, allowing Nicolas to forbid anyone else from so teaching. I have no idea why Nicolas tacked on two teachings about the Virgin to those treated by Rome, but Nicolas was a particularly vicious man, and some historians have even accused him of forging papal letters when he deemed it necessary.[9]

That Johannes de Latone received a rather mild reproof for his teaching is not really all that surprising. Although his teaching embodies a position specifically rejected by Thomas Aquinas, it had been the preferred stance of such illustrious figures as Pope Innocent III,

---

[8] "Miseratione divina Petrus sancti Eustachii et Guillermus sancti angeli diaconi cardinales Reverendis partibus Terrachonensis et Cesaraugustanensis provinciarum. Archiepiscopis eorumque suffraganeis necnon inquisitoribus heretice pravitatis a sede apostolica in ipsis provintiis deputatis. Salutem et sinceram in domino caritatem relatione religiosi fratris Nicholai eymerici magistri in theologia ac in dictis provintiis hereticie pravitatis inquisitoris ad audientiam domini nostri pape nuper prevenit quod tam in vestris quam in suffraganeorum vestrorum ecclesiis palam et publice per certos religiosos predicati fuerunt tres articuli subsequentes in effectu. . . . Idem dominus noster papa nobis ibidem presentibus vive vocis oraculo expresse commisit quatenus auctoritate sua apostolica vobis mandaremus ut omnis moris sublato dispendio in dictis vestris provintiis sub pena excommunicationis inhibentis. Nequis deinceps dictos articulos publice presumeret predicare. Nos igitur petrus et Guillermus Cardinales predicti huius mandatum apostolicum cupientes exequi ut tenemur. vobis et vestrum cuilibet in virtute sancte obedientie precipimus et mandamus. Ne ab inde in antea dictos articulos seu eorum alterum sub eisdem vel aliis verbis idem sonantibus in substantia seu in effectu in vestris ecclesiis palam seu publice predicari a quoquam permittatis: et hoc sub pena excommunicationis contra contrarium facientiem innodetis ipso facto. Notificantes vobis nihilominus simili mandato per ipsum dominum nostrum papam nobis facto quod idem dominus noster papa fratri Johanni de latone ordinis fratrum minorum qui aliquos de dictis articulis in vestris ecclesiis frequenter recitando predicaverat inhiberi fecit sub pena excommunicationis ne dictos articulos de cetero publice predicare presumat." *Directorium inquisititorum, pars* 1, n. 15 ibid.

[9] See, for example, the discussion in Grahit y Papell, *El Inquisidor Fray Nicolás Eymerich*, 47–62.

and of the Franciscan master, Alexander of Hales, *and* of St. Bonaventure *and* of the influential fourteenth century exegete, the Franciscan
Nicolas of Lyra.[10] Johannes' preaching was not only the usual teaching
of the Franciscans, it was also included in the most popular canon
law textbook of the Middle Ages, the *Glossa ordinaria* (or "regular
commentary") on Gratian's *Decretum*.[11] In short, it would seem that
Johannes de Latone was condemned for teaching Franciscan thought
in a malicious Dominican's territory; thought which would have been
orthodox anywhere else. Indeed, Nicolas may have particularly picked
Johannes for his singular attention, since Johannes was also a native
of Gerona[12] and Nicolas may have felt that the Franciscan house
in his home town ought be particularly saved from error, especially
since the Franciscan third order in Gerona had already run into trouble with the Inquisition.[13] Johannes himself, however, escaped the
Inquisitor's wrath unscathed. Earlier in his career, Johannes had been
nominated to a post at the University of Paris in 1365 by Pope
Gregory XI, the very same pope whose curia later issued the letter

---

[10] See Gary Macy, "Reception of the Eucharist According to the Theologians: A
Case of Diversity in the 13th and 14th Centuries," *Theology and the University*, Proceedings of the Annual Convention of the College Theology Society, 1987, edited
by John Apczynski, University Press of America: Lanham, MD, 1990, 15–36.

[11] *De consecratione, pars* 2, c. 23 "(*Tribus gradibus*) miscere. Sed nec species ille aliis
cibis permiscentur: non enim in stomachum descendunt: quare per secessum non
emittuntur: licet enim ex ipsis aliquis reficiatur: non tamen incorporantur: nec in
stomachum descendunt: nec per secussum emittuntur: interdum enim odore recreatur
homo: qui tamen nec in stomachum: nec in secessum dirigitur. Dici potest quod
species bene descendunt in stomachum: nam aliter quando evomerentur infra eadem.
si quis per ebrietatem (*de cons.* II, c. 28). Unde forte per sudorem emittitur de corpore:
certum est quod species quam cito dentibus teruntur tam cito in celum rapitur corpus
Christi." *Decretum Gratiani Nouissime post ceteras o[mn]es impressiones*, Venice, 1525, fol.
601v1. See also the commentary on c. 56 (Non iste panis), ibid., fol. 607v1, and
c. 94 (*Qui bene*), "Comederit. nec dicendum quod mus sumat corpus domini: statim
enim desinit esse sacramentum ex quo ab eo tangitur" ibid., fol. 613v2.

[12] Johannes is referred to as "frater Joannes de Latoni Gerundensis" in his commissioning as a master of theology as recorded by Luke Wadding, *Annales Minorum*,
vol. 8 (1347–1376), 3rd ed., Quarracchi: Florence, 1932, 389–90 under the year
1376: "Gradum Magisterii acceperunt ex commissione Pontificia: . . . Frater Joannes
de Latone Gerundensis, . . . Destinatur ei lectura Parisiensis, et magisterium conferen-
dum per Cancellarium Parisien. . . . Demum Ministro Generali concessa est speciali
diplomate facultas conferendi gradum Magisterii duobus idoneis in proximo Capitulo
Generali Aquilae celebrando: Sicut deletur, VI Idus Mai." as well as in the papal
letter recommending Johannes to a similar post in 1365; see note 14 below.

[13] See Jill Weber, *Els Menorets: The Franciscans in the Realms of Aragon From St. Francis
to the Black Death*, Pontifical Institute of Mediaeval Studies: Toronto, 1993 and John
Moorman, *A History of the Order from Its Origins to the Year 1517*, Franciscan Herald
Press: Chicago, 1988, 426.

forbidding Johannes from teaching Fransciscan eucharistic teaching in Nicolas' territory.[14] This warning does not seem to have cooled Gregory's support for Johannes, however, as Gregory again nominated Johannes to a post at Paris in 1376.[15] Johannes may eventually have taught at Paris if he can be identified with a "magister Johannes Lathomi" who signed a letter settling a dispute between the masters and the chancellor in 1389.[16]

The curial letter cited by Nicolas was not included in any medieval canon law collection of which I am aware nor quoted in any medieval theological discussions that I have read. The affair, nevertheless, continued to reverberate, though in a minor note, down until modern times. Johannes had his defender in the seventeenth century Franciscan historian, Luke Wadding, who in a lengthy discussion of this case, pointed out the many theologians, including St. Bonaventure and Pope Innocent III, who took the same position as Johannes. Wadding also pointed out that Nicolas claimed universal condemnation for what was really only a local prohibition, not to mention that fact the Nicolas accused Johannes of things he never taught.[17] Wadding's quite accurate observations, however, did not win the day.

---

[14] "(Johanni de Calore) cancellario Paris., ut Johannem de Latone de Gerunda, Ord. Min., professorem in theologica facultate in pluribus studiis juxta morem dicti Ordinis, postquam de studio Parisiensi rediit, ad legendum librum Sententiarum in vacationibus in proxime futura aestate admittat et aditti faciat, et lectura completa magisterii honorem et docendi licentiam in eadem theologica facultate largiatur, ita tamen quod ex hoc praefatus Ordo ad praestandum aliquid eidem Johanni pro suis expensis et aliis necessarius ratione dicti magisterii ultra quam antea minime teneatur, Dat. Avinione xj kal. Maii pontificius nostri anno primo." *Chartularium Universitatis Parisiensis*, vol. 3, Paris, 1894, 196–7.

[15] "Sed adhuc an. 1376, Julii 8, mandatum apost. effectu caruit, nam sub hac temporis nota Gregorius iterum scripsit cancellario, ut Johannem «in vacationibus in proxima futura estate» ad legenda Sententias admitteret." *Chartularium*, ibid. The reference is also given by Wadding in the *Annales Minorum*, ibid., 389–90. For the text see note 12 above.

[16] *Chartularium*, ibid., 480–1.

[17] The discussion occurs in the *Annales Minorum*, vol. 3, 282–7. A section of Wadding's conclusion gives the general tone of the discussion: "Videat, quaeso, candidus et sincerus lector, quanta hic rerum discrepantia, et quantum discordet haec narratio a relatione suprascripti Cardinalium diplomatis. Non alias, quam has letteras circa hos articulos ille prodicit in prima parte directorii, et ibi in margine notatur esse has ipsas: dicit tamen hic esse Pontificis litteras, et ibi referuntur missae et scriptae a Cardinalibus. Dicit aeque in illis contineri articulos de Sacramento altaris, et de beata Virgine, et nulla in eis fit mentio beatae Virginis. Dicit hic esse interdictos hos articulos per sententiam excommunicationis in Ecclesiis Cathedralibus, et illic tantum dicitur praeceptum fuissed sub excommunicatione, ne publice praedicarentur. Et subjungit, vel praemittit articulis tribus supra relatis de Eucharistia, et duobus de beata Virgine: articuli autem taliter condemnati sunt isti, ita ut aeque

Two private repositories of orthodoxy, on the other hand, include Johannes' teachings as heresies condemned by the Roman Catholic Church. Carolus du Plessis d'Argentré in his *Collectio iudiciorum de novis erroribus qui ab initio XII saeculi post Incarnationem Verbi, usque ad annum 1632 in Ecclesia proscripti sunt et notati*: . . . copied Johannes' teaching as reported by Nicolas under the year 1371, the date of the papal letter.[18] Du Plessis d'Argentré was in turn copied by Heinrich Denziger and Adolf Schönmetzer in their massive collection of "orthodox" Roman Catholic teaching, the *Enchiridion Symbolorum* under numbers 1101–1103.[19] The *Enchiridion*, now in its thirty-sixth printing, continues to be used by conservative Roman Catholics as the touchstone of acceptable teaching down to the present day. Thanks to Du Plessis d'Argentré, Denziger and Schönmetzer, Nicolas' condemnation continues to be repeated, albeit stripped of its context and limitations, while Wadding's eloquent defense is now almost completely lost.

A second instance when Nicolas condemned what appears to have been orthodox teaching presents a somewhat more complicated picture. A treatise of Nicolas entitled "On the Two Natures in Christ and on the Three Persons in God, or Whether the Symbol of the Eucharist might contain the Father and Son and Holy Spirit," now contained in Paris, Bibliothèque Nationale MS lat. 1464, is an explanation and defense of Nicolas' condemnation of Pedro Sesplanes, the rector of the village of Sella in Valencia.[20] According to Nicolas, there seems to have been a custom in Valencia of distributing the Eucharist to the sick with the formulaic question, "Do you believe this to the be be the Father, the Son and the Holy Spirit?" A three-fold affirmation was the expected reply. Sometime during the Nicolas' third and last tour of duty as Inquisitor, the question was raised by

---

condemantos hos de beata Virgine, atque illos de Sacramento altaris affirmet. At nullum video, qui ejus fidei aut auctoritati innixus asserat, aut admittat, hos posteriores articulos de beata Virgine esse condemnatos. . . ." Ibid., p. 287.

[18] Vol. 1, Lutetiae: Paris, 1728, *pars* I, p. 390 col. 1–391 col. 2.

[19] Originally produced by Denziger in 1854 the latest edition is that printed by Herder: Barcelona, Fribourg, Rome, 1976. On Denziger and the *Enchiridion*, see *The HarperCollin Encyclopedia of Catholicism*, ed. By Richard McBrien, Harper: San Francisco, 1995, s.v.

[20] Despite repeated requests for a microfilm of this text and even payment for the microfilm, the Bibliothèque nationale continues to refuse to send me a mircrofilm of this manuscript. The text has been summarized, although in slightly different fashions, by both Menéndez Pelayo, *Las Obras Completas*, vol. 36, *Historia de los Heterodoxos Españoles*, vol. 2, Aldus: Santander, 1947, 307–8 and Eufemià Fort y Cogul, *Catalunya i la Inquisició*, Editorial Aedos: Barcelona, 1973, 104–6.

local theologians whether this was, in fact, accurate. Since only the body of Christ, the second person of the Trinity, was truly present in Eucharist, perhaps a new formula should be introduced. The topic became one of general discussion. In 1389, Fr. Sesplanes wrote an address on this topic which argued that rather than references to the Father, Son and Spirit, the eucharistic formula ought to include references to the human, spiritual and divine natures of Christ. He gave the address privately, and then publicly in the Cathedral of Valencia. Nicolas transcribed part of his public sermon:

> And thus, Christian, as there are three natures in Jesus Christ, of course, the human, the spiritual and the divine, if any priest offers to you the most precious body of Christ, and asks you first concerning the human-ity, saying "Do you believe, Christian, that the bread is materially con-verted into the true Body of Christ when the priest says the same (or similar) words which Christ spoke on the day of the Last Supper?" What do you say, Christian? You say, "Yes". And if he asks you about the spiritual nature, of course, if you believe that here is the holy soul of Christ, you say, "Yes, yes". And if he asks you about the divine nature and essence, do you believe that the Father Himself, the Son and Holy Spirit are here, you say, Christian, "Yes, yes," because all three persons are there essentially.

At this point in the sermon, a merchant rose up and demonstrated one difference between medieval and modern congregations by shout-ing, "No, no". Nicolas' account then records that all hell broke loose in the church. Sesplanes was arrested and incarcerated in the Epis-copal palace until an investigation could be held. The Cardinal of Valencia and the Inquisitor called together a council of twenty-eight theologians, lawyers and physicians. Only in the third session of the council could a decision be reached concerning the case of Fr. Sesplanes. A majority of the council agreed that his teaching be condemned, while a minority held that this teaching could have an orthodox interpretation. That was enough for the Inquisitor, however. Fr. Sesplanes was forced to recant both privately and publicly under penalty of degradation and of being turned over to the secular arm. Further, he was to be perpetually imprisoned, losing his benefices and his license to preach. This sentence was subject to mitigation by either the judgment of the Cardinal of Valencia or of the Inquisitor. Neither seemed to have taken this opportunity.

The first abjuration took place in one of the rooms of the bishop's palace, on Saturday. The next day, Sunday, Fr. Sesplanes performed a solemn and public retraction at the cathedral church. The performance

was designed to be particularly humiliating. Fr. Sesplanes stood with
a burning candle in his hand, while the Inquisitor delivered a vehement
sermon on his errors. The parchment which contained the thesis of
Sesplanes was solemnly and publicly burned and its author suffered
a penitential whipping which a priest administered to him with a
leather strap.[21]

The matter did not end there, however. As soon as he was able,
Fr. Sesplanes escaped and while fleeing to Catalonia and Majorca,
he appealed to Rome against the ruling of Nicolas. The case must
have been heard in Avignon, since the only witness we have to these
events, the tract of Nicolas written in Avignon on January 31st, 1390,
was produced in order to explain and defend his treatment of Pedro
Sesplanes. The papal response to the case is not known, but one can
presume that the Pope decided against the Inquisitor, since the royal
authorities and the city council of Valencia reversed the sentence of
the Inquisitor. At least according to one commentator, the rashness
and ruthlessness of Nicolas' handling of this case was a contributing
factor to his expulsion from the kingdom of Aragon in 1392.[22]

It is hard to imagine what heresy Pedro Sesplanes could have
espoused here. Certainly to hold that Christ was composed of a body,
a human soul and the divinity of the Second Person of the Trinity
has been the orthodox opinion of the majority of Christians since
the Nestorian controversy was settled at the Council of Chalcedon
in 451. Although to hold, as Fr. Sesplanes seemed to, that there are
human, spiritual and divine natures in Christ is not quite termino-
logically correct, but it does seem to fit well with the main point he
wanted to make. It would have been more in accord with medieval
teaching to say that body, blood, soul and divinity of Christ were
present in the Eucharist rather that to say, as was the older custom
of Valencia, that each of the Persons of the Trinity was so present.

Here Fr. Sesplanes seemed to be on the firmest of grounds. While
there were theologians, notably the late twelfth century canonist,
Huguccio of Bologna, who denied that the soul and divinity of Christ
were received in the Eucharist, by the thirteenth century, the opposite
position had been universally accepted.[23] Those most famous of the

---

[21] The story is related by Pelayo, *Historia de los Heterodoxos Españoles*, pp. 307–8;
Eufemià Fort y Cogul, *Catalunya i la Inquisició*, Editorial Aedos: Barcelona, 1973,
104–6, and D. Emilio Grahit y Papell, *El Inquisidor Fray Nicolás Eymerich*, 31–33.

[22] Fort y Cogul, *Catalunya i la Inquisició*, 104.

[23] Huguccio's position is recorded (and challenged) in the *Glossa ordinaria* on the

Dominicans, St. Albert and St. Thomas, both held that the soul and the divinity of Christ were present in the Eucharist.[24] The exact way in which this was possible was certainly debatable. The Dominican master, Durand of St. Pourçain and the Franciscan master, William of Ockham, both disagreed with Thomas on how this was possible, but neither denied that the soul and divinity of Christ were present in reception.[25] Even more disconcerting for the Inquisitor would have been the suggestion by the Council of Constance (held a mere twenty-five years after Fr. Sesplanes' condemnation) that the orthodoxy of Wyclifites and Hussites should be tested by asking whether they believed that the body, soul and divinity of Christ were present in the Eucharist.[26] In short, whatever technical misgivings Nicolas Eymeric and the council he convened might have had with the teaching of Pedro Sesplanes, the rector was certainly very close to the mainstream teaching of the Parisian masters. Just as in the case of Johannes de Latone, if Pedro Sesplanes had been teaching almost anywhere else in Europe, he would have been understood as perfectly orthodox. In fact, if he had given the same sermon at the same time in England, he would probably been praised as an opponent of Wyclif and his followers.

What conclusions can be drawn from these curious cases of inquisitorial malice? First of all, and importantly at least for those

---

Decretum, de consecratione, c. 46 (*Quid est Christum*): "Casus. Duobus modis manducatur Christus. Uno modo sacramentaliter quid competit bonis et malis. Alio modo spiritualiter cum per fidem et dilectionem cooperantem accipitur: hoc est tantum bonorum. Queri autem solet hic: utrum Christi corpus sumatur cum divinitate et anima? H(uguccio) dicit quod non sumitur ibi divinitas vel anima. Alii ut B. dicunt quod sumendo corpus sumo dietatem et animam: quia tu qui accipis carnem: divine substantie eius in illo participas in alimento infra eadem *sicut verus* (c. 84)," *Decretum Gratiani Nouissime* fol. 605v2.

[24] See Thomas, *Summa theologiae*, pars 3, q. 76, art. 1, *Sancti Thomae Aquinatis, Opera omnia iussu Leonis XII P.M. edita*, Rome: 1882–, vol. 12, 178 and Albert, *Commentarii in Sententiarum*, dist. 12, Art. 4, *Opera Omnia*, Vives: Paris, 1890–99, vol. 29, 297.

[25] Durandus, *Commentaria in sententiarum*, lib. 4, dist. 10, q. 2, *D. Durandi a Sancto Porciano, . . . In Petri Lombardi Sententias Theologicas Commentariorum*, Venice: 1571, reprinted The Greg Press: Ridgewood, New Jersey, 316, col. 1 and Ockham, *Quodlibet 4*, Q. 30, *Venerabilis inceptoris Guillelmi de Ockham, Quodlibeta septem*, ed. Joseph C. Wey; vol. 9 of *Opera Philosophica et Theologica*, St. Bonaventure, N.Y., 1980, 447–8.

[26] "Item, utrum credat et asserat, quod facta consecratione per sacerdotum, sub sola specie panis tantum, et praeter speciem vini, sit vera caro Christi et sanguis et anima et deitas et totus Christus, ac idem corpus absolute et sub unaqualibet illarum specierum singulariter." *Interrogationes Wycliffitis et Husitis proonendae*, Bull "*Inter cunctas*" of Martin V, Feb. 22, 1418 promulgating the decrees of the Council of Constance (Denziger, no. 1257). This teaching was repeated by the Council of Trent, Session 13, October, 1551, *Decretum de sancta Eucharistia*, cap. 3 (Denziger, no. 1640).

concerned, as far as we know Johannes de Latone and Pedro Sesplanes both died of natural causes. Not every one who ran up against the Aragonese inquisition of Nicolas Eymeric was so lucky. Both these cases shared one important characteristic, however. Both these men had important political support, Johannes had the Franciscan Order to back him up, and Pedro Sesplanes seemed to have won civil support. Probably because of this, the appeals to the papacy appear to have been successful in both cases, but not all people had the means and the contacts to make such an appeal.

An important point to be made, then, is that there was heresy in the Middle Ages, and then there was heresy. Theologians were often accused of heresy, but few ever suffered much because of it. In my studies of theologians accused of eucharistic heresy, I have found only one example of a theologian who was burned due at least in part because of his teaching on the Eucharist. John Wyclif seemed not to have objected, however, since he had already died of natural causes some twenty years earlier.[27] In order to preach complex theological opinions which could be construed as heresy, one needed to be educated and if one were educated, one usually had the political connections necessary to survive accusations of heresy.

Secondly, and more importantly for this paper, heresy was very much in the eyes of the inquisitor. There was no "big book" of church dogma that an inquisitor could use to determine orthodoxy. Lots of tough questions remained open to debate. Two of Nicolas' chief targets, Ramon Lull and Arnold of Villanova, were both ultimately accepted as orthodox after long debate, much to Nicolas' disgust and fury. Other of Nicolas' foes, such as the beguines or the spiritual Franciscans, found themselves considered either heretics or saints depending on who happened to be pope and where they happened to live. The situation was not all clear cut. Accusations of heresy did not always mean there actually was heresy present, but merely that some local authorities thought so. Other authorities might disagree, as almost certainly happened in the two cases discussed here. In short, the fact that inquisitions existed, and that they could be vicious, is not necessarily proof that the medieval church was either monolithic nor totalitarian. In fact, it is more accurate to say there was not one medieval church. The papacy of Innocent III tried

---

[27] See Macy, "The Dogma of Transubstantiation in the Middle Ages," *Journal of Ecclesiastical History*, 45,1, 32–40.

to embody one ideal of the church in the decrees of Lateran IV in 1215. This vision of the church differs greatly from that envisioned by his opponent in England, King John. The paranoid Pope John XXII had another vision, or perhaps hallucination, of a church attacked by the devil on all sides, while one of his opponents, the Franciscan William of Ockham, worked for a church free from all material attachments. Which of these was *the* medieval church?

I raise this issue not only in the interest of historical accuracy, although this in itself would be reason enough to do so. There is a very important theological point to be made as well. If historians accept the Reformation and Enlightenment agenda, they must also, perforce, accept that "the medieval Church" must be made to be seen as a monolith, and that is only possible by reducing "the Church" to a series of canonical decisions treated as if they were Platonic forms devoid of their historical setting and significance. It is, in short, to argue that "the Church" actually was (and should be) the monolith desired by the most regressive Roman Catholics. I believe that this is not only historically inaccurate (and possibly dishonest), but it is also theologically to concede half of the history of Christianity to the most conservative elements of Christianity.

I would urge my colleagues to be very careful in attempts to find the origins of either twentieth century fascism, or totalitarian patriarchy or other forms of modern oppression in "the medieval Church." Not that there was not ruthless oppression of minorities and of women in the Middle Ages. There certainly was. No fewer people will have died by redefining persecution as local rather than international. But it is extremely dangerous theologically as well as historically inaccurate to ignore or suppress the diversity and lively debates over doctrine and practice that characterized much of the medieval church in order to buttress political agendas of the present. For if we concede that "the Church" of the past was composed only of the canonical decrees of the hierarchy, we cannot then blithely claim that the Church of the present should not be considered in the same way. If, on the other hand, the true diversity of the medieval churches (plural) can be historically demonstrated (and I am firmly convinced that it can), then it is this diversity itself that becomes an ancient and enduring Christian tradition, and any present monolithic and totalitarian understanding of Christianity can be seen for what it really is, the creation of a nineteenth century reaction to the liberation movements of Europe and an historic aberration up with which we must not put.

INDEX